Natural Rights
and the New Republicanism

Natural Rights
and the New Republicanism

Michael P. Zuckert

PRINCETON UNIVERSITY PRESS

PRINCETON, NEW JERSEY

Copyright © 1994 by Princeton University Press
Published by Princeton University Press, 41 William Street,
Princeton, New Jersey 08540
In the United Kingdom: Princeton University Press,
Chichester, West Sussex

Library of Congress Cataloging-in-Publication Data

Zuckert, Michael, 1942–
Natural rights and the new republicanism / Michael Zuckert.
p.   cm.
Includes bibliographical references (p.) and index.

ISBN 0-691-03463-X (CL)
1. Natural law.   2. Republicanism.   3. Locke, John, 1632–1704.
4. Political science—History—17th century.   5. Political
science—History—18th century.   I. Title.
JC571.Z83   1994   323′.01—dc20   94-5498   CIP

This book has been composed in Electra

This book was prepared in part under a grant from the
Woodrow Wilson International Center for Scholars,
Washington, D.C. The views expressed herein are those
of the author and are not necessarily those of the
Woodrow Wilson Center.

Princeton University Press books are printed
on acid-free paper and meet the guidelines
for permanence and durability of the Committee
on Production Guidelines for Book Longevity
of the Council on Library Resources

Printed in the United States of America

10 9 8 7 6 5 4 3 2 1

FOR CATHERINE

"Whereof one cannot speak, thereof one must be silent."

Contents

Preface   xi

Acknowledgments   xiii

INTRODUCTION   xv

PROLOGUE   3

Two Revolutions, Two Declarations   4
Contract and the Declaration of Rights   14
Locke and the Two Revolutions   15
Locke and the Americans   18

PART ONE: *Protestants*   27

CHAPTER ONE
Aristotelian Royalism and Reformation Absolutism:
Divine Right Theory   29

Dimensions of Divine Right   30
The Similitudes of Rule   34
The Reformation Attitude and the Transformation of Aristotle   39
Patriarchalism and the Reformation Attitude   43

CHAPTER TWO
Aristotelian Constitutionalism and Reformation Contractarianism:
From Ancient Constitution to Original Contract   49

The Ancient Constitution   51
The Mixed Constitution   56
Contractarianisms   64
The Original Contract and the Reformation Attitude:
    Philip Hunton   65
The Aristotelianism of the Original Contract: Henry Parker   71

CHAPTER THREE
Contract and Christian Liberty: John Milton   77

Two Revolutions, Two Contractarianisms: Milton's "Tenure"
    and the Declaration of Independence   79
Miltonic Politics and the Reformation Attitude   83
Milton's Christian Republicanism   89
Two Contractarianisms, Two Fundamental Attitudes   91

PART TWO: *Whigs*   95

CHAPTER FOUR
Whig Contractarianisms and Rights   97

The Restoration and the Emergence of the Whigs   98
Exclusion and Whig Non-Contractarianism: Grotian Legalism   101
Whig Contractarianism and the Glorious Revolution:
  Right Grotians   106
Whig Contractarianism and the Glorious Revolution:
  Left Grotians   113
Contractarianisms   116

CHAPTER FIVE
The Master of Whig Political Philosophy   119

Grotius and the Reformation of Natural Law   119
The Source of Political Power   123
The Problem of Natural Law   126
Nature and Convention in the Roman Law   129
Grotius's Break with the Natural Law Tradition   134
Nature and Convention in the Grotian Natural Law   146

CHAPTER SIX
A Neo-Harringtonian Moment? Whig Political Science and
the Old Republicanism   150

The Politics of Liberty: Bernard Bailyn   152
The Politics of the Organic Community: Gordon Wood   155
The Politics of "Zoon Politikon": J.G.A. Pocock   159
Political Philosophy and Political Science   164
Harrington and Neo-Harrington   166
In the Neo-Harringtonian Workshop   170
Whig Political Science   175

PART THREE: *Natural Rights and the
New Republicanism*   185

CHAPTER SEVEN
Locke and the Reformation of Natural Law: *Questions Concerning
the Law of Nature*   187

Grotius, Pufendorf, Locke   188
Locke and the Immanent Natural Law   195
Natural Law: Natural Sociability and Natural Morality   204
Transcendent Natural Law   207

CHAPTER EIGHT
Locke and the Reformation of Natural Law: *Two Treatises of Government*   216

The Transcendent Natural Law in "Two Treatises"   216
Thomist Natural Law and the Natural Executive Power   222
Grotian Natural Law and the Natural Executive Power   230
Natural Right and the Natural Executive Power   234
Transcendent Natural Law: Suicide   240

CHAPTER NINE
Locke and the Reformation of Natural Law: Of Property   247

Grotius, Pufendorf, Property   248
Transcendent Natural Law: Property   252
Property as Natural Right   259
Natural Law and Natural Rights   272
Natural Right as Property   275
Lockean Paradoxes   287

CHAPTER TEN
Locke and the Transformation of Whig Political Philosophy   289

Lockean Whiggism: "An Argument for Self-Defence"   291
"Cato's Letters": A Lockean Political Philosophy   297
"Cato's Letters": Natural Rights and the Old Republicanism 305
"Cato's Letters": Natural Rights and the New Republicanism 312

Notes   321

Bibliography   377

Index   391

Preface

LONG, LONG AGO, in what now seems a galaxy far, far away (actually, five years ago, in Washington, D.C.), I started out to write a study of the American founding. One thing led to another, however, and the result is the present book, devoted almost exclusively to the seventeenth and early eighteenth centuries in England. The ultimate aim remains the same: elucidating the American founding; as they might say in Hollywood, this book is the "prequel" to the one originally planned. The thesis of the original book can be quickly and easily put: with the American founding emerged a new kind of politics constituted by a new commitment to the philosophy of natural rights and dedicated to a new kind of republicanism based thereon. In a sense, that remains the thesis of the present book, although only a little is said about the way these themes work themselves out in the American materials. These two books are both parts of a broader project that bestrides two current, intertwined controversies or problems—the "America problem" and the "modernity problem."

The initial goal of my inquiry into the earlier British materials is negative—to prove that the natural rights/social contract philosophy of the American Revolution was by no means the "common sense of the subject" for the English in the seventeenth century, as Thomas Jefferson claimed it was for the Americans in the eighteenth. My thesis about the American founding runs afoul of two sometimes intermingled, sometimes opposed views. One line of thought rejects both parts of my thesis, arguing that the Americans are best understood neither in terms of the new liberal philosophy of natural rights nor as proponents of a new republicanism congruent therewith, but rather as devotees of an old classical or civic humanist republicanism much at odds with modern natural rights liberalism. The other point of view concedes the role of the natural rights/social contract theory in the thought of the American founding generation, but denies it any claim to novelty. English Whig (or opposition, or parliamentary) thought of the seventeenth century is permeated with, if not monopolized by, contractarian themes, and, as the saying goes, a contract is a contract is a contract. The Americans, according to this line of thought, were merely following in the theoretical steps of some or all of their opposition predecessors—those who made the Glorious Revolution of 1688–89; the Whigs who promoted Exclusion in the 1670s; the men who fought the Civil War in the 1640s; the leaders of the opposition to James I and Charles I before the Civil War. Both views respond to the "America problem" with an answer about modernity: either that America is not in its origins modern, or that modernity is best understood as a continuation or modification of something old.

Both views merit serious consideration, even though, as I think, both are false. The sponsors of the theory of the old republicanism have brought to the fore thinkers and styles of thought that had been neglected in the past and are undeniably important—indeed, they are important precisely for their contribution to the new natural rights republicanism. Likewise, a re-consideration of opposition thought with an eye to its contractarianism is also revealing, in part because the real differences between most of it and the late-emerging Lockean variety reveals much about the latter's modernity.

Because of this, it became increasingly clear that establishing my claims about the political innovativeness and modernity of the Americans required a much more extensive foray into what came before the American founding than I had originally planned. Thus, an introductory chapter became a thick book of its own.

St. Paul
December 1992

Acknowledgments

IT IS CUSTOMARY for an author to acknowledge help for what's good and to absolve others from responsibility for what's bad. This custom proves that the ancient distinction between nature and convention is too starkly drawn, for we scholars cannot go very long without recognizing our debts to others for insights, information, inspiration, and many other things. Nor can we go far without recognizing the stubbornness and other limits that prevent us from benefitting as much as we might from the help of others. I feel a deep obligation of gratitude to many other scholars, including those with whom I disagree. I have attempted always to turn my consideration of their work into something more positive than critique, and believe this to be a very different and better book because I have learned from them even when I have been unable to agree with them. The debts to those from whom I have more directly learned should be evident from my footnotes.

Many of the ideas in this book first saw the light of day, all squinting and blurry-eyed, in my classes at Carleton College. The intelligence, intellectual curiosity, and interest of my students have not only contributed to sharpening and improving many of the ideas here but have been a source of stimulation and sustenance to me for many years. With students like these, it remains easy to remember why teaching seemed to me all those years ago the most wonderful career choice one could make.

Professional colleagues in political science, history, literature, religion, and philosophy have read one or another part of this book and have been unfailingly generous of their time and effort, and sometimes with their criticisms. This project has been ripening over many years, so I am reluctant to single out any by name for fear of failing to mention all.

Various institutions have had a hand in this production as well. Carleton has been both a challenging and a distracting setting for scholarly work. I could mention students, colleagues, and committees, and let the reader decide which is challenging and which distracting. The Carleton administration has been committed to combining dedication to teaching with dedication to scholarship, and has gone to substantial lengths to make these commitments real. In the form of grants for time off, funds for travel and typing, and the general provision of a supportive atmosphere, Carleton has contributed a great deal to the completion of this book. The National Endowment for the Humanities supported this project with a grant that allowed me to spend a year at the University of Delaware. Although I was nothing more to the University than a faculty spouse, I was offered very fine work facilities there, and I am especially grateful for the persevering aid of the interlibrary loan department. I am also grateful to the University Honors Program for assigning to me an undergraduate research assistant, and to Greg Neff, a graduate political science student, who worked with me.

I spent another year as a Fellow at the Woodrow Wilson International Center for Scholars, a wonderful place to work. Too wonderful, perhaps. Many hours of fine conversation in the coffee lounge and lunch room probably contributed to the general quality of my life, but probably also slowed my writing. My research assistants at the Wilson Center, Steve Frazier, Barbara Blaesing, and David Morrison, were indispensable.

Far from least of the contributors to the completion of this project are those undaunted individuals who have struggled to transform my illegible script into a typed text: Hendrika Umbanhower, the typists in the Wilson Center typing pool, Helen Anctil, Terri Johnson, Larissa Zuckert, and most of all Heidi Whitmore and Rachel Zuckert. Rachel is not only a typist extraordinaire, but as a student of philosophy she also contributed more than the typist's usual share of editorial comments.

Rachel and Larissa, as well as my youngest daughter, Emily, have contributed immeasureably to the development of my dialectical skills. And finally there is Catherine. Here the conventions of the acknowledgment run out; I must let my silence stand for what only a poem I could not write well enough could say.

The *Review of Politics* has given permission to reprint material in Chapter 5 that originally appeared in its pages.

IN THE BEGINNING, all the English were Christian Aristotelians, more or less. Early seventeenth-century thought, whether royalist or parliamentary in orientation, betrays the formative marks of Aristotelian ways of thinking. By the time of the American Revolution, however, Aristotle was an almost discarded figure, among the Whig Opposition at least; the categories of political thinking resonated hardly at all with Aristotle's *Politics* and much more with Locke's *Two Treatises of Government*. Thus I defend points of view considered outdated or simply mistaken in many if not most advanced scholarly circles today. I maintain, for example, that Locke was the inspiration for the natural rights philosophy that informed American political thought and, moreover, that Locke has things to say about such fundamental matters as natural rights that are still philosophically interesting and arguably true.

This book is thus about Locke's coming to dominance within those traditions of Anglo-American thought that have come to be called Whig, and about the immense practical and theoretical significance of that event. Locke's rise to dominance occurred within the context of the English seventeenth century—a tempest of a time, marked by great political instability and intellectual innovation. Locke came along only after a buffeting succession of transforming events had already subjected political thought in England to several significant shifts in perspective.

In the beginning, all the English were Christian Aristotelians, more or less. By the early seventeenth century, however, the Reformation and its aftermath subjected those inherited ways of thought to great and transforming pressure. Part of the pressure came from the practical conflicts unleashed by the Reformation, part from the struggle of thoughtful and pious men to find the political conclusion that flowed from Protestant premises. Under pressure from Protestantism, the old accommodations between Christianity and classical antiquity embodied in the various forms of Christian Aristotelianism gave way. But they gave way to a variety of remarkably different positions. At one extreme emerged a new divine right doctrine, profoundly challenging to the inherited ways of English politics. At the other extreme emerged a variety of parliamentarily oriented contractarian doctrines, most important among which was John Milton's Christian republicanism. Although they were contractarians, neither Milton nor the other pro-parliamentary writers of the pre–Civil War era were adherents of anything like the Lockean contract doctrine. The various contractarianisms of the age, far from being more or less identical to each other, represented quite different responses to the Reformation. A Milton is not a Defoe is not a Locke.

The effort to find *the* proper political embodiment of the Protestant principle permeated the pre–Civil War era, but the variety and mutual hostility of the various embodiments promoted before and during the war showed this to be no easy task. The English Civil War, if not caused by these theoretical conflicts, nicely epitomized them. Warfare based largely on religious differences, of course, did not distinguish England very much from other European nations, for this was the era of religious warfare. However, instead of conflict between Protestant and Catholic, the English experienced mortal conflict among Protestants, each side claiming to present the correct solution to the theological-political conundrums unleashed by the Reformation.

The Reformation proved incapable of establishing a determinate politics. Thoughtful individuals during the Interregnum and in the early years after the restoration of the monarchy cast about for alternatives to the Protestant politics that had brought the country the disasters of civil strife and Cromwellian rule. Most important was the revival of politics grounded in natural law. Because of its associations with Catholicism on the one hand, and pagan rationalism on the other, the natural law philosophy had suffered an eclipse in the first half of the century. However, *sola scriptura*, or even scripture plus theology, had not only proved unable to settle politics but had contributed to the generally unsettled situation a virulence and fanaticism that led Englishmen to give new consideration to the virtues of political theories based on appeals to reason, which in principle was available to and binding on all human beings without regard to theologico-scriptural commitments.

During this period moderate natural law philosophers like Nathaniel Culverwell and Richard Cumberland wrote. It was also the moment when Richard Hooker's books became the authority to which Locke testified when he appealed to "the judicious Hooker" as nearly conclusive support for any position he could attribute to his sixteenth-century predecessor. Most important, however, was the tremendous intellectual power that the Dutch political philosopher Hugo Grotius came to exercise over the English political mind in the latter half of the century. The Whig tendency in thought crystallized at this time, and almost all Whig thought from the Exclusion Crisis through the Glorious Revolution and beyond bears the unmistakable imprint of the Dutchman's new version of natural law. Grotius developed his much reformed natural law in a Dutch context remarkably similar to that in which the English found themselves—in the wake of a period of intense and violent political and religious conflict between different varieties of Protestants. His conclusions, moreover, cohered nicely with tendencies long present in English parliamentary and anti-absolutist traditions. Grotius seems almost to have been conjured up for the occasion.

Contrary to what is sometimes said, the chief Whig writings in defense of the Glorious Revolution bore little resemblance to Locke or to the Americans' Lockean Declaration of Independence, but instead played on themes from Grotius. Grotius was the philosopher of the Whigs—a philosopher of uncommon originality, depth, and subtlety. He was not, as is sometimes said, the founder of the modern natural law or natural rights philosophy, but he introduced major changes into the existing doctrines. He broke substantially free from the revived Thomism of the late sixteenth and early seventeenth centuries as developed by Counter-Reformation thinkers like Francisco Suárez and Roberto Bellarmine. He went back to the well, to the original sources of natural law—the Roman law and the Stoics—in order to assemble an altogether new natural law doctrine. Ultimately, however, even more important than these sources for Grotius was Aristotle. His achievement could well be described as a synthesis of the philosophy of law implicit in Roman law and Aristotelian moral philosophy, in place of the Thomist synthesis of Aristotle and Christianity. The acceptance of Grotius among the Whigs thus signalled a partial restoration of the authority of Aristotle—an Aristotle much modified, it must be said, but Aristotle nonetheless.

By the late seventeenth century the fate of pre-Reformation Christian Aristotelianism was settled. Protestantism had served as a cyclotron, barraging the older synthesis with high-energy particles that split it into its constituent parts. Without being too schematic, we can identify four different patterns of successor doctrines. The Thomist synthesis did not come entirely apart; in the marvelous prose of Richard Hooker and the writings of many lesser lights who followed him, the main outlines of the Christian Aristotelianism developed before the Reformation remain discernible, although revised to meet the needs of the new context.

Popular as Hooker was, however, the more powerful currents of the day reveal the disruptive effect of the Reformation onslaught. The pre–Civil War era was dominated by modes of political thought that retained allegiance to one side of the synthesis, Christianity as understood in the Reformation, but more or less jettisoned the other side, Aristotle. The post-Restoration era was dominated by the obverse phenomenon. In Whig Grotianism we see the development of a new purified Aristotelianism, more or less freed from, although not hostile to, Protestant Christianity in its main forms.

Finally, to complete the set, there emerged new forms of political philosophy—Hobbes is the clearest case—that rejected both sides of the old Christian Aristotelianism. Hobbes' work was not the only form of this new or modernist thought, however. Pufendorf, in part, and Locke, altogether, shared with Hobbes the aspiration for a political philosophy neither Christian nor Aristotelian in character, although both also broke with Hobbes in many and important ways. In Locke's case this meant the development of a new liberal theory of political society that was constitutionalist, like the English Grotian Whigs', but differed importantly from Hobbes in its foundational theory of natural right. That difference is captured in Locke's most central teaching: all right is understood by him as property, and property is understood as natural. In both respects he diverged from Hobbes, and the differences allowed Locke's thought to become the basis for the new republicanism.

Locke differed not only from Hobbes, but from Grotius as well; although the Whigs of the late seventeenth century were mostly Grotian, and although Locke was also a Whig, Locke was not a Grotian. Indeed, his political philosophy emerges largely as a critique of Grotius, not least of Grotius's Aristotelianism. From Locke's early unpublished writings on natural law to his mature *Essay* and *Two Treatises*, Locke polemicized against the most characteristic features of Grotian natural law doctrine: the Grotian ontology that found a genuine natural law independent of all divine grounding, and the Grotian epistemology that found in the *consensus gentium* a source of knowledge of the natural law.

By the mid-eighteenth century, Grotius had been displaced by John Locke as the master of Whig thought. Nonetheless, Grotius remains an important figure, not only because he developed a philosophy of inherent interest and strength that shaped Whig thinking in the later seventeenth century but because, albeit unwittingly, he proved to be the vehicle for the further transformation of the Whig tradition by Locke. Despite the great differences between them, there were thematic similarities that made the transition from Grotius to Locke plausible if not inevitable. The greatest similarity—and the greatest difference—concerned the issue of rights. Grotius's new natural law had as one of its chief features the narrowing of natural law to the sphere of rights, and in this Locke followed him. Nonetheless, their respective understandings of rights are almost altogether different, and result in great practical differences. Paradoxically, Grotius is a rights-thinker because he attempts to adapt Aristotle to the seventeenth century situation; Locke is a rights-thinker because he breaks with Aristotle in order to respond to the seventeenth century situation.

Locke's new rights theory laid the foundation for the new republicanism, which in turn became one vehicle by which Lockean political phlosophy was disseminated. Locke did not develop the new republicanism himself, nor was it developed from materials supplied exclusively by him. He provided some of the valuable "raw materials," but others came from the pre-Lockean Whig tradition.

The seventeenth-century Whigs largely followed Grotius on the issues of political philosophy proper—natural law and natural right, political obligation, and the like. Their contractarianism was also Grotian in character. In addition to the Grotian political philosophy, however, a distinctive mode of Whig political analysis emerged. The Whigs discovered, in effect, the informal constitution, and the political dynamics that could subvert the constitution even as it was being formally honored. In this Whig political science one finds many of the themes the advocates of the civic republican thesis emphasize in their construing of the political thought of the era. They rightly emphasize these themes, because the new republicanism does partly form around them. The writers who, more than any others, put together the new synthesis that is the new republicanism were John Trenchard and Thomas Gordon, writing in the early eighteenth century as "Cato." The sponsors of the classical republican approach single out Cato for much of their attention, but mistakenly present him as an anti-Lockean. This is the opposite of the truth: Cato was a source from whom both the English and the Americans of the eighteenth century learned Lockean politics. Cato's creators are important because they built the new republicanism on the foundation supplied by Locke but incorporated in their work the older Whig political science. Trenchard and Gordon thus fused into a coherent whole two lines of thought which had proceeded in partial independence of each other previously—Whig political science and Lockean political philosophy.

The two lines of thought Cato fused together to make up the new republicanism correspond roughly to the "competing" traditions (liberal-contractarian and republican) on which recent scholars have focused in their debates over American origins. These were not so much competing traditions, even in their pre-Cato manifestations, as modes of political analysis proceeding at different levels and addressing different questions. Cato's successful synthesis proves that our contemporary scholars are quite mistaken in seeing the "America problem" in terms of an either/or. It was not.

As the American origins begin to come into focus, so does something of the modernity problem as well. America was not "founded in the dread of modernity," as one of the civic-republican historians puts it, but founded in the embrace of modernity. This modernity was neither classical nor Christian, but, as developed by Locke and Cato, it was able to make peace at some level with those elements of both traditions that had been taken almost for granted before being dislodged by the Reformation. Setting the new republicanism into the context of the seventeenth century from which it emerged helps make more intelligible not only the inner character of political modernity but also the process by which it came to power.

This book, in other words, is meant not only to elucidate something of the character and value of modernity through the analysis of Locke's political philosophy in relation to his predecessors', but also to contribute to the woefully underexplained story of how such a major reorientation of thought might have come about. In this story, Grotius, as the link between Locke and the past, and Cato, as the link between Locke and the future, play especially important parts.

Natural Rights
and the New Republicanism

GOVERNMENT, says the American Declaration of Independence, is an artifice, a made thing. A thing is properly made when its making is governed by the end or purpose it is to serve. In the realm of artifice, end or purpose dominates. In the realm of political artifice described by the Declaration, the dominating end is the securing of rights: " . . . in order to secure these rights governments are instituted among men." Important as other ideas in the Declaration may be—equality, consent, revolution—rights are thus simply central.

Although the Declaration declares government an artifice made by human beings, that is not at all the case with rights, for they are said to derive from the Creator. Rights thus precede government and result from no human making. Hence, rights are more fundamental than government in the double sense of being more original and of being the end or purpose of government.

The Declaration appears to present its chief claims, including its claims about rights, as "self-evident truths." Nevertheless, it was as obvious to the drafters of the Declaration as it is to us that not all human beings understand government as they did—as an artifice in the service of rights-protecting. One very famous example of which they were much aware was the divine right theory, which most certainly denied that government was a human artifice. Not rights, but government itself derived from the Creator. According to such theories, what were primordially given were not the rights of the people but the rights of rulers and the duties of the people.[1] Those who understood politics in terms of such theories therefore knew nothing of government as a thing made for the sake of securing rights and thus did not place rights at the center of their political thinking.

The origin of the rights-thinking articulated in the Declaration surely predated the American founding, but scholars disagree over its precise origin. Some place it as far back as the Roman law or the medieval conciliarists, while others find seventeenth-century sources like the Levellers, Grotius, Hobbes, or Locke to be more likely.[2] Knowledge of the exact origin of the rights philosophy is hardly necessary for our present purposes, however: it is certain the Americans did not discover it but took it over from preexisting sources.

Nevertheless, they clearly did have a distinct awareness of themselves as innovators. In *The Federalist*, for example, James Madison observed that the Americans had accomplished "a revolution which has no parallels in the annals of human society." And, he implied, they were about to innovate even more dramatically in the new constitution they were debating.[3] Yet more authoritatively, the Americans accepted as one of the official mottoes of the nation the phrase "novus ordo seclorum"—a new order for the ages.[4] The novel, the unprecedented, the unparalleled character of their tasks and accomplishments—this theme ran all through the founding era and well into the nineteenth century.[5] Joel Barlow proclaimed that "a new task, entirely unknown to the legislators of other nations, was imposed upon the Fathers of the American empire."[6] John Adams specified the character of that novelty with particular clarity: "The United States of America have exhibited perhaps the finest examples of government directed on the simple principles of nature." Therefore, he believed the American Revolution ought to be considered "as an era in their history" by all human beings in the future.[7] The American Revolution, according to Thomas Jefferson in his very last written statement, was to be "the signal of arousing men to burst the chains under which monkish ignorance and superstition had persuaded them to bind themselves"; because "all eyes are opened or opening to the rights of man" they will replace ignorance and superstition with "the blessings and security of liberty and free government."[8] Therein, said the founders, lies the great novelty and power of the American experiment: the regime based on nature, the regime ordered to natural rights.

Two Revolutions, Two Declarations

Not the discovery of, but the first attempt at, large-scale implementation of a rights-based politics was the chief novelty of the Americans' political actions, and the source of their other great innovations as well, including their new republicanism. Setting a new task for politics, they could not follow ways already taken by others; no existing political orders could be a model for them. "History," concluded Thomas Jefferson, "only informs us what bad government is."[9] The new end not only set new tasks but opened new possibilities for politics.

Yet the degree and character of that novelty are frequently obscured. J. G. A. Pocock claims America was founded in a "dread of modernity"; Gordon Wood says the Americans were devoted to "classical"—that is, very old—political ideals. The novelty of the revolution has been obscured not only by scholars but from the Americans themselves. The American Revolution has often been seen not so much as a novel phenomenon but as the third in a series of revolutions following on and to some degree continuing the English Revolution of the 1640s and the Glorious Revolution of 1688–89.[10] In that light, the American principles are seen as carryovers of British political ideas. The natural rights philosophy presented in the Declaration was, says historian Paul Conkin, but an "elliptical summary of a well-developed tradition, one that was rooted in both classical and Christian moral theory and was refined in the modern period by a series of legal and moral theorists. . . . No position in Locke's political writing"—and thus nothing that is Lockean in the Declaration—"was not already accepted, even eloquently defended, by Puritans who came to New England long before Locke wrote his treatises."[11]

The Americans themselves provided testimony to the continuity thesis, and thus against their own consciousness of their novelty, in the label they frequently gave themselves—Whigs. By taking this name they meant to identify with those who had made the Glorious Revolution and their political successors. The Glorious Revolution of 1688–89 was indeed glorious; almost miraculously it paved the way for an end to a long period of extensive political instability—not only a civil war, but intense conflict between kings and parliaments, threatened invasions from abroad, violent conflicts over the succession to the throne, and a persistent inability to peacefully settle the religious question. From being one of Europe's most turbulent countries during the seventeenth century, Britain went on to become celebrated for its stability.[12] The revolution settlement, Lois Schwoerer has said, provided the means for resolving "some of the basic constitutional and political issues of the seventeenth-century English history."[13] Or, as John Toland, the late seventeenth-century admirer of Locke and editor of Harrington and Milton, stated, the Glorious Revolution "settled the monarchy for the future . . . under such wise regulations as are most likely to continue it forever."[14]

Not too long ago, a generally accepted story about the Glorious Revolution went something like this: The revolution was inspired by, and was mostly understood in terms of, conceptions of politics that found classical expression in John Locke's *Two Treatises of Government*. And since the chief ideas in Locke's book are the chief ideas of the American Declaration of Independence, then, the old story went, the political understandings animating the two revolutions were much the same.[15] Like many old and comforting stories, however, this one is untenable. Despite the fact that the principles of the Glorious Revolution were contained in documents whose very names contribute to the idea that the Americans were following in the wake of their English predecessors, the Americans differed from them in their clear commitment to the idea of rights.[16] The Convention Parliament that offered the throne to Prince William of Orange and his wife, Mary, issued a Declaration of Rights in 1689, a document somewhat analogous to the American Declaration of Independence. A few months later, king and Parliament adopted a yet more official, more legal version, the Bill of Rights. Contrary to what their names might imply, however, the English Declaration and Bill of Rights not only lacked the Declaration of Independence's central focus on natural rights, they equally lacked the other ideas associated with the rights theory in the American document. The chasm between the American and the British documents can readily be seen by considering the five chief doctrines of the Declaration of Independence: (1) equality; (2) government as artifact; (3) natural rights as the foundation and end of politics; (4) consent; (5) the right of revolution.

In addition to differences on these specific doctrines, the English and American documents have an almost entirely different overall character. Surely the most prominent feature of the American Declaration is the theoretical discussion beginning, "We hold these truths to be self-evident." The English documents have no analogous presentation of the theory on which they are based. Indeed, the question arises regularly whether or not there is any discernible theory implicit in the Glorious Revolution or its justifying documents.[17] The theoretical austerity of the English statements resulted in large part from the peculiar alliance of Whigs and Tories that came together to make the Glorious Revolution. Here was a classic case of diverse groups agreeing (more or less) on what to do but unable to agree on why. In her thorough study *The Declaration of Rights*, Schwoerer shows in great detail the process by which specific claims of a more theoretical sort, which Whig and Tory politicians sought to include in the document, were carefully compromised and often excised. "The result," says H. T. Dickinson, "was a political compromise which was unintended, but surprisingly successful."[18] Another result, however, is that it becomes very difficult to discern the underlying theoretical rationale for the action they were taking.

Revolution

Nowhere is that difficulty more evident than on the crucial issue of the "revolutionary" character of the action being justified. In the Declaration of Independence the Americans were unequivocal in affirming a universal right in all peoples "to alter or abolish" governments that failed to accomplish the ends for which government was established. Quite different was the Declaration of Rights, in which King James is said to have "abdicated the government," the throne being "thereby vacant." Not only do the English pointedly fail to endorse a right in the nation "to alter or abolish" the government, insisting instead on the patently fictitious idea of a quasi-voluntary abdication by the king, but they fail even to specify wherein that abdication occurred.[19]

Given the organization of the document, one might be tempted to conclude that the abdication was a consequence of James's alleged abuses of power, which are listed just prior to the assertion that he had abdicated. That long list of actions, introduced as evidence of an "endeavor to subvert and extirpate the Protestant religion and the laws and liberties of the king-dom," is said to stand "utterly and directly contrary to the known laws and statutes and freedoms of this realm." The juxtaposition of the list of abuses and the assertion of abdication might imply, then, that the abdication con-sisted precisely in the commission of these great illegal acts.[20] If so, that might amount to something like the positing of a right of revolution—that political power is held on condition of conformity to "the known laws and statutes and freedoms of this realm" and that the people have a right to call the king to account if that condition is violated.

That conclusion, in its generality, might appear to be a rough equivalent of the affirmation made in the Declaration of Independence of a right of revolution. Yet it differs in at least two important respects: The American doctrine makes the "right of revolution" conditional on the people's judg-ment of the security of their rights, whereas the English doctrine would take its bearings by the more conservative standard of how the King's actions conform to the established laws and liberties of the kingdom. What has been historically established, rather than what is naturally right—that repre-sents the outer edge of a potential "theory of revolution" in the Declaration of Rights.[21] Moreover, the American doctrine applies not only against kings but against any governmental authorities, including an elected legislature.[22]

Yet one hesitates to infer even this much of a theory from the Declaration of Rights, for the abdication claim is not presented as a conclusion from the abuses but as a separate item. The illegalities are introduced with one "whereas" and the abdication with another, presenting the two as parallel and more or less independent facts, the one relevant to the reaffirmation of rights about to be presented and the other to the new settlement of the throne to be established thereafter. "It was never explicitly stated that James II had been deposed because of his actions."[23] As Schwoerer shows, this ambiguity and uncertainty of meaning was surely deliberate—a care-fully contrived effort to neither endorse nor deny various Whig and Tory theses about legitimate government.[24]

The Declaration of Rights not only fails to endorse a general right of revolution, it fails even to admit that the Glorious Revolution was a revolu-tion. Perhaps that event should have been known to history as "The Glori-ous Abdication." It is no surprise that the Declaration of Rights was hesitant to endorse a right of revolution or unequivocally to identify 1688 as a revolu-tion. As a rule, political societies are hesitant to admit such a right. It can be very unsettling, for it counters the old view that authority must be secure in order to be effective. The Americans, with their clear affirmation of a right of revolution, introduced a certain novelty. They were willing to take a chance with this disruptive principle, and to encourage a judgmental and adversarial attitude by the people toward their government. It constitutes no small part of the American *novus ordo seclorum*.

Equality

The first of the Declaration of Independence's "self-evident truths" and the most ringing of its political principles is the claim that "all men are created equal." This clause has been a potent touchstone in American political life. Many, if not all, of the major issues of American politics have been discussed in its terms—republicanism, abolitionism, trade unionism, civil rights, to name a few. At the same time, this clause has, been very controversial. No great consensus exists on what it means or in what respect equality may be true. But whatever the Americans meant in their Declaration it is certain the English did not mean the same. In place of "all men," the Declaration of Rights speaks of "all the estates of the people of the realm," that is, "the lords spiritual and temporal and commons." If there be a more fundamental and natural human equality, the authors of the Declaration of Rights felt no need to appeal to it. The unequal orders, or estates, of the people of the realm were the ultimate political reality to which they referred. Likewise, when they declared William and Mary king and queen, they did not speak of the nation as a sovereign body of naturally equal human beings, but again invoked the three estates. The relevant elements of political society are the differentiated and hierarchically ordered existing elements of English society cum polity.[25]

The inequality of human beings in the estates pervades the document. One particularly striking example appears in the item affirming the right to bear arms. Unlike the Second Amendment to the United States Constitution, which recognizes a general right to bear arms, the Declaration of Rights carefully limits that right to Protestants, and allows them arms only "suitable to their conditions and as allowed by law." These latter qualifications on the right refer to well-established distinctions: no one with an income under 100 pounds a year could have a gun.[26] Just as the Declaration of Rights did not contemplate natural equality, neither did it take equality of rights for granted. Rights could and did vary with one's position in the polity. Again, the Declaration of Independence puts things very differently: the rights it recognizes are possessed by "all men"; there is no shadow of an idea that rights derive from or vary according to class membership.

The Declaration of Independence is emphatic about human equality, but, because it expresses itself so concisely, the text of the Declaration is not clear on what it means by equality. Nonetheless, the structure of the text elucidates what the bare words leave obscure. The Declaration presents an idealized historical sketch of human political history. First it speaks of an original human situation: how human beings are when created—equal—and what they have from their Creator—inalienable rights. Then the Declaration speaks of the formation of government: why government is formed—in order to secure rights—and how it is formed—by the consent of the governed. Then it speaks of what happens if government goes astray: there is a right to alter or abolish it and a right to remake it. That is, the "self-evident truths" of the Declaration are not six separate points, they are interconnected parts of one narrative.

The assertion of equality comes in the section on the original human situation. That original situation precedes the existence of government. Indeed, that is what equality means: originally, or by nature, human beings are not governed, they are not subjected to the rule or authority of any other human beings. Government, in other words, is not natural, but something that human beings make. Originally, all men are equal, because none is subordinated by nature or God to another. The Declaration does not deny that there are all sorts of inequalities among human beings, but it does deny that any of these implies a right to rule. This was a very explosive claim, for most political societies proceeded on the explicit or implicit idea that God or nature had selected "the better sort" to rule; society rested on the acceptance of the propriety of "natural" rulers ruling. This is clearly the assumption of the Declaration of Rights. There the natural condition, or the relevant condition for politics, is the division of the nation into classes—lords, commons, etc.—with degree and rank order to which have been attached claims to shares in political power.

The claim about natural equality can be restated in terms of the language used by political philosophers of the age: originally human beings exist in a state of nature. A state of nature is a state where no one has rightful authority over others. This perhaps comes out more clearly in a parallel statement in the Massachusetts Bill of Rights, where it is affirmed that men are by nature equal and independent, meaning not dependent or subordinate to others.

Artifact

The Declaration of Independence takes up the issue of equality as part of its effort to explore the primeval human condition, the condition prior to established government and prior to all humanly established laws and rights. The Declaration of Rights betrays no such eagerness to uncover what pre-exists the established order; it merely attempts to discern and reassert the principles of that order. The Declaration of Rights thus contains no suggestion whatever that government is of human making. So silent is it on this question that Tory and Anglican adherents of divine right theories of politics were able to endorse the Declaration.[27]

They could never have endorsed the Declaration of Independence. Here it is very clear that government is an artifact made by human beings for their own purposes. Neither God nor nature makes government—human beings do. That means that government is like many things that people make. It can be better or worse made depending on how well the art of making is understood. This is one point of Thomas Jefferson's letter to Roger Weightman, and indeed a dominant thought in the whole founding generation: people have recently come to understand much better than ever before why and how to make governments, and therefore they can expect great improvements in their political life. Here is one origin of the frequently noted progressive attitude toward politics and society in America. Society and polity are human constructs, and as such can be made better and better. On the other hand, if political life is understood as derived from God or nature, that suggests a limit to what can be done with it. It is what it is and what it should be. One must accept it with its limits; one must take a conservative attitude towards it.

Consent

The American Declaration of Independence sees government as an artifact because it denies the naturalness of political power. How, then, does political authority come to be? The answer is simple: by "consent of the governed." When the Declaration speaks of an origin in consent, it does not necessarily mean an actual historical process; rather it refers to a kind of moral account of the origin, or, perhaps better put, a rational reconstruction of the origin. Once one understands nature properly, once one understands that neither nature nor God designates rulers or makes a government, then it is clear that humans must do it through consent—voluntarily and purposefully—with some end in view. This is not so much a thesis about the past as a vision of the present and the future; it presents a way to reconceive the nature of politics and the relationship of citizens to it.

To say that political power derives from consent of the governed is to say, in the language of political philosophers, that government derives from a "social contract." It is also to say that beneath all political institutions lies popular sovereignty. The doctrine of consent is more about popular sovereignty, about the people as the ultimate locus and source of political authority, than it is about democratic governance.

The English Declaration of Rights, on the other hand, does not see government as an artifact and therefore is not concerned with the means of making it. Thus it contains no language regarding "consent of the governed." The Declaration of Rights specifies that certain powers of government (for example, the tax power) must be exercised with the consent of the governed—or at least of some of them, those represented in Parliament. But it contains nothing of the idea that Parliament derives its powers, is constituted, via consent. That is, the Declaration of Rights does not endorse the doctrine of popular sovereignty that the Declaration of Independence asserts in its affirmation of the principle of consent.

Rights

More significant, however, than any of the other differences between the English and American documents is the difference regarding rights. The Americans appeal to rights that are bestowed by the Creator—God or nature—altogether prior to and independent of any organized political life. On the other hand, the rights declared in the Declaration of Rights can in no way be described as natural. They are, instead, "ancient rights and liberties" defined in "the known laws and statutes and freedoms of this realm." The English rights are very old, but they are not natural; they derive from "the laws . . . of this realm" and therefore belong only to the subjects of "this realm" and not to all human beings. Furthermore, they belong to those subjects according to their place in the realm, that is, according to their "condition." The rights are restricted therefore in a double sense: they are English rather than human rights, and they belong to the English differentially and unequally.[28]

Moreover, the rights in the Declaration of Rights hardly share more than the name with the rights in the Declaration of Independence. For one thing, compared to the sleek economy of the Americans' Declaration, the English list of rights is a veritable hodgepodge. It lacks the compactness and logical interconnectedness of "life, liberty, and the pursuit of happiness."[29] It seems almost a miscellaneous assemblage with no obvious principle of selection or connection. In many cases, it is not even clear what the right being declared is, or who its possessor is. Some of the rights are best described as powers of, or restrictions on, political actors. One of the "rights," for example, is the king's lack of the right of "dispensing with laws . . . by regal authority." Another affirms the right of Parliament to "authorize levies of money." Neither these nor many other rights affirmed in the document are tied to rights of individuals. Not all the rights in the Declaration of Rights even appear to be rights in the sense in which the Declaration of Independence uses that term. For example, the last of the list says that "for redress of all grievances and for the amending, strengthening and preserving of the laws Parliament ought to be held frequently." This is not so much a statement of a right belonging to anybody, not even to Parliament, as much as a declaration of a desirable state of affairs—frequent Parliaments. It is a right in the sense of "a right thing."[30]

By contrast, all the natural rights enumerated in the American Declaration are rights belonging to individuals, and all are rights in a different and quite specific sense. They are not expressions of a desirable (a "right") condition or state of affairs; they are rights that each individual can claim as his or her own—possessions to be deployed, options to be exercised at the choice of the rights-holder, rights in a permissive sense; active rights. The natural lawyers of the day defined right, according to its "strict meaning," as "a certain moral power which every man has, either over his own things, or over things due to him," and the Declaration uses the term in that sense.[31] An example might make the difference clearer. The right of free speech means that the right-holder has the option to exercise it; the right is permissive, but not obligatory. Right in the other sense would imply an obligation rather than a permission to speak. The difference is captured most commonsensically perhaps in the distinction between "rights" and "what is right." The American Declaration speaks exclusively of the former, the English Declaration speaks at least some of the time of the latter.

Most significantly, the Declaration of Rights fails to affirm the central point in the Declaration of Independence's theory of government: there is no suggestion that government exists for the sake of securing rights and only for that. Obviously, rights of the sort declared there are important, but they are not the very raison d'être of political life. Since they do not predate but derive from political life, there is no question of government's coming to exist for their sake. Rights are conditions or limits or even means of rule; they do not stand as the purpose of governance.

The difference between the conceptions of governance in the Declaration of Rights and the Declaration of Independence stands out even more clearly in the light of Schwoerer's observation that despite the claim in the former document that "all and singular rights and liberties asserted . . . are the true, ancient and indubitable rights and liberties of the kingdom," yet many of the rights lack such a clear pedigree. She concluded that more than half the rights were not, in the form declared, ancient rights at all. Parliament adopted the "time honored device" in English legal history of describing the new as the old.[32] True as that may be, it remains significant that the rights are described as "ancient and indubitable" rather than as natural. That the Declaration of Rights denominates new rights as old ones only goes to underline how distant from any doctrine of natural rights the theory of the document is. The only kinds of rights it knows of or can recognize as legitimate are historical and constitutional, not natural rights.

All the other differences that have come to light between the theories of 1689 and those of 1776 derive ultimately from their differences on this central issue of rights. Government as artifact, consent as the means of instituting and controlling legitimate political power, natural equality, and a genuine right of revolution all derive from the Americans' appeal to rights altogether prior to and independent of any organized political life. To the English, if rights are neither inalienable nor derived from nature, it follows that there is no natural right of revolution. Whether any right to resist was granted in the English version would seem to depend on the positive—and variable—content of the historical rights.[33]

Tracing rights back to a legal rather than a natural foundation, the theory of the Declaration of Rights can have no real place for a prepolitical condition.[34] On the other hand, the commitment to natural rights has everything to do with the positing of a prepolitical situation in the Declaration of Independence. If political society were a natural growth, as Aristotle had it, then the political community itself would have a natural status supervenient over, or at least rival to, the individual and his or her rights; moreover, political life under the Aristotelian conception serves a natural end that comes into sight only in the fully developed polity. Even if government in some sense naturally emerges, according to the doctrine of the Declaration its "just powers" derive only from rational consent of the governed—that is, consent to rule in the service of rights-securing. Only a rational making, not a natural growth, can produce a just or proper government. Government must therefore be a human artifice. If an artifice, then there must be a (theoretical) prepolitical situation in which and out of which the political arises. Thus the idea of government as artifice, too, is ultimately subordinate to the commitment to rights-securing.

To summarize: The rights and liberties in the English Declaration of Rights are not tied to God or nature as their source; rather they are "ancient rights and liberties"; they belong not to all human beings but "to the people of this kingdom" as arrayed in their "estates" and "suitable to their conditions." They set limits on the royal power, but their protection is not said to be the very purpose of government. The rights mentioned are not the grand human rights of "life, liberty, and pursuit of happiness," but rather, for the most part, claims that the king may not take certain actions without the authorization of Parliament. The place of rights in the Declaration of Rights shows it to have been an important document in the rise of constitutional government, but it does not express the same understanding of the nature and purposes of government as the Declaration of Independence does. It could not produce, as the natural rights philosophy was to do, the new republicanism.

Thus, the old story of a direct line of descent from the English revolutionaries of 1688–89 to the American revolutionaries of 1776 does not survive a comparison of the two declarations. "The public and authorized theory of what had occurred in 1688–89," concluded J. G. A. Pocock, "that [theory] on which the houses of the convention parliament had been able to agree and which was contained in the public documents of the time—really did base its interpretation on the doctrine of the ancient constitution, more than on the doctrines of contract, natural right and reason propounded by Sidney or Locke" (or, we might add, by the American Declaration of Independence).[35]

The revolutionaries of '88 and '76 acted out of quite different conceptions of politics and, not surprisingly, produced quite different postrevolutionary regimes. The English, in their account of things, conducted a revolution in the original sense—the restoration of an older order that had been disrupted. They reaffirmed their "ancient rights and liberties." The Americans, on the other hand, neither shrank from novelty nor feared innovation. Was not their glory, James Madison asked, precisely their willingness to innovate?[36] The most obvious explanation for the conservative character of 1688 is ready at hand: The Glorious Revolution was so glorious precisely because nearly the entire political nation was able to converge on the deed and to subscribe to the word, the Declaration of Rights, which more or less described and justified it. Controversial theories were not welcome.

CONTRACT AND THE DECLARATION OF RIGHTS

Contractarian ideas much closer to those that ultimately made their way into the Declaration of Independence did put in an appearance at the Convention Parliament as it drafted the Declaration of Rights. Their fate reveals the ambiguous status of such ideas at that time and place. The idea of an original contract was introduced into the debates by Sir Robert Howard: "The constitution of our government is actually grounded upon pact and covenant with the people," he asserted. Those who adhered to the idea of an original contract seemed to have in mind the theory that James's violation of it was the basis for his no longer occupying the throne; his misdeeds had produced a "forfeiture" of his right to rule. Not all members of the convention agreed with the forfeiture theory, however, and some who might have were clearly pleased to find in the abdication theory a way to avoid the issue altogether. At one point, the House adopted a resolution declaring the throne vacant—a resolution whose Delphic opacity probably reflects the lack of consensus on the contract issue:

> Resolved, that King James the II, having endeavoured to subvert the constitution of this Kingdom, by breaking the original contract between King and People; and by the Advice of Jesuits and other wicked persons, having violated the Fundamental laws, and having withdrawn himself out of this Kingdom, has abdicated the government, and that the throne is thereby vacant.

The grammar and structure of the resolution defy any simple analysis—only master legal minds could draft such a text—so that it remains difficult at best to ascertain the contribution the violation of the "contract" made to the throne's becoming vacant. Although the language of original contract does appear explicitly—a clear victory for the partisans of the concept—nothing explicit regarding a forfeiture resulting therefrom appears—a victory for those who had reservations about the idea.

After an even more hesitant debate in the House of Lords, the Commons resolution was accepted by the upper house. But the most revealing fact about the original contract was yet to come: despite both houses' adoption of resolutions with (ambiguous) contractarian language in them, the documents of greatest importance, the Declaration and Bill of Rights, dropped all such language.

No contractarian language appeared because the politically dominant elements of the nation were not united in a willingness to understand or publicly describe their politics in that way, nor to commit themselves to the grounds and implications of that view. Schwoerer believes that even though no explicit contractarian language appears, nonetheless Parliament "in subtle ways of organization and language in the document, implied that a contract had been broken."[37] The evidence on this point, in my opinion, is much less clear than she finds it, as I have already indicated in my earlier discussion of the "theory of revolution" of the Declaration of Rights.

Moreover, the Declaration of Rights itself "was not, as sometimes alleged, presented to [William and Mary] as a condition they had to accept before receiving the crown." That is, not only did the Declaration of Rights drop all reference to the "original contract" but it was not itself treated as a contract with the new rulers.[38]

At the key moment, therefore, the English retreated from contract. Ideas of contract were perhaps feared to be too radical, too chimerical, too unsettling of political stability and, perhaps, of social and economic arrangements as well. These hesitations about contractarianism came amid memories of the 1640s, when contract ideas were prominently used in the Civil War, in the regicide, and in Leveller proposals for a new political order. Many opponents of the king in 1688 found themselves walking the narrow line between absolutism and disorder. The political principles that might stave off the one threatened to bring along with them the other. This hesitation in England partially accounts for the novelty of the Americans' political action in the eighteenth century: the Americans did not discover the natural rights/social contract theory adumbrated in the Declaration of Independence; but they were the first to embrace it as the official basis of their most solemn and lasting political actions. Where the English feared to tread, the Americans rushed in.

LOCKE AND THE TWO REVOLUTIONS

One part of the old story, then, is surely false: the American revolutionaries did not understand politics in the same way the English revolutionaries of the preceding century did. That old story contained as a central character a thinker who stood as a connecting link between the English and the Americans—John Locke. But if the two ends of this alleged chain do not belong together, what about Locke? Does he belong with either the English or the American revolutionaries? As a historical matter, of course, Locke supported the events of 1688–89. In self-imposed exile in Holland when the revolution began, Locke returned to England with the soon-to-be Queen Mary. More significantly, he soon published his *Two Treatises of Government*, a work intended, according to its preface, "to establish the throne of our great restorer, our present King William, to make good his title."[39]

Despite his support for the Glorious Revolution, Locke's political doctrine shares almost nothing with the official theory of the "revolution" set forth in the Declaration of Rights, but instead contains all the defining doctrines of the American Declaration of Independence. Locke not only accepts the doctrine of equality, but expresses it in the *Two Treatises* in language nearly identical to the Declaration of Independence and related American documents. Human beings, he says, are "naturally in . . . a state . . . of equality, wherein all the power and jurisdiction is reciprocal, no one having more than another" (II 4). Equality is the natural or original condition of human beings, the condition prior to the institution of civil government, for it is what must be first understood in order "to understand political power right" (II 4). Human beings are equal with respect to "power" or "jurisdiction," that is, with regard to authority over one another (just as in the Declaration) but not with regard to other matters. As Locke explains at greater length, by natural equality he

> cannot be supposed to understand all sorts of equality: age or virtue may give men a just precedency: excellency of parts and merit may place others above the common level: birth may subject some, and alliance or benefits others, to pay an observance to those to whom nature, gratitude, or other respects may have made it due. (II 54)

These various human inequalities may imply inequalities of one sort or another in relations among persons, but these inequalities never extend to "jurisdiction or dominion over one another" but merely to "precedency" or "observances." Natural equality is thus nothing but "that equal right that every man hath to his natural freedom, without being subjected to the will or authority of any other man" (II 54).

Natural equality and natural liberty are almost identical. Human beings are naturally equal in their original freedom; their natural freedom implies their original equality. Such is precisely the thought contained in the Declaration as it stands, and more explicitly in Jefferson's original draft: "that all men are created equal and independent."[40] John Adams's Massachusetts constitution closely echoed this language: "all men are born free and equal" (Adams had been on the committee to which Jefferson had submitted his draft). The Virginia Bill of Rights puts it similarly: "that all men are by nature equally free and independent." Locke in several places uses language almost identical to these various American formulations: "Men being . . . by Nature, all free, equal, and independent" (II 95; cf. II 6, 7).

Locke's adoption of the view that government is an artifact coheres readily with his understanding of natural equality. The first announced topic of the *Second Treatise* is the "true original" of government in a human making, as opposed to the false original in God or nature, as presented by Filmer. The very structure of the *Two Treatises* reflects the artifactuality of the political. Locke announces as his task the proper identification of "political power," so that "the power of a magistrate over a subject, may be distinguished from that of a father over his children, a master over his servant, a husband over his wife, and a lord over his slave" (II 2). In insisting that these are all "distinct powers," Locke unmistakably echoes the opening of Aristotle's *Politics*, where the uniqueness of the political association is asserted against those who would assimilate the political to familial or despotic relations.[41]

Locke's theme may be the same as Aristotle's, but his method of developing it is entirely different. Rather than showing how nature produces different associations or relations, as Aristotle does, Locke shows that by nature human beings exist in a "state of nature"—that condition of no-rule, no-authority already described under the rubric "equality." Nature provides not the source of the relations, which Locke is concerned with distinguishing from the political, but the benchmark from which those relations depart. The opening chapters of the *Second Treatise* are devoted to the elucidation of how the various relations may justly arise from the original state of nature: lord-slave (chapter 4); master-servant (chapter 5); father (parent)-child (chapter 6); husband-wife (chapter 7); magistrate-subject (chapters 7–8). All these relations are human makings, including in decisive respects the seemingly most natural.[42]

The order of Locke's presentation differs tellingly from Aristotle's. The latter treats first the association between husband and wife, because

> in these matters as elsewhere it is by looking at how things develop naturally from the beginning that one may best study them. First, then, there must of necessity be a conjunction of persons who cannot exist without one another: on the one hand, male and female, for the sake of reproduction (which occurs not from intentional choice but—as is also the case with other animals and plants—from a natural striving to leave behind another that is like oneself).[43]

Locke, on the other hand, places the marital relationship late in his progression because he emphasizes not the naturalness but the increasing artificiality of the relations, or better, their increasing dependence on consent, compact, or conscious making. (cf. II 24, 25, 50, 68–73, 81–82).

In his account of the "true original" of the various relations, Locke presents the rational origin, an origin not always properly understood in human societies. To the degree these fundamental relations are misunderstood, the institutions made via that misunderstanding fall short of the rational order pointed toward by knowledge of the "true original." Because of such misunderstandings, for example, men like Robert Filmer fail to credit the authority of the mother over the child, equal to that of the father (cf. II 52). Locke's "history" of the origin of human relations from out of the state of nature is thus not literal history.[44] It presents, if the expression can be excused, a rationalist mytho-poetic account of the human situation in nature. Like the Declaration's, that account is essentially progressivist in character: nature leaves human beings in a situation much open to improvement through human making in the broadest sense.

Locke moves toward the political relation, and thus toward a relation dependent exclusively on consent. "Men being, as has been shown, by nature, all free, equal and independent, no one can be put out of this estate, and subjected to the political power of another, without his own consent" (II 95; cf. 119). The relevant consent, derivative from the equality of *all* men, is no once-and-for-all thing given by some distant ancestors in a moment primeval.[45] Contrary to the claims of Grotius, Hooker, and other earlier thinkers, Locke emphasizes "that *all* men are naturally in that state" of natural equality "and remain so, till by their own consent they make themselves members of some political society" (II 15; emphasis added).

The rational making of government, according to Locke, occurs for the very same reason the Declaration says it does: "for the securing of men's rights" (II 219; cf. II 124, 127, 131). Locke mostly, but not entirely, renames rights as "property"; he uses the language of rights more or less interchangeably with the language of property. Indeed, in the key place, Locke asserts the dependence of property—in the broad sense of life, liberty, and estate as well as in the narrower sense of property in things of the external world—as "founded upon the right [human beings] have, to make use of those things, that were necessary or useful to [their] being." The foundation is the right of preservation (I 86), or, as in the Declaration, the right to life.

Finally, Locke presents a teaching on resistance or revolution more detailed than, but identical to, that contained in the Declaration. He voices none of the hesitations or limitations characteristic of the English Declaration of Rights. The right belongs to the people as such and can be exercised when they judge that the rulers have "breached their trust" of rights-securing. Like Jefferson, Locke believes that this right cannot and will not be exercised frequently—in Locke's formulation, the people will tolerate "many wrong and inconvenient laws," but will or should react forcefully to "a long train of abuses, prevarications, and artifices, all tending the same way" (II 225). Jefferson incorporated into the Declaration not only the same idea but almost the very language: "when a long train of abuses and usurpations pursuing invariably the same object. . . ."

LOCKE AND THE AMERICANS

Doctrinally and verbally, then, the Declaration and the *Two Treatises* are remarkably alike. It is clear that by the time of the Revolution the American Whigs had adopted the Lockean political philosophy. A recent intellectual fashion, however, has been to challenge the strength or importance of the connection between Locke and the American Whigs, or, in the extreme case, to deny it altogether. The strongest, as well as the least defensible, challenge to the connection was entered by Garry Wills.[46] Wills attempts to dissolve the bonds between Locke and Jefferson and to weave new ones between Jefferson and the Scottish Enlightenment, especially between Jefferson and Francis Hutcheson. He presents evidence of two kinds for his claims—evidence that shows a lack of connection between Jefferson, in particular, and Locke, and more general evidence concerning the status of Locke among the Americans before the revolution.

Wills makes claims about the relationship between Locke and Jefferson so outrageous that many scholars have responded critically and sharply, showing, among other things, that Wills is simply mistaken when he claims there are "no precise verbal parallels" between the Declaration and Locke's *Second Treatise*.[47] Many have scoffed at Wills's suggestion that Jefferson's repeated practice of recommending Locke's *Treatises* as a basic reading in politics to friends and relatives, as well as for the University of Virginia curriculum is no evidence of a "close acquaintance with the text." Perhaps Wills is correct in finding "nothing dishonest" in Jefferson's so highly recommending a book he does not know well and indeed might never even have read; but it seems odd, if not rather foolish, for Jefferson to have done such a thing.[48] It certainly seems more than foolish for Jefferson to have listed Locke among the intellectual progenitors of the Declaration if he either had never read him or disagreed altogether with what he read.[49]

Whether Wills's handling of the parallel issue of the Hutcheson connection betrays more than mere foolishness is a nice question indeed. For while Wills has no difficulty dismissing the evidentiary power of a statement such as Jefferson's that "Locke's little book on Government is perfect as far as it goes," he is entirely undeterred by the fact that Jefferson not only never uttered such praise for Hutcheson but never spoke of Hutcheson at all, never once recommended Hutcheson's books to those who sought guidance on reading in politics and law, never owned Hutcheson's major work, never included Hutcheson (as he did Locke) among those authors who were sources for the Declaration.[50] Wills's Jefferson, in short, is a most odd fellow—he praises highly to all and sundry, he recommends to all who ask him, he attributes decisive influence to a work he has never read at all, or at least not with "attention and profit," and with which the deepest thrust of his thought disagrees, while he neither mentions nor recommends nor attributes any influence to the author whose work is genuinely authoritative for him.[51] Was Hutcheson so valuable that Jefferson wished to keep the Scottish philosopher all for himself?

Wills is no more persuasive in his treatment of Locke's relations to the Americans more generally. Consider his inferences from Lundberg and

May's survey of colonial library holdings.[52] "Copies of the 1714 edition of Locke's work can be found, at some point before 1776," says Wills, "in 23 percent of the known colonial libraries; but the distribution of interest in the different volumes of those works is measured by the fact that separate volumes of the *Treatise(s)* show up in 15 percent of the libraries, while separate copies of the *Essay* were in 41 percent."[53] At best this proves that the *Treatises* were less popular in America than the *Essay*, an entirely unremarkable and irrelevant finding. Even if Wills is correct in his guess about the distribution of interest in the different books contained in Locke's *Works*, the interest in the *Treatises* measured in this way (23 percent) still exceeds the distribution (20 percent) of Hutcheson's *Works* and *System of Moral Philosophy* together. If we tally distribution in a more reasonable way—additively—we find that Locke's *Treatises* appeared in 38 percent of the libraries, more than Sidney's *Discourses* (23 percent), Cato's *Letters* (37 percent), Molesworth's *Account of Denmark* (16 percent), and Hoadley's book on government (7 percent).[54] Moreover, according to the testimony of Lundberg and May, it is doubtful that Hutcheson could have formed part of the "American mind" that Jefferson was "harmonizing" in the Declaration, for the Scottish writers became popular in America only after the revolution.[55]

H. Trevor Colbourn's survey of colonial library holdings produces similar findings. Locke's complete *Works* or a separate edition of the *Treatises* appeared in a full 50 percent of the libraries (thirteen out of twenty-six), slightly more than Sidney's *Discourses*, which appeared on twelve lists, and Cato's *Letters*, which appeared in eleven.[56] Sidney's and Cato's are the only political works that appear in the libraries with anywhere near the frequency of Locke's books.

Wills also relies heavily on the findings of John Dunn about the reception of Locke in eighteenth century America. Dunn's essay itself represents a strong but not so extreme challenge to the received view of Locke's influence on the colonists. Denying neither that the colonists knew Locke's *Treatises* nor that they considered him an important thinker, he argues instead the following theses: (1) Locke's *Two Treatises* were not in fact so popular in America as their reputation would suggest. They did not achieve popular esteem until after 1750, and then largely on the basis of Locke's reputation as the author of the *Essay Concerning Human Understanding* rather than any special understanding or appreciation of the *Treatises*. (2) By the time the *Treatises* became popular "the tradition of political behavior within which the colonists conceived their relationship with England was already highly articulated." Moreover, when the colonists did begin to read Locke, they did so "with gradually consolidated political intentions and they had come to it to gather moral support for these intentions." On top of that, what use the colonists made of Locke was "conceptually uninteresting."

(3) Finally, the *Treatises* present a view of politics by no means unique to Locke. This work was "only one among a large group of other works which expounded the Whig theory of the Revolution.... The readiness with which many scholars have detected the influence of the *Two Treatises* in England and America is at least in part a product of the fact that they have read so little else of the English political writing contemporary with it."[57]

While not going so far as Wills, Dunn does go a good deal farther in minimizing the role of Locke for the American revolutionary generation than the relatively cautious revisionists, such as Clinton Rossiter and Bernard Bailyn, who preceded him. They had suggested that the revolution could not properly be seen as begotten by John Locke alone, but that other thinkers of the dissenting Whig tradition also played a formative part in shaping the Americans' political consciousness. Nonetheless, Rossiter's sober assessment remained that Locke stood "primus inter pares."[58]

It is difficult to repose much more confidence in Dunn's findings than in Wills's, however, for he consistently raises very extensive claims which he fails to support with adequate evidence, and he consistently interprets what evidence he has to tally with what look to be preconceived conclusions.[59] A particularly blatant instance is his conclusion that the *Treatises* came late to popularity, a conclusion based on his own survey of colonial library holdings. "Apart from an isolated copy to be found in [a] library . . . in Virginia in 1701, we do not even know that copies of the *Two Treatises* reached the American colonies before 1724." But we do not know that they did *not* reach the colonies either. Dunn does not make clear how few library lists dating back to 1724 there are—according to Colbourn's survey, only three for the entire thirteen colonies. In most libraries the earliest list is later than that, and just when Locke's work was acquired is usually impossible to determine from the lists we have.[60] Moreover, there is evidence to suggest that the colonists were reading Locke early and seriously. Dunn himself recounts the use of Locke's name and political doctrines in a prominent trial for seditious libel in 1724; in the same year Locke's discussion of property was used in an essay on the relations between the whites and Indians in America; by 1728 an edition with a widespread circulation was abroad in America.[61]

Both Alice Baldwin and Claude Newlin, in their studies of the clergy in America, found that Locke was indeed a "great source," and an early one for the clergy's political understanding. According to Baldwin,

> He was quoted by name as early as 1738, but his influence is to be seen in earlier works. Especially after 1763 the references to him are numerous, not only by the more prominent ministers of the larger towns but by those of country villages as well. And in many works in which no direct reference is made one finds his theories, sometimes his very phrases, and this is true for years before 1761 as well as afterwards.[62]

Baldwin further observes,

> That Locke was frequently read before 1742 seems evident from the following reference in a sermon by Thos. Foxcraft in Boston, 1740. On the title page, quoted from Dr. Watt's *Humble Attempt*, is the following: "You are not to stand up here (in the Pulpit) as a Professor of Ancient or modern philosophy, nor an Usher in the school of Plato, or Seneca, or Mr. Locke."[63]

In 1744 Elisha Williams presented an extensive and very competent summary, with attribution, of Locke's *Second Treatise*. Williams characterized his own thought as "considering things as they be in their own nature, what reason teaches concerning them." In order to present the rational teaching on politics, Williams said, he had "given a short sketch of what the celebrated Mr. Locke in his *Treatise of Government* has largely demonstrated." On these Lockean principles, Williams believed, "it is justly to be presumed all are agreed who understand the natural rights of mankind."[64] This is hardly the sort of thing one would say of a work largely unknown and of little interest. Moreover, when Williams turned to the question of what people must do to free themselves from tyranny, he referred again to Locke. "Here is a minister in 1744 using the very arguments of 1775. . . . Here is clear evidence of the transmission through the clergy of the theories of Locke."[65] Jonathan Mayhew, the liberal New England cleric, wrote that he had been "initiated in youth, in the doctrines of civil liberty, as they were taught by such men . . . as Sidney and Milton, Locke, and Hoadley." Another important colonial who later testified to studying Locke in his "youth" was John Adams.[66]

More recent and more thorough surveys than Dunn's show Locke to have been a much greater presence in colonial America than Dunn or Wills allows. Steven Dworetz "discovered a great many more citations of 'Locke on Government' in the Revolutionary writings, clerical and secular, than of any other non-biblical source." His findings match those of Donald Lutz's massive citation analysis, which found that "Locke, by a very wide margin, was the most frequently cited author in the American political writings" from 1760 to 1775.[67]

Williams, Mayhew, Adams, and other "opinion leaders" like them spread the principles they had learned from Locke to many who themselves never read Locke but who thus indirectly fell under his influence. The issue of indirect influence raises a very difficult problem for attempts like those of Dunn and Wills to read out the impact of a thinker from the distribution of his works and the mentions of his name alone. Although it is difficult to establish quantitatively, there is a great deal of evidence showing a substantial Lockean influence beyond what appears in the direct and explicit references Dunn relied on.

Limiting oneself to explicit citations systematically understates the evidence for the role of Locke in prerevolutionary writings, according to Dworetz. Even outright "plagiarism [from Locke] was not uncommon in the written political polemics of the Revolution: the rules of conventional scholarship simply do not apply under these circumstances." To the extent that this is the case, Dunn's citation-analysis methodology is necessarily flawed. "Counting citations fails to penetrate . . . the relationship between Locke's ideas and Revolutionary theory and practice." In addition to unattributed quotations or very close paraphrases, there are also important "linguistic, theoretical, or doctrinal similarities between a Revolutionary text, and, for instance, Lockean theory that are not accompanied by an explicit citation of 'Locke on Government.'"[68]

In addition to citation-counting, patient and sensitive analysis is needed. Dworetz attempts to supply this kind of supplement to Dunn's methodology through a careful study of clerical writings. That is valuable, of course, but another method has for the most part inspired the present study. I am taking especially serious note of official and quasi-official documents like the Declaration of Independence and the Declaration of Rights, King Charles's *Answer*, and the Virginia Bill of Rights, for these bespeak much more than the idiosyncratic views of one or another thinker. Yet these sorts of texts hardly ever make their theoretical roots explicit and thus especially resist Dunn's method.

Not only is there good reason to question Dunn's claim that Locke enjoyed no early popularity or influence among the Americans, there is also good reason to question his assertion that the *Treatises'* fame was entirely derivative from the greater fame of the *Essay Concerning Human Understanding*. For this claim neither Dunn, nor Wills, who repeats the point, provides any evidence whatever. We may readily concede the stature of Locke's *Essay* in the eighteenth century without necessarily accepting the view that the *Treatises* lived entirely in its shadow. The Americans relied on the *Treatises* repeatedly and quite specifically. Jefferson rated Locke one of his trinity of the three greatest men who ever lived, along with Newton and Bacon, and there is no reason to suppose, as Wills supposes, that Jefferson was referring only to the Locke of the *Essay*. After all, he and the other Americans spoke with the highest regard for Locke's productions in the realm of politics and quoted or referred to them at length. Probably as good a summary statement as can be found of the Americans' view of Locke's *Treatises* was written by Nathaniel Ames, whose almanacs are said by Rossiter to be "an especially rich storehouse of common political notions." According to one of those almanacs, "as it is unpardonable for a Navigator to be without his charts, so it is for a Senator to be without his, which is Locke's 'Essay on Government.'"[69]

Even were the facts near to what Dunn claims them to be, he is quite misleading in suggesting that Locke's alleged post-1750 impact occurred only in the context of an already "highly articulated . . . tradition of political behavior" formed entirely independently of him. The fact is, as we shall see, Locke himself was one of the great formative influences in the Whiggish tradition to which Dunn, following Bailyn, refers.[70]

By the time at which Dunn admits the Americans were paying attention to Locke, they were doing so, he says, in "conceptually uninteresting ways" (whatever that might mean) and they read him, "with gradually consolidated political intentions," only in order "to gather moral support for these intentions." Perhaps they did, but again Dunn gives us no reason to believe it so, other than, perhaps, the fact that there were others, like Peter Van Schaack, who drew different conclusions from Locke than did Adams, Jefferson, and the other American Whigs. Remarkably, it was Van Schaack and those who agreed with him who, Dunn thinks, read Locke "with deep consideration and a peculiarly close perusal," proving, one supposes, that whatever Adams and Jefferson were doing in making the revolution, they were not inspired by Locke.[71] Dworetz points out the incompleteness of Dunn's story, however. Dunn "left the theater at intermission. . . . In 1776, Van Schaack, by his own account of the event, *changed his mind, without changing his political principles.*" Earlier, he had "allowed the British government the benefit of the doubt"; more experience taught him that he had reasoned on the basis of "inadequate information concerning parliament's intentions." Van Schaack, then, provides no support for the idea that a genuinely Lockean reaction to the events of 1763–76 would produce a Tory rather than a Patriot stance: using the same "deep consideration and peculiarly close perusal," Van Schaack came to the same conclusions as Adams, Jefferson, and the others.[72] But of this, and much else connecting Locke to the American Revolution and the Declaration of Independence, we learn nothing from Dunn.

Dworetz quite sensibly concludes that although the influence of Locke on the Americans is incontestable, the real question remains, How did they understand Locke? Locke's political philosophy is beset with notorious ambiguities. Is he a philosopher of rights or of duties? A supporter of capitalism, or mercantilism, or an enemy to private property in any form? a pro-Hobbesian or an anti-Hobbesian? a bourgeois liberal or an anti-bourgeois thinker? a religious thinker at bottom or a "secular rationalist"? All of these contrasting positions have been taken in the recent literature, and the fact that contemporary scholars disagree so much about Locke supports Dworetz's contention that we cannot take for granted that we know how the Americans or any other of Locke's near contemporaries understood him or just what their embrace of him meant. Nonetheless, we cannot see how others understood him without first attempting to understand him for ourselves. And rather than attempting to understand him "backwards," so to speak, from today's viewpoint we must try to see him in an authentically historical manner, in the context of the political thought that formed the most immediate context for his work as a Whig thinker.

Dunn frames the issue sharply when he insists that Locke's *Treatises* were by no means unique in "expounding the Whig theory of the Revolution." The official document of the Glorious Revolution may not be Lockean, but "political writing contemporary with it" was more or less identical to Locke's *Two Treatises*.[73] The character of liberal modernity and the new republicanism will not stand forth until we place Locke's thought into the seventeenth century political, religious, and philosophic context from which it emerged.

PART ONE

Protestants

CHAPTER ONE

Aristotelian Royalism and Reformation Absolutism: Divine Right Theory

WHETHER Locke and the Whigs, or whether the English Whigs of 1688 and the American Whigs of 1776, spoke with one voice or not, there was surely one thing they were all agreed in—their opposition to the political doctrine of the divine right of kings. Locke's most important political writing, his *Two Treatises of Government*, contains a lengthy and detailed commentary cum refutation of one of the leading divine right theorists, and Locke's was but one of several such large-scale efforts to refute that particular thinker. Even as late as fifty years after the American Declaration of Independence— that is, more than two centuries after the emergence of the divine right position—Thomas Jefferson was still citing divine right as the enemy. He made the point with his usual eloquence in a moving fiftieth-anniversary rumination on the Declaration of Independence: "The general spread of the light of science has already laid open to every view the palpable truth, that the mass of mankind has not been born with saddles on their backs, nor a favored few booted and spurred, ready to ride them legitimately, by the grace of God."[1] Opposition to monarchy by divine right formed a stable part of every current of political thought that might be held to flow into the Whig tradition. The divine right theory stood then as probably the clearest element within the context of political thought out of which Locke's philosophy ultimately emerged.

At the same time, the very depth and breadth of the opposition to divine right monarchy obscures the variety within that context, and contributes to views like John Dunn's, that Locke, the English Whigs of 1688, and the American Whigs of 1776 all spoke with one voice.

The divine right doctrine, firmly fixed and widely repellant as it was, nonetheless was itself quite new in England in the seventeenth century. When exactly it came to England is highly uncertain, but its emergence and rise to prominence reveals especially well the underlying dynamic at work in the development and ultimate clash of systems of political thought in the seventeenth century. It has been widely noted that this was the era in which the English were engaged in strenuous efforts to discover and implement the "correct" implications of the Protestant Reformation for church organization, governance, and liturgy.[2] Having largely postponed that effort for a variety of reasons under Elizabeth, the nation set off on this task in the seventeenth century with an earnestness and intensity that surprised—and ultimately terrified—many of the participants. The transforming pressures to which the Reformation subjected issues of ecclesiology are thus widely recognized; however, the same transforming pressures, with the same disruptive results, were at work in the sphere of political thought. The first half of the seventeenth century was marked not only by the theologico-political conflict which eventuated in the Civil War but by the reworking of inherited modes of political thought, with the result that new doctrines, far more extreme and far more opposed to each other than anything that had prevailed in England to that time, emerged and vied with each other for supremacy. At one extreme lay the full-grown divine right theory as it appeared ultimately in the work of Sir Robert Filmer, at the other a variety of Protestant contractarian doctrines. Some of these doctrines, like that of Philip Hunton, were rather moderate; others, like the one that reached semi-official status in John Milton's powerful prose, were just as extreme, in a mirror-image sort of way, as Filmer's. That the development of political thought in the seventeenth century saw the emergence on English soil of these two alternative theories about the origin and nature of political authority, divine right, and contract was striking in itself; what was really remarkable was the fact that both developed as efforts to work out the authentic meaning of the Protestant principle for politics. Both had a plausible claim to having done so, and that, it turned out, was the real problem.

The divine right doctrine proved so antithetical to so many different streams of political thought in the seventeenth and eighteenth centuries that theorists who would otherwise see each other, and be seen by outside observers, as quite antithetical made common cause against it. Even today, scholars treat as altogether similar such very different thinkers as Richard Hooker, Philip Hunton, Richard Baxter, and John Locke on the basis of their common rejection of divine right doctrines.

DIMENSIONS OF DIVINE RIGHT

Although it is difficult to identify the exact origin of the divine right doctrine, Locke believed he knew "by whom this doctrine came at first to be broach'd, and brought in fashion amongst us." A contemporary historian seconds his judgment: "Both the theory and practice of absolutism came to England with James I." A monarch who prided himself on his scholarly talents, James authored and published anonymously his *Trew Law of Free Monarchies* in 1598, when he was king in Scotland, before being called south to succeed Elizabeth. Soon after his arrival in England, his book was reprinted there. Although he did not originate the doctrine, his sponsorship of it did give it a definite *éclat*.[3] There was always a nice symmetry and even some irony to the careers of the Stuart monarchs—at the head of the line James I, riding in triumphantly from Scotland to succeed Elizabeth, the murderer of his mother; two generations later, his grandson and namesake, James II, skulking off in the dark to France in order to escape the bloody fate of his father, Charles I, and about to be succeeded by his daughter and her husband. It would be not too much of a historical exaggeration to say that the divine right theory arrived in glory with James I and slunk off in shame with James II. The idea remained sufficiently alive for Whig polemicists like Benjamin Hoadley and Cato, and the American Whigs in general, to continue the assault against it until well into the eighteenth century, but after 1688 things were never the same for the divine right of kings.

Jefferson was surely correct to contrast the divine right theory, which he abhorred, with the natural rights philosophy, which he favored; but many of the former doctrine's advocates would challenge Jefferson's portrayal of it as an engine of oppression. The divine right theory, tracing the origin of political authority to a divine ordination, did indeed bestow political power "by the grace of God." But in most if not all versions of the royalist doctrine in the seventeenth century, we do not find an explicit endorsement of the most colorful part of Jefferson's denunciation—his comparison of divine right rulers and their peoples to riders and horses, respectively. Divine right theorists would deny Jefferson's implication that the doctrine justified government as entirely for the benefit of the rulers at the expense of the ruled. The power of kings, said an Elizabethan homily, was given lest "all things should come into confusion and utter ruin," as a protection against "all mischiefs and miseries."[4] Even one of the most extreme of the defenders of the divine right thesis, Roger Manwaring, identified the king as the "protector of [his subjects'] persons, lives and estates," and, more emphatically, as "the procurer of all the happiness, peace, welfare which they enjoy who are under him."[5] King James devoted the whole of the first part of *The Trew Law of Free Monarchies* to the duties kings have to their subjects: the king is to "care for his people" as "the head cares for the body." James pointedly rejected the idea that "the world [was] only ordained for kings."[6] The promoters of the divine right of kings justified it in terms of the common good of the community; this was true even of the most radical of the writers in that tradition, Sir Robert Filmer. Filmer argued, for example, that absolutist monarchies are the only regimes that can keep order and avoid those "mischiefs [that] are unavoidable and of necessity do follow all democratic [i.e., non-monarchic] regiments." Monarchies, he maintained, even when they degenerate into tyrannies, as sometimes happens, are less bloody than popular governments. "The murders by Tiberius, Caligula, Nero, Domitian and Commodus put all together," said Filmer, "cannot match that civil tragedy which was acted in that one sedition between Marius and Sulla."[7]

Much confusion, both historically and today, has resulted from a failure to make certain key distinctions regarding the divine right doctrine. That theory consisted of propositions about political power at four different levels: propositions regarding (1) the "original of political power"; (2) the ends of political power; (3) the extent of political power; and (4) recourse against the misuse of political power. Along these four dimensions one might construct a paradigm of divine right absolutism by asserting that (1) political power derives directly from God to the king; (2) the end of political power is the glory, or welfare, of the king; (3) political power is absolute and unlimited in extent, and wielded by the monarch alone; and (4) there is no recourse whatever against the misuse of political power, if it even makes sense to speak of misuse.[8]

Many critics of the theory assume that partisans of divine right automatically took the absolutist position on all four dimensions of political power. As we have seen, however, divine right theorists did not typically affirm the ends of political life solely in terms of the good of the rulers, but did affirm the common good. Moreover, the advocates of divine right did not necessarily invest unlimited power in the ruler, as is often thought: divine right and absolutism are not necessarily identical. On the one side, we can see this in the political philosophy of Hobbes, who put forth an entirely different doctrine of the origin of political power—contract or covenant—but derived from that origin an absolute power. Some of the divine right theorists, again notably Filmer, also affirmed a royal power of this extent, but not all did.[9] King James I made the point with extraordinary clarity in a discourse reported to Parliament by the Earl of Salisbury. Although James asserted that "for his kingdom he was beholden to no elective power" but instead "did derive his title from the loins of his ancestors," he admitted that his powers were by no means unlimited. "He did acknowledge that he had no power to make laws of himself, or to exact any subsidies *de jure* without the consent of his three estates," and conceded that the king may not rightfully "command anything directly contrary to Gods word, and tending to subverting of the church."[10] As Harro Höpfl and Martyn Thompson conclude in summarizing their survey of seventeenth-century writings, "Not even the most determined advocate of monarchical absolutism was disposed to deny . . . a reciprocity of rights and duties."[11] Many, if not all, of the advocates of divine right monarchy thus endorsed some version of the traditional constitution, whereby Parliament shared in certain key powers, most notably the legislative and tax powers. And so J. P. Kenyon, a keen student of the seventeenth-century Constitution, could conclude, "With remarkable unanimity early seventeenth century Englishmen believed that they were bound to abide by the ancient Constitution. . . . In the sphere of practical politics the disagreement essentially lay in how to operate a constitution of whose nature few had any doubts."[12]

Nonetheless, the limited or constitutionalist character of even the most restrained divine right royalism must not be overestimated. Although "moderates" like King James I theoretically accepted the idea of limits, they insisted that there existed no earthly agent rightly able to enforce these limits. Above all, supporters of divine right denied any right in the people actively to resist, much less to depose, their king: "What shall subjects do then? Shall they obey valiant, stout, wise and good princes, and condemn, disobey, and rebel against . . . indiscreet and evil governors? God forbid."[13] However, as James himself averred, that did not mean that kings are beyond all control:

> I [do not] mean that whatsoever errors and intolerable abominations a sovereign prince commits, he ought to escape all punishment, as if thereby the world were only ordained for kings, and they without controlment to turn it upside down at their pleasure. But by the contrary, by remitting them to God (who is their only ordinary judge) I remit them to the sorest and sharpest schoolmaster that can be devised for them.[14]

Furthermore, that sharp schoolmaster never neglected his corrective task: "Yet does God never leave kings unpunished when they transgress these limits."[15] With all correction in God's hands, subjects had no recourse against a faithless or wicked ruler and no legitimate means (other than passive resistance) of enforcing constitutional limits upon a ruler bent on disregarding them.

Moreover, those constitutional limits themselves stood on a precarious footing. According to Roger Manwaring, Parliament did not "contribute any right to kings," but merely aided in "the more equal imposing, and more easy exacting of that which unto kings doth appertain by natural and original law."[16] Parliament shared in power as a matter of convenience, not by virtue of any necessity of right. Thus, according to Manwaring, the king could levy charges against the community without parliamentary approval. In a speech to Parliament in 1628, King Charles I came very close to an outright endorsement of Manwaring's doctrine. He sought money from Parliament, "judging a Parliament to be the ancient, speediest and best way in this time of common danger, to give such supply as to secure ourselves and to save our friends from imminent ruin." But, he warned, Parliament was not the only way: "If you should not do your duties in contributing what this state at this time needs I must in discharge of my conscience use those other means which God hath put into my hands."[17]

James was more politic and never said such things openly, but he did argue that laws "are properly made by the king only"; so far as the king is limited by law (and thus by the law of the constitution) it is because the king "bound himself by a double oath to the observation of the fundamental laws of his kingdom." The obligation derives from the king's "paction made to his people." A king who "leaves off to rule according to his laws degenerates into a tyrant."[18] This is surely more restrained than Filmer or Hobbes, who saw the laws and constitutional institutions like Parliament as mere creatures of the royal will, to be disregarded by the same will that initially chose to regard them if it so desired. Nonetheless, James came very close to the same conclusion: "A good king will frame all his actions to be according to the law; yet is he not bound thereto but of goodwill, and for good example. . . . The king is above the law, as both the author and giver of strength thereto." As Charles McIlwain justly concludes, "Such a theory as this leaves no place for the law of the land or the authority of the estates of the Realm when they conflict with the king's will."[19]

THE SIMILITUDES OF RULE

By far the most revealing element of divine right theory, both of its fundamental anticonstitutionalism and of its deepest meaning, is the argument made on behalf of its characteristic theses regarding "the original of political power." It appears to be largely a biblically grounded doctrine.[20] The two classic texts of Christian politics, Romans 13 and 1 Peter 2, figure prominently in many of its defenses. According to Paul in the Epistle to the Romans, "Let every soul be subject unto the higher powers. For there is no power but of God." Especially important for the divine right doctrine was Paul's assurance that "the powers that be are ordained of God." Peter was hardly less definite: "Subject yourselves to every ordinance of man for the Lord's sake; whether it be to the king, as supreme; or unto governors."[21]

Yet these texts were far from unambiguous in their bearing on the nature of politics. It was often pointed out, for example, that Peter's letter did not necessarily support the divine right doctrine, because Peter had referred to governments as "ordinance of man," and not as directly "instituted by God." Anti–divine right thinkers also challenged the divine right interpretation of Romans by exploiting Paul's explanation of the reason for divine support of ruling authority: "For rulers are not a terror to good works, but to the evil. . . . do that which is good, and thou shalt have praise of the same: for he is the minister of God to thee for good. But if thou do that which is evil, be afraid; for he beareth not the sword in vain: for he is the minister of God, a revenger to execute wrath upon him that doeth evil."[22] From this passage John Milton concluded that "powers that do the contrary [of being a terror to bad conduct] are no powers ordained of God, and by consequence no obligation [is] laid upon us to obey or not to resist them."[23] Thus, from a passage that had been cited to support unconditional obedience, Milton extracted a lesson in the right to resistance![24]

That two plausible alternative readings of the central biblical texts were both put forward with utmost assurance suggests that some hermeneutic principle was at work guiding interpreters toward one or another reading. This turns out to be true, in that the divine right theorists grasped the biblical texts in the light of a series of images or metaphors of political life that produced their interpretation rather than Milton's. King James I expressed those images repeatedly in his analogies, or "similitudes," of politics: "The king toward his people is rightly compared to a father of children, and to a head of a body composed of diverse members."[25] To these two analogies, he added the even more daring idea that "Kings are justly called gods, for they exercise a manner or resemblance of divine power upon earth." James identified the first two "similitudes" as "taken out of . . . the grounds of policy and philosophy,"[26] which, for him, meant that they were "grounded" in the Aristotelian tradition of political philosophy. By means of these two analogies James conveyed three central, apparently Aristotelian propositions about politics: the naturalness of politics, and particularly of monarchy; the ordination of monarchy to the common good; and the irresistibility of royal authority. James was clear that these were analogies, not identifications. The king is not God; the king is not the father of his people, nor does James explicitly claim that the royal power derived from the power of a father. As Gordon Schochet rightly notes, James "never actually *identified* regal and paternal power." James's version of divine right theory thus has patriarchal elements—it is "replete with fatherly images"—but it differs significantly from Filmer's full-blown patriarchal absolutism.[27]

The political community, James implied, is natural in the same sense as the family and the human individual are natural—they are produced by nature, understood as the power of generation.[28] The royalist thinker John Maxwell gave in 1644 an especially strong version of the idea of nature as the generative source of polity:

> This *appetitus universalis* and *naturalis*, this vehement necessary propension and desire to government, is not unlike that act of the understanding by which it assenteth to the first principles of undeniable, uncontrollable truth, which are evident *ex vi terminorum*, by evident appearance in the essential connection of the terms.[29]

The polity is natural in the related but further sense that it is a natural whole in which the part, the member, is what it is by virtue of being a part. James had in mind an organismic notion of the polity. As Aristotle said in making a similar point, "for if the whole [body] is destroyed there will not be a foot or a hand, unless in the sense that the term is similar (as when one speaks of a hand made of stone), but the thing itself will be defective," that is, it will not properly be a hand, for a hand is a hand only by virtue of being a part of a whole human body.[30] Moreover, just as nature produces human bodies and families with a guiding element—the head and the father, respectively—so, James concluded, nature has produced political communities with a ruling element of the same sort, the king. Since human individuals, families, and kingdoms are natural organismic wholes, there is no inherent conflict between the ruling element and the ruled.[31] They are not separate things, but parts of one whole whose good is genuinely a common good. The common good is not unrelated to the good of the parts (members), but is at bottom different from the sum of the goods or interests of the parts. James drove that point home when he explained the operation of the directive element in the organismic whole:

> As the judgment coming from the head may not only employ the members, every one in their own office, as long as they are able for it, but likewise, in case any of them be affected with any infirmity, must care and provide for the remedy, in case it be curable, and if otherwise, gar cut them off for fear of infecting the rest, even so is it betwixt the prince and his people.[32]

The prince's "care" for the whole extends both to the ordering of all the parts to the good of the whole, and to "cutting off" any part which might "infect the rest." This understanding of the common good in terms of whole and part reveals as well as any other single element of divine right theory how far it stands from the natural rights philosophy, which understands the common good in terms of individuals and their rights.[33]

The similitudes also reveal how absurd and wicked resistance to the prince would be: "It may very well fall out that the head will be forced to gar cut off some rotten members . . . to keep the rest of the body in integrity. But what state the body can be in if the head, for any infirmity that can fall to it, be cut off, I leave to the reader's judgment." James actually does not leave it to the reader's judgment, but makes everything quite explicit: "Whereas a Prince being the Head, cannot bee loosed in the proper jount, not dismounted; like a cannon when the carriage whereof is unlockt, without a sore shaking and a most grievous dislocation of all the members, yea, without subverting the whole bodie of the State, whereby private persons without number are inwrapped together in the same ruine."[34] The viciousness of resistance to the ruler appears further via the analogy of the family:

> Consider, I pray you, what duty his children owe to him, and whether, upon any pretext whatsoever, it will not be thought monstrous and unnatural to his sons to rise up against him, to control at their appetite, and when they think good to slay him, or to cut him off and adopt to themselves any other they please in his room.[35]

Thus the similitudes would appear to settle the question of how to read the ambiguous biblical texts: God has ordained kingly rule in the same way he has ordained nature and the natural process of generation. The development of the Aristotelian doctrine of the naturalness of the *polis* would seem, therefore, to be more foundational for the divine right doctrine than any strictly biblical or Christian ground; or, perhaps better, divine right theory appears to nestle easily within the synthesis of biblical and Aristotelian themes characteristic of Thomas Aquinas and Richard Hooker. But that impression is misleading, for the Aristotelian foundations were greatly transformed in their migration to the similitudes. A comparison between the Aristotelian original and the similitudes is most useful, however, for pointing toward the true grounds and for making clearer than the explicit teaching does what the real character of the divine right doctrine is.

Aristotle, it is true, did speak of the polity as natural in the way a human individual is natural, and, like James, he also concluded that "the whole must of necessity be prior to the part."[36] Yet Aristotle notably failed to develop the parallel between polity and body in the way James did. According to the latter,

> The proper office of a king towards his subjects agrees very well with the office of the head towards the body and all members thereof, for from the head, being the seat of judgment, proceeds the care and foresight of guiding. . . . As the discourse and direction flows from the head, and the execution according thereunto belongs to the rest of the members, every one according to their office, so it is betwixt a wise prince and his people.[37]

But in Aristotle, the mode of rule that James described is the mode characteristic of master and slave, not of political rule! As Aristotle explained,

> There are many kinds both of ruling and ruled. . . . For whatever is constituted out of a number of things—whether continuous or discrete—and becomes a single common thing always displays a ruling and a ruled element; this is something that animate things derive from all of nature. . . . An animal is the first thing constituted out of soul and body, of which the one is the ruling element by nature, the other the ruled.

Thus far, James and Aristotle concur; they are both concerned with composites, wholes made of (dissimilar) parts in which there is perforce a ruling element. But Aristotle parted ways with the divine right argument in his recognition that while all composites require rule, there are different types of rule appropriate to different kinds of wholes, or to different parts within the whole: "There are many kinds both of ruling and ruled," a proposition he illustrated as follows:

> It is then in an animal, as we were saying, that one can first discern both the sort of rule characteristic of a master and political rule. For the soul rules the body with the rule characteristic of a master, while intellect rules appetite with political and kingly rule.

That is, the kind of rule of the head over the members of the body that James affirmed as the model for kingly rule was identified by Aristotle with despotic rule: "For that which can foresee with the mind is the naturally ruling and naturally mastering element, while that which can do these things with the body is the naturally ruled and slave."[38]

Aristotle's "slave by nature" is the one who is appropriately ruled with James's sort of rule. But, Aristotle said, "it is evident . . . that mastery and political [rule] are not the same thing. . . . For the one sort is over those free by nature, the other over slaves. Political rule is over free and equal persons."[39] It is easy to understand, therefore, how, in a generation well versed in Aristotle's political philosophy, many might find the divine right doctrine alarming: it amounted to a relegation of the community to the status of natural slaves. The parliamentary leader Henry Parker observed that "if all nations . . . can neither set limits or judge limits set to sovereignty, but must look upon it as a thing merely divine . . . then all nations are equally slaves; and we in England are born no more by the laws of England than the asinine peasants of France are there."[40]

James's other similitude—the family—represents a similar transformation of the Aristotelian doctrine of the naturalness of the *polis*. The *polis*, said Aristotle, came into being naturally as part of a series of natural associations, of which the family is one. Aristotle used the family as an example of how nature produces human communities, yet he was also very clear that the political community is different from the family, that it represents the operation of nature in a different way and with a different kind of product. "Rule over children," Aristotle agreed, "is kingly, for the one who generates is ruler on the basis of both affection and age."[41] But, since the kingly rule over children depends on their age, that is, on the incompleteness in them of the "deliberative faculty," that rule can only be temporary and surely cannot be the model for rule in the commonwealth. "From the children," said Aristotle, "come those who are partners in the regime," that is, citizens. That ultimate fate not only sets a period to their subjection to the paternal kingly rule, but also sets the goal in terms of which the father's rule is to be exercised: adult freedom and share in rule.[42]

The divine right theory thus built on, but transformed in altogether decisive ways, the Aristotelian doctrine of nature. Those transformations reveal better than the explicit claims raised by most of the writers themselves the real character of the doctrine they defended—a form of rule that, according to Aristotle at least, was fit only for natural slaves and perpetual children, a form of rule at the opposite extreme from genuine political life. In other words, Jefferson was quite correct in seeing the absolutist implications of the divine right theory.

James I and the other divine right authors made much of the similitudes; they were surely not unique to James but were so common as to be called "a conventional set of comparisons" by one scholar of the era.[43] This was, in general, an age of metaphor, analogy, similitude.[44] Not only the divine right theorists, but political writers of quite different persuasions, reasoned in terms of similitude. James himself took note of these competing images: "Whether these [i.e., his] similitudes represent better the office of a king, or the offices of masters or deacons of crafts, or doctors in physic (which jolly comparisons are used by such writers as maintain the contrary proposition), I leave it also to the reader's discretion."[45] These other similitudes—the statesman as physician of the polity or master artisan—are in fact much closer to Aristotle's conception of politics: witness his discussion of politics as the architectonic science, the master art of the other arts.[46] Unfortunately, James did not present his own reasons for judging his set of similitudes superior to the other set, but his challenge to his readers does pose the question of what might make *his* similitudes so apt. To put it another way: it appeared for a moment that the foundation of the divine right position was Aristotle's doctrine of nature, but on examination it has become clear that Aristotle was greatly modified in being appropriated by the partisans of divine right. What governed that modification?

The Reformation Attitude and the Transformation of Aristotle

> God gives not kings the stile of Gods in vaine,
> For on his throne his scepter doe they swey:
> And as their subjects ought them to obey,
> So Kings should feare and serve their God againe
> If then ye would enjoy a happie raigne,
> Observe the statutes of your heavenly King,
> And from his Law, make all your laws to spring:
> Since his lieutenant here ye should remain,
> Reward the just, be stedfast, true, and plaine,
> Represse the proud, maintaining aye the right,
> Walke always so, as ever in his sight,
> Who guardes the godly, plaguing the prophane:
> And so ye shall in Princely virtues shine,
> Resembling right your mightie King Divine.
>
> James I to his son Henry[47]

If the Aristotelian intimations of the first two similitudes have proven inconclusive, then perhaps the key to the grounding of the divine right position is the third similitude: "In the Scriptures," said James to Parliament in 1609, "kings are called gods, and so their power, after a certain relation compared to the divine power." In his *Basilikon Doron*, a treatise of "instruction" to his eldest son, James reminded his supposed heir that God "made you a little God to sit on his Throne, and rule over other men." Kings, James wrote, represent "the image of God in earth and Gods place." Kings exercise "a manner or resemblance of divine power upon earth."[48] In his speech to Parliament in 1609, James carried this daring argument very far:

> God has power to create, or destroy, make, or unmake at his pleasure, to give life, or send death, to judge all, and to be judged nor accountable to none; to raise low things, and to make high things low at his pleasure, and to God are both soul and body due. And the like power have kings.[49]

Remarkable as this claim is, it was not entirely uncommon, although not often put forward so blatantly as James did here.[50] John Maxwell, for example, had argued that "it proveth the excellency of monarchy above all governments because it approacheth nearest the government of God, and God himself who is the author of all government." The divine similitude resonated throughout English society in the early seventeenth century. At the opening of Parliament, for example, the Speaker would echo the similitude: "Kings were visible gods and God an invisible king." Members were heard to say such things as, "Because the king is a God upon earth I would answer him as we should answer God in heaven, that is with a prayer."[51]

An early expression of the divine similitude, a homily preached in 1570, helps explain these remarkable claims. According to the anonymous author,

> For that similitude that is between the heavenly monarchy and earthly kingdoms well governed, our Saviour Christ in sundry parables says that the kingdom of heaven is resembled unto a man, a king, and as the name of the king is very often attributed and given unto God in the Holy Scriptures, so does God himself in the same scripture sometimes vouchsafe to communicate his name with earthly princes, terming them Gods, doubtless for that similitude of government which they have or should have, not unlike unto God their king. Unto them which similitude of heavenly government, the nearer and nearer that an earthly prince does come in his regiment, the greater blessing of God's mercy is he unto that country and people over whom he reigns.[52]

The homily reveals more about the divine similitude than James did because it sets it in an especially enlightening context. The homily opens briskly by identifying the fundamental relationship between God, "the Creator and Lord of all things," and humanity: "It was his will that man, his chief creature upon the earth, should live under the obedience of his Creator and Lord." Not only human beings, but the angels too are to live under obedience; obedience is the law of the whole, the chief expression of the creatureliness of all creatures. From the very outset, God put humanity under a law of obedience; the lower creatures, in turn, were to express their obedience to God by being obedient to human beings. Had humans and angels remained in a condition of obedience, they would have remained in a condition of "favor and grace" with God, "which to enjoy is perfect felicity." Since "perfect felicity" follows from "obedience," the homilist concludes, "it is evident that obedience is the principal virtue of all virtues, and indeed the very root of all virtues." Here the homilist indicates a clear break with any Aristotelianism, for Aristotle does not even list obedience (or piety) among the virtues, much less as the chief and root virtue.

As obedience is the root of all virtue, so "rebellion" is "the first and greatest, and the very root of all other sins." The first great act of rebellion brought much misery on mankind, but changed not at all the fundamental fact—that obedience is the "virtue of all virtues." After the Fall, "God . . . repaired again the rule and order of obedience." But now this "rule and order" was multiplied and made earthly; as God withdrew from the direct relationship with humanity that had predated the Fall, he made earthly authorities who were to be the recipients of the obedience that originally went directly to him. Just as at the beginning the lower animals expressed their ordination to obedience by rendering obedience to human beings as intermediaries, so in the postlapsarian world there are intermediaries within the human sphere—husbands, fathers, masters, and, above all, kings. These sets of rulers serve a useful function in this new world in which "confusion and utter ruin" so pressingly threaten, but even more than that, they express the fundamental moral fact that human beings are to live in obedience: God "has ordained and set earthly princes over particular kingdoms . . . [so that] the majesty of heavenly things may by the baseness of earthly things be shadowed and resembled."[53]

The grounding element of the divine right theory, which governs the interpretation of the relevant biblical passages and shapes the reinterpretation of Aristotle and the tradition of political philosophy, is, we might say, an attitude—an attitude that the fundamental human stance in existence is, or should be, obedience.[54] Human beings stand existentially as beings under obligation to a superior. They are most human when they most surrender to the will of their superior. The Stuart poet George Herbert captured this attitude extraordinarily well in his poem "Discipline":

> Throw away thy rod,
> Throw away thy wrath:
>   O my God,
> Take the gentle path.
>
> For my heart's desire
> Unto thine is bent:
>   I aspire
> To a full consent.

Not a word or look
I affect to own,
  But by book,
And thy book alone.[55]

The divine right teaching about obedience owed to the king is an expression of that fundamental attitude. To give expression to the attitude of obedience requires having something to obey. What is required must be specific and knowable, otherwise there can be no certainty of how to render obedience. That which is to be obeyed must arise from a source altogether external to the obedient: it must be a command. That command can take the form of an externally given set of laws or it can be the living will of a ruler. In either case, the authoritative element is the quality of command; otherwise it is not obedience but self-rule. The commendatory quality of the law or command inheres not in its usefulness but in its arbitrariness. If the law or command were binding because it served the interests of the ruled, then the chief quality expressed in conforming would not be obedience.

If God ruled directly, as he did before the Fall, then human beings could express their attitude of obedience through direct obedience to God. Or, if God ruled through his positive laws, as he did the Jews, then human beings could express their attitude of obedience through reverential honoring of the law. The Reformation interpretation of Christianity dwelt upon the abrogation of the laws through Christ; but at the same time, it dwelt upon the majesty and sovereignty of God and the concomitant utter creatureliness of humanity. Human beings are entirely unfree vis-à-vis God, at the same time that they are free from the law.[56] How then can they live within the still obligatory stance of obedience? The divine right absolutist king steps into the breach caused by the insistence on the continued requirement of obedience coupled with the insistence (within certain strands of the Reformation) on the unbindingness of the law.

Thus, it appears, divine right absolutism is preeminently a development of the Reformation, or at least of a certain interpretation of human existence within Christianity. That conclusion comports with the claim raised by seventeenth-century thinkers like Sir Robert Filmer and John Maxwell that the divine right doctrine was the appropriate embodiment of the Reformation in the political sphere and that the alternatives to that doctrine were either "papist" in inspiration or, worse yet, pagan or atheistic. In his classic study *The Divine Right of Kings*, J. N. Figgis endorsed Filmer's view, as does much recent scholarship.[57] Figgis and the others present a somewhat different, but not incompatible, account of the relation between Protestantism and divine right theory. Divine right theory, they say, was an almost necessary response to papal pretensions to power in temporal affairs, whether direct or indirect. As Filmer saw quite clearly, Catholic apologists frequently patronized contractarian accounts of the origins of political authority as a way of lowering the dignity of the political vis-à-vis the directly divine origination of papal power. The divine right doctrine, quite simply, countered with an equal claim to direct derivation of secular authority in the divine will.[58]

The divine right doctrine was, of course, not the only political doctrine characteristic of the Reformation. There certainly were others, including those most forcibly opposed to divine right monarchy. That fact does not derogate from the connection between divine right and the Reformation, however, but reveals what gave shape to the seventeenth-century struggles in England and elsewhere. These were, in part, contests over the question of what the proper political embodiment of the Protestant principle was.

PATRIARCHALISM AND THE REFORMATION ATTITUDE

The most famous and most widely discussed theorist of divine right was not yet out of his teens when James became king, and his chief works were composed during the reign of James's son, Charles I, and during the Interregnum. Robert Filmer's doctrine is not identical to that of James and the earlier divine right monarchists, but he has come to be taken as the quintessential spokesman for that point of view. Filmer's preeminence within the divine rights tradition is only partly deserved. So far as his argument is indeed different from the other *jure divino* royalists, he is given undue credit for influence or representativeness. Nonetheless, Filmer brings out especially well the underlying thoughts and attitudes in the divine right doctrine. By bringing these to near perfect expression, Filmer exposes himself to certain obvious logical and practical objections, which helped doom his position; yet, for the same reason, he does earn the preeminence he achieved.[59]

Filmer seems to be a considerably less supple thinker than James; for example, he takes James's similitudes absolutely literally. The king is not only *like* a father to his people, he *is* the father, or the heir of the father. Since royal power is fatherly power, it must have belonged originally to the first father, Adam. Thus Filmer comes to center his doctrine on the account of Adam in Genesis in a way that James surely never did. Filmer transforms the earlier divine right theory until the similitudes disappear, leaving in their place a yet more direct expression of the grounding Reformation attitude that inspired earlier divine right thinking. Nonetheless, the proper context for appreciating his work is precisely the earlier theory he remade.

Ever since Locke's devastating critique of Filmer, however, it has been difficult to approach the latter in any context other than the one Locke supplied for him. At the same time and for the same reason, it has been difficult to take Filmer seriously enough to grasp the serious core of his position. Locke has disserved Filmer not only in general ways, by wrenching him from his proper context and making him appear utterly ridiculous, but more particularly by bequeathing us a diluted version of his predecessor's argument. Having set off on a diligent search for Filmer's "full sense", Locke informs us, he discovered in Sir Robert's essay on Hobbes "all those arguments" for his divine right patriarchalism "which in his writings I find him any where to make use of." The key passage that Locke quotes states:

> If God created only Adam, and of a piece of him made the Woman, and if by generation from these two, as parts of them all mankind be propagated: If also God gave to Adam not only the Dominion over the Woman and the children that should issue from them, but also over the whole earth to subdue it, and over all the Creatures on it, so that as long as Adam lived, no Man could claim or enjoy anything but by Donation, Assignation, or permission from him . . .

The most important tactical move in Locke's assault on Filmer occurs at this moment, in his comments on this Filmerian passage:

> Here we have the sum of all his Arguments, for Adam's Sovereignty, and against natural freedom, which I find up and down in his other Treatises; and they are these following; God's creation of Adam, the Dominion he gave him over Eve: And the Dominion he had as Father over his children.[60]

Locke's restatement is so important because it serves more or less as the program, the table of contents, for his investigation and critique of Filmer's argument. In a succession of chapters he considers *in seriatim* the various grounds for Adam's sovereignty he had extracted from the passage he quoted. But right at the outset, and in this definitive place, Locke has distorted Filmer's position to such a degree that the latter's central thought is no longer visible in Locke's explicit presentation.

Most obviously, Filmer had not identified three separate reasons in support of Adam's authority, as Locke said, but only two, as even the punctuation makes clear: the two are divided by a colon, and the second is introduced by an "also." Filmer's first argument is this: God made only Adam at first, and all others, including Eve and their children, derive from him as their origin and source. From this fact derives Adam's "dominion" over all other human beings. Filmer's second argument concerns Adam's dominion over the nonhuman parts of the world. Adam's dominion over humans derives from his being their source; his dominion over the rest of the world derives from positive divine grant. Although Filmer does not make his point perfectly explicit, he is clearly echoing and extending the most daring of James's similitudes. Just as God has dominion over his creation because he is its source, so Adam has dominion over his progeny, because he is their source. Adam is a kind of surrogate begetter of the human world; he is

God's lieutenant on earth not merely by appointment, but through his rib and his loins.

The singular creation of Adam and the derivation of all others from him stands for Filmer as the single most significant fact about humanity. It proves, he concludes, that all human beings are born into a state of subjection, for if they were born free and equal, as Hobbes and the contractarians believe, they would have had quite a different origin:

> I cannot understand how this [Hobbesian] right of nature can be conceived without imagining a company of men at the very first to have been all created together without any dependency one of another, or as mushrooms (*fungorum more*) they all on a sudden were sprung out of the earth without any obligation one to another: the scripture teaches us otherwise, that all men come by succession, and generation from one man: we must not deny the history of the creation.[61]

Filmer does not mean to trace Adam's authority to any particular grant or command by God, but rather to the general pattern or plan revealed in creation. God expressed his will in his deed; the authority of Adam results from and constitutes the very point of the version of the origins of humanity in Genesis.

Filmer's derivation of the authority of kings thus shares much with James's; the traces of two of the similitudes remain visible, if much metamorphosed. The king is father, and the king is Godlike. Yet all lingering echoes of the Aristotelian doctrine of nature vanish from Filmer's version. In place of nature is the biblical doctrine of Creation. This is not to say that Filmer did not occasionally cloak himself with the authority of Aristotle, but in the final analysis the Greek philosopher could not be a proper guide in politics: "We cannot much blame Aristotle for the uncertainty and contrariety in him, if one considers him as a heathen; for . . . it is not possible for the wit of man to search out the first grounds or principles of government . . . except he know that at the creation one man alone was made. . . . This point can be learnt only from the scriptures."[62] Filmer makes quite explicit what had lain implicit and partially concealed in the earlier forms of divine right theory: nature, and thus philosophy, no longer played any essential role in its depths.[63]

Filmer appears to rest everything on his reading of the account of creation in Genesis, but that reading contained at least two difficulties, which Filmer's Whig critics did not hesitate to emphasize and which pointed to the deep-lying agreement between Filmer and the earlier divine right thinking. In the first place, Filmer's reading of Genesis was by no means compelling in itself. Does it necessarily follow from the single origin of mankind in one man that kings rule by divine right and possess absolute, illimitable power? The second difficulty with Filmer's doctrine related not so much to the interpretation of Genesis itself as to the effort to bring it to bear in the present. Even if one accepts the Filmerean interpretation of the creation of Adam, no actual king could trace his lineage, and thus his authority, back to Adam. Far from settling political power more firmly in an already unsettled age, Filmer threatened to unsettle all power by establishing a principle of legitimacy nobody could meet. "The skill used in dressing up power with all the splendor and temptation absoluteness can add to it, without shewing who has a right to have it, will serve only to give a greater edge to man's natural ambition," commented Locke. The result, he concluded, can only be a "scramble" leading to "endless contention and disorder" (I 106).

What in Filmer's system either blinded him to the force of these objections or served as a reply to them was an implicit appeal to the same Reformation attitude of obedience and subjection we have already seen underlying the other divine right theories. Filmer read the story of creation as implying the subordination of humanity to Adam and his heirs because he began with the premise of subjection to God the Creator, to be carried over to the begetter-surrogate, Adam.[64] Human beings are not mushrooms, he said; they do not spring up spontaneously and with no forebears. To have a source is to be under obligation to that source; if that were not so, then where would be the obligation to God himself? And human beings have a source: "We must not deny the history of the creation."

As to the gaping chasm separating Adam and all reigning monarchs over which Filmer's critics gleefully held him, Sir Robert admitted to it easily enough. "It is true, all kings be not the natural parents of their subjects, yet they all either are, *or are to be reputed,* as the next heirs of those progenitors who were at first the natural parents of the whole people."[65] Contrary to what one would expect on the basis of a superficial grasp of Filmer's scheme, he did not believe it made any difference whether the prince actually possesses the Adamic paternal power or is merely "reputed" to do so:

> In all kingdoms or commonwealths in the world, whether the Prince be the supreme Father of the people or but the true heir of such a Father, or whether he come to the crown by usurpation, or by election of the nobles or of the people, or by any other way whatsoever, or whether some few or a multitude govern the commonwealth, yet still the authority that is in any one, or in many, or in all of these, is the only right and natural authority of a supreme Father.

In other words, no matter who possesses authority, and no matter how it was acquired, that authority is the authority of the fatherhood, ultimately the authority of Adam. (As Locke, Sidney, and others insisted, there is something quite absurd in such a claim: if the power derives from fatherhood, it surely would appear that only fathers can possess it, and then only over their offspring.) Filmer is even willing to defend the authority of the hardest case, the usurper: "If it please God, for the correction of the Prince or punishment of the people, to suffer Princes to be removed and others to be placed in their rooms . . . in all such cases, the judgment of God, who hath power to give and take away kingdoms, is most just."[66]

Filmer is untroubled by the inability of any princes to trace their authority back to Adam, for three reasons. In the first place, he means to say that the Pauline affirmation that all authority is of God finds its explication in Genesis, in the creation of Adam. This is where and how God has "appointed" rule; all rightful authority is nothing but the subjection owed to the original source, God, and derivatively to the derivative source, Adam. God could have provided for human beings to come into being in some other way, but he did not. The most common fact of nature, generation, when understood in light of the revealed creation, proves fathers to have sovereign authority in the human world. The objections of Locke, Sidney, and the others to the contrary, this "fatherly" authority can be transferred, or held by others, for it is the original of all authority. Certainly no authority can arise from individual consent, for no individual is free, no man has the moral authority to subject himself because he is already caught within a web of subjection and lacks the truly creative power of God.

According to Filmer, rulers can exercise the power of fathers and of the heirs of Adam, even if they are usurpers of that power. From the point of view of the subject, it matters much less who possesses the power than that it is recognized and obeyed; the relevant fact is the same whether the ruler he faces is Adam or Richard III: the king is he to whom he can render his obedience. Calvin made more or less the same point: "It belongeth not to us to be inquisitive by what right and title a prince reigneth . . . and whether he have it by God and lawful inheritance. . . . To us it ought to suffice that they do rule. For they have not ascended unto this estate by their own strength, but they are placed by the hand of God."[67] For the subject, it is enough to know he lies under the obligation to obey those he finds in positions of authority. The subject is concerned only with his own duties, not with the duties of the authorities to God. What is common to all such authority relations is precisely the obligation of obedience. For Filmer, this is the decisive matter, and it makes possible his acceptance of the apparent absurdities his Whig critics denounced. Filmer's doctrine derives coherence, in other words, precisely from the way the Reformation attitude toward obedience radiates through every part of it.

It is indeed possible, Filmer concludes, that the true heir to Adam no longer exercises power, or even that great criminals do so, but this is thoroughly compatible with God's ways. God is not bound even by his own ordinations. If he chooses to use evil men to rebuke Princes or peoples, that "is most just." "God doth but use and turn men's unrighteous acts to the performance of His righteous decrees."[68] Not only is the power that rulers possess an embodiment or reflection of God's creative power, but so is their loss of power. The other side of human subjection is the supervening sovereignty of God, uncontained and uncontainable. The authority of the usurper does not contradict Filmer's system but completes it.

The surpassingly sovereign God lying in the background of Filmer's royalism is also a part of the Reformation dispensation. As Calvin, for example, insisted, God's Providence is no lazy thing. The Reformation God is active and assertive, not leaving the world to run on its own. He is no divine watchmaker.[69]

The divine right doctrine, extreme and even absurd as it may have been in some respects, nonetheless derived its power from its derivation from and connections to some of the deepest strains of the Reformation. On the surface, the natural rights philosophy of Locke and the American Declaration of Independence differ so much from the divine right doctrine that nothing at all needs to be said at that level; yet, since the natural rights philosophy is also sometimes treated as a version of Reformation political thought, a comparison at a somewhat deeper level is worthwhile. The natural rights philosophy is very far from embodying or endorsing the fundamental attitude of obedience. The original condition is not one calling for obedience, but a situation of "no-rule"; human beings enter a status where obedience becomes important only through an act of their own reason and will, deployed in their own self-interest. And, according to the natural rights philosophy, human beings never enter a sphere of unconditional obedience, but always retain the right to disobey in a pinch, or in situations they judge may turn into a pinch—that is, in circumstances where their rights become insecure. Lacking a fundamental commitment to the attitude of obedience, the natural rights doctrine has no resonance with the "similitudes"; the family is distinctly not the model of political life, and the political good is not conceived in such a way that the political whole is ontologically and morally prior to the individual. The fundamental attitude expressed or endorsed in the natural rights philosophy is, in a word, almost the reverse of that in the divine right doctrine—not quite self-assertion or rebelliousness, but far closer to these than to obedience.[70] If the natural rights philosophy expresses something in Reformation Christianity, it is something quite different from what found expression in the doctrine of divine right of kings.

Aristotelian Constitutionalism and Reformation Contractarianism: From Ancient Constitution to Original Contract

THE DIVINE RIGHT THEORY reveals one of the significant processes at work in seventeenth-century England—the Protestantization of political thought. However, just as a sumptuous variety of strains and forms of Protestant theology emerged, so did a plethora of versions of Protestant political thought. Although it is not altogether fruitful to directly correlate major Protestant theologies with the variants of Protestant political thought, some important parallels exist. The divine right doctrine, with its emphasis on the divine ordination of public authority and its focus on human subjection, shares much with Luther's own version of reformed Christianity and of its authoritarian political implications. This is not to say that Luther was a divine right thinker or that theorists like Filmer agreed with Luther in detail; there were many and significant differences. There were, moreover, significant enough echoes and parallels with Calvinist theology in the divine right thinkers to foreclose any simple Luther-Calvin dichotomy.[1]

Neither Lutheran theology nor Luther-like political thought monopolized the scene. In England there had always been a traditional understanding of political life, largely rooted in Aristotle and expressed by such writers as Fortescue, which was very distant from both the practical and theoretical claims of the emergent divine right position. In the face of the development of the new divine right doctrine parliamentary writers in the seventeenth century appealed to this earlier line of thought, first in the form of the doctrine of the ancient constitution, and then in the form of the theory of the mixed regime or mixed monarchy, as it was most frequently called in England.

These versions of Aristotelian constitutionalism finally gave way in the 1640s to parliamentary contractarian doctrines. With the acceptance of contractarian doctrines, the parliamentary writers made an important break with Aristotle himself and with the forms of Aristotelianism that had prevailed in England to that point. The emergence of parliamentary contractarian thought occurred in response to three somewhat separate kinds of pressure to which the older Aristotelian constitutionalism was subjected. One was the dialectical necessity of responding to novel challenges posed by one or another version of the divine right alternative. Secondly, events in the ongoing struggle between king and Parliament combined with these novel theoretical issues to face the old constitutionalism with unprecedented tasks to which it did not seem able to respond in its inherited form. Contract was a plausible but by no means a necessary response to both these challenges. Finally, the parliamentary thinkers, like their royalist opponents, faced the ongoing challenge of altogether rethinking politics in the light of the Reformation. Precisely because Aristotelian constitutionalism was so old, predating the Reformation by many years, it was subjected to reconsideration in the light of the new truths and new attitudes of reformed Christianity.

Parliamentary contractarianism emerged in the 1640s as the result of these various forces. It, too, was in its most important formulations a version of Protestant political thought (or theology), but it was a different Protestantism. I will not attempt in this chapter, any more than in the last, to correlate this other form of Protestant political thinking with formal Protestant theological doctrines; but it is surely no accident that contractarianism emerged among those associated with the so-called Puritan wing of English Christianity. The difference between this form of Protestant politics and the royalist form derives from divergent understandings of the role of Christian liberty in the matters of this world. In Luther himself and in doctrines leaning in Luther's direction, Christian liberty freed humanity from earlier forms of bondage but remained abstract and highly indeterminate in its contact with the world. At the extreme opposite pole from Luther, antinomians attempted to take Christian liberty more seriously as a force within the world. The Puritans and parliamentary writers of the 1640s surely were no antinomians, but they attempted to find a more determinate presence for liberty in ethical and political life. Contractarian politics became the vehicle by which Christian liberty found a positive presence in the world without falling into the antinomian stance of fundamentally challenging or even overturning the fact of subjection or the attitude of obedience.

With the emergence of contractarian thinking, the English political tradition came to contain a form of thought that resonates far more with Locke and the American Declaration of Independence than with the divine right doctrine, the political understanding implicit in the Declaration of Rights, or the various forms of Aristotelian constitutionalism favored by parliamentary writers of the early seventeenth century. In this case, as in so many others, however, superficial similarities can be misleading. The contractarianism of the parliamentary thinkers was in fact almost as distant from Lockean thought as was divine right theory itself. Indeed, parliamentary contractarianism and divine right theory shared more with each other than even the former shared with Locke. We cannot, in other words, understand Locke or his American successors as standing in some single line of succession to an already established tradition of political thought tracing back to the early years of the Civil War or before. Change occurred between the early 1640s and Locke, the recognition of which fact is indispensible to any further attempt to understand the nature and significance of that innovation—that is, any attempt to deal with the modernity problem.

THE ANCIENT CONSTITUTION

Even before his accession to the throne of England in 1603, James had published his views on the source and nature of royal power, a practice that the greater eminence and more visible "bully pulpit" of his new position encouraged him to continue. Moreover, partly under the sway of his theories and partly under the press of necessity, he asserted his powers into gray areas of the constitution. He seldom, if ever, took actions that were clearly illegal, but in many areas where the constitution was less than decisively settled, he stated his claims to authority. In 1604, for example, after the Hampton Court conference convened to consider Puritan calls for reform in the church, James issued a proclamation defending his power to make policy for the church, a position that had been opposed in Parliament earlier in the year. "Our duty towards God," asserted James, "requireth at our hands that what intractable men do not perform upon admonition they must be compelled into by authority, whereof the supreme power resting in our hands by God's ordinance we are bound to use the same in nothing more than in preservation of the church's tranquility, which by God's grace we are fully purposed to do."[2]

At almost the same time, James acted in another equally controversial area. Perpetually short of funds and unable to prevail upon Parliament to vote him sufficient supplies, the king moved to increase his revenue from the impost by levying new duties on goods without any authorization from Parliament. In *Bate's Case* of 1606 James was upheld in this action by the courts, but he clearly was trenching on an area very dear to Parliament, and in a constitutionally questionable manner.[3]

From the very earliest moments of his reign, Parliament reacted negatively to both James's theory and his practice, and in that context put forward a competing conception of politics.[4] Parliament was quick to challenge the particular powers exercised by the king. In June 1604, even before James issued his proclamation on the church, Parliament denied him the powers he claimed: "For matters of religion, it will appear by examination of truth and right that Your Majesty should be misinformed if any man should deliver that the kings of England have any absolute power in themselves either to alter religion, . . . or to make any laws concerning the same otherwise than as in temporal causes, by the consent of Parliament."[5] Parliament also firmly asserted its role in the exercise of the taxing power: "The policy and constitution of this your kingdom appropriates unto the kings of this realm, *with the assent of Parliament*, as well the sovereign power of making laws, as that of taxing or imposing upon their subjects' goods or merchandises"—notwithstanding the judges' decision in *Bate's Case*.[6] Not only did the king possess but a portion of the legislative power, but also—contrary to the right he claimed to decide legal causes personally—James was told by Sir Edward Coke in no uncertain terms that he was severely limited in his judicial powers. "The king in his own person cannot adjudge any case, either criminal . . . or betwixt party and party . . . but this ought to be determined and adjudged in some court of justice according to the law and custom of England."[7]

Even more broadly, the Parliamentary spokesmen rejected James's theories on the source and nature of his (and Parliament's) power. He was king hardly a year before Parliament spoke out against the view (which they associated with him) that Parliament "held not our privileges of right, but of grace only, renewed every Parliament by way of donature upon petition, and so to be limited." On the contrary, said the House of Commons, "our privileges and our liberties are our right and true inheritance, no less than our very lands and goods. . . . These rights and liberties of the whole commons of [the] realm of England . . . they and their ancestors from time immemorial have undoubtedly enjoyed."[8] The great parliamentary leader John Pym, leading the effort to impeach Roger Manwaring for his sermons favoring divine right absolutism, insisted that "the law of England, whereby the subject was exempted from taxes and laws not granted by common consent of Parliament, was not introduced by any statute, or by any charter or sanction of princes, but was the ancient and fundamental law, issuing from the first frame and constitution of the kingdom."[9] At the time of the contest over imposts, Parliament contended that "the law of property be originally and carefully preserved by the common laws of this realm, which are as ancient as the kingdom itself." Any proclamations by kings or statutes of Parliament affirming these rights of subjects and Parliament were merely confirmations of the preexisting law.[10]

This appeal to a set of parliamentary privileges and subjects' rights "as ancient as the kingdom itself" had two aspects. First, it served to reject the very idea of an "original of political power." There was no such thing; the beginning was itself originless. Therefore, there was no original authority that ordained the constitution and the rights it embodied, and if no authority in the past to establish the constitution, then no authority in the present to disestablish or override it.[11] The early parliamentary position thus differed from the divine right theory, not in offering a popular or social contract in place of the king as source of the constitution, but in refusing to credit any original authority. The Commons Journal for 1604 (the first Parliament under James I, and the one that registered the very strong objection to James's divine right theories quoted above) reported that the House rehearsed a theory of "the true original pedigree of government." This theory could identify no specific origin of the English regime, and surely was no theory of popular sovereignty:

> Order, the lustre of Nature, guided by a First Essence, put all government into form: First, in two, who, by procreation, . . . made a Family, with one Head; by propagation, a Tribe or Kindred, with one Elder, or Chief; by multiplication, a Society, a Province, a Country, a Kingdom, with one or more guides or leaders, of spirit aptest, or of choice fittest, to govern.[12]

The Commons no more affirmed that political society arises from an agreement of the people, as an exercise of some original popular power, than did the more clearly royalist formulation in the unlicensed canons of 1606:

> If any man shall affirm that man at first . . . ran up and down the woods and fields, as wild creatures . . . acknowledging no superiority one over another . . . until . . . they chose some among themselves to order and rule the rest, giving them power and authority to do so; and that consequently all civil power, jurisdiction and authority was first derived from the people, and disordered multitudes or either is originally still in them, or else is deduced by their consents actually from them, and is not God's ordinance originally descending from him and depending on him; he doth greatly err.[13]

Likewise, Pym, in his major attempt at refuting Manwaring's doctrines, did not endorse an original power in the people but held only that the powers of Parliament and the rights or immunities of subjects were "the ancient and fundamental law, issuing from the first frame and constitution of the kingdom"—that is, as old as, but not older than the "the first frame and constitution," derivative from and not the source of the constitution.[14]

As the passage from the Commons Journal suggests, the Parliamentary theory of the "ancient constitution" was an attempt to say something Aristotelian—or rather, two things: the constitution is natural, and the constitution cannot be understood by reducing it to its parts or elements. Political society is natural because it grows up naturally out of the lower human associations of family, tribe, and so on, just as Aristotle traced the process in the first book of his *Politics*. Human beings naturally constitute such associations, and these associations always have a principle of rule as a part of them.[15]

Some scholars—for example, J. G. A. Pocock—have speculated that the emphasis on the antiquity of the ancient constitution reflects the authority of the old as such: the old, ultimately old custom is the only legitimate authority.[16] Echoes of such a view surely exist in the documents, but these scholars have perhaps overemphasized this theme at the expense of the more significant nonreductionist point the Parliamentarians were making. Pocock is led by his view of the authority of antiquity as such to assimilate the argument regarding the ancient constitution to the argument made by the seventeenth-century common lawyers in favor of the common law over statutory law, an argument (complexly) resting on the antiquity of the former. As Sir John Davies put it in what is usually considered the classic formulation of the common lawyer's point of view, "The customary law of England . . . does far excel over written laws, namely over statues or acts of Parliament: which is manifest in this, that when our Parliaments have altered or changed any fundamental points of the common law, those alterations have been found by experience to be so inconvenient for the commonwealth, as that the common law has in effect been restored again, in the same points, by other acts of Parliament in succeeding ages."[17] But the Parliamentary doctrine of the ancient constitution contained no such hostility to legislation as this common lawyer voiced. Parliamentarians merely insisted that Parliament shared that power and had always done so. Even Fortescue in the fifteenth century, a common lawyer himself, accepted the legislative power and welcomed its capacity to change the common law.[18]

The doctrine of the antiquity or even immemoriality of the constitution seems rather a way of expressing in temporal terms an Aristotelian conception of the nature of constitutions as such: they are not merely the sum of their parts; although they grow out of prior elements, they cannot be reduced to those parts.[19] King, Parliament, subject—all are co-constitutively original elements of the constitution. Without the constitution there is no king, no subject. The part is a part only in relation to the whole, which is exactly coterminous with the part and not derivative from it. Thus Pym said that the "ancient and fundamental law"—and therefore Parliament, King, and subjects, with their respective rights and powers—"issue from the first frame and constitution of the kingdom." As Aristotle put it, the whole is prior to the parts, or, as Fortescue said, "A people does not deserve to be called a body while it is acephalous, that is, without a head. Because, just as in natural bodies, what is left over after decapitation is not a body, but is what we call a trunk, so in bodies politic a community without a head is by no means a body."[20] This was Fortescue's way of denying popular sovereignty, but the general principles hold more broadly for all the elements or parts of the polity. The body politic is in this sense what Fortescue called a *corpus mysticum*. The doctrine of the ancient constitution thus takes Aristotle's organic image of the polity just as seriously as does the divine right doctrine.

None of the elements or parts of the constitution can be prior to the whole; certainly none can be the cause of the whole, in the sense in which the divine right theory makes the king the cause of the constitution. And therefore, the theory of the ancient constitution takes Aristotle's organic image of the polity *more* seriously than does the divine right theory. Anything prior to the constitution is simply external to it, in essence irrelevant to it as a constitution. The ancients expressed that externality in terms of the great Founder, who brought the constitution into being but was no part of it, and whose only "representative" in it was the whole. Within the doctrine of the ancient constitution, the immemorial past served exactly the same role. Even if the origin of the constitution were not, strictly speaking, beyond the memory of man, that would not matter. Nothing prior to the origin has any further authority over the present; only the ongoing constitution itself has authority.

Like the divine right theory, the parliamentary doctrine of the ancient constitution thus came to expression in Aristotelian language.[21] More than the divine right theory, the doctrine of the ancient constitution remained close to its Aristotelian roots, as became clearer later, when efforts were made to articulate the doctrine in a yet more fully Aristotelian way. The Aristotelian provenance of this pristine version of parliamentary theory is one indication of how far it stands from the philosophy of the American Declaration of Independence. The theory of the ancient constitution does not conceive human beings as equal in the sense that by nature they are born owing no subjection; rather, it is natural that they be born into a community, and it is natural that every community have a principle of rule. In this respect the theory of the ancient constitution and the theory of divine right monarchy are far more like each other than either is like the Declaration. The parliamentary theory of the early seventeenth century, in fact, is most like the parliamentary theory of the late seventeenth century embodied in the Declaration of Rights. The notion of the ancient constitution, despite some setbacks later in the century, had remarkable resilience and power to define political reality for large and important segments of the political class.

In almost all respects the early parliamentary conceptions matched those of the chief documents of 1688–89. Under the parliamentary theory subjects are said to have rights, and the king is bound to respect these, but the rights are not natural rights. They do not precede the constitution but "issue" from it, in Pym's term. Referring to the "rights" of king, commons, peers, and other entities is another way of identifying the powers and immunities each has under the constitution. The rights differ according to the place of the rights-holder in the constitution. Thus the rights of king, commons, and peers are all different, not universally human.

These rights, of course, must be respected. According to Pym's account, "the form of government is that which doth actuate and dispose every part and member of a state to the common good."[22] Rights must be respected, for they keep each part in its proper relation to the whole and thus to the common good. In this view, the common good is the ultimate source of rights, rather than the security of rights being more or less the sum and substance of the common good, as in the Declaration of Independence.[23] If rights are not respected, said Pym, "the whole frame will quickly be dissolved, and fall in pieces, and instead of this concord and interchange of support . . . they will miserably consume and devour one another."[24]

Regard for constitutional rights thus stands as a central means to the successful conduct of political life; but security of rights is not affirmed as the very end for which government exists. Many generations earlier, Fortescue had made the point very clearly: the end of the laws (and constitution) of England is "the perfect virtue that is called by the name of legal justice," which "eliminates every vice and teaches every virtue, so that it is itself rightly called the whole virtue."[25] That is to say, Fortescue endorsed the classical Aristotelian idea that the political association exists for the sake of the most comprehensive human good, complete virtue: the political may come into being for the sake of mere life, but continues to exist for the sake of the good life.[26] The political as comprehensively ordered to all the requirements of the good life, or of "perfect virtue," is a far cry from the relatively narrow Lockean conception that government exists solely for the sake of securing rights.

We have no reason to doubt that the parliamentary writers of the seventeenth century saw the ends of political life much as Fortescue, and before him, Aristotle, had done. Accordingly, the original parliamentary theory endorsed none of the most typical of the American Declaration's set of truths—no state of nature, no artificial construction of government through a social contract, and therefore no popular sovereignty, no natural rights, no understanding of rights as the end of political life, no right of revolution. In sum, the ancient constitution differed from the American Declaration in just the same places as did the Declaration of Rights of 1688.

The Mixed Constitution

Between 1629 and 1640 no Parliaments met. The first Parliament after that long hiatus, known to history as the Short Parliament, met for only three weeks before King Charles I dissolved it. Seven months later a new Parliament, the Long Parliament, was convened. By that time even the avid proponents of the doctrine of the ancient constitution had been pressed by events and the logic of their fundamental commitments to abandon, or at least to modify extensively, the doctrine of the ancient constitution as they had previously articulated it.

For eleven years Charles had attempted to rule without Parliament, and for a time his effort bid fair to succeed. The immediate incitement toward such a course was provided by the Parliaments of the early years of his reign, which turned toward him an Oppositionist face—refusing to vote him the traditional revenues, insisting on "redress of grievances" as a precondition for further funding, and in general asserting their desire for different policies in both church and state. The high point of Parliament's success came in 1628 with the adoption of the Petition of Right, affirming or reaffirming much of the parliamentary view of the constitution. The height of contention between king and Parliament came in 1629, when members of the House of Commons forcibly held the Speaker of the House in his chair in order to carry on further business rather than comply with the king's order to dissolve.

The precondition for Charles's effort to govern alone lay in his powers, conceded generally to be part of the ancient constitution itself, to control the meetings of Parliament. The king issued writs for the election of members of the House of Commons, set the date for opening, and had the power to conclude all sessions. Armed with those powers, Charles could ensure that there would be no Parliament. He still needed to find alternate ways to furnish himself with the fiscal resources Parliament had traditionally supplied. Despite his acceptance in the Petition of Right of the proposition that parliamentary consent was required for all taxation in the kingdom, the king and his ministers resourcefully exploited all existing sources of funds and cultivated new or extended old ones.[27] Most ingenious was the laying of ship's-money levies against all the counties of England; port towns were traditionally liable to such levies, but never before had inland counties been required to pay. Since this was simply an extension of an existing valid tax, the king argued that parliamentary consent was not necessary.

In the *Ship's Money Case* (*Rex v. Hampden*) of 1638 the judges upheld the king. That decision was but one in a series that supported the monarch. Much earlier, *Bate's Case* had endorsed the king in his levying of new imposts. *The Five Knights' Case* of 1627 supported the king's practice of holding men without charge (arguably contrary to the Magna Charta) in service of his efforts to extract a forced loan from the merchants. Those decisions reflected in part the ambiguity of the constitution, the fact that much of it truly was unsettled and thus genuinely controvertible; but they also reflected the fact that the judges held office at the pleasure of the king—and prior to the decision in the *Ship's Money Case* he had vented his displeasure on several occasions by dismissing judges who disagreed with him.[28]

Charles's efforts to govern without Parliament fell afoul of his war in Scotland over the structure of the Scottish Church. To fight this war he required funds that even his creative finance measures failed to provide. Charles's hopes that in the emergency conditions of war Parliament might vote him the supplies he required proved baseless. By the time the Long Parliament convened in November 1640, positions had hardened among the members: there would be no quick granting of supplies to the king with a "thank you very much" in return. No, Parliament most recalcitrantly insisted that all the rubs in policy and constitution that had accumulated over eleven years would be raised. As Pym thundered within four days of the opening of the new Parliament, "There is a design to alter the kingdom both in religion and government. This is the highest of treason." Therefore there must needs be "a reformation," there must needs be a "finding out the authors and punishment of them."[29] In a word, there would be no business as usual, no voting of revenues for the king until the constitution was secured.

Parliament indeed went forward on both the tracks Pym announced: villains (or scapegoats) were identified and punished, and legislation was introduced with the intention of reforming the political system. In the course of things, the ancient constitution was so modified as to leave the king, plausibly, as its champion and Parliament as the sponsors of innovation.

During the period 1641–42 parliamentary leaders advocated and at times succeeded in enacting a series of measures that clearly would change the terms of the ancient constitution. Traditionally, the king possessed the power to convene and dismiss Parliaments, a power he had been using to prevent any Parliaments. In 1641 Parliament passed, and forced Charles to accept, the Triennial Act, which began with the concession that the power "to appoint the time and place for the holding" of Parliaments had always belonged to the monarch, but then went on to provide for other ways to call a Parliament if the king failed to do so. In addition, reacting to the recent experience of the Short Parliament, it also set stringent limits on the king's power to dissolve Parliament.[30] In rapid succession, Parliament passed statutes abolishing the Star Chamber and the High Commission, two well-established if not ancient courts.[31] These acts were followed by the Grand Remonstrance, which, among other things, demanded that the bishops, many "corrupted" by "Jesuits and other engineers and factions for Rome," be deprived of their traditional seats in the House of Lords, and that Parliament be conceded the right to approve the king's ministers.[32]

Other novel demands soon followed, most of which were collected in the Nineteen Propositions issued in June 1642. Parliament pressed for control over so many matters in the conduct of government that it would "have made the two houses masters of the state." Parliament demanded involvement in appointment to the government, control over the education and marriage of the royal children, the right to reform the church as it wished, that all judges serve for good behavior, that Parliament have a say in the selection of military officers and a share in powers over the militia, and so on.[33] There was no question that Parliament was pushing well beyond the boundaries of the ancient constitution, even in the most pro-parliamentary interpretation of that uncertain institution.

Now the king, only yesterday the great innovator, was able to appear in the guise of defender of the ancient constitution. In 1641 he expressed his entire willingness to join in a reformation of the government, by which he meant a routing of "all innovations in church and commonwealth." He vehemently distinguished that from "alteration of government," which he would not abide. Therefore, he felt compelled to resist many of Parliament's most ardent wishes. For instance, on the issue of the bishops and the House of Lords, Charles demurred, saying that he could not "consent for the taking away of their voice in Parliament, which they have so anciently enjoyed, under so many of my predecessors, even before the Conquest, and ever since." As J. W. Allen rightly observed, by 1642 "the Royalist party was essentially a constitutional party."[34]

Thus Parliament abandoned the conservative position to the royalists. The parliamentarians were driven to this for at least one fairly obvious reason: the events of the past eleven years had proven the ancient constitution to be more or less a failure. Its failure lay especially in its non-self-executing character. The constitution armed the king with prerogatives that enabled him to circumvent it in both letter and spirit. Even where the king stepped into relatively clear unconstitutionality—for instance, on ship's money—the constitution failed to provide adequate means of redress for subject or for Parliament, especially if, as Charles showed was possible, Parliament could be prevented from coming into session. That is why so many of the most persistent efforts during the early years of the Long Parliament were directed toward ensuring that Parliament could come into session even against the king's will. That is also why Parliament pressed so hard on its demand for a hand in the appointment of those who surrounded the king, so that he could have no independent agents bent on dishonoring the constitution. Structural changes like these were seen as preconditions for the preservation of the ancient constitution.

If the ancient constitution required alteration for its salvation, then its mere antiquity, the merely inherited character of its elements and features, could no longer suffice as a way of identifying the desirable constitutional order. Thus parliamentarians were forced to develop a new conceptualization of the old constitution.

Thoughtful parliamentarians themselves recognized that the recent changes threatened a crisis of authority. Henry Parker, for example, reported that "some lawyers doubt how far the Parliament is able to create new forms and precedents and [whether] it hath a jurisdiction over itself."[35] Paradoxically, one of the earliest and best statements of a doctrine meant partly to justify recent deviations from the ancient constitution issued not from Parliament but from the king. In 1642 Charles I promulgated his *Answer to the Nineteen Propositions of Both Houses of Parliament*. He made no mention of divine right absolutism;[36] instead, he defended the ancient constitution, as he had been doing since 1640, but he also defended the legitimacy of the constitutional innovations recently adopted. The new arrangements agreed to by king and Parliament, he said, went "beyond the examples of any of our ancestors," but he justified the changes as "better enabling" Parliament to play its proper role in the constitution.[37]

Charles's *Answer* still conceived of the constitution in Aristotelian categories, this time as a variant of the classical mixed regime, a doctrine developed by Aristotle, adumbrated by Cicero, Polybius, and others, and possessing much currency in Europe thereafter. According to Corine Weston, "during the conflicts of the seventeenth century" this theory of the mixed regime "became the leading theory of the English constitution." Although the theory had classical origins and appeared in England as early as Elizabethan times, it was "rarely used" until the 1640s; the "metamorphosis in public opinion" that made it so prominent began with Charles's use of it in his *Answer*.[38] Each of the three pure types of government—monarchy, aristocracy, and democracy—has its "particular conveniences and inconveniences," Charles wrote. The ancient constitution of the English is good not because it is ancient but because their "ancestors . . . so moulded [it] out of a mixture of these [pure forms] as to give this kingdom (as far as human prudence can provide) the conveniences of all three, without the inconveniences of any one, as long as the balance hangs even between the three states, and they run jointly on in their proper channels (begetting verdure and fertility in the meadows on both sides), and the overflowing of either on either side raise no deluge or inundation."[39] Charles implicitly conceded that his efforts to rule without Parliament represented such an "overflowing," and thus accepted the innovations Parliament had managed to impose on him as a means of restoring the balance.

The House of Commons, as late as 1646, put forward a very similar account of its aims in promoting constitutional innovation:

> We are so far from altering the fundamental constitution and government of this kingdom by king, lords, and commons, that we have only desired, that with the consent of the king, such powers may be settled in the two Houses without which we can have no assurance but that the like or greater mischiefs than these which God hath hitherto delivered us from may break out again.[40]

Just as the innovations were presented by both sides as preservative of some underlying balance or mixture contained in "the fundamental law," so the doctrine of the mixed constitution was used to oppose some of the proposed innovations. Charles appealed to the doctrine in his rejection of Parliament's demands to share in the choice of the king's ministers. "The House of Commons," said he, is "an excellent conservator of liberty, but [was] never intended for any share in government, or the choosing of those that should govern." Likewise the king objected to Parliamentary efforts to control the militia and to preempt his share of the legislative power.[41]

Although the theory of the mixed regime emphasized somewhat different themes than the theory of the ancient constitution—above all, the goodness, not the oldness, of the constitution—nonetheless the two doctrines had much in common. The constitution as described in the one theory was recognizable, more or less, as the constitution described in the other. Granted, the theory of the mixed constitution had a more logical or theoretically satisfying sense of coherence to it. The constitution was not merely an inheritance, nor even merely an organic whole prior to its parts, but was a particularly well-made whole in general and could be made even better with some judicious reform.

Not insignificantly, both theories proceeded largely within an intellectual framework supplied by Aristotle's *Politics*. The closeness of the two is visible in the writings of earlier thinkers like Fortescue, whose treatments of the constitution contained elements of both. Another factor common to both is their distance from the theory of the American Declaration of Independence: neither constitutional doctrine evokes the political universe of natural rights, consent, and right of revolution. Despite the fact that the American founders would retain a great concern with balance in the constitution—witness two such magnificent statements as John Adams's *Thoughts on Government* and *The Federalist*—yet the Americans transformed the theory of the constitution drastically and attached it to a doctrine of the foundations of politics that had few precedents in this earlier theorizing.

The constitutional vision of Charles's *Answer* was, of course, far closer to the earlier parliamentarian ancient constitution than it was to the earlier royalist commitment to divine right. That the document was chiefly authored by a group of moderate parliamentarians helps explain that otherwise paradoxical fact.[42] The dominant emphasis of this theory was on the balance among the constitutional elements and the indispensability of all to the proper functioning of the regime. That notion of balance served, in turn, as a criterion by which to impose or resist changes in the ancient constitution. The constitutional debate turned not so much on whether some practice or power was immemorial custom, but on whether it would contribute to the desirable constitutional balance.[43] The ongoing debate revealed a fundamental indeterminacy at the root of the theory, however. In the view of Charles's advisors, the theory implied that further augmentation of parliamentary authority would be deleterious to the future health of the constitution. In the view of parliamentary partisans like Henry Parker and William Prynne, however, the preservation of the constitution required the very augmentation rejected by the king's supporters.

The mixed constitution analysis proved, moreover, to stand in a certain tension with the onrush of events in the 1640s. If at first the question was what might justify innovations in the ancient constitution, after 1642 the question became instead what might justify Parliament in resisting the king and claiming the authority to act legally on its own, independent of the king's concurrence—for with the outbreak of war between royalist and parliamentary forces this became the actual situation in England. The theory of mixed monarchy, with its emphasis on shared, concurrent powers, was not congruent with the situation facing Parliament.

Accordingly, Parliament was driven to modify the doctrine of the mixed constitution in novel ways. Perhaps the most striking fact about those modifications was Parliament's continued failure to adumbrate anything like a theory of revolution, or even of resistance. True, Parliament did emit a defense of its various acts of resistance to commands of the king, and of its open warfare against his supporters, but it did so in terms of a distinction between the king's own person and his legal person. In the Militia Ordinance of March 1642 Parliament in effect acted to take control of the military power of the kingdom from Charles. The king reacted strongly, denying the legality of Parliament's action, and by the ancient constitution he surely was on strong ground there, as even Parliament admitted: "It is acknowledged that the king is the fountain of justice and protection." That is, under normal circumstances the power over the military resides in the king; but, Parliament asked, "if the king shall refuse to discharge that duty and trust, whether there is not a power in the two Houses to provide for the safety of the Parliament and peace of the kingdom, which is the end for which the ordinance concerning the militia was made." Parliament's answer to its own question was yes, because although the king has the power, these "acts of justice and protection are not exercised in his own person, nor depend upon his pleasure, but by his courts, and by his ministers, who must do their duty therein, though the king in his own person should forbid them." And in a daring sweep to a conclusion, Parliament declared that even if it delivered judgments against the king's will and personal command, "yet are they the king's judgments. . . . What they do herein hath the stamp of royal authority, although his majesty, seduced by evil counsel, do in his own person oppose or interrupt the same; for the king's supreme and royal pleasure is exercised and declared in this high court of law and counsel, after a more eminent and obligatory manner than it can be by personal act or resolution of his own."[44]

Parliament claimed no right to overturn or act against the constitution. The constitution as coaction of king, lords and commons remained operative—except lords and commons now played the role of king as well. In the case of a reprobate king, Parliament could speak more truly for him than he could for himself. The incoherences of the parliamentary position are clear enough, but it is nonetheless worth noticing that Parliament is saying something quite important here.[45] The king is not so much a person as a public function. Political life is in no sense the private preserve of a person, the king, but is a public thing. Thus the kingdom is not in any sense his private property.[46] In a word, Parliament has here extirpated all remnants of the feudal mingling of public and private authority, an intermingling that persisted, in modified form to be sure, in the royalist divine right doctrine. In this respect, the parliamentary doctrine shares something very important with the philosophy of the Declaration of Independence, for the latter understands all political power as public in nature.

Nonetheless, the parliamentary doctrine remains far from Locke and the Declaration for the same reasons the more pristine doctrine of the ancient constitution was remote from them. One measure of that distance is the lengths to which Parliament went to remain within the theory of the mixed constitution—by repairing to the distinction between the king's "own person" and his legal or properly royal status, a distinction whose chief vice is its contradictory stance in relation to the theory of the mixed monarchy, of which it is a part. The theory of mixed monarchy holds that the common good is served through separated yet shared powers; the parliamentary application of the theory, on the other hand, implies that the common good is reached through the artificial maintenance but actual overcoming of the separation.[47] The parliamentary doctrine fails not because it has recourse to a legal fiction, but because that fiction is so purely fictitious. Julian Franklin, who has reviewed the parliamentary doctrines of this early period of the Civil War with great care, found the parliamentary theory "inconsistent," in that under it Parliament affirmed its right to appropriate the king's "true" royal powers but rejected any right to depose the king. That observation, surely just in some respects, also misses a central point—that Parliament failed to claim a power to depose the king because it remained committed to the doctrine of mixed monarchy.[48] It failed to claim for itself a power over the constitution on grounds of either parliamentary or popular sovereignty, but instead doggedly attempted to remain within the mixed constitution. The effort proved just how great was Parliament's official commitment to some version of the mixed constitution. And, as we have seen already, the doctrine of the mixed constitution, like that of the ancient constitution, contained within it great powers of resistance to the move toward the preconstitutional power that constituted it. Thus Parliament was attempting to do quite the opposite of what J. W. Allen has accused it of doing: "In spite of confusion and ambiguity it seems the House was really claiming sovereignty for themselves as the representatives of the nation." That is just what Parliament, at this moment, twisted itself into awkward and clumsy positions to avoid doing.[49]

Nonetheless, despite the great force of the Aristotelian resistance to the preconstitutional, in 1642–43 writers sympathetic to the parliamentary cause (although not Parliament itself) were to take the momentous step of introducing into Opposition discourse the notion of a preconstitutional contract. Such ideas were not invented at this time, of course, but from this point onward contractarian thinking of some sort or other became and remained centrally important to Anglo-American political thought. Although it was far from carrying the day, as we have already seen, a form of contrac-tarian thought was a strong contender for favor at the time of the formula-tion of the Declaration of Rights. With the acceptance of contractarianism, moreover, English political discourse appears to draw much closer to the Lockean style of thought. Nonetheless, before discussing these parliamen-tary doctrines further, we must pause to consider more generally the theme of contractarianism in political thought.

CONTRACTARIANISMS

From the 1640s on, contract was a powerful theme in parliamentarian thought, and later in Whig thought. Recent research in the history of polit-ical thought has made it increasingly clear, however, that not all contractar-ian doctrines are identical; nor are all best understood as efforts to achieve some paradigmatic or standard doctrine. Most of the earlier scholarship was more or less "permeated by the belief that there is, as it were, *a* or *the* theory of contract, a model to which actual writers more or less conformed." The appearance within a political statement of any "allusion to consent, consen-sus, or mutual obligation" was taken as indication of the presence of this more or less uniform contract theory.[50]

Historians like John Gough, Ernest Barker, and their mutual source, Otto von Gierke, often drew distinctions among contract ideas, but the assimila-tive result remained. These writers frequently differentiated types of con-tract—for example, a government contract from a social contract proper—but they identified the full-blown social contract theory as paradigmatic and other contractarian ideas as "anticipations" or "approaches" to this ma-ture "fulfillment" of the contract idea. Whatever differences there may be, Gough, for example, still spoke of *the* contractarian theory.[51]

Instead of the old "unicontractarian" approach (to borrow a phrase from the literature of totalitarianism), Höpfl and Thompson advocate greater sensitivity to particularity and difference.[52] They insist that at least two very different types of contract theory need to be distinguished as relevant to political discussion in seventeenth-century England. Both deployed the lan-guage of covenant, contract, or compact, but this common language ap-peared in a context and with a function that made the overall doctrines importantly different from each other. One variant—the older, and in the seventeenth century the practically more important version—was "constitu-tional contractarianism." It "set covenant within the terminological context of 'fundamental law', 'fundamental rights' or 'liberties', 'original contract', and 'ancient' or 'fundamental constitution'." This form of contractarian-ism would then appear to have a prima facie connection to the types of parliamentary thought under consideration in this chapter. "In constitu-tional contractarianism particular positive laws and the institutional in-heritance of specific polities were most relevant and important, rather than universal propositions about all men and all polities." The other tradition, "philosophical contractarianism", had much greater "theoretical ambitions and [intended] generality of thought"; it "spoke of 'natural right', 'natural liberty', 'natural equality', 'condition [state] of nature', 'covenant', and 'sovereignty'."[53]

Applying their distinction specifically to the period after 1660, Höpfl and Thompson observe that the Whig polemicists of the age remained almost entirely within the constitutional contractarian tradition, in that they "placed emphasis almost exclusively on justifications in constitutional law for political action and the historic rights of Englishmen." The Whig appeal to the "original contract" in the Convention Parliament deployed this language of constitutional contractarianism, not of philosophical contractarianism—a "contract that had established the ancient English constitution, that had been rendered in each coronation oath, and that was embodied in English fundamental laws."[54]

An alternative view is John Dunn's, who spoke of Locke's *Two Treatises*, and their influence in America, as follows:

> Above all, it was only one work among a large group of other works which have expounded the Whig theory of the revolution. . . . The readiness with which many scholars have detected the influence of the *Two Treatises* in England and America is at least in part a product of the fact that they have read so little else of the English political writing contemporary with it.[55]

Dunn's is a good example of unicontractarianism, for, according to Höpfl and Thompson, Locke and "only Locke, it appears, produced a treatise . . . that relied solely upon notions of natural right, natural law, state of nature, and social contract"—a treatise, that is, wholly of the philosophical type. "Locke's uniqueness . . . helps account for the initial failure of his *Two Treatises of Government* to achieve the task Locke set himself in publishing: the justification of the Revolution of 1688."[56]

Just as Höpfl and Thompson's distinction between constitutional and philosophical contractarianism serves to separate Lockean theory, and thus the American Declaration, from other sorts of Whig political thought in the period 1688–90, so their categories bring out the same sort of fundamental difference between Lockean contractarianism and the appeals to contract that began to appear in parliamentary writings on the mixed monarchy in the early 1640s.

THE ORIGINAL CONTRACT AND THE REFORMATION ATTITUDE: PHILIP HUNTON

Contract became part of the theory of the mixed regime in the early 1640s, and its meaning was much determined by the context of thought in which it emerged. Part of that context was set by the rush of events that led Parliament to assert for itself the powers of the monarchy; possession by Parliament of such powers was in fact incompatible with the original form of the theory of the mixed regime. More thoughtful writers thus sought a rationale that would do less damage to underlying parliamentary theory. For a whole group of writers between 1642 and 1644—Charles Herle, Henry Parker, William Prynne, John Goodwin, Philip Hunton, and Samuel Rutherford—contract was the answer. However, more than the need to find a better way to justify parliamentary actions in the superheated setting of civil war promoted contractarianism's rise to prominence. The mixed regime analysis was also subjected to theoretical pressure by royalist writers attempting to integrate the theory of Charles I's *Answer* with earlier doctrine to support the king's stance in the increasingly escalating conflicts of the day.

The royalist writer who attracted most attention from writers on the other side was Dr. Henry Ferne, a royal chaplain and one of the more prolific polemicists on behalf of King Charles. Ferne introduced a distinction into the controversy that proved to be of capital and long-lasting significance: as the *Answer* said, England had a mixed constitution with shared powers, but that was only at the level of the exercise of power. The supreme power or sovereignty "belonged wholly to the monarch." Such powers as Parliament had—and Ferne did not deny it had them—derived from the king. Ferne differed from the earlier forms of divine right theory chiefly in emphasizing more strongly the political desirability of the sharing of powers, and thus he endorsed, to a degree, the mixed regime. For example, he stated his desire "to take off that false imputation laid upon the divines of this kingdom and upon all those who appear for the King in this cause that they endeavour to defend an absolute power in him, and to raise an arbitrary way of government: this we are as much against on his part as against resistance on the subject's part."[57] Yet Ferne gave nothing on the principle-in-chief: where power primordially resided, whence it derived. Thus Ferne introduced into the heart of the debate precisely the sort of consideration the mixed regime analysis had in principle avoided—an insistent resolution of the constitution into a preconstitutional source of power. Ferne derived a series of conclusions from his conception of the preconstitutional origins of the English mixed monarchy. Two were particularly important. First, Parliament shared in the legislative power, but had no call to share in governance itself; thus Parliament's demands to approve the king's ministers or control the militia were way out of bounds. Equally important in the context, Ferne concluded that since all legitimate power originally belonged to the king, resistance such as parliamentary forces were offering was wholly unjustifiable.[58]

The most obvious response to Ferne was that put forth by Charles Herle, rector of Winwick in Lancashire, in a series of pamphlets in 1643–44. England's government "is not simply subordinative and absolute," he argued, "but a co-ordinative and mixed monarchy. This mixture or co-ordination is in the very supremacy of power itself," which implies that Parliament is not "subordinate to the king. . . . Every member . . . taken severally is a subject; but all, in their Houses, are not."[59] From this premise, Herle articulated a doctrine of parliamentary power that came relatively close to expressing the views officially adopted in parliamentary actions. "If the king violated the law or failed to provide for the safety of the kingdom, the other estates would have to supply the necessary co-ordination to carry on the government and form 'virtually the whole.'"[60]

Similar to Herle's work, but more thoughtful and ultimately more revealing, was the development of the theory of mixed monarchy from a parliamentary perspective by the Puritan divine Philip Hunton in his work of 1643, A *Treatise of Monarchy*. Hunton's marvelously systematic treatise avoids some of the most obvious defects of Herle's (and Parliament's) position, and at the same time more thoroughly brings out the basis, nature, and goals of parliamentary contractarianism. According to Hunton, "The sovereign power must be originally in all three, viz. the composition be of all three, so that one must not hold his power from the other, but all equally from the fundamental constitution; for, if the power of one be original, and the other derivative, it is no mixture, for such a derivation of power to others is the most simple monarchy."[61] Hunton's language is instructive: he attempts to trace all power back to "the fundamental constitution" itself, revealing thereby the continuing power of Aristotelian nonreductionist constitutionalism, even when, as we shall see, he was moving away from it under the joint pressure of events and theoretical challenge.

From the premise he shared with Herle, that the mix resided in the "sovereign power" itself, Hunton drew the more consistent conclusion that Parliament's claims, too, required trimming. As Weston observes, Hunton was "abler and more moderate than Herle." Allen comments on Hunton's "cool detachment and . . . unusual fairness to opponents."[62] Hunton took it to be the principle of "every mixed government" that "there must be necessity of concurrence of all three estates in the production of acts belonging to that power which is common to them. Else . . . you put it in the power of two by a confederacy at pleasure, to disannul the third, or suspend all its acts, and make it a bare cipher in government." Hunton shared Charles's concern that the king not be overborne, no more than he should overbear. Thus even in the hands of this important parliamentary writer the mixed monarchy theses came to stand against certain of the more innovative and unbalancing of the parliamentary demands. Hunton insisted that Parliament share the power of constituting "courts of judicature," for example, but conceded that "the choice of persons" to staff these courts "is entrusted to [the king's] judgment."[63]

Hunton nonetheless grounds the whole on a doctrine of contract. The English constitution establishes a limited and mixed monarchy—that is, a monarchy in which the powers of the ruler are constrained by limitations derived from a source other than the will of the monarch. The sovereign power itself is shared and held independently and directly from the constitution by those who share in it. The English constitution derives this character from the consent of the people, as does even the most absolute monarchy. Both the type of government in any place—that is, the constitution—and the particular persons or family holding power under the constitution derive from "the tacit and virtual, or else express and formal consent of that society of men they govern."[64]

Hunton relishes complexity. In a system like the English one there are four levels of political authority, each requiring more or less separate treatment. The very "constitution or power of magistracy in general" derives from God himself. "It is God's express ordinance that, in the societies of mankind, there should be a magistracy or government." At this level, Hunton finds the relevance of classic Christian texts like Romans 13. But God does not normally mandate any particular form of government; that is up to each human society to do for itself. At this second level, in all societies except those few in which God directly ordains a particular constitution, a presovereign power of the people rules. The people exercise this power to establish a third level of authority, the constitution, which establishes where sovereign power resides for that society. Finally, in the fourth sphere are those who actually exercise power within a given constitution. A great variety of permutations and combinations are theoretically possible, but for England the four levels are marked respectively by the rule of God, the people of England, and, for the final two, the mix of king and Parliament.[65]

The more purely Aristotelian theory of the mixed regime provided only for Hunton's third and fourth levels; Hunton has added onto the idea of the autonomy of the constitution a supervening prepolitical power in the people and, supervening over that, the power of God. At Hunton's second level, then, contractarian ideas make their entrance into parliamentary constitutionalism. The most obvious reason for that entrance would appear to be the need to counter Ferne's claim that the mixed monarchical constitution itself derives from the monarch; the constitution derives instead from the nation. But why does Hunton say so, and why could he have not remained within a more purely Aristotelian frame and denied Ferne's assertion about the origin of the constitution and, more to the point, denied the very relevance of that origin?

The answer to these questions is suggested in the form in which Hunton poses the question to which his *Treatise* is addressed: "Government and subjection are relatives; so that what is said of the one, may in proportion be said of the other." The question of government is strictly correlative to the question of subjection, or obligation, of subjects; the question of political philosophy resolves itself into the source, nature, and degree of subjection.

This is surely foreign to the approach of Aristotle himself, for to the ancients the question of obligation or degree of subjection is no thematic part of political science. Hunton's deviation from classical Aristotelianism in developing a doctrine of contract is paralleled by the deviation of putting at the center the question of subjection.

Hunton's two innovations are related. In bringing the issue of subjection to the fore, Hunton shares more with the divine right theorists than he does with Aristotle himself. Both Hunton and the monarchists *jure divino* seek to discern to what degree humans are conscience-bound to obey political authorities. Ultimately, political philosophy for both is but a branch of moral philosophy, or better yet, moral theology. As Hunton put it, "government is . . . the exercise of a moral power," but that power is defined by the moral subjection of those over whom the power is exercised.[66] The most immediate or obvious source of that approach to politics is the common Christian context in which Hunton and the royalists thought about politics: "Ye must needs be subject, not only for wrath, but also for conscience sake."[67]

Hunton and the divine right theorists take a fundamentally different approach to the issue of subjection, however. For the latter, unconditional obedience to the ruler is the means whereby the peculiar Reformation combination of freedom and subjection may find expression in the political sphere. Hunton's superimposition of contract onto an Aristotelian constitution represents an alternative attempt to discover the political embodiment of the Reformation.[68] The chief function of contract or consent for Hunton is to generate obligation or subjection. Subjection is not natural and universal, something one is simply born into, but is undertaken voluntarily. "An oath to a lawful thing is obligatory," indeed is one of the ways, if not the prime way, in which obligation as such is incurred. "Man, being a voluntary agent, and subjection being a moral act, it does essentially depend on consent. . . . A bond of subjection cannot be put on him, nor a right to claim obedience and service acquired unless a man became bound by some act of his own will." The generation of obligation through an act of will—that is, through consent and contract—is another way of conceiving the copresence of human freedom and human subjection. God ordained that humanity be subject: to him in general and to public authority in particular. But God does not ordinarily place human beings within a complete structure of authority; their free coaction is required to complete the subjection they are to be under. Human will cocreates the moral ties that bind the species. Not merely does Hunton's political science culminate in a teaching of the goodness of mixture in the constitution, but in its deepest grounds it is committed to a mixture of divine and human coaction as well.[69] Thus humanity can be both free and subject at once.

Contrary to what many present-day scholars believe, Hunton's contractarianism differs substantially from the version more familiar to us from the

Declaration of Independence or the political philosophy of John Locke.[70] The keynote of Hunton's Protestant theory is the power of human will to cocreate moral obligation. To express that morally creative power it is not sufficient that human beings merely consent to an authority already completely established.[71] Human will not only freely accepts but partly creates the structures of moral obligation. According to Hunton, there is no paradigmatic contract. For Locke and for the Americans it is impossible, both logically and psychologically, to conceive the contract as one of unlimited subjection: there are always inalienable natural rights to serve as an end and limit to all subjection. But Hunton knows nothing of natural rights or of the contract of subjection as the means to secure them. His contract is perfectly open-ended. Human beings may as well establish an absolute monarchy as a limited and mixed constitution. Absolute monarchy results "when people . . . resign up themselves, to be governed by the will of one man. . . . This is a lawful government. . . . Therefore where men put themselves into this utmost degree of subjection by oath and contract . . . it binds them and they must abide it." Limited monarchy derives from precisely the same source. "Kings have not divine words and binding laws to constitute them in their sovereignty, but derive it from ordinary providence; the sole means thereof is the consent and fundamental contract of a nation or [sic] men, which consent puts them in their power, which can be no more or other than is conveyed to them by such contract of subjection." Or, as Hunton put it yet more generally, "In the first original monarchy, yea, any individual frame of government whatsoever, is elective; that is, is constituted and draws its force and right from the consent and choice of that community over which it sways."[72]

The constitution, as well as the actual ruler, is determined by this positive act of will: the moral power of human freedom is very great. This power is so great that it can bind whole communities and even the future. The consent is not the consent of individuals but of the community. Hunton neither explores how this can be so nor looks very carefully into how the contract might be executed. Moreover, the contract is not made anew by each generation, much less by each person: future generations are morally bound by past generations. People have no right to complain of their political condition, whatever it may be, if "they or their ancestors have subjected themselves to such a power by oath or political contract."[73] Hunton's point is to establish the quasi-sovereign coactive power of human will as such, not the power of each individual. Only in a certain sense does government "derive its just power from the consent of the governed."

Positive, historical consent founds the constitution. The character of the constitution, defining the rights and duties of rulers and subjects, is to be found out by reference to the actual historical terms of the constitution, as established in the original contract. "Thus," Hunton asserts, "the community, whose consent establishes a power over them, cannot be said universally to have an eminence of power above that which they constitute: sometimes they have, sometimes they have not; and to judge when they have, when not, respect must be had to the original contract and fundamental constitution of that state."[74] There is no abstract "natural constitutional law," as one finds in Hobbes, Locke, or Jefferson; there is no universal natural right of revolution, as one finds in Locke and Jefferson.[75] Hunton's contractarianism is thus most closely related to Höpfl and Thompson's category of constitutional contractarianism, for in it contract is conceived as historical and constitutional.

Hunton uses some of the same terms as Locke and the American Declaration, but, it should now be clear, his doctrine lacks all five of the defining elements of Lockean contract theory. Hunton recognizes no general right of revolution, and even when resistance is legitimate, as in the English limited and mixed monarchy, sets severe limits on the kind of resistance allowable.[76] The equality of all human beings also forms no part of Hunton's scheme. The ultimate reference is the nation, which he conceives as organized in its classes and orders in more or less the same way as did the authors of the Declaration of Rights. Hunton does not understand government as an artifact; it is divinely ordained. Consent is required to complete the ordination, and thus a degree of human making enters into the process, but this is not a consent which in its nature constitutes public authority out of some preexisting authority residing only in individuals. Consent for Hunton is connected to an "original contract"; consent is given at some discrete historical moment, but not by each and every individual human being. Finally, and most important, natural rights play no part in Hunton's political thought.

THE ARISTOTELIANISM OF THE ORIGINAL CONTRACT:
HENRY PARKER

Like the divine right theory it opposed, Hunton's mixed monarchy contractarianism emerged as a Reformation-inspired and -infused modification of an essentially Aristotelian line of thought. One of the other mixed monarchy theorists of the day, the parliamentary leader Henry Parker, made the Aristotelian dimensions of mixed monarchy contractarianism even clearer, and in so doing clarified some otherwise inexplicable elements of Hunton's theory.

Parker, like Hunton, willingly accepted Charles's description of the English constitution in the *Answer* as a mixed monarchy, but he rejected far more forcefully than Hunton the proroyalist implications drawn from that characterization.[77] In Parker's *Observations upon Some of His Majesty's Late Answers and Expresses* (1642), contractarianism takes on much greater importance at the expense of the loss of authority of the similitudes of rule, so important to divine right political doctrine. He does not deny the similitudes altogether, but he strips them of most of their evocative power by making them mere analogies, perhaps true to some degree but more often than not misleading or even outright false. The divine similitude, if taken in the way James and the royalists did, is "a kind of blasphemy." The familial similitude does no better at capturing the nature of the political relationship. "The father is more worthy than the son in nature, and the son is wholly a debtor to the father, and can by no merit transcend his dutie, nor chalenge any thing as due from his father. . . . Yet this holds not in the relation betwixt King and Subject, for its more due in policie, and more strictly to be chalenged, that the King should make happy the People, than the People make glorious the King." Parker also rejects the similitude of the body. "The head naturally doth not more depend upon the body, than that does upon the head, both head and members must live and dye together; but it is otherwise with the Head Political, for that receives more subsistence from the body than it gives, and being subservient to that, it has no being when that is dissolved, and that may be preserved after its dissolution."[78]

Even though Parker dismissed the similitudes, and with them the organic polity of Aristotle, nonetheless the remarkable power of Aristotle as a political thinker remains visible in Parker. Unlike Hobbes (who at almost the same moment was developing a contractarian version of politics that, in its mature form, was meant to effect a root-and-branch break with the Greek philosopher's long-lived and, as he thought, baleful doctrines), Parker quite comfortably set out his contractarianism in essentially Aristotelian terms.

"In this contestation between Regall and Parliamentary power," Parker states at the very beginning of his essay, "for method's sake it is requisite to consider first of Regall, then of Parliamentary Power, and in both to consider the efficient, and finall causes."[79] Parker begins, in a word, with the recognition of "contestation" among the elements of the constitution. In that respect, he begins in the same way Charles did in his *Answer*: the authority of the ancient constitution provides inadequate guidance for the present. The difference between Parker and Charles's moderate parliamentarian ghostwriters centers on the issue of where to look instead. The *Answer* had proposed as a standard of the constitutional order the mixed regime and thus the balance of the constitution: the goodness of the constitution lies in its balance. For the sake of that balance, Charles concluded, parliamentary demands for greater power must be rejected. Parker, on the contrary, formulates the issue in terms of the efficient and final causes of the elements of the constitution. How can we settle the proper balance of the constitution except in terms of the purpose or end of the constitution? Aristotle himself had pointed the way by distinguishing the regimes from one another not only in terms of the social-political elements dominant in each but in terms of the goodness of each. The theory of the mixed regime was indeed derivative from this primary consideration—an attempt to reap the positive and avoid the negative qualities of each pure regime. Parker sees the "balance" as too formulaic; the point of the mix is to achieve some good beyond the mix itself. Parker attempts to discern the good of the mix by raising the question of the final cause of the constitution, or of its chief elements. "The finall cause of Royal Authoritie," Parker concludes, is "the people"—that is, the welfare of the people and not the greatness or fame of the ruler. Parker's understanding is identical to Aristotle's: the good regime aims at the good of the community rather than the good of the rulers.[80]

Parker and the Opposition writers of the time, however, drew an inference from the Aristotelian thesis about the final cause that produced a real amendment to Aristotle's own political philosophy. If the good of the people is the final cause of the constitution, Parker insisted, the same people must be the efficient cause of the constitution as well. "Power is originally inherent in the people, and it is nothing else but that might and vigour which such or such a societie of men containes in itselfe, and . . . by such or such a law of common consent and agreement it is derived into such and such hands."[81] The "original" of political power resides in the people and passes from them to the actual ruling authorities. Parker is so certain of this precisely because he knows the natural end of politics even more certainly: "the paramount law that shall give law to all humane laws whatsoever, and that is *Salus Populi*." According to J. W. Allen, with this move Parker becomes the first clear-cut contractarian thinker in England.[82]

In drawing a contractarian conclusion regarding the efficient cause, Parker breaks with Aristotle on the basis of their common premise regarding the final cause of government. Parker's essay suggests several reasons for the insertion into parliamentary theory of an Aristotelian contractarianism at this time. First, the broad context of Parker's ruminations made the issue of the "original" of political power far more pressing than it had been for Aristotle and most of his followers. Parker, like Hunton, was opposing the pretensions of the monarchy, and behind these still hovered the doctrine of divine right—not only that the king's authority was *jure divine*, but, à la Dr. Ferne, that the source of the constitution in its entirety was the king's more primordial power. That claim had implications for the issues in immediate contention. Two visions of what properly could or should be done about the constitution were in conflict, and the party that could claim an originating power over the constitution could surely use that as the basis for a claim to settle the present conflict. That immediate context certainly must have pushed Parker and the others in contractarian directions. If the king has final say on the shape of the constitution, then the constitution can hardly accomplish its final end or purpose, the welfare of the people. If the king retains the kind of supremacy within the mixed constitution that was urged by royalists like Ferne, then the entire notion of mixture and limit was for naught, as was the practical significance of the idea that regal power was for the sake of the people. In case of conflict between king and Parliament, "we must retire to the principles of Nature, and there search, whether the King or the Kingdom be to be lookt upon as the efficient, and finall cause, and as the proper subject of all power."[83] Precisely because the people are the final cause, one must also conceive them to be the efficient cause. If nature ordains the good of the people, then the natural original and ultimate locus of political power must be the people as well. Any other arrangement would be self-contradictory and self-defeating. Parker agrees with Hunton that political authority is ordained prior to any contract, but the one looks to a divine ordination to be completed by human free action, where the other looks to nature for the original and end of political power.

Parker's context forced him to struggle with the very same problem Herle and Hunton did: In case of conflict over powers in the mixed monarchy, who has the right to define the constitution and what powers exist to enforce any rightful definition?[84] Hunton had answered that the nature of the mixed constitution allows no legal answer to that question: if one or another part of the constitution had this legal power, then the constitution would not be truly mixed in its foundation. Hunton conceded this to be an imperfection, but "a frame of government cannot be imagined of that perfection, but that some inconveniences there will be possible for which there can be provided no remedy."[85]

Parker attempted to avoid Hunton's "imperfection" by taking a different tack from both him and Herle:

> If we allow the king to be the sole, supream competent Judge, . . . we resigne all into his hands, we give lifes, liberties, laws, Parliaments, all to be held at meer discretion? For there is in the interpretation of law upon the last appeal, the same supremacy of power requisite, as in making it; And therefore grant the King supream interpreter, and its all one, as if we granted him the supream maker of law; and Grant him this, and we grant him above all limits, all conditions, all humane bonds whatsoever.[86]

Parker is, in a real sense, more practical than Hunton. Some real supremacy must be somewhere, and Parliament is the place. In the final analysis, Parker is only a tentative spokesman for the mixed constitution. "In matters of law and state both, . . . some determination must be supreme, . . . and there can be nothing said against the arbitrary supremacy of Parliaments."[87] Parker accepts, that is to say, the ultimate sovereignty of Parliament. "Parliaments have the same efficient cause as monarchies, if not higher, for in truth, the whole kingdom is not so properly the Author as the essence it selfe of Parliament."[88] Since Parliament embodies or stands as "the essence" of the whole kingdom, any judgments about the character of the constitutional balance can rightly and safely be left to it. "It is indeed the state itself. . . . We had a maxime, and it was grounded in Nature, . . . that a community can have no private ends to mislead it, and make it injurious to itselfe, and no age will furnish us with one story of any Parliament freely elected . . . that ever did injure a whole Kingdome, or exercise any tyranny, nor is there any possibility how it should."[89]

Parker's approach to the problem of the origin of power thus allows him to assimilate the newly developing theory of sovereignty, which had posed extreme difficulties for earlier forms of Aristotelian constitutionalism.[90]

> That there is an Arbitrary power in every State somewhere is true, 'tis necessary, and no inconvenience follows upon it. . . . Every State has an Arbitrary power over itself, and there is no danger in it. . . . If the State intrusts this to one man, or few, there may be danger in it; but the Parliament is neither one nor few, it is indeed the State itself.[91]

Except for the conclusion that supremacy accrues to Parliament, Parker's contractarianism was nearly identical to Hunton's in its main elements. Like Hunton's, it is an "original contract," and not, like that in Locke, in effect made and remade by all human beings. Parker also takes for granted that the consenting agent is the community, not the individual; accordingly, he does not begin with natural rights of individuals. Parker has no notion of an abstract and universal right to revolution, but instead a much restricted notion of a right of resistance.[92]

Parker, however, is far less emphatic in allowing for the legitimacy of absolutist monarchy than Hunton was, and this reflects the stronger role within his system of Aristotelian theory. Absolutism does not comport as well with the final cause of the polity—the welfare of the people—as other forms of rule. Thus, Parker concludes, it is not rational for a people to have authorized absolutist rule and they should not be presumed to have done so.[93]

For Parker, the moral purpose of the polity is the defining feature of his contractarianism; for Hunton, it is the moral source of the polity in consent. For Parker popular consent or contract is a non-Aristotelian means to an Aristotelian end; for Hunton, consent is posited as the requisite mode for entering into moral obligation.[94] In these two forms of parliamentary contractarianism the dominant elements of prior political discourse—Christianity, as understood in the English Reformation, and Aristotelianism—are pulling away from each other but still coexist in a viable form. Indeed, Parker's more Aristotelian form of the doctrine clarifies an element of Hunton's more Protestant form.[95] Hunton, it will be recalled, conceived the contract as communal, not individual; but his doctrine was grounded in a notion of the relation between consent and moral obligation that would seem to point toward, if not require, a more individualistic consent. Parker's view indicates why parliamentary contractarianism looked to the community. For Parker, contract and consent are inferences from the final cause of the polity, the welfare of the community, the common good. The required consent is, therefore, the consent of the community. Consent of individuals is not only unnecessary, it is not even to the point.

CHAPTER THREE

Contract and Christian Liberty:
John Milton

BY THE LATE 1640s the universe of parliamentary political thought had changed almost entirely from what it had been at the time of Hunton and Parker. Parliament—by now a rump of the House of Commons—no longer accepted the ancient constitution, no longer took pains to remain within the bounds of the regime of mixed monarchy, and no longer resisted the effort to find an authority for the constitution back behind the constitution. As a prelude to putting King Charles I on trial, the House of Commons issued an all-important resolution in January 1649. No shadow of the theory of mixed monarchy remained, for the House declared that "whatever is enacted or declared for law, by the Commons, in Parliament assembled, hath the force of law; and all the people of this nation are concluded thereby, although the consent and concurrence of king, or House of Peers, be not had thereunto."[1] This was not merely an extension of the legalist version of the mixed monarchy theory Parliament had been deploying since 1642. Parliament no longer made recourse to the claim that it temporarily spoke for the king, but they put him on trial and then to death. This was no momentary setting aside of the personal will of the king in favor of his "real" will.

In March 1649 the House of Commons took the even more momentous step of abolishing the monarchy and the House of Lords. The Constitution was no longer the mixed monarchy described so lovingly by Hunton. Not king, peers, and commons but commons alone composed the new constitution. The ancient constitution, the mixed regime, was, for the time being, dead. Not merely did the Commons destroy the mixed constitution, but it no longer refrained from claiming a power over the constitution, as the Long Parliament had earlier done. In the declaration of January 1649, the Commons succinctly made their point: "The Commons of England, in Parliament assembled, do declare, that the people are, under God, the original of all just power." But the holder of that power, for all practical purposes, is "the Commons of England, in Parliament assembled." They, "chosen by, and representing the people, have the supreme power in the nation."[2]

The mature parliamentary position was thus almost entirely different from any of the versions of the ancient constitution or mixed monarchy that Parliament and its defenders had described for most of the 1640s. In addition to the three important differences already noted—the jettisoning of the mixed constitution, the recourse to a preconstitutional source of political authority in the people, and a locating of the supreme power in the House of Commons by virtue of its representative relationship with the people—the new parliamentary position broke with most other elements of the older orthodoxy. For one, the earlier view, as defended by Hunton and Parker, set stringent limits on the type of resistance that could be made to a king. Hunton held resistance of any sort to be proper only in cases of "exorbitant" illegality. In these "exorbitant" cases, Hunton defended active resistance against the "instruments or agents in such commands," but rejected any actions against "the person of the sovereign."[3] Where there is a genuine monarchy, whether absolute or mixed, as in England, the person of the monarch, "invested with . . . a sovereign politic power," is "sacred, and out of reach of positive resistance or violence."[4] Henry Parker took the same line: "The king in his own person is not to be forcibly repelled in any wrongdoing. Nor is he accountable for ill done. Law has only a directive but no coactive force upon his person."[5] This limit on the power of resistance flows directly from the authorization of resistance. As Hunton put it, "By the foundation of the government they are bound to prevent the dissolution of the established frame."[6] Resistance is legitimate in the service of the "established frame" and therefore can extend only so far as to maintain it. To act against the person of the king is to overturn the "frame" and therefore to go beyond any authorization for resistance. The limit on resistance therefore reveals once again that parliamentary writers before 1649 hesitated to claim an extraconstitutional power, in Parliament or elsewhere, to control the constitution. Nor did they affirm a universal right of resistance of even the limited extent they allowed for England. Hunton finds perfectly legitimate an absolute monarchy in which no rights of resistance are to be found. The rights of resistance depend entirely on the terms of the original contract.[7]

The parliamentarian doctrine of the late 1640s thus compares more closely to the Lockean doctrines of the Americans with much better reason than to the thought of Hunton, Parker, and the like. The later parliamentarian texts show much less commitment to the continuing sway of the inherited constitution and the terms of the "original contract" and thus are much more like the "philosophic contractarianism" of Locke and his American followers.

The most authoritative and powerful version of the parliamentary argument of the Civil War era—said to have been "the most eloquent expression of [philosophical] contract theory of the day"—was John Milton's *Tenure of Kings and Magistrates*, a work first written to justify the trial of King Charles in 1649. So germane did Milton's work appear to be for the post-Restoration Whig tradition that two different versions of his treatise were reissued during the Glorious Revolution; Miltonic ideas also seem to have had an impact on other pamphleteers of the age that cannot be measured merely by the explicit references to his book that occasionally appear.[8] Milton is an instructive writer to consider, not only because he was widely read and influential but also because he so clearly presented a version of radical contractarianism on a natural, or at least nonlegal, foundation, justifying resistance and even regicide and endorsing the right to change the constitution. In this he carried the project of Protestantizing political thought to a far more radical conclusion than Hunton had done. Yet he differed greatly from Locke and the Declaration of Independence. He thus illustrates, even better than Hunton, Parker, and later writers like Gilbert Burnet, how apparent similarities and parallels can mislead.

TWO REVOLUTIONS, TWO CONTRACTARIANISMS: MILTON'S "TENURE" AND THE DECLARATION OF INDEPENDENCE

Milton's *Tenure* attained quasi-official status, although retroactively, so to speak. He wrote The *Tenure* as a private individual in 1649 and rushed it to press—it appeared only two weeks after the execution of Charles I. On the strength of his essay, Milton was appointed the following month "Secretary for Foreign Tongues," a position which was to involve him in justifying the ways of the English Revolution to foreigners.

Lois Schwoerer has much in her favor when she classifies The *Tenure* as a work of "philosophic contractarianism." It surely does not meet Höpfl and Thompson's criteria for constitutional contractarianism: it does not affirm contract solely in the context of "particular positive laws and the inheritance of specific polities." Milton's work has the "theoretical ambition and generality of thought" which they identify with philosophical contractarianism. The character of Milton's doctrine—in relation to Höpfl and Thompson's categories, as well as to earlier Parliamentarian contractarianism and the Americans' Lockean contractarianism—stands forth most clearly on the issue of the right of resistance. "Since the king or magistrate holds his authority of the people, both originally and naturally for their good in the first place, and not his own, then may the people, as oft as they shall judge it for the best, either choose him or reject him, retain him or depose him, though no tyrant, merely by the liberty and right of freeborn men to be governed as seems to them best."[9] Milton's argument is thoroughly universal; when he speaks of "the people" he means "any people." When he traces the people's power to reject or depose their rulers to its source, he makes no reference whatever to the positive laws or constitution of England or of any country. "What the people may lawfully do" to a tyrant, "as against a common pest and destroyer of mankind, I suppose no man of clear judgement need go further to be guided than by the very principles of nature in him."[10]

English law and history hold no privileged place in Milton's scheme; the English merely example the general point: peoples of all times and places "have deposed and put to death their kings."[11] Contrary to the practice of his predecessors, Milton regularly denigrated the inherited law and consitution. In the *Tenure* he spoke of those who looked back to old law and custom as men caught up in "that old entanglement of iniquity, their gibberish laws . . . the badge of their ancient slavery." In a much earlier work, he had taken up the argument of those who thought that bishops were to be retained because "the government of episcopacy is now so woven into the common law." But the authority of the received law hardly impressed John Milton. "In God's name let it [episcopacy] weave out again. . . . It is not the common law, nor the civil, but piety and justice that are our foundresses." Custom, and therefore customary law, is a "tyrant" that begets further tyrannies.[12]

Milton, then, hardly qualifies as a partisan of the original contract. The people may reject or depose their rulers "merely by the liberty and right of freeborn men to be governed as seems to them best." Since "all men were naturally born free," all power in the hands of "kings and magistrates is nothing else but what is only derivative, transferred and committed to them in trust from the people"; the power thus transferred, however, "yet remains fundamentally and cannot be taken from them without a violation of their natural birthright."[13] Milton's "freeborn men" retain a freedom at least sufficient to empower them—all of them—to replace their rulers whenever they like. To revert to the language of the Declaration of Independence—Milton's freedom is inalienable.[14] Thus on two principles Milton stands with Locke and the authors of the Declaration, where Hunton, for example, did not: (1) the right of resistance has a natural and thus universal base, and (2) that base is the inalienability of the primal human liberty.

Yet Milton's right to choose or reject, retain or depose rulers differs dramatically from the doctrine of the Declaration of Independence, in that Milton insists that the people retain this right against any ruler, whether a tyrant or not. The Declaration affirms a far more limited right: only when faced with a government "destructive of those ends"—that is, of the security of inalienable rights—does a people have the "right to alter or abolish" their government. A ruler who threatens rights in this way is said in the Declaration to have "a character . . . marked by every act which may define a tyrant." The Declaration thus differs from Milton as much as it does from Hunton, Parker, and the others, although in precisely the opposite way. Whereas Hunton's alienable liberty undercuts any natural right of resistance, Milton's completely inalienable liberty generates a right of resistance of such potency it can no longer properly be called merely a right of resistance or of revolution. Rather it becomes a nascent or covert transconstitutional republicanism: the people always have the right to change their government for whatever reason seems good to them. Such a right inheres in freedom.

Since the people have the right to change their rulers at any time, all constitutions are republics, in a manner of speaking. Perhaps it is better to say that Milton collapses the people's constitutive power and their governing power. The popular origin of political power in the Declaration implies popular sovereignty, but not the direct rule of the people. The people ordain and establish a government, that is, make a constitution, and unless that government becomes threatening to rights, it governs. The people have neither a right nor an interest in interfering in any other way. In the gap between popular sovereignty and governance proper arises the possibility of constitutionalism, a set mode and structure of government established by a higher authority than the government and expressly providing for the people's rights. The higher authority does not rule or attempt to rule as a matter of course, but stands in the wings, ready to reassert its original power if government fails greatly in its ordained task.

None of this holds for Milton. Inalienable freedom means the people always possess the right to rule, or, as Milton more moderately leaves it in The *Tenure*, the right to be governed by rulers of their choice. No constitutional arrangement can finally restrict this power; the people have a right to assert it at any time and for any reason. Thus it is not possible to draw and retain a stable distinction between ordinary governing power and popular sovereignty. The latter stands not as an ultimate check and recourse but as an omnipresent possibility. Milton's later overt republicanism is already implicit here.

Milton's doctrine seems to fulfill the kinds of fears enemies of contractarianism like Sir Robert Filmer expressed regularly: tracing the original of all power to the people openly invites anarchy. Milton certainly is more open to that charge than is the moderate Hunton, who himself would probably have recoiled in fear from the doctrine of The *Tenure*. But the American founders, much less conservative and fearful than Filmer and Hunton, also found the Miltonic version of contract unacceptable. It is difficult to imagine Milton's version producing the kind of commitment to a constitution—any constitution—that the Declaration's did.

The American founders might even have endorsed one of Filmer's major charges against Milton: although the people are the "original of political power" and therefore have the ongoing power to choose or reject, retain or depose their rulers, Milton nowhere makes clear who the people are or who speaks for them.[15] He clearly cannot mean the whole people acting together; he does not even mean the majority, for, as Filmer pointed out, he speaks of "the better and sounder part"—perhaps something like a revolutionary vanguard. To the degree Milton was attempting to justify the deeds of the English Revolution, he was more or less forced into a doctrine of this sort (such as it was) regarding the identity of the people, for by the time he wrote, the Parliament that had initiated the revolution had been much diminished in size through the ministrations of the army. Thanks to Pride's Purge, the more conservative Presbyterian elements of Parliament had been "sequestered," leaving all the power with a relatively small remainder—the so-called Rump Parliament. Even the original Parliament had little claim to represent the entire people, given the restrictions on suffrage in the seventeenth century, but the Rump had much less claim than the Long Parliament it succeeded.

However, there was an even deeper reason that made Milton so indistinct on the identity of "the people." Since he looked at the power of the people as an extraconstitutional, extragovernmental force, he perforce had to consider modes of popular action outside normal or organized channels. The people as such, at least in a nation of any size, cannot act as a body and spontaneously. Thus the people must act via smaller groups that can achieve the organization and energy to act and that put themselves forward as representatives of the people. In 1649 Milton was willing to accept the army as such a body. But there exists no way to identify in advance who is authorized to speak for the people; thus Miltonic contractarianism has the appearance of inviting the regular intervention of (armed) organized minorities into politics. It does not promise stability.

Moreover, the inability to clearly define the people suggests another important difference with the theory of the Declaration. In a sense, Milton accepts the Declaration's formula that government derives its just powers from the consent of the governed, but his utter openness in principle to minority intervention in the name of the people makes it quite impossible to specify in practice what consent actually amounts to. The extraordinarily elitist republicanism he advocated in his treatise *The Ready and Easy Way to Establish a Free Commonwealth* testifies in part to this very quandary: there, a very small and even permanent group can speak for the whole people.

These difficulties in Milton's doctrine—which, from the perspective of the Declaration of Independence, appear to be grave defects—might themselves seem to point up difficulties in the philosophy of the Declaration as well. The beginning point for Milton in his account of politics, as it was for Hunton and Parker, as well as for the Declaration, was liberty. "No man who knows ought, can be so stupid to deny that all men naturally were born free."[16] For all, the same questions thus arose: if human beings were originally free, how came they to be subjected to political authority, and what degree of subjection are they in? There seem to be two and only two possible answers: either liberty is alienable, in which case Hunton's form of original contractarianism (or perhaps even a more absolutist version) would follow, or liberty is inalienable, in which case Milton's form would follow. If that is true, then the Declaration's middle way would be untenable, and the differences between Milton and the Declaration would express no more than the

Americans' inconsistent application of the doctrine Milton put forward with greater rigor and coherence.

The authors of the Declaration clearly believed there was a third way, but their document is too brief and concise to indicate what they took that to be. Locke gives a more extended presentation of the third way, however—indeed, that was precisely one of the tasks he set himself in the *Second Treatise*. Locke's solution, briefly, is as follows. In the state of nature, human beings possess "a title to perfect freedom, and an uncontrolled enjoyment of all the rights and privileges of the law of nature." This implies that everybody has "by nature a power, not only to preserve his property, that is, his life, liberty, and estate, against the injuries and attempts of other men; but to judge of and punish breaches of that law in others." Locke calls that latter power "the executive power of the law of nature." To form a political society, human beings do not give up their rights to life, liberty, and estate, but they "wholly give up"—that is, alienate—this executive power of the law of nature. They give up the powers that accrued to them as means of securing their primary rights under the conditions of the state of nature, and through that renunciation establish government, which is a surer and more reliable means to secure their rights. But they do not alienate the rights themselves, "for no rational nature can be supposed to change his condition with an intention to be worse." Thus Locke shows, formally at least, how a middle way is possible.[17]

One might be tempted, then, to understand Milton's position as an imperfect anticipation of Lockean contractarianism, falling short because he had not the wit to think up Locke's solution of an alienable executive power of the law of nature, coupled with inalienable natural rights. But that would be a mistake, a version of the unicontractarianism Höpfl and Thompson warned against. The differences we have already noted between Milton and the Declaration (or Locke) stem rather from the more fundamental point that the Declaration puts natural rights and the securing of them at the center, where Milton puts freedom.[18]

MILTONIC POLITICS AND THE REFORMATION ATTITUDE

Milton does say that "all men naturally were born free," but he adds that the reason for this is that men were "the image and resemblance of God himself, and were, by privilege above all the creatures, born to command and not to obey." Moreover, he continues, the need to overcome or cancel this original condition arose "from the root of Adam's transgression," leading men "to do wrong and violence."[19] The knowledge Milton possessed of original humanity is knowledge he learned from the Bible—knowledge of God the Creator, man the divine image, and the Fall. Milton differs from the Declaration of Independence, in that the latter appeals only to the "laws of nature and of nature's God." Nature's God is the God known in and through nature, that is, known through natural faculties, available to humanity as such and not only to believers in any particular revelation. That is very different from Milton's appeal to biblical knowledge. In his treatise *De Doctrina Christiana*, Milton makes the point very explicitly: "That the world was created, must be considered an article of faith."[20] In *Paradise Regained* he is even more emphatic. Offered the wisdom of the ancients by Satan, Christ replies with this query:

> Alas what can they teach, and not mislead,
> Ignorant of themselves, of God much more,
> And how the world began, and how man fell
> Degraded by himself, on grace depending?[21]

Lacking the Bible, dependent on reason alone, the pagan philosophers lacked knowledge of the very items from which Milton constructed his political theory. Milton's political thought, like divine right theory, is thus better described as political theology than as political philosophy.[22]

That immense doctrinal differences between Milton and the Declaration exist should not, therefore, surprise. The authors of the Declaration and Locke speak of the Creator; apparently they believed that natural knowledge of creation is available to reason, but neither the Declaration nor Locke speaks of human beings as created in the image of God, nor do they speak of a fall. The principles of political life can be construed without reference to a fall. By contrast, Milton's scripturally grounded knowledge of nature teaches him of freedom, but not of rights. Both the Bible and Milton are silent on the subject of natural or inalienable rights.[23]

The original human condition is one of freedom, Milton asserts, and in this he seems close to the Declaration and Locke. The Declaration asserts equality as the natural condition, meaning that no human beings have a natural claim to rule any others, a thought very similar if not identical to Milton's notion of original freedom. Milton derives natural freedom from humanity's creation as "the image and resemblance of God himself." According to the Declaration, the endowment human beings receive from their Creator is not the divine image, but inalienable rights. These rights can be readily seen to serve as the foundation of natural equality, the Declaration's equivalent to Milton's original freedom. Each person's life, liberty, and happiness (the ultimate goal of human action), belong emphatically to him or herself. One's life and one's actions, one's hopes and one's satisfactions—these are one's own-most in the strongest sense. Thus Locke calls them "property."[24] No virtue, no quality of any sort in one human being can give rightful possession of another's own-most belongings—his or her rights. But political power is just the power to make rightful claims against the life and actions of others; political power cannot, according to the Declaration, derive from any natural quality of rulers; there can be no natural ordination to rule; political power must derive from the consent of the governed and come to be for the sake of securing these own-most possessions called rights. The original or natural juridical condition, then, must be one of equality.

This accounts for the more conservative and stable version of contract that we find in the Declaration.[25] Political power exists for the sake of, or as a means to, securing rights, or as a means to liberty. Rights are less secure without government than with it, and therefore it is both rational and rightful to establish and retain stable government, so long as it plays its rights-securing role. Government being entirely a means to the end of rights-securing, there is nothing else at stake in it.

Milton's natural freedom belongs to an entirely different universe of thought. In the first instance, it signifies the human situation before the Fall. Human beings are originally free in two different senses, both related to and derivative from a yet more fundamental sense in which they are not free: they are under the rightful rule of God. From the start, he rules through "the nature which was so implanted and innate in [man] that he was in need of no command." That is, human beings were subject to the divine commands, or rather promptings, of the law of nature; because it was natural, this law required no positive command to actualize or effect it. Human beings were subjected also to divine positive command, the command to eschew the fruit of the tree of knowledge of good and evil. This command is an instance of God's positive law: "Positive law comes into play when God, or anyone else invested with a lawful power, commands or forbids things."[26] The key point is the last: despite their freedom, God has "lawful power" over human beings in the prelapsarian condition and has used it in his promulgation of both the natural and the positive laws. Being obligated to the lawful power of God, human beings in this condition are thus under a moral subjection to God, and in this sense are not free at the beginning. Indeed, God promulgated his one positive command in order to emphasize human subjection to the Creator: "So, that there might be some way for man to show his obedience, God ordered him to abstain only from the tree of knowledge of good and evil."[27]

And yet moral subjection to God does not imply complete unfreedom, for human beings were originally altogether free metaphysically. As God explains in *Paradise Lost,*

> I formed them free . . .
> I made [them] just and right,
> Sufficient to have stood, though free to fall.
> Such I created all the eternal powers and spirits. . . .
> Not free, what proof could they have giv'n sincere
> Of true allegiance, constant faith or love,
> Where only what they needs must do, appeared

> Not what they would? What praise could they receive?
> What pleasure I from such obedience paid,
> When will and reason (reason also is choice)
> Useless and vain, of freedom both despoiled,
> Made passive both, had served necessity,
> Not me.[28]

This "metaphysical freedom" is thus intimately related to human subjection to God—indeed, is in the service of it. Both human subjection to God and human freedom from God are compassed in the notion of the "image of God." The free will human beings are endowed with—that is, the power to be the cause of their own actions—is a function of the more fundamental human moral subjection derived from creatureliness: human beings need freedom in order to obey, in order to do their duty, in order to express the truth of their situation as creatures vis-à-vis their creator. Human beings are created free because freely given obedience is superior to the dumb or necessary obedience rendered by the lower orders of creation.

> Thrice happy men,
> And sons of men, whom God hath thus advanced,
> Created in his image, there to dwell
> And worship him, and in reward to rule
> Over his work, on earth, in sea, or air,
> And multiply a race of worshipers
> Holy and Just.[29]

As the freely obedient beings, humans are above the rest of creation—"made to command not to obey". Like their metaphysical freedom, their earthly dominance derives from their moral subjection.

But dominion over the other creatures does not extend to dominance over other human beings. In the prelapsarian condition and by nature, human beings are morally subject only to God; no human beings stand intermediate between God and other human beings, as human beings do between God and the lower creatures. The direct moral subjection of all humans to God implies the moral freedom of all humans from each other:

> He [God] gave us only over beast, fish, fowl
> Dominion absolute; that right we hold
> By his donation; but man over man
> He made not lord; such title to himself
> Reserving, human left from human free.[30]

This is not to say that human beings in the prelapsarian state owed no natural duties to each other; they did indeed—the duties specified by the law of nature.[31] But they owed no political subjection to another, and that is the second, and most political, sense in which human beings were originally free.

Before the Fall humanity could, according to The *Tenure*, "live so"—could live exclusively under the law of nature, with no political subjection of one person to another. The Fall changed that, however: afterward only "a kind of gleam or glimmering of the [law of nature] still remains in the hearts of all mankind."[32] Under the new postlapsarian conditions, human beings were driven to abrogate their initial status of political freedom, they now must create human authorities to which they are subjected, because it is no longer possible to live within the law of nature without government.

Compared to earlier thinkers like Hooker, Grotius, and Parker, or to later ones like Locke, Burnet, or Rousseau, Milton in the *Tenure* presents a very blurry doctrine of the political contract. He passes over the contract with barely a word as to who the parties or what the terms of the contract are, or how the contract serves to generate rightful authority.[33] In other political statements, Milton put even less weight on contract. In his *Doctrine and Discipline of Divorce*, written well before the trial of King Charles, Milton had already affirmed the right to overthrow a ruler, not because of a contract, but absolutely—"against any authority, covenant, or statute."[34] Later, in *Paradise Lost*, Milton restated the history of political society and there gave a different (more biblical) account from the one limned in The *Tenure*, with no role for contract.[35] The burden of his argument really does not lie on what passes in the moment of covenanting; as we have already seen, the agreement made has no particularly binding power on the people in any case.[36] Milton, in fact, rides the contract idea very little distance, only to bridge (rather inadequately) the gap between the original human freedom and the later (quasi-) subjection to specific rulers. The gravamen of his argument lies elsewhere. He derives principles for the guidance of political life not from the terms of an original contract but from his three most fundamental ideas about humanity, contained in the image of man as the free but fallen creature. Everything in Milton's politics flows more or less directly from the conjunction of freedom, fallenness, and creatureliness.[37]

Despite fallen humanity's existence in partial estrangement from God, creatureliness remains the species' defining feature. As creature, humanity stands over and against God the maker; in the fallen condition human beings are even less godlike than before—the image of God in them is partially effaced—but as fallen they are more and more likely to forget their creatureliness, their dependence on the Being from whom they have their source and whose eternal nature surpasses theirs in ways they, as finite beings, cannot begin to grasp.[38] In their fallen condition they are most apt to fall into one or another form of idolatry—to worship false gods and establish false dependencies, to seek false security and to make of and for themselves false absolutes.[39]

Reason clouded, passion unleashed, sin on the prowl, and, above all, death lying in wait for all, fallen men—even the best of fallen men, like the ancient philosophers—remain ignorant of themselves (as creatures), of God (as Creator), and of their own inability to elevate themselves without grace.

> Much of the soul they talk, but all awry,
> And in themselves seek virtue, and to themselves
> All glory arrogate, to God give none.[40]

Radically insecure in the face of death, fallen human beings seek their security within the human sphere, falsely place their hopes on themselves or other men, falsely seek and falsely find human self-sufficiency. Only God is self-sufficient, but the more distant humanity is from God, the more it aspires to divine self-sufficiency.[41]

Such are the idolatrous principles that more often than not animate politics. The first king, who was also the first tyrant, was a man "of proud ambitious heart . . . not content with fair equality, fraternal state."[42] Only God deserves glory and rightly stands above the "fraternal state," but "man, proud man, most ignorant of what he's most assured," constantly and mistakenly attempts to seize for himself, the creature, "that which to God alone of right belongs."[43] In place of that pride should stand humility, "the virtue which makes us acknowledge an unworthiness in the sight of God."[44]

The "proud and ambitious heart" that began politics was still at work in Milton's England. He saw it everywhere. It was at work in the prelatical structure of the church. Rather than the humble life preached and led by Christ, the bishops had their "pompous garb, . . . lordly life, . . . wealth, . . . haughty distance."[45] It was "hateful thirst of lording in the church, that first bestowed being upon prelaty." Christ came to regenerate man, to "restore the whole mind to the image of God, as if he were a new creature," to restore him to his full creatureliness. But "prelaty, both in her fleshy supportments, in her carnal doctrine of ceremony and tradition, in her violent and secular power, [goes] quite counter to the prime end of Christ's coming in the flesh."[46]

The "proud and ambitious heart" was at work in the state, too, especially in those pretentions to divinely ordained, absolute and unbounded power in which the Stuart kings and their supporters indulged. These rulers, in claiming to be "accountable to none but God," were reaching for a status itself godlike, "not a mortal magistrate"; the Roman emperors openly "deified themselves," but Christian princes who raise absolutist claims tacitly do the same when they "arrogate so unreasonably above the human condition, or derogate so basely from a whole nation of men, [their] brethren, as if for [them] only subsisting."[47]

Milton's nascent republicanism in The *Tenure* derives directly from his rejection of all royal idolatry. The people must have the power to call to account "lawless kings and all who so much adore them," in order to "teach" them "that not mortal man, or his imperious will, but justice, is the only true sovereign and majesty on earth. . . . And justice it is most truly, who accepts [sic] no person, and exempts none from the severity of her stroke. . . . But if a king may do among men whatsoever is his will and pleasure, then neither truth or justice but the king is strongest of all other things."[48] The freedom of the people that inalienably empowers them to judge—and re-place—their rulers merely expresses in different form the fundamental fact of human creatureliness. That power, always retained, is no means to an ulterior end, as it is according to the understanding animating the Declara-tion, but is itself the expression of the human situation. Unconditional human subjection to God leaves no room for unconditional subjection to any other human beings. As Milton very succinctly put it, "Being therefore peculiarly God's own . . . we are entirely free by nature."[49]

MILTON'S CHRISTIAN REPUBLICANISM

In his *Ready and Easy Way*, written on the very eve of the restoration he feared of the monarchy he hated, Milton reiterated and radicalized his point. All monarchy, not just the "unaccountable" kind, is "regal bondage"; Christ himself "expressly declared that such regal dominion is from the gentiles, not from him, and strictly charged us not to imitate them therein." Only a "free commonwealth" comes near to Christ's precepts. In a republic "they who are greatest, are perpetual servants and drudges to the public, . . . neglect their own affairs yet are not elevated above their brethren." But a king—he "must be adored like a demi-god." Republican leaders live sober and moderate lives, while courtiers live in "pride and profuseness." By recog-nizing any hereditary ruler, a people "concede themselves his servants and his vassals, and so renounce their own freedom." No good Christian could even be a king, "with such vanity and ostentation [displaying] his regal splendor, so supereminently above other mortal men." No Christian "can assume such extraordinary honor and worship to himself."[50]

The main elements within Milton's thought are thus few and their con-nections clear-cut. Fallenness requires government, but human creature-liness requires liberty; liberty in turn requires quasi- or even complete republicanism.[51] But it would be easy to misunderstand Milton's republi-canism and his concern for liberty—to be misled, for example, by the com-mon words into finding more common ground with the American founders than there is. Rather remarkably, with the egalitarian and libertarian atti-tudes we have already seen so much in evidence, with the affirmation of a retained freedom that constantly threatens to erupt into and unsettle all settled political life, Milton combines profound elitism and authoritarian-ism. Milton is both far more radical and far more conservative than the

Americans. That strain of his thought that appears conservative to a modern eye so overwhelmed one scholar that he suggested that "if any conception was paramount" for Milton, "it was the conception of aristocracy." And, he went on, "this aristocratic idealism was not anything democratic."[52] That is very true. In *The Ready and Easy Way*, his most republican work, Milton went out of his way to exclude the people from real power in the constitution. His ideal constitution would differ from the ancient English constitution in lacking both a king and a recurrently elective parliament. "The ground and basis of every just and free government . . . is a general council of ablest men." Once selected, "this grand or general council, being well chosen, should be perpetual." Milton had only contempt for the constitutional provision most often sought by the parliamentarians before the Civil War and by the more reformist Whigs after it—frequent Parliaments. "Ask not, therefore how we can be advantaged by successive and transitory parliaments." To empower the people at all is to invite " a licentious and unbridled democracy." The people are to be excluded because experience has shown that no element is "more immoderate and ambitious to amplify their power than such popularities." Milton thus altogether reversed Machiavelli's prescription for a popular republic on the model of Rome. In his republic, Milton sought a different ethos from the expansionist and greedy popular regimes of antiquity.[53]

Milton's antimonarchism and his advocacy of liberty thus did not prevent him from supporting Cromwell. "Nothing in the world is more pleasing to God, more agreeable to reason, more politically just, or more generally useful, than that the supreme power should be vested in the best and wisest of men."[54] And along with his support for Cromwell went support for the army's actions against Parliament.

On the basis of evidence such as this, Perez Zagorin concluded that "even the idea of liberty, important as it was for Milton, had its content and its claims determined at all times by his aristocratic principle."[55] This, I think, gets Milton backwards: his aristocratic politics emerged from his concern for liberty. From his earliest to his latest works Milton conceived the end of politics in terms of the moral end of liberty. "To govern well is to train up a nation in true wisdom and virtue, and that which springs from thence, magnanimity . . . and that which is our beginning, regeneration and happiest end, likeness to God, which in one word we call godliness."[56] It is significant that Milton thought the end of politics in terms of "likeness to God"— how different, indeed, from thinking the end of politics in terms of rights-securing. The Fall, in fact, changed little, according to Milton, or at least much less than might first appear. As Milton said in The *Tenure*, after the Fall human beings could no longer live exclusively in their original freedom without political authority to supplement the direct rule of the law of nature within them. The Fall required the supplement of government, but it was a supplemental means to the same end as was originally set for humanity—to live as the image of God, to live as the free creature, freely obedient to the laws of nature and to the God beyond nature. Human freedom, vis-à-vis God and vis-à-vis other human beings, never was merely freedom from restraint, freedom to follow one's arbitrary will or desires. Will, reason, and freedom exist for the sake of free *obedience*. The moral end of politics privileges those who embody the virtues at which it aims:

> Unjustly thou deprav'st it with the name
> Of servitude to serve whom God ordains,
> Or nature, God and Nature bid the same,
> When he who rules is worthiest, and excels
> Them whom he governs.[57]

And yet to Milton the other side of freedom always remains the right of freeborn people to be governed as seems good to them. It is not that one view succeeded the other in Milton's mind (although one did achieve greater expression at one time and the other at others), but that Milton's political thought is caught in a tension inherent in his notion of liberty. Liberty, properly understood, is merely the special form of human creatureliness; liberty can have no end but obedience, that is, virtue; but God will not and others cannot make human beings virtuous. Obedience must be free and virtue freely won, but the coercive authority of the state can have no end but the virtue and true worship that is the business of human beings in this life.[58]

TWO CONTRACTARIANISMS, TWO FUNDAMENTAL ATTITUDES

I need not belabor the chasm that separates the political understanding of the Declaration of Independence from that in Milton's work. At bottom the Declaration is more like those ancient philosophers Milton's Christ dismissed: eschewing specific guidance from the Bible, it articulates a doctrine of freedom, of contract, and of politics at once less godly and less paradoxical, and hence more practical, than Milton's.

Behind all the specific differences we have noted, however, lies the crux, the differing commitments at the center of each theory—for Milton, the "image of God" that is humanity, for the Declaration, the rights-possessor that is humanity. Not merely is Milton (like his Bible) silent about natural rights, but his doctrine of the divine image implicitly denies them. Not merely is the Declaration silent about the image of God in human beings, but it tacitly rejects that way of conceiving the fundamentals of politics.[59] To understand the human endowment as the rights to life, liberty, and the pursuit of happiness is to affirm that human beings are not in the image of God, for their rights express their deepest needs; rights express not human godlikeness but human vulnerability and mortality, human distance from any divine character. Only a needy being, a mortal being, a being shot through with vulnerability to death and pain, a being radically insecure, can be a rights-bearer and make rights the basis for its existence. Neither gods nor brute beasts define themselves in terms of rights. To immortal gods the right to life is simply superfluous. Beasts, who have a natural orientation toward survival, never posit a right to life, although some human beings may do so on their behalf. Rights testify to humanity's thoroughly human character.

Milton's human beings as *imago dei* were not rights-bearers in their original condition because they were neither needy nor mortal. Only with the Fall did they become both and thus even potential bearers of the Declaration's natural rights. But for Milton the mortality and neediness that human beings incurred in the Fall never became the defining features of their being or of their politics. Milton's way of expressing that is to say that "traces of the divine image still remain in us, which are not wholly extinguished by this spiritual death."[60] The task for humanity never is to live entirely in the realm of need and death opened up by the Fall, but rather to live in the light of God's gracious offer of reparation and reconciliation.

The Declaration represents the decision to understand human mortality and needfulness not as a fallen or derivative quality but as the ground or foundation, as the real endowment supplied by the Creator. It represents the decision to give humanity over to the realm of need and death, even if that means positing these as enemies to be overcome or conquered. Mortality and need are not the product of sin and therefore matters for guilt. The way forward cannot be to strive to recover an original innocence now lost, or to accept reconciliation now offered. Milton, on the other hand, has his Adam and Eve walk together "hand and hand" out of Eden in a hopeful finale to his epic. "The Golden Age," concluded Christopher Hill, "lies not in the past, but in the future of men and women who understand their destiny."[61] Nonetheless, the hope for the future that the two exiles from Eden share is the hope for the coming redemption, that is, restoration of the original relationship between human beings and God, albeit at a different and higher level.[62] Milton essentially looks backward; the future is a restoration.[63]

Milton's version of contractarianism, ironically, reminds one more than a little of the political position apparently at the very opposite pole from his, the divine right doctrine he abhorred. Both make gestures toward the idea of retaining the main elements of the Thomistic synthesis of rational and revelatory politics. Both speak as though Aristotle and reformed Christianity equally constitute the foundation of their politics. Yet Milton and Filmer both concede in crucial places that the ancients cannot be proper guides to politics, for they lack knowledge of the one most necessary fact, the Creation, and thus human creatureliness. In Milton, as in Filmer, the conjunction between Aristotle and Protestant Christianity that still holds in Hunton and Parker has definitely split apart.

Milton and his arch-opponents both take the fact of the Creation with the utmost seriousness.[64] Although they stand at opposite extremes of the seventeenth-century political spectrum, both Milton and Filmer are Reformation political theologians rather than Christian political philosophers. Each represents a deep-going attempt to find the political embodiment of the Reformation; each seeks the political and moral forms that flow from the Reformation attitude—as each understands that. Their differences with regard to the latter appear to be quite small—and as immense as the universe itself. For Filmer, as for King James and the other divine right thinkers, the fact of human creatureliness, and thus the attitude of pious obedience, dominates. The same can be said for Milton. For the divine right thinkers, worldly authorities constitute an earthly locus for the expression of the obedient attitude. For Milton the majesty of God and the requirements of free obedience so surpass the earthly authorities that only his oddly unstable Christian republicanism can follow.

Both are plausible versions of a Reformation politics. In the realm of thought they express and reproduce the impasse—the violent impasse—that developed in post-Reformation English practice. A civil war and a regicide made much the same point on the field of battle that the Battle of the Books between Milton and his opponents made on the shelves of the libraries: the Reformation had unleashed ways of constituting politics that not only unsettled previous ways but seemed unable to resettle them. The English Civil War, after all, was not a war between Protestants on the one side and Catholics on the other, but between different kinds of Protestants. That was true of the war between Milton and Filmer as well. The seventeenth century in England served to prove that the Protestant principle would be incapable of finding an authoritative political expression. Instead, it produced that splendid variety of principled and uncompromising systems that the names Filmer, Milton, and even Hunton represent.

PART TWO

Whigs

CHAPTER FOUR

Whig Contractarianisms and Rights

THE SEARCH for the "one true Protestant politics" produced a civil war, the regicide, the Commonwealth, Cromwell's Protectorate—and, finally, a general and widespread revulsion against the whole enterprise. The ultimate outcome was then a restoration of the monarchy and the Stuart line of monarchs, of the old church, and of the old House of Lords. Given the astounding fragmentation and conflict of political opinion during the preceeding half century, the degree of unanimity of opinion favoring the Restoration was truly remarkable. By 1660, Milton's eloquent voice protesting the return of kings could no longer raise an answering echo; blind and unhappy, he returned to private life and poetry.

That unanimity was not, in the event, to last very long; well before the 1660s had run their course, many of the grave issues arose once again to shake the nation. Despite resemblances to the earlier conflicts, the post-Restoration political world was subtly transformed as well. Two external facts indicate some of the differences. The whole process culminated, it is true, in another revolution, and another displacement of a king, but this time the process was relatively peaceful and restrained, and surely did not bring the kind of radical tearing at the bonds of social life that occurred in the 1640s. A second difference between the post-Restoration crises and those of the first half of the century lay in the nature of the opposition. The opposition to the king, centered once again in Parliament, was this time led by a group of men known as Whigs rather than by a group known (loosely) as Puritans. "Whigs" is a purely political category; although it is not entirely devoid of religious content, that is not at its center, and it is not marked by the effort to find the "one true Protestant politics."

The Whigs remained as opposed to royalist absolutism as their predecessors had been (perhaps more single-mindedly so), but they just as firmly opposed the descent into chaos and tyranny their predecessors had produced. Recognizing the search for the "one true Protestant politics" as a major source of the problem, the Whigs shifted the grounds of their political thinking. Nobody had succeeded in finding the "one true Protestant politics," and the Whigs turned their backs on the attempt. True Protestantism (in politics) came to be well enough defined as non- or anti-Catholicism, and non- or anti-absolutism. During this era of Whig opposition, contentious and undecidable conflicts over theological politics gave way to more moderate and more rationalist modes of political thought. The post-Restoration world thus saw political men turning to the rationalist and universalist principles of natural law and natural religion. Although he had written decades earlier, Richard Hooker's moderate natural law writings made their mark during these years. Even more significantly, the new natural law philosophy of Hugo Grotius immigrated from Holland and came to the center of Whig consciousness.

In appealing to natural law and natural reason—that is, to rational principles—the post-Restoration Whigs certainly approached much more closely to the kind of thought Locke and the American Declaration of Independence represented. The latter, for example, spoke of "the laws of nature and of nature's God," not the law or principles of Scripture as understood by one or another Christian sect—not *sola scriptura*, but *sola ratio*. This fact gives plausibility to a revised version of the old story of "immemorial continuity" in Anglo-American political principles from Magna Charta to Pym and Milton to Locke and Jefferson: Perhaps the pre–Civil War opposition was more committed to constitutionalist contractarianism or to reformation political theology than to a doctrine like the American Declaration; perhaps the ambiguous consensus won for the Glorious Revolution and "contained in the public documents of the time" differed from Locke and the American Declaration; yet the post-Restoration Whigs, who had been unable to entirely carry the day in the Convention Parliament of 1688–89, did understand politics much as Locke and later the Americans did. The Americans, according to this story, adopted a mode of political thinking that had failed to win official recognition in the Glorious Revolution, but was nonetheless well established and traditional within English politics. "It was left to Locke," said J. R. Jones, "to publish . . . after 1688 the classical Whig exposition of the origin, nature, and purpose of political institutions."[1] From the Whigs to Locke to the Americans—a chain of transmission of well-worn and widely, if not universally, accepted political ideas.

Even this revised story has met with much criticism of late, criticism that will be accepted and even extended here. The Whigs, rationalist as they were, were neither uniformly contractarian nor were they contractarians of the sort Locke and the Americans were. They represented a distinct and quite different style of political thought both from Locke and from their parliamentary predecessors. They differed almost entirely from Locke, but such are the ironies of history that their political thought went some way toward making possible the ultimate emergence of modern—that is, Lockean—contractarianism, and that fact helps to account for the preeminence it later attained.

THE RESTORATION AND THE EMERGENCE OF THE WHIGS

Whiggism was a product of the post-Restoration world. Despite a continuing commitment to Protestantism and an opposition to divine right absolutism, Whiggism differed in important respects from pre-Commonwealth Opposition thought. After the Restoration everything was the same, and yet everything was different. The Stuarts were on the throne again, and on very favorable terms. So hungry was the nation for a return to "the good old days," so discredited was the immediate past by civil war and Cromwellian military rule, by Presbyterian oppression and Independent rebellion, by Levellers, Muggletonians, and a clutch of other eccentrics scheming to reconstitute England's social, political, and economic life that with no apparent regrets the political nation made every effort to pretend that most of the whole period after 1642 had been but a bad dream.

"The Restoration Settlement was based on the undertakings given [by Charles II] in the Declaration of Breda, and on the legislation of 1641 and 1642 to which Charles I had given his assent."[2] At Breda, Charles had committed himself to a general pardon, to a degree of "Liberty to tender consciences," to a parliamentary settlement of all property claims brought into confusion by the war and the Interregnum, and even to full pay for the army that had marched out against his father.[3] The established church, which had been unbearable to Parliament only a few years before, was restored, complete with bishops. Not even the gestures toward a more liberal ecclesiastical policy that Charles had pledged at Breda were adopted. In 1662 Parliament passed the Uniformity Act, premised on the belief that "nothing conduceth more to the settling of the peace of this nation . . . unto the honour of our religion and the propagation thereof than a universal agreement in the public worship of Almighty God." Accordingly, the law mandated that all ministers acting in any "place of public worship" use the Book of Common Prayer and required of them an oath declaring their "unfeigned assent and consent to the use of all things in the said Book" on pain of being deprived of their positions. Perhaps two thousand out of nine thousand clergy did surrender their livings because their "tender consciences" would not allow them to take the pledge.[4]

The Cavalier Parliament tripped over itself in its eagerness to denounce its predecessors' constitutional pretensions. Parliament's earlier efforts to curb the royal prerogative were denounced as being "in derogation of his Majesty's just rights and prerogatives inherent to the Imperial Crown of this realm for the calling and assembling of parliaments." Those attempts by Parliament to establish independence from the King were denounced as productive of "manifold mischiefs and inconveniences," and repealed, every jot and tittle of them. In their place, Parliament "humbly beseeched" the king to call Parliaments frequently.[5] The king's full power over appointment of his own ministers was reaffirmed; Parliament's efforts to say otherwise were renounced, disowned, and abjured. The king had the right to command the military, when and how he liked; Parliament's efforts to say otherwise were denounced as misguided, mistaken, and mischievous.[6] At the same time, the Restoration Settlement endorsed an unequivocal duty of obedience to the king and rejected all theories of the right of resistance— Hunton's moderate theory as much as Milton's more untrammeled views.[7]

Yet not even the Cavalier Parliament accepted an absolutist monarchy. They sought a return to the ancient constitution, more or less: Parliament had to agree to taxation bills, Parliament had a share in the legislative powers. Englishmen did have certain rights the king must respect. Not even the Cavalier Parliament was willing to sign on to a Filmerean royal absolutism.

As an attempt to restore a status quo that had produced all the evils the Cavalier Parliament wished to renounce, the Restoration seemed to set the stage for a replay of the first half of the century. It almost happened that way: years of intense religio-political conflict between king and Parliament; efforts by the king to rule without Parliament; efforts by parliamentary leaders to outfox the King; charges of royal usurpation, charges of parliamentary usurpation; deep-going social unrest, centering largely on conflicts over religion; and all culminating in a revolution—not a regicide this time, but a new king set on the throne and the old king, despite the ironclad oath, dependent on the hospitality of the French king.

Yet it was not quite a return of the same. Instead of the chief line of cleavage lying between those who supported the orthodox or established church and those who wished to make the church yet more Protestant, the main divide this time lay between those who supported the established church and the "papists," a relatively small but well-placed minority.[8] In part, the new placement of the barricades represented a deliberate effort by some Opposition leaders to shape a different, perhaps less explosive politics for the second half of the century. Except for the fact that the Duke of York was an avowed Catholic who favored other Catholics, fomenting conflict with the Catholics was surely a lower risk policy domestically than the religious conflicts of the first half of the century had been. Anti-Catholicism was one thing all the different sorts of Protestants could underwrite, even if they could agree on little else.

The Whigs arose as a party, or at least as an identifiable and identified group, in the struggle of the late 1670s and early 1680s to prevent the Catholic James, Duke of York, from succeeding Charles II as king.[9] The effort slightly followed and slightly overlapped the notorious and malodorous affair of the Popish Plot. Much if not all of the plot was fabrication—complete with perjured witnesses, religious fanatics, and manipulative politicians. The plot—the main charge was that the Catholics intended to kill Charles so that his brother could succeed and thence lead the nation back to the Roman church—directly inspired Exclusion. If a Protestant succession could be guaranteed, it was said, there would be little point in a Catholic attempt on Charles's life.

The leader of Exclusion, the leader of the Whigs, was the Earl of Shaftesbury, a politician extraordinaire and the patron of John Locke, who lived in
the earl's household as physician, political confidant, and resident intellectual. Despite Locke's closeness to Shaftesbury and thus to the center of
Whig activity, recent scholarship on Whig political thought of the era from
Exclusion to the Glorious Revolution draws a picture of a body of thought
remarkable un-Lockean. Neither before, nor during, nor for a long while
after the 1680s were Lockean ideas dominant within the Whig party. The
recent scholarship finds that Locke's *Treatises* was not "very influential during the Revolution period." It did not "become straightaway the principal
authority of the Whigs."[10] That may have been because "Locke was unlike
. . . all the other leading Whig theorists." Whatever the cause, the outcome
was that "in supporting the Revolution Settlement of 1689 . . . few men
justified their actions by reference to such radical concepts as the original
contract, the sovereignty of the people or the natural rights of all men."[11]
Locke as spokesman for the Whigs, the Whigs as Lockeans—two illusions
of historical judgment produced by an overly anachronistic reading of the
seventeenth century. The "remarkable lack of immediate response to *Two
Treatises* seems to indicate that hindsight has inflated our sense of Locke's
importance as a political writer during the late seventeenth and early eighteenth centuries."[12] From the dominance Locke later came to have over
Whig thought, historians had read him backwards into history.[13]

Not merely did "the Whigs who came to power in the wake of the Glorious Revolution . . . *not* rush to embrace the ideas of Locke," but they "went
to considerable lengths to disassociate themselves from the . . . opinions
contained in the *Two Treatises*."[14] Locke-like views were seen by the Whigs
as a liability. "The strength of support [in the nation] for Toryism drove the
Whigs to abandon some of their more liberal views and to stress their commitment to conservative principles."[15] More fundamentally still, recent historians argue, "contractarian thought had fallen into general disfavor . . . as
a result of the 'murder' of Charles I and the 'tyranny' of Oliver Cromwell."
Whig defenders of the Revolution like Benjamin Hoadley "eschewed all
mention of Locke and Sidney, preferring to base his case on Hooker and
St. Paul." In so much "disfavor" were Lockean principles, concluded J. P.
Kenyon, that "the Whigs were not anxious to be associated in the public
mind with what we now regard as the fathers of Whig political thought."[16]

Locke and the relatively few Whigs who agreed with him returned the
favor. In a recently rediscovered commentary on the aftermath of the Revolution, Locke denounced the reasoning by which most men were endorsing

the Revolution. If one rested one's acceptance on mere possession of the throne, without recognizing explicitly the rightfulness of removing James and of replacing him with William, then the distinction between lawful king and usurper is no more. The only path to safety and national unity, thought Locke, lay along the lines of public avowal of the principles he had defended in the *Two Treatises*. [17]

The new story about the Whigs and the Glorious Revolution thus has the following elements: The Whigs were not sole begetters of the Revolution, dominating the political landscape with their ideas; moreover, the Whigs themselves splintered into conservative, moderate, and radical blocs. Accordingly, says one scholar, "rather than an approach to the political theory of the Whigs that is premised upon a consensus, we require a framework that highlights and explains the importance of a split within Whig political theory in the 1680s and 1690s." Seen in that light, "Locke's *Two Treatises* expresses a distinctive radical perspective, and . . . it does so in language that contemporaries clearly perceived to have those qualities."[18] That "distinctive radical perspective" was also distinctly a minority perspective. In addition to the testimony we have already seen regarding Whig reluctance to endorse Lockean theory, there is Mark Goldie's careful tally of the types of arguments made in the political pamphlets of the revolutionary era: no more than ten percent endorsed a view of politics at all like Locke's. Lockean argument, concluded Goldie, was "utterly uncharacteristic" because it was "unusually abstract."[19]

The previously prevailing consensus that pegged Locke as a mainstream Whig and the Whigs as nascent or actual Lockeans, so far as it was not mere anachronism, arose from the presence of contractarian language within the writings of many Whigs and in *Two Treatises* as well. This is a double mistake, however; in the first place, the idea of contract was by no means universal or entirely dominant within Whig thought, and second, as we have already seen, not all contractarianisms are the same.

Post-Restoration Whig thought not only continued to be un-Lockean in character, but it also differed noticeably from pre-Restoration Opposition thought. Its continuing tie to the Reformation lay not in an effort to find "the one true Protestantism" but rather in its virulent anti-Romanism. "There is no question but that anti-popery feeling was the glue that held together the various constituencies comprising the political movement that emerged during the Exclusion crisis." The Whigs appealed to "a deeply ingrained cultural prejudice against Catholicism."[20] And to a fear of it: in 1681 one of the Whig pamphleteers demanded to know "what Mercy, Favour, or Compassion would a Popish prince exercise over Protestant subjects,"[21] stirring memories of Bloody Mary, of St. Bartholomew's Day, of the Irish Massacre. As bad as a Catholic king would be in himself for the Protestant interest of England, the Whigs also feared that Catholicism led—

perhaps inevitably—to political absolutism.[22] "Where Popish lords are in power, there rages tyranny," raged the Exclusionist author of the pamphlet "Percat Papa."[23] The most visible themes in Whig writings of the Exclusionist period were thus themes centering on the Catholic threat and the evils of absolutism. "No Popery, No Slavery" was the chief slogan of the day.[24] The Earl of Shaftesbury probably captured the fear most picturesquely in a 1679 speech to the House of Lords: "Popery and Slavery, like two sisters, go hand in hand, sometimes one goes first, sometimes the other, in a door, but the other is always following close at hand."[25]

The Whigs proposed to exclude James via ordinary legislation—a bill to be passed by Parliament and signed by the king. The question naturally arose whether it was possible for Parliament and king to alter the laws of inheritance in this manner.[26] Although O. W. Furley is correct in asserting that the Whigs attempted to establish "that Exclusion was constitutional and not innovatory," he overstates the case when he implies that they tended to limit themselves to measuring the lawfulness of Exclusion in terms of "their ideas of the ancient constitution."[27]

A new sort of legalism appeared in Whig thought, different in emphasis from anything before the Civil War. Even those Whigs who refused to follow Hunton and Parker into an original contract anterior to the constitution tended to place their consideration of the lawfulness of Exclusion in the context of this broader legalism. There was now not only an appeal to the laws and constitution of England but also a systematic canvassing of the provisions of the laws of nature, of nations, and of God. These other laws were important to the argument in two ways. First, the Whigs sought to address the issue not only of the legality but of the justice of Exclusion. Exclusion seemed just under the laws of God, for example, because the Scriptures show instances of God displacing one ruler in favor of another ruler in Israel itself. "Now if God permitted and allowed of this in his own commonwealth, no doubt but he approveth also the same in other realms, viz., that the ordinary line of succession be altered, when just occasions are offered."[28] Likewise, concluded the same pamphleteer, "that it is lawful for king and Parliament to alter succession is evident from the Law of all Nations," as evidenced in the fact that the nations do this very thing when the occasion arises.[29]

The appeal to the broader context of law served another function as well: it supplied an interpretive principle for construing the laws and constitution of England. The chief legal arguments under the laws of England were precedential ones; king and Parliament had together regulated the succession in the past.[30] But the opponents of Exclusion denounced such precedents as "unconstitutional, . . . null and void."[31] The Whigs had to have some sympathy for this objection, because they were unwilling to concede that every historical precedent had the force of law. Many times kings had taken actions that the Whigs considered usurpations. The Whigs therefore appealed to the broader context of law in order to establish a version of the law and constitution beyond mere precedent. Once again, the ancient constitution in itself proved inadequate. "It is contrary to the Law of Nature and Reason to suppose that the King and Parliament together cannot alter the succession." According to the law of nature, "government being ordained for the benefit of the publick and not for its destruction," there must exist a power in the political authorities—king and Parliament—to do what the public benefit requires.[32] The standard for measuring the power of king-in-Parliament is "the safety of the nation," and therefore they "may for weighty causes refuse the Heir presumptive"; given the very great potential harm to the whole public, this is not at all the same case as an ordinary inheritance.[33] "No government can want power to preserve itself and obtain its great end, *viz*, the preservation of the community and the polity itself."[34] Those laws that transcend the positive laws of England provided the Whigs the key to construing the positive laws and constitution. "In the last analysis," the Whigs "rested upon an interpretation of the Law of Nature."[35] On the basis of that interpretation, they pronounced (their) legal precedents sound. The noncontractarian Whig position outlined here combines appeal to the constitution, even the "ancient constitution," with appeals of a less historical and less narrowly English character. Richard Ashcraft thus counsels wisely when he advises against "positing a dichotomy between" ancient constitution and natural law arguments. The Whigs used both, and used them together with no sense of incompatibility between them.[36]

It was just this appeal beyond mere English law and history that distinguishes this type of Whig theory from the doctrines of the Declaration of Rights of 1689. The Declaration resolutely resisted any transconstitutional, translegal reference, a resistance made possible by James II's convenient "abdication." The Declaration of Rights was clearly a legalist document, and it remained entirely within the ambit of the English positive law. The new Whig legalism, even in its noncontractarian form, appealed outside the positive law to a trio of laws: the laws of nature, of nations, and of God. That trio in turn betrayed the influence of the Dutch political philosopher Hugo Grotius, whose 1620 treatise *The Law of War and Peace*, a work of great popularity in mid-century England, proceeded precisely in terms of the systematic and orderly appeal to these three types of law. The prominence and parallelism of the three serve as a marker for the presence of Grotius: earlier natural law writers, like Richard Hooker, either did not deploy all three or did not use them in this parallel form.[37] In most of his substantive discussions of topics like "the rights of captives in war" and "the rights of killing enemies in lawful war," Grotius first lays out the mandate of the law of nature, then of the law of nations, and finally of the law of God, just as the Whig Exclusionist writers increasingly did.[38] Thus, even when they did not mention Grotius explicitly, his signature was clearly visible; many did in fact cite Grotius as an (or the) authority.[39] The details of the argument did not always strictly adhere to the Grotian original, since the Whig writers often misconstrued Grotius on the law of nations, yet the style of argument was unmistakably Grotian. Moreover, in order to establish the content of the various laws, the Whig writers followed Grotius's empirical method: the uniform or common practice of the nations points to the content of the relevant laws.[40] Although earlier writers like Hunton showed more than a few signs of a Grotian presence in their thinking, it is really in the post-Restoration context that Grotius became the overwhelming force that led to the conclusion that in the second half of the seventeenth century he was "the master of Whig thought."

The Whigs' Grotian appeal to the triumvirate of laws beyond the English positive law brought this noncontractarian Whiggism closer to the doctrines of Locke and of the American Declaration of Independence than the Declaration of Rights was. As in the American Declaration, there are natural standards to guide, shape, and judge political life. As in the Declaration, there is clear recognition of a naturally established public good as the defining end for political life. Even so, this Whig theory remains notably different from the American doctrine. The Whigs affirmed the primacy of the "public benefit," but left that almost entirely unspecified and surely made no suggestion that it ought to be understood in terms of securing individual rights. While the Whig theory deploys the law of nature, it contains no notion of a prepolitical condition or of original equality. Accordingly, this Whig theory knows nothing of the political as artifact, constituted through "consent of the governed"—rather the contrary, in fact, for the mandates of the law of nature are applied directly to government, implying its naturalness. That is, the "just powers" of government do not "derive from the consent of the governed" but from the law of nature.

In the period leading up to and beyond the Glorious Revolution, noncontractarian arguments remained prominent among the politically active elements of the nation and even among the Whigs. Goldie's thorough survey of the pamphlet literature shows that more than fifty percent of those who wrote in defense of the Revolution failed to make a contractarian argument of any sort; among the Whigs a full one-third failed to do so. Moreover, Goldie suspects contractarianism to have been even less widespread than these figures suggest. On the basis of "observations of contemporaries" regarding the prevalence of different sorts of political principles, he thinks "the printed frequencies of arguments . . . with their large contractarian Whig wing may well provide a misleading picture."[41] Goldie's suspicion coheres with the conclusion of H. T. Dickinson, who, on the basis of his own resurvey of the literature, believes that the appeal to contract was less prevalent among the Whigs than the various appeals to law, natural, and positive.[42]

Whig Contractarianism and the Glorious Revolution: Right Grotians

Notwithstanding the many Whigs who avoided contractarian arguments, prominent Whig writers did commit themselves to contractarian political docrine. An especially important instance of Whig writing, said by some to "coincide with ideas expounded by Locke," to "present ideas that were strikingly close to those of Locke," is Gilbert Burnet's "Enquiry into the Measures of Submission to the Supream Authority" (1689).[43] Burnet, a Scot living in exile in Holland at the time of the Glorious Revolution, had been something of a prodigy in his time; he had mastered Latin, Greek, Aristotelian philosophy, civil law, and theology by the age of eighteen. His Whig leanings had caused him difficulties with Charles after the Exclusion Crisis, and, under ban in England, he became a member of the large English exile colony in Holland in the 1680s, a colony that then also included John Locke. By 1687 he had become a political advisor to Prince William of Orange and spiritual advisor to his wife, Princess Mary. When William invaded England toward the end of 1688 Burnet accompanied him. So did Burnet's "Enquiry," "printed in large numbers for distribution at William's landing."[44] In its original form, it bore the imprint "by authority," and "was surely published with the approval of William," and almost as surely "written after consultation with distinguished English emigrés in Holland."[45] Burnet's "Enquiry" thus comes as close as we can get to an official theory of their actions by those who actually made the Revolution.

At first glance, Burnet's "Enquiry" is not easily placed into any of the categories in terms of which Whig thought is usually discussed. It surely is neither exclusively a rationalist nor exclusively a legal-historical argument, for although it appeals to the English constitution, it also appeals to the "law of nature," "natural religion," and the teachings of the Bible. Indeed, what characterizes Burnet's argument most decisively is just the way he combines constitutionalist and philosophical arguments. His inquiry in the pamphlet—prepared, it must be recalled, at the moment of William's march on England—is into "the measures of submission to the Supream Authority," by which he means the extent of obedience due to rulers, or alternatively, whether and when "it may be lawful or necessary for subjects to defend their religion, lives and liberties."[46]

The answer to those questions, he says, is not determined by natural or divine laws, but by the particular laws and history of particular polities, and accordingly the answer will vary from place to place. That is, one nation, such as England, may owe only a limited degree of submission to its king and may possess a right of resistance under some circumstances, whereas another nation may owe unlimited submission and retain no right of resistance.

> The measures of power, and by consequence of obedience, must be taken from the express laws of any state or body of men, from the oaths they swear, or from immemorial prescription, and a long possession, which both give a title. . . . The degrees of all civil authority are to be taken either from express laws, immemorial customs, or from particular oaths.[47]

Thus far, Burnet fits the model of the constitutional contractarian; his concern is with "particular positive laws and the institutional inheritance of specific polities."[48] The "laws, customs, and oaths" to which he looked are all taken as evidence of the content of a specific and positive original contract that empowered the rulers and subjected the ruled: a human being "becomes in the power of another, only so far as it was provided by the contract."[49] Burnet thus assimilated the themes of ancient constitution ("immemorial custom") and original contract in a way that belies those who see them as distinctly different modes of argument.

The constitution provides the authoritative answer to the question of what degree of submission a particular human being is under, but Burnet deploys a very different, rationalist or philosophic, argument in order to establish the authority of the constitution. Indeed, his philosophic-theological arguments function precisely to establish the authority of the constitution, and only that. "We are then at last brought to the constitution of our English government: so that no general considerations from speculation about sovereign power, nor from any passages either of the Old and [sic] New Testament, ought to determine us in this matter; which must be fixed from the laws and regulations that have been made among us."[50] Natural and divine law carry him only so far as the positive law and then set him down before it. For Burnet, therefore, the rational principles run out at a particular moment, but they nonetheless perform a crucial function: they provide the normative ground for the positive constitution. Burnet combines philosophic and constitutionalist contractarianism just enough to validate the authoritativeness of the appeal to the constitution. He may legitimately be classified as a constitutional contractarian, but only with a major proviso regarding the universalistic philosophic ground that gets him there.

The significant dimension of rationalist or philosophic contractarianism in Burnet does not, however, bring him very close to Locke or the Declaration of Independence. The important difference lies not merely in the commonplace observation that Burnet deploys historical-legalist arguments in addition to his philosophic arguments, which Locke does not. Much more important is the fact that Locke and the Declaration insist that natural principles of right settle the question regarding the "measures of submission" for all peoples, and for all peoples affirm a right to revolution. "Whenever *any* government becomes destructive of these ends"—that is, the securing of the rights that all men everywhere possess—then it is the right of all men "to alter or abolish" their government. It matters not at all what the particular positive law and constitution of the place may be.

Nonetheless, there is a certain plausibility in identifying Burnet as the source of "ideas that were strikingly close to Locke's." There is at least an arguable case for attributing to Burnet three of the five doctrines at the heart of the theory of politics in the Declaration: natural equality, the artificiality of government, and consent.[51] (There is no comparable case to be made for the other two doctrines, the centrality of natural rights and the right of revolution.)

According to Burnet, "The law of nature has put no difference nor subordination among men, except it be that of children to parents, or of wives to their husbands; so that with relation to the law of nature, all men are born free."[52] That is, the law of nature puts no one under political subjection. Men are "born free" under the law of nature in the sense of being born equal, free of the authority of any other human being. It is surely plausible to see a parallel here to the doctrine of the state of nature, even if (significantly) Burnet never used that term.

Natural religion does not disturb the mandate of natural law: "It cannot be supposed, by the principles of natural religion, that God has authorized any one form of government, any other way than as the general rules of order and of justice, oblige all men not to subvert constitutions nor disturb the peace of mankind, or invade those rights with which the law may have vested some persons."[53] Natural religion mandates peace, order, and justice, and does so by commanding obedience to the positive laws and constitution of one's polity, but it does not establish any particular government or any possessors of political authority. It establishes certain natural duties of obedience toward one's rulers, but it does not establish those rulers or the extent of their authority.

Positive religion also confirms the mandate of the law of nature. The Old Testament presents the story of the Jews, a people ruled by kings "that were immediately designated by God." No other rulers "can pretend to such designation." Thus "all that was done in that dispensation, either for or against princes, is not to be made use of in any other state."[54] The New Testament has a more abiding relevance, but extends no further than the teaching of natural religion in the content of its political commands: "All Christians are bound to acquiesce in the government, and submit to it, according to the Constitution that is settled by law."[55] But the New Testament does not settle the constitution nor designate the holders of power, nor place any obligations on anyone beyond those imposed by the settled constitution.

Human beings are born free under the law of nature, "and this liberty must still be supposed to be entire, unless so far as it is limited by contracts, provisions, and laws." This seems a plausible rendering of the Declaration's doctrine of the artificiality of government: it exists only as made by human beings, the natural condition being one of no-rule. The means by which government is made is contract—again plausibly parallel to the Declaration's assertion that consent of the governed is the origin of the "just powers" of government.

Despite these apparent similarities, Burnet's position is in fact very different, on all counts, from that of Locke and the Declaration. According to Burnet, the law of nature has put no orders of political subordination among men, but that does not imply that *all* men are born free and equal, that is, outside political subordination, for each man who is born under a political constitution is subject to that constitution, the governors designated by it, and the "degree of submission" ordained in it. The original or natural freedom and equality applies, or is relevant, only to those who lived before the constitution was established. They who founded it ended not only their own condition of nonsubjection but also that of all subsequent human beings born under the constitution they established. The positive law entirely supersedes the law of nature for all later human beings, as is evident in the fact that nobody in 1688 could look to the law of nature to ascertain the limits of his or her subjection, but only to "the laws and regulations that have been made among us."[56]

The Declaration insists quite otherwise: "All men are created equal," not only those who lived at some moment of founding, but even those living here and now, in 1776, or in 1994. Thus "all men" retain the right to appeal to "the laws of nature and of nature's God" and to assert their rights, which precede and do not derive from government. Locke states the point at greater length than the Declaration does, but it is the same point: "Men being, as has been said, by nature, all free, equal and independent, *no one* can be put out of this state and subjected to the political power of another, without *his own consent*." That later human beings are born into already existing political societies does not change matters: "'Tis true, that whatever engagements or promises any one has made for himself, he is under the obligation of them, but cannot by any compact whatsoever, bind his children or posterity." Since "every man" is "naturally free . . . nothing [can] put him into subjection to any earthly power, but only his own consent."[57]

It should be obvious, therefore, that the doctrine of consent in the Declaration is quite different from what appears to be a similar idea in Burnet. For Burnet, consent or compact occurs but once; for Locke and the Americans consent must occur as often as human beings come to take up a place within a polity. The most obvious token of the abiding relevance of consent is the right of revolution: when government no longer does what needs to be done, then the subjects may withdraw their consent and alter or abolish it.

The important differences between Burnet and the Declaration ultimately come back, as might be expected, to the issue of rights. The agreement or contract to which Burnet traced political subjection differs from the equivalent idea in the Declaration in at least two respects. As we have already seen, Burnet assumed that the contract could and did bind future generations entirely; and Burnet explicitly affirmed the unlimited power of human beings to contract away the entirety of the liberty (nonsubjection to other men) that the law of nature bequeathed them:

> As a private person can bind himself to another man's service, by different degrees, either as an ordinary servant for wages, or as one appropriate for a longer time, as an apprentice; or by a total giving himself up to another, as in the case of slavery: in all which cases the general name of master may be equally used, yet the degrees of his power are to be judged by the nature of the contract: so likewise bodies of men can give themselves upon different degrees to the conduct of others: and therefore though all those may carry the same name of king, yet every ones power is to be taken from the measures of that authority which is lodged in him.[58]

Or, to use the language of the Declaration, according to Burnet liberty is alienable, entirely alienable, to the extent that an individual may give it all up and become a slave and a people may give it all up and become entirely subjected to an absolute ruler. But the Declaration pronounces liberty to be an "inalienable right": no individual can voluntarily give it all up and become a slave; no people can voluntarily give it all up and become subjected to an absolute king.

Since human beings can, under Burnet's law of nature, resign themselves up entirely to their ruler, there is an openness about the end of the political societies thus created. Since they can alienate their liberty, it cannot be insisted, as the Declaration does, that government exists solely for the sake of securing their inalienable rights to that selfsame liberty. Burnet thus has nothing whatever to say about the universal purposes of rightful government. In other words, despite some surface similarities, Burnet's version of Whig contractarianism is almost as far from that in the Declaration of Independence as the Declaration of Rights was. It is also, as should be apparant, very distinct from Milton's Christian "contractarianism."

Thus, it appears, Burnet was not learning his politics from Locke during those years the two spent in Holland. Nonetheless his Dutch exile was far from irrelevant to the "Enquiry," for in its main outlines it closely follows the political thought of the greatest Dutch thinker of the time, Hugo Grotius. Grotius had published his masterwork, *De Jure Belli ac Pacis*, the founding work of the field of international law, about two generations before Burnet and Locke involuntarily found themselves residing in his homeland. By the late seventeenth century it was an acknowledged classic, widely read and extraordinarily influential in England as well as on the Continent.[59] Burnet's Whig contractarianism was shaped by Grotius to an even greater degree than was the Whig noncontractarianism surveyed above.

The traces of Grotius's thought appear everywhere in Burnet's pamphlet, but most importantly in his central argument. Grotius, like Burnet, argued for the origin of political power in the people, but he incisively rejected "the opinion of those . . . who hold that everywhere and without exception sovereignty resides in the people, so that it is permissible for the people to restrain and punish kings whenever they make a bad use of their power." Grotius found this doctrine not only untrue but dangerous: "How many evils this opinion has given rise to, and can even now give rise to if it sinks deep into men's minds, no wise person fails to see." The doctrine of popular sovereignty, understood as a general right under the law of nature to resist or punish kings, is untrue, he said, for the following reason:

> To every man it is permitted to enslave himself to any one he pleases for private ownership, as is evident both from the Hebraic and the Roman Law. Why, then, would it not be permitted to a people having legal competence to submit itself to some one person, or to several persons, in such a way as plainly to transfer to him the rights to govern, retaining no vestige of that right for itself? . . . A people can [originally] select the form of government which it wishes.[60]

Grotius does not take the opposite position—that resistance is never justified—but precisely the one taken by Burnet: it all depends on the positive constitution of the country in question. "It may happen that a people, when choosing a king may reserve to itself certain power; but may confer the others on the king absolutely." The rights and duties of king and people depend entirely on what was actually established. When the people "enjoins upon the future king something in the nature of a perpetual command . . . it is understood that the king can be constrained or punished." Grotius goes on to list the cases in which "resistance [may] rightly be made to those who hold the sovereign power." In all cases, the standard Grotius uses is "the purpose of him who laid down the law"—that is, the law of the constitution as fixed at the establishment of the constitution.[61]

Burnet's Grotian doctrine contained features that made it very well suited indeed to the situation in which he proffered it. First, it was a serious and very thoughtful effort to give normative ground to the constitution. The Whigs almost universally accepted the authority of the historical constitution (as they interpreted it), but thinkers like Robert Filmer and Dr. Ferne not only challenged their specific interpretation of it but also posited natural or divine principles of politics that, in effect, superseded the authority of the constitution. In general, the theory of the original contract, most of the tenets of which Burnet captured very well, was the answer to this challenge. The constitution was binding because it had been made via a binding promise between the people (or rather, their ancestors) and the king (or rather, his ancestors).

Burnet presented an especially conservative version of the original contract; he went so far as justifying resistance to James, perhaps justifying replacing James with another (William), but no further. Everything turned on the terms of the inherited constitution and there was no hint that further remodelling of the English polity or society was justified by the theory. As a quasi-official statement, it served William's needs admirably well; as a conservative version of contractarianism, it spoke well to those who wished to resist the innovatory (as they saw it) aims of King James but who feared and distrusted the kinds of innovations instituted under the auspices of Reformation contractarianism between 1642 and 1660. Burnet's was, in every way, as reassuring a version of contractarianism as the context could have required or allowed.

The same animus Burnet shows against the 1640s is more explicit in a pamphlet written some months after William's success by the great publicist and novelist Daniel Defoe. Defoe's "Reflections upon the Late Great Revolution," one of his very early works, repeats Burnet's arguments exactly, although somewhat less incisively, at greater length, and with more attention to biblical history. But on essentials it is just the same: "The magistrate's power and the measures of the subjects subjection, are only to be judged of by the particular laws and constitutions of the kingdom; for that may be very lawful in one place which is not so in another." The ground for this judgment is also just the same as in Burnet. "The power of kings" derives "being" from "that original contract which is made between the people and the person or family they shall think fit to advance to the kingship. . . . The people at the first institution and setting up of monarchy among them make over so much of the power, and such and such rights and privileges to the king, which if afterwards they refuse to make good, they are and ought to be looked upon as rebels and traitors." But just as the people become "rebels and traitors" when they fail to live up to the terms of the original contract, so the king "forfeits" his authority when he exercises power beyond his legal bounds. All covenants are "conditional," all obligations established by covenant are "mutual." According to Defoe, 1689 did not in the least reprise 1642 or 1649, which "was the most open and notorious rebellion that ever was rendered in story." Charles I, "that good king and true martyr," had but one fault—"complying too much with his people," in contrast with the character of his son James, who had launched a concerted attempt to subvert the laws.[62]

The character of the American Declaration of Independence stands out by way of contrast. Burnet's form of contractarianism was in principle oriented to the past, and to history: not merely were the standards for political action in the present to be found exclusively by reference to historically established laws and principles, but the past remained exclusively authoritative over every future. Burnet's theory could never preside over the inauguration of a "new order for the ages"; it could only restore, over and over, the old order—quite without regard, by the way, for the inherent goodness of that past order. The Americans, by contrast, affirmed the ever-present right "to alter or abolish" their government "and to institute new government, laying its foundation on such principles, and organizing its powers in such form, as to them shall seem most likely to effect their safety and happiness." The Americans were thus, in principle, progressive, or open to the future.[63]

The daring of the Americans stands out when contrasted with the discernible conservatism of Burnet, Defoe, and Grotius. Surely the latter group would have seen the doctrine of consent in the Declaration, as well as the ever-open appeal to nature—over the head, so to speak, of history and law—as potentially unsettling of all political life. Surely they would have seen the Declaration's openness to an open future as potentially unsettling of all political life. The very suitability of Burnet's "Enquiry" to his situation reveals the truly radical bearing of the American Declaration.[64]

WHIG CONTRACTARIANISM AND THE GLORIOUS REVOLUTION: LEFT GROTIANS

Popular as Burnet's type of contractarianism was,[65] there were other, much less conservative versions put forward in the late seventeenth century. In addition to using contractarian arguments to justify resistance to and replacement of King James, this strain of thought also promoted changes in the constitution, some more and some less far-reaching, but all less committed to the continuing sway of the inherited constitution and the terms of the "original contract." Like Milton, and unlike Burnet, these Whigs endorsed the right to change the constitution, to modify the terms of the original contract; but, like Burnet and unlike Milton, they did not transform this right into a cryptorepublicanism, to be opened up for use whenever the people or some part of the people cared to. Like Burnet, like Hunton, like Locke, and like the authors of the Declaration of Independence, they limited the occasions on which a people may have recourse to this power.

This relatively large group of Whig thinkers would appear, then, to be most like Locke; so far as the Whigs served as antecedents for the theory of politics contained in the Declaration of Independence, these are the predecessors we might identify. With the exception again of Locke, however, that seems not to be the case. This group of Whigs, surprisingly perhaps, turns out to be Grotians as much as Burnet and Defoe were. Although they emphasized certain of the Dutch jurist's themes ignored by Burnet, and thus produced a somewhat less conservative version of the contract doctrine, they nonetheless differed from Lockeanism almost as much as Burnet himself.[66]

In some of these Whig writers the Grotian connection is even more obvious than in Burnet, for Grotius is explicitly quoted as the authority on the law of nature and on the right of subjects to resist kings.[67] In other cases the Grotian presence is less explicit—in the seventeenth century authors were not always generous in citing by name authorities from whom they borrowed ideas—but nonetheless discernible. For example, a pamphlet frequently attributed to the former Leveller John Wildman affirmed Grotian doctrines we have already noticed in Burnet: "All power is originally or fundamentally in the People"; government is set up by the people and they "may set up what government they please . . . a monarchy absolute or limited; or an aristocracy or democracy." The present situation of the people, with respect to their relationship to government, must therefore be ascertained not by reference to abstract principles of natural law, but by reference to the constitution.[68] Another pamphlet, usually attributed to the clergyman John Humphrey, not only endorses the same Grotian ideas but adds the following, which captures the center of the Grotian position in language almost directly taken from the Dutchman:

> Whatsoever reservation of liberty the people make in their agreement, these are to be looked upon as their rights by the laws of the constitution, and essential thereunto, and consequently inviolable by any of these governments whom they set up for the administration.[69]

The doctrine of the "left Grotians" differs from Burnet's in but one essential: Not only may the king forfeit his rightful power, or exceed his authority and therefore ask more submission of the people than they owe him, but the government may be "dissolved," in which case "the supreme authority . . . does escheat or fall to the community." When that happens the people may remake government in whatsoever way seems desirable to them, for the old constitution, which "lay in the original agreement of the people," is then "at an end."[70] Because 1689 was such a moment of dissolution and reversion, the "left Grotians" argued, the opportunity for revision of the constitution was at hand. With the memory of the Commonwealth and the Protectorate behind them, few in 1689 proposed truly radical reformation, such as aboli-

tion of the monarchy, but a few did recommend fairly substantial reshuf-
fling of the powers of government between king and Parliament.

The ideas of royal forfeiture and reversion of sovereign powers to the
people affirmed by this group of Whigs can also be traced to Grotius. The
Dutch jurist, even though he rejected a general right of resistance, developed a lengthy table of cases in which resistance to the king was justifiable
and in which the king was dethroned, or dethroned himself. Whig writers
appealed to almost all the possibilities Grotius listed, singly or in combination, and although they seldom mentioned him by name in this context, he
was clearly the source of Whig thinking about forfeiture and the resultant
dissolution. One pamphlet that did mention Grotius by name on the subject, and that was also very thorough in charging King James with all the
offenses deserving resistance that Grotius had discovered, was "Some Short
Considerations Relating to the Settling of the Government." The anonymous author found the government to be dissolved, because two parts of
the constitution—the King and the House of Commons, which depended
on the king to call it into session—were not operative. The writer found that
the king had forfeited his power in "several ways," including his effort to
"alienate the kingdom" by accepting subjection to the Pope; his "desertion"
of the kingdom; his "abdication," which the Convention Parliament had
made so much of (with Grotian warrant); and, most interesting, his forsak-
ing of his true constitutional powers and attempt to usurp powers not his.
The English constitution "allows no such king."[71]

Not all the Whigs were as eclectic as the author of "Short Considerations," and there were frequent disagreements among them as to just what
"brought things back to their first original," but the details of these controversies are not important here. Beneath these disagreements was a more
fundamental consensus on the point Grotius had argued: under certain circumstances the sovereign power reverts to the people and thus makes possible a new "original contract."[72]

Even though the "left Grotianism" of the Whigs is less conservative than
Burnet's "right Grotianism," nonetheless all the differences between Burnet's Grotianism and the American Declaration that we have discussed earlier also apply to theirs. It, too, remains very close to Höpfl and Thompson's
"constitutional contractarianism." The "left Grotians" continue to speak of
"the original contract" as an historical and historically binding event; they
conceive the contract as occurring between the ruler and the people; they
trace the power given to the ruler to the community, to which it reverts
in case of dissolution, instead of to individuals; the actual historical legal-
constitutional arrangements of particular peoples remain the indispensable
point of reference for deciding major questions of political right and obligation. On all of these matters, as we have seen above, the Declaration of
Independence takes a different position.[73]

CONTRACTARIANISMS

Despite the usefulness of Höpfl and Thompson's classification of contractarianisms, their typology now appears in need of some refinement. For one thing, the distinction between constitutional and philosophic contractarianism is too rigidly drawn. As the Whig Grotians of both left and right reveal, this particular version of constitutional contractarianism contained a heavy dose of philosophic matter. Moreover, their dichotomy is not fine enough to pick out the kinds of differences that exist between, say, Burnet and Wildman.

Höpfl and Thompson's claim about the relative uniqueness of Locke is well borne out, however. The differences between Locke and his American followers, on the one hand, and the English Whigs of the seventeenth century, on the other, are far more striking than the similarities, although judgments of that sort must always be made with a context of comparison in mind. Despite the differences we have just emphasized, Locke and the Americans *were* Whigs and rightly saw themselves as making common cause against divine right monarchy, against absolutism, and for constitutionalism. Despite the changes, that common heritage remains important; despite the changes and the differences, there is something valid to the idea of a tradition of Anglo-American constitutionalism reaching back to Magna Charta if not earlier.

Höpfl and Thompson also treat philosophic contractarianism too narrowly. They wish to challenge the unicontractarianism of past scholarship, but substitute for that a notion of philosophic contractarianism too closely tied to Locke's coattails. Locke is taken as paradigmatic, but, as we have seen, the Grotians, Hunton, and Milton all proffered versions of contractarianism with strong claims to the title "philosophic" (or at least nonconstitutional), but that differ greatly from Locke. Had we extended our survey of Whig literature a bit, we could have discussed yet other modes of philosophic contractarianism, versions that share little with Locke, Grotius, or Milton.[74] Some of the limits of Höpfl and Thompson's scheme reflect the fact that they developed their categories largely through the study of, on the one hand, Protestant thinkers who developed a doctrine of resistance in the sixteenth century (in particular the treatise *Vindiciae Contra Tyrannos*), and, on the other hand, Locke. They thus failed to see that most Whig contractarianism differed from both of their two chief sources, in that it had a heavy infusion of Grotian political philosophy. Indeed, the story of seventeenth-century Whig thought is the story of the rise to dominance of Grotius, who by 1689 had gone far toward supplanting earlier natural-law or purely legal-constitutional political theory. It might be more accurate to say that Whig contractarianism represented an amalgam of an earlier contract/resistance doctrine, which found its best expression in the *Vindiciae*, and of

Grotius. The *Vindiciae* supplied a more sharp-edged notion of contract than Grotius, while the latter supplied the natural law grounding, including the materials out of which the doctrine of dissolution was constructed.[75] The *Vindiciae* itself had incorporated a doctrine of the law of nature taken over from the old Roman law and developed it toward conclusions inconsistent with its own foundations. Grotius began his great work with a withering critique of the Roman-law version of natural law and supplied a new doctrine that more or less swept the field and shaped the broad contours of the various Whig theories that drew on it.[76]

Grotius, in turn, was supplanted by Locke, who became so much the quintessential thinker of the Whig tradition that it has taken a generation of scholars a great effort to recapture a truer perspective within which Locke appears as quite unrepresentative of trends of thought in 1689. But the story of Locke's triumph is a story that does not become at all visible unless we take a more fine-tuned approach to contractarianism than even Höpfl and Thompson did. As Julian Franklin has well said, "an impression of blandness is conveyed" by Locke's *Second Treatise* because he "makes no attempt to distinguish his own position from that of the writers whose political objectives were similar to his." But, says Franklin, that "blandness" is deceiving: "subtle and acute distinctions often lie beneath the surface."[77] Locke's politically inspired reticence has for too long had too great an impact on scholars.

The story we must note first, however, is the story of the relative failure of both Lockean and "left Grotian" contractarianism in 1689: both positions remained minorities within a minority, unable to achieve the official recognition of the legalist-historical doctrine of the Declaration of Rights or even the quasi-official recognition of Burnet's conservative version of Grotius. They were, in Franklin's mild term, "unwelcome," because they were seen as potentially unsettling and therefore dangerous. A Whig admirer of Locke, William Atwood, captured the Whig concern very clearly when he insisted, as Franklin says, that the Revolution "required a defence that did not rest upon an appeal to natural law, natural rights, and the dissolution of government, but one which appealed instead (or as well) to the constitutional rights of Englishmen and which restricted the limits of constitutional change to the 'restoration' of the Ancient Constitution."[78]

The Whigs were happy with the ancient constitution—or their version of it anyway—and were not eager to set off toward whatever "brave new world" the appeal to the dissolution and thus possible remaking of government might lead to. Atwood's formulation makes perfectly clear how much more unsettling Lockean contractarianism was than even "left Grotianism"; the latter doctrine posed far less challenge to the received order, for it only opened the possibility of a remaking; and once a new "original contract" was made, "left Grotianism" would be entirely indistinguishable from the conservative Grotianism of Burnet. But as Atwood clearly saw, this was not so with Lockeanism.

That "brave new world," that "new order of the ages," is what the Americans embraced when they embraced the natural rights doctrine of government—even though they were not entirely clear themselves what that new world would look like and spent many years disagreeing, first with the British and then among themselves, over the appropriate terms of the new order.

CHAPTER FIVE

The Master of Whig Political Philosophy

GROTIUS dominated seventeenth century Whiggism—and with good reason.[1] His *De Jure Belli ac Pacis* (1625), known generally as the founding treatise of international law, is far more comprehensive than that description suggests.[2] It also presents a full-blown theory of the law of nature and the civil law. It treats such topics as the origin of political power and private property, the relations among the natural, divine, and human laws, and the powers of rulers and the liberties of peoples. Moreover, the *De Jure* is a work of nearly unparalleled erudition. Probably not since Thomas Aquinas had an author displayed such a grasp of all the literature relevant in even the slightest degree to his topic. Philosophers, poets, and historians, as well as jurists and legal codes, found a place in Grotius's synthesis. The book's "index of names" by itself runs the length of a very long chapter in an ordinary book. Grotius not only drew on standard authors such as Plato and Aristotle, Bartolus and Livy, but showed a remarkably fluent knowledge of Jewish writers like Maimonides and Abravenal, of very recent theorists like Bodin and Suárez, and even of commentators on the English common law like Fortescue and Littleton.

GROTIUS AND THE REFORMATION OF NATURAL LAW

The comparison to Thomas Aquinas seems especially apt, for Grotius fulfilled a function in his day somewhat akin to what Thomas had done three and a half centuries earlier. Thomas had showed perplexed Christians how the pagan philosophy of the ancients could be intergrated with Christianity. But Thomas had integrated pagan philosophy with a version of Christianity that, in Grotius's time and place (and in seventeenth-century England), had become suspect, or worse, hated. Early Protestantism struck out not only against the Roman Church but also against its characteristic modes of thought. Thus early Protestant political thinkers like Luther, and later ones, like Milton, turned not to Thomist natural law for guidance about politics, but to the Scriptures. Protestant political thought was initially political theology, not political philosophy. Grotius paralleled the achievement of Thomas, in that he developed a Protestant version of the law of nature—a doctrine that had been developed and nurtured by "popish" writers and, even in the seventeenth century, remained mostly the property of counter-Reformation thinkers like Francisco Suárez and Roberto Bellarmine.[3]

In a sense, the "Protestantization" of the natural law meant no more than the sponsorship and restatement of the doctrine by a writer with recognizably reformed credentials. It also meant the excision of obviously pro-papalist components from the theory. From Thomas through Bellarmine and Suárez, the natural law theorists had tended to support at least some papal claims to authority in both the sacred and the secular spheres.[4] Needless to say, there was not a spark of such ideas in Grotius's version of the natural law. Indeed, so contrary to Church doctrine was Grotius's book that it was placed on the Index soon after publication, there to remain until the early twentieth century.[5]

Moreover, although Grotius did not merely restate what all "right-thinking" Englishmen already believed, what he said readily converged with what many of them did think. His teaching about the authority of the original contract cohered with English tendencies to think about politics in terms of the ancient constitution. His version of contractarianism coexisted easily with English antiquarianism, and appears to have been an important force in accustoming the English to think in terms of contract. This habit of thought later on—in Locke, Sidney, and others—became attached to doctrines less readily congruent with the ancient constitution and the authority of history; thus Grotius, in retrospect, appears to have functioned as a transitional force in the Whig tradition. Furthermore, although Grotius was far from an unambiguous proponent of liberty and constitutionalism, his theory as applied to England readily became a support for these causes, because, as we have seen, it supplied a natural law endorsement for the historic (Whig) order.

The history of the reception of Grotius in England has yet to be written, but the publication history of *De Jure* may suggest it. The first edition appeared in 1625 in Paris, followed by at least fourteen editions before 1680 at Amsterdam and yet another at the Hague.[6] Given the pattern of intellectual interchange between England and the Netherlands throughout the seventeenth century, the early presence of Grotius's text among English readers of Latin may be easily surmised. Locke, for example, posessed the 1650 Latin edition of *De Jure*, published at Amsterdam, as well as another edition he purchased in Holland during the 1680s. He also owned Grotius's *De Veritate Religionis Christianae*, apparently also purchased in Holland.[7] Beginning in 1654 English translations of *De Jure* began to appear, the earliest of which was titled, significantly, *The Illustruous Hugo Grotius of the Law of Warre and Peace*. Grotius and his book were clearly already of wide fame. Another edition of the same translation appeared in 1655, and a new translation in 1682.[8] The fact that it was retranslated so soon suggests it was considered a vital book. The English-language presence of *De Jure* began during the Protectorate, and the new edition of 1682 suggests a particular relevance of the text to the growing conflicts between Whig opposition groups and the court.[9]

The events of mid-century no doubt gave Grotius a great boost. England suffered from religious conflict of a similar intensity to that found elsewhere in post-Reformation Europe, but with a somewhat different focus. The most important English battles occurred not between Catholics and Protestants, but between different varieties of Protestants. That did not make the battles less serious, or less violent, however. The conflicts of the seventeenth century proved that Protestantism could not easily and peacefully settle the theological-political problem. A generation earlier, Grotius had lived through a similar situation in his native Dutch Republic. There the theological-political conflicts between the Arminian Remonstrants, with whom he was aligned, and the partisans of the more orthodox Calvinist doctrine led to civil violence for the country and great personal suffering for Grotius himself. The Synod of Dort in 1618–19 rejected the Remonstrant doctrine and prepared the way for Grotius's arrest in 1619. His arrest inaugurated a long period of imprisonment and exile, during which Grotius wrote his *De Jure* and most of his other important writings.[10]

Grotius thus understood at first hand the particularly unsettled character of politics under the Reformation dispensation. His effort to restate the traditional doctrine of the natural law must be seen as one response to this situation.[11] That response took the form of a doctrine consonant with dominant Protestant principles but free from the vagaries of theological-scriptural doctrines and commitments. In the *De Jure*, Grotius is quite insistent: the law of nature is common for all human beings without regard to religion.[12] However, "there are those who urge the Old Law in itself as the law of nature." Grotius strongly disagrees, "for much of [the Old Law] comes from the free will of God." That part of the Old Law that derives from the free will of God must be distinguished from the law of nature. In order to know the difference, one must know the law of nature altogether independently of the Old Law.[13] Knowledge of the law of nature does not derive from the Old Testament, but stands as a measure of it.

Likewise, Grotius distinguishes the New Testament from the law of nature, and in doing so, goes "contrary to the practice of most men. . . . We are admonished to a greater holiness" by the New Testament than "the law of nature alone would require." The New Testament does not supply binding principles for the governance of political life; its precepts are commended rather than strictly enjoined.[14] Knowledge of the law of nature is through "right reason," not through divine revelation.[15]

Grotius goes even further: the law of nature is accessible as wholly natural and would have "some place even if one posited that there were no God." He hesitates to follow this last thought out, but it has a certain consistency with the dismissal of the Scriptures as a source of knowledge of the law of nature.[16] Accessible directly to right reason, knowledge of the binding or obligatory principles of politics, in Grotius's account, thus promises an escape from the sphere of sectarian conflict and undecidability characteristic of the Protestant era and most especially of the Civil War era in England.

Grotius's concern to free politics from Scripture seems to have had a yet broader end. In his view, politics in the entire Christian age showed a marked decline from pre-Christian days. The Greeks and Romans lived in "better times" and were "better peoples" than those who lived after. Therefore, "examples" taken from their histories have special "authority." No less than Machiavelli, Grotius looked to the model of antiquity as a corrective to the degenerate politics of his own era.[17] This degeneracy was especially visible in the international sphere. To Grotius, the Christians of his time fell short not only of the civilized pagans but of the barbarians as well. The Thirty Years War and other religion-inspired warfare formed the larger backdrop for Grotius's life and career and furnished much of the inspiration for his book. "I saw throughout the Christian world a license in waging war that would shame barbarous nations. . . . For light or even no causes" nations rushed to arms, and once in arms, they showed reverence for neither divine nor human laws. When most ostensibly inspired by reverence, the nations showed less reverence than ever. Grotius saw, therefore, greater need for his undertaking than ever before.[18]

In his own age, an age riven by uncertainty—or by too many conflicting certainties—Grotius displayed the same striving for mathematical (i.e., non-controversial) certainty as did Descartes, Hobbes, and Spinoza shortly after him. He sought to ground the propositions of the law of nature in "notions so certain that no one can deny them without doing violence to himself." The "principles of natural law [are] therefore patent and evident." So determined is the law of nature that God himself could not change it. No matter how powerful God is, "there are certain things over which his power does not extend." Just as for Descartes, the model for utterly immutable truth, a truth immune from all unsettling by any act of even an omnipotent will, is mathematics. "Even God cannot bring it about that twice two is not four."[19] The "intrinsic qualities of acts," apparently, have the same inevitable character as mathematical truths. The identification of the law of nature with certain and immutable propositions stands as Grotius's most extreme, but not his only, effort to escape all arbitrariness, all interpretation and contention, all possibility of contamination by will. Even where Grotius introduced a role for will, he strove for the same kind of certainty, as we shall see below. His attempt to move political discussion to this different and more promising plane of discourse (more promising because available in principle to all human beings qua human) must have formed a large part of the appeal Grotius had for people long wearied of interminable polemics based on obscure, ambiguous, or controversial texts.[20]

In his dedication of the *De Jure* to the French King, Louis XIII, Grotius signalled his intent to adumbrate a new kind of doctrine of the law of nature and of nations as part of an effort to pacify post-Reformation Europe. That act of dedication was natural in one respect, for Grotius was living in France at the time he wrote *De Jure*, and he received a small pension from the king. But it was also a significant and bold deed: a Dutch Protestant dedicating his masterwork to a very powerful Catholic monarch. In the dedication, Grotius, on behalf of "the peoples of Christian lands," urges Louis that "through his initiative peace may come again, not only to the nations but also to the churches, and that our time may learn to subject itself to the discipline of that age which we all who are Christians acknowledge in true and sincere faith to have been Christian." That age, Grotius's editor reminds us, was "the period of the early church, before there was a division into sects." Grotius found the seventeenth century, by contrast, an age "of partisan passions, fired by hatreds which blaze more fiercely day by day." Writing in the midst of the Thirty Years War, with memories of many other religion-incited controversies in mind, Grotius confessed that "our hearts [are] wearied with strifes."[21] "The Law of War and Peace" was meant as a contribution to peace and, should that fail, to more moderate war.

THE SOURCE OF POLITICAL POWER

The Whigs who found Grotius so attractive were, for the most part, quite adequate interpreters of his position. Even their intramural disagreements found their basis in ambiguities in his text. Let us recall, then, some of the more significant dimensions of Whig Grotianism, left and right. First, Grotius and the Grotians were indeed contractarians, but they differed in very many and very important ways from the natural rights contractarianism of Locke and the American Declaration of Independence. Second, there is an ambiguity in Grotius regarding the dissolution of government in those cases where resistance is valid, and this ambiguity produced important differences among Whigs. Third, Grotius and the Grotians developed a strikingly peculiar doctrine of resistance. This last deserves special attention, for it provides an admirable entrée into the core of Grotius's doctrine. The Grotians, true as they may have been to the master, did not themselves allow more than a glimpse of the theoretical foundation of the doctrine they espoused. For that, we must turn to Grotius himself.

The Grotian resistance doctrine, like most else in Grotius, is meant to be moderate, no doubt reflecting both his conscious effort to strike an Aristotelian note and his perception that the political ills of his day were exacerbated if not caused by the thoroughly immoderate approach to politics fostered by reigning theologico-political commitments.[22] The Grotian doctrine can be briefly restated: There is no universal right of resistance under the law of nature, just as there are no universally established principles of limitation set for the powers of rulers by the law of nature. Instead, the existence of a right of resistance and of limits on rulers are matters to be ascertained under the constitution or original contract or civil law of each individual polity. Grotius is entirely nondoctrinaire. Such rights and limits are matters not of *jus naturale* but of *jus civile*.[23] The Grotian doctrine thus establishes a remarkable power in the original or constitutional act of human will or agreement that establishes politics. The Grotian doctrines of resistance and its limits betoken the role in Grotius of human will, vehemently disconnected from the *jus naturale* but admitted to great power in this and other key places. Human will—or, perhaps better, human covenanting or promising—establishes much, perhaps most, of the binding guidance for political and ethical life. As Leon Ingber says, in Grotius "consensualism is deployed without limit and liberated . . . from formalism."[24]

Grotius was surely not the first political philosopher to incorporate covenant or agreement in his doctrine, but, I would venture to say, he elevated it to a role it had never previously held in the tradition of natural law philosophy.[25] By comparing Grotius to Francisco Suárez, whose *On Laws and God the Legislator* appeared barely a decade before Grotius's work, we may see how far Grotius deviated from the more standard approach. Suárez provides an instructive contrast, for he himself went very far toward developing a voluntarist perspective on the natural law. As close as Suárez and Grotius appear to be on many issues, the depth of their disagreement on the theory of resistance points toward the limits of their concord.[26]

Suárez's doctrine on the right of resistance is as follows:

> If a legitimate king is governing tyrannically, and no other remedy is at hand for the self-defense of the kingdom but to drive out and depose him, then the whole commonwealth by means of a public council of the citizenry, of the commons and of the nobles, may depose him. This would be allowed both by the law of nature which permits one to resist force with force, and also because this case requiring [action] for the very salvation of the commonwealth is always understood as excepted in that first compact by which the commonwealth transfers its power to the king.[27]

To mention but two of several importantly different features of the two doctrines: First, Suárez found the right to resist and depose a tyrant to be a universal right, which Grotius and the Grotians denied. Second, Suárez found the source of this right just where Grotius and the Grotians pointedly did not, in the law of nature and in an idealized or constructive version of the "original compact."[28]

Although Suárez accepted a version of the original compact, his understanding of this, and of the origin of political power, differs from Grotius's in ways that produce their differences on the right of resistance. The beginning point appears to be much the same: "Man is in his nature free and subject to no one but the Creator." But, Suárez hastens to add, "it must first be said that civil magistracy together with temporal power for ruling human beings is just and altogether in accord with human nature."[29] Suárez seeks to harmonize natural freedom and natural subjection to the civil power: natural freedom does not imply that human beings are in any sense apolitical by nature.

According to Suárez, human beings are by nature subject to the civil magistrate and at the same time "subject to no one," because neither nature nor God vests the civil power "in some rather than others." Political subjection is not "immediately from nature," but "it is not against the directive law of nature." Here, then, is the place of compact: "Natural law by itself does not effect political subjection without the intervention of human will." Human will establishes the locus of political authority, but not whether it exists nor whence it comes. "From the nature of the thing alone it does not exist in any individual human being, but in the collective body of mankind." Nature establishes the power, and the people vest it in particular persons so that it may be exercised for its purpose, the common good of the community.[30] Human choice, not nature, determines who has political authority and thus is responsible for the form of polity, that is, for the constitution. Any of Aristotle's three pure forms—or, perhaps better, a mixed form—is eligible. Constitutions accordingly may assign different powers to the king; monarchical absolutism is no requirement of the natural law.[31]

Political power is not created from any power preexisting it in the individual human beings; the political community is "a mystical body," a "unity."[32] Human agreement or human will plays an important, but subordinate and far from constitutive, part. Suárez appeals to the analogy of marriage: An act of will is necessary for the parties to enter into the marriage, but the relation of authority that exists in it is not the product of that will; it is rather from "the author of nature himself." The parties can "contract the marriage of their own will" but they cannot construct marriage itself.[33] Both marriage and the political, according to Suárez, are natural and have natures.

Suárez's near contemporary, Roberto Bellarmine, taught nearly the same thing. Political power is natural, but "the divine law has not given this power to any particular man." Rather, it "resides immediately in the whole multitude as in an organic unit. . . . The power belongs to the whole multitude." "The community," however, "being unable to exercise this power itself, is obliged to communicate it to one or to several." The community can choose the form and powers of government.[34] Thus, for Bellarmine as for Suárez, compact has a definite but limited role in supplying the foundation of a political society.

For Grotius human compact is far more potent. Grotius, in a word, understood the relationship between the *jus naturale* and the *jus civile*, between the law of nature and human will, altogether differently from his predecessors.[35] It is tempting to attribute the differences between Grotius and his predecessors to the Dutchman's announced aim of developing, more fully and more consistently than had ever been done before, a code of the "law of nations"—the legal rules that prevail among, rather than within, political communities. Since none of his predecessors had put that concern at the center of his thinking, it is plausible to think that Grotius's new concern led to his new teaching on the nature and origin of political authority: his concern with the law of nations led him to pose the question of the basis (if any) for the use of force, the waging of war, by one community against another. Since Grotius was convinced that war is sometimes just and therefore justified, he concluded that the rightful use of force by some against others cannot be limited to the situation in which all the people in question are fellow citizens or members of the same political community. Therefore, he surmised, there must be a basis for rightful use of force which derives from something else than Suárez's "mystical unity."

Grotius found that source in a natural and individual power to punish that was entirely different from anything affirmed by Suárez or the earlier natural law philosophers. "Victoria, Vazquez, Azor, Molina, and others [Thomas Aquinas and Suárez among them] . . . claim that the power of punishing is the proper effect of civil jurisdiction [alone], while we hold that it is also derived from the law of nature." The power of punishing, which is the power exercised by political authorities within a community and in a just war of one community against another, "originally rested with individuals," because, "according to the law of nature, . . . punishment . . . may be exacted by anyone at all."[36] This direct power to act under the law of nature supplies a foundation for the application of rightful force against persons not members of one's own community, and thus for the rightful use of force in international relations. Having generated a new doctrine on the power of punishment under the law of nature for the sake of his interest in international relations, Grotius might have been led to posit a new account of the original of political power as well, a new account which produces the novel hypervoluntarism visible in his teaching on resistance.

THE PROBLEM OF NATURAL LAW

The above account of Grotius's revision of the traditional theory of the origin of political power tempts, but does not ultimately persuade. The single consideration most decisively against it is this: Suárez himself had paid much attention to international relations (as had Bellarmine), and had even presented a doctrine of the just war. His approach to the origin of political power did not disbar him from treating issues of right among nations: the civil authority that inheres in the community as a "mystic unity" can be deployed externally as well as internally.[37]

In the prolegomenon to the *De Jure* Grotius suggests another, more radical reason for his revision of the natural law tradition. He seeks in his work, he says, to treat "the law that holds between several peoples or rulers of peoples whether effected by nature itself or established by divine laws or introduced by customs and tacit covenant." Others have written on this law, he says, but none satisfactorily. In the course of his treatise Grotius returns often to the inadequacies of his predecessors, but early in the prolegomenon he emphasizes a truly major deficiency: "In our age, as in the past, there are not lacking those who contemn this part of right (law) as though it were nothing more than an empty name." In this context he mentions by name only ancients and none of the men of his own age who so believe, but he gives a good hint as to the identity of at least one of the more recent doubters. Two of the objectionable sayings he quotes recall more than a little that notorious contemner Machiavelli: "For those whom fortune favors might makes right," and "A republic (commonwealth) cannot be governed without injustice."[38]

Machiavelli and others in Grotius's day doubted the very existence of the law Grotius sought to treat; more than that, they held that there is no *jus naturale*. The greatest deficiency of the natural law tradition, Grotius says, is that it has failed to convince the scoffers; he must revise the tradition not only because he seeks to treat more adequately a relatively undeveloped branch of law, but more fundamentally because the tradition has hitherto failed to meet the challenge of men like Machiavelli. The full-blown adumbration of the natural law theory within Christendom has not made these "hard-nosed" men any more believers in natural law than were their pagan predecessors millenia ago.[39]

Grotius refers to a saying of the Roman playwright Terence to bring out one aspect of his problem. The matters with which he is concerned are "so uncertain" that one could just as well "make them certain by reason" as "go insane with reason." Grotius's subject matter, in other words, appears not to have the certainty and definiteness to bear a scientific treatment. So far as that appears to be true, it is in turn one ground for those who believe there is no natural law, or any law, governing war. To meet this kind of skepticism, Grotius says he must demonstrate that the law he seeks has sufficient certainty and clarity so that rational treatment of it is possible.[40]

Another central dimension of the problem was brought out in the challenge to the *jus naturale* as formulated by Carneades, the skeptical head of the Third Academy. Grotius avoids giving aid to the cause of injustice by merely sketching in briefest outline the Carneadean argument, which he and others found to be among the most powerful ever made against natural right:[41] Nature is not the source of laws (*jura*) because laws vary "according to the customs" of different peoples, and even among the same people laws often change over time. If nature were the source of laws, their content would be invariable, as nature is everywhere the same and unchanging. The true source of law is not nature but human beings, who "impose it on themselve for their own benefit." Law, according to Carneades, embodies human will or agreement. His argument depends on the central distinction between nature and convention: fire burns everywhere the same, but the just and the unjust vary from city to city. In the light of nature—of what truly is, never varies, and is generally effectual—the conventional loses its authority.[42] Even so far as there is a universal character to law (jus), it remains contrary to nature. So far as *jus* is universal it prescribes justice, the good of others, or the common good; but both men and other animals are led by nature to their own benefit. To follow justice is therefore to go against nature and engage in the "highest folly."[43]

Several implications of great importance for Grotius's enterprise follow from the Carneadean argument. If the source of law is not nature but mere human convention, there is no genuine obligation to obey law; under some conditions, there may be advantage in doing so, but there is no obligation. So, in order for law to function as it is set up to do, it must have a sanction attached to it, making it potentially more advantageous to obey than to disobey the law. Where there is an effective sanction, it may not be mere folly to adhere to justice. The sanction, therefore, is not merely crucial, but one might say definitive for law. However, there is no sanction, at least not of the sort attaching to the civil law, in the international sphere. There is, therefore, no international law. Carneades challenges the existence of not only the law of nature, but along with it the law of nations. Grotius was quite right to see that he must refute Carneades in order to be confident that the subject matter of his treatise exists. The absence of a sanction in the international sphere would appear to make it double folly to adhere to the principles of justice in dealing with other peoples. But the greatest folly of all would be Grotius's: he would be like the man who brought ridicule upon himself by offering commentaries on justice to Antigonus while that general was attacking cities belonging to others.[44]

The Carneadean challenge was the old challenge of conventionalism: law and justice are not by nature but are indeed against nature. Grotius apparently believed this old doctrine had not been sufficiently refuted, despite the centuries of political philosophy devoted to the effort and despite the immensity of the treatises on natural law by men like Suárez. Grotius thus faced a war on two fronts, so to speak, in his effort to establish the law of nations. Both ancient conventionalism and the Reformation posed deepgoing challenges to his enterprise.[45] In the course of meeting those challenges, in the course of securing the laws of nature and nations against them, Grotius substantially modified a tradition that had hitherto failed to accomplish its appointed task.

Nature and Convention in the Roman Law

The conjunction of the two challenges to the natural law led Grotius to take with special seriousness one of the founding texts of the whole tradition, the sixth-century codification of the Roman law, the *Corpus Juris Civilis*. The Roman jurists were grappling with the same challenge of conventionalism that Grotius addressed, but the Roman law was not at all implicated in Reformation-era sectarian squabbles. Even though it was prepared in Christian times, its roots predate Christianity and its treatment of the *jus naturale* bears no marks of having been shaped by Christian motifs.

The massive presence of the *Corpus Juris Civilis* in Grotius's book is well testified to by his "index of authors cited," according to which the Roman law is more frequently mentioned than any of the standard philosophical or theological authors in the natural law tradition—more often than Thomas, Suárez, Vazquez, and Victoria together. More fundamentally, Grotius's entire presentation of law is shaped by the Roman jurists' classification of laws into the three types *jus naturale*, *jus gentium*, and *jus civile*.[46] To say that Grotius recurs to the Roman law is not to say, however, that he entirely agrees with it. The *Corpus* is present in *De Jure* as much an object of criticism as one of inspiration. Indeed, Grotius's modification of the tradition comes to light initially as a modification of the Roman law's version of the various types of *jus*.

The *Corpus* is remarkable for the prominent place it gives to the notion of natural right—*jus naturale*, a philosopher's concept—in an actual legal code. Both the *Institutes* and the *Digest* begin with discussions of the *jus naturale* and refer to it at various strategically important places as well.[47] Equally remarkable is the *jus gentium*, the law of nations or peoples. This concept, it is now widely believed, also owes its origin to philosophic speculation, in the Roman context most especially to Cicero, who is credited with coining the term; and behind Cicero stands Aristotle, who developed a similar concept under the rubric "common law" in his *Rhetoric*.[48]

The understanding of the three types of law, and especially of the *jus naturale*, that animates the *Corpus* is not easy to discern, however, for the presentations of those ideas are always brief and not always consistent. The problem comes to view in the very opening section of the *Corpus*. The *Institutes*, following the jurist Ulpian, place the *jus naturale* within the now familiar tri-partite categorization of types of *jus*. However, yet other authorities, in the *Digest*, adopt only a twofold classification, and the elements in it differ from one source to another. The highly authoritative Gaius speaks of *jus gentium* and *jus civile* as the two types of *jus*, as Hermogenius also appears to do. Paulus, on the other hand, appears to contrast *jus naturale* and *jus civile*.[49] The authorities seem to be of two minds about the relative status of the *jus gentium* and the *jus naturale*: are they different from each other, or are they the same, and if the same, are they to be considered more properly as *jus gentium* or as *jus naturale*?

One finds this ambivalence not only between different authorities (whose opinions were supposed to be harmonized in the *Digest*), but even within the *Institutes* itself. In the very important discussion of the origin of private property, for example, it is claimed that *jus naturale* "is called" *jus gentium*. The identification of the two here is asserted to be "sicut *diximus*" ("as we said"); but that is not at all what is said in the initial discussion. There the *jus naturale* is said to be "that which nature has taught *all* animals". Justinian, following Ulpian, emphasizes its universalistic character, "for that *jus* is not peculiar to the human race, but is for all animals which are born in the sky, on the land, or in the sea."[50] The *Institutes* and Ulpian in the *Digest* emphatically disagree with the position taken within the Stoic natural law teaching that natural law (right) pertains especially to human beings, to the reason, and to social life. As Cicero, for example, recounts the Stoic view, natural law is "right reason applied to command and prohibition." Justinian and Ulpian indicate further deviation from Stoic conceptions in the example they give of *jus naturale*: "the union of male and female, which we call matrimony, and also the procreation and education of children: for we see that other animals are also moved by acquaintance with this *jus*."[51]

The *jus naturale* is thus natural in a readily cognizable sense: it is the natural, as the universally operative force in human and all other animal beings. As most common, or most universal, or universally effective, it is most natural. As natural in this sense, it is not the best or the highest; contrary to both earlier and later theories, *jus naturale* does not stand at the top of some hierarchy of right.[52]

The other two types of law are characterized by progressively less universality. The *jus gentium* is that which "natural reason has established among all men, and that which is observed equally among all peoples." The *jus civile* is narrower yet: it is the law peculiar to each political community.[53] Although it is less universal, nonetheless it is the Roman *jus*, composed of *jus naturale* (precepts shared universally with all animal nature), *jus gentium* (precepts shared universally with all other peoples), and *jus civile* proper (precepts peculiar to the Romans), that is the subject of the *Corpus*. There are no indications, it should be noted, that *jus civile*, although less universal, has less dignity or validity than the other forms of *jus*.[54]

The *jus gentium* and the *jus civile* are less universal, and therefore less natural, than the *jus naturale*, but they differ from the natural law in yet another way: both involve the intervention of human reason, or human making; they are both products of human agreement or establishment. The ambiguities in the discussions of the three types of *jus* in the *Institutes* and the *Digest*, especially the ambiguity about the relation between *jus naturale* and *jus gentium*, derive from an ambiguity in the notion of the natural at work in the texts. On the one hand, the natural is the "not artificial," the not conventional; it is that which is, independent of and apart from all human agreement. According to this understanding of nature the *jus gentium* belongs with the *jus civile* as not natural. The *jus naturale*, in this view, includes the basic desires or instincts and the human situation prior to any artificial agreements. According to the former aspect, the union of male and female is *jus naturale*; according to the latter aspect, human freedom and the nonexistence of private property are natural.[55]

But nature is also taken to mean the universal or the common. The most natural is the most common, so that what human beings share with all living, animate beings is emphatically *jus naturale*, but what all humans share with each other is also natural, at least natural for the human species. Thus, in this sense *jus gentium* is *jus naturale humanum*, and all such universal principles, along with the yet more universal *jus naturale* itself, are distinguishable from the *jus civile* as the particular and variable. Thus the *jus gentium* is both natural and non-natural, both a separate or third type of *jus* and assimilable to either *jus naturale* or to *jus civile*. Likewise, *jus naturale* can be assimilated to it, as Gaius did. The in-between or variable status of the *jus gentium* thus accounts for the equivocality of the texts on the classification of *jus*. The *jus gentium* is somehow the most interesting, certainly the most problematical, element of the classificaton of *jura* in the Roman law.

In line with its philosophic origin in Cicero and Aristotle, the real significance of the *jus gentium* comes to light when we reflect on one of the senses of "natural" employed in the overlapping classification schema adopted by the jurists. The categorization that distinguishes *jus gentium* and *jus civile* from *jus naturale* evokes the familiar distinction between nature (*physis*) and convention (*nomos*). The jurists were concerned with the same conventionalist challenge that later engaged Grotius. That challenge not merely leads to the denial of a law of nature, or natural right, it also leads to the sapping of authority from the civil law, for it robs the civil law of the authority of nature. Once the philosophic thesis of conventionalism was posited, the philosophically minded Roman jurists—those "priests of *jus*," those seekers of "the real not a pretended philosophy," as Ulpian called them— perforce had to take account of it.[56]

The definition of law clearly bears the marks of the conventionalist critique. The whole reflects the nature-convention distinction; the natural is presented emphatically as the universal. The human institutions that are law or right are modifications of the natural, and thus arguably against nature. The jurists go a long way toward presenting law in Carneades' terms. Yet they contain no hint that the conventionalist thesis undermines law.

They do not accept a simple opposition between law and nature. Instead they speak of *jus naturale*, which is related, somehow, even if only as a point of departure, to the civil law. It seems fairer to conclude not that the Roman lawyers accept the conventionalist critique but that they respond to it.

They were not, of course, the first to attempt to do so. The political philosophy of the Socratic school sought to salvage law in the face of the challenge of nature. To some extent the effort to discover a right by nature which is compatible with the *nomoi* of actual political communities succeeded, but not altogether so. In Plato, for example, the teaching about natural right culminated in a best regime in speech, utopian or nearly so, which transcends and calls into question the justice of every political regime in the here and now: it calls into question almost every legal institution in actual cities, including such core institutions as the family and private property. Stoicism, with its commitment to a universal natural law of right reason—to the cosmopolis rather than to individual, particular cities—and its relatively uncompromising commitment to natural as opposed to legal right, to the rule of the wise, and so on, radicalized the Platonic transcendence of the here and now.[57]

The doctrine of law in the *Corpus Juris Civilis* was an attempt to meet the challenge of Carneadean conventionalism but also to avoid the opposite yet equally subversive challenge represented at its most radical by Stoicism. The Roman lawyers were teachers of natural right—that is, they adopted a form of the Socratic political philosophy to guide them in their rationalization of the Roman legal order—but they were not Stoics. They opposed Carneades from a position apparently much closer to him than to the Stoics, but they did oppose him. They seemed to regard both Carneadean conventionalism and Stoic natural law as forms of the "pretended philosophy" they eschewed.

The center of their doctrine was the *jus gentium*. It was, as we have seen, the in-between or variable status of the *jus gentium* that accounts for the equivocality of the texts on the classification of *jus*. The *jus gentium*, in turn, was developed as it was as an attempt to mediate the conflict between *physis* and *nomos*; in the *Corpus*, *jus gentium* appears as a type of *nomos* or convention that has a claim to being natural. To be conventional is not necessarily to be variable. There exists a (more or less) universal or common set of conventions (*nomoi*), agreements, or practices established by human reason, the very universality of which testifies to their naturalness. Thus the distinction between *physis* and *nomos* is far too starkly drawn. In itself, the fact that something is established by human agreement does not rob it of authority and validity, or even of a sort of naturalness.

The real value of the doctrine of the *jus gentium*, however, lies in its validation of the variably conventional, and thus highly vulnerable, *jus civile*.

The key text is the passage by Ulpian in the *Digest* in which he relates the *jus civile* to the other two:

> The *jus civile* neither wholly recedes from the *jus naturale* or *gentium*, nor is it altogether subordinate to it either; so that when we add something, or subtract something from the common *jus*, we make our own *jus*, that is, *jus civile*.[58]

Ulpian speaks most concisely here and his words thus require interpretation. It is relatively easy to understand what he means when he says that the *jus civile*, differing in some way from the common *jus*, is not altogether subordinate to the latter; he seems to mean "subordinate to" both in the sense of "determined by" and "in need of validation by." On the other hand, he affirms that the *jus civile* does not altogether "recede from" the common *jus*, employing the same word (*recedere*) he used to describe the relationship between *jus gentium* and *jus naturale*, when he said that the former "recedes from" the latter because it is common to all human beings only and not to all animate beings. But the degree to which *jus gentium* recedes from *jus naturale* does not prevent Ulpian from referring to the two together as *jus commune*, even though he has emphasized also in the meantime that the *jus gentium* on occasion changes the *jus naturale*; slavery is brought in by *jus gentium*. For the jurists, that does not invalidate slavery.

Just as the *jus gentium*, the human agreement that adds to or subtracts from (that is, changes) the *jus naturale*, remains valid despite its deviations from the latter, so does the *jus civile*, the more restricted agreement, remain valid. The origin of a *jus* in convention, even in a convention against *jus naturale*, neither necessarily undermines the validity of the *jus* nor even prevents Ulpian from assimilating the two kinds of *jus* to each other. That idea is extended to the *jus civile* on the basis of the following explanation of the reasons for the *jus gentium*: "*Jus gentium* is common to the whole human race. For under compelling use and human [*humanis*] necessities, the peoples of mankind [*humanae*] have instituted certain things."[59] The *Institutes'* point, apparently very close to Ulpian here, is that *human* needs led human beings to add to or alter the arrangements they shared in common with all animals (i.e., the *jus naturale*). By extension, the specially Roman, or Sabine, or Athenian needs led these peoples to alter the arrangements they shared with all other human beings and to produce thereby a *jus civile* specific to each of them. Each requires different *jus* because all peoples exist under different circumstances.

The necessity under which they operate, or the benefit to be realized from the alteration, justifies and explains the change and implicitly introduces another standard of nature different from the two we have already seen. Human benefit or the good is the natural, in terms of which both the nonartificial, or noninstituted, and the universal as such are abrogated, or challenged as standards of the natural. In this sense, the *jus civile* can be the most natural and the most valid. But in opening out toward the good or benefit as the natural, the jurists move back toward the philosophic transcendence of the political here and now, although not in so obvious or thoroughgoing a way as in the pre-Socratic distinction between *physis* and *nomos* or in the Stoic emphasis on the simply universal and rational.

The jurists' doctrine represents an attempt to retain the guiding force of a philosophic grasp of nature as a standard, but to blunt the force of nature as a solvent. Thus *jus naturale* in the strict and explicit sense is narrow and even crabbed; it is the lowest, not the highest. It is so unauthoritative that it may be and even needs to be changed by human convention. But the jurists themselves understand, and point their readers on the road to understanding, those conventions as potentially rooted in nature, otherwise understood.[60] The task of the jurist is to bring *jus civile*, that is, the effective law, as close as possible to the natural standards, or the *jus naturale*, in the most extended and exalted sense. Nonetheless, the *jus naturale* in the extended and exalted sense has not at all the quality of law; it is surely not categorically and universally valid; nor is it specific and determinate enough to be lawlike. The jurists' understanding of the need for a tamed, watered down *jus naturale* means that they cannot expect their legal code, or any legal code, simply to embody the just order. Not the one who has the best natural claim, but the one who legally owns, must have right.

The Roman lawyers thus proposed a teaching on the natural law that seems able to satisfy the twofold requirement Grotius identified. It replied to the Carneadean challenge and did so in a way perfectly free from the theologico-political wrangling of reformed Europe. Nor was Grotius the only writer of his age to feel the attraction of the Justinian synthesis; the very important *Vindiciae Contra Tyrannos*, as we have already noted, attempted to work out a theory of political obligation and resistance on the basis of the Roman law doctrine. But, attracted as he was to the Romanists, Grotius, in his own reformation of natural law, broke fundamentally with them, a break which led him to his own peculiar way of blending nature and convention.

GROTIUS'S BREAK WITH THE NATURAL LAW TRADITION

The Roman law supplied a solution of sorts to the very problems Grotius set for himself: the abiding problem of conventionalism and the more recent set of problems posed by post-Reformation sectarianism. Although Grotius departed from the Roman jurists in quite a few important respects, nonetheless his text reminds more of their work than of any of the intervening texts. Indeed, some competent scholars have concluded that Grotius represents an unreserved "return to the Roman law." Besides the frequent appearance of the *Institutes* and the *Digest* among the profusion of learned citations in *De Jure*, probably the most visible presence of the Roman lawyers lies in Grotius's central use of their classification of laws into *jus naturale*, *jus gentium*, and *jus civile*.[61] To the compilers of the Roman codes, Grotius admitted, he "defers much, for they often supply the best reasons for showing what is the right (law) of nature and they also often furnish evidence for this right (law) no less than for the *jus gentium*."[62]

Despite his admiration of and deference to the Roman jurists, Grotius does not hesitate to signal his disapproval as well. No less than other writers on law, they confuse the different types of law, Grotius says, and they are particularly confused about the law that stands near the center of his concern with international law, the *jus gentium*. They do not clearly see its character as a law between peoples, but sometimes treat as *jus gentium* matters which are strictly speaking civil laws of particular peoples. And, like all other legal writers, they "indiscriminately mix together maxims of the *jus naturale* and the *jus gentium*."[63] Grotius, on the other hand, is most eager to keep the different kinds of law clearly and distinctly separate from each other.[64]

These complaints of Grotius against the Roman law cut very deep. It was not mere carelessness of analysis or exposition that led the Roman lawyers to "confuse" matters in the manner he so disparages. Both the way in which they conceived of the *jus gentium* (as a common law of peoples rather than a law between peoples) and the way they vacillated on the relation between *jus naturale* and *jus gentium* derive from their general solution to the problem conventionalism posed for the status of law. Grotius's differences with the Roman law on these matters thus suggest a more fundamental difference in the way he relates nature and convention: in his view the Roman lawyers failed because they did not properly separate the natural from the positive law.[65] Whereas the Roman codifiers hesitated on the principle of the *jus gentium*, and by implication even on the principle of the *jus civile*, Grotius is certain that both belong together as positive law, "depending on human will" or "common consent" over and against the natural law, depending only on "correct inference from the principles of nature." The law of nature is everywhere the same and unchangeable; the other laws depend on human will and are thus changeable if not arbitrary.[66] The Roman lawyers responded to Carneades by mingling the various kinds of law; Grotius responds by rigidly separating them.

Despite his explicit critique of the Romanists, Grotius suppresses the true depth of his disagreement with them. In his response to Carneades, Grotius plants an argument which is as much directed against the jurists as against Carneades himself. Carneades had denied natural right because nature drives all creatures, both human beings and other animals, to pursue their own benefit. Nature is the same for human beings and all other animals.[67] As we have seen, the Roman lawyers' doctrine of *jus naturale* accepted that Carneadean claim: what is natural is what human beings share with all animate nature. Grotius's reply to Carneades thus tells as much against the jurists' conception of *jus naturale* as against Carneades' attack: "Man indeed is an animal, but an exceptional animal, far more distant from all other animals, than the other kinds of animal are from each other." Even if all other animals were as Carneades said, which Grotius denies, humanity is sufficiently different that the *jus naturale* cannot come to light on the supposition of a uniform animate nature. The Roman lawyers, therefore, can hardly supply genuine knowledge of the *jus naturale*.[68]

Instead, Grotius reverts to Stoic doctrine: there are "many traits peculiar to the human species," chief among which is "the desire for society." Thus, he continues, Carneades erred when he claimed that all animate beings seek their own benefit, if by that he meant that they seek their benefit at the expense of others. For human beings, living together peacefully with other human beings is precisely the benefit that nature drives them to seek.[69] Their good is inextricably intertwined with that of others. But even that formulation is subject to Carneadean misinterpretation. Human beings desire social life not merely in order to realize mutual aid in securing their private benefit; rather, "human nature itself is the mother of *jus naturale*," for human beings would be sociable even if they lacked nothing that social cooperation could help them secure. Here Grotius agrees with Aristotle: "Human beings are by nature political animals. Hence they strive to live together even when they have no need of assistance from one another."[70]

Grotius concedes there are other social animals. The human uniqueness lies not merely in the end—social life—to which nature impels, but in the specific means wherewith nature equips human beings for that end. Alone of all the animals, humanity has the special instrument of speech. Grotius in part has in mind the familiar point that the faculty of speech, so constitutive of *human* being, testifies to human sociability, for it is only in society that language thrives and it is through speech that the common or social human world exists. If speech is a unique and therefore particularly revealing quality of the nature of the human animal, then clearly that animal is a social being, and the law of its nature necessarily must reflect that fact.[71]

Grotius has a further and yet more precise point in mind as well. Only human beings possess "the faculty of knowing and acting in accordance with general rules." It is the nature of mankind, and only of mankind, to formulate and act in terms of laws. Both Carneades and the Romans were wrong in seeking the dictates of nature in what humans share with other animals. Only human beings raise the question of natural law; only they seek that kind of standard and guidance. Human beings are by nature not merely rational animals, but legal animals as well. That fact points to the character of *jus naturale* as well as to its existence. Human beings seek to direct their behavior in accordance with general rules, and therefore do not seek merely their own benefit, for, as Rousseau and Kant later developed Grotius's point, the quality of generality in a rule prevents one from exclusively seeking one's own benefit. And, contrary to the Roman jurists, what is natural for human beings does not appear in the instinctive promptings ("extrinsic intelligence," as Grotius puts it) by which nature directs the animals.

Grotius thus identifies as "the source" of the *jus naturale* the "care for society consistent with (or appropriate to) human intellect."[72] Both parts are important: the natural law springs from natural human sociability, but as expressed rationally, in the mode of "a dictate of right reason."[73] It is, in other words, part of nature, part of *jus naturale* that human beings be governed by law or lawlike rules. "Only a nature using general rules is properly capable of law (*jus*)." That implies in turn that not only is the *jus naturale* not that which is common to mankind and the lower animals, but that the latter are not properly speaking governed by law at all. *Jus naturale* is not like the law of gravity or the biological laws to which all animate beings must conform. Therefore, when Grotius finally makes explicit his views on the Roman jurists' treatment of the *jus naturale* it is no surprise that he is very harsh: the way the Roman lawyers treat *jus naturale* (and *jus gentium*) "has hardly any usefulness."[74]

Despite the fact that Grotius is a contractarian, his clear and even strident affirmation of natural sociability distinguishes him from the later contractarianism of Hobbes, Rousseau, and even Locke and the American Declaration of Independence. Contrary to what some readers of Grotius have concluded from his contractualism, he has no doctrine of a state of nature.[75] Indeed, Grotius explicitly rejected Hobbes's idea of a state of nature.[76] Grotius himself uses the phrase on a few occasions, but his meaning is far different from that with which his successors endow it. He cites Cicero, for example, on the duty we have "to preserve ourselves in a state of nature." He means by that not a duty to persevere in a prepolitical condition of some sort, but rather to preserve one's body in a state "that is sound and perfect in all its parts." This state of nature is the state of natural perfection. Elsewhere Grotius refers to the state of nature in regard to laws regulating marriage; there he interprets the state of nature as the state governed by the law of nature, contrasting it with the "norm of greater perfections" brought in by the "law of Christ," that is, the positive divine law of Christianity. Neither of these usages has any connection to the later idea of the state of nature.[77]

Contract and state of nature are not correlative concepts for Grotius or for the Whig thinkers who followed him. Unlike Hobbes, for example, who builds on natural asociality, Grotius understands human beings to be not merely naturally sociable, but also naturally political: it is rational for human beings to live under laws of human discovery or devising, that is, to live

politically. Grotius thus rejects the premises about human nature characteristic of theories on the state of nature. He approvingly quotes Plutarch: "By
nature no man is or was a wild and unsociable animal." He approvingly
quotes Aristotle: "Man is an animal by his own nature tame." If human
beings do not always show themselves to be gentle, that is due to falling
beneath their nature; but, as Grotius paraphrases Aristotle, "what is natural
must be seen in those things which hold themselves well according to nature and not in the perverted."[78]

The state of nature, according to Hobbes, is the home of the right of
nature (*jus naturale*), or the right of all men to everything, including one
another's bodies. The right of nature implies that the state of war exists not
merely factually but rightfully in the state of nature. Somewhat like Hobbes,
Grotius concedes the natural rightfulness of deploying force. War, or use of
force aimed at preservation, "altogether agrees with the first principles of
nature." Reasoning uncomfortably like the Roman lawyers, Grotius points
to the lower animals, among whom nature has distributed weapons for defense, weapons frequently in use. But Grotius avoids the subhuman natural
law of the Romans by calling attention to "right reason and the nature of
society"; these are "more important than the testimony of the lower animals, and establish the point that nature prohibits not all force but only that
which is against society, that is, what takes away the right of others." The
standard for judging the bounds of natural right is "the nature of society";
that both authorizes and limits the permitted use of force. Thus, for example, Grotius denies the universal rightfulness of rebellion under the natural
law: even though human beings possess a right by nature to resist threats
to their lives and property, yet the polity can inhibit that right "for the sake
of public peace and order." The "nature of society" and its needs simply take
precedence over an individual's right of preservation.[79] How different from
Hobbes and Locke!

With no state of nature to overcome, Grotius's contract serves a function
different from analogous concepts in the thought of his Enlightenment successors. It is not the means whereby human society is made for purposes of
mutual benefit, but it fulfills the far more limited, although still important,
function of establishing the constitution, the governing authorities and
their powers, and the "degree of subjection" of the populace.[80] Grotius supplies the theoretical grounding for the contract as "original contract"; he
does not, as we have already noted, develop the notion of consent of the
governed in the Lockean direction, ultimately so explosive of the notion of
the original contract and so powerfully fraught with republican, or even
democratic, implications.[81]

Grotius revises the Roman law doctrine of *jus naturale* more or less in the
same direction as did the Catholic natural lawyers, who themselves followed

the Socratic philosophers, especially the Stoics: natural law takes its bearings from the nature of humanity. And humankind is, by nature, sociable and rational. So far as he develops *jus naturale* in terms of those themes, Grotius remains firmly within the older natural law tradition, despite some apparent similarities to his more "modern" successors, Hobbes, Locke, and Rousseau.

Yet Grotius also made an important break with the precedent tradition, a break based in part on his intimate connection to the Roman lawyers, a break that in turn unintentionally helped prepare the later triumph of the modern natural rights philosophy. The difference between Grotius and his Socratic predecessors becomes visible in his treatment of the theme of natural rationality. Although Grotius identifies rationality as part of human nature and as highly relevant to the *jus naturale*, he forbears from developing that theme in the direction Plato, Aristotle, and especially the Stoics had done. For all of those ancient thinkers, rationality pointed toward political life, but also pointed beyond it, or even against it—toward philosophy or wisdom as the natural end of humankind. Since the majority of the inhabitants of political communities are neither wise nor seekers of wisdom (philosophers), the political community is only in an equivocal sense in accord with *jus naturale*. It was the tendency of natural right thus understood to transcend every actual political community that led the Roman lawyers to develop their universalistic, and therefore subhuman, notion of *jus naturale*. Grotius rejected that conception of *jus naturale*, but his reticence about the transpolitical implications of rationality suggests that he may have shared something central with the Roman lawyers.

Grotius appeals to Socratic, especially Stoic, principles in order to respond to the Carneadean (or Machiavellian) challenge and thus breaks with the Roman lawyers and draws much nearer to the Thomist natural law doctrine. But at the same time he retreats from the latter in a way that reflects his continuing debt (despite his criticism) to the Roman lawyers. The Socratic doctrine culminated in claims like the following: Natural justice requires the allotment to human beings of what is proper for them, according to their characters (or natures) and their actions. For example, the wise should rule, or the best flute player should have the best flute. Justice or natural right involves the distribution of goods in proportion to the natural merit or desert of the recipient; justice so understood was accordingly called "distributive justice" by Aristotle.[82]

Grotius, however, denies that this kind of distribution has anything to do with *jus* "properly so called." He does not deny that such judgments may rest on or point toward what is right by nature in some sense, but not in a legal sense. Natural *law*, strictly speaking, does not deal with those sorts of claims of distributive justice, nor with the full range of natural virtues. *Jus* strictly and properly so called is not the same as a "dictate of right reason": there are such dictates that are not law.[83] Grotius narrows the range of *jus* substantially from what it was in the Socratic and Thomist traditions.

Thomas himself had worked a kind of synthesis of the Socratic and the Roman law traditions. The Roman lawyers had retreated to a narrow and crabbed or low version of natural law in order to accommodate nature to their actual legal code. Thomas replaced that with the more elevated Socratic conception of nature and endowed it with the full legal status the Roman texts had found in all laws. Grotius, in turn, revised the Thomist revision in the spirit of the Roman law: Thomas was largely correct as to nature, but mistaken as to law; the natural standards of virtue and distributive justice are not, strictly speaking, law. Thus Grotius approvingly quotes the famous passage from the *Education of Cyrus*: The coat belongs to the boy who legally owns it, not to the one for whom it is most suitable.[84]

Grotius distinguishes his law (right) in the strict and proper sense from the enlarged idea of right in terms of a number of differentiating marks.[85] It is, first of all, essential to law in the proper sense that it carry along with it an obligation: *jus* is "a rule of moral acts obliging to what is right (*rectum*)."[86] Nonobligatory counsels or precepts do not qualify as law, even though they may point to what is right or good. Grotius is attempting to distinguish the kind of rightfulness in the claim the best flute-player has to the best flute from the kind of claim the flute's owner has to it. Although the best flute player has some sort of right—it would be right, fitting, proper for the best player to possess the best instrument—yet there is no clear obligation on the part of any other person to see to it that the best player has the best flute. Law in the strict sense is not equivalent to distributive justice, for the latter does not impose clear obligations on specific parties.

Thus for Grotius obligation becomes the defining feature of law. That distinguishes his view from one alternative that would make law coextensive with sanction. According to Grotius, sanction gives law its outward effect but is not crucial for its existence. Thus both the law of nature and the law of nations, both of which lack sanctions in the ordinary sense, qualify as law without any difficulty. But Grotius does not go as far as many of his theoretical predecessors; mere rightfulness, merely being a "dictate of right reason," is not sufficient to endow a proposition with the quality of law.[87]

Secondly, law properly so called has as its source the "care for society" that Grotius identifies as an important distinguishing characteristic of the human species. Human beings are by nature sociable beings and the natural law (properly so called) is what conduces to social life. There is, Grotius concedes, another and "larger signification" of law or *jus*, again unrelated to the Roman jurists' universal nature, but rooted instead in specifically human qualities. *Jus* in this larger sense rests on the human ability to judge and weigh what will conduce to an individual's thriving or harm in the present or in the future. It includes, in other words, the full range of the natural virtues, so far as the virtues specify what conduces to human thriving. For example, moderation is part of natural right in this larger sense, for it is good for the person who possesses it.[88]

Law properly so called is not concerned with the full range of virtues, however, but only with those relating to society, and preeminently with justice. Of the cardinal virtues that formed so central a part of ethical thinking within the Platonic-Stoic philosophic tradition, only justice is a matter of natural law. And not all of justice, for from *jus* in the larger sense derives that notion of distributive justice that Grotius rejects as no part of *jus*. From the judgment of what contributes to the thriving or harm of persons derives the notion of distributive justice as "the allotment to human beings of what is proper for them, according to their characters and their actions"— allotments, that is, of the things they naturally deserve or benefit from.[89] What is naturally right or lawful according to this understanding is what naturally benefits; it is the Platonic-Stoic notion of natural right that the Roman jurists attempted both to incorporate in their law and to tame. Grotius is more emphatic in rejecting it: "*Jus* properly and strictly so called has a very different nature." It is "to leave to another what is his or to give to another what is owed." Law properly so called deals only with others— and not with their good in some abstract sense, but with what is actually theirs or concretely owed them. Grotius comes very close to saying that law (and *a fortiori* natural law) concerns only the rights of others. "Justice . . . consists entirely in abstaining from what is another's."[90] The kind of right (*jus*) Grotius has in mind here, the right to one's own, which he considers to be right in the proper sense, is said by him to be a "faculty" or a "moral quality of a person fitting him to have or to do something justly." Right for Grotius is entirely "subjective right" and "active right," a possession of its holder or subject, something to be exercised (or not) at the discretion of the right-holder; it is no longer objective right, a rightful state of affairs.[91] Grotius's *jus* has become the sort of right the modern natural rights doctrine affirms.

In reserving the term *jus* for subjective rights, Grotius innovated only mildly. The ancients, including the Roman lawyers, never clearly distinguished objective from subjective right, but it is clear that objective right was the primary meaning the term had for them. The same is true for the Thomist natural law tradition up to but not including Suárez, who, as we saw earlier, identified *jus* with *facultas*—subjective right—in just the same way Grotius did.[92] Nonetheless, Grotius differed from Suárez just as much as from others in the Thomist tradition in insisting that *jus* so understood was the sum and substance of law properly so called. Suárez did not identify *jus* with all the law there is: he distinguished *lex* from *jus* and denominated the natural law *lex naturalis*.[93]

Grotius's doctrine of natural law thus differs from his predecessors' in these two ways: *Jus* in the proper sense has become solely *facultas*, or subjective right, and it concerns only that relatively narrow sphere Aristotle called commutative justice.[94] These are innovations of first rank importance. One's first impression is of a greatly diminished natural law. The differences between Grotius and Thomas, for example, could hardly be clearer, for according to the latter "all virtuous acts belong to the natural law." Thomas's affirmation involved an anticipation of the position Grotius later would take, and an explicit rejection of it: Since "it is of the nature of law that it be ordained to the common good," and since "some acts of the virtues are ordained to the private good of the individual, as is evident especially in regard to acts of temperance," it might seem to follow, Thomas says, that "not all acts of the virtues are the subject of natural law." But Thomas dismisses that Grotian thought because "to the natural law belongs everything to which a human being is inclined according to his nature."[95]

The more comprehensive character of Thomas's version of the natural law appears with especial clarity in his quite different manner of relating the Roman lawyers' version of natural law to that of the Stoics. The natural law, says Thomas, contains a variety of precepts, which correspond to "the order of natural inclinations." Human nature reveals three levels of such inclinations, levels which, like the jurists' discussion of nature, have progressively less universality. There is, first, "an inclination to good in accordance with the nature which human beings have in common with all substances, inasmuch, namely, as every substance seeks the preservation of its own being, according to its nature."[96] Self-preservation (and the means thereto) thus is a dictate of the natural law. There is also a human inclination to "those things . . . which nature has taught all animals, such as sexual intercourse, the education of offspring, and so forth," that is, those things that involve the reproduction and continuation of the species and not just the preservation of the individual.[97] Finally, there is a third level of inclination, pertaining to what is humanly unique: reason. "Thus man has a natural inclination to know the truth about God, and to live in society; and in this respect, whatever pertains to this inclination belongs to the natural law: e.g., to shun ignorance, to avoid offending those among whom one has to live, and other such things regarding the above inclination."[98] Grotius's treatment of the natural law truncates it, directly retaining only the third of Thomas's three levels as part of it, and of that third, only the part about social life.

Both the identification of *jus* with *facultas* and the drastic shrinkage of the natural law in Grotius have reminded readers of Hobbes's natural rights teaching. Richard Tuck, for example, finds Grotius the real orginator of the kind of natural rights doctrine promulgated by Hobbes, and many other commentators have pronounced Grotius the true founder of modern natural law.[99] These scholars are surely correct to see parallel developments in the thought of Grotius and Hobbes, but the transformations of natural law effected by the two are in fact quite different; they proceed from different motives and they involve different philosophic commitments. Both limit the Thomist natural law by simplifying Thomas's tripartite scheme of law-generating natural inclinations. Where Grotius drops the rest and grounds natural law entirely in one-half of Thomas's third-level inclination, Hobbes grounds his entirely in the first-level inclination toward preservation. Hobbes finds the nature that grounds natural right in the most universal inclinations human beings share with all beings as such (thus the large role of the law of inertia in Hobbes's thought).[100] Grotius, on the contrary, finds the nature that grounds natural law only at the highest and most humanly unique level. Thus Hobbes presents his revision of the natural law as a major break with the Aristotelian tradition of political philosophy, requiring a full-scale rejection of the "darkness from vain philosophy," particularly "the vain philosophy of Aristotle."[101] Grotius, on the other hand, modifies both the tradition and Aristotle, but admittedly remains within an Aristotelian orbit. "Among the philosophers Aristotle deservedly holds first place, whether you consider the order of his treatment or the acumen of his distinctions, or the weight of his reasoning." Most significant, Grotius remains firmly within the Aristotelian framework of the tradition, no matter how much he revises it, by taking his bearings from human rational sociability.[102]

The immense differences between Hobbes and Grotius show up in the very place in which the two thinkers draw closest together: the notion of *jus*. "Right strictly so called" for Grotius "signifies the faculty of acting in sole respect to society." Social nature, and ultimately the social duty to others, grounds right. Thus, for Grotius, a (or even the) defining feature of law (*jus*) is obligation. But for Hobbes, natural right is solely grounded in the individual's striving for preservation; as right of every man to everything, the *jus naturale* necessarily fails to carry with it a correlative duty of any sort.[103]

Grotius innovates, but withal remains firmly attached to the tradition. To describe his innovations, especially his innovations regarding the meaning and place of *jus*, in terms of modern natural rights philosophy is to risk missing the inner character of Grotius's thought. Grotius combined the natural law teachings of the Roman lawyers and the Thomists in an altogether novel way. As we have seen, he takes his bearings to a large extent from Justinian's jurists, but he rejects their understanding of nature on the grounds that since universal nature cannot reveal the nature of human beings it cannot reveal the human natural law. In that he agrees more or less with Thomas and his followers. He balances his acceptance of a broader and more elevated notion of nature characteristic of the Thomists with a much diminished and narrowed notion of law. What he gives with one hand, he takes with the other. The spirit of that diminution seems, moreover, to be very much the spirit of the Roman law. Grotius shares with the jurists a desire to tame nature and natural justice for the sake of law. For Grotius only a small corner of the realm of the right by nature constitutes the law of nature.

Neither the Roman jurists nor the Thomists had successfully negotiated the Scylla and Charybdis of the natural law—the Carneadean collapse of all law into unnatural or antinatural law and the Stoic transcendence of all actual law by the ideal or abstract law. To avoid foundering in the Stoic manner, the Roman jurists explicitly took their bearings by an untenable (because too low) understanding of nature. So far as they implicitly supplemented that with a more elevated conception of human good as such, they were threatened with a return to the quandary of the Stoics; at the very least they were unable to promulgate a doctrine of natural law of a specific and precise character. The natural law, caught somehow in a tension between two different aspects of nature, is not determinate or lawlike. It has nothing of the character of a legal code, and thus, at the least, depends on wise lawmakers or law compilers for its efficacy. More likely, the exalted natural law will most of the time collapse too readily into the civil law. The civil law, at best, possesses only a hazy relation to the *jus naturale*. In other words, the Romanists' solution fails to measure up to the demands set by the post-Reformation context. It does not produce clear and distinct, determinate and certain natural law. Political good remains a matter for the prudent judgment of wise men.

The Thomist solution succeeds no better. It posits a more adequate doctrine of nature, but proves unable to transform that into a genuine law of the sort Grotius sought. One place in the Thomist scheme where that is especially visible is in Thomas's three levels of natural inclinations. Although they clearly exist in a hierarchy—the inclinations associated with specifically human reason are higher than those shared with all entities—there is still no clear principle of priority implicit in that hierarchy. Thomas implicitly concedes as much when he makes no effort to adumbrate a definite natural code of law. The Thomistic natural law does not achieve the definiteness and certainty of a genuine law.

From Grotius's point of view, the Thomist version of natural law is especially deficient in the post-Reformation context. Not only are its historical associations difficult to shake off, but it contains principles that exacerbate the characteristic troubles of the age. Thomas ranked at the peak of the natural inclinations those that take their bearings from human rationality: the desire to know God and the desire for social life. Not only does he not specify how the precepts flowing from these inclinations are to relate to precepts flowing from the other inclinations, but he neglects to specify the relation between these two goals of the rational faculty. If, as seems plausible, we understand the orientation to God as specifying simply the highest demands nature places on human beings, then Thomas has in effect enfranchised within his natural law the very theological-political uncertainties that racked Grotius's age. In the name of such an ordering, various natural law thinkers before Grotius had unrestrainedly urged socially unsettling practices—for example, the assassination of "heretical" rulers—in the name of obedience to higher precepts.[104] Grotius's truncated natural law, absolutizing the demands of social life and of justice, placed all such counsel outside the bounds of the natural law. Grotius's simplifying surgery was based on an important insight, parallel in many ways to Hobbes's. According to Hobbes, all natural standards that justify resistance against the ruling authorities jeopardize the peaceful preservation that is the end and purpose of political life. The fundamental point seems to have been discovered by Grotius, however, and adapted by Hobbes to his own preservationist philosophy. According to Grotius, nature dictates social life and social peace. Grotius (unlike Hobbes) does not deny that nature prompts to other ends as well. As a modified follower of Stoic doctrine, he can easily accept Thomas's version of the three levels of natural inclination, but only the prompting to society is to be understood as law. Social life is facilitated by the existence of definite, specifable rights and duties.[105] As opposed to natural goods of individuals, the duties of justice—that is, the social duties relating to others—require the enforcement power that attaches to law in the proper sense, for human beings are more inclined to ignore what is owed to others than what is good for themselves. Thus Grotius strongly endorses Aristotle's claim that "a community cannot be preserved without law."[106]

Not only do the duties of social life require legalization in ways that the other virtues do not, but the treatment of the other virtues as legal unsettles the specific legal duties and rights that attach to the requirements of social life. Every assertion that the best flute should belong to the best flute player rather than to its legal owner unsettles settled rights and threatens social peace. Every assertion that some more naturally deserving set of rulers merit rule more than the legal rulers unsettles politics. Grotius goes so far as to exclude not only the higher claims but also the lower ones. The individual right of preservation, Thomas's first order of natural inclination, makes no natural and universal claim against existing legal duties of subjection. The other parts of natural right potentially conflict with natural requirements of social life. The latter, as the most necessarily legal (as for the most part witnessed by actual legal practice), is therefore given by Grotius a uniquely privileged position. He does not deny other dimensions of natural right, but he denies them the status of law, for, among other reasons, they can thrive without that status.

Nature and Convention in the Grotian Natural Law

Grotius's category of law (or right) properly so called represents his attempt to take the legal character of the natural law very seriously. The post-Reformation situation prompted that attempt, but in making it he was facing up to a problem that had been implicit all along in the idea of a natural law: does natural right have the character of a law?[107] The post-Aristotelian natural lawyers had answered yes, but in various ways their versions of natural law had fallen short of presenting an authentically legal code. In so doing, they left a theoretical and a practical opening for both the Reformation's unsettling of politics and the renewal of the Carneadean-Machiavellian cynical-realist rejection of natural right. Having reformulated the natural law as he did, Grotius could claim to be the first to present the true art or science of law.[108]

Grotius's reform of the tradition was meant to repair these deficiencies by producing a doctrine far more precise and lawlike and at the same time more realistic and effective. A key part of his effort in both directions lay in his new teaching on the relation between nature and convention, or human agreement. As we have already noticed in the Grotianism of Gilbert Burnet, as well as in Grotius himself, one of the most characteristic features of this new natural law doctrine was the strongly determinative force of human agreement, a feature that came to underlie Whig theories of the original contract and gave shape to various alternative Whig approaches to 1689.

It is a frequent, but not for that reason just, complaint against Grotius that he leaves the natural law vague and hazy at best, almost contentless and merely subjective at worst.[109] I question the justice of these charges, because compared to Thomas, for example, Grotius is quite specific in his presentation of the natural law. He states the natural law provisions regarding the very broadest matters (such as the origin of political power and private property), as well as the most detailed and specific ones (such as whether a declaration of war is required, or when promises are naturally obligatory). Grotius's most comprehensive statement of the tenets of the law properly so called occurs early in his text: "abstention from what belongs to others, and if we have what is another's, we should restore it or any gain we made from it, the obligation of fulfilling promises, the reparation of loss done through fault, and the rightfulness of punishing human beings who deserve it."[110] Much of this list is familiar from our earlier discussions, but especially important for Grotius's scheme is the central item, the obligation of fulfilling promises: "It is [a precept] of the law of nature to stand by pacts." Grotius's explanation is especially revealing. "It was necessary among human beings that there be some way of obligating themselves, and no other natural way can be framed." Recall the beginning point of our discussion: the unusually powerful role that agreement, or convention, plays in Grotius's theory, such that the terms of the "original agreement" definitively set forth the powers of rulers and the liberties of subjects. The obligaton to fulfill promises is not merely one among many natural law obligations, but stands preeminent. From it derives the validity of all positive law, both the *jus gentium*, based on mutual consent of states or peoples, and the civil law, the internal law derived from constituted authorities.[111]

It stands at the same time as Grotius's answer to the problem of nature and convention. Grotius goes even further than the Roman lawyers in validating convention. Convention (agreement) is not contrary to nature, but it carries with it an obligation derived from nature. Grotius explicitly grounds his refutation of Carneades on this point. The "mother of justice" is not utility, as Carneades and others had said, but natural law, or, ultimately, human nature. Compacts (mutual promises) are to be kept not solely because they are useful (presumably they are useful or else human beings would not make them), but because they are genuinely obligatory. They are obligatory, it appears, because this kind of mutual engagement is one major mode by which human beings relate to each other socially; through mutual engagement and compact human beings enter into fixed relationships with each other, setting terms of cooperation and interaction. Compact, contract, promise, and related modes of voluntary engagement set the terms for, facilitate, and even make possible much of the social life of beings who are rational. More than that, such engagement is a suitable way for rational beings to interact, for it involves the guidance of life through the exercise of reason and choice.

Compact, contract, and promise can fulfill their facilitating function for society only if the undertakings agreed to in them are faithfully fulfilled. Since they are efforts to bind the future and to condition some present actions on other future actions, they can never fulfill their function if there is no regular and reliable expectation that the obligations expressed in them will be carried out. But there can be no such expectation if the fulfilling of compact is merely a matter of utility, if there is no moral obligation beyond usefulness. The futural character of contract implies this: since agreement binds future actions, not all of which are to occur at the same time, it may be the case that after one party fulfills the terms of the agreement it is no longer useful to the other party to do so. Only an obligation essentially independent of usefulness can secure the general practice of compact. Thus, Grotius concludes, the law of nature that dictates society dictates the obligation to fulfill promises. Hence George Sabine was really quite off the mark when he concluded that Grotius shared in an assumption Sabine identified in "nearly all thinkers of the natural law tradition in the seventeenth century"—that "an obligation to be binding must be freely assumed by the parties bound," that is, that "obligation is always self-imposed."[112] The obligation to fulfill compacts is not self-imposed, but is imposed by nature.

Sabine confuses here the further obligations incurred via agreements with the obligation, so to speak, to fulfill obligations. As Grotius says, "That promises should be performed comes from the nature of immutable justice, which is . . . common to God and all those who make use of reason."[113]

Most but not all of the obligations human beings live under turn out to derive in one way or another from human agreement—either the private agreements that are contracts and related acts, or the public agreements that produce the various sorts of positive law. The law of nature, while certainly not contentless, in many cases merely brings us up to, but not beyond, the threshold of positive undertakings and gives them moral validity. Natural law is relatively silent, and leaves much (although certainly not all) to positive determination. Both Grotius's rigorous distinction between natural and voluntary law and among the different kinds of law reflects his desire to keep the content of obligation-generating acts of agreement relatively pure; this segregation in turn serves the purpose of keeping the content of *jus* as precise and definite as possible. In Grotius, therefore, consent comes to hold a far more determinative position than it had ever held before. The *jus gentium* is to be found entirely in the realm of consent, and the authority of the civil process is decisively determined by consent.[114]

All this accords with the deepest thrust of Grotius's thought, toward both a very determinate and specific standard of right, a standard beyond the vicissitudes of religious and political controversy, and an effective standard, one that can stand up to the sneers of the Machiavellis of the world, who say that the natural law is "weak and unarmed." The role of positively generated obligations in Grotius promises well on both counts. Grotius provides a method to produce a definite answer to the question of where to look to find the ruling obligations—in specific promises, contracts, agreements, and statutes. Not the socially contentious and ever-interpretable Bible, nor a vague and indeterminate nature, but empirical or historical reality is the locus for searching out most authoritative obligations.

Moreover, if agreement of one sort or another generates most obligations, then there must be some ultimate congruence between the interests of human beings and their duties, for they will not make agreements that do not promise some good to themselves. Law remains for Grotius an ideal, often standing against the immediate interests of individuals, but the gap between the real and the ideal is meant to be much narrower under the Grotian dispensation than under earlier versions of natural law. Thus Grotius hoped to avoid the position of those ridiculous men who preached an otherworldly justice to unjust men or who preached pacifism to the bellicose, without at the same time falling into the moral cynicism of Carneades and Machiavelli.[115]

Grotius's sweeping success in England and elsewhere in Europe proves that he had succeeded, to some degree at least, in fashioning a political doctrine that political men found worthy and useful. Nonetheless, some-time in the eighteenth century in England the authority of Grotius came to be supplanted by that of Locke. In retrospect, it is difficult not to see Grotius as a transitional figure, in effect although certainly not in intent. Grotius contributed to the ultimate triumph of the natural rights philosophy not because, as some scholars claim, he propounded a philosophy of that sort himself, but because from his different Aristotelian principles he accustomed political men to thinking about politics in terms that the natural rights philosophy would later adopt. Most important was Grotius's notion of "law (jus) properly so called," a narrower doctrine of law and politics than had prevailed theretofore and one that shared much with Lockean natural rights philosophy. Had Grotius not (so successfully) reinstated and then transformed the natural law tradition, it is difficult to imagine writers like Locke succeeding in their more far-reaching break with the tradition.[116] Grotius, therefore, is part of our story of the emergence of the natural rights republicanism of the American founding in a twofold way. Because he was the deepest expression of the Whig thought that dominated in 1688–89 in England and yet was so different from the later Lockean thought, he serves as a point of contrast. But he also helped prepare the way for the coming of the new natural rights philosophy.

Grotius thus contributed to the coming of modernity, even if he was not part of its creation himself. It is tempting to view that process in reverse-Hegelian terms. English political thought as it entered the decisive seventeenth century was much like that in the rest of Europe (allowing for specific accents and emphases associated with English political history)—some form or forms of Christian Aristotelianism. The various emergent doctrines of the seventeenth century—royalist divine right theory, parliamentary contractarianism, Whig Grotianism—all betray the prior sway of Christian Aristotelianism. Those forms of Protestant political thought that have figured in part 1 of this study were all constituted through a negation (or extreme diminution) of the Aristotelian element in the inherited synthesis. Aristotelian nature gave way to more strictly biblically or theologically grounded modes of political thought as the English political nation set off on its quest for the Holy Grail of the true political Protestantism. Grotius and the Whigs negated the Christian Aristotelian synthesis in the opposite direction. A modified yet still reconizable and vibrant Aristotelianism set aside the biblical-theological dimensions of the synthesis in favor of a rational philosophic politics aimed at setting political life on a more certain, stable, and universalistic foundation. The chief marker of this second movement in seventeenth-century thought was the reemergence and reformation of natural law philosophy, and especially the dominance of Grotius's theologically neutral natural law.

CHAPTER SIX

A Neo-Harringtonian Moment?
Whig Political Science
and the Old Republicanism

THAT THE WHIGS of the seventeenth century were Grotians rather than Lockeans undermines the version of the story of Anglo-American political thought that told of continuities between 1649, 1689, and 1776, or some set of points in between. Insight into the Grotianism of the Whigs helps highlight the role the very un-Grotian doctrines of the state of nature and natural rights came to play for Locke and his American successors, and thus to highlight the essential differences between Locke and the Americans, on the one hand, and the Grotian Whigs, on the other. Insight into the Grotianism of the pre-Lockean Whigs thus also shows something about the "modernity problem." In adopting natural rights/state of nature theory the Americans were not merely reaffirming an old—that is, a premodern—approach to moral and political matters. Something centrally important changed between 1688–89 and 1776.

Whether appreciative of the modernity of rights or not, discussion of the thought surrounding the American founding premeinently in terms of rights would have been almost a matter of course not too many years ago.[1] That is no longer so. A prevalent new approach emphasizes instead of rights the idea of republicanism, and thus is often referred to by historians as "the republican synthesis."[2] Scholars now find themselves "admitting, often grudgingly, the incontestable reality of America's republican roots." That recognition has led to "a dramatic reorientation . . . in interpretation of the Revolutionary and early national periods,"[3] and of later American history as well. The discovery of republicanism has, according to Joyce Appleby, "produced a reaction among historians akin to the reaction of chemists to a new element. Once having been identified, it can be found everywhere."[4]

Scholars have often been "grudging" in their willingness to recognize "America's republican roots," because this required a major shift away from the older emphases on natural and constitutional rights and individual liberty, from the older identification of Locke as the chief if not sole intellectual influence on the Americans, and from the Toquevillian claim that America was quintessentially modern in and from its origins—"the first new nation."[5] As Appleby put it, "Republicanism has come to represent a declaration of independence from older scholarship."[6] Earlier scholars had passed over the significance of republicanism because they had "assumed that republicanism represented simply a form of government." Within the republican synthesis, on the other hand, republicanism is "a dynamic ideology assuming moral dimensions and involving the very character of . . . society."[7]

Although the republican synthesis represents "a new consensus" among scholars,[8] there are distinct differences in the way republicanism is understood within that school of thought.[9] The "republican synthesis," in a word, is not so monolithic as to deserve the appellation "synthesis." The failure to recognize or admit this has led many scholars who deploy the idea of republicanism to rely on a very general conception that papers over the fissures in the synthesis by discussing it in terms of "themes," usually presented in a list of items only loosely and partially related to each other.[10]

The discovery of republicanism is of undeniable importance, for it can help us understand the new republicanism of the American order, but not in the form of the current "republican synthesis." Much of what is said of republicanism is useful and true, but much is not, and even the true must be set more carefully into its context before it can be useful. The notion of the "republican synthesis" does not conduce to that kind of sorting and judging. I propose first, therefore, to unravel the separate strands from which the synthesis has been constructed. The result will supply not only a clearer sense of the different theses that make up the synthesis, but will supply also a form of the arguments that will facilitate judgment on what in the whole set of conceptions is sound and what is not. Most important, it will allow us to grasp the relationship between natural rights and republicanism.

On one issue there is perfect agreement among all scholars of the republican synthesis: although it had many forerunners and many contributors, three men in particular "established the . . . perception of republicanism that has become so familiar"—Bernard Bailyn, Gordon Wood, and J. G. A. Pocock. "Bailyn was the progenitor" who "established a new paradigm for interpreting the Revolution."[11] Wood's most obvious contribution was to carry the story of republicanism beyond the revolution and into the era of constitution-making. Pocock extended the story in the other direction, back into its roots in English thought, and from there back to Italian Renaissance humanism and classical political philosophy. (Pocock is thus of most interest here.)[12] At the same time, he attempted to deepen as well as broaden the republican idea by supplying it a richer philosophic meaning than it had received from the pens of Bailyn and Wood. However, this sequential description is only superficial, and threatens to mislead in the same way that the idea of a republican synthesis itself does; the three only partly relate as a series of contributions to one progressively unfolding adumbration of a singular conception.

THE POLITICS OF LIBERTY: BERNARD BAILYN

Bailyn "established a new paradigm" by setting himself simultaneously against both previously prevailing modes of "interpreting the Revolution." He rejected the progressive approach that focused on economic interests and dismissed the colonists' theorizing as propaganda.[13] But he also rejected the chief alternative view, which took the colonists' intellectualizing more or less at face value and traced the revolution to the influence of Enlightenment philosophers like Locke, or to the complex constitutional argumentation of the likes of John Adams.[14] He agreed with the intellectualizers that the Americans "were led by the force of ideas," but he shared the Progressives' skepticism that ideas as "abstruse" or high-flown as Enlightenment philosophy, "abstractions" as "disembodied" as those of the "philosophes," or "the formal arguments of the constitutional lawyers . . . could constitute motives."[15] "Formal discourse" is not by itself so important, he said, but it "becomes politically powerful when it becomes ideology."[16]

Bailyn devoted a good deal of attention to the question of the source of American ideology, and he found the answer to be complex. At least five different kinds of writings helped shape the American mind: writings of the ancients, especially ancient historians; writings by the Enlightenment philosophers, such as Locke and Voltaire; writings deriving from Protestant, and especially Puritan, sources; writing on the English common law by such as Edward Coke; and finally, writings in the Whig Opposition tradition, by the likes of John Trenchard and Thomas Gordon (as "Cato"), Walter Moyle, and James Burgh. The last group was most important, because it "dominated the colonists' miscellaneous learning and shaped it into a coherent whole"; all the other "clusters of ideas" floating about in the American mind "did not in themselves form a coherent intellectual pattern."[17]

Bailyn credited the other four strands of thought with only a tangential shaping role. Least important were the classics: they "are everywhere in the literature of the revolution, but are everywhere illustrative, not determinative of thought"; they were "not the source of political and social beliefs."[18] He found that the common law tradition was "manifestly influential" but that "it did not in itself determine the kinds of conclusions men would draw in the crisis of the time."[19] Puritan ideas were important, but "limited and parochial . . . restricted . . . to those who continued to understand the world, as the original Puritans had, in theological terms."[20] Contrary to many of his predecessors and many of his successors, Bailyn believed that "the efforts . . . to discount the influence of the 'glittering generalities' of the European Enlightenment" are misplaced. "Their influence remains and is profusely illustrated in the political literature." Those writers "were quoted everywhere in the colonies, by everyone who claimed a broad awareness. . . . In pamphlet after pamphlet," Bailyn found, "the American writers cited Locke on natural rights." After almost a page of examples, he gave up: "Examples could be multiplied without end."[21] The Enlightenment writers, he concluded, "contributed significantly to the thought of the Americans." And yet, with the major exception of Locke, "their influence, though more decisive than that of the authors of classical antiquity, was neither clearly dominant nor wholly determinative."[22] In contrast, it will be recalled, Bailyn asserted that the Whig Opposition writers "dominated." The Americans cited the Enlightenment writers all the time, but "the knowledge they reflect . . . is at times superficial." Yet he failed to inform the reader wherein their knowledge was superficial. Locke, he said, "is cited often with precision on points of political theory, but at other times he is referred to in the most off-hand way, as if he could be relied on to support anything the writers happened to be arguing."[23] The one piece of evidence Bailyn produced to support that last claim does not appear to do so, however. He made reference to a sermon in which the author had cited Locke on the state of nature in order "to validate" the use of the state of nature idea; that seems perfectly appropriate, in that Locke did put forward a doctrine of the state of nature and did defend the state of nature against those who doubted its existence or relevance.[24]

Bailyn, in other words, was hard put to give a persuasive reason for his reorientation away from Locke and the other Enlightenment authors. He was, in fact, more modest in the reorientation he proposed than later scholars who claimed to follow him. He did not put it as an either/or: either Locke or the Whig Opposition writers. Indeed, he conceded that ideas typical of Locke, like natural rights and "the contractual basis of society and government," were pervasive in the Opposition literature itself.[25] The question Bailyn led up to, but did not quite address, was this: What is the relationship between his Whig Opposition tradition and the natural rights tradition of Locke? The evidence available thus far would seem consistent with the thesis that the Opposition was itself Lockean.

Bailyn did not deny that conclusion, but he leaned in another direction. He identified the Whigs as "distinctive," and while their thought "overlapped" that of the other traditions, especially Locke, it "was yet distinct in its essential characteristics and unique in its determinative power." Its essential distinctiveness seems partly a function, in turn, of its source, for "the ultimate origins of this distinctive ideological strain lay in the radical social and political thought of the English Civil War and of the Commonwealth period."[26] Bailyn devoted precious little effort, however, to detailing the character of that earlier thought, or of its echoes in the Opposition tradition. For that he relied mainly on Caroline Robbins's loose discussion in *The Eighteenth-Century Commonwealthmen*.[27] That particular lacuna has since been addressed at length by J. G. A. Pocock, and I will return to it below.

Although Bailyn concedes that Lockean and Enlightenment ideas appeared frequently, they were set in the context of other ideas of a content and temper quite different. Where the Enlightenment produced "glittering generalities," the Americans, like the Opposition writers, had a quite specific political analysis that explained the events they were experiencing and gave specific guidance on how to respond to them. This other set of ideas was not only more specific and practical, it was more simplistic, vulgar, and crude. Accordingly, it was more suited to serve as an ideology, to marshal the emotions and energies of a people, than the merely philosophic musings of a Locke or a Montesquieu.[28]

Thus Bailyn did not deny the presence of the themes of natural rights that had so dominated earlier scholarship, though he self-consciously identified other terms as more central. Natural rights were "all-important," but, he deprecatingly said, "they are defined in a significantly ambiguous way. They were understood to be at one and the same time the inalienable, indefeasible rights inherent in people as such, and the concrete specifications of English law."[29] That ambiguity seems to have justified for Bailyn his search elsewhere for the "triggering" and "organizing" components of the beliefs of the Americans, for a "significantly ambiguous" idea could hardly provide clear and decisive guidance.[30]

According to Bailyn, the political understanding of the Americans was not organized so much around the ideas of natural rights, social contract, consent of the governed, and the other doctrines epitomized in the Declaration of Independence, but rather around a quite different set of concepts, the most important of which probably were liberty, power, and conspiracy. Americans of the revolutionary era considered organized political life to be a steady and unremitting contest between liberty and power: rulers strive to encroach on the sphere of liberty carved out by the ruled; political history is the record of the oscillating fortunes of one and then the other force. Opposition thought thus shared "the traditional anti-statism of seventeenth century liberalism." But it "was yet distinct in its insistence that all power—royal or plebiscitarian, autocratic or democratic—was evil: necessary, no doubt, for ordered life, but evil nevertheless in the threat it would always pose to the progress of liberty."[31] In the contest between liberty and power, liberty most often has the worst of it—witness the rarity of free polities in the world. Clever rulers regularly mount conspiracies against liberty.[32] The colonists were prepared by their theory to interpret the events after 1765 as yet another instance of a dread conspiracy. Opposition thought gave them a ready-made frame within which to interpret British actions, a frame more determinative and energizing than generalities and slogans like "no taxation without representation."[33]

Bailyn did not rid himself of natural rights, for they remain ensconced in a central place in his account. The good for the sake of which the colonists contended was liberty, which, said Bailyn, is "the capacity to exercise 'natural rights' within limits set not by the mere will or desire of men in power but by non-arbitrary law."[34] Liberty, in other words, is security in one's natural rights. In the final analysis, Bailyn's opposition-Whig-inspired Americans sound much like Locke, and this is so even though Bailyn omitted any discussion of the Declaration of Independence, an omission for which some critics have legitimately berated him.[35]

Bailyn no doubt unearthed an important dimension of the intellectual orientation of the Americans circa 1776, but he was not helpful in relating what he discovered to what was already visible. Bailyn did not pose his new tradition as a genuine alternative, in the sense of an either/or, to the Lockean or liberal tradition, but he opened the way to that development, which occurred very soon after his *Ideological Origins* was published.

THE POLITICS OF THE ORGANIC COMMUNITY: GORDON WOOD

Gordon Wood not only carried Bailyn's story forward in time, but in doing so he changed much of it, adding along the way a much fuller specification of the nature of the "non-Lockean tradition" Bailyn had haltingly invoked. The modification of Bailyn's work is not the most striking feature of Wood's analysis, however, for he opens his *Creation of the American Republic* with an acknowledgment of an "incalculable debt" to Bailyn, and much of his discussion obviously echoes Bailyn's book. Wood's first chapter, for example, "The Whig Science of Politics," contains as its centerpiece a section titled "Power against Liberty" that restates some of Bailyn's main arguments.[36] Yet for all the echoes and common ground, there is a major difference, captured summarily in the fact that Bailyn called the ideology he found at the core of the Americans' revolutionary political culture an Opposition Whig tradition, whereas Wood called the ideology he found at the core of the Americans' revolutionary political culture a classical republican tradition. Bailyn and Wood had in mind the same tradition, but Wood redescribed it in a significantly different way.[37]

Both the "classical" and the "republican" parts of Wood's label indicate important differences. Where Bailyn had dismissed classical influences as indecisive, Wood was more impressed with "the appeal of antiquity"; it was "a source of republican inspiration"—indeed, "the deepest origin" of their political thinking.[38] Wood firmly connected the Whig or Opposition tradition Bailyn had identified to the Renaissance and, behind that, to classical authors like Cicero and Aristotle.[39] That closer link to classical-Renaissance republicanism probably accounts for Wood's somewhat more summary dismissal of Locke: the English Whigs on whom the Americans depended "perhaps owed more to Machiavelli and Montesquieu than [they] did to Locke."[40]

The classical roots came to the fore because, according to Wood, "republicanism was the basic premise of American thinking—the central presupposition behind all other ideas."[41] This is quite different from Bailyn, for despite the frequency with which Bailyn is invoked as one of the trinity of the republican synthesis, Joyce Appleby was nonetheless correct when she observed that "curiously the word, republicanism, does not figure prominently in his text."[42] "Republic" receives only one entry in Bailyn's index, and that pretty fairly suggests its place in his book. Bailyn's book is not about republicanism but about the dialectic of liberty and power.

Wood's book is not only about republicanism, but about an old republicanism: for Wood's Americans, republicanism was a pervasive and deep-going commitment:

> Republicanism meant more for Americans than simply the elimination of a king and the institution of an elective system. It added a moral dimension, a utopian depth, to the political separation from England—a depth that involved the very character of their society.[43]

Wood emphasized the "moral dimension" and the "utopian depth" of American republicanism because he saw "the essence of republicanism" in the call for "the sacrifice of individual interests to the greater good of the whole." The "public good," or "common interest," was understood "not, as we might today think of it, [as] simply the sum or consensus of the particular interests that made up the community," but rather as "an entity in itself, prior to and distinct from the various private interests of groups and individuals." This public good was the center of Wood's republicanism.[44] From that conception came the chief requisite of the old republican regime: "Virtue is the lifeblood of the republic." The republic required the individual to be willing "to sacrifice his private interests for the good of the community." This willingness was "public virtue," which "was primarily the consequence of men's individual private virtues." Only private virtue could produce public virtue; thus the republic of virtue "demanded an extraordinary moral character in the people."[45]

Such notions of virtue and the common good rested in turn on a more fundamental presupposition about political life. "Most English colonists did not conceive of society in rational, mechanistic terms; rather society was organic and developmental." The Americans were attempting "to realize the traditional commonwealth idea of a corporate society, in which the common good would be the only objective of government." The Americans continued to endorse the "traditional conception of the organic community."[46] Here is Wood's ground for calling this republicanism classical: it rested at bottom on a classical conception of an organic or natural polity. In such an organic society the good of the whole is not only higher than, but to some degree independent of and separate from, the goods of the parts. Just as the parts of a living body have a good only so far as they contribute to the good of the whole, so the members of an organic community have a good subordinate to that of the whole. Just as a limb may have to be sacrificed on occasion for the health of the whole, so may the interests of an individual be submerged or denied for the sake of the community. "The ideal republicanism was beautifully designed to express was still a harmonious integration of all the parts of the community," on the model of a well-functioning, healthy organism.[47]

Wood's reconceptualization of the "ideological origins" in terms of classical republicanism not merely led him to bring to the fore notions like virtue that had not figured prominently in Bailyn's text ("virtue" has no index entry at all in Bailyn), but it led him to redefine even the terms that had figured prominently for Bailyn.[48] Most revealing is the fate of liberty. Bailyn's notion of liberty as security in one's natural rights was at its core an individualistic idea, but, said Wood, "ideally republicanism obliterated the individual." Wood therefore could hardly understand liberty individualistically; he salvaged it by claiming that the "important liberty in the Whig ideology was public or political liberty," which was "equivalent [to] participation by the people in the government."[49] Liberty is thus itself the corporate involvement of the people in ruling, and not the individual security of natural rights.

Wood's classical republicanism stands as a thorough alternative to the kind of commitment to natural rights contained in the Declaration of Independence. We find an either/or we did not find in Bailyn; it is an either/or because the Declaration denies almost all the theses most characteristic of Wood's classical republicanism.[50] Polity is not natural and organic but artificial and constructed. The Declaration does not set as an ideal "the obliteration of the individual," but rather the security of his or her rights. Liberty is not "in the first instance public liberty," but prepolitical individual liberty, a right with which "all men are endowed by their creator." Gary Schmitt and Robert Webking put the issue very clearly: according to the standards of rightful government voiced in the Declaration, "both the monarchy of George III and Wood's republicanism in which the individual is obliterated must be judged to be illegitimate governmental forms."[51] Wood's classical republicanism is not a supplement to the theory of rights, but a full-blown alternative to it.[52]

Wood not only reconceived the original tradition of American politics as classical republicanism, but he effectuated one other major shift from the Bailyn version of "the ideological origins." Not merely did he sketch the rise, but he also traced the "death of classical politics." The Americans "constructed not simply new forms of government, but an entirely new conception of politics, a conception that took them out of an essentially classical and medieval world of political discussion into one that was recognizably modern."[53] This "recognizably modern" conception found its embodiment in the federal constitution of 1787 and the Federalist political science that generated and explained it.[54]

This modern conception, said Wood, was the antithesis of the tradition it replaced. "The Americans of 1787 shattered the classical Whig world of 1776." All of the old ideas were now reversed. Within the new understanding, "the public good could not be the transcending of the different interests, but the reconciling of them. . . . The public good could not be an entity distinct from its parts; it was rather 'the general combined interest of all the state put together, as it were, upon an average.'" With the public good no longer seen as distinct and opposed to private interests, the old republican virtue was no longer required. "The aim of instilling a spartan creed in America thus began to seem more and more nonsensical." Another consequence of the shift lay in a new definition of liberty: "The liberty that was now emphasized was personal or private, the protection of individual rights." This in turn dismantled the organic conception of society that had stood at the base of the earlier classical republicanism:

> Once the people were thought to be composed of various interests in opposition to one another, all sense of a graduated organic chain in the social hierarchy became irrelevant, symbolized by the increasing emphasis on the image of a social contract. The people were not an order organically tied together by their unity of interest but rather an agglomeration of hostile individuals coming together for their mutual benefit.[55]

The American political tradition was "transformed" into its opposite: from organic to individualistic, from classical to modern, from individual-obliterating to individual-affirming—a transformation of some magnitude. According to Wood, "by 1787 Lockean liberalism [came to] overshadow republican sentiment."[56] The process leading from the Revolution to the Constitution entailed, for Wood hardly less than for Charles Beard before him, "the repudiation of 1776." That repudiation brought a new "alliance of power and liberty," exactly the forces Bailyn had seen as inalterably opposed to each other in the Whig Opposition political science. At the same time, said Wood, "the Constitution was intrinsically an aristocratic document designed to check the democratic tendencies of the period."[57]

One measure of Wood's distance from Bailyn's version of the founding is Bailyn's denial of Wood's theory of the "transformation": "The Constitution was neither a repudiation of '76, nor an instrument devised to protect aristocracies threatened in the states. . . . It is a second generation expression of the original ideological impulses of the Revolution applied to everyday, practical problems of the 1780s." According to Bailyn, there was in fact no shift away from the viewpoints of 1776. The "earlier opposition ideology survived intact and fundamentally shaped the emerging state."[58] Because he revised Bailyn's Opposition ideology in the direction of classical republicanism, Wood was driven to find the Constitution and what succeeded it further removed from what preceded it than Bailyn did.

THE POLITICS OF "ZOON POLITIKON": J. G. A. POCOCK

J. G. A. Pocock, the third in the trinity of the "republican synthesis," had much to do with Wood's move away from Bailyn. Pocock's work stands in ambiguous temporal relation to that of the other two. His major work, *The Machiavellian Moment*, appeared after and drew from theirs, yet several shorter preliminary studies had appeared before Bailyn and Wood wrote, and both scholars were obviously influenced by at least one of these earlier studies.[59] Some of the differences between Bailyn and Wood stem from the greater degree to which Wood allowed Pocock's conceptions to shape him. Pocock developed far stronger connections between Whig Opposition thought and classical republicanism than either Bailyn or Robbins before him had done.[60] Nonetheless, neither Bailyn nor Wood saw the full scope of Pocock's project when they wrote, and his conceptions differ even from Wood's in two very important respects.

Perhaps the most significant difference is again the one signalled by a shift in terminology. Although Pocock was not averse to the phrase "classical republicanism," he gravitated more naturally to "civic humanism."[61] He accepted "classical republicanism" because he too traced the Opposition Whig tradition back to the ancients, especially to Aristotle. Pocock described the thought of James Harrington, whom he saw to be the main figure in the Anglo-American version of the republican tradition, as "essentially Greek"; Harrington put forward a "fundamentally Aristotelian theory of citizenship." In modified form, Harrington's "classicism" founded the Whig Opposition tradition that Bailyn and Wood traced into the American founding.[62]

Yet Pocock's adoption of the label "civic humanism" signifies two major differences from Wood. First, Pocock understood the ancient—that is, Aristotelian—foundation of the republican tradition in a humanistic rather than a naturalistic manner; and secondly, he believed that Renaissance humanism produced an important modification in "classical republicanism," such that the American founding is better understood as occurring at a "Machiavellian" rather than an "Aristotelian moment."[63]

Wood had interpreted classical republicanism in a naturalistic manner, for he had found at its ground the old notion of an organic or natural community. That notion in turn gave meaning to the republican ideals of the common good and virtue. Aristotle's doctrine of the naturalness of the *polis* is the obvious origin of Wood's organic conception in which the whole has an unconditional priority over the parts. The political community, Aristotle suggested, is just the sort of natural whole the human body is.[64]

Pocock emphasized different Aristotelian themes. At its most general, he said,

> civic humanism is a style of thought . . . in which it is contended that the develop-
> ment of an individual toward self-fulfillment is possible only when the individual
> acts as a citizen, that is, as a conscious and autonomous participant in an autono-
> mous decision-taking community, the polis or republic.[65]

Pocock's conception was peculiarly political: he emphasized citizenship and political participation, not ontological subordination of part to whole. The latter idea, Wood's idea, leads to a conception of man as a social animal, but not to the *zoon politikon* that Pocock found at the center of the civic humanist tradition. Participation in shaping the public good, not subordination to it, became for Pocock the highest expression of one's humanity.

The beginning point for Pocock's humanistic interpretation was the observation that for Aristotle "every human activity was value-oriented in the sense that it aimed at some theoretically identifiable good." In this view, such "valuing" is always social, for the goods are sought with and in reference to others. Human sociability requires that some "common valuing" be arrived at. The *polis* is the universal association, for it encompasses all the particular individuals and associations and their "values" or goods. Since human beings are defined by their valuing activity, "participation in the value-oriented direction" of the universal association, the *polis*, "forms both a means to an end," the achievement of one's particular values or goods, "and an end—or good—in itself."[66] Pocock's Aristotle recognized an indefinite number of values that might be pursued by citizens, but found that the good of the whole takes priority over those of the particular members. "Having entered the political process in pursuit of his particular good, [the citizen] now found himself joining with others to direct the actions of all in pursuit of the good of all; the attainment of his private good was not lost but must take a lower priority"[67] (a lower priority—not, as with Wood, extinction). Participation in decisions regarding the values that should rule, and to what degree, is most important as an end in itself, for sharing in the determination of the ruling values is the decisive way of expressing one's human character as a valuing being. To be human, therefore, is preeminently to be a citizen.

Certain specific political imperatives followed from this conception. Each group or individual, having a particular good, "was to have power to pursue" it, but only "in such a way as to involve it in the pursuit of other goods by other groups." Each group and individual, therefore, was to share both in ruling and in being ruled. "The evil to be avoided was the situation in which any group was able to exercise an unshared power over the whole"; this was "despotism."[68] Politics involves blending and sharing powers among groups in varying and flexible patterns.[69] In the hands of Polybius and later theorists this took the form of a concern, deep and abiding with the republicans, for the "balance" of the constitution.

Virtue came to light for Pocock's Aristotle as an eminently political quality: not so much self-sacrifice, but participation as a citizen, is the core of virtue. "The polity must be a perfect partnership of all citizens and all values since, if it was less, a part would be ruling in the name of the whole." The "perfect partnership" imposed the duty of "perfect citizenship," for without this a man would fall short of his own virtue and "tempt his fellows . . . to injustice and corruption." Apolitical retreat was not the only mode of falling short of "perfect citizenship":

> To become the dependent of another was as great a crime as to reduce another to dependence on oneself. The dereliction of one citizen, therefore, reduced the others' chances of attaining and maintaining virtue, since virtue was now politicized; it consisted in a partnership of ruling and being ruled with others who must be as morally autonomous as oneself. In embracing the civic ideal, therefore, the humanist staked his future as a moral person on the political health of his city.[70]

Corruption, or loss of virtue, then, was above all "loss of autonomy."[71]

Pocock's Aristotle is humanistic precisely because the core of humanity is said to consist in the non-natural and uniquely human activity of "valuing." He is "civic" because the valuing is done in a political and not just a social setting. Politics, or republican citizenship, is more an end in itself than a means to other ends. Virtue is the active and independent participation in political life. Liberty is "freedom from restraints upon the practice" of political life.[72] All of this differs substantially from Wood's version of classical republicanism, even though there are overlapping elements and common terms.[73]

According to Pocock, the Aristotelian foundations of this republican tradition were modified during the Renaissance, especially by Machiavelli. In part because of their Christian roots, the Italians of the fifteenth century were more concerned with the problem of time than Aristotle had been. The civic humanist ideal made the republic, the particular city existing in the here and now, the locus of all virtue and fulfillment; but the Christian heritage made the here and now, the whole temporal sphere, an arena of irrationality, particularity, and mortality. In the form of *fortuna*, history—that is, existence in time—threatened the very existence of the republic. One typical response was the attempt to raise barricades against change—to recur to extremely static models of republics that would resist the depredations of time. Machiavelli followed the bolder and newer path of proposing that the republic attempt to dominate rather than hide from history.

But the problem he addressed was just the same as that addressed by his more conservative peers: how to realize and guarantee the continued existence of the republic in time. A dynamic rather than a static internal ordering—Rome, not Sparta or Venice—and a popular, not an aristocratic, republic (again, Rome, not Sparta or Venice) stood at the center of Machiavelli's revision of the civic humanist tradition. As part of his drive for a popular dynamic republic Machiavelli placed unprecedented emphasis on the citizen-soldier; the virtuous city became the one with the armed citizenry. This was a major shift from Aristotle, who placed the pursuits of peace ahead of the pursuits of war, and it became the basis for the abiding concern within Opposition literature about standing armies.[74]

Despite Machiavelli's revisions, the modified republican tradition maintained a negative view toward time, which continued to appear as the realm of the particular, the irrational, and the mortal. Change, therefore, continued to be viewed with suspicion. Change was regress, corruption, decay; it either had to be resisted altogether or countered with a "return to first principles."[75]

A number of consequences flow from Pocock's reconceptualization of republicanism. First, the American founders as carriers of the republican virus faced not forward, to modernity, but backward, to antiquity. Not only did they act on the basis of an old, thoroughly traditional understanding of politics, but that understanding was itself distrustful of change, of time, of the future. "The American Revolution," Pocock decreed, was "less the first act of revolutionary enlightenment than . . . the last great act of the Renaissance." America was founded in a "dread of modernity."[76]

Another consequence was the deepening of the chasm between natural-rights-centered ideas and the republican tradition. As much or even more than Wood did, Pocock presented the republicanism of the Americans in opposition to an alleged "Lockean liberalism." Kramnick surveyed some of Pocock's most colorful claims regarding the place of Locke:

> Pocock has seen the history of political thought "dominated by a fiction of Locke," whose importance "has been wildly distorted." . . . To understand the debates of eighteenth century politics does "not necessitate reference to Locke at all." Pocock has applied this revisionist verdict about Locke to an alternative reading of America and its founding. . . . The proper interpretation "stresses Machiavelli at the expense of Locke."[77]

"It is clear," said Pocock, "that Locke played no predominant role in the formation of what Caroline Robbins has called the Whig canon. . . . [Those] seventeenth-century writers . . . are defined by their relation to the classical republican tradition, with which Locke had little if anything to do."[78]

When Pocock attributed the inspiration for the American founding to his civic humanism he was explicitly intending to depreciate the role and importance of rights, natural or otherwise, for, as he said, liberalism "is a matter of law and right." The language of law and right has a separate "vocabulary" from that of civic humanism; "they are markedly discontinuous with one another because they premise different values, encounter different problems, and employ different strategies of speech and argument." Even though some scholars seem inclined to blend the two traditions together, Pocock found it "highly important to stress that the two modes remained incommensurate. Virtue was not reducible to right."[79]

Having reconceived republicanism in a richer and more supple manner than either Bailyn or Wood had done, Pocock proceeded to reject Wood's story about the "end of classical politics": The republican tradition, in somewhat modified form, perhaps, lived on well beyond 1787, argued Pocock and his followers (although just how long has become a matter of great controversy).[80] Civic humanism was composed of a more complex amalgam of ideas than Wood had realized, and therefore the changes effected in early "Whig political science" by the Federalists did not move beyond the older republicanism, to say nothing of the persistence of the latter in Jeffersonianism and elsewhere. Moreover, Pocock implied, republicanism was a far more flexible, changeable tradition than Wood had realized. By the time of the American Revolution it had undergone a number of significant transformations, and to undergo further modification was not foreign to its protean nature.

Pocock's rejection of Wood's "death of republicanism" thesis spoke to one of the most troublesome features of Wood's whole construction. Not only did the Americans, according to Wood, "shift paradigms" in the years between 1776 and 1787, but the shift was of momentous proportion. The earlier ideology turned nearly into its opposite. Not only is such a shift implausible on its face, but nobody at the time seemed quite aware of having made it. As Wood himself admitted in a later restatement, "None of the Founding Fathers had any sense that he had to choose or was choosing between Machiavelli and Locke."[81] Pocock's claim that they did not choose, that they did stay with Machiavelli, could account for their failure to notice that they faced a significant choice.

It is now possible to draw some conclusions from this unraveling of the republican synthesis: (1) One feature of the synthesis remains intact; all three agree that the formative tradition for the Americans of the founding era was not the Lockean, or natural rights, tradition, but the English Whig Opposition tradition of the eighteenth century, represented by writers like Trenchard and Gordon and James Burgh. (2) Beyond that, however, agreement breaks down, in that all three understand that tradition differently. For Wood and Pocock it is essentially a republican tradition, but not so for Bailyn. (3) Wood understands it as "naturalistic" republicanism based on an organic conception of society, whereas Pocock understands it as "humanistic" republicanism. The all-important notion of republican virtue differs accordingly. (4) Two of the three understand the formative tradition as a clear alternative, as quite different from the natural-rights-centered doctrine of the Declaration of Independence; Bailyn does not appear to view the two as an either/or. (5) Wood sees a real shift in the "reigning paradigm" during the founding era; the other two do not.

The differences among the trinity, and the even more diverse positions that have emerged more recently among later scholars, ultimately trace back to the (largely unacknowledged) different fundamental conceptions of republicanism brought to the materials. The questions that require reconsideration are What was the real nature of that "other" tradition, and how did it relate to the natural rights doctrine? The Declaration of Independence, conveniently ignored in the republican literature, insistently points toward natural rights; Bailyn and the others have established a case for something like republicanism. But the two themes have nowhere been brought adequately into conjunction with each other. Having sorted out the different strands of the "synthesis," we are now favorably situated for the attempt to address these issues, and ultimately to bring out the relationship between natural rights and (the new) republicanism.

POLITICAL PHILOSOPHY AND POLITICAL SCIENCE

No matter how much they may differ from each other on some matters, the republican synthesizers nonetheless agree both in what they ignore and about the surface of the tradition with which they are concerned: there was a line of British political thinkers (called by some commonwealthmen, by others the Whig or country Opposition or classical republicans) to whom the Americans of the founding generation looked for their political education. Influential as the British thinkers were in America, they were decidedly less so at home. During the period of Whig ascendancy in the aftermath of the Glorious Revolution, these men were "voices in the wilderness," mostly a permanent and more or less radical opposition. They thus carried on the original Whig tradition of opposition to the government, but now in a new context, because the government they opposed was controlled by self-professed Whigs. As Opposition Whigs they were far less visible than their more successful counterparts, and that accounts, in part, for the historians' slowness in catching sight of them.

The synthesizers are perfectly correct to emphasize the role this Whig or country Opposition had in shaping the frame of political mind with which the Americans entered what proved to be the founding era. But the synthesizers have misunderstood the character of this British Opposition tradition, and their misunderstandings have set in motion false debates and unproductive controversies based on false dichotomies and unproductive categories.

A better ingress to the Opposition tradition lies along a path marked out by a distinction that John Locke (and many others) have drawn regarding political knowledge. "Politics," Locke said, "contains parts very different the one from the other, the one containing the original of societies and the rise and extent of political power, the other, the art of governing of men in society." He placed his own *Two Treatises of Government* in the first class of political works.[82] Just a century later, Thomas Jefferson repeated Locke's distinction, this time in terms of "theory" and "practice." The first kind of book, according to Jefferson, considers "the general principles of liberty and the rights of man, in nature and in society."[83] He apparently considered the character of the second so self-evident as not to require a description, but he provided examples of each—again Locke's *Treatises* in the first class, and *The Federalist* in the second. In terms of current academic discourse we might state this distinction as one between political philosophy (or theory) and political science.[84] However best described, that distinction will be indispensable in the effort to relate natural rights to the political themes discussed by the republican synthesizers.

My central contention, in brief, is as follows: The synthesizers have more (Pocock) or less (Bailyn) confused political thinking at these two levels and construed lines of thought that differed in level as though they were at the same level and opposed to one another. That confusion has led in turn to the synthesizers' postulation of "gog-and-magog" battles between liberals and republicans—of which, one of the synthesizers now admits, the alleged "participants" were quite unaware.[85] They were unaware of these battles because the reality was quite otherwise than the one described by the synthesizers. Most of what is currently discussed as classical republicanism is political thought at the level of political science; most of what is discussed as liberalism is reflection at the level of political philosophy. Lines of thought at these different levels, as both Locke and Jefferson implied so clearly, do not necessarily conflict.

Of course, they *can* conflict. Some "political science" may be more congruent with one "political philosophy" than with another. Likewise, a political science originally connected to a particular understanding of the issues of political philosophy may be taken over and adapted to another. That happened in the seventeenth and eighteenth centuries. During the Restoration there was a Whig political philosophy—essentially one or another form of modernized natural law philosophy (e.g., Hooker or Grotius)—and a Whig political science. Over the course of the eighteenth century Locke, and to a lesser but still important degree Algernon Sidney, replaced Grotius as the chief authority in political philosophy, but many of the elements of the older Whig political science were carried forward, assimilated to and at least somewhat transformed by their connections to the new Lockean political philosophy.

The creation of a new and comprehensive Whig politics was the work of several generations of British political thinkers—indeed, it was a process that never came to a clear completion. But an unended process is not necessarily a shapeless process, nor one without its markers and monuments. The synthesizers themselves have called attention to these moments. Although their republican tradition is very old, and has roots at least as far back as Aristotle, there was a moment when the Opposition tradition emerged on English soil. According to Pocock, that moment was almost identical to the moment of birth of the Whig Party itself; at least, the parents of both were the same: the first Earl of Shaftesbury and his "circle." The second well-noted marker in the tradition is the series of articles written by John Trenchard and Thomas Gordon, *Cato's Letters*, published almost half a century after Shaftesbury's alleged formulation of the themes of the classical republican tradition. This marker has more the character of a monument; so far as the Whig Opposition produced a masterpiece, most of the synthesizers agree this was it. Certainly none of the writers said to be part of this tradition was more admired or read in America than "Cato."[86]

HARRINGTON AND NEO-HARRINGTON

All the synthesizers agree on the importance of the Whig Opposition tradition, but all except Pocock take its existence for granted. Pocock sets for himself the explicit problem of explaining how a way of thinking that originated in pagan Greece and was revived and refined in Renaissance Florence came to be planted and then to thrive in England. A consideration of the origins of the Whig Opposition tradition becomes, perforce, a reconsideration of Pocock's narrative of the English tradition of civic humanism.

Post-Reformation but prerevolutionary England had been marked by ways of conceiving politics very distant from Machiavellian civic humanism. "As long as these modes of consciousness held, it would be difficult if not unnecessary to envisage the Englishman as Machiavellian citizen." The latter "mode of consciousness" exists only "where a political society becomes highly conscious that its *vita* is *activa* to the point of creating its own morality." The English "defined . . . a public realm and a mode of action therein," but they did so "in traditionalist terms," meaning that "the liberties of the subject were rooted in custom and birthright, property and inheritance—the mechanisms of antiquity." The resultant view of politics fell well short of the republican *polis*. Viewing politics as an inheritance, they did not view themselves as "creating their own morality."[87]

English political consciousness began to change in response to the conflicts preceding the Civil War. "The English, monarchical and customary animals by nature, took up the rhetoric of balance and republic only because their traditional constitution was threatened by disorder in such a form—a dispute over the sharing of power—as to make this an appropriate response." During the years of the Interregnum, Machiavellian and civic republican themes appeared with some frequency; but the decisive moment came in 1656, when James Harrington published his *Oceana*. That book, declared Pocock, "marks a moment of paradigmatic breakthrough, a major revision of English political theory and history in the light of concepts drawn from civic humanism and Machiavellian republicanism."[88]

Harrington stands literally at the center of Pocock's story of "Florentine political thought and the Atlantic republican tradition" (Pocock's subtitle to *The Machiavellian Moment*), for through him Machiavellianized civic humanism flowed into England in a form that took hold, and, even though not himself "a specially visible figure in the rhetoric of opposition," the Opposition tradition that constituted "Atlantic republicanism" derived from him.[89] Pocock's Harrington transmitted the republican tradition by "anglicizing" it. Harrington both retained and modified the chief elements of the previous tradition. He kept the founding Aristotelian theme of the primacy of citizenship in the constitution of human personality and the Machiavellian addition of "the possession of arms as necessary to political personality." His modification was relatively simple, but of immense significance for (Pocock's picture of) what would happen later in England and America: Harrington adapted a previously urban tradition of politics to England's rural and historically feudal situation. On that basis he introduced the idea of property—landed freehold property—into the republican tradition. "The bearing of arms, once it was seen as a function of feudal tenure, proved to be based upon the possession of property." One who possessed property in freehold had the means to be armed and the basis for the independence that constituted civic virtue in the humanist tradition. "The function of free proprietorship became the liberation of arms and consequently of the personality, for free public action and civic virtue." And so, with Harrington "the politicization of the human person had now attained full expression in the language of English political thought; God's Englishman was now *zoon politikon* in virtue of his sword and his freehold."[90]

Property for Pocock's Harrington was thus not the dynamic, productive, plenty-producing entity of capitalism or protocapitalism—of Locke or Adam Smith or Marx—but the means whereby a man could take his place as a full citizen of the English extended rural republic. Property was not an economic but a political phenomenon.[91] "As with Aristotle, the end of land is not profit, but leisure: the opportunity to act in the public realm, . . . to display virtue. . . . Harrington's economics and his politics were alike essentially Greek."[92] This theory of landed property provided "a means whereby the country free-holder could equate himself with the Greco-Roman *polites* and profess a wholly classical and Aristotelian doctrine of the relations between property, liberty and power."[93]

This new interpretation of Harrington supplied Pocock with markers, rather like radioisotopes, whereby he could trace the presence and permutations of civic humanism. Property, arms (or militia), and independence (or virtue) became for Pocock indicators of the presence of the republican tradition. It was not that any or all these things self-evidently signified republicanism, but that in the Harringtonian version of that tradition—or rather, in Pocock's rendition of it—these elements were attached, as means or condition, to the yet more fundamental core of citizenship, of participation in republican politics as the defining human act. Pocock's Harrington displays the almost complete chain of the anglicized version of republicanism: freehold (Harrington)—arms (Machiavelli)—balance of political power (Polybius)—citizenship, independence, sharing in political power (Aristotle).[94] When Pocock espies one or another of the elements of this chain in later political thought, he infers the entire chain even when the other elements are not explicitly present. As I shall argue below, this procedure turns out to be the source of much misinterpretation by Pocock of political thought subsequent to Harrington.

According to Pocock, the Anglo-American republican tradition was generated from Harrington, but it was a transformed Harrington, a "neo-Harrington." To the untutored eye, however, Pocock's neo-Harringtonians appear far more "neo" than "Harringtonian."[95] The master himself had been a full-fledged republican, or commonwealthman, because he thought England had decisively left behind the "ancient constitution," the "Gothic" or feudal order, the mixed constitution that had been its historical legacy. The destruction of the monarchy and the abolition of the House of Lords were the natural and inevitable results of long-term trends in the distribution of property. Harrington shed no tears for the passing of this "Gothic" order: it was an inherently unstable system, full of conflict and irrationality. The ancient constitution was "incoherent," a vice it shared with all monarchies. Harrington argued "that there can be no such thing as a stable monarchy," for a monarchy cannot successfully solve the problem of the role of force in politics. Harrington therefore rejected "any return to the traditional 'ancient' or 'balanced' constitution."[96] The balance he sought was no longer the balance of the "orders" represented by king, lords, and commons.

Yet Pocock's "neos" wrote in the very context Harrington had insisted could never recur; after the Restoration there was once more a monarchy and a House of Lords. Moreover, the "neos" accepted this return of the ancient constitution. Rather than seeing the Gothic order as irrational and unstable, they affirmed it as "free, stable, and natural." They embraced the monarchy and rejected the republic.[97] They seem very distant indeed from James Harrington.

Pocock therefore emphasizes the transformative character of their thought. "The neo-Harringtonian interpretation . . . involved a complete reversal of the historical order found in Harrington's own account of English government, the reconciliation of his norms . . . with the Ancient Constitution." This reversal constituted the very "essence of neo-Harringtonianism":

neo-Harringtonianism emerged when Harringtonian themes were adapted to the situation of the continued and accepted existence of the ancient constitution.[98] The neo-Harringtonians "reconcile Harrington with the historical complacency of the English"; they effect a synthesis or "uneasy marriage" of two heretofore separate traditions.[99]

Despite the non-Harringtonian elements of this synthesis, "the root idea was Harrington's," according to Pocock, for "it was he who first stated in English terms the theses that only the armed freeholder was capable of independence and virtue, and that such a proprietor required a republic in which to be independent and virtuous." Put another way, "If the end of property was independence, the end of independence was citizenship and moral personality." These Harringtonian (or neo-Harringtonian) isotopes mark the presence of civic humanist thinking within traditional rhetoric about the ancient constitution.

> The central Harringtonian idea is that property confers independence, and the central idea of the Harringtonian balance is that power must not be so distributed that it encroaches on the independence of property. In neo-Harringtonian hands this was transformed to read: the English constitution consists of an ideal balance between the powers of the Crown and those of Parliament, which stands for property and independence.

Counter to Parliamentary independence, resting on land and arms, are the encroaching forces of the Crown. It "has not only a tendency to encroach, but a means of doing so. The particular means is what we collectively call corruption."[100]

Thus Pocock adds some links to the chain we have already identified, some further "markers" signalling the presence of civic humanist politics: fear of standing army (or enthusiasm for militia), praise of parliamentary independence based on property (or blame of parliamentary influence and corruption), encouragement of parliamentary opposition to the executive (or rejection of parliamentary cooperation with or dependence on the executive). The ear trained by Pocock hears civic humanism in discourse containing those ideas even if that discourse is otherwise and mostly couched in the traditional language of the constitution.[101]

Harrington's commonwealth, or republican, commitment thus metamorphosed into a country position "in the full sense of the term." As the ideology of the country gentry discontented with change and progress sponsored by or associated with the court, the neo-Harringtonians were not "liberal" forces, but rather reactionaries. "Neo-Harringtonian ideas . . . provided . . . an ideology for 'ancients' who would have none of the 'modern' world that was emerging." They found their "political norm . . . in the past" and saw all change as decline, as "corruption." Thus, this ideology "sounded an unmistakably paranoic note at times." Its doctrines and concerns were "bogeys intended for country gentlemen." As a reactionary doctrine it was "barren," for it could conceive no positive uses for power. As reactionaries, the Opposition theorists were nowhere as near to "constitutional reality" as were their court counterparts.[102] Pocock, in other words, is no partisan of the republican tradition he has unearthed.

From the early neo-Harringtonians of the 1670s, to the full-blown Whig Opposition of the eighteenth century, to the American founding generation—in one more or less continuous and smooth sweep Pocock's neo-Harringtonians complete the chain linking Aristotle at one end to Jefferson, Madison, and Adams at the other. That chain provides him with the decisive means of characterizing the later links. His neo-Harringtonians were not liberals in any sense. The neo-Harringtonians, including the American founders, consistently took the side of "participatory ideals. . . . Harrington and his successors will be found invariably ranged on the side of participation, in defence of a republican ideal of virtue against those who would lessen it in the name of other [liberal] values."[103]

IN THE NEO-HARRINGTONIAN WORKSHOP

The foundations of the country ideology were laid, says Pocock, in the mid-1670s by the Earl of Shaftesbury and men close to him politically, especially the poet Andrew Marvell. Pocock identifies the very beginning of the neo-Harringtonian transformation in some parliamentary speeches by Shaftesbury in 1675 and in a pamphlet of that year, "A Letter from a Person of Quality to His Friend in the Country."[104] The thought in the pamphlet, its language, even its metaphors are extraordinarily close to the thought and language of Shaftesbury's speeches, so it is at least plausible to suspect the same authorship for both sets of statements.[105] For convenience's sake, I am going to call that author Shaftesbury, recognizing full well that his authorship of the pamphlet, much less of the speeches he delivered, has not been definitively established.[106] It is a bit like the problem of Homer: if Homer was not the author of Homer's works, it must have been some other poet or poets whom we might as well call Homer.

Our question is this: What have these so-called neo-Harringtonians to do with civic humanism? The link, according to Pocock, is Harrington, but he concedes there is little in the way of a direct and explicit tie. Harrington was barely mentioned by Opposition writers, and "there is no sign of contact between Shaftesbury," the supposed founder of this branch of Harringtonians, and the master himself, who still lived in 1675. The "relation between what Shaftesbury now began to say and Harrington's writings" must, therefore, be inferred entirely from "textual analysis."

The "textual analysis" does not appear very promising for displaying those "relations," however. Not only does Shaftesbury differ from Harrington in the broad ways discussed above, but the three specific themes that Pocock finds in Shaftesbury supposedly linking him to Harrington are themselves foreign to the latter. According to Pocock, Shaftesbury was contending against the use by the Earl of Danby, the king's minister, of "patronage, places, and pensions," known collectively as "corruption," in order to control Parliament. But, he admits, "in Harrington neither Court, corruption, nor office had been major elements of political analysis. . . . Corruption had not been a prominent term in Harrington's vocabulary."[107] Secondly, Shaftesbury and after him the other "neo-Harringtonians" had been greatly exercised over the question of a standing army. Pocock admits Harrington had not much considered such a possibility, and so far as he had, he "had flatly declared it impossible."[108] Finally, says Pocock, the third Harringtonian theme in Shaftesbury is the crucial role of the House of Lords, but, he admits, Harrington had "no place for them [the Lords]."[109]

Given all these concessions and admissions by Pocock, how does he yet connect Shaftesbury to Harrington and through him to civic humanism? The answer, I am compelled to say, is not well; on examination, the textual evidence of connection is remarkably thin, and Pocock processes what evidence there is through a screen so beset with a priori judgments as to amount to question-begging.[110] Not only does he squeeze Shaftesbury into a mold foreign to him, but he misses what is actually there.

Pocock's best evidence—really his only textual evidence linking Shaftesbury to Harrington, linking Shaftesbury's praise of the House of Lords to Harrington's rejection of the same—is this: When Shaftesbury spoke of the Lords, he conceived of it as an alternative to monarchical military rule. "There is no Prince that ever governed without nobility or an army." Now, according to Pocock, this "language is unmistakably Harringtonian, . . . for *Oceana* had expressed the thought that the monarchy had been driven to attempt military rule when the feudal power of the peers had failed it." Pocock concedes, as he ought, that Harrington's point was different, that he was describing the already accomplished changes (as of 1656) that had impelled the king to attempt military rule. Shaftesbury's rejection of this Harringtonian context of the argument (that is, the view that the nobility was no longer available as a potential prop for the monarchy) amounts to a rejection of what really was Harrington's point, the explanation of the appearance in England of a commonwealth.[111]

The pairing of the peerage and the military is not by itself sufficient to decree this "neo-Harringtonianism," however. Shaftesbury made his own point clear enough and it has little to do with Harrington. Peers and army are alternate means to monarchical rule, in that the prince, being but one person, requires agents—subordinate powers—in order to actualize, localize, and particularize his rule; these powers, moreover, must have a coercive presence. Two very different kinds of subordinate powers have been deployed historically: powers more or less independent of the prince and powers dependent on him. We might be more inclined to call the latter sort bureaucratic rather than military, but Shaftesbury thereby emphasized the coercive, and thus threatening, aspect of this political alternative. The evil that the Whigs constantly feared arising from a monarchy—absolute and arbitrary power—is obviously more likely to arise where the king's agents are entirely dependent on him and possess a monopoly of coercive authority than where they are independent powers with a stake in their own and others' freedom. "A standing force can be for nothing but prerogative, by whom it hath its idle living and subsistence."

Moreover, "history shows the power of peerage and a standing army are like two buckets, the proportion that one goes down, the other exactly goes up." Why? That same history shows that "standing forces, military, and *arbitrary government* came . . . plainly in by the same steps that the nobility were lessened." When the nobility was "in power and greatness," they did not "permit the least shadow of any of them." Not merely did the nobility stand as a safer mode of governance than military or bureaucratized rule, but it had the power and incentive to resist attempts by rulers to introduce the devices of "arbitrary government."[112] Shaftesbury here voices precisely the point Montesquieu and then Tocqueville later made when they called attention to the role of independent intermediate powers in society as a mode of resisting despotism.[113] Nothing in this idea requires or implies anything of civic humanism.

As violent as Pocock's interpretation of the role of the House of Lords is, even more so is his treatment of the fear of a standing army. According to Pocock, "the threats of military dictatorship . . . form the small change of standing army debate: . . . The more immediate threat [is] the corruption of Parliament: . . . The standing army appears in this context as an instrument of corruption rather than of dictatorship. The threat of rule by the sword is there, but it is muted." The real problem is "the presence of military men in Parliament as a specially dangerous form of placemanship." The army provides places with which the Crown can subvert the independence of Parliament, and once having done that, can prevail upon Parliament to support the very army that supplied so many of its members their places. "The professional officer is the cause as well as the effect of this corruption."

Evidence we have already seen strongly counters Pocock's claim that fears of military rule were "the small change" of the debate: they were rather, to escalate Pocock's metaphor, the Brinks trucks of Shaftesbury's concern. "If ever there should happen in future ages (which God forbid)," thundered Shaftesbury in the House of Lords in 1675, "a king governing by an army, without his Parliament, 'tis a government I own not, am not obliged to, nor was born under."[114] Not a corrupted Parliament, but no Parliament, not an army which offers places and positions to compromise the independence of

the *polites*, but genuine, no-fooling-around military rule—these are Shaftesbury's real fears.[115] They are little different from the fear that animated
those who spoke out on the army issue both before and after Shaftesbury.[116]
The issue underlying all such concern was "whether government should
move toward the absolutism of the continent or not."[117]

Pocock's tack on the army issue reveals extraordinarily well the truth of
the old adage "context is all." He comes to Shaftesbury with Harrington
filling his mind. Harrington said standing or professional armies are impossible, never to be achieved; Shaftesbury must, thinks Pocock, be responding
to Harrington, must be trying to show how a standing army is possible.
Pocock is certain, in other words, that Shaftesbury is answering a question
implicitly posed by Harrington: "A standing army is possible, Mr. Harrington, because the king can use it to corrupt Parliament and then induce the
corrupted Parliament to support it." This is not so much wrong as it is
wrong-headed, missing Shaftesbury's point and concern. The same can be
said for Pocock's treatment of the militia, the alternative to the professional
army. "The militia . . . could be seen as a means to the reactivation of
virtue"—thus says Professor Pocock, neatly attaching the supporters of the
militia to civic humanism. "The militia must, and can never be otherwise
than for English liberty, because else it destroy itself"—thus said the Earl of
Shaftesbury, neatly attaching his support for the militia to his opposition to
absolutist rule.[118] What Pocock sees as "most purely Harringtonian in all
this [are] the associated ideas of propertied independence and the militia,"
which are the center of "Harrington's theory of citizenship." Now, this may
or may not be Harringtonian, but it is not what Shaftesbury was saying. The
earl knew that the militia, composed of and under the control of the nation
itself, could not be used as an instrument of oppression. There is nothing
here of virtue, of *vivere civile*, of *ridurre ai principii*, of *polites* or *cives*. Instead, there is a hard-headed and realistic politician who appreciated the
role of force in politics, and who took his bearings politically not from Harrington but from the precedents "of former times," from "privileges" and
"rights" inherent in birth into the orders of English life, from the "rights,
privileges, and freedoms, which men now enjoy by the laws established,"
from "the great liberty we enjoy as Englishmen," from "the law and constitution of the government," which do not support "an absolute and arbitrary government." Shaftesbury thought in terms of the ancient constitution and customary rights, not Pocock's Harringtonian tradition of civic
humanism.[119]

The same distortions, deriving from the same causes, appear in Pocock's
discussion of parliamentary corruption. This last is, in his eyes, the truly
central issue, for it is the ultimate point of both the other two and provides
the link to civic humanism through the idea of citizen independence.
Pocock, as we have seen already, identifies court patronage through place-

men in Parliament as the chief threat to his Harringtonian affirmation of civic independence as the precondition for "the liberation . . . of personality, for free public action and civic virtue." It was the center, he says, of Harrington's "politicization of the human person."[120]

Shaftesbury's texts cohere very little with this reading of them, however. For an issue supposedly so much at the heart of his concern, he spent remarkably little space on it—perhaps one-half column out of nearly thirty columns in the "Letter from a Person of Quality." What he did say of it had none of the neo-Harringtonian overlay Pocock consistently gives it. Shaftesbury complained, for example, that "all places of profit, command, and trust [were] only given to the old Cavaliers." This sounds, in part at least, suspiciously like the kind of partisan complaint familiar to all students of political parties, for Shaftesbury coupled that complaint with the whining observation that "no man that had served or been of the contrary party, [was] left in any [offices]." The complaint was not about office holding as such, but about the exclusion of him and his supporters. More important, he saw this pattern of appointment as evidence for the conspiracy he saw afoot, a conspiracy to revive the old Civil War cleavages, to set aside the Act of Oblivion, to restore the Cavalier party and secure for it a victory in politics that it could not win in battle.[121]

Shaftesbury's other significant mention of the pensioners and placemen occurred in the context of his account of the "dread" many felt in anticipation of the parliamentary session of April 1675:

> The officers, court lords, and bishops were clearly the major role in the lords house; and they assured themselves to have the commons as much at their disposal, when they reckoned the number of courtiers, officers, and pensioners, increased by the addition of the Church and Cavalier-party, besides the address they made to men of the best quality there, by hopes of honour, great employments, and such things as would take.[122]

Shaftesbury's worry here was much simpler, and more obvious, than Pocock's high-falutin notion of citizenship. The influence the court had in Parliament would allow it to carry majorities there for principles and policies that Shaftesbury was convinced were nefarious. Dependence on the court was not presented here as an evil in itself, as a denial of the very *telos* of the human personality or anything of that sort, but because it could be a means to the accomplishment of very bad things. Shaftesbury's concern was not much different from that of present-day political analysts who point to the politics of pork and patronage as means whereby whoever controls those prizes can control outcomes in Congress, often to the detriment of the public good and contrary to the nation's true interests. There is nothing remotely "neo-Harringtonian" in this. So far as it was different from concern over pork-barrel politics, the difference lay in the more serious threat

Shaftesbury thought he discerned in the court policy that was being thus supported. The members of Parliament who succumbed to court blandishments were not merely supporting a misappropriation of public funds, they were furthering a policy aimed at "introducing an absolute and arbitrary government." That fear provided the context for Shaftesbury's denunciation of these practices.[123]

WHIG POLITICAL SCIENCE

One would never know from Pocock's account that Shaftesbury and his fellows foresaw so ominous an outcome as "absolute and arbitrary government." One would never realize from Pocock's account that passions ran very high on both sides, that some men, including Shaftesbury himself, ended up in the Tower, or in exile, or on the scaffold for what they said and did in the decade or so prior to the Glorious Revolution. One would hardly suspect from Pocock's account, in other words, that all this political "discourse" was related to politics. Instead of the passion of politics or the passion of philosophy, Pocock serves up colorless and odorless "paradigms," coupling and decoupling silently in the night.

All of this is done in the name of a more historically adequate account of political thought, which, Pocock insists, means one properly contextual.[124] But, ironically, it is precisely context that is lacking from his version. Or rather, he supplies his own context—his Harringtonian civic humanism— and pays altogether too little attention to what Shaftesbury and the others understood about their own context and how they understood their thought and action in relation to that context.

The arbitrariness of Pocock's treatment of context glows like neon if we consider the remarkably selective account he gives. He claims to present the thought of the Whig Opposition, but hardly mentions Milton. Nowhere does he mention Hugo Grotius. Nor does Algernon Sidney figure much in his story of "the Atlantic republican tradition," even though later Whigs, both English and American, looked to Sidney frequently and explicitly.[125] And of course there is Pocock's depreciation of Locke.[126]

Yet more telling is his omission of the political context proper.[127] The chief expression of the Shaftesburean position came in the "Letter from a Person of Quality," which announced its own occasion quite clearly in its subtitle: "Giving an account of the debates and resolution in the House of Lords, in April and May, 1675, concerning a bill, entitled, 'A Bill to Prevent the Dangers which may arise from Persons disaffected to the Government.'" The measure proposed in that bill to "prevent dangers" was an oath, drafted by Danby, to be subscribed by all officeholders, including members of both houses of Parliament, which would commit the subscriber to denying the legitimacy of all armed resistance to the king or any of his agents, and promising never to "endeavour the alteration of the government either in Church or State." Fifteen years after the Restoration and more than thirty years after the outbreak of the Civil War, the bill was attempting to commit the entirety of the political community to positions that would have made the Civil War impossible. It might thus be seen as a genially ineffective example of the "barn-door" phenomenon, common enough in politics not to require much comment.

Shaftesbury and his colleagues, however, saw it in a much less benign light, not as a foolish attempt to prevent an event that had occurred a generation in the past, but as an effort to revive the old battle lines and refight the old battles. Understood "in its whole extent," the oath was an effort

> to make a distinct party from the rest of the nation of the high Episcopal Man, and of the old cavalier; who are to swallow the hopes of enjoying all the power and office of the kingdom; being tempted also by the advantage they may receive from overthrowing the Act of Oblivion; and not a little rejoicing to think how valiant they should prove, if they could get any to fight the old guard over again, now they are possessed of the arms, forts, and ammunition of the nation.[128]

Despite what may appear to be hyperbolic rhetoric, there were, concludes Shaftesbury's biographer, "concrete issues at stake. . . . If Danby's test had been applied to all office-holders, justices of the peace and members of Parliament, it would have made difficulties for many conscientious people; it could have been the basis for a government purge; and it could have seriously embarrassed any attempts at "alterations" in the existing order."[129]

The oath, thought Shaftesbury, was a piece of a plot motivated by the twin forces of interest and revenge.[130] The plot was both subtle and complex: in forcing all men to swear the government of the church to be unalterable, the bill would "tacitly own it to be of Divine Right," even though that was contrary to the Oath of Supremacy that conceded the authority of the king over the church. For this grant of independence from king (and Parliament), the church would in turn "declare the government absolute and arbitrary, and allow monarchy, as well as episcopacy, to be *Jure Divino*, and not to be bounded or limited by any human laws.—And to secure all this they resolve to take away the power and opportunity of parliament to alter anything in the Church or State." The solemn declaration against nonresistance would play a major role in rendering the monarch absolute and unlimited, for the option of resistance was necessary to the preservation of the specific limits set to the powers of the king: "It is not out of the way to suppose, that if any king, hereafter, contrary to the Petition of Rights, demand and levy money by privy seal, or otherwise, and cause soldiers to enter and distrain for such illegal taxes, that in such a case any man may by law defend his house against them."[131] That is, unless he is bound by Danby's oath never to resist any agents commissioned by the king.

The plot was, then, in the first instance, a straightforward trade: the Crown "parts with its supremacy" over the church, and "in requital" the church supports the Crown's claims to divine right and absolute powers. The clergy, Shaftesbury asserted, had never been champions of "the rights and liberties of the people," either in England or elsewhere, if they had first been able to extract the independence they would acquire here.[132]

But there was a yet further step to this scheme: "As the top stone of the whole fabric, a pretence shall be taken from the jealousies they themselves have raised, and a real necessity from the smallness of their party, to increase and keep up a standing army." With the acquisition of a standing army, however, "the Cavalier and the Churchman will be made greater fools, but as arrant slaves as the rest of the nation."[133] The king and his very narrow circle of favorites (including, presumably, the Earl of Danby) would be the real beneficiaries; The original "party" of Cavaliers and churchmen would be thrust aside soon after the parliamentarians they would have helped defeat. Resistance to the plot, Shaftesbury implied, was in the interest of all.

The oath was the chief means (to that point) to effectuate a regime in which Parliament would be reduced to a nullity and the monarchy elevated to an absolutism; but the chief means whereby the oath was to be effected was Parliament. The forces of absolutism in the post-Restoration era operated differently, more subtly than in the pre–Civil War era. In the days of Charles I, the constitution itself was in contest; the question of who had what powers was directly raised, as the Crown attempted to rule without Parliament—attempted, for example, to raise money without parliamentary authorization. Shaftesbury did not identify that kind of outright unconstitutionality as the real danger posed by Charles II. (Unlike some other Whigs, he made light, for example, of the constitutional issues raised by the Declaration of Indulgence.)[134] Charles II and his minister Danby posed the far more subtle threat of subverting the constitution and the rights and liberties of Englishmen through actions themselves formally constitutional—adopted by Parliament—at least up to the last moment when, according to the scenario, the standing army would put an end to the very forms of liberty. This is the context in which Pocock's themes of corruption, standing armies, and the place of the House of Lords became important. According to the logic implicit in the constitution, Parliament is to guarantee the liberties of the community and to restrain the monarch.[135] Danby's devices for managing Parliament through the use of patronage, pensions, and outright bribery meant that Parliament could play its formal role in the constitution, but could yet fail to play its substantive role. "The oath rendered Parliament but a snare, not a security to the people."[136]

Danby provoked the new departure in Whig political analysis because "he strove to [accomplish] something which no one had previously achieved, control on the king's behalf of the House of Commons."[137] Danby's policies were demonstrating in practice, and Shaftesbury was attempting to demonstrate in theory, that the formal constitution was not enough. So far as Shaftesbury and the Whigs of the 1670s introduced any novelties into political analysis, it is here. So far as there is something Harringtonian or Machiavellian to this Whig political science, it is this appreciation of the politics—in contrast to the formal legal arrangements—of the constitution, and has nothing to do with Pocock's civic humanism.

The Shaftesbury Whigs were quite traditional in their political theory: they accepted either a historical-legal-traditionalist account of the ancient constitution or one or another form of Grotian (or Hookerian) contractarianism that cohered readily with the ancient constitution. They moved beyond that in the development of a political science that probed beneath the formal realities and presumptions of constitutional law to the actual operations of institutions. They injected this political analysis into an English political discourse that had been largely formalist, historical (in the sense of precedent-obsessed), and theological-moralistic (in its concern for the moral and scriptural grounds of obedience and resistance).

The Shaftesbury Whigs, in other words, accomplished in the seventeenth century what American political science claimed to have discovered for the first time in the twentieth—a "realistic" analysis of politics that does not take formal structures at face value but insists that the reality of politics is both more informal and more fluid than the formal or constitutional prescriptions suggest. Unlike the American "new" political science, however, the Whigs made no break with the prescriptive constitutional order; theirs was no "value-free" political science. The constitutional order as the Whigs understood it prescribed a "bounded" monarchy and the Whig political science took its bearings at all points from that prescription. Thus Shaftesbury objected to the effort on the part of the sponsors of the oath to remove all fear of popular resistance from the mind of the king. "There can be no distinction left between absolute and bounded monarchies, if monarchs have only the fear of God, and no fear of human resistance to restrain them. . . . They overthrew the government that propose to place any part of it above the fear of man."[138]

The Whig political science attempted to rally those in positions of power within the formal institutions to operate them so as to secure a limited rather than an absolutist monarchy for England. For the most part, that rallying took the form of exhortation: those in Parliament (especially) should do their duty to the country and not succumb to the private benefits proffered by the court. As Shaftesbury made clear in his warning to the Cavaliers and churchmen who were the instruments of the Crown in 1875, public duty to the constitution was identical with long-term self-interest as well. Shaftesbury did not call for a superhuman commitment to civic virtue or the public good.

But it was not all exhortation. Shaftesbury sought to reinforce those parts of the constitution that could be especially immune to the informal devices that threatened absolutism. In this context the House of Lords loomed large in his thinking, for the lords, independently possessed of wealth and position, might resist the court more readily than the commons, so long as the authority of their constitutional institution was maintained. That is one reason he rallied his fellow lords to repudiate any suggestion that peers could be denied their right to sit in the House for *any* reason, much less the failure to accede to Danby's test oath. With somewhat less success he attempted to persuade the House to preserve all its privileges, including the right of free debate, the right of supreme judicial appeal, and the right to be free from intimidation by the king or his agents.[139]

By jamming Shaftesbury into a civic humanist context foreign to him, Pocock has thus missed the structure, motives, and grounds of Shaftesbury's position. Not attending much to Shaftesbury's indication of his own concerns, but instead deploying his radioisotopic markers, he transforms Shaftesbury into his kind of Harringtonian. But the whole enterprise is based on a logical failure: Even admitting (*arguendo*) that these markers (e.g., independence of Parliament from the king) might be part of a civic humanist structure of thought such as Pocock assembles, it does not follow that the presence of any one (or more) of them necessarily implies the whole structure. As is the case with Shaftesbury, these elements can be part of quite other structures of thought and action as well. One can identify the character of a given body of thought only by attending to it and not to isolated fragments of it. Pocock, here as elsewhere, fails to adhere to the crucial maxim that we must first attempt to understand a thinker as he understood himself.

Many of the same difficulties vitiate Pocock's interpretation of Andrew Marvell's *Account of the Growth of Popery and Arbitrary Government*. Marvell's lengthy pamphlet contains many of the same themes and concerns as Shaftesbury's "Person of Quality" essay. Like Shaftesbury, Marvell took his point of departure from "a design" he had discovered "to change the lawful government of England into an absolute tyranny," and in this case, "to convert the established Protestant religion into downright Popery." The stakes, Marvell believed, were "as great and weighty as ever was any in England," because they "concerned our very being, and included our religion, liberty and property."[140]

The details of the "design" Marvell discovered differed somewhat from what Shaftesbury described. Writing more than two years later, he had many more events to sweep up into the pattern of duplicity, including a foreign-policy dimension that Shaftesbury had ignored. The conspiracy aligned king and court with the French king, the most powerful ruler in Europe, champion of Catholicism and the very model of the type of absolute monarch the Whigs dreaded. Contrary to his own public statements and the more or less settled policy desires of Parliament, Charles was duplicitously supporting Louis in his designs on the Dutch republic—a bastion of liberty and Protestantism—rather than allying with the Dutch to oppose Louis.

Like Shaftesbury, Marvell saw both political and religious dimensions to the conspiracy, but again the details differed. Marvell insisted that the conspiracy aimed to reintroduce Catholicism in England, although not for reasons of religious conviction. In fact, he praised those Catholics, including James, Duke of York, who acted sincerely on the basis of their faith, despite his own certainty that no religion was so "false and unreasonable," so "absurd," so marked by "cruelty" as "popery." The "persons that have . . . taken the work" of the conspiracy "in hand, are such as lie under no temptation of religion." As Marvell presented it, the aim of these plotters was somewhat obscure, but that apparent obscurity may have had more to do with limitations on what might and might not be said about the king than with any unclarity in his mind. Explicitly, he stated that the designers were "obliged by all the most sacred ties of malice and ambition to advance the ruin of the king and kingdom";[141] that is, the king was the chief victim and sheer malice the chief motive for the conspiracy. But Marvell regularly expressed allegiance to the convention that the king could do no wrong: if wrong was being done, it must be by others and against the will and interests of the king. Yet, like many of the Whigs we have previously encountered,[142] he implied that these unbelievers were promoting popery because, entirely unlike reformed Christianity, it was "compiled of terrors to the phancy, contradictions to sense, and impositions on the understanding," all of which fit men for slavish obedience. Thus the aim of the plot would be the institution of a religion of slavishness that would prepare the way for a political regime of slavishness.[143] The ultimate sponsor of such a plot therefore could be none other than Charles himself, or those in his circle who sought to please him. The instruments of the conspiracy included both foreign policies—for example, the machinations on behalf of Louis—and domestic policies—for example, Danby's test oath.

Marvell gets filed away in the neo-Harringtonian pigeonhole, however, because Pocock finds in him "the clearest of this group of statements of the theme of corruption by the executive."[144] Marvell did, indeed, devote a few pages to that subject, but Pocock leaves his readers with a misleading impression of its role in his treatise. Corruption, placemen, and related themes are but a few among a large set of evils that came under fire from Marvell's pen, and, as with Shaftesbury, his concern with them must be set into the broader context of his objections to royal policies aimed at overcoming the constitutional limits on the monarchy and imposing a new and objectionable religion on the nation. Those policies, to repeat, include many other practices that Marvell found equally or more objectionable.[145]

Indeed, Marvell called the discussion of parliamentary corruption (in the broad sense) a "digression"; it surely was not the center of his concern. Moreover, he presented it in such a way as to reveal very clearly that he grasped it altogether differently from Pocock's civic humanism (*vivere civile*). The problem with corruption is not the way it compromises or undercuts the specifically public or citizenly character of political actors, but rather the way it produces a potential conflict of interest. "No honorable person," concluded Marvell, "related to his Majestie's more particular service, but will in that place and opportunity suspect himself, lest his gratitude to his master, with his self-interest, should tempt him beyond his obligation there to the publick." The problem is not one peculiar to public life or public obligation, but is altogether parallel to conflicts of interest in the private sphere: "The same [consideration] excludes him that may next inherit from being guardian to an infant." This last could not be said if Pocock's special brand of republican virtue were the issue.

Once again, attention to the more specific context of Marvell's discussion clarifies its genesis and function in his argument. The discussion was provoked by the opening of the parliamentary session of February 1677. Parliament had been prorogued since November 1675, and the Whigs in Parliament raised the question whether such a long prorogation did not amount to a dissolution and whether, therefore, new elections were not necessary. The king and his supporters resisted this constitutional interpretation. Both groups were acting consistently with their overall strategies regarding Parliament. The court sought to get by with the minimum number of meetings of Parliament and therefore attempted to keep it out of session as much as possible. At the same time, the king sought to prevent new elections, for the Parliament of the mid-1670s was still the one elected in 1660, at the time of the Restoration. This Cavalier Parliament was relatively well disposed to the cause of the king and hostile to that of the king's opponents. The Whigs sought a new election because they were certain that opinion in the country was much more favorable to their cause by the mid-1670s than it had been in 1660; the King's efforts to avoid elections indicated that he agreed with this assessment.

In February 1677, after a prorogation of over a year, the Whigs attempted to declare the session illegal. They were eager not only to force elections, but also to assert the rights of Parliament to share regularly in governance. The Whig effort failed, however, and that failure stimulated Marvell to reflect on the role of officeholders and placemen in the House of Commons. His point was nearly identical to that of Shaftesbury: Parliament had an opportunity to assert its proper role in the constitution, but declined to do so because of the private benefits that some members received from the king. The court's ability to appeal to private interest prevented the constitution from operating properly in this case, and, Marvell feared, would prevent it from operating properly in general.

> How improper would it seem for a privy-counsellor if in the House of Commons he should not justify the most arbitrary proceedings of the council-table, represent affairs of state with another face, defend any misgovernment, patronize the greatest offenders against the kingdom . . . and extend the supposed prerogative on all occasions, to the detriment of the subject's certain and due liberties! . . . And whatsoever they may commit in the House of Commons against the national interest, they take themselves to be justified by their circumstances.[146]

Thus Marvell, too, missed Pocock's neo-Harringtonian moment.[147] If Harrington was the civic humanist Pocock presents him to be, then these early Whigs have nothing much to do with Harrington. They were, it is true, as little natural rights thinkers as they were civic republicans. But Pocock's interpretation of their thought in terms of the republican idea systematically stands in the way of understanding the development that soon occurred—the amalgamation of the Whig political science we have just discussed with a political philosophy of Lockean natural rights. By the time of *Cato's Letters* such an amalgamation had taken place, and it was in that form that Whig political science came to be a force in the era of the American founding. Pocock would make that amalgamation impossible, for he understands Whig political science to be part of his civic humanist tradition which, he insists, differs essentially and thoroughly from natural-rights-oriented politics.

Pocock's "neo-Harringtonian" Whig thinkers hold up no better as classical republicans à la Gordon Wood than they do as Pocockian civic humanists. They displayed little of what Wood identified as the central themes of the Opposition tradition. They were not republicans, much less classical republicans dedicated to self-abnegating public virtue and the organic polity. Natural law and the original contract, the ancient constitution and the historic rights of Englishmen—and virulent public anti-Catholicism—held the loyalties of these founders of the Whig movement, and remained the chief commitments of the Grotian Whigs of 1688–89.

Of the synthesizers, Bernard Bailyn is the only one whose characterization of the Opposition tradition truly reverberates with those early Whigs: They do believe in a conspiracy of power against liberty. They do sense the fragility of liberty, and they do assume that those in authority seek to destroy it. Above all, they do (emphatically) believe in conspiracies.

Of the three synthesizers, Bailyn is also best able to accommodate to the later emergence of a new comprehensive mode of Whig political thought (as in Cato), replacing the seventeenth century's Grotianism with the new

Lockean political philosophy and combining that with the Whig political science developed in the early days of the movement. Since Cato and his successors were indeed germinal for the eighteenth-century Americans, the synthesizers are correct to call attention to the Whig Opposition as an important ingress to the frame of political mind of the colonial and revolutionary Americans. Pocock and Wood, however, mischaracterize the political orientation they explored as an older republicanism, and thus miss its modernity. As a consequence they leave us with unintelligible events, such as the synthesis of incompatible liberal and classical positions, or implausible events, such as the transformation of one kind of political thought into its opposite with hardly anybody noticing.

Bailyn makes no such error, and thus he has no difficulty acknowledging the Lockean liberal dimension of the new republicanism. Nonetheless, he never adequately integrates the Lockean and other elements of his opposition tradition, and thus never provides a full portrayal either of the Opposition tradition itself or of the American thought supposedly built upon it. Bailyn points in the right direction, in other words, but his work must be supplemented with a more serious attempt to make Locke part of the story, and then to reinterpret the Opposition tradition the light of what comes into view with Locke. To the first of these tasks we must now turn.

PART THREE

Natural Rights
and the New Republicanism

CHAPTER SEVEN

Locke and the
Reformation of Natural Law:
Questions Concerning the Law of Nature

In 1688–89 the most Whiggish of the Whigs were Grotians; by 1750 or so, they were Lockeans.[1] The obfuscating theory of unicontractarianism has concealed the fact of this change so effectively that we have no real idea of how it came about or what it signifies.[2] But by the time the Americans began their serious thinking about politics, at the end of the Seven Years War, Locke was so firmly ensconced as the Whig theorist of the revolution that his immigration to America had been natural and easy.[3]

Only in the last half of the twentieth century are we in a position to piece together the first part of the story of Locke's Whig ascendancy, for only since mid-century has Locke's sole extended writing on the law of nature been available to scholars. In the early 1660s, while still a rather young scholar at Oxford, Locke offered a series of lectures in moral philosophy in connection with which he apparently prepared the untitled manuscript now known as *Essays on the Law of Nature* or *Questions Concerning the Law of Nature* (I shall refer to it by the latter title).[4] That manuscript presents what Locke assumed, but never developed or explicated fully in his published works: a relatively comprehensive theory of natural law. As Locke said at an especially pregnant moment of his *Second Treatise on Government*, "It would be besides [sic] my present purpose, to enter here into the particulars of the law of nature." As his editor, Peter Laslett, commented, "It was always beside his present purposes."[5] Although the *Questions* does not clear up every question one might wish to raise about Locke on the law of nature, it does go a long way toward remedying this so-noticeable omission in his published works.

The *Questions on the Law of Nature* not only presents Locke's views as of 1664, but it presents his considered judgments on the many important natural law theorists who preceded him, in particular Hugo Grotius. Close study of Locke's *Questions* reveals a deep and thoroughgoing critique of the Grotian natural law doctrine. Despite this, Locke incorporates certain emphases in his own doctrine that parallel themes in Grotius and that help begin to account for how Locke replaced Grotius as the leading Whig authority on politics over the course of the half century following 1688.

188 · Chapter Seven

Grotius, Pufendorf, Locke

It may seem quixotic to treat Locke's *Questions* as a critique of Grotius, for Grotius never once appears by name in Locke's book. Nonetheless, Grotius has an unmistakable presence there. For example, in Question I, Locke twice quotes Grotius at length, and without acknowledgment, a practice not at all uncommon in the seventeenth century, and one that Locke followed in the *Questions* fairly regularly, with respect not only to Grotius but to most of the other earlier writers on natural law. Locke quotes or refers to recent writers like Richard Hooker, Thomas Hobbes, and Samuel Pufendorf without mentioning their names or citing their books.[6]

Grotius appears, then, to be but one among many of the natural law writers considered by Locke in his *Questions*. Grotius nonetheless has a certain primacy among Locke's predecessors, a primacy reflected in the very structure of the work. Locke's *Questions* is divided into three parts, each devoted to a central issue concerning the natural law. The first section (Question I) addresses the existence of the natural law, the second section (Questions II–VII) the knowability of the natural law, and the third section (Questions VIII–XI) the obligatoriness of the natural law.[7] Grotius is so strong a presence in Locke's *Questions* that the latter's treatment of the knowability and obligatoriness of the natural law are largely but not exclusively critiques of the Grotian positions on the same topics.

The most obvious difference between Locke and Grotius on the law of nature is this: Where Grotius had daringly said that the law of nature would be even if there were no God, Locke insists that God is simply indispensable to the law of nature. Locke signals his dissent from Grotius from the first sentence of his book. The beginning point of his consideration of natural law is his recognition of the near universal recognition of the existence of God (fol. 9).[8] Locke's point in beginning there becomes clear shortly thereafter, when he proffers his definition of the law of nature as "the command of the divine will, knowable by the light of nature, indicating what is and what is not consonant with a rational nature, and by that very fact commanding or prohibiting" (fols. 11–12). Locke thus emphatically rejects the Grotian *etiamsi*. For Locke, no God, no natural law.

Moreover, immediately after providing his own definition, Locke explicitly challenges the definition Grotius had offered. Where the Dutchman had identified the law of nature as "a dictate of right reason," Locke pointedly insists that "less accurately some say it is a dictate of reason; for reason does not so much lay down and decree this law of nature as it discovers and investigates a law which is ordained by a higher power" (fol. 12). Locke's rejection of the *etiamsi* and of the Grotian idea of "a dictate of reason" are, of course, related, for (human) reason cannot in any sense be the source of the law if God necessarily is.[9]

Locke's insistence on the necessity of God signals a shift away from Grotius in one important respect, but not necessarily in the underlying concern that pushed Grotius toward his famous affirmation in the first place. Locke shows the same desire to find a natural law entirely independent of the particular—and variable—theological-scriptural politics of the various parties in post-Reformation Europe. The law of nature, Locke emphasizes throughout, is "a law which each individual can discover by that light alone which is implanted in us by nature." Revelation has nothing to do with it, "since we are inquiring, not into what man has the power to know when filled by the divine spirit, [nor] what he has the power to behold, illuminated by a light come down from the heavens, but what, by the power of nature and his own sagacity, man, equipped with mind, reason, and sense, can unearth and investigate" (fols. 11, 23–24). The God who stands as the source of natural law for Locke must be accessible entirely to the unassisted human reason; natural law depends on natural theology. The centerpiece of Locke's argument, therefore, is a rational proof for the existence of God, and thence of the existence and content of the natural law.

Locke announces the necessity of God very early in his work, but it is only rather late in it that the point of his insistence becomes clear: God is required for the law of nature to have obligatory force. That in turn is crucial, for the distinguishing feature of law as such is obligatoriness. "The formal definition of law seems to consist in its being the declaration of a supreme will" (fol. 12). Law, as opposed to mere advice or inauthoritative commendation, contains a "bond," that bond being "obligation," or "duty."[10] In the case of the law of nature, the "duty" is what "is incumbent on each individual as something which must be performed by reason of one's own nature" (fols. 12, 83). But nature itself cannot impose obligation: "No one can oblige or constrain us to do anything unless he has a right and power over us." Only if one can find in nature the will of a superior can there be said to be a law of nature, as opposed, say, to a natural good. Obligation, and thus law, can ensue only when there is an antecedent superior/subordinate relationship (fol. 83).[11]

In identifying obligatoriness as the core of what makes law law, Locke follows a very old tradition; as he himself says, this is the way the Roman lawyers saw it (fol. 83). Although they referred in particular to the civil law, Locke extends the point to the natural law. In so doing, Locke assimilates natural law to ordinary law, a procedure generally reminiscent of Grotius, even if Grotius did not make quite the same specific move regarding the obligatoriness of the natural law.

Grotius, it must be said, was far from satisfactory in explaining the obligatoriness of the natural law.[12] On the one hand, he and Locke appear to agree that obligation is a necessary feature of law: "We require obligation, for even the best counsel, if it is not obliging, comes not under the name of law (*lex*) or right (*jus*)." On the other hand, Grotius is seriously unclear when he attempts to specify the source of the obligatoriness of the natural law. "Natural law," he says, "is a dictate of right reason, indicating that any act, from its agreement or disagreement with a rational nature, has in it moral turpitude or a moral necessity, and consequently that such an act is either forbidden or commanded by God, the author of nature." The obligation, or "moral necessity" (logically) precedes, rather than, as in Locke, necessarily follows from the divine command. Although Grotius does not reject God as the source of obligation, he clearly does not agree with Locke that only God can oblige to the natural law. As Grotius says in the immediate sequel, "Acts for which such a dictate exists are either owed [obligatory] or unlawful *in themselves*, and are therefore understood as necessarily either commanded or forbidden by God." He distinguishes the natural law from the divine positive law precisely on the ground of the per se obligatory or forbidden quality the commands and prohibitions of natural law: the divine positive law "does not command or forbid acts which are *in themselves and by their own nature owed [obligatory] or unlawful*, but by forbidding makes them unlawful, by commanding makes them owed [obligatory]."[13]

Grotius blurs his own position by constantly conjoining the divine command or prohibition with the purely natural apprehension of the rational quality of the acts, but his point is clear enough: the obligation exists (logically) prior to and independently of the divine command; indeed, the divine command is posited only on the basis of the prior grasp of the natural law obligation. That the divine command reinforces the natural obligation in no way compromises Grotius's basic thesis: the obligation of the natural law would exist "even if there were no God." Nature is the sufficient condition for the natural law.

Although Grotius insists that obligation is a necessary condition for law, and that nature is the source of the obligation of the natural law, he hardly explores how. So far as he has an answer, it is something like this: The natural law expresses the requirements of human rational, social life, and to be true to their nature human beings are obliged to conform to the natural law.[14] Grotius's answer, then, is that the obligatoriness of the natural law derives from the content of the natural law, a position altogether different from Locke's, who finds legal obligation not in the law's content but in its source. The dispute between Grotius and Locke reproduces the long-lived dispute between legal rationalists and voluntarists.[15]

It is not difficult to identify at least one reason that held Grotius back from finding the defining quality of law in the will of a superior, as Locke did. The kind of law Grotius had most interest in developing was the law of nations, the law that prevailed between nations. But between nations there is no superior, and therefore, if the will of a superior is necessary for a law, there is no law of nations and no subject matter for Grotius's treatise.

Locke, of course, was not the only natural law writer to reject Grotius's derivation of obligation from the content rather than the source of the law. Writers like Thomas Hobbes, Samuel Pufendorf, and Nathaniel Culverwell also refused to follow Grotius on this issue, for his position was exposed to a very grave difficulty. Grotius appears able, at best, to generate a hypothetical obligation: to live according to one's nature, one ought to obey the natural law. But where is the obligation to live according to nature? What if one understands one's nature in the manner of Carneades? As Grotius concedes in a key place, perhaps the best one can really say is that it is "wise" to live according to the promptings of nature; he cannot establish the obligatoriness of the natural law.[16] Grotius is caught in a bind: he seeks a truly lawlike natural law, but his position on obligation prevents him from accomplishing his goal. Locke's strong affirmation of the voluntarist alternative reflects the failure of the Grotian rationalism.

Locke thus clings to and better fulfills the Grotian aspiration to a genuinely lawlike natural law. Indeed, in positing the source of law as the locus of its lawfulness, Locke surely does bring the natural law closer to law as we ordinarily experience it. Normally it is sufficient to identify a law as the duly expressed will of the appropriate authorities in order to recognize it as law.

At first sight it appears that Locke's break with Grotius is based on the influence of the German natural law writer Samuel Pufendorf. In 1660, only a few years before Locke began the *Questions*, Pufendorf published his first major work, *Elementorum Jurisprudentiae Universalis*, a new treatment of natural law aiming to synthesize the philosophies of Hobbes and Grotius. "No small debt . . . do we owe to Thomas Hobbes," Pufendorf conceded, "whose basic conception in his book *De Cive*, although it savours somewhat of the profane, is nevertheless for the most part extremely acute and sound."[17] At the same time, Pufendorf decreed Grotius "incomparable" and admitted to having "drawn much from that marvelous book, *De Jure Belli ac Pacis*."[18]

Despite his admiration for Grotius, Pufendorf was apparently sufficiently moved by Hobbes's notion of law as the will of a superior to endorse a definition of law that left no room for Grotius's *etiamsi*: "A law is a decree by which a superior binds one subject to him to direct his actions according to the command of the superior."[19] Just as in Locke's definition, no superior, no law. Although Pufendorf retains the Grotian formula of "dictate of right reason," nonetheless he silently corrects this in the direction of Locke's comment that reason does not "lay down and decree" law so much as "discover and investigate" it. Echoing Hobbes again, Pufendorf proclaims the laws of nature "to be merely certain conclusions, perceived by the reason" (i.e., not laid down by it), "touching things to be done and to be avoided."[20]

Pufendorf's influence on Locke's definition is even more visible in the latter's attempt to justify his definition in terms of criteria essential to all

law, criteria clearly adapted from Pufendorf's discussion of law. Locke identifies three, or perhaps four, such characteristics of law in Question I, all
taken from Pufendorf. As Robert Horwitz observes, Locke's definition of the
law of nature "seems fashioned to meet these criteria."[21] Later, in Question
VII, Locke adds another criterion, this too an essential aspect of law as presented by Pufendorf. The four- (or five-) part definition of law that Locke
takes over from Pufendorf is: (1) It is "the declaration of a superior will";
(2) it "prescribes what is to be done and what is to be avoided"; (3) "it is
binding upon men" in being (a) derivative from a superior and (b) properly
promulgated; and (4) it has sanctions attached to it.[22]

A final indication of the role of Pufendorf, again embodying a Hobbesian
theme, is the hard distinction Locke draws between natural law and natural
right: like his two most recent predecessors, but unlike Grotius and the rest
of the precedent tradition, Locke insists on the difference—amounting to
opposition—between natural right (*jus naturale*), as "free use of something," and natural law (*lex naturale*), as "that which either commands or
forbids some action" (fol. 11).[23] As Hobbes put it, law and right "in one and
the same matter are inconsistent."[24]

At the same time, there are definite limits to Locke's dependence on
Pufendorf. These, too, come to sight as early as the first Question and per-
vade the entire work. As eclectic as Pufendorf is in his effort to synthesize
Grotius and Hobbes, Locke appears to be much more so in his endorsement
of a variety of arguments on the natural law that even Pufendorf had found
too diverse to affirm. Almost two-thirds of Locke's first Question is given
over to five "arguments" that, he states, "persuade that a law of this kind
exists" (fol. 13). Locke's survey of arguments made on behalf of the law of
nature again interestingly echoes some passages in a parallel place in Pufendorf's *Elementorum*. Pufendorf introduced his consideration of the natural
law with the observation that "as to what the law of nature properly is, what
its fountain-head, as it were, and by what indication a matter is recognized
as pertaining to the law of nature, there is no complete agreement among
the learned."[25] That comment prefaces a survey by Pufendorf in which he
recognizes the differences between the various doctrines he reviews, and
takes a critical stance toward most of them. Locke, on the other hand, appears to endorse uncritically all five of the arguments he restates, many of
which were identical to ones rejected or much revised by Pufendorf.

One noticeable difference between Locke's list and Pufendorf's is that
Locke cites conscience as an argument for natural law and Pufendorf does
not, while Pufendorf cites the Roman lawyers' notion of natural law and
Locke does not.[26] The presence of conscience and the absence of Roman
law in Locke's version point to one feature of Locke's treatment that tends
to distinguish it more generally from Pufendorf's: echoes of Christian, or at
least theological, themes are much stronger right on the surface of Locke's

discussion than Pufendorf's. In addition to his explicit incorporation of Christian themes, Locke leaves the overall impression of retaining clearer and stronger ties with the natural law tradition as a whole than Pufendorf does. The latter clearly incorporates crucial Hobbesian elements in his doctrine, and either openly or tacitly departs from traditional (e.g., Thomist) natural law theory; Locke, as we have seen, also incorporates important Hobbesian elements in his assimilation of Pufendorf, but he blunts the effect of that by combining it with a more eclectic approach to the natural law. For example, the five arguments Locke endorses are an argument openly taken from Aristotle; an argument from conscience, supported by a quotation from the Roman poet Juvenal, but clearly reminiscent of passages in the New Testament;[27] an argument explicitly supported by a quotation from Thomas Aquinas, quoted earlier by Hooker; an argument concerning the relation between the law of nature and "the foundations of society," attributed to no specific earlier writer but distinctly reminiscent of Grotius; and finally a fifth argument, again unattributed, but reminiscent of Pufendorf's doctrine.[28]

Locke presents himself, then, as agreeing with Aristotle, Juvenal, the New Testament, Thomas Aquinas, Hobbes, Grotius, and Pufendorf. On the basis of such things, many scholars have concluded that Locke's "version of natural law is a continuation of the classical natural-law philosophy; . . . his conception of natural law is continuous with the classical Stoic and Christian tradition represented by Cicero and St. Thomas and coming down to Richard Hooker." Those scholars who emphasize Locke's continuity with the tradition are normally eager to parry any suggestion that Locke's philosophy represents "a deviation from [the tradition], as Hobbes's certainly is."[29]

Just how Locke's understanding of the natural law relates to various traditional notions is more difficult to say than these scholars make out, however. The most obvious difficulty, implicit in the contrast between Locke's treatment of these traditional views and Pufendorf's, is the fact that few, if any, of Locke's arguments ostensibly going to prove the existence of the law of nature deploy a notion of that law consistent with his own definition of it. The first argument appeals to a combination of Aristotelian points, one to the effect that "the function of man is activity according to reason," from which Aristotle, or Locke, concludes that "man must necessarily perform those actions which are dictated by reason" (fol. 13). But Locke has on the preceding page explicitly rejected the idea of law of nature as "dictate of reason," and therefore it does not appear that the "law of nature" Locke attributes to Aristotle can be the same as the law Locke seems to accept. Likewise, he imputes to Aristotle a notion of natural law as "certain principles of conduct which the entire human race recognizes and which men everywhere embrace with unanimous agreement" (fol. 13). Whether Aristotle recognized such a law has been questioned by many readers of Locke's

Questions, but the decisive point here is that whatever Aristotle may have thought, the universal natural law Locke attributes to him falls short of being a natural law in the Pufendorf-Locke sense: Locke's "Aristotelian" doctrine explicitly identifies "the origin" of this law as "nature" and not, as in Locke's own definition of natural law, the divine will (fol. 13).

Locke's second argument "persuading" to the existence of a law of nature "can be derived from men's consciences." The kind of law implicit in this argument also seems not to satisfy Locke's definition of the law of nature, for it does not satisfy that definition's requirement that the law be "knowable by the light of nature," where the "light of nature" appears to be reason, understood as "that faculty of the intellect by which it articulates and deduces arguments" (fol. 11; cf. fols. 12, 48, 49). Locke's own discussion, that is, is very like Pufendorf's, according to whom reason discovers laws of nature via discursive reasoning to conclusions.[30] For neither Pufendorf nor Locke, would conscience be an example of such reasoning.

Locke's third argument fails to embody the final clause of his own definition of the natural law. In the argument he cites "the very fabric of this world, in which all things observe a fixed law of their operations . . ." He quotes Hippocrates in support of this notion of law: "Each thing in both small and in great fulfilleth the task which destiny hath set down" (fol. 18). His definition of the law of nature points to a very different kind of law, however, for the law Locke has in mind "commands or forbids some action" (fol. 11). Locke's law of nature is prescriptive, not determinative. Pufendorf is quite explicit in his consideration of those "who call the law of nature that order implanted in all things by the Creator, whereby each thing does what is in accord with its nature and moves toward its destined end." He does not accept this as an adequate account, for he is "seeking such a law of nature as will direct the action of the rational man." Among other things, that means law "touches actions only through the intellect"; natural law addresses "voluntary actions," that is, "those actions placed within the power of man, which depend upon the will, as upon a free cause."[31]

Locke's final two arguments in favor of the existence of the law of nature do not so much say what the law is as describe what it does: it provides the foundation for social life by setting bounds to the power of rulers and establishing a ground for the obligation of pacts—a Grotian idea—and it establishes the basis for all morality. "Without the law of nature there would be no virtue, or vice, no praise for probity or punishment for wickedness" (fol. 20). Without law, there would be only human will, or human pleasure and interest, or blind impulse to guide action. Properly adumbrated, these two arguments could indeed be consistent with Locke's definition, although they neither imply it, nor it them.

At least three of Locke's five traditional arguments, therefore, rest on a notion of natural law inconsistent with his own definition. It is difficult not to be puzzled by Locke's procedure in Question I. Can he indeed be presenting five arguments from the tradition he accepts, arguments that betoken his essential continuity with the tradition? What, moreover, does it mean to affirm a continuity with a "tradition" that is quite disparate in itself? How can Locke both follow Pufendorf in rejecting important elements of the Grotian natural law and reaffirm the Grotian natural law?

Some scholars consider Locke to have been confused, but perhaps closer attention to his text can make his intention clearer without necessitating a last-resort explanation of that sort.[32] Locke introduces his five arguments in the following quite precise manner: "The following arguments persuade that a law of this kind exists" (fol. 13). But whom do they persuade? Locke does not say that they persuade him, and the lack of fit between his own definition of the law and most of these arguments suggests that it is not he whom they persuade. As we shall see later, there are yet stronger reasons to conclude that Locke does not in fact endorse these five arguments for the existence of a law of nature, but rests his acceptance of the law on an entirely different kind of reasoning.

LOCKE AND THE IMMANENT NATURAL LAW

If these arguments do not persuade Locke, then whom do they persuade? Let us suppose, as a hypothesis, that these are the arguments Locke finds persuade most or all of those who accept the natural law. These are the generally persuasive arguments; they help account for the widespread belief in natural law. As such, they pose a question to Locke the young philosopher: Are they worthy of credence? That is the question he will more or less follow out in the remainder of the *Questions*, especially in the next section of disputation, where he investigates the issue of how the law of nature is known and along the way reconsiders and rejects the "persuasive" arguments he presented in Question I.

Questions II–VII constitute by far the longest section of the manuscript, both in the number of questions and in the number of pages. The section is devoted to the issue of "by what means the law of nature is known," a question of utmost importance because of its central relation to the problem of promulgation: in order for the law of nature to be a law, it, like all law, must be promulgated—known or knowable (fol. 22). If the law is not sufficiently promulgated, it cannot be obligatory, for humanity cannot be bound to follow a law insufficiently declared to it. Likewise, an unpromulgated law is contrary to the very nature of law as a rule for governing voluntary actions.[33] Within the tradition, a variety of answers had been given as to the precise mode in which the natural law is promulgated. Many argued that through conscience or some kind of innate knowledge the law of nature is "written in the hearts of men." Some argued that the principles of the natural law are self-evident truths of the practical reason. Most followed Thomas in seeing the natural inclinations as indications of duties under natural law.

Surely the most striking and unique feature of Locke's *Questions Concerning the Law of Nature* is his treatment of the theme of promulgation. Whereas much of the rest of the discussion retains close ties to one or another of his predecessor natural law writers, he breaks almost completely with all his predecessors, including Grotius, on promulgation.[34] His positive argument on promulgation is, to say the least, disappointing. Less than a short paragraph suffices to contain it all, and in that short passage he says little that is truly helpful in understanding how the law of nature, as a set of substantive rules, is promulgated (fols. 60–61). His negative, or critical, argument, on the other hand, is lengthy, acute, and deep-going. The John Locke who was to explode on the world almost three decades later in the *Essay Concerning Human Understanding* is unmistakably present in this part of the *Questions*; Locke the epistemologist clearly has found his voice here. In a series of arguments reminding very much of Book I of the later *Essay*, Locke succinctly and successively rejects all the modes of promulgation that had been identified by earlier theorists.[35] Not tradition, not conscience, not innateness or inscription, not self-evident principles of reason, not natural inclinations—none of these constitutes a promulgation of the law of nature.

While exploring the various modes of promulgation in the second section of the *Questions* Locke also reconsiders those arguments favoring the existence of the law of nature he had sketched in Question I.[36] The connection between the arguments presented in Question I and Locke's investigation of the promulgation issue derives from the fact that most of the arguments for the existence of the law of nature in Question I take as their point of departure some claim about the way in which natural moral principles are present for or given to human beings. The arguments proceed from a claim about the presence of moral standards to the existence of a natural law; the discussion of promulgation proceeds in the reverse direction, but the relevant considerations are just the same.

Most striking in Locke's second treatment of the ways in which the law of nature may be present to human beings is the vehemence with which he denies the premises from which the arguments in Question I proceeded. This is especially clear with regard to the first argument, allegedly taken from Aristotle. Locke attributes to Aristotle the view that "'this natural law is that law which has everywhere the same force' from which it is rightly inferred that there exists some law of nature, since there exists some law, which obtains everywhere" (fol. 13). Locke's elucidation of the reasoning according to which the law of nature is inferred, however, reminds far more of Grotius than of Aristotle, who is famous for having said not what Locke puts into his mouth but rather that all natural right is changeable.[37] Locke's

Aristotle reasons, however, that "there exist certain principles of conduct which the entire human race recognizes and which men everywhere embrace with unanimous agreement; which could not have come about unless it had its origin in nature" (fol. 13).

Whether Locke understood this to be a distortion of Aristotle or not is difficult to say with any certainty; it is far easier to judge that Locke most likely came into contact with this argument in this form in the pages of Grotius. Locke may have meant to signal Grotius's Aristotelian roots, but whatever his intent, he quite accurately reproduced an important part of Grotius's position regarding the promulgation of the natural law.

Grotius had innovated on the question of promulgation, just as he had on other issues. He identified two methods for determining whether something "is or is not part of the law of nature," that is, whether it is known as a law of nature. The first method, the a priori method, is the more philosophic, the more "subtle"; it requires showing the "necessary agreement or disagreement of anything with the nature of a rational and social being." The a priori method, in other words, expresses the core ground of the Grotian law of nature. The a posteriori method is "more popular" than the other; it identifies the law of nature in terms of what is accepted as such "among all, or among all the more civilized nations." This latter method has less "certainty" than the former, for it does not display the inner necessity that makes something part of the law of nature, as the a priori method does. Nonetheless, it has a real measure of authority for Grotius, for, as he says, "a universal effect requires a universal cause"; universal agreement must derive from "the common sense of mankind," or from nature, or from "correct inference from nature." This is the Grotian argument Locke brings into Question I. Although Grotius gives a privileged position, in theory, to the a priori method, in practice he relies heavily on the a posteriori or popular method. What is generally or widely accepted is both more effective and more known; "subtle" reasonings such as the a priori method involves are not the stuff by which practical life is governed, and Grotius's intentions are importantly practical.[38] Locke's first argument in Question I refers to Grotius's a posteriori method, even while anomolously attributing it to Aristotle, and his Question VII contains an extended discussion of the validity of this method.[39]

Although Locke fails to mention Grotius by name, he paraphrases the relevant Grotian text: the consensus on moral rules must point to the law of nature, Locke hypothesizes; "since they [the rules of conduct] are the same in all men, [they] can have no other author than god and nature" (fol. 67).[40] Yet, Locke insists, there is in fact no such universal agreement on conduct or on the standards according to which conduct is judged.[41] The "consensus of mankind" does not indicate the content of the natural law because "there exists among men no common consensus concerning right conduct. . . .

There exists virtually no vice, no violation of the law of nature, no vicious-ness, which will not be quite evident to anyone who consults and observes the human events [of his own time] as not only something allowed privately somewhere in the world, but also ratified by public authority and practice. Nor has there existed anything so disgraceful in its own nature that it has not in some place been sanctioned by religion or considered as a virtue and exalted with praise" (fol. 68). Since there is no practice that is universally held to be part of the law of nature, or morally correct, Locke concludes, "were the consensus of mankind to be considered the rule of morals, there would either exist no law of nature, or this law would vary from place to place; one thing is considered virtuous in one place and vicious elsewhere; and vices themselves are transformed into duties" (fols. 69–70).

Grotius had sought and claimed to discover a natural law which was in-deed effective in the world, as witnessed by its widespread acceptance. Grotius's law of nature, like that of the Thomists before him, is natural, in that it is present in the world—in Grotius's case, in actual universal or very widespread practices and opinions. Locke severs the natural law from nature in that sense. It lacks immanence; it is neither known nor practiced in the world; surely it is not universally practiced. It is, at least up until Locke's own revelation of it, definitely not an "effective truth."

Although Locke cannot have been persuaded of the existence of the natu-ral law by the "unanimous agreement of the entire human race," because he is very far from believing that there is such a consensus among humanity, he nonetheless affirms his knowledge of both the existence and content of the law, presumably on quite other grounds, because he pronounces many of the practices of mankind to be in "violation of the law of nature" (fol. 68). The clear implication of Locke's statements in Questions I and VII is that the practices to which he refers in VII do not derive from nature. As he puts it in Question I, "If the laws were positive, and established by men at their pleasure, without any prior notion of law itself or of obligation, they would not so resemble one another everywhere, nor would they be in such close agreement with one another" (fol. 14). But they do not resemble one an-other; they are not in close agreement, and thus these human laws and practices bespeak not natural but positive law.

Even in Question I Locke retreats from his affirmation of universal con-sensus, in this following Grotius again, up to a point. He concedes that the law is not known universally, and that "therefore, we must consult not the majority of mankind"—to say nothing of the universality—"but the sounder and more perceptive part" (fol. 17). The majority will not do, for, as Locke brings out later, in Question II, "most mortals have no knowledge of this law, and nearly all have different opinions concerning it" (fol. 33).

Locke retreats even further, however. Even the "sounder part" cannot be all taken as knowers of the law of nature, because "this sounder part of mankind does not fully agree what the law of nature is, what its certain and known edicts are" (fol. 17). The law of nature is immanent neither to all mankind, nor to the majority, nor to the "sounder part," for the empirical reality is massive disagreement. If we look to established practice, we see only relativity.

Locke has yet one further fallback position within the dialectic of his first argument for the existence of the natural law. Although the only uniformity in what human beings take the natural law to be is variability, nonetheless "concerning this law all hold the same opinion, and differ only in its interpretation; for all recognize that vice and virtue exist by nature" (fol. 17). The nearly universal variation in what people take the content of the law to be is less important than the universal agreement that nature is the source of moral distinctions; the differences are mere differences of "interpretation" of a universally recognized law. Locke thus retreats to a second-order immanence: the law's content is not present in universal or widespread or even elite opinion and practice, but the law's existence is.

Yet even this fallback position must also be among those arguments that persuade others and not Locke, for again he denies in his own name the premise upon which it is built. In Question IV he reiterates the relativist themes we have already noted, repeating the claim that "when it comes to this law, men depart from one another in so many different directions" (fol. 38). The problem is not only the familiar one conceded in Question I, that "in one place one thing, in another something else, is declared to be a dictate of nature and of right reason; and what is held to be virtuous among some is vicious among others." More significant in our present context than that "some recognize a different law of nature" is that "others [recognize] none." Locke claims to know of people, those closest to nature in fact, who "live ignorant of any law, as if they needed to take no account at all of what is right and virtuous" (fol. 42; cf. fol. 9). Human beings do not agree even on the second-order immanence of the natural law.

So, Locke's first argument for the existence of the law of nature not only evokes a conception of law at odds with the one he himself endorses, but it also rests on a premise he explicitly denies, even when he restates that premise to make it less vulnerable to objections that can be raised against it in its original (Grotian) form. The same, more or less, must be said for his second argument for the existence of the law of nature. The second argument looks not to the uniform practices of humanity, but to the phenomenon of conscience. The argument from conscience almost begins where the argument from universal consensus leaves off: it recognizes that human beings act in ways contrary to the law of nature, but notes that when they do so, the conscience pronounces a verdict of guilty. "That verdict which each pronounces upon himself is evidence that there exists a law of nature" (fol. 17; cf. fols. 67–68).

Again, however, as the manuscript proceeds, Locke denies the premise on which the argument from conscience is built. In the all-important Question VII, Locke considers at somewhat greater length the theses raised in Question I about the conscience. Not only "is one thing considered virtuous in one place and vicious elsewhere; and vices themselves . . . transformed into duties," but when men perform "actions which seem . . . vicious and impious . . . they have felt none of the lashes of conscience" (fol. 70). Human beings feel the "lashes of conscience" not when they violate the law of nature but when they violate the standards set by "dominant opinion" (fol. 70). No matter how vicious an action may be, no matter how much it runs counter to the dictates of the law of nature, "that internal goad of the heart, which usually wounds and torments those guilty of a crime," will not operate unless the action counters settled social opinion about morality. If it does not do so, transgressors will "consider their action, whatever it was, not only permissible but even something praiseworthy" (fol. 70). Conscience, another potentially immanent mode of the presence of the natural law, betokens not that law, but rather "the power of custom and opinion," and these, we have already seen, do not derive from or indicate the presence of the law of nature.

We have already noticed that Locke's third argument for the existence of the law of nature appears almost irrelevant to the law of nature understood as a moral law governing the voluntary actions of human beings, for it refers to a directive law from which all things "depart . . . not as much as a nail's breadth" (fol. 18). Nonetheless, this third argument cannot be passed over quite so quickly, for the chief authority, unusual because cited by name here, is Thomas Aquinas, the most important thinker in the entire Christian natural law tradition. As several astute readers of Locke's *Questions* have pointed out, the passage Locke quotes from Thomas refers to the eternal law and not the natural law, perhaps confirming its irrelevance to the natural law understood as a moral law.[42] However, since Thomas understands the natural law to be a subclass of the eternal law, what is true of the genus eternal law must also be true of the species natural law. The "participation of the eternal law in the rational creature is called the natural law." Human beings partake in the eternal law governing all of creation "in an intellectual and rational manner."[43] Thus the eternal law has for human beings the character of a voluntary or moral law. Locke obscures this sense of Thomas's law in the way he brings it into his first question, and especially by his quotation from Hippocrates, but it lurks somewhere beneath the surface.

According to Thomas, "all things partake somewhat of the eternal law, insofar as, namely, from its being imprinted on them, they derive their respective inclinations to their proper acts and ends." Most of created being partakes in the eternal law in a nonrational manner—the law merely sets the principles of their action, and they unknowingly obey it. The law of gravitation satisfies this notion of eternal law, for it formulates the "inclination" of material bodies in their motions vis-à-vis each other.

The law of gravitation is not a Thomistic natural law, however, for beings do not participate in it rationally; No more than the oceans or the planets have human beings any choice about obeying the law of gravitation. The eternal law "imprints" on all beings "their respective inclinations to their proper acts and ends," and human beings are no exception to this. "The rational creature . . . has a share of the eternal reason, by which it has a natural inclination to its due act and end." The natural inclinations do not determine human actions so much as set the proper ends for actions that human beings rationally and voluntarily pursue. The natural inclinations are thus the means by which the Thomistic natural law is promulgated to humanity. So far as Locke's third argument, his Thomistic argument, points to the Thomistic natural law theory, it points to the natural inclinations as the way in which the natural law is known or knowable.[44]

Locke treats the Thomist argument in much the same way as he treated the two previous arguments on behalf of the natural law: it may persuade some, but it apparently does not persuade him, for he denies its central tenet. According to Question VI, the law of nature "cannot be known from the natural inclinations of mankind" (fol. 61). This claim appears in one of the Questions in which Locke does not explain his answer at length, but its importance is no less—indeed, is much greater—than many of the questions Locke addresses at great length. Its importance is so great, to repeat, because Locke's denial of the natural law implications of the natural inclinations amounts to a rejection of the Thomist natural law and thus of the third argument cited on behalf of the natural law in Question I.

Although Locke does not expand on his brief denial of the Thomist theory of the natural inclinations in Question VI, his argument elsewhere allows us to reconstruct the main outlines of his reasoning against the Thomist view. The relevant reasoning is similar but not identical to the reasoning used to reject the Grotian argument from consensus and the Christian argument from conscience. The Thomist view is relatively secure against the arguments used against the other two positions, for Thomas merely affirms that there are natural inclinations pointing to the proper ends. These require completing by human rational and voluntary acts, and therefore the mere failures of agreement or of conformity to the natural law of which Locke made so much, relative to the consensus and conscience arguments, are not so relevant to Thomas. Such empirical failures do not ipso facto speak against the Thomist claim that the natural law can be known through the natural inclinations. According to Thomas, human beings can fail properly to obey their natural inclinations, because those address the human intellect rather than determine human actions.

Seeing the Thomistic doctrine in this manner suggests a pattern to Locke's "arguments" on behalf of the natural law: they move from the doctrine holding the natural law to be most immanent in the world, the argument from universal consensus, through a variety of reformulations that posit lesser degrees of immanence, culminating now in Thomas's natural inclinations, nowhere near as immanent as universal consensus or conscience. Nonetheless, the Thomistic doctrine does posit a mode of immanence for the natural law, for the inclinations are given, present, and more or less effective forces in the world.

Implicit in Locke's standard response to all the other arguments for an immanent natural law lies the likely basis for Locke's firm conclusion that the natural inclinations do not supply any knowledge of the law of nature. Although the fact of dissensus does not of itself refute the Thomist position, it, together with widespread ignorance and disobedience, speaks strongly against it. If the natural inclinations point to the precepts of the natural law, one would have to expect a real presence of the natural law in the world, in human actions, and in human standards of praise and blame. But the absence of such natural law standards is precisely what Locke devotes Question VII to showing; moreover, he argues in Question IV that those closest to nature behave least in conformity with the law of nature (fols. 40–42).

Locke's truly decisive reason for rejecting the Thomist doctrine stems from his very different reading of what the natural inclinations actually incline toward. "Those who have no other guide than nature herself, among whom the dictates of nature are least corrupted by positive regulations concerning morals, live ignorant of any law, as if they needed to take no account at all of what is right and virtuous." Among these natural peoples "there appears not even the slightest trace of piety, gentleness, good faith, chastity, and the other virtues, but they spend their lives wretchedly in rapine, theft, debauchery, and murder" (fol. 42). In Question XI, Locke responds to those who "seek the principles of morals and the rule of life from the natural appetites and inclinations of men . . . as if what is morally best is the object most men strive for" (fol. 116). Although Locke here explicitly addresses other theorists than Thomas, nonetheless the position described is Thomas's. Locke finds this a defective approach, because if this is the ground for the law, that is, for the duties of human life, then "the condition of human life is such that it would not be lawful for a man to yield anything of his own right or to benefit another without the certain expectation of profit" (fol. 116). The point of Locke's rebuttal is this: The natural inclinations cannot be the source of a natural law of the type Thomas commends because the natural inclinations impel toward one's own profit, advantage, or benefit only. Such is the lesson Locke draws from his observation of human customs and human history. The natural inclinations are self-regarding and thus cannot be the source of the social virtues Thomas identifies as simply crucial parts of his law of nature. If the law of nature provides for the sorts of things Thomas says it does, the natural inclinations cannot be the source of its precepts. Locke states the very same point in much starker terms in his later *Essay Concerning Human Understanding*: "Principles of action indeed there are lodged in men's appetites, but . . . if they were left to their full swing, they would carry men to the overturning of all morality. Moral laws are set as a curb and restraint to these exorbitant desires."[45] Locke affirms that there are "natural inclinations," but they are not moral in character, that is, they do not point toward a moral law of nature.

Ultimately, Locke is driven toward this manner of treating the natural inclinations not only by his observations of the inclinations at work, but by his adoption of a conception of nature according to which "in her working nature is the same and uniform" (fol. 40). Nature is pure immanence—what works everywhere the same. Thomas, following Aristotle, was deploying a conception of nature of a different sort: nature exists as tendencies and ends; nature often fails in her operations.[46] For Locke that would be impossible; nature is the manifold of effective causes. In his conception of nature, in other words, we see tracks of the new science, traces of the influence of Descartes, Bacon, and even of Machiavelli. This conception of nature is nearly the deepest element in Locke's doctrine of natural law, because it is the very immanence of nature as he now understands it that compels him to reject all immanentist versions of the natural law.

The very structure of the second major section of the *Questions* reflects the concern with the immanence of the natural law as we have discerned it in following out the arguments posed in Question I. The law of nature, to be natural, must be knowable "by the light of nature," that is, it must be "the kind of truth whose knowledge man can, by the right use of those faculties with which he is provided by nature, attain by himself and without the help of another" (fol. 23). Locke examines "three means of knowledge," which might be considered natural ways of coming to know the law of nature. The first, inscription, is a clear instance of the kind of immanentism we have seen Locke to be rejecting throughout his *Questions*: "There are some who judge that the law of nature has been born in us and so graven in the minds of all men that there is no one who comes into the world whose mind does not carry these very characters and marks of his duty graven within him" (fols. 24–25). Of course, all the evidence of a relativist sort that Locke cites and that we have already noticed in other contexts directly refutes this kind of claim for the presence of the natural law in the "hearts of men" in an immediate and innately given manner.

Tradition, the second "means of knowledge" Locke takes up in his second section, likewise affirms an immanent natural law: its content is present to humanity in the body of opinions and precepts "handed down to us by others" (fol. 21). Although Locke emphasizes the power of tradition to shape human opinions of virtue and vice, he strongly denies that tradition provides knowledge of the law of nature. "In such a great variety of traditions, warring among themselves, it would be impossible to establish what the law of nature is, difficult even to judge what is true, what false; what is law, what opinion; what nature commands, what interest, what reason persuades us of, what civil society teaches" (fols. 28–29). Locke thus denies to the law of nature another mode of immanence. Such is the dominant thrust of the *Questions*: he shows that most, perhaps all, of those who have accepted the teaching of a law of nature have understood that law to be immanent in one way or another. Locke goes out of his way both to bring out that fact and at the same time to criticize sharply all the forms he knew of in which the law was held to be immanent.

NATURAL LAW: NATURAL SOCIABILITY AND NATURAL MORALITY

Locke's last two arguments allegedly persuading of the existence of the natural law also raise the kinds of issues of immanence we have been considering, but the real focus shifts to other matters. In his consideration of the themes raised by these arguments Locke attempts to supply an account of why people so persistently but unjustifiably posit a natural law of the immanent sort. By disposing finally of the immanent natural law, Locke completes his preparation of the ground for his introduction of his more Pufendorfian transcendent natural law.

The fourth argument Locke brings forward for consideration "derives from human society": the law of nature appears to be prerequisite to the possibility of "association or union of men among themselves," for society depends, on the one hand, on a "constitution of a regime" whereby the powers of rulers and the duties of subjects are specified and, on the other, on "the keeping of covenants" (fols. 18–19). The law of nature, according to this argument, supplies the moral glue of obligation to ground these two all-important sets of practices grounding human society. Echoes of Grotius's law of nature, making for or deriving from human sociability, are very apparent here. The Grotius connection points to the broader theme implicit in this argument: the law of nature as thus understood confirms or assumes that human beings are sociable by nature.

Locke himself is no more persuaded by this Grotian argument regarding the character of the law of nature than he was by the Dutchman's argument regarding consensus. In order to appreciate the force of Locke's reply to this argument, one must note that Locke takes for granted that human society, "association or union among men," does exist. That is not at issue; all that is at issue is whether that fact implies or depends upon the existence of natural law. Horwitz pointed out one key fact—"Locke's acknowledgement"

(I would add, insistence) "that natural law is hidden from men and therefore is, at best, known to very few."[47] If most human beings do not know the natural law—if, in fact, there are some societies in which no human being knows it—then knowledge of the natural law must not be necessary for the cohesion of society (fols. 33, 38, 41–42, 64–66, 68–72).

The kinds of human agreements or consensus that ground regimes or support contract do not, according to Locke, necessarily point to or rely on the law of nature at all. In the important seventh Question, the chief locus of his response to Grotius, Locke not only denies the existence of general consensus, but such consensus as he admits to exist rests on an altogether different foundation. He divides consensus into two types—"positive" and "natural." According to Locke, "a positive consensus [is] one which issues from a compact, either tacit, as when some common human necessity or advantage draws men to it, . . . or expressed" (fol. 63). Locke denies any natural law connections to such compacts: "Neither of these kinds of agreements proves the existence of a law of nature at all, since they both depend on a compact, and issue from no principle of nature whatsoever" (fol. 63). If such compacts have nothing to do with the law of nature, then the law of nature must not be necessary for their force, as the fourth argument in Question I implied. The force of contract, Locke suggests, derives not from the law of nature but from the "common human necessity or advantage" that drew men to make it in the first place.[48]

The independence of constitution and compact from the natural law not merely undermines one of the standard arguments for the existence of natural law, it also removes one of the props for the doctrine intimately associated with the law of nature in the thought of Locke's most important recent predecessor, Grotius. According to Grotius, natural sociability and the law of nature are two sides of the same coin, more or less. Locke traces the grounds of compact not to the natural law but to "common human necessity or advantage." Locke, in other words, opens up the possibility of a thoroughly individualistic interpretation of social life: human society does not imply natural sociability. Here Locke appears to break not only with Grotius but with Pufendorf as well, for the German thinker had insisted on the necessity of natural sociability in his attempted synthesis of Grotius and Hobbes.[49]

Locke drives home the anti-Grotian and implicitly individualist bearings of his observations by introducing into Question VII a thoroughgoing critique of Grotius's entire enterprise of a law of nations built upon a law of nature grounded on natural sociability. "It is clear," Locke says, "that the common agreement on the treatment of envoys which has obtained among all nations is . . . positive agreement and does not imply a law of nature" (fol. 63). The right of envoys was, of course, a major theme in Grotius's treatise, and although the Dutchman for the most part treated the relevant laws as derivative from the *jus gentium* and not from the law of nature itself,[50] yet the reason Locke provides against a natural law grounding the "treatment of envoys" speaks very broadly against Grotius's doctrine as a whole: "By the law of nature all men should be friends to one another and joined together" (fol. 63). If, Locke is saying, the law of nature derives from and expresses the principles of human sociability, then the very division of mankind into separate and potentially warring nations is itself contrary to the law of nature. If so, then it makes no sense to derive a law of nations—which includes, among other things, rules for regulating the relations among separate and potentially or actually hostile nations—from the law of nature. The Grotian enterprise, in other words, is self-contradictory.

Locke suggests in this context, as an alternative to Grotian natural sociability, the possibility "that in the state of nature war is common, and there exists among men a perpetual, mutual, and internecine enmity" (fol. 63). This is, I believe, the sole reference to the state of nature in the *Questions*. Although Locke explicitly leaves it an open question as to which alternative view of the natural condition—a natural sociability or a natural separateness—is truer, nonetheless he quite unmistakably suggests that the latter view fits the phenomena better, including especially the phenomena of compact and legation.[51]

The fifth and final argument that Locke brings forward for inspection in Question I serves as a kind of culmination to the entire line of discussion those five arguments set off. "The fifth argument is that without the law of nature there would be no virtue or vice, no praise for probity or punishment for wickedness; where there is no law [there can be] no wrong, no guilt" (fol. 20). As stated, Locke clearly and decisively rejects this argument. As we have already seen, he traces human practices of identifying virtue and vice—praising and punishing them respectively—to forces quite other than the law of nature.

Yet, Locke says, "I hardly think that these opinions [about morals] are derived from nature, but they spring from some other source." Even if they happen to coincide in content with the law of nature, nature is not their source: "Men are not instructed by nature, but by men" (fol. 42). Nature is not the source of the human positing of virtue and vice, and yet human beings regularly consider it to be, and thus are readily persuaded of the existence of a natural law. The moral instruction human beings receive is such that they easily fall into the error of attributing to nature what they come to believe as a result of the influence of other human beings (fol. 42):

> These opinions concerning what is right and virtuous which we embrace so firmly are, for the most part, the kind which are infused into our minds, at an age when our minds are little on their guard, when we are still of a tender age, before we can

yet form a judgment concerning them or notice how they insinuate themselves. They are instilled by our parents or teachers and by others with whom we associ-ate. . . . And so, when these opinions have slipped into our minds in this way . . . without our noticing it, they take root in our hearts. . . . And they also strengthen their authority by the common custom, agreements and praise of those men with whom we associate. (fol. 43)

The result of this process of youthful social indoctrination is that "we think we must conclude, that, since we observe no other origin for them, these opinions are inscribed in our hearts by God and nature" (fol. 44). Along the way, Locke insinuates that "all hope for a future life" is acquired in the same manner (fol. 43).

Once these opinions of morality and religion have been acquired in this unwitting manner, there is a continuing reason to cling to them all the more firmly and to insist on their natural or divine origin. "And inasmuch as we establish these as rules in the daily course of our life, were we to doubt that these constitute the law of nature, we would be unsure both of our future life and repent of our past" (fol. 44). On moral matters, then, human beings commit a widespread theoretical error, but one with grave practical conse-quences for the way they shape their lives. "We embrace with all our might those opinions of our earliest youth, . . . set a high value on them, stubbornly believe in them"; and perhaps most relevant to Locke's own enterprise, "nor do we suffer anyone to call them into question" (fol. 44).

Locke's five arguments, then, do not persuade him of the existence of the law of nature, but they are designed to reveal to the attentive reader why Locke retreats from all versions of the immanent natural law of the tradi-tion. At the same time, he shows how deep-going and, so to speak, natural it is for human beings to attribute their moral notions to nature, and how risky it is to do what Locke himself is doing, to question that attribution.

Transcendent Natural Law

Locke does not refute the immanentist version of natural law for the sake of rejecting natural law altogether. He insistently identifies himself as a devo-tee of natural law. He rejects the traditional forms of natural law in favor of a new transcendent kind of law. Pufendorf had already paved the way, but Locke develops his version of natural law quite differently from the way taken by his distinguished predecessor. Locke's natural law is transcendent because both the knowledge and obligatoriness of the natural law are abso-lutely dependent on rational knowledge of the existence and will of the transcendent God; the precepts or contents of the law are nowhere present in the world, but are available only to one who can ascend the heights of Locke's rational proof. The law of nature properly understood has thus hardly been known among human beings prior to Locke, but, being firmly rooted in rational truth, it apparently remains a natural law despite the widespread or near universal ignorance of it.

The centerpiece of his doctrine of natural law is thus a rational proof for the existence of God, a proof that must establish not only that there is such a God, but that God has a will and what that will is. From the "wonderful art and order" of the world, Locke infers the existence of a "powerful and wise creator of all those things . . . to whom we are necessarily subject." "Decidedly, the Creator has right and power" over us, for is not "the clay subject to the potter's will," and "cannot the pot be destroyed by the same hand that shaped it?" (fols. 54, 56, 58).[52] It is this "potter's sovereignty," this "right and power" that is the source of the obligatoriness of the natural law, once we discover the Creator's will. Since we infer the Creator's wisdom from his creation, we can infer that God did not "make this world random and to no purpose." God must "want man to do something"—he must have a will for humanity (fols. 59–60).

But how can we discover by our unaided reason what the Creator has willed? Locke's answer is unfortunately very brief, but its general point is straightforward enough. "We can infer the principle of our duty and its certain rule from the constitution of man himself and the equipment of the human faculties. God's will is that we use our faculties and that we honor God" (fol. 60). But whatever we do involves using our faculties, so this is less than determinate as a legal command. One can only wish Locke had said more about the reasoning by which the dictates of the natural law are to be derived from human faculties. At this point, for example, the Thomist appeal to the natural inclinations would seem relevant and helpful, but Locke has clearly cut himself off from Thomas's version of teleology, even though Locke seems to be making some sort of teleological gesture himself.[53] That difficulty aside, however, it is clear how far Locke's natural law teaching strays from the Grotian pattern and how much it rests on a critique of some of the most characteristic features of Grotius's system, most especially the Dutchman's conception of a nontheistic natural law and his refusal to equate the full moral good with the natural law.

Locke's law of nature is entirely transcendent; it has no natural manifestation in the world. The burden of Locke's *Questions* is to show that the natural law must be such a transcendent thing or no natural law at all. Only as transcendent can the natural law retain its quality as law, which requires both that the law be sufficiently promulgated and that it be properly binding. It must be promulgated—somehow rationally known or at least available—and yet Locke, in accord with his epistemological turn, insists that the law is not promulgated in the standard ways posited in the immanentist tradition. The transcendent natural law allows one to conceive the law as promulgated and yet to honor the facts about the moral dissensus and disobedience that Locke's empirical investigations convince him are so pervasive. The transcendent natural law must also be obligatory; unequivocally tracing it to God serves, as we have noted, to find a source that promises to make it properly obligatory and not merely commendatory.

We are now in a position to state quite precisely Locke's relation to his two most immediate predecessors on the issues of promulgation and obligatoriness. He differs from Grotius on both counts. Grotius's thoroughly immanent natural law failed to adequately secure either one of the two key requirements. He premised promulgation only by distorting the facts; he never did supply an even vaguely satisfactory doctrine of the obligatoriness of the law. Pufendorf had fastened his attention on the latter problem; he had followed Hobbes in requiring that the law of nature be seen as transcendent for the sake of securing its obligatoriness. Locke endorses this move, but he extends it drastically in his far more searching treatment of the question of knowledge of the law of nature. The move leads him to jettison pretty thoroughly all Grotian remnants in the Pufendorfian synthesis.

Locke's transcendent natural law gives him a position of security—intellectual, political, and moral—from which to launch what is really a devastating critique of the natural law as understood by his predecessors. Locke can be so critical of all the naturally immanent manifestations of natural law precisely because he stands on the very firm ground of his transcendent natural law, a law apparently unshaken by all the failures of promulgation he details.

Locke's law of nature is "hidden" and "secret," mostly if not entirely unknown by other human beings (fol. 33). It most definitely does not lie out in the open like Grotius's law of nature, available for discovery by the interested observer in what most people praise or blame. But approaching the natural law in Locke's own spirit, we must ask, Is a "hidden" or "secret" natural law really sufficiently promulgated? What if a human lawmaker followed the example of Caligula, "who had his laws written in small letters and posted at some distance above the ground"?[54] Surely such a practice would not count as adequate promulgation, and Locke's hidden natural law bears a marked resemblance to it.[55]

Locke argues, however, that the analogy is false. The widespread or even universal ignorance of the natural law is not an innocent ignorance, as it would be if the hiddenness of the natural law were the fault of the legislator. This universal ignorance is a blamable or guilty ignorance, for the natural law is accessible in principle to all rational creatures—or at least to the very intelligent who apply themselves assiduously to the task (fols. 15–16).[56]

Not merely is it accessible to human reason, but there is an obligation to make use of human faculties in order to discover it. Accessibility to human effort is not sufficient to make human beings blamable for their own ignorance; they must have a duty to engage in the search. Otherwise their ignorance of the natural law is no more blamable than, say, their ignorance of astrophysics. As Locke says, "Some make no use of the light [of nature] but love the darkness. . . . They are nurtured in vices and scarcely distinguish between good and evil" (fol. 16; cf. fols. 34–36). Human beings fail to discover the natural law, fail even to engage in the open-minded and fully devoted search for it, for morally blamable reasons. They turn their backs on their duty to find the law.

This moral blameworthiness makes human ignorance the fault of human beings; in this case, ignorance is no excuse for disobedience. This almost willful ignorance, afflicting all or almost all human beings, prevents them from engaging in the Lockean reasoning about God and nature that establishes the natural law on its proper foundations and in its proper content. Universal ignorance does not imply that the law has not been sufficiently promulgated.

Yet to claim that ignorance of the natural law is guilty ignorance is to imply that human beings can be pronounced guilty and blamable prior to their knowledge of the natural law. Locke shows us, in other words, that there is a deep incoherence in the idea of transcendent natural law. The natural law must be already binding (meaning promulgated and known) in order to effectuate its promulgation. It must be binding or promulgated before its promulgation. The immanent natural law as understood in the tradition is untenable; as Locke shows, the revised version, the transcendent natural law, is equally so.[57]

Locke further shows that the law's obligatoriness can be no more established on the basis of the reformulated natural law than it could be on the basis of the immanent natural law. Obligation to law must derive from the law's origin in the will of a superior—in the case of natural law, in the will of the creator-God. In a number of different ways, however, Locke severely undercuts the authoritativeness of the creator-God. At a key place in his proof for the existence of God, Locke purports to demonstrate that man must be created by God because

> if man were creator of himself, someone who could bring himself into the world, he would also have granted himself an eternal duration for his existence. . . . For it is impossible to imagine anything so hostile and inimical to itself which, though it could grant itself existence, would not at the same time preserve it, or which would be willing to readily abandon it once the course of its brief life had been spent; without life, all other things, dear, useful, pleasant, blessed, cannot be preserved and are sought in vain. (fol. 55)[58]

Human mortality is an expression of "hostility" and "inimicability." It is the gift of an enemy. One of two things must be true: there is no such creator-being as Locke has posited, or there is such a being and it is hostile to humanity. Whichever is true, the Lockean natural law cannot exist, for either way one destroys the premise-in-chief for the natural law—that there is a superior whose will we are obliged to obey by right. A supremely power-ful enemy may force us to obey, but he cannot oblige us to obey. We would appear to arrive at the unavoidable conclusion that there is no natural law, were it not for a yet unnoted dimension of Locke's treatment of the relation between human beings and their alleged Creator.[59]

Locke does not treat the claims of the Creator to obedience as claims exclusively rooted in the benevolence of the Creator. He insists on the Cre-ator's power: the potter surely has the power to crush the pot. His notion of subjection to the Creator seems not to be an entirely moral subjection. If there is a Creator who stands to his creation as a potter does to his pots, then surely he can impose whatever conditions he wills for the continued existence of his creatures. The obligatoriness of the law of nature strictly follows from the fact that the Creator can or does attach sanctions to the law. The sanctions not only potentially supply a motive for obeying the law, they constitute the very obligatoriness of it: no sanctions, no law.

Yet as Locke makes clear in his voluminous arguments against the imma-nent law of nature, the sanctions are not in any evident manner attached to the happenings of this world. Thus, toward the conclusion of his demonstra-tion in Question VII of the lack of consensus on morals, Locke notes that "immortality of the soul . . . must . . . necessarily be assumed for the exis-tence of the law of nature" (fol. 16). Some readers have found Locke's intro-duction of a new criterion of law into his work at this late stage to be puz-zling, but it follows from the necessities of his transcendent law.[60] In this very place Locke points out that human opinions are as diverse regarding the question of immortality of the soul as they are regarding other matters relevant to the law of nature. If there is natural knowledge of immortality of the soul, a prerequisite of the law of nature's being natural, by analogy with the rest of his argument from dissensus it must be demonstrative and not inscribed or innate in any sense (fol. 76). But in the decisive place, Question V, where Locke presents a demonstrative argument regarding God and the content of the law of nature, he makes no effort to include a demonstration of the existence of an afterlife, which could serve as sanction for the law of nature. Perhaps he is foreclosed from such an argument by his suggestion in Question V that God is hostile to humanity. In any case, what Locke later says quite explicitly in his *Essay Concerning Human Understanding* and *The Reasonableness of Christianity* is entirely consistent with what he implies but leaves unsaid in the *Questions*: reason cannot establish the existence of an afterlife.[61] With reason's failure to establish immortality of the soul falls the transcendent natural law. No more than the immanent law can the tran-scendent law satisfy the all-important dual requirements of promulgation and obligatoriness.

If there is no natural law, are human beings left with no natural guidance whatever? Early in his essay Locke had contrasted the natural law with natu-ral right. "This law [of nature] should be distinguished from natural right;

for right consists in the fact that we have a free use of something, but law is that which either commands or forbids some action" (fol. 11). If there is no natural law, properly speaking, no limit human beings are naturally obliged to keep, then it would seem to follow that they possess by nature the opposite, a natural right of "free use." Although Locke can find no evidence of natural law, i.e., command or prohibition of actions, he does not find that nature has left human beings entirely without guidance. Locke does not deny that there are natural inclinations, he denies only that these are directed to the natural law as taught in the tradition. Instead, he shows, they point to self-preservation, or more broadly, self-interest. "Human beings are impelled to this . . . and more than impelled, by an inner instinct" (fol. 61; cf. fol. 14). Like Carneades before him, Locke is impressed with the fact that nature's guidance leads not to justice or the common good, but to "one's own advantage" (see fol. 42). That is probably why Locke lavishes so much praise on Carneades (even while appearing to disagree with him): "[His] extremely acute intelligence and [his] powerful eloquence left nothing intact, virtually nothing unshaken" (fol. 105). To say that human beings are driven by nature to seek their preservation, and to say that there is no natural law, is to say that people are endowed by nature with a permission (a right) to pursue that goal toward which nature willy-nilly drives them. Human beings, in other words, begin with a natural right to life (see fol. 82).

If the driving force for human beings is their "instinct for preservation," then their defining or driving quality is not their rationality or sociability, à la Grotius, but their mortality. It is no accident that in the key place in his "proof" for God Locke emphasizes human mortality and the inimicality that implies if some intelligent being is responsible for it. Locke not only breaks with Grotius, therefore, but with Christian political thought as exemplified by Milton's approach to the Fall and redemption.

To say that Locke's argument, extrapolated along Lockean lines, leads to the natural right to life as the ground might seem to contradict Question XI.[62] Locke there considers the question "Does the private interest of each individual constitute the foundation of the law of nature?" He answers the question in the negative; since the natural right to life is a "private interest of each individual," this Question does seem to counter the position taken thus far. But Question XI is far from straightforward. It begins, as I have noted already, with reference to the doctrine of Carneades and with an implied promise of a refutation of the ancient skeptic. (Worth noting is that Locke clearly takes over the reference to Carneades from Grotius; also worth noting is the fact that Grotius responds to Carneades at the outset of his treatise, and quite forthrightly, whereas Locke raises the specter of ancient conventionalism only at the end.) Instead of attempting to refute Carneades, Locke praises him and turns his philosophic powers against a rather different position. Carneades had argued, it will be recalled, that "there exists no law of nature, or, were such a law to exist, it would constitute the height of folly, since . . . both humans and animals are moved to their own advantage at nature's guidance" (fol. 105; cf. fol. 112).[63] Locke, it must be repeated, does not directly attack Carneades' own position, which, as far as it goes, bears a partial resemblance to what he himself has argued thus far. Instead, he reformulates the issue as follows: "whether what each private individual judges to be useful to himself and to his own affairs as the occasion arises conforms to the law of nature and, by this title, [whether] it is not only lawful for him but even necessary" (fol. 108). Locke thus substitutes for Carneades' rejection of so-called natural law, on the ground that nature guides toward self-interest, a quite different doctrine—that human beings are obliged by natural law to pursue only their own interest. That, of course, is not what Carneades had argued for, nor is it what Locke's own arguments had established. Locke easily and decisively refutes this new natural law teaching, but that refutation reaches neither Carneades' nor his own earlier arguments.

We can best capture Locke's critique of this "neo-Carneadeanism" in terms of the conceptual distinction between right and law developed in Question I. The "neo-Carneadeans" turn self-interest into natural law, that is, into a morally obligatory mandate, whereas Locke showed it to be a right, a morally permissible liberty. According to the neo-Carneadean natural law, it would be morally unlawful to renounce one's pursuit of self-interest for any reason; according to the Lockean natural right, it would be perfectly permissible to renounce immediate self-interest for longer term self-interest, or even for the sake of the common good. Lockean natural right would be perfectly compatible, for example, with "a compact, either tacit . . . or expressed," aimed at achieving "some common human necessity or advantage." Such compacts may establish rules of conduct placing moral limits on human actions, limits that may look very like the precepts of the traditional natural law, but they do not "prove the existence of a law of nature at all . . . and issue from no principle of nature whatsoever" (fol. 63).[64]

Observance of those law-of-nature-like rules is conducive to one's self-interest; indeed, "nothing is as conducive to the common advantage of the individual, nothing so protective of the safety and security of men's possessions" as that observance. "From the keeping of this law peace arises, concord, friendship, freedom from punishments, security, the possession of our own property, and, to embrace all these in a single word, happiness." None of these goods can arise, however, unless the natural-law-like rules are kept, and that cannot be if human beings are free, much less obliged, to obey or not as they decide in each instance on the basis of a calculation of "present advantage." For the law to serve interest, interest cannot be the "foundation of law or basis of obligation" in the way neo-Carneadean doctrine tries to make it (fols. 108, 117, 118, 119).[65]

The necessity for natural-law-like rules provides the key to Locke's odd procedure in the *Questions*. He both reveals and conceals the failure of the natural law tradition. He reveals that failure without admitting that is what he is doing; he reveals it while continuing to say he is adhering to the tradition. Locke, in other words, is somewhat deceptive, but the reason for his deception is not far to seek. Whatever its defects, the natural law tradition has something crucial to say, and Locke does not want to demolish its hold on the minds of his compatriots. Nature may guide human beings to pursue their own advantage, but the result of a "natural" life is not pretty. Those human beings who have "no guide other than nature" are discussed by Locke in Question IV:

> How far removed are the morals of these men from virtue, how alien are they to any sense of humanity! Nowhere is there such fickle faith, so much perfidy, such monstrous cruelty; and, by murdering men and shedding kindred blood, they sacrifice both to their gods and to their own "genius."

Those people who live exclusively under the guidance of nature "spend their lives wretchedly in rapine, theft, debauchery, and murder." They do not, in a word, achieve that "happiness" promised by the natural-law-like-rules Locke endorses (fol. 41; cf. fols. 116–19).[66] In other words, morality, more or less of the sort endorsed in the natural law tradition, is part of the answer to the problem nature poses for human existence. Thus Locke wishes to retain the law of nature, or some version of it, at the same time that he levels a very powerful theoretical critique against it.

Locke wishes to retain the natural law, but at the same time he transforms it. Morality in the post-Lockean version is in the service of natural right and derivative from it, rather than primary and underived. Morality is not the first principle of human action, as the Thomists and Grotius had it. The ground of "natural law," or morality, is now understood by Locke as natural right, and therefore the main requirements of morality can be restated in terms of rights. It becomes possible, for example, to formulate the purpose of political life entirely in terms of the mandate "to secure these rights."

Morality continues to be required, but its content is subtly redefined. The primary precept becomes Respect the rights of others. Duties to others can be captured in these terms, and other desirable moral qualities can be understood as suitable means to producing a society in which habitual rights-respecting occurs. One example of this kind of redefinition occurs in the *Questions*. Locke at one point launches an almost passionate tirade against the Romans as bellicose predators: "The Romans themselves, who are held up as having displayed examples of virtue for the entire world, how did they acquire for themselves honors, triumphs, glory, and an immortal memory for their own name, if not from robbery and rapine by which they laid the entire world to waste? What else is that great 'virtue' so celebrated among them with so many panegyrics, what else is it, I ask, but violence and wrong?" As Locke puts it in his *Second Treatise*, his new moral understanding favors not the bellicose Romans but "the industrious and rational" (fol. 71).[67] A substantive moral shift follows from Locke's new understanding of the nature of morality.

As should now be clear, Locke rejects the natural law doctrine of Grotius, but he comes to rest at a place where his doctrine and the Dutchman's overlap considerably—on the centrality of rights and the importance of compact. It would not be too much to say that Locke and Grotius differ entirely, but in their difference is a similarity that allowed the Grotian natural law to prepare the ground for Locke. The *Questions* was not, of course, the vehicle on which Locke rode to his Whig ascendency, and therefore it does not express exactly the historical form in which Locke supplanted Grotius. The important negative themes of the *Questions* were carried forward in the *Essay Concerning Human Understanding*, while the construction of an alternative (to) natural law teaching was most visibly presented in the *Second Treatise*.

CHAPTER EIGHT

Locke and the Reformation of Natural Law: *Two Treatises of Government*

LOCKE'S unpublished *Questions Concerning the Law of Nature* reveals much of his thinking about the natural law tradition—far more than the later *Two Treatises of Government*, and more even than the *Essay Concerning Human Understanding*. The *Essay* reproduces much of the critical reasonings of the *Questions*, but does not make their application to the natural law tradition so clear. Nonetheless, the *Questions* itself fails to do more than hint at the political teaching that might be implied by Locke's new understanding of the law of nature. The *Questions* helps one understand the innards of Locke's political philosophy, but *Two Treatises* remains indispensable.[1] There the implications of Locke's break with the tradition, and especially with the most important representative of it at Locke's time, Grotius, become clear. Thus it forms a central part of the story of Locke's supplanting Grotius, as the authoritative thinker for the Anglo-American Whig tradition.

THE TRANSCENDENT NATURAL LAW IN "TWO TREATISES"

Two Treatises of Government carries forward the main themes of Locke's confrontation with the tradition and particularly with Grotius, as developed earlier in the *Questions*. The two-step argument of the *Questions* reappears: first a version of the new transcendent law of nature Locke tentatively developed in the *Questions*, then a dissolution of the transcendent law of nature into natural rights.[2] As in the *Questions*, Locke is content to have the whole remain rather blurry; he attempts to leave the impression that even his transcendent natural law, to say nothing of natural rights, fundamentally harmonizes with the very different Thomist natural law of traditional writers like Richard Hooker.[3] Nonetheless, Locke's trajectory in *Two Treatises* becomes very apparent by the time he comes to draw the chief political implications of his natural law: government for him comes to be solely for the sake of rights, renamed "property." Human beings, he says, agree to a compact to make civil society and government for the sake of "the material preservation of their lives, liberties, and estates, which I call by the general name, 'property'" (II 123), a conclusion no Thomist natural law theorist like Hooker could accept.

The natural law doctrine Locke begins with in *Two Treatises* is a simplified version of the natural law explicitly presented in the *Questions*. He again deploys a version of his very anti-Grotian "God the artificer" argument, although significantly in *Two Treatises* he makes no effort to prove the existence of such a God. *Two Treatises* is a less philosophical work than the *Questions*.[4] "Men being all the workmanship of one omnipotent, and infinitely wise maker; all the servants of one sovereign master, sent into the world by his order, and about his business, they are his property, whose workmanship they are" (II 6). Made by God, human beings belong to God—the paradigm case, it appears, of a labor theory of property. Although his argument is slightly different, Locke in *Two Treatises* rejects Grotius's *etiamsi* as he had done in the *Questions*. The transcendent natural law is known entirely through knowledge of God the Creator. Locke thus not only holds the creating God to be indispensable, but he deduces the content of natural law from the relation of humanity to God as creature to Creator.

As in the *Questions*, the natural law derives from the human relation to the transcendent creating God, but in *Two Treatises* the central idea is the human being as property of God the maker. Filmer, perhaps, suggested the idea to Locke, for he had argued, in effect, that all human beings were originally the property of Adam, because Adam was their source or origin.[5] Even if Filmer's major premise is correct, that the one "who gives life and being" has authority over the ones to whom life and being are given, Locke piously insists that Filmer was quite mistaken in his identification of the prime "begetter": "They who say the father gives life to his children, are so dazzled with the thoughts of monarchy, that they do not, as they ought, remember God, who is the author and giver of life" (I 52).

Locke's opening argument in the *Second Treatise*, then, carries forward the main line of his critique of Filmer. The "workmanship argument" saves him from reliance on the kind of teleological argument that still found a place in his transcendent natural law in the *Questions*.[6] The workmanship argument thus allows Locke to present an even more untraditional argument than he had deployed in the *Questions*. His first inference from the Creator-creature relation is the natural freedom and equality of human beings, that is, the natural condition as a state of nature. If God has given no explicit sign of "appointment" or precedence to one over another of the creatures, then their "independence" would follow (II 4).

Human beings by nature are free and equal, in that they do not "depend upon the will of any other man," but they nonetheless remain "within the bounds of the law of nature" (II 4). The natural law prescriptions described in the early chapters of the *Second Treatise* essentially have the character of limits on an otherwise existing natural freedom. Locke derives these limits from the workmanship argument as well. Human beings "are his property, whose workmanship they are, made to last during his, not one another's pleasure." If human beings belong to God, they cannot belong to one another, or even to themselves. Since God is the true proprietor, no one else has the right to damage or destroy his property. From this thought Locke derives a general "no-harm" principle.[7] They may not "take away, or impair the life, or what tends to the preservation of the life, the liberty, health, limb, or goods of another" (II 6). From this general limit, Locke infers limits on what human beings may appropriate from "that which God gave to mankind in common. . . . The same law of nature, that does . . . give us property, does also bound that property too" (II 25, 31). Likewise, "a man [has] not . . . power over his own life," presumably for the same reason, that God owns us all.

Contrary to Grotius, then, Locke unqualifiedly affirms inalienability.[8] No one can "by compact, or his own consent, enslave himself to anyone nor put himself under the absolute, arbitrary power of another to take away his life, when he pleases." Or, as Locke summarily puts it, "he that cannot take away his own life cannot give another power over it" (II 23). Thus from the workmanship argument via the "no-harm" principles apparently follows many of the most characteristic strands of Lockean liberalism, particularly his rejection of absolutism and his reservation of a natural right of resistance.[9]

Even the central doctrine of natural rights would seem to follow. The natural law limitations that follow from God's proprietorship set out the natural duties that primordially govern human life. Natural rights would seem to be the duties of others as they appear to the individual toward whom the duties are owed.[10] For example, if all others have a duty not to take my life, I can be said to have a right to life vis-à-vis them. To have a right, then, is merely to be the beneficiary of the duties of others. Rights, according to this view, are clearly not primary but derivative.

Locke's natural law in *Two Treatises* thus has a remarkably narrow content. It is not clear that the principle Locke identifies as standing behind that natural law does or ought to produce such a narrow content. Humankind, Locke says, is "sent into the world by [God's] order, and about his business," but why is this "business" exhausted by mere forbearance from harming self and others, as Locke has it (II 6)? Might not "God's business" have more to it? What, after all, is "his business"?[11] Although Locke supplies more specific details about the content of the law of nature than he had in the *Questions*, he gives little of the reasoning that generates this content from the first principles of the natural law. It is not evident, in other words, that the content of the law of nature in fact follows from the creator-God thesis with which Locke ostensibly begins. He is certainly more definite about that content than his explicit reasonings warrant.

The workmanship argument parallels Filmer's argument about fatherhood, in holding that the progenitor retains property rights in the generated. God's rights over human beings exhaust the field of possible rights;

there can be no other rights-holders, except in the secondary and derivative sense that each comes to possess the right to the forbearance of the others that is the obverse of the universal lack of rights over mankind in any but the real owner, God. Human beings are "made to last during his, not one another's pleasure" (II 6). God's proprietary rights extend to the right to destroy his workmanship.[12] As Locke asks more than once in his writings, Has not the potter the right to destroy the pot? The core of Locke's transcendent natural law comes to view just here: God gives life, and God may take it back—and only God may do so. The sovereign and ultimately arbitrary God of Protestant theology lurks just beneath the surface of Locke's argument. Is God's "business" the mere exercise of arbitrary power? Ironically, Locke attempts to use this transcendent, sovereign, arbitrary God to lay the groundwork for nonarbitrary human order. It is as though God is to be the scapegoat for the community; on his head is to be laid all the arbitrariness that humans can conceive and with him it is to be driven out of this worldly sphere.[13]

The tie that binds the first and second treatises together, then, appears to be the notion of God as maker, or, more important, as owner. The negative implication of God's proprietorship rules out Filmer's doctrine of Adam and his heirs as owner; the positive implications constitute the main outlines of the transcendent natural law teaching of the *Second Treatise*. The most important of those implications can be stated succinctly in terms of one proposition—human beings are by nature free and equal—and three limitations imposed on humanity: (1) human beings are not morally free to harm one another; (2) human beings are not morally free to harm themselves, that is, they may not commit suicide; (3) human beings are not morally free to harm each other indirectly by appropriating more than their share of the external world. At times Locke summarizes these three limitations under natural law in terms of an obligation to "preserve mankind" (II 6).[14]

Locke's three limitations show his distance from Hobbes as well as from Filmer. Although Hobbes agrees that human beings are free and equal by nature, he interprets that freedom and equality in a much more radical way than Locke does in the early pages of the *Second Treatise*.[15] For Hobbes the primary and original fact is the possession of "the right of nature," defined as "the liberty each man hath, to use his own power, as he will himself, for the preservation of his own nature; that is to say, of his own life; and consequently, of doing anything, which in his own judgment, and reason, he shall conceive to be the aptest means thereunto." The original moral (or quasi-moral) fact is not a set of limits, as in Locke, but a liberty to do what each considers necessary for preservation. That liberty amounts to a "right to everything, even to one another's body."[16] So far is Locke from affirming a right to the bodies of others that he denies even a right over one's own body and life. From this very important difference flows the oft-noted dissimilarity between the two philosophers' conceptions of the state of nature. Locke refuses to accept Hobbes's identification of the state of nature as a state of war. "However some men have confounded" them, they "are as far different, as a state of peace, good will, mutual assistance, and preservation, and a state of enmity, malice, violence, and mutual destruction are from one another" (II 19).

Just as in the *Questions*, however, Locke substantially modifies his position as he proceeds through his argument. Indeed, by the time he finishes he has reversed the relation between natural rights and natural law with which he began, and pointed toward an altogether different account of the natural foundation of politics than his transcendent natural law. Surely the most telling point is a simple, yet absolutely central, terminological matter: Locke affirms unequivocally that "every man has a property in his own person. This nobody has a right to, but himself" (II 27; cf. II 44). This assertion directly counters the ostensible foundation of the law of nature in God's proprietorship, according to which God owns all human beings, and no one owns him or herself.[17]

It might appear that this shift makes little difference, for some of the key implications of self-ownership are indeed the same as, or parallel to, the implications of God's proprietorship. In particular, the all-important denial that any human being belongs by nature to any others, including rulers, holds as well under the one claim as under the other. Filmer's notion of the natural proprietorship of Adam and his heirs makes as little sense if each owns himself as if God owns all. The parallel implications of the two claims tempt the conclusion that Locke does not understand the two formulations as saying anything different from each other. The assertion of self-ownership might be understood as a restatement of the divine-ownership thesis from a slightly shifted point of view. If we look at human beings vis-à-vis God, they all belong to him; if we look at human beings vis-à-vis each other, they do not belong to any other, and therefore might be said to belong to themselves. This, in any case, is the solution various scholars have suggested in order to account for Locke's surprising shift in terminology.[18]

Nonetheless, this proposed interpretation fails to make sense of many other features of Locke's text that we must soon discuss, and it also does not work in its own terms. Let us posit a society in which slavery is legally recognized. All the slaves of a given slaveholder can be said to belong to that slaveholder, and as the property of that owner, they surely have limited rights vis-à-vis each other. It would be a violation of the slaveowner's proprietary rights for one of his slaves (or any other person, for that matter) to murder or injure one of the other slaves. Each slave thus derives some measure of protection, or of secondary rights vis-à-vis other slaves, from the primary rights of the slaveowner. Nonetheless, it would be incorrect to say that the slaves are therefore self-owners. To be the property of A (in this case myself) involves more than having certain immunities from actions by B, but that is all that the claim of self-ownership could amount to in our hypothetical case. Since there is no relevant difference between our hypothesis and Locke's postulation of God's proprietorship, Locke's shift in terminology must be either the product of very loose thinking or the expression of a shift in conception of some significance.

As was true in the *Questions*, Locke only gradually shifts his position. He presents the workmanship argument near the opening of his second chapter, and the self-ownership claim for the first time in the fifth chapter. Between the two come two very important discussions of topics highly relevant to the limits on natural law that Locke attaches to the God-as-owner thesis: the nature of the state of nature, with an emphasis on the role of the executive power of the law of nature, and slavery. The former bears directly on the natural law's no-harm-to-others limitation on human freedom, the latter on the suicide prohibition. The meaning and significance of Locke's shift to self-ownership from divine proprietorship can only be grasped via a close analysis of these two transitional arguments.

The law of nature mandates not harming others, and in Locke's argument this is not left a mere moral desideratum; the law of nature also makes available a mechanism to make this command effective.[19] "And that all men may be restrained from invading the rights of others, and from doing hurt to one another, and the law of nature be observed, which willeth the peace and preservation of all mankind, the execution of the law of nature is in that state, put into every man's hands." This so-called "executive power of the law of nature" necessarily follows, for without it that law "would, as all other laws that concern men in this world, be in vain" (II 7). Just as in the *Questions*, the sanctions for the law of nature constitute an essential part of it. In *Two Treatises*, however, these sanctions appear to shift entirely to the worldly sphere; the absence of rational knowledge of the soul's immortality does not appear to vitiate the natural law in *Two Treatises*, as it did in the *Questions* and will do again in the *Essay Concerning Human Understanding*. Nonetheless, the reason for the introduction of the executive power of the law of nature appears to be quite similar in spirit to the discussion in the *Questions*. Recalling both Machiavelli and Grotius, Locke demands an effective law; yet he denies the law immanence. To be anything but "vain"— that is, without effect—it must depend upon external enforcement; human beings do not inherently or spontaneously obey it, at least not universally, or sufficiently.[20]

The law of nature necessarily implies the existence of some enforcement power; since all human beings are equal in the state of nature, it cannot belong to some and not others; therefore "every one must needs have a right to . . . prosecute that law" (II 7).[21] The executive power fills out the endowment human beings have in the state of nature: to a set of natural law limits or duties is added a right or power to execute the law. This natural executive power turns out to be crucial to Locke's purposes in *Two Treatises*. As he explains later, the executive power is "the true original of political power," for which the second essay has been in search from the outset. "Where-ever therefore any number of men are so united in one society, as to quit every one his executive power of the law of nature, and to resign it to the publick, there and there only is a political, or civil society" (II 89).

As that which makes the natural moral order effective, the natural executive power would seem to perfect the state of nature: not only is there a moral command not to harm others, but there is a device to keep human beings obedient to the law. So far as the state of nature is not a state of war but a state of peace, the executive power would appear to make a major contribution. Despite the executive power's intimate relation to the law of nature, and despite its indispensable function within his political philosophy, Locke suspects many will find it a "very strange doctrine," a judgment in which he himself concurs (II 9, 13). He appears to mean that it is strange at least in the sense of being novel or unusual. Although Locke directs attention to the strangeness or novelty of his executive power of the law of nature, to many readers this appears just another place in which Locke remains in close contact with the precedent natural law tradition. Peter Laslett finds that "Locke's doctrine on the point differs only by a twist of emphasis from that of Pufendorf and Cumberland."[22] Hans Aarsleff finds that on the natural executive power, "Hooker says the same as Locke."[23] Quentin Skinner thinks Jacques Almain developed "a theory which was later characterized by John Locke . . . as the 'very strange doctrine' that each individual in his proper political state must be pictured as the 'executioner of the law of nature.'"[24] At stake here, of course, is more than the petty question of Locke's originality, for his signals about the natural executive power stand in marked contrast to the overall tone of the early parts of the *Second Treatise*, where Locke for the most part suggests that his position is anything but novel, claiming agreement with Hooker, and through Hooker with a long tradition of Christian natural law philosophy going back at least to Thomas Aquinas. Given Locke's effort to establish continuity with the past, his insistence on "strangeness" requires some attention.

Thomist Natural Law and the Natural Executive Power

Hooker is the traditional natural law source to whom Locke most clearly directs our attention in *Two Treatises*, but Hooker's position represents a development and modification of the Christian natural law teaching of Thomas Aquinas.[25] Now, it is absolutely clear that Locke's doctrine of the executive power of the law of nature is an innovation from the point of view of Thomas's doctrine: private individuals, Thomas says, do not possess the power of punishment.[26] The power to punish, according to Thomas, serves "the welfare of the community," and therefore, he concludes, "it belongs to him alone who has charge of the community's welfare." If one were to ask where this power resides in the absence of civil authorities, that is, in a "state of nature," Thomas would reply that there is no such thing: government is natural.[27]

The counter-Reformation natural lawyer Francisco Suárez developed the Thomist alternative to Locke's natural executive power more fully. Following Thomas, Suárez affirms that "the punishment of malefactors" and "the infliction of punishment for injuries done to individuals" are powers that "transcend human authority as it exists in individual men."[28] This is not to say, however, that this power is not a human power; it, like the more general powers to make civil law and to choose a form of government, resides in the community as a whole, not in individuals. "Such power must dwell in men inasmuch as they are not naturally governed in a polity by the angels, nor directly by God Himself."[29] The legislative and executive powers are natural, according to Suárez, but only "in mankind viewed collectively; . . . the power resides not in individual men separately considered, nor in the mass or multitude of them collected, as it were, confusedly, in a disorderly manner, and without union of the members into one body; therefore such a political body must be constituted, before power of this sort is to be found in men."[30]

The Thomist position, as explicated by Suárez, is therefore almost exactly the opposite of Locke's. For Locke, human beings begin in a state of nature, that is, a state of no government, where each person possesses the executive power of the law of nature. That power is "the original of the legislative and executive Power of civil society," brought into existence when the individual executive power is resigned to the community (II 87–89). Thomas and Suárez emphatically deny the derivation of the community's power from the individual's power: the community's power derives from the very existence of the community. "Once this body has been constituted, however, the power in question exists in it"; political power "exists as a characteristic property resulting from such a mystical body."[31]

The denial of an individual executive power, then, is the converse of the Thomistic affirmation of the naturalness of the political community under the natural law. That naturalness is meant in a dual sense, at least. Adapting Aristotle, the Thomists affirm that human beings are destined by nature for social and political life, because the dictates of the natural law—the natural virtues and vices, the natural perfections—include and require social existence, which in turn includes political life. Secondly, the Thomist position affirms the naturalness of the political, in the sense that it has a reality beyond the sum of its parts. The political community is a genuine whole, with characteristics and a genuine good not simply reducible to those of its component human parts. As Suárez says many times, the political community, although brought into being by the wills of its member human beings, forms "a mystical body" or "unity." We may recall from an earlier discussion Suárez's use of the analogy of marriage: although marriage is entered into consensually by the two parties, yet the marriage relationship, in particular "that the husband is the head of the wife," follows from the nature of the marital unity, not from the wills of the parties or the consent of the wife to the power of the husband.[32] The political, like the marital, is natural, and also has a nature.

By contrast, Locke treats the political as artificial and therefore lacking a nature in the full sense. Locke's political philosophy—indeed, the social contract tradition as carried on even by present-day theorists like John Rawls and Robert Nozick—is purely reductionist, in that it looks at the political in terms of what rational human beings would construct, on the basis of the thought that the political must be reduced to the sum of the wills of its members. Locke's executive power, in other words, is so much different from the Catholic Thomists' conception that it signifies a shift in the very roots of the respective philosophies.[33]

Hooker develops and modifies the Thomist natural law in directions that are indeed reminiscent of Locke on the two central issues of the state of nature and the "strange" executive power of the law of nature. Hooker affirms a prepolitical condition suggestive of Locke's state of nature, and along with that a power in each individual apparently similar to Locke's executive power of the law of nature.

Hooker's shifts in doctrine reflect new Reformation motifs in political thought. Thomas and Suárez had followed Aristotle rather than Augustine in finding the political so thoroughly natural that it would exist even in the "state of innocency." Hooker, on the other hand, is much closer to the Augustinian position: "there being no impossibility in nature considered by itself, but that men might have lived without any public regiment. Howbeit, the corruption of our nature being presupposed, we may not deny but that the law of Nature doth now require of necessity some kind of regiment." Hooker therefore speaks of "those times wherein there were no civil societies, . . . no manner of public regiment established."[34] He speaks of natural laws that "do bind men, absolutely even as they are men, although they have never any settled fellowship, never any solemn agreement amongst themselves."[35] Hooker's statements are so unambiguous in affirming the derivation of the political from a prepolitical condition that Locke might well seem justified in referring to Hooker as authority for his own state of nature against those "that say, there were never any men in the State of Nature" (II 15).

Since Hooker puts some weight on the generation of civil society from a prepolitical condition, the question of the "original of political power" plausibly arises, and it is in this context that the Hookerian precedent for Locke's executive power of the law of nature comes to view. According to Hooker,

> In those times wherein there was as yet no manner of public regiment established . . . men always knew that when force and injury was offered they might be defenders of themselves; they knew that howsoever men may seek their own commodity, yet if this were done with injury unto others it was not to be suffered, but by all men and by all good means to be withstood.[36]

Where the Thomists denied the right of individuals to act against "malefactors" under all conditions, Hooker affirms such a right under certain conditions. He introduces this right as part of his minor modification of, or addition to, the Thomist teachings. As in Locke, this doctrine in Hooker forms part of the transition between the prepolitical and the political. In the condition without "public regiment," Hooker argues,

> to take away all such mutual grievances, injuries and wrongs, there was no way but only by growing into composition and agreement amongst themselves, by ordaining some kind of government public, and by yielding themselves subject thereunto; that unto whom they granted authority to rule and govern, by them the peace, tranquility, and happy estate of the rest might be procured.[37]

Although human beings could in principle guide their lives according to the law of nature alone, with no need of either human law or civil government in a state of innocence, "the corruption of human nature" through the Fall guarantees that life under the natural law alone leads to "mutual grievances, injuries, and wrongs," to which the only solution is "public regiment." However, a private solution, one in which individuals rather than government remedy those injuries and wrongs would be more natural, because "public regiment" means that some few are specially designated to rule, whereas in nature there is "no reason that one man should take upon him to be lord or judge over another." Or, if there is such a reason in the "natural right in the noble, wise and virtuous, to govern," the assertion of that right is not so universally accepted by fallen men as to lead to "peaceable contentment."[38] "Public regiment" requires an act of agreement, consent, or convention in order to designate who will have the power to make and execute human law; it is therefore less strictly natural than the situation in which all persons act to protect their own and others' just right. The power to defend and withstand that Hooker affirms, then, stands intermediate between the prepolitical, fallen condition and civil government.

The individual power to defend and withstand is merely a moment in Hooker's dialectical account, however. Although men "knew . . . they might be defenders of themselves," they also "knew that no man might in reason take upon him to determine his own right, and according to his own determination proceed in maintenance thereof, inasmuch as every man is towards himself and them whom he greatly affecteth partial."[39] Hooker presents a more detailed and nuanced treatment of the Fall and its consequences than we find in Thomas or even in Suárez, and the power of self-defense is part of that. The difference again reflects the impact of the Reformation, in this case particularly the polemical context of Hooker's discussion, the attack on the Puritans and their inherent suspicion of all human authority in favor of private judgment. The individual power to defend and withstand is Hooker's concession, at the level of the natural law, to the Puritan preference for individual judgment. The intermediate position of the individual right to defend and withstand is intended to show the self-contradiction of the Puritan position.[40] That power is required because of "nature corrupt," but precisely the fallen nature that makes that power necessary makes it impossible as well. Thus the otherwise puzzling paradox in Hooker's statement: on the one hand, "men always knew . . . they might be defenders of themselves," but on the other hand, "they knew that no man might in reason take upon him to determine his own right." What Hooker gives with one hand he takes away with the other. The right of individual judgment appears only long enough to show its self-contradictory, self-cancelling character, its inability to satisfy the natural law dictates of peace and justice.

That right of individual judgment most emphatically does not serve as the source for political authority itself. Hooker's view on this is much the same as Suárez's and Bellarmine's. The power inheres in the political community; consent or convention does not bring the public power into existence, as in Locke, but rather agrees to its placement somewhere. "By the natural law . . . the lawful power of making laws to command whole politic societies of men belongeth . . . unto the same entire societies."[41] Or as he says in another place, "The case of man's nature standing therefore as it doth, some kind of regiment the Law of Nature doth require; yet the kinds thereof being many, Nature tieth not to anyone, but leaveth the choice as a thing arbitrary."[42] The collectivity, or the corporation, is the original home and source of political power, just as in Thomas and Suárez, and not the individual, as in Locke.

Hooker's limited and self-cancelling right of individual judgment differs from Locke's executive power of the law of nature in at least three ways. First, Hooker's affirmation of this right is extraordinarily equivocal; Locke's natural executive power, on the other hand, is entirely unequivocal. Where Hooker says "no man might in reason . . . determine his own right," Locke contends quite the contrary: so long as there is no one else to do so, a man has the right under the law of nature and reason to do just that. Hooker does not merely say what Locke admits, that such individual judgment will not work well; for Hooker the right of individual judgment is cancelled whether there is or is not "a common judge," while for Locke only the common judge cancels the power.

Second, Hooker's analog to the executive power does not have the same central function in his theory that Locke's does, for he follows the Thomist tradition and derives political authority directly from the law of nature and the inherent power of the community, and not from the prepolitical powers of the individuals who compose political society.

Finally, for Locke the power in question is that without which the law of nature itself would be "in vain."[43] Hooker disagrees. Hooker's treatment of the sanctions that make the law of nature effective follows by and large the outlines of the traditional Thomist position. The "rewards and punishment" attached to the laws of reason are two- or even three-fold in character.

> Now the due observation of this Law which Reason teacheth us cannot but be effectual unto their great good that do serve the same. For we see the whole world and each part thereof so compacted, that as long as each thing performeth only that work which is natural unto it, it thereby preserveth other things and also itself.

The natural law carries its own reward and punishment with it. A being that keeps the law is operating well and properly, and therefore thrives. Conversely, failure to keep the law brings its own punishment, the frustration of the natural operation of the being and its consequent discontent.[44]

But Hooker's law of nature is a law in the full sense. Human beings are not merely benefited by keeping the law, they are obliged to do so and held blamable if they fail to do so. Thus there are other sanctions to the law of nature besides the "felicity" of a being working in its proper manner. Quoting Paul (Romans 2:9), Hooker looks to that "tribulation and anguish unto every soul that doeth evil" through "transgressing the Law of Nature."[45] That is, he looks to conscience, and behind that the ultimate sanction of the divine judge:

> Sith every man's heart and conscience doth in good or evil, even secretely committed and known to none but itself, either like or disallow itself, and accordingly either rejoice, very nature exulting (as it were) in certain hope of reward, or else grieve (as it were) in a sense of future punishment; neither of which can in this case be looked for from any other, saving only from Him who discerneth and judgeth the very secrets of all hearts; therefore He is the only rewarder and revenger of all such actions; although not of such actions only, but of all whereby the law of Nature is broken whereof Himself is author.[46]

Hooker most emphatically differs from both the Locke of *Two Treatises* and the Locke of the *Questions*. The law of nature is not "in vain," but has the

support of a number of natural and supernatural sanctions. Not coinciden-
tally, those sanctions are the very forces Locke dismisses in the *Questions*.

Hooker is only apparently a forerunner of Locke on the natural executive
power. Locke's "strange" doctrine reveals the same chasm that separates his
overall natural law theory from Hooker's and from the Catholic Thomists'.
Given Locke's thoroughgoing break with Thomistic philosophy in the *Questions* and in the *Essay*, it should be no great surprise that this central doctrine of *Two Treatises* bespeaks that same break.

As with the Catholic Thomists, the essential difference between Locke
and Hooker that manifests itself in Locke's "strange" natural executive
power concerns the state of nature. Despite Hooker's recognition of a prepolitical condition, which Locke attempts to assimilate to his own state of
nature, his understanding of the prepolitical condition is very distant from
Locke's state of nature.

Hooker actually has two conceptually distinct senses of a prepolitical
state. The first involves only a mere shade of difference with the Thomists.
Like them, Hooker sets his political teaching within the context of a full-
blown teleology. Nature is most revealed in the end, or perfection, of a being
rather than in its origin.

> God alone excepted, who actually and everlastingly is whatsoever he may be . . . all
> other things besides are somewhat in possibility, which as yet they are not in act.
> And further cause there is in things an appetite or desire, whereby they incline to
> something which they may be; and when they are it, they shall be perfecter than
> now they are.[47]

For Hooker, as for Thomas, those same "natural inclinations" that Locke
had dismissed in the *Questions* point to the "perfecter" or truly natural state
of a being. Following Aristotle, Hooker applies this scheme to the origin of
political society: the naturalness of the political does not imply its temporal
primacy. Thomas, Suárez, and Hooker all see the political as prior in nature,
but posterior in time, to the family. Thus Hooker's time "before civil society" is not Locke's equal and independent state of nature. "To fathers
within their private families nature hath given a supreme power; for which
cause we see throughout the world even from the foundation-thereof, all
men have ever been taken as lords and lawful kings in their own houses."[48]
While Locke adopts some of this, he denies the central claim—that nature
has given the fathers a supreme power (e.g., II 64, 75). The beginning for
Hooker is surely not an individualistic condition of "no-rule" but a state of
organized and naturally authorized rule in the fathers. Hooker no doubt
comes uncomfortably close to Filmer in passages such as this, and that may
be one reason why Locke so distorts Hooker's genuine position.[49]

And distort him he does, for it is this Aristotelian sense of the prepolitical
that Locke, misleadingly, quotes into his text; Hooker's once-existing pre-

political condition is not in any sense natural, nor could it be said to be one in which "all men are naturally" (II 15). Locke's fairly casual extension of Hooker in fact transforms Hooker's fairly standard restatement of the Aristotelian derivation of the political from the subpolitical into his own very different state of nature.[50]

The second sense in which Hooker speaks of a prepolitical state deviates further from the Thomist doctrine. More strongly than the Thomists, and certainly more than Aristotle, Hooker insists that nature be taken in a double sense—nature before and after the Fall. Government is natural and necessary to the perfecting of a being with a fallen nature, but it is not natural to humanity prior to the Fall. Hooker's deviation from Thomas, so far as he does deviate, is partly based on his Protestant echoes of Augustinianism and partly based on an effort to be more consistent in his adherence to the Thomist position than Thomas himself was. If there exists a natural law, of which human beings have knowledge and the ability and will to obey, then in a state of innocence the natural law by itself should be sufficient for the ordering of human life. Thus, concludes Hooker, there is "no impossibility in nature considered by itself but that men might have lived without any public regiment." Only "the corruption of our nature," which affects both the ability to know the whole of the law of nature and the ability to obey that law, makes "public regiment" and human law necessary as supplements to the natural law. Hooker reconciles his claim that the law of nature does not require "regiment" with the claim that it does by introducing a distinction between "primary and secondary laws; the one grounded upon sincere, the other built upon depraved nature."[51] Political society is natural under the one, even if not under the other. For Hooker, therefore, there is no state of nature.

Locke's executive power of the law of nature is an emblem within his philosophy of his rejection of the central premise of the Thomist political philosophy—the naturalness of the political, and thus the direct provision for political authority by nature or natural law. That is why it is "strange" relative to the theories of all the Thomists, including Hooker. Although Locke does not spell things out in the same detail as in the *Questions*, the overall shape of his argument is almost the same. The naturalness of political authority for the Thomists reflects the same reliance on the natural inclinations to indicate the mandate of nature—in this case, political life—that Locke rejected in the *Questions*.

Locke's transcendent natural law does not rely on natural inclinations in order to establish nature's mandate. Locke doubts that natural inclinations account for political life for at the center of political life is coercion—the power of punishment (II 3). Political life must somehow go against the grain of human beings if violence is its defining character. The natural law must be independent of the natural inclinations for the same sort of reasons as in the *Questions*: the natural inclinations left to themselves would overturn order and justice.

The executive power of the law of nature is the link between Locke's nonimmanent, nonpolitical natural law and political society. The executive power of the law of nature moderates what might otherwise appear to be a radical break by Locke with traditional natural law—the positing of a state of nature. The state of nature was no part of previous natural law philosophy, because natural law mandated and provided for political life. The moderating role of the executive power of the law of nature is visible if we compare Hobbes and Locke on the state of nature. In Hobbes the assertion of a state of nature is accompanied by a rejection of the law of nature altogether. "These dictates of reason, men use to call by the name of laws; but improperly; for they are but conclusions, or theorems concerning what conduceth to the conservation and defence of themselves."[52] Locke's transcendent natural law in *Two Treatises* is emphatically not that—it is the expression of will of the maker and owner of nature, the divine law-giver. The executive power of the law of nature, then, allows Locke to affirm both the state of nature and the natural law, albeit quite differently from the Thomists. The executive power is an innovation precisely because the law of nature and the state of nature it accompanies are innovations also.

GROTIAN NATURAL LAW AND THE NATURAL EXECUTIVE POWER

Grotius was no Thomist, and therefore it is not strange that a much closer parallel to Locke's natural executive power appears to occur in his *De Jure*. Grotius goes much further even than Hooker in affirming that "punishment . . . may be exacted by anyone at all according to the law of nature."[53] While Grotius agrees with Hooker in emphasizing the difficulties partiality for self makes for such a power, he does not go as far as Hooker and find that this difficulty cancels the power in question, nor does he believe the existence of civil authorities altogether supercedes that power.[54]

Nonetheless, in the key respects Grotius's position is far closer to Hooker or Suárez than to Locke. Again, given the depths of Locke's divergence from the Grotian natural law philosophy, this is not a surprising conclusion. Yet the surface similarities must have been among the factors allowing Locke to ride in on Grotius's popularity among the Whigs.

Like Hooker, Grotius cloaks his doctrine in a series of qualifications that Locke does not accept. Grotius is curiously of two minds as to the location of the right of punishment. He often says the right belongs to all, but immediately qualifies that to "anyone of sound judgment who is not subject to vices of the same kind or of equal seriousness," or to "the good man" or "the wise man."[55] His most general statement on the right to punishment holds that "reason declares that the criminal may be punished. It does not, however, declare who ought to inflict the punishment, excepting so far as this, that nature makes it clear enough that it is most suitable that punishment be inflicted by one who is superior."[56] Locke neither endorses the idea that nature or reason leaves unsettled the holder of the power (he unhesitatingly affirms that it belongs equally to everyone), nor does he equivocate in the slightest between "everyone," on the one hand, and "the good" or "the wise" or "the superior," on the other.

Moreover, Grotius agrees with Hooker that the law of nature is not "in vain" without the natural power of punishment. "Nevertheless, law, even without a sanction, is not wholly void of effect. For justice brings peace of conscience, while injustice causes torments and anguish. . . . But, most important of all, in God injustice finds an enemy, justice a protector. He reserves His judgments for the life after this, yet in such a way that He often causes their effects to become manifest even in this life."[57] Like the Thomists, Grotius sees the content of the law of nature in (some of) the natural inclinations, and therefore the frustration or satisfaction of these also serves as a "sanction" for the law.[58] Perhaps most significant, however, he does not understand sanction to be an essential or defining characteristic of law, as Locke does.

For Locke, the executive power of the law of nature functions as the source of the political power that rulers hold in trust; for Grotius it has no such task:

> For liberty to serve the interests of human society through punishments, which originally, as we have said, rested with individuals, now after the organization of states and courts of law is in the hands of the highest authorities, not, properly speaking, in so far as they rule over others but in so far as they are themselves subject to no one. For subjection has taken this right away from others.[59]

Grotius seems to agree with Locke, as he must, that subjection to government requires the surrender of the individual power to punish violations of the law of nature—generally speaking, at least—but it is not the source of political authority. The source of political authority is rather the agreement of subjection supported by natural law. In this, Grotius differs from the Thomists as well; the law of nature that provides for social life gives a weight to human agreement the Thomists do not recognize.

Grotius's doctrine differs so much from Locke's because it fulfills a much different function within his theory. He posits a natural law power to punish violations of the law of nature in order to complete his teaching on the law of war and peace. The pre-Grotians, like Suárez, had managed to develop natural law doctrines of the just war, but they did so on the basis of conceiving political society as a "mystical body." Grotius rejected that part of his predecessors' doctrine, and thus had to find an alternative source of the power a state might rightfully use in warfare against other states, as well as the natural standards that govern that use. The natural power of punishment supplied Grotius's alternative to the "mystical body" as the source of the power to wage war. It did not supply the source of domestic political power, however.

This shift by Grotius had practical consequences for the just conduct of international relations. Those natural lawyers who deny a natural power of punishment, he said, also deny "that war may be waged upon those who sin against nature," and rather "seem to demand that he who undertakes it should have suffered injury either in his person or his state, or that he should have jurisdiction over him who is attacked. For they claim that the power of punishing is the proper effect of civil jurisdiction [only,] while we hold that it is also derived from the law of nature."[60] For Grotius, the naturally derived power of punishment supplies ground for a somewhat more muscular theory of just war than he found in his predecessors.

> Kings, and those who possess rights equal to kings, have the right to impose punishments not only on account of injuries committed against themselves or their subjects, but also on account of injuries which do not directly affect them but excessively violate the law of nature or of nations in regard to any person whatsoever.[61]

Grotius would be more interventionist than his Thomist forerunners, in that he does not limit rightful use of force to defensive or restorative actions but also admits modest efforts to enforce the law of nature on behalf of third parties. The vehicle for this, of course, is the natural power of punishment.

The implicit reasoning that leads Grotius to modify the traditional doctrine in the direction of the natural power of punishment seems to be the following: The law of nature is a law for a naturally sociable, rational being, aiming at the just social life of that being. Since wrongs may be committed, the rightful use of force must be included as valid under the law of nature.[62] Rightful force cannot be limited to self-defense or to the restoration of one's own, because the root of the law is human rational sociability. One is justly concerned not only with injuries to oneself, but also with injuries to others. Thus, all have a power to use force rightfully in order to punish those who harm others in contravention of the law's dictate of human sociability and peace. However, people being what they are, the claim of protecting someone else's right is often merely a pretense disguising a far more selfish intent; thus one of Grotius's main themes becomes the distinction between a truly just cause of war and a mere pretense of a cause—a theme that Locke does not pursue. The abuses of the power of punishment are behind Grotius's odd vacillation regarding the location of that power as well. The "good," or the "wise," or the "superior" are those who will prosecute the natural power of punishment so as to keep it in harmony with its end, social peace.

Locke's differences with Grotius can be understood in terms of themes we have already explored in the confrontation between them. Of all the differences, probably the most significant is the tight link Locke forges between his executive power and the original of political authority. Grotius draws no such connection between his power of punishment and the foundation of political authority in the pact of subjection. On the one hand, this powerful link in Locke stands as the very feature of his theory that forefends any possible absolutism; the Grotian grounding of political authority in compact has no such result. Locke's executive power finds its limits in the same place it finds its authorization, in the transcendent natural law. Political power has grounding in the executive power, but because of the natural law's no-harm principle, the executive power does not contain a quantum of power sufficient to authorize absolutism.

Although Grotius rejects the Thomistic notion of the "mystical body" in which political power directly inheres under natural law, nonetheless the difference between him and Locke also turns on the status of the state of nature. As we have already noticed, Grotius never affirms a state of nature in his own name, and when confronted by one in Hobbes's work turns explicitly against it. For Grotius, the obligations upon which political life is built exist directly under the law of nature, in the social duties that, for example, ground the obligation of compacts. Although human will, as we have seen, makes an enormous contribution to the Grotian theory of the constitution of political authority—too much, perhaps, from Locke's point of view—yet prior natural law obligations grounded in sociability in turn ground all human agreement. For Locke, human beings are driven into society or government by the "inconveniences" of the state of nature, but this neither requires nor implies any fundamental sociability within human nature or the natural law. As Locke insists, political society is constituted entirely in order to secure the property (in the broad sense) of each of the contractors individually.

Locke's executive power of the law of nature is "strange" relative to the precedent modes of natural law thinking because it is attached to the state of nature and the concomitant denial of the naturalness of political life— itself a "strange" doctrine, as Locke testifies by his great efforts to assure readers that there was or is such a state, and to distinguish his version of that state from the only precedent for it in Hobbes (II 15, 19). Not only is Locke's state of nature more peaceful than Hobbes's, but it is governed by Locke's transcendent natural law. As in the *Questions*, Locke's new type of natural law keeps his otherwise novel doctrine in touch with the tradition, for novel as it is, it surely has much more in common with the old natural law than Hobbes's so-called natural law.

Once the state of nature finds acceptance within political philosophy, that which seemed to differentiate Locke most clearly from his predecessors disappears. Pufendorf, for example, who has been heralded as the propounder of something very like Locke's executive power of the law of nature, accepts the state of nature in his effort to synthesize Grotius and Hobbes. Pufendorf's position still differs a great deal from Locke's, but it will be best to return to Pufendorf only after we have seen what the executive power of the law of nature does to Locke's transcendent natural law.

NATURAL RIGHT AND THE NATURAL EXECUTIVE POWER

Locke's executive power of the law of nature is "strange" because it holds together two things, the law of nature and the state of nature, that previous political philosophy, as witnessed by the Thomists and Grotius, on one side, and Hobbes, on the other, had held apart. The executive power of the law of nature not merely coexists with the state of nature but appears to perfect it, by supplying a device for making the natural law effective in the state of nature. On the other hand, the executive power of the law of nature represents a break in the character of the state of nature. "And thus in the state of nature, one man comes by a power over another" (II 8). Contrary to the initial impression that in the natural state no person holds rightful power over another, under the natural executive power some may do so. To hold rightful natural power over another as authorized by the executive power of the law of nature means, above all, to possess the right to apply force—that is, the right to harm others.[63] Contrary to the initial and unequivocal command of the law of nature that "no one ought to harm another in his life, health, liberty or possessions," the law of nature authorizes this exception: To "do justice on an offender . . . one man may lawfully do harm to another" (II 6, 8). Locke concedes not merely that there will be violence in the state of nature, but that at least some of it will be rightful, authorized by the law of nature itself, or by "reason, which is that law" (II 6).

The executive power may overcome what had first appeared to be categorical natural law limitations, yet Locke very carefully delimits the scope of this new power.[64] It is by no means an "absolute or arbitrary power." The power extends only "to retribute" to the offender, "so far as calm reason and conscience dictates, what is proportionate to his transgression, which is so much as may serve for reparation and restraint," which constitute "the only reason why one man may lawfully do harm to another" (II 8). Yet in the very same section Locke restates his point in much harsher terms: "Every man . . . may bring such evil on any one, who hath transgressed that law, as may make him repent the doing of it, and thereby deter him, and by his example others, from doing the like mischief" (II 8). To reparation and restraint, Locke adds deterrence as a legitimate object of use of force under the law of nature. Locke hesitated to mention deterrence at first. Although deterrence consists well enough with the underlying rationale for the existence of the natural executive power—to make the law of nature effective—it does not comport as well with the main limitation Locke had first asserted, proportionality. A theory of punishment limited to reparation and restraint can more readily remain within the bounds defined by proportionality than one open to deterrence.

The introduction of deterrence in effect repeals the proportionality requirement as initially stated and greatly expands the scope of lawful use of force in the state of nature. The severity of natural law punishment becomes visible only gradually in the course of Locke's argument: although he mentions in passing in section 8 that "every man . . . may restrain, or where it is necessary, destroy things noxious to them," it takes him a discussion spread out over two chapters to bring out the full implications of his deterrence doctrine. For one thing, "every man in the state of nature, has a power to kill a murderer, both to deter others from doing the like injury . . . and also to secure men" against very vicious criminals (II 11). The natural executive power authorizes not merely the use of force, but great force. The force allowed in the state of nature is thus far greater than the force allowed in antediluvian times in Genesis.[65] The teaching of reason goes well beyond the teaching of revelation.

The lawfulness of the death penalty for murder coheres with Locke's initial emphasis on proportionality, but his extension of that penalty to "lesser breaches" evidences the difference the introduction of deterrence makes. "Each transgression may be punished to the degree and with so much severity as will suffice to make it an ill bargain to the offender . . . and terrifie others from doing the like" (II 12). Locke's deterrence principle would appear to overturn proportionality almost entirely, for under the law of nature one could inflict any level of punishment one wanted, as long as some lesser penalty had failed to deter.

To the deterrence doctrine, moreover, Locke adds a new principle, the "enmity" doctrine, that extends the executive power ever further. "It being reasonable and just I should have a right to destroy that which threatens me with destruction . . . one may destroy a man who makes war upon him, or has discovered an enmity to his being" (II 16). Clearly, this covers attempted murders—one need not wait until the fatal blow has been struck to take note of "enmity" of this sort—but it also covers those who attempt to interfere with one's liberty: "Reason bids me to look on him as an enemy to my preservation, who would take away that freedom which is the fence to it." Those who attempt to "take away the freedom . . . must necessarily be supposed to have a design to take away everything else" (II 17).

Locke propounds a doctrine of "constructive enmity"; it is "lawful for a man to kill a thief, who has not in the least hurt him," nor declared any design upon his life" (II 18). Both the offering of force and interference with the means of preservation are evidence of the sort of enmity that might in principle threaten one's preservation. Victims or potential victims are given great leeway in determining whether and when another has enmity toward them. The logic of the doctrine of enmity allows the application of the most extreme form of coercion against persons who directly challenge one's preservation. Moreover, the right to execute the law of nature operates not merely on actual crimes committed but on crimes planned or intended, of which the intended victim appears to be the sole judge.[66] Locke concedes that under such circumstances "self-love will make men partial to themselves and their friends," with the result that "ill nature, passion and revenge will carry them too far in punishing others" (II 13). Contributing to the resulting "confusion and disorder" will be a factor we have not yet taken sufficient notice of: not only actual or potential victims have the right to execute the law of nature; everybody does. They may do so not only on their own behalf, but on behalf of the law of nature itself, or of "preserving all mankind" (II 11). Any person may rightly "punish" any offender or potential offender. Predictably, this will produce "confusion and disorder." Locke describes this not as wrong or unlawful, but rather as "inconvenient" (II 13). The violent and unacceptable character of the state of nature follows as much from the use of rightful force as from the use of unlawful force. Indeed, under the conditions of the state of nature, the difference between the two becomes exceedingly difficult to ascertain, for the law of nature in effect sanctions preemptive strikes against those in whom one has "discovered enmity."

By the time Locke completes his early discussion of the executive power of the law of nature it is clear that the "no-harm principle" is, to an important degree, inoperative. The law of nature, via the natural executive power, validates an extensive right to harm others. Contrary to the initial impression, there will be much violence in the state of nature, much, perhaps most, of it morally allowable under the law of nature. Given all the force used in the state of nature, it is not so clear how different Locke's version of the natural condition is from Hobbes's. As Robert Goldwin has shown, careful attention to Locke's efforts to distinguish his state of nature from Hobbes's reveals that Locke is not in fact claiming his state of nature to be a state of peace, the opposite of Hobbes's state of war. The state of nature and the state of war "are not to be confounded," not because peace prevails in Locke's nature, but because "their difference lies in the fact that they are not things of the same kind." The defining characteristic of the state of nature is "no common superior"; the defining characteristic of the state of war is "force without right" (II 19). The state of nature is thus a condition in which, in principle, there can be either a state of peace or a state of war; the state of war, obversely, can exist either in nature or in civil society. As Goldwin concludes, "However clearly we have distinguished the state of nature and the state of war one from another [conceptually,] we have not at all disposed of the essential question: will there be war in the state of nature?"[67] Locke's answer, we see, is yes. Indeed, because "civil government is the proper remedy for the inconveniences of the state of nature" (these "inconveniences" being the tendency to the use of force), it follows that the state of nature is much more likely to be marked by use of force than the civil state. So far as peace exists somewhere, it is in civil society. "Civil society [is] a state of peace . . . from [which] the state of war is excluded by the umpirage they have provided in their legislature, for the ending of all differences that may arise amongst them" (II 212). No "umpirage," no peace. The state of nature lacks umpirage and therefore lacks peace.

Locke's executive power of the law of nature at first appears to be the completion and the perfection of the natural human endowment, for it is the mechanism God has supplied to make the moral law effective. Yet this mechanism provides a far from adequate system. Much better would it have been had God, or nature, supplied government more directly. Despite the law of nature, the natural endowment is very defective. In a word, Locke's presentation of the executive power of the law of nature undermines the premise-in-chief of his argument for the transcendent natural law early in *Two Treatises*, the provident Creator, and it undermines the first command of the transcendent law of nature, the no-harm principle. Under the law of nature all may harm the guilty, the threatening, or the presumed threatening. Under the law of nature the guilty and the innocent are difficult to distinguish. Under its executive power the law of nature authorizes something very close to the war of all against all.[68]

Grotius hedges his natural law power of punishment with equivocations and restrictions that Locke in the end does not, precisely because his law of nature mandates social peace. Locke is not tempted, for example, to restrict the natural executive power to the "superior," because he fully accepts the fact that the executive power cannot be limited to "good means" or "good men"; for Locke it has a naturally expansive character Grotius's designedly lacks. Indeed, Locke's ever-encroaching executive power stands as much as anything as a critique of Grotius on just this count. Locke's analysis points to the highly unsatisfactory status of Grotius's position as intermediate between Hooker's and Locke's own. Hooker posited a natural power to punish as a moment in an analysis going to show the simple unviability of that power, the need to cancel it. Locke insists on maintaining the power, but accepts the consequences: the means of enforcing the law of nature becomes itself a great threat to the peace that the law of nature presumably mandates. Grotius notices less than either Locke or Hooker the destructive effects of the natural power to punish. Because of his deep commitment to a voluntarist origination of political society, he is foreclosed from following Hooker into cancelling the power of punishment; because of his deep commitment to the natural law as effecting peaceful social life, he is foreclosed from following Locke into fully recognizing the anarchic, or rather bellicose, consequences of the "executive power of the law of nature."

Once the full terror of Locke's executive power comes out, parallels to Pufendorf's position appear. In his effort to synthesize Grotius and Hobbes, Pufendorf moved away from Grotius in ways that definitely remind of Locke. Grotius, for example, insisted on proportionality between crime and penalty. "No one is to be punished beyond desert." In general, Grotius emphasized moderation and limitation in punishment.[69] Much more like Locke, however, Pufendorf admits the right "of exercising force against [a violator] without stint or limit. And this not merely if he attacks my life, but even if he should knowingly and willingly direct some lesser evil against me."[70]

Yet at the very points where Pufendorf appears most to draw close to Locke, a very great gap between them persists: for Pufendorf, proportionality is not necessary because proportionality "has place only in tribunals where punishments are inflicted by superiors." The premise for Pufendorf's discussion, as for Locke's (although not for Grotius's), is a state of nature. "All this is in place between those who do not recognize a common judge among men, whether they be individual moral persons, or composites, in other words, societies."[71] Applications of force against malefactors in the state of nature, according to Pufendorf, "do not properly have the character of punishment." The power Pufendorf speaks of, therefore, is not what Locke calls the executive power of the law of nature. Explicitly rejecting Grotius's view, and implicitly Locke's, Pufendorf claims to be "entirely convinced that the power to exact penalties is part of sovereignty [alone,] and so no one can impose upon another a penalty, properly speaking, unless he have sovereignty over him." Pufendorf expressly grounds his denial of a right of punishment on the thought that "men have need of sovereignty, but not merely anybody can and should exercise it over any and everyone else."[72]

The power Pufendorf speaks of is rather the direct exercise of a natural law power under which "any one whatsoever should protect his own life and limbs, as far as he can, and save himself, and what is his own."[73] This power is not a power to enforce the natural law, but is the embodiment within Pufendorf's system of the Hobbesian right of nature. Locke's explicit law of nature, however, starts out by striking off in a very different direction from Hobbes's; it does not make room directly, as Pufendorf's does, for the Hobbesian right of nature, yet, starting off with a natural law apparently closed to the Hobbesian right of nature, it ends up embodying something very like it in the guise of the executive power of the law of nature.[74] The comparison to Pufendorf is thus especially revealing of the character of Locke's natural law.

The executive power of the law of nature is a step along the way in the movement of Locke's argument from the initial affirmation of divine proprietorship to the later restatement in terms of self-ownership. As Locke first presents the moral mandate of nature, it stands at the farthest extreme from what Hobbes presented as the right of nature, and thus even from

Pufendorf's first law of nature, adapted from Hobbes. According to Hobbes, human beings have a right, that is, a moral liberty, to do what is necessary for their preservation even if that means harming others. According to Locke, human beings have a moral duty to start with: a duty to forbear from harming others. But his doctrine of the executive power of the law of nature emphasizes more and more their right to harm others, whenever and to the degree they judge it appropriate for preserving themselves and others. The executive power of the law of nature makes Locke's law of nature nearly indistinguishable from Hobbes's right of nature.

Does the discussion of the natural executive power then provide the grounds for understanding Locke's shift from divine to self-ownership? In two important ways it helps bring out the reason for and implications of that shift. In the first place, as we have already noted, the development of the character of the state of nature via the explication of the executive power works to undercut the central premise of the divine-ownership argument, a benevolent and provident God. In this respect it parallels Locke's Cartesian argument on God and mortality in the *Questions*.

The emergence of a right of preservation and the executive power of the law of nature is not, however, thoroughly inconsistent with the divine-workmanship argument. From God's ownership derives a duty of preservation, and from that, presumably, a right of preservation. Such a right of self-preservation is, of course, also consistent with self-ownership. On the whole, in fact, it is more consistent with self-ownership than with divine ownership as Locke develops it in chapters 2 and 3 of the *Second Treatise*. Divine ownership would produce a doctrine far more like those of Hooker or Grotius, for the duty or right to self-preservation is always joined with an equally binding duty to others. In Hooker, that conjunction implies the cancellation of any individual right to punish others under the law of nature; in Grotius it produces a consistently moderated doctrine with a far greater insistence on proportionality and restraint than we find in Locke. Locke underlines for his readers how much the right (or duty) to self swallows up the duties to others by initially stating the latter in the very uncompromising terms of the prohibition of all harm to others. Locke derives a right to harm others via what may be perfectly legitimate inferences from the workmanship premises, but he allows the legitimacy of the right to harm others to overwhelm what Hooker and Grotius more firmly retain as limitations on that right. In this sense, Locke's argument is more consistent with self-ownership.

Locke's odd procedure may be understood as follows: He does not move right away to settle the controversy between the two theses, divine or self-ownership. He begins instead with the more conservative, more traditional hypothesis: human beings live in a created whole, governed by a benevolent and provident deity; they are themselves creatures, subject to their Creator. From this hypothesis Locke develops the various forms of the "no-harm" principle. Locke shows that these various principles are in greater conflict than they might at first appear to be. Locke shows that under natural conditions, that is, under conditions of no public authority, permission to harm will overwhelm the prohibition against harm, for human beings are much given to being partial to themselves, a partiality the law of nature cannot remedy under the terms of the state of nature. Thus, even if we begin from the very different premises and implications of divine ownership, we end up with the same, or nearly the same, results as if we began directly with the competing thesis of self-ownership.

If we take the law of nature seriously as a law, Locke suggests, we arrive via the natural executive power at something quite different from what the law of nature had been understood to be. The executive power is both a necessary implication of the transcendent natural law and the executioner of it. Despite his initial derivation of it from a version of the traditional view, the natural executive power stands as an emblem and offspring of Locke's break with the ontology, metaphysics, and theology that animated the tradition's understanding of the status of the political.

To underscore the implications of the undermining of the transcendent natural law by the natural executive power, Locke in a later restatement retracts his initial specification that the state of nature has a law of nature to govern it. "In the state of nature there wants an establish'd, settled, known law, received and allowed by common consent to be the standard of right and wrong." Just as in the *Questions*, the transcendent natural law stands so far from human beings that they have no knowledge of it. "For though the law of nature be plain and intelligible to all rational creatures"— we've heard that before—"yet men [are] biassed by their interest as well as ignorant for want of study of it." In the state of nature, human beings do not know the law of nature. They therefore cannot understand their actions vis-à-vis each other as efforts to execute a law of which they know nothing. Their actions can be understood, however, as based on "a strong desire of self-preservation the . . . planted in them, as in all other animals" (I 86). Just as in the *Questions*, the transcendent natural law gives way to a natural right of preservation.

TRANSCENDENT NATURAL LAW: SUICIDE

Locke's transcendent natural law in *Two Treatises* begins with the thought of divine ownership and derives from that a series of natural law limitations or duties that apply to human beings even in the state of "perfect liberty" that is the state of nature. The chief limitations are a series of variations on the theme of no-harm: under the law of nature we may not harm ourselves or others, directly or indirectly. The discussion of the executive power of the law of nature shows how little the no-harm-to-others principle can be honored under natural conditions. That result accords well with Locke's stunning reversal of claims about ownership: human beings own their own persons, he later says. More than any other aspect of Locke's political philosophy, that reversal calls for thoughtful understanding.

The next stage of Locke's argument, his discussion of slavery, bears directly on the divine vs. self ownership issue; indeed, in this place he settles the question definitively in favor of self-ownership. Slavery would appear to be contrary to both ownership theses, for slavery involves the ownership of some human beings by others. Slavery can become a rightful condition only because human beings can "forfeit" their "preservation and life together" by violating the law of nature, that is, by threatening the life, liberty, or property of another (II 23). The person who possesses the right to execute the law of nature against the offender—actually, anyone—has a right to mitigate the full punishment that could be inflicted and take the malefactor's liberty rather than his or her life. Ruth Grant thus observes that "Locke's discussion of slavery in chapter 4 is the culmination of the discussion of the natural executive power."[75]

Slavery, the first of the five human relationships Locke presents in the series of chapters following the adumbration of the baseline state of nature, is a rightful relation in a sense, but not wholly. As Locke insists, it is the only one of the five that has nothing of consent mixed in with it; indeed, human beings do not have the power to constitute themselves slaves even if they so desire. "For a man, not having the power of his own life, cannot, by compact, or his own consent, enslave himself to any one, nor put himself under the absolute, arbitrary power of another, to take away his life, when he pleases" (II 23). Locke differs from Filmer, then, in denying that human beings are, in effect, born slaves; he differs from Grotius in denying that human beings can make themselves slaves.

Whatever right there is in slavery comes wholly from the right of the master; since the master has the right to kill the slave, he has the lesser right to enslave him as well. Yet the right is, in important respects, very imperfect. As Locke says, "Slavery . . . is nothing else, but the state of war between a lawful conqueror and a captive" (II 24). Yet Locke has defined a state of war as "force without right," although he also defines it as "force or declared design of force upon the person of another where there is no common superior on earth to appeal to for relief." Locke systematically vacillates on the rightfulness of the force that constitutes the state of war: either it is force without right, or it is force of any sort in the state of nature. Locke's presentation of the executive power of the law of nature points to the grounds for that vacillation. In a state of nature, it is operationally impossible to distinguish between rightful and unrightful force. Only in civil society, with its common judge and standing rules, does it become feasible to distinguish rightful from wrongful use of force.

The force with right/without right exercised by the master over the slave does not bring the state of war between them to a conclusion. Only a compact can do that, and a compact would at the same time undo the master-slave relation (II 24). In a state of war "there is no appeal but to Heaven," which in Locke's lexicon means an appeal to force (II 21). The point of Locke's insistence on the state of slavery as a state of war is that even if the origin of the master's power lies in a rightful use of force, the slave lies under no obligation to accept the authority of the master. Locke's understanding of slavery, as of many other matters, is very close to Pufendorf's, whose parallel discussion makes more explicit some of Locke's main points: "Out of an antecedent war arises the society of slave-masters, that is to say, when I grant life to the man I could licitly have slain." The master-slave relation has no basis in compact and "since passage is made from war to peace only by means of compacts, a state of war is understood to be still enduring between us." That means "there is no obligation on [the slave] to serve." A slave may rightly "not merely run away, but even, when the chance has come to him, treat his captor as an enemy."[76] The relation of slavery, then, is juridically asymmetrical and unstable. The master's right generates no corresponding obligation in the slave.

Obligation derives from consent, and Locke firmly teaches that no one can consent to slavery. His reasoning would seem to support the divine-ownership premise, for we cannot give a power over our lives to another that we do not ourselves possess, a claim Locke traces directly to God's ownership. And yet in the very section in which Locke denies the possibility of consent-based slavery, he rejects the premise from which this argument has proceeded. "Whenever [a slave] finds the hardship of his slavery outweighs the value of his life," Locke says, "'tis in his power, by resisting the will of his master, to draw on himself the death he desires" (II 23). On this passage, Locke's editor, Peter Laslett, comments that "Locke seems to contradict himself . . . by justifying indirect suicide."[77]

Admitting indirect suicide, directly contrary to the suicide taboo derived from the premise of divine ownership, is exactly what Locke does here. At least three different ways of understanding Locke's surprising move suggest themselves. The first, and I think correct, way is that Locke is here retracting the no-harm-to-self consequence of the divine-ownership thesis and substituting the directly contrary implication of the self-ownership thesis. Since a person "may even destroy the thing, that he has property in," suicide would be permissible on the premise that human beings are self-owners. According to this reading, Locke would be signalling the true grounds of his natural law or natural right doctrine, self-ownership.

Two other interpretations of Locke's apparent admission of suicide are possible, however, both of them more easily reconcilable with the divine-ownership thesis and the resultant suicide taboo. Perhaps the key point is the indirectness of the suicide in the case of Locke's slave; courting death at the hands of another may differ sufficiently from death at one's own hands to avoid running afoul of the suicide taboo. An alternative line of reconciliation of the suicide taboo and the slave's right to seek death might lie in Locke's claim that the slave has already "by his fault, forfeited his own life, by some act that deserves death" (II 23). Having forfeited his life, perhaps he is no longer bound by his duty to God not to harm himself, and especially not to take his life.

Neither interpretation that attempts to reconcile the slave's right to indirect suicide with the suicide taboo works, however. The indirection argument maintains, in effect, that courting death, as Locke concedes the slave may do, is not suicide, and therefore not prohibited by the suicide taboo;[78] it is the master and not the slave who takes the slave's life. In his formulation and application of his natural law limits, however, Locke has made room for such indirect harms. One may not, for example, "take away, or impair the life, or what tends to the preservation of the life . . . of another" (II 6). But since under the workmanship argument the duties to self and to others are simply parallel, one may not destroy oneself indirectly either. John Simmons is justified, in other words, in concluding from these passages that one "may not do that which 'tends to' his own destruction, either."[79] But that is surely what Locke's slave is doing. Moreover, in the way he describes the actions of the slave, Locke stresses the slave's agency. He not only makes no appeal to an indirection argument, he emphasizes the slave's resistance to the master as an act "in his power"; thereby the slave can knowingly and intentionally "draw on himself . . . death" (II 23).

Locke's contemporary Pufendorf addresses the question of suicide in his *Elementorum Jurisprudentiae Universalis*, a book Locke admired. Pufendorf supports rejecting the indirection argument. With regard to the rightfulness of suicide, Pufendorf explicitly takes up the issue of indirection. "Whether a person falls by his own hand, or in any way whatsoever forces others to put him to death seems not to have any bearing." If, Pufendorf concludes, one is morally bound not to take one's own life, then one "is not excused if one has used the hands of another in bringing about death, since forsooth, one is reckoned to have done oneself that which one does through the instrumentality of another."[80]

The more serious alternative to recognizing Locke as withdrawing the natural law prohibition against suicide is the forfeiture argument. The slave may commit suicide because he has already "forfeited his own life by some act that deserves death"; the suicide taboo remains intact for those who have not so forfeited their lives. Perhaps by forfeiting his right to life he also relinquishes his duty to life.

More careful analysis of the logic of God's proprietorship, however, reveals that the forfeiture argument cannot make divine ownership consistent with Locke's waiver of the natural restriction on suicide. Suicide is initially declared illicit because God owns human beings; therefore, being the property of another, they do not have the right to destroy themselves. For the same reason, human beings lack the right to destroy (or harm) other human beings. In a derivative sense, thus, we can say that John possesses a right to life vis-à-vis Thomas because Thomas is barred from destroying him. If John violates the natural law prohibition, however, and threatens the life of Samuel, then Thomas, among others, is empowered to harm or even destroy him. Thomas no longer has a duty to refrain from harming John, and therefore we could rightly conclude that John no longer possesses a right to life vis-à-vis Thomas or others in a position to punish him for his violation of the law of nature. To have rights against other human beings, rights understood as derivative from the primary natural law duties, means to be the beneficiary of the others' natural law duties. When the duty ceases, so does the right. This is what, under the workmanship argument, it must mean to "forfeit" a right.

But does this argument for "forfeiture" also imply that John loses his duty to preserve himself, one implication of which is the prohibition on suicide? This duty is owed directly to God: John belongs to God, and has no right to destroy God's property. This relation to God, and this limit on John's rightful actions deriving therefrom, are not affected at all by any change that may occur when Thomas's duty not to destroy John is lifted.

The only way suicide could be justified in such a case would be to interpret it as an enforcement of the law of nature under the executive power. John as enforcer kills John as criminal. Locke surely gives us no reason to understand the slave's suicide in this way, and indeed goes out of his way to foreclose such an interpretation. Locke expressly denies the slave the right to end the state of war with the master by compacting into slavery, for "no man can, by agreement, pass over to another that which he hath not in himself, a power over his own life" (II 24). If John's forfeiture of his right to life vis-à-vis Thomas includes a repeal of his duty to preserve himself through an empowerment of himself to murder himself, then clearly John would possess the right to compact himself into slavery also.

Locke's winding comments can make sense on the basis of an alternative hypothesis, however: Locke is subtly shifting the ground of his argument from divine proprietorship to self-ownership. Self-ownership either rests on, or implies, or includes a right to life. A right to life, as opposed to a duty to life, includes a right to end one's life when it becomes too burdensome, for a right is a liberty, not a duty (see I 92, II 123).[81]

This interpretation of Locke's ground as self-ownership and the right to life threatens to make even more havoc in Locke's system, however, than the workmanship argument. Surely the fixed destination of his argument is the rejection not only of the Filmerian notion of absolute government by nature, but also of the Hobbesian (and even the Grotian possibility of) absolutism by compact.[82] The ground for reaching this destination appears to be precisely the divine-ownership-derived denial of self-ownership, setting specific and apparently unbreachable limits on the compacts one may make. If, on the contrary, human beings are self-owners, and possess a right to life that incorporates a right to suicide, what is there in Locke's philosophy to foreclose the Grotian opening toward absolutism?

The complete answer to these troubling questions cannot be reached until we have resolved the meaning and importance of Locke's affirmation of self-ownership, or his construal of rights as "property." Nonetheless, a tentative answer can be put in terms suggested by Thomas Jefferson's reformulation of Locke's position in terms of inalienable rights. John Simmons is correct to remind us that Locke barely deploys the language of inalienability in the *Treatises*.[83] Nonetheless, Jefferson and the authors of other of the founding American documents did not hesitate to translate Locke into the language of inalienable rights. Not only the well-known Declaration of Independence, but the Massachusetts Declaration of Rights of 1780 in its very first sentence after its preamble pronounced that "all men . . . have certain natural essential, and unalienable rights." The Vermont and the Pennsylvania constitutions used almost the same language. The Virginia Declaration of Rights said almost the same in more words: "all men . . . have certain inherent rights, of which, when they enter into a state of society, they cannot by any compact, deprive or divest their posterity."

The concept of inalienable rights allows us to make good sense of Locke's apparent vacillations on slavery. If the right to life is an inalienable right not derivative from a prior duty, as stated in the workmanship argument, then both the licitness of suicide and the illicitness of absolutism would be intelligible. "To have a right is more than to be a recipient of certain duties, it is to exercise one's sovereignty. . . . An active right expresses that a person is sovereign over a part of his moral world."[84] It means one has a certain set of choices respecting the object of one's rights. For instance, one's right to free speech incorporates the moral power to choose not to speak out. The dimension of choice distinguishes a right to speak from a duty to speak. The right over an object, then, includes the right to use it as one will (abstracting for the moment the claims of other rights-holders and other moral limitations imposed on one's actions). It even includes, as Locke says, the right to destroy the thing in which one has a right.

Applied to the right to life, this view of rights implies a right to suicide: one may licitly destroy the object of this right, one's own life. Yet Locke insists we cannot surrender to another our right to life. This paradox may be readily resolved by distinguishing between the right itself and the object of the right. We may alienate (or destroy) the object of an inalienable right, but not the right itself. For example, to take the easier case of the right to property: Surely our right to property includes the right to dispose of it through sale or gift, that is, the right to alienate it. Yet the right to alienate property does not imply the right to alienate the right to property itself, that

is, the moral capacity to be a property holder. Indeed, the very act of alienation of property is an exercise of the right to property.[85]

The paradoxical implication of the notion of an inalienable right is that
a person may give up life but not the right to life. Should a person succeed
in committing suicide, then the distinction, of course, means little. Yet we
might consider one who attempts suicide; Locke might argue that this person had a right to attempt suicide, and yet did not, for all that, therefore lose
the right to life. A failed suicide retains exactly the same right to life all
others have. The attempt at suicide represents neither a forfeiture nor a
surrender of right.

As a rights-holder, one may exercise one's right by renouncing the object
of the right. One may, for example, give away all one's external goods and
eschew the possession of private property. This does not amount to a renunciation of the right to property; one would be free to change one's mind and
later exercise one's capacity to hold and own property. The recognition of
the inalienability of the right in a state of nature would be the continued
possession of whatever moral right of appropriating external goods others
had. In civil society the embodiment of inalienable right would be the continued recognition of the agent as a potential rights-holder to whom the
"protection of the law" would be available. The inalienable right stands as
a persisting standard of justice. Since in civil society civil laws "regulate"
matters such as property or the protection of persons, the rights held under
such law are not purely natural. Locke's point, however, is that the natural
inalienable rights set requirements that any just political society must meet.
Likewise, one may, like Sir Robert, accept the terms of absolute rule. This
does not amount to an alienation of right either, for, according to Locke,
whenever one understands things better, one is free to reclaim one's non-
slave condition. This is Locke's point: No compact we may make for ourselves or others can morally disbar us from rejecting a condition of slavery or
servile political subjection. We are always morally justified to reject such
conditions, and prudentially counselled to construct the institutions of our
common life so as to guard against the de facto exercise of absolute power.

Locke's repeal of the suicide taboo does not endanger his liberal anti-
absolutism, then, for the two positions are consistent with the affirmation
of a natural inalienable right to life—and only with that. It does, however,
plant him unreservedly on the side of self-ownership: human beings possess
a right but not a duty to life.

CHAPTER NINE

Locke and the Reformation of Natural Law: Of Property

LOCKE CONTINUES his systematic consideration and revision of the original natural law limitations on natural liberty in the *Two Treatises* with his famous discussion of property. This discussion stands in an obviously important place in Locke's thinking, for his argument has been moving to the claim that "every man has a property in his own person"—a claim that not merely contradicts the ostensible initial grounding of the law of nature in God's ownership of all persons, but one that reverberates with one of the most striking features of Locke's doctrine of rights, his tendency to cast the whole in the language of property. "Lives, liberties and estates . . . I call by the general name property" (II 123; cf. II 135, 137, 173). All the rights, or all the objects of our rights, are "property." Government is for the sake of securing property, so understood (II 139). Here, in the discussion of property, we might expect Locke to clarify and defend his notions of self-ownership and rights as property. Perhaps this is the reason Locke chose to single out his discussion of property for special commendation in a letter written while *Two Treatises* was still anonymous: "Property, I have found nowhere more clearly explained than in a book intitled, *Two Treatises of Government*."[1]

Clear as Locke pronounced the explanation of property to be, hardly anything in his political philosophy has produced more controversy in interpretation. One reason for the controversy is the failure of most readers to keep clearly enough in mind the place of the chapter on property within the structure of Locke's argument. The guiding thread through the first seven chapters of the *Second Treatise* is the list of five relations presented almost at the very opening of the book. Locke means to show how the political relation differs from the other four, or how "the power of a magistrate over a subject" differs from all other sorts of power (II 2). The chapter immediately preceding the one on property explains the master-slave relation; the chapter following elucidates the power of parents over children. Later chapters outline the husband-wife and magistrate-subject relations. The chapter on property does not fit as obviously into the sequence because Locke does not make the "master-servant" relation explicitly thematic in it, as he does the other relations in the chapters devoted to them. Only a few times in the entire chapter does Locke mention a "servant" or "day worker" (II 28, 29,

41). One could thus easily overlook the centrality of the master-servant relation, yet grasping the chapter in terms of its location within Locke's overall structure brings to the fore its ultimate destination: an explanation of how master-servant relations arise and what they are in contrast to the political relation.[2]

Both slaves and servants labor for others, but the latter sell their labor rather than having it seized forcibly (II 85). Since the slave relation is inherently asymmetrical and unstable, the master-servant relation promises to be a more successful arrangement for providing labor. No state of war inherently exists between master and servant.

The servant is "a freeman" who sells his "services" to another (II 85). But why should a man sell his labor power to another, especially given the original "perfect freedom" of the state of nature? The chapter on property is to answer that question, and how it does so becomes clear in its final section. With the introduction of money, land became entirely private, and none of it remained part of the original common. At the same time, money produces great inequalities in possession of land. Although Locke does not dwell on the point, the harsh fact emerges that one may legitimately own a great deal of land, far "more land than he himself can use the product of," while others, legitimately, own nothing but their "persons" (see II 35). That situation explains the rise of the master-servant relation, and gives it its decisive character, for some must sell their labor to others in order to survive. In a word, the chapter on property begins with a world belonging in common to all, where one aspect of natural equality consists in "sharing all in one community of nature," and moves to a situation in which nothing is common and some are excluded from any ownership of what was common, the whole discussion having the aim of showing the rightfulness of this course of development.[3]

GROTIUS, PUFENDORF, PROPERTY

As is typical of his procedure in *Two Treatises*, Locke does not begin by calling attention to his ultimate destination; rather, he announces his task as follows: "I shall endeavour to shew, how men might come to have a property in several parts of that which God gave to mankind in common, and that without any express compact of all the commoners" (II 25). Locke chooses not to emphasize the end result of the process whereby some are dispossessed and thus relegated to the role of "day labourer," but rather the conundrum of how the originally common could become private at all. As Laslett rightly emphasized, Locke has set his problem up in terms of his ongoing confrontation with Filmer, on the one hand, and Grotius, on the other.[4] Grotius, like the Roman lawyers, had affirmed an original community of property transformed through compact to private possession. Filmer, in turn, had challenged Grotius's concession of an original community of property: If the law of nature mandated community of property, how can it consist with the "providence of God almighty" for the natural law mandate to change? How can human beings have the power to introduce private ownership? Grotius, said Filmer, "doth thereby . . . make the law of nature changeable, which he saith God cannot do." Filmer found the mechanism Grotius identified to effect this change in the natural law doubly problematical: Is it reasonable to surmise that all human beings came together to make such a compact? Even if they did, can one generation disinherit later generations from their share in the natural community of property?[5]

In his essay on property, then, Locke means to save the Grotian thesis, or something like the Grotian thesis, against the criticism of Filmer. He will do this without recourse to an "express compact" and thus avoid at least some of Filmer's strictures against Grotius. Locke does not merely restate the Grotian doctrine with the minor modification of substituting tacit for express consent, however; in the first instance, he appeals to his transcendent natural law to develop a quite different account of the "original of property."

Locke attempts to defend Grotian theses against Filmer, but it would be a mistake to conclude that Locke's modifications in the Grotian property doctrine are determined solely by the effort to lift the Filmeran siege.[6] Peter Laslett rightly called attention to the imprint of anti-Filmerism throughout both treatises, but not everything in Locke's revisions of the natural law thinking prior to him—perhaps nothing of real importance—results from his efforts to shore it up against Filmer.

This is especially clear in the case of the Filmerian critique of property, for Pufendorf had already responded to a critique of Grotius almost identical to Filmer's. Pufendorf both pointed to places where the critics seriously misunderstood Grotius and modified those Grotian theses that were genuinely vulnerable. He produced a philosophy of property only slightly different from Grotius's that was proof against Filmer's blasts. If Locke were only or chiefly concerned to fend off the Filmerian critique, he could stick with a doctrine much closer to Pufendorf's modified Grotianism. However, he departs substantially from both Grotius and Pufendorf.

When Filmer challenged Grotius on the grounds that the Dutchman had derogated from the majesty and providence of God and changed the immutable natural law by allowing human convention to abrogate the initial community of right, he touched on probably the most characteristic feature of Grotius's natural law doctrine. Just as Grotius, in his doctrine of political authority teaches that the natural law empowers human will and human convention to a surprising degree, so he does regarding property.[7] According to Grotius, "the common and undivided possession by all men" of all things that prevailed at the beginning allowed "each man" to seize whatever he could, as he wished, for his own use, and "to consume whatever could be consumed." This "universal use was then a standard of right, as [private] property is now"; no one could seize what another had already seized without committing an "injustice."[8]

Nature's original dispensation could have been maintained if human beings had continued to live very simply, that is, if they had been satisfied to take only what they needed. The simple life of cave-dwelling, nakedness, and nuts and berries did not suffice; as Glaucon put it in Plato's *Republic*, human beings desire "relishes" as well as necessities. Grotius cites Cicero's example of the theater as a model of the original common right: although the theater is common, a seat is properly said to be his who occupies it. The change disrupting this common right occurs when some people decide they need backrests, or built-in cushions, or shade from the sun. To "improve" their seats, they need to apply their industry to them and thus to have a steady relation to them beyond mere use when needed. The need for an abiding relation to things gave rise to the need for property, but not "by the act of one alone"; it is not sufficient for the would-be claimant merely to begin improving the seat unilaterally. Since the property relation implies an abstention by non-owners, and thus an abrogation of original common right, a compact of some sort is necessary to establish property. A compact allows each to know what another considers his or her own and thus to know what should be abstained from.[9] In a now-familiar Grotian move, the compact grounds the obligation to abstain from what another possesses, and thus is essential to constituting property as such. Occupation of land does not itself give a right, but the tacit agreement that occupation is to be taken as signalling ownership does so.[10] A better understanding of Grotius than Filmer showed would appreciate that Grotius does not endorse changing what he had indeed affirmed as an immutable natural law. The natural law decreeing social peace suited to rational beings remains the same; what changes is the application of it in different circumstances. As Pufendorf later said, the demarcation of mine and thine serves social peace by making clear what belongs to whom and thus reducing conflict.

Filmer, however, interprets Grotius differently, not only as allowing human will to change natural law, but as allowing it to contradict or reverse natural law. To the Reformation attitude of human obedience to an overwhelming divine will out of which Filmer's thinking proceeds, this Grotian theory is altogether intolerable. "Grotius saith, that by the law of nature all things were at first common, and yet teacheth that after propriety was brought in, it was against the law of nature to use community."[11] Grotius thus "makes the law of nature contrary to itself," first requiring common right, then requiring private right.

Although I know of no evidence that Pufendorf knew Filmer's critique, nonetheless he responds in *De Jure Naturae et Gentium* to a position very like Sir Robert's: Another critic of Grotius had insisted that whatever right in the things of the world human beings have, the first man, Adam, must have had directly from God, and had fully. If private property was not the initial mandate, then the later introduction of property must be condemned as a "greedy" deviation from right.[12] The point of this objection, as of Filmer's, was to challenge not the rightfulness of private property but the Grotian method of justifying it, and especially the Grotian beginning point in common right. Grotius's natural law is problematic, that is, not because it allows property but because it threatens to destablize it by resting it on a merely human practice, introduced with no authority and contrary to the alleged original natural law ordination.

Pufendorf dismisses this objection because it rests on a confusion between positive and negative community. The critics take Grotius as establishing an original positive community, whereas he really only establishes a negative community.[13] Things held in positive community "differ from things [privately] owned, only in that the latter belong to one person while the former belong to several in the same manner." Negative community, on the other hand, holds things "to be common, according as they are considered before the interposition of any human act, as a result of which they are held to belong in a special way to this man rather than to that."[14] Positive community is thus a kind of joint ownership; negative community is non-ownership: things "are not yet assigned to a particular person, not that they cannot be assigned to a particular person."[15]

Filmer understands Grotian community in the positive sense: natural law prescribes joint ownership and thus the devolution of the things of the world into the exclusive possession of individuals would indeed represent a reversal of the natural law.[16] The original common right as a negative community in Pufendorf's interpretation is not open to the same objection as positive community, however. It merely means that according to natural law, the world is originally unowned—that is, not assigned to particular persons, but ownable. Since the Grotian natural law mandates sociability and peace above all, the assigning of the world to particular persons, so far as that conduces to human peace and welfare, is permissable.[17] "Some arrangements that are permitted, but not enjoined by natural law," comments James Tully, "come to be backed by natural law once . . . introduced."[18]

Pufendorf defends Grotius against his Filmer-like detractors, but he also modifies the Grotian doctrine on property in ways that prove relevant to Locke's discussion. More strongly even than Grotius had done, Pufendorf emphasizes the role of compact in constituting property. Grotius had introduced compact at the second stage of the human relation to the things of the world. In the first stage of common right, human beings could seize whatever they needed, and Grotius does not suggest that this right of taking involved compact. Only at the next stage, in which a more or less permanent relation is developed with external things, required by the improvement of them through the arts, does Grotius expressly introduce compact. Pufendorf, in the guise of a gloss on Grotius, introduces a "tacit convention" in the first stage. "So long as the actual bodies of things were not yet assigned to certain individuals, there was a tacit convention that each man could appropriate for his own use, primarily of the fruits of things, what he wanted, and could consume what was consumable."[19] Pufendorf interprets Grotius in this somewhat questionable manner because he and Grotius agree that the initial appropriation of "the fruits of things" established a right, in respect of which it would be unjust to interfere with what another had seized. An "antecedent pact was required . . . to produce [this] moral effect."[20] Pufendorf distinguishes the kind of use human beings make of the things of the world from the use animals make of them precisely on the ground of this moral obligation. "Brute creatures use and consume things . . . although no dominion is recognized among them." None of the animals "can claim a special right above others to anything, but every one takes for his own nourishment everything he first happens upon." Animals, in effect, share in the same negative commons, but they lack the power to make what they seize property, "for the reason that there is no convention among animals which confers a special right over a thing to the one that first got it." Pufendorf concludes, "It is clear that before any conventions . . . existed there was a community of all things."[21]

Pufendorf concedes that a tacit pact suffices at first, but this must give way to express agreements, a claim that also goes beyond anything Grotius had said. "There was need of an external act of seizure, and for this to produce a moral effect, that is, an obligation on the part of others to refrain from a thing already seized by some one else, an antecedent pact was required and an express pact."[22]

Transcendent Natural Law: Property

Locke is so far from accepting Pufendorf's defense of Grotius against Filmer-like critique that he takes Pufendorf's version of the rationale for property as the account he will avoid: he will make much less, rather than more, of convention or compact than Grotius had done, and thus move in exactly the opposite direction from his synthesizing contemporary. Locke's difference from Pufendorf can be captured in a single phrase: not compact or consent, but labor, supplies "the beginning of property" (II 30). Before property, "the earth and all that is therein . . . belong to mankind in common" (II 26). Contrary to James Tully's assertion that the negative commons "differentiates Pufendorf's [and Grotius's] theory from the theory of Locke," Locke understands this commons as negative—ownerless, but capable of being owned.[23] He illustrates his notion of the original commons with a homely example his contemporaries could understand from their own experience. "Amongst us the hare that any one is hunting, is thought his who pursues her during the chase. For being a beast that is still looked upon as common and no man's private possession, whoever had imploy'd so much labour about any of that kind, as to find and pursue her, has thereby removed her from the state of nature, wherein she was common, and hath begun a property" (II 30; cf. the reference to the oceans as common in II 30 and to running water in II 29).

Locke differs from Pufendorf not on the character of the hypothetical point of origin, but on what gives title to property. "Will any one say he had no right to those acorns or apples he thus appropriated, because he had not the consent of all mankind to make them his?"[24] Of course not, Locke says, because "if such a consent as that was necessary, man had starved" (II 28). Pufendorf's theory of compact is at odds with the very point of property. Since Pufendorf posits a tacit convention, which does not require the actual consent of all mankind, Locke's criticism should perhaps be stated differently: not so much that men would starve if Pufendorf is correct, but that Pufendorf's approach does not sufficiently bring out why property is needed and what the real title to it is. Pufendorf had accentuated the need for consent because he was eager to account for the exclusive character of property rights, and compact seemed the only thing that could generate such an obligation. Locke on the other hand, asserts that "labour . . . excludes the common right of other men" (II 27).[25] Contrary to Pufendorf, then, Locke believes he has another basis—labor—on which to generate the moral obligation to abstain from what another has come to possess. So far as Grotius agrees with Pufendorf on the role of compact in generating that obligation, Locke's rejoinder applies to him as well. So far as Grotius affirms a property right independent of consent, as he seems to do in his first stage of property, Locke dissents for a reason that much parallels his stance toward Grotius in the *Questions*. Just as Grotius insists that obligation is essential to law but has no adequate account of the obligation-generating features of the natural law, he likewise holds obligation to be essential to property but again has no adequate account of the obligation-generating features of the original seizure of property. The closest he can come is to appeal to general duties toward others grounded in rational sociability as the overall mandate of the law of nature. This appeal, however, has, from Locke's point of view, the difficulties presented in the *Questions*. Both in the *Questions* and in *Two Treatises*, Locke appeals to his own transcendent natural law against Grotius in order to supply an account of the right or obligation Grotius required but could not supply.

We must trace out the reasoning whereby Locke finds in labor the power to originate property as an exclusive right in order to appreciate the role Locke's transcendent natural law plays in the critique of Grotius and Pufendorf. Locke's argument is relatively straightforward: "Men . . . have a right to their preservation" (II 25). They must, "consequently," also have a right "to make use of those things, that were necessary or useful to [their] being" (I 86). Human beings require things from the external world in order to survive. Repeatedly Locke calls attention to how deeply our "use of those things" must go. Our first need is food. "The fruit or venison which nourish" us must be "ours and so ours, i.e., a part of us" (II 26). "He that is nourished by the acorns or the apples he gathered . . . has certainly appropriated them to himself. No body can deny but the nourishment is his" (II 28). Locke takes appropriation—the taking of the external world—very literally. The most revealing process of labor is digestion. Locke thus makes clear why property necessarily includes the right to destroy what is owned.[26]

Labor is the human activity that allows the external things to become our own; it is that "without which the common is of no use" (II 28). By a kind of law of transitivity, therefore, Locke concludes that labor must originate property, for it is the sole means by which our right to life can be made effective. The appropriating power of labor is in effect equivalent to the executive power of the law of nature, a necessary inference from our fundamental right to life, because a necessary means to it. The title conferred by labor, then, "does not depend on the express consent of all the commoners" (II 28)—nor, for that matter, on the tacit consent of any of them.[27] Locke seems to have found a way to move from the original (negative) commons to subsequent exclusive property without reliance on consent or compact, and thus to have accomplished what Grotius and Pufendorf failed to accomplish.[28]

Locke himself raises a difficulty with his argument, however. "It will perhaps be objected to this, that if gathering the acorns, or other fruits of the earth etc. makes a right to them, then any one may ingross as much as he will" (II 31). This objection might well be the response of Grotius or Pufendorf to Locke's abandonment of agreement as a means of constituting property. The requirement of agreement embodies the social imperative animating Grotian natural law, because the need for agreement means that individuals lack the power to make property unilaterally, so to speak; the requirement of the consent of others guarantees that property will be (more or less) to the benefit of all. As Pufendorf put it, "Natural law clearly advised that men should by convention introduce the assignment of such things to individuals, according as it might be of advantage to human society." It is to be kept to the "advantage of human society" by being done "in such a way that no one might claim them for himself alone," or by himself alone.[29] Locke, however, has given to individuals through their own labor the power to do this very thing—to "claim them for himself alone," and by himself alone.

The objection Locke raises on behalf of the Grotians to his theory of the power of labor under the law of nature shows again just how parallel that power is to the executive power of the law of nature. Just as the latter was an innovation, so Locke, more quietly to be sure, suggests that this is an innovation, too—as indeed it was. Just as the executive power seemed "strange" compared to earlier natural law doctrines because it empowered individuals to do what individuals had been held morally incapable of doing, so the power of labor to originate property does the same. Finally, just as Locke derived the executive power from the natural law and along with it derived limitations on the power (soon to be overcome, of course), so he now discovers natural law limitations on the power of labor to appropriate the things of the world. "The same law of nature, that does by this means give us property, does also bound that property too" (II 31). Locke's argument loses texture at this point, for he identifies the limitations by quoting a passage from the Bible, apparently a deviation from his task of giving us what the "law of reason" teaches about property (II 30). This is not to say that reason might not confirm what Locke takes from revelation, but in fact he makes little effort to show how his natural law limits derive from reason (see II 25). In particular, he does not here explicitly derive the natural law limitation from the God-as-owner thesis, just as he had not traced the right to life, which grounded the right to appropriate, back to that thesis.

Many scholars take for granted that the right to life Locke depends on is nothing other than his old right derivative from the duty to preserve or not harm self, presented early in his essay. Since Locke has undercut that argument in numerous ways by the time he comes to discuss property, this is not to be so readily taken for granted.[30] Nonetheless, the most plausible construal of the discussion of the natural law limitations places the discussion back in the context of the God-as-owner thesis, and thus suggests that the whole argument about property to this point rests on or is meant to be congruent with the workmanship argument. In the first part of his discussion of property, Locke is presenting an alternative to both Filmer and Grotius in terms of his novel transcendent natural law.

In II 6, Locke had announced the no-harm principle in very general form. Because all human beings belong to God, no one has the liberty to harm another, or to "take away, or impair the life, or what tends to the preservation of the life . . . of another." The argument in chapter 5 identifies the external things of the world as items "tending to the preservation of life." To leave no external goods for others would surely qualify as the sort of indirect harm Locke pronounces to be contrary to the natural law. Unless one left "enough and as good in common for others," or at least enough to support their preservation, one would be guilty of violating the no-harm principle, itself the chief command of the transcendent natural law (II 27).[31]

When he comes to supply an explicit formulation of the natural law limit on appropriation, however, he retreats from his earlier "enough and as good" language and lays down another formula for the limitation:

> As much as any one can make use of to any advantage of life before it spoils; so much he may by his labour fix a property in. Whatever is beyond this, is more than his share and belongs to others. (II 31)

The "spoilage limitation" replaces both the Grotian compact requirement and Locke's "enough and as good" limit, but it fulfills the same function: to set a limit for the sake of others on what any individual may appropriate. Although Locke does not explicitly relate the spoilage limitation to the general no-harm principle, it can be interpreted as a form thereof: one may not appropriate so much as to harm others gratuitously through having things spoil (i.e., lose all usefulness) while in one's possession.

The spoilage limitation is surprisingly less stringent than other possible formulae embodying the general no-harm principle. For example, it is less stringent than the restatements of it one finds in some of the recent literature on *Two Treatises*: "God may have given the earth to everyone to enjoy, but He did not give them a natural right to property beyond the level of subsistence," says Richard Ashcraft.[32] This interpretation runs directly counter to Locke's text, however: "As much as any one can make use of to *any advantage* of life before it spoils; so much he may by his labour fix a property in." Ashcraft's "subsistence rule" would perhaps be more consistent with the transcendent natural law as initially presented, but nonetheless Locke quite explicitly endorses the one and not the other.

The spoilage limitation might at first appear to be less stringent than the "enough and as good" rule, in part because it is less directly responsive to the needs or claims of others. These needs have no direct presence in the rule, as they do in the "enough and as good" proviso. One can indeed satisfy the spoilage limitation and yet violate the "enough and as good" rule—and vice versa, of course, but the latter possibility is much less significant than the first, because if enough and as good is left for others, allowing some of what one had appropriated to go to waste would not harm anyone. Yet Locke describes the conditions under which the spoilage rule holds in such a way that it would not be materially less stringent than the "enough and as good" rule. "Considering the plenty of natural provisions there was a long time in the world, and few spenders, and to how small a part of that provision the industry of one man could extend itself, and ingross it to the prejudice of other," it follows that there was "little room for quarrels or contentions about property so established" (II 31). If the original condition was one of plenty, as Locke says it was, then the spoilage limitation is not in practice less stringent than the "enough and as good" rule. Under conditions of plenty, the spoilage limitation is an adequate embodiment of the original natural law mandate of no-harm; the assumption of plenty is required to make the spoilage limitation a valid—that is, a sufficient—limitation under the natural law.[33] Of course, under those conditions, it is not necessary.

Locke's assumption of natural plenty in the beginning not only allows the spoilage limititation to fit under the original natural law, but it coheres well with the workmanship argument in general. The creator-God who made us also provided for us. As Locke regularly says, quoting a passage from the New Testament, "God gave us all things richly to enjoy."

The spoilage limitation, understood as a special case of the no-harm principle, and the postulate of natural plenty tie the whole argument on acquisition through labor to the God-as-creator-and-owner argument. That in turn allows us to understand how labor can create an exclusive right in things, that is, how the moral dimension of property, the obligation in others to abstain from what one has appropriated, arises under his labor theory. Property, via labor, is a means to preservation; to interfere with property is to do that which tends to harm others.[34] Therefore, individuals possess a right of property in two senses—that of possessing a liberty to appropriate and that of possessing a claim such that others have a correlative duty to abstain.

Locke's procedure may be confusing, so a few words of recapitulation are in order. Despite having already undermined two of the chief tenets of the transcendent natural law—the no-harm-to-others principle and the suicide prohibition—Locke opens his discussion of property by reverting to the transcendent natural law as grounded in the God-as-owner thesis and contained in the general no-harm principle. By the end of section 31, somewhat more than one-fourth into the chapter on property, Locke has presented the general outlines of an approach to appropriation through labor that stands as a critique and alternative to the Grotian approach he evoked in the very opening section of the chapter. As opposed to the Grotians, Locke cuts the origin of property loose from all connection to human agreement; he does this by generating a natural right to exclusive property from the altogether self-regarding right to preservation. The link to the law of nature is maintained, however, through Locke's affirmation of limits to what any individual may rightfully appropriate from the natural common. That link invites us to understand the right to preservation, the ground for the power of labor to appropriate, as itself derivative from the duty to self-preservation under the original no-harm principle. Nonetheless, the attentive reader can hardly help but notice that Locke's discussion of the executive power of the law of nature and of suicide have pointed to a very different grounding for his political philosophy—not the right of preservation as an implicate of divine ownership of humankind, but the right of preservation as a primary and underived right compatible with self-ownership. Locke's procedure is confusing because he keeps reverting to what appears to be a preliminary position—the transcendent natural law—even though he has already moved beyond it. He has moved beyond it, and yet, just as in the *Questions*, he leaves it (more or less) standing as a presence in his finished philosophy, perhaps much for the same reasons as he did in the *Questions*.

The transcendent natural law remains always an important moment in the unfolding of Locke's position. Although it is itself quite different from traditional natural law doctrines, it resembles them far more than his own natural rights theory does. His transcendent natural law not only resembles various traditional doctrines in one respect or another, but it allows him to maintain closer ties to biblical views than Grotius's less theistic natural law was capable of doing. Indeed, to many readers who fail to penetrate Locke's procedure, he appears to be mainly or solely a theologian, resting his entire political philosophy on revealed truths.[35] Locke's transcendent natural law gives him a secure footing from which to launch a critique of traditional natural law.

In the early part of the presentation of his doctrine of property, then, Locke supplies a purely (transcendent) natural law grounding for the right to appropriate and the duty to abstain. Grotius was at best too hazy on the former and—in Pufendorf's gloss, at least—dependent on consent for the latter. Locke generates a different and arguably more focused account on both scores.

Both Grotius and Pufendorf conclude with a definition of property bearing a heavy conventional element, one implication of which is that their theory leaves property remarkably open to political control. Once again, the issue of property presents substantial parallels to the issue of the natural extent of political authority. According to Grotius, the original compact can create an absolutist regime as rightfully as any other form of rule. Locke contests that claim on two levels, one of which was within hi. teaching of a transcendent natural law via the executive power of the law of nature and the inherent limits on compact established by the natural law no-harm principle. Locke derives the same kind of protection for property that he asserted for rights of life and liberty. Human beings come to possess property prior to and independent of political society, which indeed comes into being for no other reason than to protect property in his extended sense, which of course includes property in the narrow sense. Locke concedes the right and power of the civil law to regulate property, but the natural origin of property and the conventional origin of civil government combine to produce a set of important constraints on law and on what the legal authorities may do vis-à-vis the property of their subjects. Perhaps the best known of these can stand as shorthand for all the rest: as the Americans later so eloquently put it, "No taxation without representation." The Lockean state, of course, may tax, but the authorities can never have a "power to take to themselves the whole or any part of the subjects [*sic*] property, without their own consent"

(II 139). This means, of course, that the sole legitimate taxing body is a representative assembly of some sort (II 140). This is, for Locke, a matter of universal constitutional law: no regime may rightly tax in any other manner, no matter what its previous practice was.

This Lockean insistence on a natural and universal constitutional requirement runs in the face of the general thrust of Grotius's thought on the subject. According to the Dutchman, the powers of authorities depend on the variable positive constitutions, or original compacts. The location and extent of the tax power may vary from polity to polity, just as the general quantum of power held may vary from polity to polity.[36]

Grotius was serviceable to the Whigs because he gave legitimacy to the traditional polity, which in England provided that Parliament alone had power to raise taxes—at least as the Whigs interpreted the constitution. But both they and Grotius left that as a positive law mandate, which could, in the nature of things, just as well be otherwise. Locke's transcendent natural law came out in the same place as the Whigs', but in his case the principle of "no taxation without representation" is freed from all contingency, from all uncertainty resulting from the possibility that tomorrow some new document or court case will turn up to challenge the received version of the constitution. Serviceable as Grotius was to the Whigs, Locke was potentially far more so. The very features of his argument that were foreign to typical Whig historical argumentation were the same features that in the long run promised greater and more solid support for Whig positions. Locke's critique and revision of the Grotian natural law of property was, in other words, an important part of the story of Locke's rise to prominence as *the* Whig philosopher. The transcendent natural law, as the respectable vehicle for that critique, thus contributed more than its share to Locke's ultimate triumph. There is good reason to doubt that the transcendent natural law stands in Locke's mind as the true ground for the conclusions to which his political philosophy tended; but he managed to derive—or to appear to derive—those conclusions from that transcendent natural law while at the same time challenging it and subtly supplying indications of an alternative grounding for his conclusions.

PROPERTY AS NATURAL RIGHT

Having established the right of property in the fruits of the earth on the basis of his transcendent natural law, Locke proceeds to consider property in "the earth itself as that which takes in and carries with it all the rest" (II 32). This analysis apparently merely extends the former analysis, for, Locke believes, "it is plain that property in that too is acquired as the former" (II 32). The necessity of that extension is apparent from the place of the discussion within the structure of the *Second Treatise*; the elucidation of the master-servant relation requires the demonstration of the process and legitimacy of the appropriation of the land. That being Locke's task, there can hardly be a more serious misreading of his text than the claim by a recent Locke scholar that "the only form of property in land which he endorses in the *Two Treatises* is the English commons."[37] To the contrary, Locke concludes very explicitly that "we see how labour could make men distinct titles to several parcels of [land] for their private uses; wherein there could be no doubt of right, no room for quarrel" (II 39; cf. II 36).

Locke's explanation of rights in land is, or appears to be, a simple and straightforward extension of his labor theory of acquisition of the fruits of the land. "As much land as a man tills, plants, improves, cultivates, and can use the product of, as much is his property" (II 32). Yet with the example before us of Grotius, who also discussed the origination of property in two stages roughly comparable to Locke's, it is tempting to ask why human beings would or could extend their claims from the fruits to the land itself. If the world originally contained a "plenty of natural provisions," why would human beings start to claim the earth itself? Why would they not remain content with taking from the plentiful commons the "fruits" they require or desire?

When he comes to answer that question, Locke indicates that the turn in the argument to property in land is no simple extension of his earlier discussion. Human beings appropriate land because they need somewhere to labor, and they labor because "the penury of [their] condition requires it" (II 32). The world is not plentiful, but scant, and labor is the means to make it less so. With these thoughts Locke has introduced a major revision of his previous presentation.[38]

He blunts the impression of innovation by reference to divine injunction. "God, when he gave the world in common to all mankind, commanded man also to labour" (II 32). If Locke intends by this to refer to the various biblical injunctions recorded in Genesis, then he presents here a highly truncated and thus highly questionable interpretation of the relevant texts, for God commanded to hard labor only after the Fall, not at the Creation, when he "gave the world in common to all mankind." Locke thus collapses two phases of biblical history and entirely overlooks the key event, the Fall. The condition of penury that requires labor is, according to Locke, the condition of the beginning in itself, not a punishment or curse. In the very act of suggesting biblical support for his doctrine, he shows instead the severe difference between himself and the Old Testament authors.

In fact, Locke does the very same thing at the opening of the chapter on property. He assures us that "whether we consider natural reason, which tells us that men, being once born, have a right to their preservation, and consequently to meat and drink, and such other things as nature affords for their subsistence: or revelation, which gives us an account of those grants

God made of the world to Adam, and to Noah and his sons," reason and revelation teach the same (II 25). Locke has stated the point in such a way, however, as to bring out the very opposite of the ostensible claim. Reason teaches that human beings "have a right to ... meat and drink and such other things as nature affords for their subsistence," but in the *First Treatise* Locke made it one of the chief points of his refutation of Filmer to insist that revelation teaches no such thing about human right. To Noah, long after the Creation and even long after the Fall, God said, "'every moving thing that liveth ... shall be meat for you,' which was not allowed to Adam in his charter" (I 39). Human beings at the beginning—that is, Adam and all who lived before Noah—had no right "to have taken a kid or a lamb out of the flock to satisfie his hunger." Lacking that right, Locke concludes the biblical Adam had at best "a very narrow and scanty property" (I 39). Locke's reason and biblical revelation do not teach the same thing. Locke's reason draws the full implication of the right of preservation; the Bible does not, but, much more like Locke's transcendent natural law, presents God as the owner and master of nature who grants or reserves rights to humanity as he chooses.

Locke follows a complex tactic: he blurs the difference between reason and revelation by exaggerating parallels or even wrongly asserting identities; but at the same time, although somewhat more subtly, he draws the differences. The transcendent natural law itself manifests Locke's blurring strategy, for he leaves the ready impression that God the creator and owner, who is the center of that theory, is the very God known through the Bible. "Deblurring"—bringing out the differences between reason and revelation—is part of the next phase of Locke's argument, the undermining of the transcendent natural law. Reason's conclusions do not coincide or even (for the most part) parallel the authentic teaching of the Bible. Locke's transcendent natural law recapitulates the post-Christian drive within Western civilization to find common ground between its Greek and its Hebrew inheritances, a drive visible in the most important Christian theologies since Thomas Aquinas and especially present in such English thinkers as Richard Hooker, Nathaniel Culverwell, and Richard Cumberland, all of whom attempted to reconcile biblical and rational teachings within the context of a natural law theory. The Reformation surely disrupted this drive for harmony, but even radical Christian thinkers like John Milton made important gestures toward this reconciliation.

Locke officially aligns himself with this mainstream Christian theology, both in his transcendent natural law and in the formal doctrine of his *Essay*, that reason and revelation teach the same, except for matters such as immortality of the soul, where revelation goes beyond but does not contradict reason. However, if we pay attention to what Locke actually shows us, rather than what he says he is showing us, we see a rather different picture. Reason and revelation frequently conflict, and therefore a thoughtful person must somehow choose between them. Locke makes clear what he chooses in the face of conflict: "Reason is [our] only star and compass" (I 58; cf. II 57).[39]

Despite the differences between the teachings of reason and the commands of revelation, and despite Locke's commitment to reason, he consistently and persistently blurs the differences. He blurs differences in order to conceal his innovativeness. He would leave the impression, to return to the example at hand, that the need to labor that grounds the new kind of property in the earth itself is a mere recognition of a divinely imposed duty. He makes no effort to trace this duty to the transcendent natural law, and it is difficult to see how he could do so. It does not follow from the fact that human beings are the "workmanship" and therefore the possession of God that "in the sweat of their brows they should eat bread." Surely the Bible itself does not understand human creatureliness in this way. Were it not for the Fall, humanity could have survived on the spontaneous fruits of the garden. Labor arrives as a punishment for humanity's disruption of the initial relation to God through disobedience.

If, on the other hand, Locke intends the command to labor to be understood as following from the Fall, and thus from explicit biblical doctrine, we have his interpretation of the Fall in the *First Treatise* to show that he does not understand the command to labor as a moral obligation of any sort. There, Locke had rendered the parallel punishment laid on Eve as "no more a law to oblige a woman to such a subjection [to her husband,] if the circumstances either of her condition or contract with her husband should except her from it, than there is that she should bring forth her children in sorrow and pain, if there could be found a remedy for it" (I 47). The curse on Eve, and by extension the "command" to Adam to labor, lays no obligations but only "foretells" how things will be. As there is a "foundation in nature" for woman's subjection to man (greater male strength, female vulnerability through pregnancy and motherhood), so there is a foundation for Adam's labor—the penury of the human situation in nature. By Locke's method of interpretation, then, the "command" to Adam to labor is nothing other than "his condition," which "required it of him." In a word, there is no basis in Locke's appeal to the "command" to labor for inferring that "everyone now has an obligation to labour," or for concluding that "labour as an activity, and its end product, private property, have become a fulfillment of man's natural law obligations, expressed as the will of God."[40]

Human beings must labor, not to fulfill an obligation but to cope with the insufficiency of nature. The need for labor produces the need for property in land. Locke's extension of the labor principle is more than a mere extension of his earlier argument, because it is premised on a reversal of the presumption that informed the earlier discussion of property in the fruits of the earth: not plenty but scarcity is the divine, or natural, endowment for human beings.[41] Most of the remainder of chapter 5 is devoted by Locke to expounding on the theme of natural scarcity and, in that context, to substantially modifying his earlier treatment of labor.

Locke begins his thematic discussion of natural scarcity with the observation that, like the novel executive power of the law of nature, it may at first appear "strange . . . that the property of labour should be able to overbalance the community of land" (II 40). It is "stranger" that labor should be able to create property in land than in the consumable items Locke had first spoken of. The rationale he originally presented for labor does not directly hold for land. There is no need to absorb or digest it, as there is with food, the paradigmatic instance of the first sort of property. The case for land in property, especially if it has the consequence of dispossessing many (or most) human beings from their original right to appropriate the fruits of the natural common, is much harder to make than the case for appropriating acorns and venison. This case can be made only in terms of natural scarcity.

Locke's most thematic statement on natural scarcity is his almost shocking claim that "nature and the earth furnished only the almost worthless materials, in themselves" (II 43). Neither God nor nature "has given us all things richly": men have neither been given "all things," nor were they given "richly."[42] Locke invites us to consider "the ordinary provisions of life"— bread, wine and cloth. These "are things of daily use," yet none is produced by God or nature. "Unassisted nature" does not give us "all things" (e.g., bread, wine, and cloth), but instead provides acorns, water, and leaves, skins, or moss (II 42). The "commodities" nature does not provide are far the "more useful"; they far "exceed in value" the natural ones.

Neither does nature supply "richly." In a series of almost comical restatements, Locke progressively diminishes nature's contribution. Unimproved land produces, not one tenth not one one-hundredth finally not even one one-thousandth of what improved land does (II 40, 43; cf. II 37). When nature produces abundance, Locke reminds, even much of that is useless. "The greatest part of things really useful to the life of man, and such as the necessity of subsisting made the commoners of the world look after . . . are generally things of short duration; such as, if they are not consumed by use, will decay and perish of themselves" (II 46). In sum, nature provides few things, most unpalatable in themselves, ordinarily small in quantity or, when more profuse, rotting. Locke would first have us believe that humanity finds itself set in a world designed for it by a kindly father; later he shows it to be the sort of place a wicked stepmother might produce. Therefore, he observes, in the world as nature gave it, the inhabitants are "needy and wretched" (II 37).

Since nature is so niggardly, human labor must make up the deficiency. "Labor makes the far greatest part of the value of things, we enjoy in the world" (II 42). Unimproved or natural land scarcely has any more value than nature's spontaneous products. "The ground which produces the materials, is scarce to be reckon'd in, as any, or at most, but a very small, part of [value,] so little that even amongst us, land that is left wholly to nature, that hath no improvement, pasturage, tillage, or planting, is called, as indeed it is, wast[e]; and we shall find the benefit of it little more than nothing" (II 42; cf. II 36).

Labor's contribution goes beyond the relatively simple "ploughman's pain," but includes the entire complex of a division of labor, including "invention and the arts," skills and effort, and the very social organization of labor itself (II 44). Perhaps thinking of the Lord's Prayer—"give us this day our daily bread"—Locke traces out the amount and complexity of human labor required to "give us" a loaf of bread:

> It's not barely the ploughman's pains, the reaper's and thresher's toil, and the baker's sweat, is to be counted into the bread we eat; the labour of those who broke the oxen, who digged and wrought the iron and stones, who felled and framed the timber imployed about the plough, mill, oven, or any other utensils, which are a vast number, requisite to this corn, from its being seed to be sown to its being made bread, must all be charged on the account of labour, and received as an effect of that. (II 43)

Locke's new treatment of labor replaces both the earlier view, associated with his transcendent natural law, of a provident Creator, and his earlier account of labor. Human beings require labor not merely to appropriate for their own use products already available but also to bring forth the products themselves. Labor, Locke now shows, contributes far more than he had first suggested. Nonetheless, the two presentations place the same feature at the center—labor's transformative power. The original appropriative labor that takes digestion as its model is the power of living beings to appropriate the being of other beings and assimilate it into their very being itself. The second kind of labor, productive labor, is just as transformative. Things that were never in the world are produced from what was there. The natural endowment, far from being the support and ground of human life, becomes mere raw material, "almost worthless material" at that. It is tempting to view Locke's theory of labor as a forerunner of Heidegger's theory of technology as the human power to reveal all being as "standing reserve," that is, raw material of an especially abstract and interchangeable sort.[43] Heidegger's theory of technology, indeed, appears to be a generalized and hostile version of Locke's theory of labor. What Heidegger decries, Locke celebrates.

As the comparison to Heidegger suggests, there is a vision of being as a whole underlying Locke's doctrine of labor. It is not the view often attributed to Locke—the great chain of being, a world composed of distinct and graded beings, ordered into a whole.[44] Certainly Locke sometimes supplies evidence for such a conception, yet his theory of labor evokes an altogether different world, one with fluid boundaries, matter organized temporarily now this way, now that, and "being" an artifact of a particular temporary organization. In this world, the beings become . . . raw material. And standing above this world of flux is one being, somehow capable of ordering the rest around itself, engaging not merely in the constant transformations of animal labor—appropriation, digestion, growth, death, decay—but in a different sort of labor altogether: human labor, transformative, like animal labor, but self-consciously so, based on arts and knowledge, and consciously setting itself and its purposes ("conveniences") as the end for the sake of which the rest of nature is to be transformed. It is no accident that the society that above all others has drunk from the Lockean cup has been more at home with the technological transformation of the world than any other.

If nature (except for humanity) is reduced to raw material, then the being of the beings (to borrow a phrase from Heidegger), cannot be defined in terms of their whatness, their essences, or species beings. Animals are potential food, metals potential tools or weapons, plants potential clothing. Such a view of the beings has already been prepared in Locke's doctrine of natural species as presented in the *Essay Concerning Human Understanding*. The species are not, in fact, natural, but constructs of the human mind. Substance as such is a posit of the mind, the particular substances certainly unknowable.[45] Behind his epistemology and his doctrine of labor stands precisely the same Lockean insight: the immensely creative power of human labor, understood either as the labor that constructs a world of use and convenience from almost worthless raw material or as the labor that constructs a world of things with qualities from sense data that do not and cannot vouch for this world. Tully is correct to notice a parallel between human creative labor power and divine workmanship, but Locke's point is far more daring than Tully sees: because the divine workmanship lacks inherent character—is not a "world"—the human workmanship is possible.[46]

Given the wonders of labor as Locke delineates them, one puzzles over the Bible's perception of it as a curse or a punishment. Despite his enthusiasm for it, Locke acknowledges that labor is "pain," "toil," "sweat" (II 34, 37, 42, 43). The world, not made for human use as the race would wish it to be, resists human efforts to refashion it. The world is body and the defining quality of body is solidity, that is, the "resistance which we find in body"— resistance, not Descartes's purely intellectual extension. Locke's world is a solid, resisting world that makes itself known through its ability to inflict pain. To the skeptic who doubts the existence of the external world or the adequacy of the senses' testing of it, Locke replies, "He that sees a candle burning, and hath experienced the force of its flame, by putting his finger in it, will little doubt, that this is something existing."[47]

The world, not made for us, can be remade to suit us better, but it requires expenditure of effortful labor. Most human beings would prefer to suffer less pain; not all are "industrious and rational" (II 34). Labor is required to overcome human neediness and wretchedness, but it involves its own wretchedness. Only if one has some assurance of reaping the rewards of one's labor is one likely to expend it. The phenomenal productivity of labor can show itself only if there is something for it to work on and only if others are excluded from the fruits of its efforts. Exclusive property in the land or, more generally put, in the means of production is a necessary condition for productive, transforming labor, which is a necessary condition for comfortable preservation. Under conditions of natural scarcity and productive labor, the right to life implies the right to property, with labor as the intermediate term. "The conditions of human life, which requires labor and materials to work on, necessarily introduces private possessions" (II 35).

Locke thus accepts and goes beyond Grotius's point that the application of labor requires a more stable and ongoing relation to the object of one's labor. Labor requires and constitutes a link over time between a person and a part of the external world entirely different from that involved in gathering spontaneous natural products. For Locke the unstable or raw-material-like quality of the things of the world is the precondition for the fashioning by human beings of a new kind of stability through property.

As should now be clear, the whole drift of Locke's teaching on property is away from the structure of thought captured in his transcendent natural law. The whole can be restated in terms of a chain of reasoning with a primitive right of preservation as its first member (see esp. I 86, II 25). As his argument proceeds, Locke shows why the natural right account is superior to the natural law account: the notion that there are natural limits preceding and grounding natural rights rests on untenable premises of a beneficent and provident God or nature.

The replacement of the transcendent natural law grounding of property by natural right is reflected, as might be expected, in the fate of the natural law limits on acquisition Locke first articulated. The same transcendent law of nature that allowed property also bound it; with the demise of that law of nature comes the demise of the limits as well.

As he does throughout, Locke proceeds in stages. He begins, let us recall, with his transcendent natural law. As God's property, human beings are both obliged to maintain themselves, and thus to use the things of the world necessary for survival, and obliged not to harm others, even indirectly, and thus not to take so much of the things of the world that others are imperiled. Locke formulates the limitation on appropriation first as the "enough and as good" rule then as a spoilage rule. He asserts the same pattern of limitation for the appropriation of land as he had earlier asserted for the appropriation of fruits: first a requirement of leaving enough and as good, then a spoilage or use limitation (II 33, 34, 36, 37). "Before the appropriation of land," human beings were free to take from nature what they could use without spoilage; if goods spoiled in their possession, they "had offended against the law of nature," for they had "invaded [their] neighbour's share" (II 37).

> The same measures governed the possession of land too: whatsoever he tilled and reaped, laid up and made use of before it spoiled, that was his peculiar right; whatsoever he enclosed, and could feed, and make use of the cattle and product was also his. But if either the grass of his inclosure rotted on the ground, or the fruit of his planting perished without gathering, and laying up, this part of the earth, notwithstanding his inclosure, was still to be looked on as waste, and might be the possession of any other. (II 38)

The meaning of the limitations must be reconsidered not only on the basis of the extension to land itself but even more on the basis of the new information about natural scarcity. The discussion of the limitations on acquisition of the "spontaneous products of nature" was premised on natural abundance. In a situation of scarcity the rules look rather different. The "enough and as good" constraint directly protected the interests of others; the scarcity limitation did not, but if there is plenty the shift means little. Under conditions of scarcity, however, the shift to the spoilage limitation means a great deal. Under the latter rule, neither the quantity of goods appropriated nor the needs of others limit the right of appropriation. "He that gathered a hundred baskets of acorns or apples, had thereby property in them." The only limit was that he "used them before they spoiled." But to barter perishables like apples for less perishable items like nuts is "no injury . . . so long as nothing perished uselessly in his hands." The key term is "perished," for the actual use of the item is not essential. So long as the goods do not perish, Locke does not believe any one has taken too much, no matter how much others may lack—"the exceeding of the bounds of his just property not lying in the largeness of his possession, but the perishing of anything uselessly in it" (II 40).[48] Under conditions of scarcity, the spoilage limitation does not satisfy the no-harm principle, for one person may hoard so much as he or she can (eventually) use without regard to whether this indirectly imperils others. Locke's point is this: one's own preservation has an absolute priority over the needs of others under the principles of nature. One has a right to whatever might be useful to one's preservation as long as it actually can be useful. Gratuitous harm to others is ruled out, but all forms of self-benefit are legitimate. With regard to property, Locke affirms the same expansive notion of the right to self-preservation as he did in his discussion of the executive power of the law of nature.[49]

The extension of the limiting principle to property in land raises only slightly different issues. Ironically, perhaps, the "enough and as good" rule appears easier to satisfy for land than for "fruits" under the posited condition of the beginnings. As Locke emphasizes, unimproved land is so unproductive that there is a great deal more of it than of "fruits." Nonetheless, the general point of the shift from an "enough and as good" restriction to the spoilage rule is the same as it was with regard to fruits. Whatever one person can usefully take, he or she has a right to, quite without regard to the needs or concerns of others. This appropriation is potentially more harmful to others, for it amounts to a more serious dispossession. The nonowner not only may not seize the hoard of nuts the owner has gathered, but may not use the owner's land as a locus for hunting and gathering activities, so long as the spoilage limitation is satisfied, anyway. Under conditions of scarcity, in other words, the spoilage limitation indicates a severing of the link between Locke's substantive teaching on property and the mandates of the transcendent natural law. The latter accounts for less and less, and a pure right to preservation accounts for more and more.

Accordingly, Locke treats the spoilage limitation less and less as a moral limitation and more and more as a prudential one. "Indeed it was a foolish thing . . . to hoard up more than he could make use of" (II 46). It is foolish because it is wasted labor.[50] "As a man had a right to all he could imploy his labour upon, so he had no temptation to labour for more than he could make use of" (II 51). Locke here reinterprets his own spoilage rule in the same way he reinterpreted the biblical curses on Adam and Eve—as statements of how things will be rather than normative requirements, natural laws in quite another sense than his transcendent natural law.

The link between Locke's reinterpretation of the biblical curses and his own natural law rule suggests that just as woman would be under no obligation to suffer the pain of labor in childbirth if a way around it could be devised, so human beings would be under no obligation to appropriate only what is useful in the near term if the tendency of the things to spoil or the wasteful (of labor) consequence of this could be arrested. That is just what Locke teaches. The invention of money frees humanity from the limitation of the spoilage rule. "A man may fairly possess more land than he himself can use the product of, by receiving in exchange for the overplus, gold and silver, which may be hoarded up without injury to any one, these metals not spoileing [sic] or decaying in the hands of the possessor" (II 50). If the surplus product of one's labor can be stored in money, then it is no longer "a foolish thing . . . to hoard up more than he could make use of." Before money, Locke had said, the one who hoarded more than he could use was "dishonest" as well as foolish, for "he took more than his share, and robb'd others" (II 46). Since the introduction of money, it is as little dishonest as it is foolish.

In early times "different degrees of industry" were "apt to give men possession in different proportions," a tendency the invention of money much accentuated, ultimately resulting in a "disproportionate and unequal possession of the earth" (II 48, 50). In civilized (money-using) countries it "can scarce happen" that "tracts of ground are to be found, which . . . still lie in common" (II 45) Put more directly than Locke does, the invention of money eventually produced that situation of possession and dispossession in which some own more than they can use and others own nothing but themselves. Locke, in other words, finally arrives at his destination, an account of the conditions that produce and make possible the master-servant relation. Masters and servants, employers and employees, rightfully exist because human beings have within themselves the capacity to overcome the natural limitations on appropriation. The waiving of the limitations signals or reflects the passing of the transcendent natural law that first generated them. It is not merely that the natural property right is one of unlimited acquisition, as Strauss and Macpherson insisted, but that that right is grounded in the natural right of preservation and not in the workmanship based natural law.[51]

The right to appropriate land, even to the point of private ownership of the entirety of what was common, follows from the right of preservation of the appropriators, and the rights of those who are excluded from ownership set no limit on what may be appropriated. But what of those who are excluded? Is not their right to appropriate, and thus their right to preservation, endangered by the transformation of the common into wholly private property? Locke devotes much attention to their situation, for the rightfulness of their being consigned to selling their labor for wages depends on showing that their rights have not been violated in the process of appropriation. It is not enough, in other words, to show the rightfulness of this process from the point of view of the rights of the appropriators; it must also be shown to be right from the point of view of the dispossessed.

In the early stages of appropriation of land, the amount of land is far greater than the number of persons who might appropriate it (II 33). "He that had as good left for his improvement, as was already taken up, needed not complain, ought not to meddle with what was already improved by another's labour" (II 34). In the long run, however, more important than the surplus of land over people is the productivity of improved land. "He who appropriates land to himself by his labour, does not lessen but increase the common stock of mankind" (II 37). Locke refers, of course, to the power of labor to produce ten or a hundred or a thousand times more than nature herself. "He that incloses land and has a greater plenty of the conveniencys [sic] of life from ten acres, than he could have from a hundred left to nature, may truly be said to give ninety acres to mankind" (II 37). The cultivator of land can support himself on far fewer acres than when the land was left to nature and thus, by taking a small portion of the land for his exclusive use, he no longer shares the natural commons with the others; by removing himself from competition with them for sustenance in the common, he has, paradoxically, benefited them. He uses the product of less land now, and therefore leaves the others more than he did before. Thus Locke's paradox:

by taking, he gives. Not merely do the others have no just ground for complaint against the appropriator, they have reason for gratitude.[52]

This reasoning no longer holds, in this form at least, in the world remade by money. Here the appropriators have taken all the commons and thus it is no consolation to the excluded that the appropriators are feeding themselves on the product of less land than they would have required if all were common. Moreover, Locke's rejoinder that land remains for them to do the same with no longer holds. This is the moment when the process of appropriation would seem to rob them of their right to appropriate and thus would endanger their survival.

Locke denies both points. The dispossessed, he maintains, have consented to their own dispossession. The process could never reach this point without money, and money "has its value only by consent of men." In consenting to the use of money, "men have agreed to disproportionate and unequal possession of the earth" (II 50).[53] Locke's recourse to consent here is no return to Grotian or Pufendorfian notions, however. On the one hand, the consent shows that the dispossessed are themselves participants in the process that led to their situation; it is not something merely imposed on them by outside predators. The consent to money is needed for the process of appropriation to run to completion, but it is not necessary in any other way to its rightfulness. The rights of the dispossessed are not violated, because their right was merely to take from the unappropriated commons what they needed for their survival. The right to appropriate land or goods was contingent on there being unowned land and goods.[54]

The right they undeniably have that might appear endangered is the primary right of preservation. With no land of their own and no natural common to glean, they are potentially at great risk. Yet Locke also denies that their right to life is violated. The appropriation of the land makes possible the great increase in production Locke celebrates. The use of money makes possible the complete appropriation of the land. While money excludes some from owning land, it also makes possible a yet greater increase in productivity. Money allows hoarding, but it also allows commerce, and commerce supplies an incentive for the production of surplus. Without commerce, the potentially great creative power of labor cannot be fully expressed (II 48).

The complete enclosure of the natural common, then, potentially makes for even more plenty, but only if goods can be exchanged for money and there is effective demand for the surplus that could be produced. As a result of the development of large holdings, proprietors can no longer work all their land themselves. It produces more than they can consume and requires more hands than they can supply. They must hire (or otherwise procure) the labor of others. The very circumstances that dispossess some from all land ensures demand for their labor. In place of the natural foraging of the beginnings arises a system of ownership, wage labor, commerce, and, most important of all, plenty. The so-called dispossessed are not truly dispossessed. They lack land, but "by being masters of themselves, and proprietors of their own persons, and their actions of labor [they have] still in themselves the great foundation of property" (II 44). Their right to property receives recognition in their ability to sell their labor and derive the fruits of it. They share in the distribution of goods produced in the new system, not at the same level as the owners, perhaps, but they live better (in terms of the goods necessary for survival and comfort) than even the best off in a natural common. "A king of a large fruitful territory [in America] feeds, lodges, and is clad worse than a day-labourer in England" (II 41). Everyone, even the nonowner, is better off under the advanced economy of private ownership and wage labor.[55]

Locke's theory is not exclusively of either the deontological or the consequentialist variety, to use the jargon of contemporary political and moral philosophy.[56] The system of property he describes is justified both in terms of the natural rights of individuals and in terms of its consequences—the material improvement of life, the better satisfaction of the natural desires than is otherwise attainable. Locke implicitly concedes that not everyone is equally better off; the owner of the means of production will be best off, no doubt, but everyone does benefit.[57] The proper standard for judging the distribution of benefits is not equal distribution of the existing stock, as many of our contemporary theorists of social justice assume, but the original situation before the human economic system improved it. Locke's treatment is, of course, only a rough one. He takes for granted, for example, something like a full-employment economy. In a less than full-employment economy, the unemployed would be genuinely threatened in their right to life and would have the right to seize what they could to survive. In the *First Treatise*, Locke describes this right as "charity," which, he says, "gives every man a title to so much out of another's plenty, as will keep him from extream want when he has no means to subsist otherwise" (I 42). This charity, it must be noted, is not the old duty to charity, binding on the wealthy, but a right to charity—that is, to the necessary means to subsistence when such can be gotten no other way—inhering in the destitute. Even when sounding most traditional, Locke is radically innovative. The implication of this right under conditions of modern economy is a modest welfare—or better, security—state, one that guarantees a job for all, or, that failing, subsistence.[58] It does not justify redistribution for its own sake or in order to produce a more equal distribution of wealth per se.

Rather than welfare, charity, or redistribution, Locke identifies as "the great art of government" the promulgation of "established laws of liberty to secure protection and incouragement to the honest industry of mankind" (II 42). The principle underlying the whole process of appropriation, from the natural common to the wholly owned world—the unleashing of that incredibly productive, creative force, human labor power—is to govern societies now rationally aware of the process.[59] Political economy becomes "the increase of lands and right imploying of them" and Locke identifies that, in turn, as "the great art of government" (II 42). Locke thus becomes the first to define political economy as the central task of politics.

The centrality of political economy and economic growth came to be one of the central features of the new post-Lockean natural rights republicanism, in contrast to the old republicanism. No genuine partisan of the old republicanism, such as Plato, Aristotle, or Livy, would say what James Madison said, very much in the spirit of Locke's new "natural law" teaching: "The protection . . . of the diversity in the faculties of men, from which the rights of property originate . . . is the first object of government."[60]

NATURAL LAW AND NATURAL RIGHTS

Let us recapitulate. Without any doubt Locke is a rights theorist who initially presents rights as derivative from the transcendent natural law that affirms natural limits or duties based on divine ownership as the primordial moral reality. As Locke's discussion proceeds, the status of the natural law comes more and more into question, however. To say nothing of many other relevant considerations, Locke gradually denies the limitations that are the primary expressions of the transcendent natural law. Locke thus withdraws his support for the transcendent natural law. He does not withdraw his support for rights at the same time, however. Contrary to the initial impression, rights are not derivative from the natural law, but somehow independent of it.

We are perhaps to understand the natural law somewhat as Hobbes did, as "a precept or generall rule, found out by reason, by which a man is forbidden to do that, which is destructive of his life, or taketh away the means of preserving the same."[61] Locke nowhere argues systematically for such a position, but there are numerous suggestions that tend in this direction, among the most important of which is his frequent identification of the law of nature as the law of reason, or even more suggestively, his claim that "reason . . . is that law" (II 6, 30, 31, 56, 57, 96, 118, 172).[62] Since he never retreats from the view of reason taken in the *Questions*, that it is a "discursive faculty" for moving from premises to conclusions and contains no substantive principles or apprehensions of truth in itself—that is, has no innate knowledge of any kind—we could easily understand him to mean that the law of nature states reason's conclusion in the mode of Hobbesian natural law.[63]

Much about the way Locke treats rights also coheres with the Hobbesian formula for "natural law." Locke thinks in terms of the famous triad, life, liberty, and property; he understands the right to life to be the primary right and understands the others as rights because they are conducive to "preserving the same," to use Hobbes's phrase. "Freedom," Locke says, "is the fence to my preservation" (II 17). "Freedom," he says in another place, "is . . . necessary to, and closely joyned with a man's preservation" (II 23). Locke derives the core of the property right from the right to life in a passage very reminiscent of Hobbes's discussion as well: "Natural reason . . . tells us that men . . . have a right to their preservation, and consequently to meat and drink and such other things, as nature affords for their subsistence" (II 25). Preservation, for Locke as for Hobbes, is the primary right, and liberty and property are derived rights. "Law in its true notion, is not so much the limitation as the direction of a free and intelligent agent to his proper interest, and prescribes no farther than is for the general good of those under the law" (II 57). This description of law does not much correspond to the transcendent natural law as Locke developed it early in *Second Treatise*. The transcendent natural law did not take its bearings from the "interests" or the "general good" of humankind, but from the sovereign fact of divine ownership. It surely set "limitation" on human action. On the other hand, Locke's restatement does coordinate well with an understanding of the law of nature as a set of rules not primarily aiming to limit but rather to achieve the interests—that is, preservation and what is useful to preservation, that is, rights—of humanity. In this restatement, therefore, Locke puts no emphasis on the obligatoriness of law, but mentions only the utility of law. As he says in the immediate sequel, "Could they be happier without it, the law, as an useless thing would of itself vanish" (II 57). The law is only if it is useful, and it is useful only if conducive to happiness. More broadly, the law is a means to an end variously described as "interest," "good," "happiness," and finally "freedom" (II 57). The point of the transcendent natural law is to express the human creature's relation to the divine Creator; the point of law as discussed here is "to preserve and enlarge freedom." Locke goes further: "Where there is no law there is no freedom, because liberty is to be free from restraint and violence from others which cannot be where there is no law" (II 57). Freedom is either the "interest" or "good" of human beings or the comprehensive means to these things and more generally to "happiness," and law, in turn, is the means to freedom. Locke's focus on freedom is especially helpful, for he has affirmed throughout that freedom is a right (II 17). All of this leads to the conclusion that the law of reason, that is, the (non-transcendent) natural law, far from being primary and the source of rights, is secondary and derivative from rights.[64]

In a passage that reminds more than a little of the just-completed discussion of the improvement of land through labor, Locke identifies law as what "hedges us in only from bogs and precipices" (II 57). The chief danger ("bog and precipice") from which law saves us is "violence from others." Such "rules of reason" as Hobbes identifies would seem to fit Locke's description as well; for example, Hobbes's first and fundamental natural law is "that every man ought to endeavour peace, as far as he has hope of obtaining it; and when he cannot obtain it, that he may seek, and use, all helps, and advantages of warre."[65] The first part of the rule would be the rough equivalent to the kind of natural law limitations Locke speaks of in his no-harm principle, the second the authorization of use of force via the executive power of the law of nature. From the first, Hobbes derives a second law of nature—to contract into civil society when possible. Again, Locke endorses this view: reason suggests civil society as the remedy for the evils of the state of nature.

So far as Locke retains a law of nature, it appears to be very close to Hobbes's. In terms of the criteria of genuine law set forth in the *Questions*, Locke's "law of reason" does not qualify as genuine law. It is neither the product of the authoritative lawgiver, nor, therefore, truly obligatory, nor, finally, properly promulgated. As Locke reconfirms in *Two Treatises*, "no body can be under a law, which is not promulgated to him; and this law [is] promulgated or made known by reason alone" (II 57). But it is not promulgated or made known in the state of nature: in the state of nature, human beings are "ignorant" of the law of nature (II 124).

The law of nature, or the law of reason, as the set of rules that state the means for the security of rights, differs in content very little from proper civil laws, which aim at that same preservation of rights. Thus Locke can say, "The obligations of the law of nature cease not in society, but only in many cases are drawn closer, and have by humane laws known penalties annexed to them, to enforce their observation." The natural law becomes genuine law at the moment it comes to be embodied in the civil law, for then all the qualities of law are present: lawgiver, promulgation, obligation, and sanction (II 135). Since the law of nature sets the standard all properly made civil societies aim for—the security of rights—Locke perfectly appropriately insists that "the law of nature stands as an eternal rule to all men, legislators as well as others" (II 135).

Locke's natural law teaching appears to be very similar to Hobbes's. This is admittedly a very controversial conclusion within the scholarly literature on Locke. A justly controversial conclusion, I would add, for even though there are important similarities to Hobbes lurking not too far beneath the surface of Locke's text, the surface impression of important dissimilarities also points to important truths about the character of Locke's political philosophy. The two philosophers differ, of course, on the important practical outcomes of their philosophies, Hobbes siding with absolutism (royalist or not, he didn't care too much) and Locke agreeing with the Whigs in their rejection of absolutism. Behind—and in a way the source of—these very important practical disagreements lies an even more important disagreement on fundamentals, however. Both Hobbes and Locke may understand so-called natural law as in reality a series of rules derived from and in service of the more fundamental moral reality of natural right, but Locke understands natural right substantially differently from Hobbes.

NATURAL RIGHT AS PROPERTY

The difference between Hobbes and Locke on natural right appears with greatest clarity in the cluster of issues surrounding Locke's treatment of property—the argument for a natural right to property, the establishment of self-ownership, and the treatment of all rights or objects of rights as property.[66] To say there is property by nature is to say there is justice by nature, for, in the common understanding of the day, "justice is the constant will of giving to every man his own." As Hobbes explains the point, "Where there is no *own*, that is, no propriety, there is no injustice." Or, as Locke puts it, "Where there is no property, there is no injustice."[67] Thus natural property, or natural "own," is the ground or prerequisite for natural justice.

Hobbes strongly insists there is no natural justice. "Before the names of just and injust can have place, there must be some coercive power, to compell men equally to the performance of their covenants." Only with the establishment of civil society does justice come to exist. In the state of nature "there is no propriety," for "all men have right to all things." Hobbes understands property just as Locke does, as a claim with an implication of exclusivity, or a duty of forbearance and abstention on the part of others. Hobbes's right of nature lacks any such duty of forbearance: the natural right of one individual imposes no duties whatever on others and therefore is a right, but not property.

Pufendorf had mounted an astute critique of Hobbes's right of nature as contrary to the nature of rights as such. A "real right" involves a "moral effect" in others, that they "may not hinder him, against his will." To a right "in the strict sense," Pufendorf says, "there must always be some obligation in another corresponding."[68] According to this notion of the necessary correlativity of right and obligation, Hobbes's right of nature is not a proper right. Thus, according to Pufendorf, all proper rights have the character of property.

Pufendorf concedes, however, that "the word 'right' is highly ambiguous."[69] Hobbes's use of the term "right" to signify a liberty with no correlative duty of any sort is one of the primary instances of the sort of ambiguity he has in mind, and Locke's recourse to the language of property represents his effort to avoid some of these ambiguities. Whether Hobbes's right of nature deserves to be called a right or not (in the *Questions*, Locke suggests yes), Locke uses the language of property to signal that he is thinking of right in the Pufendorfian manner, as entailing a concomitant duty in others. Property is what is ours, and that, by definition, means it is not others'.

Where Hobbes affirms no natural property, or a right with no correlative duty, Locke insists on natural property and thus on natural justice. "Every man has a property in his own person"; in this and every case, that in which a man has property "nobody has a right to but himself." However much Locke's natural ownership may approach Hobbes's right of nature, it still does not amount to Hobbes's unequivocal right of nature, the right of every man to everything. Even in the state of nature, Locke has grounds for saying certain actions are wrong. The practical differences between Hobbes's absolutism and Locke's liberalism derive not merely from different judgments the two make regarding the political means to the natural end, but, more important, from a difference in their understandings of the end, or of natural right. Natural property, in Locke's extended sense, sets the purpose for and serves as standing guide and limit to political power.[70]

The claim to property in one's own person is thus simply central to Locke's enterprise. On the one hand, it points toward his break with the entire premodern tradition. He had initially brought that tradition into *Two Treatises* in the form of his assertion of divine ownership, but now shows that human beings are self-owners. That implies a certain sovereignty, or in Hobbes's sense, a liberty they possess with regard to their persons and actions, including the liberty to commit suicide. On the other hand, the claim to property in one's own person points toward his break with Hobbes: accompanying the primordial right is a claim to exclusivity that distinguishes Locke's natural property from Hobbes's right of nature. If, as I have argued, Locke's natural property does not follow from, but rather precedes, the so-called law of nature (reason), then whence derives the exclusive character of the property right? What is the origin of that in the Lockean notion of natural right that goes beyond Hobbes's natural right as pure liberty? For Hobbes, as for Locke in the *Questions*, it was, after all, the very fact that natural right precedes natural law that led to the conclusion that there is no property by nature.

Hobbes's right of nature, like Spinoza's, represented the result of his attempt to set human beings into nature in a way earlier thought did not. The same mechanistic principles that account for nature as a whole also account for humanity. The same principles of motion that account for the actions of all animals account for human beings as well. The differences between human beings and other beings are mere matters of degree.[71] Locke, on the other hand, draws a much stronger line of demarcation between human and other beings. Whereas all animate being seeks preservation and is directed "to the use of those things . . . serviceable for . . . subsistence [via] the desire, the strong desire of preserving . . . life and being," only human being is "taught" and "assured" that he "had a right to make use of those creatures, which by his reason or senses he could discover would be serviceable thereunto" (I 86). Where Hobbes wavers on the question of whether natural right is unique to human beings or universal to all or all animate being, Locke clearly asserts that right is only human, for only humans formulate the claim to right.[72]

He returns to this same theme in the very place he announces the self-ownership thesis. "Though the earth, and all inferior creatures be common to all men, yet every man has a property in his own person. This no body has any right to but himself" (II 27). The earth and all the lower animals are "common," yet the human person is property of the human self, that is, private to themselves, possessing a claim of right not to be interfered with. This distinction between human beings and other animals accounts for the fact Pufendorf had earlier pointed out, that only human beings generate property, despite the fact that other animals also interact with the world and must seize and digest other beings in order to survive. Self-preservation sets the need that appropriation serves, but it cannot fully account for property.[73]

Locke and Pufendorf raise the same objection to Hobbes: human beings alone have property, and what is unique cannot be accounted for by what is universal. In the first instance, Locke, like Pufendorf, merely wishes to reconsider the phenomenology, so to speak, of human-rights claiming. They have two points: first, human beings raise claims of right, whereas other beings merely act with the liberty ascribed to them; second, according to Locke, the claim of right is not merely a claim of liberty. My claim of my right to my life as a matter of observed fact includes a claim of exclusivity. My life, my body, my actions—being mine means they are not yours. All things equal, this is a claim that it is wrong for you to interfere with them. At the very least, it means that if our preservation does not come into competition or conflict, it would be injustice for either of us to harm the other. If we do come into competition, or if we are in such a situation of uncertainty that we do not know whether we are in conflict or not—that is, if we are in the situation typical of the state of nature—it is no injustice for us to harm each other. Even if in the state of nature it is difficult, if not impossible, to distinguish rightful from wrongful violence in practice, it nonetheless remains true in principle that gratuitous harm to others is wrong. Locke has a clearer answer than Hobbes to the problem posed by the Marquis de Sade.

The claim of right is thus more than and different from Hobbes's claim of liberty. So far as I raise a claim to property, in myself or my belongings, I raise by definition a claim with implications of exclusivity. On that basis I expect of right that others ought to respect my claim and forbear from my property. Locke does not, as Shapiro claims, "adopt . . . the Hobbesian tactic of separating rights from obligation."[74] This does not necessarily mean I expect they will so forbear, but if they do not, I will consider their actions unjust. This is an analytic truth, implicit in the very notion of property I am deploying. If I raise this claim, and do so not on the basis of some exceptional feature of myself (for example, divine donation to myself alone) but on the basis (somehow) of my bare humanness, then the logic of my own claim for myself leads me beyond the claim I raise for myself to recognize like claims of others. If my being owner of myself gives me a rightful expectation that others will not gratuitously harm me, I am led to see that their claim to be owners of themselves gives them the same rightful expectation that I and others will not gratuitously harm them.

My claim and the limits on others implicit in it implies a system of rights and concomitant duties for all, a system of mutual claims and recognition. The duty or quasi-duty of forbearance from gratuitous harm is not derived from some antecedent law or duty, it is the indirect consequence of the very claim I and others raise on our own behalf. Duty or quasi-duty follows from right, rather than the reverse. Given the way in which the system of rights is generated, it is no accident that the example Locke uses of how morality could be deductive is the proposition "where there is no property, there is no injustice." If there is property in self, and by extension in the things appropriated as discussed in chapter 5 of the *Second Treatise*, then there is injustice—violation of right—in interference with this property.

Locke never believed that the logic of rights sufficed, of course. Civil society, the coercive force of authorities, and the authoritativeness of the civil law are absolutely required to make natural rights effective and secure. In this respect Locke surely resembles Hobbes, but he nonetheless affirms a preexisting normative right, which, ineffective as it may be in itself, grounds the entire edifice of political life and political philosophy.

If there is property, there can be injustice. The first or primary property is the person him or herself. Locke announces that theme in chapter 5 in order to explain how property in the things of the external world is possible; the discussion of the things of the external world also helps explain how there can be property in the person. The chief point of Locke's discussion of property in nature is the role of labor in the making of property, both as appropriating power and as transformative power. Through labor, what was not me becomes me, or at least mine. Labor transforms and appropriates; it remakes the given world, the almost worthless raw material, into new and humanly valuable things. If the "great foundation of property" is labor, then Locke is suggesting that the person is himself the product of transforming and appropriating labor. Human making, not divine making, is the primary moral fact. The chapter on property leads up to the suggestion that human beings are self-owners because they are the makers of their selves and they own what they make.

That suggestion is developed further in Locke's more philosophical *Essay Concerning Human Understanding*. Wherever Locke speaks of self-ownership in *Two Treatises* he carefully employs the same precise formula: men have property in their persons (II 27, 44, 173). "In the ordinary way of speaking," Locke notes in the *Essay*, "the same person, and the same man, stand for the same thing." He disagrees, however; man and person are terms or ideas that refer to quite different things. "The idea in our minds, of which sound man in our mouths is the sign, is nothing else but of an animal of such a certain form." Thus the identity or sameness of a man is of precisely the same sort as the identity of an animal. "An animal is a living organized body, and consequently, the same animal . . . is the same continued life communicated to different particles of matter, and they happen successively to be united to that organized living body."[75] A man is an animal, and as animal the identity of a man resides in the same continuity of life over time. Nonhuman animals are incapable of personhood, however, for a person is "a thinking intelligent being, that has reason and reflection." The term person "belongs only to intelligent agents capable of a law and happiness and misery."[76] Personhood is something non-animal-like.

The distinction between man and person parallels Locke's distinction in *Two Treatises* between animals and human beings. All animate beings share in life and in the strong drive to preservation, but only in human beings does this drive become a right. Likewise, all animate beings share in digestion, the process by which "different particles of matter" come to be "united" to "one organized living body," yet only human beings are proprietors. Human beings have property in their persons, and have property because they are persons.

Locke defines a person as "a thinking intelligent being, that has reason and reflection, and can consider itself as itself, the same thinking thing in different times and places."[77] A person is a "thinking being" precisely because it is "that consciousness which is inseparable from thinking." Consciousness is inseparable from thinking because it is "impossible for any one to perceive, without perceiving, that he does perceive. When we see, hear, smell, taste, feel, meditate, or will any thing, we know that we do so." Locke's language can be misleading, however, as the case of nonhuman animals makes clear. What does it mean to say we perceive that we are perceiving, or know that we are, say, smelling? Do I know I am smelling so far as I am smelling? Is my perception, my knowledge of it, the perception itself? Or is it further knowledge of a reflective sort, such that I might be able to utter the proposition "I know that I am smelling"? I can be smelling, perceiving an odor, and therefore knowing it in one sense without at the same time knowing it in the other sense. I may be smelling but have no separate idea that I am smelling, that is, be conscious of a smell but not of smelling.[78]

Only in the first sense is it "impossible for anyone to perceive, without perceiving that he does perceive." Animals certainly perceive and have consciousness in this first sense; to perceive is to have that consciousness which is the perception. At times, Locke is willing to call perception "thinking," but his more considered judgment is that it is not: "Thinking, in the propriety of the English tongue, signifies that sort of operation of the mind about its ideas, wherein the mind is active; where it with some degree of voluntary attention, considers any thing. For in bare perception, the mind is, for the most part, only passive."[79] Thinking, properly speaking, is like labor—active and productive.

Not consciousness as such—what is present in "bare perception"—but self-consciousness constitutes the person. To be more precise: "Person is the name for [the] self. Wherever a man finds, what he calls himself, there I think another may say is the same person."[80] To recognize another as a person is to recognize the other as a self. So far as one's touchstone for recognizing another as a self must be one's consciousness of one's self as a self, the structure of the self-person relation already suggests something of the reciprocal recognition of claim and limit present in the very notion of property. In any case, to understand person and therewith one's property in one's own person, we must, it is clear, understand self.

Person "considers it self as it self, the same thinking thing in different times and places." That is to say, person is a structure of consciousness of the sort that identifies itself as a self persisting over time and as the persisting and unifying element amidst a variety of perceptions, passions, and actions: as the person experiences experience as his or hers, actions as his or hers, pleasures and pains, happiness and misery as his or hers, the self—the "I"—stands alone and partially outside the perception, passions, and actions it experiences or undergoes.[81] The experiences and actions of the self pertain to the self, belong to the self, but do not exhaust it. The relation of the self to its life is exactly the reaction of a person to his or her property—property is both other and own. If, as Locke says, the self supplies the identity, that is, continuity, of a person over time, the self must both be present in and stand outside any, and therefore all, of its experiences.[82]

The self is not, however, a natural thing; it is not a substance either material or immaterial. It is "the same consciousness that makes a man be himself to himself." Self is merely consciousness—consciousness of self. "Personal identity consists not in the identity of substance, but . . . in the identity of consciousness." More bluntly put, "Consciousness alone makes self." Locke goes so far as to say that the same consciousness, even if (somehow) united to different substances, would constitute the same self or person. Self is emphatically not soul. Locke can imagine the same soul inhabiting or informing two different human beings, "for souls being, as far as we know any thing of them in their nature, indifferent to any parcel of matter, the supposition has no apparent absurdity in it." In such a case the soul would have consciousness of the actions and experiences only of that person to whom it belonged, and therefore neither person could conceive himself the same person with the other.[83]

Self is consciousness of self, but the self that comes to consciousness is not a preexisting, self-subsisting entity. Consciousness of self is either an idea of sensation or one of reflection. It might appear to be an idea of reflection, that is, a "perception of the operation of our own minds within us, as it is employed about the ideas it has got."[84] It is not, for example, like the idea of sensation, an operation of the mind that occurs independently of our forming an idea of it. Self differs from sensation and other primary ideas of reflection in being self-constituted. Self-consciousness is both consciousness and cause of self.

The more active faculties of the mind are required for the consciousness or construction of self precisely because it is self-constituting. Locke does not give us a detailed analysis of the generation of self, but it is clear that it involves a number of "higher" or more complex mental faculties, which the brutes either altogether lack or possess to a much smaller degree than human beings. Nonhuman animals are not persons, and thus not rights-claimants and rights-bearers, because they lack the intellectual powers to constitute themselves as selves. One such necessary power is the power of retention in both its forms as contemplation ("keeping the idea, which is brought into it, for some time actually in view") and in the form of memory ("the power to revive again in our minds those ideas, which after imprinting have disappeared, or have been as it were laid aside out of sight"). Since self unites past and present actions and experiences, memory is central to it. Without memory, "an intellectual creature . . . in [its] thoughts, reasonings, and knowledge, could not proceed beyond present objects." Retention is thus a necessary—but, Locke insists, not a sufficient—condition for personhood. "This faculty of laying up, and retaining the ideas, that are brought into the mind, several other animals seem to have, to a great degree, as well as man."[85] He gives the example of birds that remember tunes and attempt to imitate them. Nonetheless, human powers of retention far outstrip those of other animals, in part, it would appear, because of other mental powers that more clearly differentiate humanity and enhance human memory.

Human beings most clearly surpass the brutes in their far greater facility at comparing and composing ideas, and altogether differ from the brutes in being able to abstract ideas. Comparing ideas depends on the prior power of discernment, that is, the power to "distinguish between the several ideas . . . in our minds." Once the mind distinguishes ideas it can "compare them one with another, in respect of extent, degrees, time, place, or any other circumstances." Brutes have this latter power "not in any degree." It is, Locke believes, "the prerogative of humane understanding, when it has sufficiently distinguished any ideas, so as to perceive them to be perfectly different, and so consequently two, to cast about and consider in what circumstances they are capable to be compared." Animals compare ideas as they present themselves, but humans "cast about." The human power is far more active; human beings are far less immersed in the given world than the brutes are.[86]

The same freedom that makes possible active comparison of ideas also reveals itself in the power of composing, "whereby [the mind] puts together several of those single [ideas] it has received from sensation and reflection, and combines them into complex ones." Here, too, "brutes come far short of men." They "take in and retain together several combinations of ideas," yet "they do not of themselves ever compound them, and make complex ideas." The power to compound grounds the mind's ability to form complex ideas. These instance the mind's active, laboring character extremely well. "The mind is wholly passive in the reception of all its single ideas," but "it exerts several acts of its own, whereby out of its simple ideas, as the materials and foundations of the rest, the others are formed."[87]

Most important, however, is the mind's abstracting power, "whereby . . . the mind makes the particular ideas, received from particular objects, to become general; which is done by considering them as they are in the mind such appearances, separate from all other existences, and the circumstances of real existence, as time, place, or any other concomitant ideas." In the process of abstraction, "ideas taken from particular beings, become general representatives of all of the same kind." Only because of this power can human beings give names to ideas, and thus abstraction serves as the germ of language. Locke partially agrees with Aristotle—human being is the speaking being—but he traces the power of speech to this yet more fundamental power. For Locke it is a power, not an insight into being. Human intellectual power makes and remakes ideas, with little necessity that they conform in any particular way to reality.[88]

While Locke had spoken very tentatively about the relative power of humans and animals with respect to the other powers of the mind, he states firmly that he "may be positive in that the power of abstracting is not at all" in the lower animals. "The having of general ideas [produced by this power] is that which puts a perfect distinction betwixt man and brutes; and it is an excellency which the faculties of brutes do by no means attain to." Locke speaks with such certainty, for he can find "no foot-steps in them, of making of general signs for universal ideas," especially no "use of words."[89] The power of abstracting is "that proper difference wherein [brutes] are wholly separated [from man], and which at last widens to so vast a distance. Speech and reason are thus not equivalent for Locke, as they had been for Aristotle. Animals, Locke concludes, possess "some reason," but no speech or power of abstraction.[90]

The abstracting power appears to be a major contributor to human excellences. For example, memory is stronger in human beings because they can abstract from the mass of particulars and fix their general ideas with names. Likewise, the power to abstract much enhances the power to compound, because the general ideas, purified of the accompanying din of other ideas served up by the mind, can more readily be combined with others, for two reasons: they are more readily focused on and made stable and, perhaps more important, the process of abstraction frees the mind of the givenness with which ideas first are received. Abstracting lifts the mind out of the given flow of sensation and allows it to stand in semisovereign sway over its own contents.

These active intellectual powers, especially the power of abstracting, distinguish human beings from animals and thus must stand somewhere behind the fact that humans constitute themselves selves or persons, as animals never do. Surely these powers are necessary conditions for the constitution of the idea of the self. The abstracting power, especially, bears on the self, for the idea of the self involves precisely an act of abstracting self from the other contents of consciousness. Powers of combining also have their place. Reflection gives a series of ideas of mental faculties—perception, discerning, and so on[91]—and the mind assembles these to form an idea of mind, and ultimately of consciousness as such.

Although Locke forbears from presenting an analysis of the generation of the idea of the self in terms of the operation of the faculties of the mind on the raw materials contained in the simple ideas of sensation and reflection, he does make a few pregnant suggestions that point toward the nerve of his understanding of the essentials of generation of the self. We must look somewhat more carefully now at Locke's discussion of the person and the self. "Person . . . is the name for this self." What is the self to the self is person to another. Almost at the very end of his discussion of person and self, Locke presents a brief description of what "founds" the process whereby the self "appropriates" to itself its actions and thereby, in effect, constitutes itself as well, for that appropriation requires or implies the positing of self as that which takes responsibility for its "owns" as its own. "All which is founded in a concern for happiness, the unavoidable concomitant of consciousness: that which is conscious of pleasure and pain desiring that that self that is conscious should be happy."[92] Locke had employed this same theme in his definition of self: the self is "sensible or conscious of pleasure and pain, capable of happiness or misery, and so is concerned for itself, as far as that consciousness extends."[93]

Pleasure and pain, and then happiness and misery, are central to the constitution of the self. The self cannot be understood solely in terms of the faculties of the mind. Pleasure and pain are pervasive, near-universal experiences, for "one or other of them join themselves to almost all our ideas, both of sensation and reflection: and there is scarce any affection of our senses from without, any retired thought of our mind within, which is not able to produce in us pleasure or pain."[94] From the near-universal experience of pleasure and pain the mind's capacity to distinguish ideas from one another, and then to abstract them from their accompaniments, produces general ideas of pleasure and pain. We never experience pure pleasure, or at least never for any length of time. The evanescence of pleasure is a source of unease that, together with the human capacity for composition of ideas, produces the idea of happiness and that of its partner, misery. "Happiness and misery are the names of two extremes, the utmost bounds whereof we know not." We do experience "several instances of delight and joy on the one side, and torment and sorrow on the other," but happiness is "what eye hath not seen, ear hath not heard."[95] Since we never experience it, happiness is an idea the mind compounds for itself from the "raw materials" furnished by sensation and reflection. "The lowest degree of what can be called happiness, is so much ease from all pain, and so much present pleasure, as without which any one cannot be content." At a higher degree, "happiness . . . consists in the enjoyment of pleasure, without any considerable mixture of uneasiness."[96]

Since happiness as defined by Locke is unattainable, it exists as an object of pursuit: human beings devote their lives to the pursuit of happiness. This special kind of pleasure and absence of pain has a naturally compelling force for human beings once its idea has been formed. Not merely do human beings separate out the ideas of pleasure and happiness, pain and misery, but they delight in the one and dislike the other. As opposed to other ideas, in which the consciousness is buried in the idea itself, so to speak, pleasure and pain, especially in their alternation, and happiness and misery as states to be pursued or avoided call attention to the very consciousness that experiences these affects. The consciousness is not lost in the idea, but stands as attracted to one and repelled by the other. Consciousness thus comes to consciousness as other than its ideas because of the non-neutrality of the ideas of pleasure and pain. Consciousness is constituted as the seat of pleasure and pain, and thus of the ideas and volitions. Consciousness thus becomes self-consciousness.

Locke's self has two dominant features. First, it is a consciousness of itself as itself, and second, it is that which posits itself as persistent or continuing or unifying of "existence" over time. The temporal dimensions of the self also follow from happiness and misery. "Since our voluntary actions carry not all the happiness and misery, that depend on them, along with them in their present performance; but are the precedent causes of good and evil, which they draw after them, and bring upon us, when they themselves are passed, and cease to be; our desires look beyond our present enjoyments, and carry the mind out to absent good, according to the necessity which we think there is of it, to the making or increase of our happiness."[97] Contrary to a common impression often left by Locke's discussion, self and person are not essentially constituted by memory of the past. The past, operating via memory and the other active powers of the mind, is necessary for the formation of the ideas of pleasure, happiness, and so on, and thus of self and person, but the self thus formed is essentially futural. For the self, happiness, the unavoidable object of its existence, never present to consciousness, always exists as a goal to be moved toward; the unease caused by its absence serves as a goad toward action. The self extends itself forward and backward in time. It posits itself as the same self that will be the beneficiary or loser of happiness or misery in the future for actions taken or projected in the present. It posits itself as the source of past actions and experiences from which it has been or presently is the beneficiary or loser.[98]

The self is constituted around happiness and misery and therefore the self is always "self-concerned." "Self is . . . conscious of pleasure and pain, capable of happiness or misery, and so is concern'd for itself, as far as that consciousness extends." The self is decidedly self-interested, "happiness and misery being that, for which every one is concerned for himself."[99] Self-interest is to be understood in the first instance as securing pleasures for the self or avoiding pains and discomforts. Locke's ontology of the self points in this way, too, toward a politics of the realist rather than idealist sort and an orientation toward existence of the kind he reveals in his teaching on property: the search for comfortable preservation through labor.[100]

Even more important, however, is the very structure of the self Locke uncovers; the self is not merely disposed toward property, but is itself property. Locke appears more certain of this than of the mechanism by which it produces itself. The self is that form of consciousness that posits itself as owner and master of itself—of "its" body, for one, those bodily things "joined to or affected with that consciousness." A dismembered limb, no longer involved in the community of consciousness that is the self, no longer counts as part of the self.[101] Above all, self is owner and master of its ideas and its actions. The mode by which ideas and actions come to be owned and mastered is precisely the same as the way in which unowned parts of the external world come to be owned—by appropriation, that is, by finding them ours, by finding the self in them as acting or suffering power. The self is just that empty center of consciousness that contains and possesses all its appearances. The self as empty center of consciousness—pure ego—is owner; the self as array of possible ideas and actions is owned.

Self-ownership has the character both of right and of inalienable right. The claim to ownership over one's self implies the claim to personal sovereignty over the field of the self to the exclusion of others. To be a self is to be owner of self, proprietor of one's actions, and actor in terms of one's own happiness, that is, one's pleasures and pains. So far as we are owners of our selves, we claim the right to dispose of our actions in our own self-ish way in pursuit of our own happiness. So far as we recognize our claims to life, liberty, and property as resting on our self-ownership, we are logically (if not practically) impelled to grant or recognize the same claim in other persons. As persons, the others are selves, constituted in the same manner, implicitly raising exactly the same claim. The rights, moreover, are inalienable because they inhere in the very structure of the self. There is no way they can be given away, for the self cannot deconstitute its own basic structure as self-owning consciousness.

Self by its nature is a rights-bearer and free, but Locke emphasizes almost as much the other side of rights and liberty; person, the self gone public, refers "only to intelligent agents capable of a law." Indeed, Locke emphasizes that person "is a forensick term appropriating actions and their merits." Self is that consciousness that appropriates one's own actions to one's own happiness; person is that which is held responsible to legal rules, and thus answerable to "reward and punishment on account of any such action."[102]

Self grounds rights; person grounds morality proper, because "moral good and evil . . . is only the conformity or disagreement of our voluntary actions to some law, whereby good or evil [pleasure or pain] is drawn on us, from the will and power of the law-maker."[103] Critics often find Locke's emphasis on reward and punishment as essential to morality either meretricious or simply confused about the distinction between motivation and obligation. The role of the idea of happiness in the constitution of the self reveals why reward and punishment are so essential to the person, law, and morality. Action for which we can be held responsible is action that the self appropriates to itself via its assimilation to its happiness or misery. Reward and punishment—the happiness or misery that results not from the natural consequences of actions but from the artificial interposition of other human voluntary action—is required to make human beings capable of law, that is, of morality.

Locke's self is necessarily self-interested, even self-ish, but for all that not antisocial. Society suits Locke's individual, even if human beings are not naturally sociable.[104] The analysis of the state of nature and of property reveals how much human beings benefit from and rationally desire society. The social connections run even deeper: the mental faculties most constitutive of human being, especially the power of abstraction and thus, eventually, the power of language, point toward society, for language is an essentially social phenomenon. Locke's analyses aim to show, however, that human sociability, as opposed to animal sociability, is not a natural endowment but an acquisition. His political analysis proper is meant to show that government, the coercive authority that supplies reward and punishment, is indispensably necessary for the successful establishment and stable maintenance of social life.

LOCKEAN PARADOXES

Locke traces right, or property in the extended sense, straight back to the very structure of the self, in that the basic or grounding principle of his political philosophy, self-ownership, follows more or less directly from that structure. Yet human beings do not regularly—perhaps not at all, prior to Locke—understand themselves in this way. The self is self-deceived. Some, like Grotius, see no difficulty in human beings belonging to others; many, like those appealed to by Locke's transcendent natural law, are quicker to see divine ownership than self-ownership. Others, like Plato or Aristotle, do not see the question in terms of ownership at all, either self or divine, and think in terms of soul rather than self-consciousness. But if Locke has uncovered the very structure of the self, constituted by self-consciousness itself, then the critical idea and its political-economic implications should be clear to all, one would think. Locke clearly does not agree: the self may be constituted so, and yet may misunderstand itself, understanding neither its own constitution nor the moral and political implications thereof. A curtain, woven mostly from words that systematically mislead, stands between the mind and its own grasp of itself. Before Locke, human beings thought of themselves as substances—soul or the like—not self-constituting consciousness. Complete access to the true structure of the self is available only through Locke's "new way of ideas," a radical and profoundly disruptive reorientation of thought.[105]

Lockean political philosophy has a double task made doubly difficult by the paradoxes above: Locke's truth is a truth embedded in reality, and yet to be fully effective it must be known. The freedom of the mind and the self-defining character of happiness imply that human beings are free within some range to live their lives in ignorance of the truth:

> Thus far can the busie mind of man carry him to a brutality below the level of beasts, when he quits his reason, which places him almost equal to the angels. . . . The imagination is always restless and suggests variety of thoughts, and the will, reason being laid aside, is ready for every extravagant project. (I 58)

And, Locke speculates in an uncharacteristically poetic passage, it can hardly be otherwise, "in a creature whose thoughts are more than the sands, and wider than the ocean, where fancy and passion must needs run him into strange courses, if reason, which is his only star and compass, be not that he steers by" (I 58).

But reason is not what most steer by and, as he saw very early on in the *Questions*, most resist it. The truth is needed in order to set things to rights, and yet the truth cannot be served up straight. Locke's solution is his transcendent natural law, a teaching that compromises his understanding of the truth with an understanding more at home among those whose imagination carries them into insupportable but comforting hypotheses.[106]

If Locke had to present his teaching in a form quite different from the truth as he understood it, then what difference does his truth make? Steven Dworetz raises a form of this question in his thoughtful study of the impact of Locke on the American founding generation. Let us say, he says, that there are various plausible ways to read Locke. Let us even say that the Locke who rejected the workmanship argument and its theistic premises is the real Locke; yet the Locke who made an impact on history is not that one, but rather Locke as understood by those who took him up. Here Dworetz believes the evidence is overwhelmingly in favor of a theistic Locke.[107]

Let us say that is true, that most readers of Locke failed to penetrate the heart of his philosophy and, therefore, that the historical task of transforming Whig thought was accomplished in the main by Locke the theist, promoter of the idea of divine workmanship and ownership. Dworetz's reasonable point overlooks a matter of great importance, however. Locke may present an argument with echoes and more than echoes of traditional views, and may appeal and more than appeal to traditional habits of thought and commitments of opinion, but nonetheless his transcendent natural law argument was made to order according to specifications provided by his underlying understanding of rights as property. Locke deploys quasi-traditional forms of argument to lead readers to conclusions mostly congruent with and ultimately derivative from his wholly untraditional premises. Readers who buy the theistic Locke are victims of bait-and-switch marketing. Locke struggles to minimize the impression of breaking with accepted views, but such a break is present and willy-nilly makes itself felt. It is no accident, I suspect, that readers like Dworetz and Geraint Perry find the divine workmanship-ownership grounding of Locke's political philosophy unconvincing and irrelevant, and yet find his political philosophy still vital and important.[108] They find themselves, it would seem, in the position of Filmer surveying Hobbes: Filmer liked the Hobbesian building, the absolutist state, but he disliked the foundation, the right of nature. In the case of Locke, however, the building stands while the "foundation" crumbles, because the apparent foundation never was the basis on which the building was actually constructed.

CHAPTER TEN

Locke and the Transformation of Whig Political Philosophy

NOT ONLY DID Locke's *Treatises* differ from other Whig defenses of the Glorious Revolution, but Locke failed to set his name to the work until he acknowledged it in his will. Those two facts together help account for its relatively marginal place in English political thought in its early years. "Contrary to many textbook accounts, the early defenders of the Revolutionary Settlement" did not see *Two Treatises* "as an expression of the principles upon which the revolutionaries acted in 1688."[1] Many scholars now agree that "the majority of writers who supported the Revolution failed to say that they had found the arguments they were seeking in the *Second Treatise*, but they also *presented* arguments which were very different in kind from those to be found there."[2] Locke's book became "a major authority for Whigs and liberals in the eighteenth and nineteenth centuries," but it "was taken into the canon of Whig authorities later than many historians have supposed."[3]

Nonetheless, some scholars—John Dunn, for example—overly minimize the role Locke's book played in postrevolutionary English thought.[4] In 1690, for example, very shortly after *Two Treatises* itself was published, there appeared in England a political pamphlet, *Political Aphorisms*, that tendered Locke that most sincere form of flattery—outright plagiarism. "*Political Aphorisms* contains numerous passages copied word for word from the *Two Treatises*. These passages are reproduced without acknowledgment, without quotation marks, without any indication whatsoever as to their original source."[5] *Political Aphorisms* "reappeared in 1709 under a new title, *Vox Populi, Vox Dei*," with some new materials, most of which were plagiarized from other Whig writers of the revolutionary era. In 1710 *Vox Populi* was again reprinted, this time with the title *The Judgment of Whole Kingdoms and Nations. Vox Populi* "proved to be one of the best-selling pamphlets of the eighteenth century," as did the *Judgment*. "It was through the means of [the] influence [of these pamphlets] that not only Lockean principles, but also actual phrases taken from the *Two Treatises*, entered into the political consciousness of many Englishmen."[6] Despite their heavily Lockean character, Dunn altogether misses these pamphlets as indicators of the spread of Lockean ideas, precisely because they do not mention Locke by name. As a victim of unicontractarianism he does not recognize as Lockean those arguments that do not explicitly deploy Locke's name.

Richard Ashcraft and M. M. Goldsmith appear to be the first scholars to appreciate the importance of *Political Aphorisms* and its progeny; if their conjecture as to the author of the pamphlets deserves any credit, then we have some suggestive evidence regarding the transition from Grotian to Lockean Whiggism. According to Ashcraft and Goldsmith, an eighteenth-century tradition attributed one of this family of pamphlets to Daniel Defoe. They find no clear evidence supportive of this attribution, although they find none against it either. They do find verbal and thematic similarities to known pamphlets by Defoe, especially his "Original Power of the Collective Body of the People of England, Examined and Asserted," a 1701 production characterized by them as "one of Defoe's most radical and Lockean tracts." In sum, they find Defoe a "plausible candidate" for author of *Political Aphorisms*.[7]

The suggestion of Defoe as author is intriguing, for, as we have already seen, Defoe penned an earlier, Grotian pamphlet in defense of the revolution. If Defoe authored both the Grotian and the Lockean pamphlets, it would suggest that an adherent of the one set of principles could easily segue into the other, despite the considerable theoretical differences between them. Several similarities between the two philosophies, as well as some important features of the practical situation in which the pamphlet were written, would help account for the ease of transition. As already noted, Grotius and Locke both give central place to rights and to contract, although their doctrines on these matters differ in many important ways. Perhaps more immediately important, the Lockean argument, once available, had certain advantages over the Grotian argument in the polemical circumstances. The Grotian doctrine requires that the revolution be defended in terms of many historically contingent and hotly contested issues. What was the character of the "original contract"—if it made sense to speak of such a thing—in English history? What powers were reserved to the people under it? Locke's doctrine does not require any such dependence on the historically contingent in order to defend the revolution. The powers conveyed to rulers in Locke's theory are not ascertained via actual historical investigation but via a conjectured rational reconstruction. The historically *eigentlich* is more or less irrelevant. Thus Locke makes available a rationale for resistance much more within the reach of all peoples, no matter what their particular histories might have held. Locke's position, precisely because of this universality, was decidedly less appealing to some, but it held an obvious attraction for those facing the polemical task of propounding a persuasive defense of 1688 in the face of the historical ambiguities of the English past exploited by some and the theoretical countermoves exploited by others.[8] In any case, whether Defoe was the author of *Political Aphorisms* et.al. or not, the basic point is the same; he initially wrote a pamphlet stamped with Grotianism, but sooner or later he started to make Lockean arguments instead, or in addition. By 1701, in "The Original Power of the Collective Body of the People of England," Defoe had embraced Lockean principles. Moreover, the strong presence of Locke in Defoe's most famous product, *The Adventures of Robinson Crusoe*, has been frequently noted.[9]

The flurry of excitement that prompted the reprinting of these various plagiarisms was the continuing controversy over the "revolution principles" of 1688–89, brought to a head by a sermon preached on November 5, 1709, at St. Paul's Cathedral—in the heart of London, a center of Whig sentiment—denouncing 1688 and reasserting the old doctrines of "the utter illegality of resistance."[10] Not merely the location but the timing of Dr. Henry Sacheverell's sermon was bound to make Whigs take notice: the fifth of November was traditionally celebrated as the anniversary of the arrival of William of Orange and was thus an occasion for prorevolutionary sentiment. It was as though an American orator had used the Fourth of July to denounce the Declaration of Independence. The Whigs who controlled Parliament began impeachment proceedings against him that culminated in a trial in February 1710. This trial sparked a more intense debate over the principles of 1688 than had occurred since the revolution itself. A "pamphlet war, pro and con, raged throughout this period, and indeed for many months following the trial."[11]

LOCKEAN WHIGGISM: "AN ARGUMENT FOR SELF-DEFENCE"

Among the pamphlets that appeared during the Sacheverell uproar was one that along with *Political Aphorisms* and its reprints, forms an instructive part of the story of Locke's rise to prominence among the Whigs. The pamphlet, entitled *An Argument for Self-Defence*, contains many curious features, chief among which is its uncertain authorship and date of composition. The title page announces that it was "written about the year 1687, [and] never before published." The original published version bears the date 1710. The pamphlet is prefaced by an anonymous note purporting to explain the discrepancy in dates: "You are busy at present inquiring whether any manner of resistance to the supreme magistrate is lawful, which will excuse me in publishing the remains of a manuscript discourse of a worthy person deceased"[12] (the reference to the Sacheverell controversy is unmistakable). We would appear to have, then, a manuscript written before the Glorious Revolution by an anonymous "worthy person," now dead, published in 1710 by another anonymous (and presumably worthy) person, whom we might call the pamphlet's sponsor. The subtitle of the pamphlet, furthermore, presents it as "offered to the consideration of the gentlemen of the Middle-Temple," one of the inns of law in London. The invocation of the Middle Temple was especially apt in 1710, for it was a traditionally Whig establishment and some of its members were heavily involved in the Sacheverell trial, including four of the seventeen members of the Articles Committee that brought charges against Sacheverell.

It is obvious that the title of the work, written from the perspective of 1710, is the product of the sponsor, not the author. At least some of the footnotes must be likewise. For example, one note quotes a passage from a sermon delivered in 1705, well after the purported date of composition. Another note says, "If the author had been so happy as to have lived to the Revolution . . ." This note not only proves that the sponsor added notes to the text, but perhaps supplies some of the basis on which the sponsor dates its composition to 1687; if he knew that the author died before the revolution, it surely could have been written no later than 1688. Likewise, it could probably have been written no earlier than 1687, for it contains a reference to abuses by a king that might justify resistance: "There are . . . instances in which 'tis possible for a king to betray his trust, endeavouring to subvert and extirpate the laws and liberties of his people, by assuming and exercising a power of dispensing with the laws he is to govern by, and making use of the force of the community in standing armies, against the liberty of the subject, back his own arbitrary proceedings."[13] The dispensing power and the use of standing armies became an issue under James II only in 1686–87, when he dispensed with the laws against dissenters and Catholics.[14]

The sponsor must then have composed some of the notes, but probably not all of them. Toward the end of the pamphlet, the author states, "I know I ought not to cite any more authorities; but . . ." All the earlier citations of authority appear in footnotes, and therefore the author must have written most of the notes. The sponsor apparently does not fulfill the standards of modern editorial practice, for he leaves us uncertain what is original and what has been added. There is even a passage in the text itself that must derive from later than the putative date of composition:

> But to be better satisfied, that the happiness of one people becomes the envy of their neighbours; from this difference, that one has good laws duly executed, the other none at all, or at least subject to the prince's pleasure; why are we here in England in a better condition than the subjects of France or Denmark? . . . We here enjoy the fruits of our honest industry, every one under his vine and fig tree, solicitous for nothing but the happiness of her that derives these blessings on us. In short, . . . peace and quietness [are] the effect of good laws, and a just temperament of power.[15]

The "her" from whom these blessings derive can, in the context, be no one other than the "prince" whose "just temperament of power" supplements the effects of "good laws." But England had no female "prince" in 1687. Indeed, only with the accession of Queen Anne, in 1702, does this reference make sense. More than that, the entire passage, of which only an excerpt has been quoted here, points not toward 1687, with its superheated atmosphere of disorder and sense of threat to English liberty, but to the more settled and prosperous postrevolutionary period; it is hardly likely, for example, that a writer of the temperament of the author of the *Argument* would speak of the 1680s as a period of "success abroad," but the decades after the revolution might well be so described.

Either our sponsor falls very far short of proper editorial standards, or, perhaps, the whole business is a kind of hoax. Although I cannot definitively rule out the first alternative, I believe the second the more likely. A composition date of 1687 can make sense for this pamphlet only if its author was John Locke or somebody who had access to Locke's *Two Treatises*, for this pamphlet, no less than *Political Aphorisms*, *Vox Populi*, and *The Judgment of Whole Kingdoms*, contains a thoroughly Lockean argument. It is unlike any Whig writings of the revolutionary period other than *Two Treatises*.

The Argument for Self-Defence shares with Locke not only the superficial similarities that more standard Whig contractarian writings do, but goes almost as far as *Vox Populi* in its borrowing of language from *Two Treatises*. It begins with the same transcendent natural law principle of "no harm" with which Locke began his argument in the *Second Treatise*. It nonetheless derives, just as Locke did, a natural law right to use force against others. Although the author does not use the term, clearly he has in mind Locke's "strange" executive power of the law of nature. Such a power existed, the author affirms, "before the forms of government were fixed in the world." The law of nature mandates not political life but rather the executive power of the law of nature. Where everyone had this power was "a state of equality [that] I call a state of nature." A little later in the pamphlet the author defines the state of nature more precisely as "such a state of equality where there is no superior power on earth, to which a man on any injury received or threatened may have recourse for relief," precisely the way Locke defined it in *Two Treatises*. Therefore, for the author of the *Argument*, as much as for Locke, the state of nature is not primarily a condition existing in the mists of time, but rather exists wherever "two men are without this common judge."[16]

The state of nature is a condition "which had abundance of inconveniences"—strikingly, the very term Locke used to so describe it. The reasons for those "inconveniences" are precisely the same as the ones Locke details in sections 124–26 of the *Second Treatise*, and presented in the very same order as Locke's version. According to Locke, "self-love will make men partial to themselves." According to the *Argument*, "self-love is apt to make us partial." The solution is to "fix on some standing rule which should be the nature of right and wrong between man and man"—a clear echo of Locke's "standing rules . . . by which every one may know what is his." Human beings enter civil society "the better to be preserved in their lives and properties"; Locke uses almost the same words in *Two Treatises*: "Men . . . enter into society only with an intention in every one the better to preserve himself his liberty and property."[17]

Given all the premises they have in common, it is no wonder that the author of the *Argument* draws the same conclusions as Locke does regarding the impossibility of absolute and arbitrary power and the legitimacy of revolution when rulers violate their trust. It is lawful, the *Argument* concludes, for the people "to resist unlawful force with force . . . when their laws are cancelled or in apparent danger of it; and consequently their estates, lives, liberties, and all that is valuable in this world, subjected to the arbitrary decrees of one person, armed with the force of the society." In this, the *Argument*'s author briefly restates some of Locke's main conclusions in his chapter "Of the Dissolution of Government."[18] Both authors affirm the right to resist rulers quite without regard to any specific constitutional provision or original contract.

The *Argument*, in sum, differs altogether from the mass of Whig writings discussed earlier; unlike them, it takes the Lockean approach to the issues of 1688. Even the brief summary presented here shows that, like Locke, the *Argument* endorses the five doctrines later adumbrated in the American Declaration of Independence but mostly absent from the Grotianist Whig writings more characteristic of the English revolutionary moment.

The parallels in doctrine and especially in language and terminology between Locke and the *Argument* are so precise that it is unthinkable that the author was not either Locke himself or someone who wrote with Locke's text at hand. Locke surely did not write the text as it comes to us, for it contains references which postdate his death; even assuming that the sponsor added these later materials, it still seems unlikely that Locke wrote the *Argument*. Although the text contains many phrases similar, if not identical, to phrases in *Two Treatises*, nonetheless, in style the pamphlet differs quite markedly from Locke's writings. The syntax is far simpler and more straightforward than Locke's highly Latinate prose. The *Argument* employs a stylistic device that I cannot recall seeing in Locke, the conclusion of paragraphs with partial sentences that are completed at the beginning of the next paragraph. Quite apart from any consideration of this sort, the sponsor affirms that the "author" did not live to see the revolution. That of course leaves Locke out of it, if anything the sponsor says deserves credence.

It is even more unlikely that someone else wrote the *Argument* before *Two Treatises* was published. Peter Laslett has convincingly demonstrated Locke's secretiveness with the manuscript of *Treatises* in the years just before the Glorious Revolution. He probably did not have the text with him in the Netherlands, but had left it behind when he went into exile, under a code name with some trusted Whig friends. If Laslett's conjecture about the history of the manuscript is correct, very few men knew of its existence, and they and Locke considered it something dangerous, not the sort of thing to be adapting for casual inclusion in one's papers. This was not long after the trial and execution of Algernon Sidney, an event that Locke apparently watched from a distance, and his friends from a bit closer.[19] Moreover, in its reference to events from 1686–87 the text echoes parts of the *Second Treatise* that were most likely added after Locke reclaimed his draft on his return to England after the revolution. The *Argument*, in other words, mimics the entire text of the *Second Treatise*, which was not completed until after 1688, thus suggesting strongly that 1687 is an impossible date of composition, even by someone who had Locke's manuscript in his desk. Of course, the possibility that one of Locke's friends prepared the *Argument* cannot be entirely excluded, but the weight of probability seems much against it.

Far more likely as author than Locke or some person using Locke's manuscript is the so-called sponsor as author himself. The *Argument*, I think, is a great hoax, composed, probably in 1709–10, by someone with a fine knowledge of *Two Treatises* and backdated to 1687. The feature of the pamphlet that ties it most clearly to the sponsor also speaks forcefully against Locke. As already noted, the title and dedication of the work must derive from the sponsor rather than the putative author of 1687, for the title is written from the vantage point of 1710. The most striking feature of the text, apart from its very Lockean argument and phraseology, is its practice of appealing to legal writers, especially writers on common law, as authorities for the arguments put forward. By far the most widely cited authority in the text is John Fortescue, author of the fifteenth-century dialogue on the common law, *De Laudibus Legum Angliae*. This is a book Locke refers to in passing in section 239 of the *Second Treatise*, but, as Laslett comments, "there is no evidence that [Locke] ever possessed or read" Fortescue or other legal writers mentioned by Locke in his published writings. The use of these writers in the *Argument* far surpasses anything in any of Locke's known works; it fits perfectly well, however, with the addressees of the pamphlet, the Whig common lawyers of the Middle Temple.

Locke himself argues far more like a natural lawyer than a common lawyer. He is much more likely to invoke the authority of Richard Hooker than of Coke or Fortescue; he eschews history and precedent in favor of nature and reason. He has little use for the original contract or the ancient constitution so often embraced by Whig lawyers. The author of the *Argument*, in other words, manipulates a genre of literature for which Locke apparently had little sympathy, and of which he perhaps had little knowledge. And that genre just happened to be the very genre best suited to appeal to the audience to whom the pamphlet was dedicated. It is difficult not to conclude that the same person who dedicated the pamphlet to the men of the Middle Temple in 1710 also wrote it for them, and in the same year.

The strongest evidence linking the *Argument* to 1687 is the reference to the controversy over the dispensing power and the standing army. The former was not at issue in 1710 and the latter was no longer so clear an issue, for William had instituted a standing army and most of the Whigs had acquiesced. The historical reference is clearly to the years just before the Glorious Revolution, and that suggests the *Argument* was composed then. However, such references are also consistent with the hoax hypothesis. James's use of the dispensing power and his efforts to build a standing army were among the most notable abuses charged against him, and it would require no more than passing knowledge of the events of 1687–88 to incorporate these concerns into the pamphlet in order to give it an air of historical authenticity.

But why the great hoax? That the author left the pamphlet anonymous is no surprise, for most of the pamphlet literature of the age was. A composition date of 1687 not only predates the revolution but, interestingly, also predates the publication of *Two Treatises*. The dating points toward a reasonable conjecture as to the purpose of the hoax. If Locke's chief style of thinking—rationalist, ahistorical, and nonlegalist—meant that he was relatively untouched by the common law tradition, the obverse was true as well: the common lawyers found Locke's mode of thought uncongenial, even if they shared some of his conclusions.[20] The author of the *Argument*, however, reproduces the main lines of Locke's political theory, with one important addition—the implicit claim that this line of argument is consistent with or founded in some of the greatest authorities on the common law, Fortescue and the anonymous authors of *Doctor and Student* and *The Book of the Mirror of Justices*.[21] The *Argument*, it seems, was written by someone trained in the law, most probably a member of the Middle Temple, and yet one thoroughly familiar with and sympathetic toward Locke.[22] Its aim: to contribute some Lockean thoughts to the renewed debate on "revolution principles" stirred by the Sacheverell trial and, more significant in the long run, to win the lawyers to Lockean principles by convincing them of the congruity of those principles with their beloved common law writers. The careful backdating of the text to 1687, several years before *Two Treatises*, would leave the impression that the political principles defended therein stand entirely independent of any Lockean rationalism.

Although Locke's philosophical style ran counter to common law modes of thinking, there were elements in Locke's thought that made a reconciliation with the lawyers seem promising. Both Locke and the lawyers, for example, affirmed the rule of law, and tended to oppose royalist absolutism. Locke, moreover, framed his political teaching in terms of the triumvirate of rights—life, liberty, and estate—that already played a major role in the common law. By the time Blackstone became the most authoritative voice of the common law tradition about a half century later, Lockean principles had clearly made great headway in penetrating the common law mind, for Blackstone, if not a strictly orthodox Lockean, took much from his philosophic predecessor.[23]

The *Argument* itself is part of the story of how Locke came by 1750 to be *the* Whig thinker, and it points toward another sphere in which Lockean principles could and did spread, the common law. It appears, in this case, at least, that the triumph of Locke was accomplished by something like a conspiracy, but however much that may have been the case here, that cannot have been so altogether. Nonetheless, it is certainly striking that among the earliest writings adopting and spreading the Lockean philosophy were these anonymous pamphlets, at least one of which, *Political Aphorisms* and its clones, was exceedingly popular in the eighteenth century, and which never once mentioned Locke's name, despite their clearly derivative character.

"CATO'S LETTERS": A LOCKEAN POLITICAL PHILOSOPHY

A decade after the Sacheverell controversy, the most remarkable piece of English political writing since Locke's *Two Treatises* exploded on the scene. Here was testimony to Locke's success in giving form to a major statement of Whig theory by 1720. In that year John Trenchard and Thomas Gordon, writing as "Cato," began the newspaper series known as *Cato's Letters*. It ran in the press into 1723, went through several bound editions, and came to stand as a key document in the development of Opposition or radical political thought in both England and America. It was unprecedentedly popular in its own time, to judge by Cato's own testimony in his "farewell" letter in July 1723: "I have with a success which no man has yet met with (if I regard the number of my readers, and the sale of these papers) carried on a weekly performance, under this and another title for near four years."[24] Trenchard and Gordon's estimation of their success has been confirmed by scholars. "The letters themselves were immensely popular, occasioning a huge amount of applause and criticism and 'were to prove for nearly three years among the most troublesome thorns that pricked the vulnerable sides of the British ministry,'"[25] Cato attracted such a wide audience, and vexed the Walpole ministry so painfully, because he set his thoughts before the public in the wake of the great South Sea Bubble Scandal of 1720, a scandal that implicated political personages up into the higher reaches of the court and that Walpole did his best to stonewall. Topical as the provocation for beginning the Cato series was, Trenchard and Gordon did not limit themselves to issues immediately related to it, but allowed themselves to range over the full field of "civil and religious liberty." Their audience, moreover, may have come to hear denunciations of the South Sea Company's directors, but it stayed to hear the rest. Unlike many topical political writings, Cato's *Collected Letters* remained a vital work for many years after the directors met their final reward (or punishment), and it appealed to readers as far-flung, and in as different circumstances, as the colonial Americans. In

England *Cato's Letters* remained a work with a steady, if insular, readership. As late as 1774, for example, substantial excerpts from Trenchard and Gordon went into James Burgh's manual of reform and opposition, *Political Disquisitions*.[26]

It would not be too much to say that the revolution in the historiography of the American founding captured by the phrase "republican synthesis" was triggered by the rediscovery of the role of Cato in helping shape the political vision of the Americans.[27] Cato was, according to Bailyn, "most important" within the Opposition tradition that "dominated the colonists' miscellaneous learning and shaped it into a coherent whole," giving it a "coherent intellectual pattern." According to Bailyn, "the writings of Trenchard and Gordon ranked with the treatises of Locke as the most authoritative statements on the nature of political liberty and above Locke as an exposition of the social sources of the threats it faced."[28] To support his claims, Bailyn supplied a long list of pamphlets produced by the Americans during the revolutionary era in which Cato figured as a prominent authority. Bailyn likewise discovered many instances of the extensive use of Cato without attribution, a common eighteenth-century phenomenon we have already noticed.[29] Pocock found the writings of Trenchard and Gordon to be "some of the most widely distributed political reading of the contemporary American colonists." Shalhope, speaking for the synthesizers as a whole, found Cato to be "of the utmost importance in the creation of American republicanism."[30]

Recognition of the role of Cato is not limited to partisans of the new republican historiography, either. Forrest McDonald found that Cato was "widely read by the Americans" and was an "important . . . source of republican thought" for them. Ronald Hamowy, a critic of the republicans, nonetheless concedes that Cato had a "position of preeminence . . . as revolutionary tracts in the colonial struggle against the Crown." Thomas Pangle, another strong critic of the synthesizers, conceded that Cato was an important bridge by which political ideas crossed the Atlantic.[31]

The republican sponsorship of Cato's revival indicates that the issues surrounding Trenchard and Gordon are complex. Although historians sympathetic to a non-Lockean interpretation of Cato are responsible for calling him to our attention, Cato is nonetheless important to the story being told here precisely for the opposite reason, that he is a major figure in the rise of Lockean Whiggism. Nonetheless, there are features of Cato's thought that, if not anti-Lockean, are not particularly Lockean either. It is these that have led Pocock and the others to find Cato a bearer of the very different classical republican or civic humanist tradition of political thought. This, I will argue, is a quite mistaken grasp of Cato's thought, but the *Letters* do provide an apt test case for the republican hypothesis in its various forms. Cato does not stand for the triumph of republican over Lockean or liberal thought, but rather for the development of a genuine and immensely powerful synthesis between Lockean political philosophy and the earlier Whig political science. The infusion of the latter elements misled Pocock et.al. into believing Cato to be an alternative to Locke. Trenchard and Gordon were, on the contrary, above all syncretistic thinkers who were able to solidify a new kind of Whiggism by creating the aforementioned new combination. They thus produced the form of Whiggism that became authoritative for the Americans preceding and immediately following 1776.

Cato's credentials as a partisan of the revolution are entirely unimpeachable. Trenchard had himself been one of the main supporters of William in 1688, going so far as to lend the new monarch a very large sum of money. Moreover, Cato regularly and persistently defends the legitimacy of 1688. The "late Revolution" stands on the [true] "principles of government," which "lie open to common sense." Only "hirelings" who would "betray" their country "for a sop" would deny the "maxims" of the revolution.[32] Cato never hedges, as the Bill of Rights did, as to the deposition of James; it was no "abdication," but rested on the "principle of people's judging for themselves, and rejecting lawless force."[33] He has no patience for doctrines of divine right monarchy[34] or absolute and unbounded submission, or absolute and arbitrary monarchical power.[35] The claims of the Jacobites move him only to rage. Cato can think of no better examples of factious and treacherous actions than the string of policies pursued under the Stuart monarchs.[36] To him James II clearly exampled a tyrant who attempted to exercise "usurped powers."[37]

On occasion, one finds in Cato language reminiscent of the old Whig arguments—the deeds of 1688 defended in the manner of 1688: "The late King James did . . . violate and break the fundamental laws and statutes of this realm, which were the original contract between him and his people."[38] But for the most part we find a thoroughly Lockean defense. Surely there is nothing of the Grotian themes so prominent in the literature of 1688–89. Even when Cato deploys the concept of the original contract, as above, he does not use it in the Grotian way typical of the 1680s; the very question of whether a right to resistance exists at all depends not on the original contract but rather on whether the king has done something deserving of resistance, or even of overthrow.[39] Apart from these rather un-Grotian echoes of the doctrine of the original contract, moreover, we see nothing of the most characteristic Grotian themes. In nearly one thousand pages of essays, Cato never once betrays the kind of interest in the law of nations that forms the very core of Grotius's concerns.[40] Indeed the central Grotian doctrine of the *jus gentium* never appears in Cato; accordingly absent is Grotius's characteristic manner of treating the natural law. As opposed to the clear tracks of Grotianism in most of the literature of 1688–89, there is, in fact, no compelling reason to suspect that Trenchard and Gordon had ever read the Dutch jurist's magnum opus. (Trenchard, a very widely read man, probably had, but Grotius leaves no stamp on Cato's thinking.)

Cato adheres to an "unquestionably Lockean" political philosophy. As Ronald Hamowy points out, Cato's style of argumentation is definitely Lockean, for it employs the "kind of speculative reasoning" characteristic of Locke.[41] Although Cato frequently cites historical examples, he does not use history in the manner of the seventeenth-century parliamentary or Whig thinkers, as a source of standards of right, nor does he appeal to the closely related common law arguments. As striking as the use of common law authorities by the author of the *Argument for Self-Defence* is Cato's failure to give them any place at all. He never once mentions the heroes of the common law, Fortescue, Bracton, and Coke, nor does he appeal to common law cases or principles. He proceeds in nothing like the manner of the author of the *Argument*. Cato is a Lockean not merely in the general sense that he endorses ideas of contract and so on—what Bailyn calls "the commonplaces of the Whig tradition."[42] He is a Lockean in the much more specific sense that he endorses the same five Lockean doctrines contained in the American Declaration of Independence but not in the non-Lockean Whig literature of the seventeenth century.[43]

Cato's political philosophy begins exactly where Locke's does: "All men are naturally equal." Locke, almost identically, begins his attempt "to understand political power right" with the observation that "the state all men are naturally in [is] a state . . . of equality."[44] The Declaration of Independence echoes both in its "all men are created equal" passage. Locke and Cato surely understand human equality identically; in Locke's words, it means that "all the power and jurisdiction is reciprocal, no one having more than another"; no one has authority over another by nature (or divine appointment). That is, exactly Cato's explication of equality, too: "None ever rose above the rest but by force or consent: no man was ever born above all the rest, or below them all."[45] Cato suggestively identifies "nature" as the "kind and benevolent parent" of humanity, an anticipation perhaps of the "nature's God" the Declaration seems to identify as the "Creator." Cato— in this case Gordon—appears to have Locke's *Treatises* open before him as he writes his essay "Of the Equality and Inequality of Men," for he paraphrases rather closely the immediate sequel in Locke's text. Locke supports his claim about equality with the following reason:

> There being nothing more evident, than that creatures of the same species and rank promiscuously born to all the same advantages of nature, and the use of the same faculties, should also be equal one among another without subordination or subjection.

That passage becomes this in Gordon's text:

> Nature is a kind and benevolent parent; she constitutes no particular favorites with endorsements and privileges, above the rest; but for the most part seeds all her offspring into the world furnished with the elements of understanding and strength, to provide for themselves.

Cato's restatement shows a more original mind than those at work in *Vox Populi* or the *Argument*, but the connection to Locke's text is just as clear.[46]

This condition of equality, affirmed in Locke, Cato, and the Declaration, is explicitly called by Locke and Cato a "state of nature," that state being precisely the condition in which there is no authority, no regular government.[47] Moreover, both Locke and Cato identify the original state, the natural state of equality, with a state of freedom. According to Locke, the "state all men are naturally in . . . is a state of perfect freedom to order their actions, and dispose of their possessions, and persons as they think fit." Cato says much the same: "All men are born free."[48]

Cato explicitly endorses the corollary of human equality or the state of nature, government as artifact—as he titles one of his essays, "All Government Proved To Be Instituted By Men." No government comes from nature or God. "It is certain, on the contrary, that the rise and institution or variation of government, from time to time, is within the memory of men or of histories; and that every government, which we know at this day in the world, was established by the wisdom and force of mere men." Locke's point in his discussion "of the beginning of political societies" is just the same; the only way that government comes to be is that men make it.[49] The result for both is the desacralization and demystification of politics. "Most of those who manage" government, says Cato, "would make the lower world believe that there is I know not what difficulty and mystery in it, far above vulgar undertakings." This, however, is mere "craft and imposture." In Cato's view, government is "of all the sciences . . . the easiest to be known." The people may be ignorant of the "principles of government," but they are easily grasped once one understands government as artifact. "What is government, but a task committed by all, or the most, to one or a few, who are to attend upon the affairs of all?" Political society is an artifact produced by originally free and equal human beings; it follows that "the publick" is nothing "but the collective body of private men." The public is not the *corpus mysticum* of Fortescue, Suárez, or Filmer.[50] No trace of Aristotelian organicism remains in Cato, nor much of theocentric natural law.

About one hundred years later, Thomas Jefferson made many of the same points, in language that contained traces of Cato's earlier polemic. On the fiftieth anniversary of the Declaration of Independence, he expressed his commitment to the Cato-like project of "arousing men to burst the chains under which monkish ignorance and superstition had persuaded them to

bind themselves." Like Cato, Jefferson called for "the free right to the unbounded exercise of reason and freedom of opinion."[51] Cato, following out
the implications of the thought that government is nothing but an object
made for the purposes and interests of the governed, had been one of the
first great champions of freedom of speech, including the freedom to speak
critically of rulers. For Cato, the people have every right to look into the
conduct of their governors, for the world of politics is a human affair
through and through and does not reflect the hand of God.[52]

If government is an artifact, its makers construct it for a purpose. Cato
follows Locke and anticipates the Declaration of Independence in finding
the standards for measuring government in the purposes implicit in its "institution": "To know the jurisdiction of governors, and its limits, we must
have recourse to the institution of government, and ascertain those limits by
the measure of power, which men in the state of nature have over themselves and one another." Cato understands the purpose behind the institution of government in the familiar Lockean manner: the securing of rights.

> The entering into political society, is so far from a departure from his natural right,
> that to preserve it was the sole reason why men did so; and mutual protection and
> assistance is the only reasonable purpose of all reasonable societies. To make such
> protections practicable, magistracy was formed, with power to defend the inno-
> cent from violence, and to punish those that offered it; nor can there be any other
> pretence for magistracy in the world.[53]

In the preceeding, Cato reproduces the essentials of the teaching on the
"ends of political society" found in Locke:

> But though men when they enter into society, give up the equality, liberty, and
> executive power they had in the state of nature, into the hands of the society, to
> be so far disposed of by the legislative, as the good of the society shall require;
> yet it being with an intention in every one the better to preserve himself his lib-
> erty and property; (for no rational creature can be supposed to change his condi-
> tion with an intention to be worse) the power of society . . . can never be supposed
> to extend further than this common good; but is obliged to secure every one's
> property.[54]

Cato thus accepts three distinctively Lockean thoughts that together distinguish him from the pre-Lockean Whigs. The standards for judging government are to be ascertained from the performance of making it. The
performance, however, is not some actual historical event, but a rational reconstruction of "the true original" of government, based on a theoretical
grasp of the "natural condition" of humanity and of what rational beings
would do in that situation. The claim is not that actual historical humankind, perhaps blinded by "monkish ignorance and superstition," did make
government in the way described. Finally, both Locke and Cato understand

the end of the making in terms of rights-securing (or in Locke's idiosyncratic terminology, the preservation of property). In Cato's succinct phrase, "No government ought to take away men's natural rights, the business and design of government itself being to defend them."[55]

Unlike the Whigs, who spoke in terms of the ancient constitution or of an historical original contract, history has little to do with Cato's theory of the origin of government. The chief reason for that is the same as Locke's: rights are inalienable, and human beings, no matter what they may actually have done, can never subject themselves or their descendants to a more extensive, absolutist, or arbitrary power. "Liberty is a gift which [human beings] receive from God himself; nor can they alienate the same by consent." Again, Cato (this time Trenchard) must have been writing with Locke's text open before him, for he loudly echoes Lockean language. "No man has power over his own life, or to dispose of his own religion; and cannot consequently transfer the power of either to anybody else: Much less can he give away the lives and property of his posterity, who will be born as free as he himself was born, and can never be bound by his wicked and ridiculous bargain."[56]

The natural rights for the sake of which "governments are instituted among men" also provide the foundation for political power. "Every man in the state of nature had a right to repel injuries, and to avenge them; that is, he had a right to punish the authors of those injuries, and to prevent their being again committed." Cato thus follows Locke in affirming a natural executive power of the state of nature. "The right of the magistrate arises only from" this natural right to enforce the law of nature.[57]

As should be clear from the discussion thus far, Cato also accepts the fourth Lockean doctrine enunciated in the Declaration of Independence. "Consent," says Cato, is "the only foundation of any government." Cato understands the consent in the Lockean and not in the old Whig way: it is not the consent of some ancestors at the beginnings of the regime, but the consent of each and every human being, for each is "born as free" as every other and can only accept the burden of government for him or herself.[58]

Since government is made by consent, it can be unmade by withdrawal of consent, upon proper cause. "When [the magistrate] exceeds his commission, his acts are as extrajudicial as are those of any private officer usurping an unlawful authority, that is, they are void." Again, Cato-Trenchard develops his theme not merely in a generally Lockean way but by directly paraphrasing his philosophic authority: "But here arises a grand question, which has perplexed and puzzled the greatest part of mankind. . . . The question is, who shall be Judge whether the magistrate acts justly, and pursues his trust?" The parallel to Locke's formulation is apparent: "Here, 'tis like, the common question will be made, who shall be judge whether the prince or legislature act contrary to their trust?"[59]

Cato does not merely raise the question in a directly Lockean way, but he answers it in that manner as well.

> If neither magistrates, nor they who complain of magistrates, and are aggrieved by them, have a right to determine decisively, the one for the other; and if there be no common established power, to which both are subject; then every man interested in the success of the contest, must act according to the light and dictates of his own conscience. . . . Where no judge is nor can be appointed, every man must be his own; that is, where there is no stated judge upon Earth, we must have recourse to Heaven.

Cato has here followed Locke not only in answering, in Locke's phrase, that "the people shall be judge" but in describing the act of judgment as an "appeal to Heaven."[60]

Cato, in other words, is not merely repeating "commonplaces of the Whig tradition" or employing "traditional contractual terms," but is giving quite precisely Lockean versions of doctrines that differ considerably from those in the Whig tradition. On the important issue of dissolution, for example, Cato also follows Locke and differs from most of the Whigs. Cato refers to an instance of the "recourse to Heaven" and says of it, "The government becoming incapable of acting, suffered a political demise: the constitution was dissolved; and there being no government in being, the people were in the state of nature again."[61]

Cato's understanding of the central concept of rights parallels, even if it does not quite reproduce, the philosophic subtleties of Locke's discussion. Although Cato has much of Hobbes in him, especially in his understanding of human psychology, he accepts the Pufendorf-Locke view that rights inherently raise a moral claim. His most important consideration of rights occurs in a letter titled "Inquiry into the Source of Moral Virtue." His approach to morality is exactly like that of Locke and not at all akin to earlier writers. "Morality or moral virtue, are certain rules," not habits or perfections of character, as Aristotle or Thomas would have it. Those moral rules provide for the "mutual convenience or indulgence, conducive or necessary to the well-being of society." Like Grotius, and Locke after him, the sphere of morality is the relatively narrow sphere of social virtue, or justice. The content of morality is social, but the beginning point is not: "Every man knows what he desires himself." In this context Cato calls attention only to the relatively harmless desires "to be free from oppression, and the insults of others, and to enjoy the fruits of his own acquisitions, arising from his labour or invention."[62] Visible in this list, of course, is the Lockean triad of rights.

Cato fails to mention in this place the other, less benign desires he elsewhere details, however. Men are the source of evil for each other because "every man loves himself better than he loves his whole species." Like Hobbes, he believes that self-love takes the form of a "natural passion for superiority. . . . All men have an ambition to be considerable, and take such ways as their judgments suggest to become so. Hence proceeds the appetite of all men to rise above their fellows, and the constant emulation that always has been, and always will be, in the world, amongst all sorts of men." Whatever any man possesses, he "would have more" and not necessarily feel bound to be too nice in how he acquired it. "Men are very bad where they dare, and . . . all men would be tyrants, and do what they please."[63]

Human desires, if simply left to themselves, would overturn rather than promote the "well-being of society." The natural desires must undergo a transformation before they can become moral rights. "Since he can have no reason to expect this indulgence to himself, unless he allow it to others, who have equal reason to expect it from him," the desires one has for oneself must be checked, in effect, for the possibility of mutual acceptance, or "mutual convenience." Only those desires that others could "indulge" can become moral right. Desires must be trimmed to the mutually acceptable; what is left is moral right. The desire to dominate others thus cannot survive this process, but the desire to "be free from oppression" can.[64]

The natural right that Cato uses as shorthand for all the others is liberty, which he understands as "the power every man has over his own actions, and his right to enjoy the fruit of his labor, art and industry." But this power and right, subject to the process of mutual recognition, is right only "as far as it hurts not the society, or any members of it, by taking from any member, or by hindering him from enjoying what he himself enjoys." More than a century before John Stuart Mill, Cato formulates Mill's libertarian principle. "Thus, with the above limitations, every man is sole lord and arbiter of his own actions and property."[65]

The requirement of potential mutuality not only reveals which desires can be affirmed as rights, but also reveals "the common interest of all, who unite together in the same society, to establish such rules and maxims for their mutual preservation, that no man can oppress or injure another, without suffering by it himself." The same asocial character of the desires that requires mutual recognition also requires, for the establishment of right, government with the power to rule and enforce rules in order to secure the rights so discovered. It is not enough to identify which desires can be mutually validated; there must also be a device to keep the unvalidated desires in check.[66] Human beings thus came to understand rights and the proper ground of government simultaneously.

"CATO'S LETTERS": NATURAL RIGHTS AND THE OLD REPUBLICANISM

Despite Cato's Lockean understanding of the issues of political philosophy, the chief sponsors of the various forms of the new republicanism claim Cato for their own. Pocock finds Cato "unmistakably Machiavellian and neo-Harringtonian." Wood identifies Trenchard and Gordon as preservers and transmitters of "classical republican . . . ideals."[67] If, as Pocock and Wood appear to believe, their civic humanist or classical republican tradition is very different from Lockean liberalism, then either Cato must not be one of their republicans, or he must be very confused indeed, for he is most definitely a Lockean. Although Pocock and Wood claim Cato, it must be said, neither presents a very strenuous case for classifying Trenchard and Gordon among the classical or civic humanist republicans. Indeed, it is quite easy to show that Cato does not share the core commitments of Pocock's and Wood's republicans.[68]

Despite the long series of modifications Pocock traces in his civic humanist tradition, as it wended its way from Aristotle and Polybius to Machiavelli, Harrington, and the neo-Harringtonians, the spine holding it together as a tradition is its Aristotelian core. "Civic humanism is a type of thought . . . in which it is contended that the development of an individual toward self-fulfillment is possible only when the individual acts as a citizen; that is, as a conscious and autonomous participant in an autonomous decision-taking community, the polis or republic."[69] It is striking, however, that Cato never says anything to this effect, and says a great deal that does not sit well with it. For example, this notion of citizenship as the arena for "fulfillment of the self" comports poorly with Cato's acceptance of the Hobbesian-Lockean doctrine that the "natural state of man" is a "state of nature," that is, a state without political life of any kind. That doctrine was, and was intended to be, a denial of the Aristotelian doctrine of the *zoon politikon*, man as political animal. For Cato, accordingly, the foundations of political life are not high and "self-fulfilling" but necessitous and defensive. Cato endorses the view of a certain "great philosopher" who "called the state of nature, a state of war" and concludes that because that is true, "human societies and human laws are the effect of necessity and experience."[70] For Cato, government is extraordinarily important, but not extraordinarily high. Far better is the private life. "Happiest of all men, to me, seems the private man." Human happiness requires not active citizenship but "manumission" from the many "impositions, frauds, and delusions, which interrupt" it. Happiness has more to do with liberty, understood as negative liberty, than with citizenship.

Cato nowhere endorses Pocock's idea of liberty as "freedom from restraints upon the practice" of political life. Cato's idea of liberty, it will be recalled, is really quite different and quite Lockean: "By liberty, I understand the power which every man has over his own actions, and his right to enjoy the fruit of his labour, art, and industry, as far as by it he hurts not the society, or any members of it." To say that Cato does not endorse the core concerns of the civic humanist interpretation is, of course, not to deny that Cato does contain many of the elements Pocock, in his chain-reasoning way, assimilated to his civic humanist tradition. Cato clearly does contain themes such as the mixed and balanced constitution, the balance of property, the various threats to the constitution deriving from standing armies and parliamentary corruption, and, finally, the preference for republicanism itself. These elements are better understood in Cato as parts of his synthesis and extension of Lockean political philosophy and Whig political science.

Bailyn was far closer to the truth when he placed Cato among the extreme libertarians. "True and impartial liberty is therefore the right of every man to pursue the natural, reasonable, and religious dictates of his own mind; to think what he will, and act as he thinks, provided he acts not to the prejudice of another." Private liberty is primary; "free government," or public liberty, "is the protecting the people in their [private] liberties by stated rules." According to Cato, "public happiness [is] nothing else but the magistrate's protecting of private men in their property and their enjoyments." Public happiness resolves itself into private, domestic happiness, and the public sphere itself is merely instrumental to the private. The public, in other words, is not the sphere of human self-realization, but the means to protect and preserve the private, which is the sphere of happiness, so far as there is such.[71]

At a deeper level yet, the entire sphere of public and private liberty serves "the great principle of self-preservation, which is the first and fundamental law of nature." Liberty serves preservation because "where liberty is lost, life grows precarious, always miserable, often intolerable. Liberty is to live upon one's own terms; slavery is, to live at the mere mercy of another; and a life of slavery is . . . a continual state of uncertainty and wretchedness, often an apprehension of violence, often the lingering dread of a violent death."[72] All this has even less to do with Pocock's *vivere civile* than Shaftesbury's or Marvell's earlier opposition to absolutism.

In accord with his understanding of life and liberty, Cato appreciates property in the purely Lockean manner Pocock denies was part of the civic humanist tradition as modified by Harrington. According to Pocock, property for Harrington and Harringtonians was not dynamic, productive, or capitalist, but existed for the sake of political participation. Property was to provide "the opportunity to act in the public realm or assembly, to display virtue."[73] On the contrary, Cato emphasizes the role of political liberty in encouraging labor and commerce, which in turn produce plenty. His understanding of the contribution of labor is not only like Locke's, but cast in Locke's very language. "An hundred men . . . employed [in agriculture] can fetch from the bowels of our common mother, food and sustenance enough for ten times their own number. . . . Without labor the human condition [is] abject and forlorn." Security of property is crucial for Cato for the same reasons it is for Locke: it is the means to preservation and it is the means to induce human beings to engage in productive but painful labor. "Men will not spontaneously toil and labour but for their own advantage, for their

pleasure or their profit, and to obtain something which they want or desire."
Liberty, which leaves people free to labor and in possession of the fruits of
their labor, serves the cause of "making life easy and pleasant. . . . There will
be always industry wherever there is protection." Liberty also secures commerce as the means whereby people can voluntarily exchange what they do
not want for what they do.[74]

All the vices of commercial society that Pocock's civic republicans excori-
ate are quite acceptable to Cato, including the great bugbear, luxury. It is
good that people be induced "to believe, what they will readily believe, that
other things are necessary to their happiness, besides those which nature has
made necessary." The freedom from necessity that human labor power can
bring about soon leads, in "very quick progression," to the so-called vices of
luxury: "emulation, ambition, profusion and the love of power." Unlike
Pocock's republicans, Cato is far from damning those developments. "All
these, under proper regulation, contribute to the happiness, wealth, and
security of societies." Even without the general benefit acquisitive commerce brings with it, Cato pronounces it to be "natural to men and societies, to be setting their wits and hands to work, to find out all means to
satisfy their wants and desires, and to enable them to live in credit and
comfort."[75]

It should be apparent also that Cato gives no brief to Wood's conception
of classical republicanism and the organic polity. Cato is a throughgoing
individualist, methodological and ontological. He has no doubt that individuals and their rights are the reality, that society, government, and political
power are derivative and, in a sense, artificial. Organismic notions such as
Wood attributes to his classical republicans and, by extension, to Cato
would be considered by the latter to be the kind of obfuscation or "impositions" that interfere with the proper realization of human liberty.

An especially revealing test case for Wood's conception of classical republicanism lies in his notion of that kind of public good that correlates with the
republican ideal. According to Wood, "the sacrifice of individual interests
to the greater good of the whole formed the essence of republicanism."
According to Wood, "this common interest was not . . . simply the sum or
consensus of the particular interests that made up the community." Consistent with "the traditional conception of the organic community," he finds
instead that the common good "was rather an entity in itself, prior to and
distinct from the various private interests of groups and individuals." Wood
caps off his description of the chief political aspiration within the so-called
Catonic tradition with the claim that "ideally, republicanism obliterated the
individual."[76]

Apart from the commitment to the public good, Cato accepts none of
this, as he announces in the title of one of his essays, "Every Man's True
Interest Found in the General Interest." The common interest is not some-

thing different from or opposed to the interest of the individual, but is just what Wood said it was not, "the sum or consensus of particular interests"— so long as we qualify that with the distinction between real and long-term interest, on the one hand, and merely apparent and short-term interest, on the other.

> The publick very often suffers by their not consulting their real interest, and in pursuing little views, whilst they lose great and substantial advantages. A very small part of mankind has capacities large enough to judge of the whole of things; but catch at every appearance which promises present benefit, without consider- ing how it will affect their general interest; and so bring misfortunes and lasting misery upon themselves to gratify a present appetite, passion or desire.[77]

How could it be otherwise for the Lockean Cato, in whose conception human beings voluntarily accept the bonds of political life solely for the sake of the benefits that accrue to them? "The entering into political society, is so far from a departure from his natural right, that to preserve it was the sole reason why men did so. . . . The sole end of men's entering into political societies, was mutual protection and defence." And Cato's decisive response to Wood's common good separate from and even opposed to individual goods: "Mutual protection and assistance is the only reasonable purpose of all reasonable societies. To make such protection practicable, magistracy was formed . . . nor can there be any other pretense for magistracy in the world." "The business of government," Cato affirms, is "to secure to every one his own," not to require its sacrifice.[78] Because he understands republi- canism as asserting an anti-individualist ideal, Wood identifies the "impor- tant" liberty in his Whig-republican tradition primarily as "public liberty." But as we have already seen, this does not correspond to Cato's view, in which the primary meaning of liberty is individual, and public liberty is but a means to the securing of that.

Wood's notion of the requirements of the common good not only runs counter to Cato's normative theory regarding the rightful ends of political power, but against his considered judgments on the motives of human ac- tion: "The chief inducement which men have to act for the interest of one state before another, is, because they are members of it, and that their inter- est is involved in the general interest." Patriotism, the devotion to one's particular polity, is collective self-interest. "Men will be men, in spite of all the lectures of philosophy, virtue, and religion."[79] At times Cato speaks as if he decries these hard facts about human nature,[80] but the first principle of his political science requires that he make peace with them. Cato con- cludes his essay "Of the Weakness of the Human Mind; How Easily It Is Misled" with a paraphrase of a famous Machiavellian dictum—not the soft civic humanist Machiavelli, but the tough-minded realist: "I shall take the liberty of considering man as he is, since it is out of our power to give a model to have him new made by. . . . We must not judge of men by what they ought to do, but by what they will do." Given "man as he is," Cato resolves that "all wise and honest men are obliged, in prudence and duty, not only by lectures of philosophy, religion, and morals, to fashion this sovereign of the universe into his true interest, but to make use of his weakness to render him happy, as wicked men do to make him miserable."[81] Not preachments about self-sacrifice, but prudent indulgence of self-interest.

Cato goes very far in his accommodation of self-interested passion. "Dry reasoning has no force"; nor does the common moral advice to "subdue our appetites, and extinguish our passions." Advice like that comes "from men, who by these phrases shewed . . . their ignorance of human nature." The passional root of the human situation appears to be this: "Every man loves himself better than he loves his whole species." Cato is perhaps more self-ish than Locke: "Of all the passions which belong to human nature, self-love is the strongest, and the root of all the rest; or, rather all the different passions are only several names for the several operations of self-love." Human beings are "naturally innocent," yet because of the passions, they "fall naturally into the practice of vice." Yet, Cato pronounces with all his authority, self-love is not only "the parent of moral . . . evil," but the sire of "moral good" as well.[82] Cato, in other words, bears little resemblance to, and has not much respect for, Wood's self-denying and moralistic republicans.

Cato's Lockean or even Hobbesian conception of humanity forecloses for him the kind of moral position attributed to him by Wood. Not only are human beings moved primarily by self-love, but, as Cato shows in a remarkable analysis, they are driven by nature to be thoroughly "selfish and restless." The key is the familiar Lockean idea of pursuit of happiness. "Men are never satisfied with their present condition, which is never perfectly happy; and perfect happiness being their chief aim, and always out of their reach, they are restlessly grasping at what they can never attain. Just as with Locke, the idea of happiness constitutes human being as futural being. "His content cannot possibly be perfect, because its highest objects are constantly future." That is to say, human beings are driven by their hopes, expectations, and anticipations; "it is the enjoyment to come that is only or most valued. . . . The only real happiness that we have is derived from non-entities."[83]

The present always falls short of the happiness we seek, and therefore "every man would have more." The goods we possess are not only insufficient in themselves, but insecure in present possession. Not even "the possession of all [would] quiet the mind of man, which the whole world cannot fill." The desires are ever expansive: "He who has most wants most; and care, anxious care . . . is the close companion of greatness." Cato's human nature is acquisitive, insecure, consumed by desire and anxiety. "Human life is a life of expectations and care." Cato develops yet more strongly than Locke himself the theme in Locke that Strauss captured in the memorable expression, "Life is the joyless quest for joy."[84]

Not surprisingly, Cato draws conclusions from his conception of human nature far removed from Wood's notion of virtuous citizenship: "Men are very bad where they dare, and . . . all men would be tyrants, and do what they please." Cato's politics, accordingly, is a politics not of virtue but of laws and institutions. Neither morality nor religion by themselves have much effect in making men good. Therefore, they "ought to establish their happiness, by wise precautions, and upon solid maxims, and, by prudent and fixed laws, make it all men's interests to be honest."[85] Good behavior requires laws with teeth, and these require government. Government, the concentration of society's coercive power, can in its turn be a source of great danger. Cato's ultimate solution is not the public-spiritedness of the classical republicans, but devices more familiar to those who have grown up under the theory of the American constitution.

> The power and sovereignty of magistrates in free countries was so qualified, and so divided into different channels, and committed to the direction of so many different men, with different interests and views, that the majority of them could seldom or never find their account in betraying their trust in fundamental instances. Their emulation, envy, fear, or interest, always made them spies and checks upon one another.[86]

On the whole, among the trinity of chief synthesizers, Bailyn's account of the Opposition tradition holds up best next to Cato's text. Cato does indeed reveal a concern for the opposition between power and liberty, does express suspicion of the motives of power in its dealings with liberty. On the other hand, Bailyn's account also falls short. He asserts, for example, that Cato "insisted, at a time when government was felt to be less oppressive than it had been for two hundred years, that it was necessarily—by its very nature—hostile to human liberty and happiness."[87] Bailyn is far too single-minded in this claim. It could equally well, perhaps better, be said of Cato that government was—by its very nature—*necessary* for human liberty and happiness. Let us recall Cato's approving quotation of Hobbes: a state of nature is a state of war. "Were all men left to the boundless liberty which they claim from nature, every man would be interfering and quarreling with another; every man would be plundering the acquisitions of another; the labour of one man would be the property of another; weakness would be the prey of force." To prevent universal warfare governments arose. "Men quitted part of their natural liberty to acquire civil security," and Cato considers it a good and necessary exchange. Power is not unequivocally bad and dangerous, but "is like fire; it warms, scorches, or destroys." Properly conducted, governments can make a "people great and happy."[88] Without it, there is only the misery of endless quarrel and war. Thus Cato suspects government and governors, but he sees nothing more valuable than them.

Cato's point is not so much to denounce any and all possible governments, but to delineate a political science that will help construct governments that warm but do not scorch. Given his pessimistic view about human nature, Cato is remarkably optimistic in his hopes for what can be accomplished with sufficient political intelligence and skill. Self-interested and mostly regardless of virtue, "men are the materials for government. . . . The art of political mechanism is, to erect a firm building with such crazy and corrupt materials," a task about which Cato is far from despairing. "The strongest cables are made out of loose hemp and flax; the world itself may, with the help of proper machines, be moved by the force of a single hair; and so may the government of the world, as well as the world itself."[89]

The difference between free and arbitrary governments does not lie in the fact "that more or less power was vested in one than in the other." The difference has more to do with the way power is "qualified and . . . divided into . . . channels." The structure, not the quantity, of power is Cato's concern; he is far from being an unrelieved enemy of power. Bailyn's emphasis on the critical and Oppositionist themes in the Opposition literature too much ignores this side of Cato as hopeful projector of "new modes and orders," of a political science of liberty that can teach "how free governments are to be framed so as to last."[90]

"Cato's Letters": Natural Rights and the New Republicanism

Cato does indeed devote much more space to the presentation of the chief tenets of such a political science than Locke does. But this is no indication that Cato differs from Locke. As both Locke and Jefferson made clear, *Two Treatises* was not intended to be a work in political science of this sort; it was rather to be an effort in political philosophy.[91] Cato's book, twice or three times as long as Locke's, is in a certain sense more comprehensive than Locke's, including both the main themes of Lockean political philosophy and Cato's political science of liberty.

The republican synthesizers have been attracted to those features in Cato's thought that present the elements of this political science. For interpreters like Pocock and Wood, these elements express a mode of thinking about politics different from and opposed to Lockean liberalism; for Cato, they represent the means to accomplish the ends of political life as delineated in the Lockean political philosophy. The political science of liberty shows how to maintain free government, and free government, in turn, provides for private liberty and security of rights. Again, none of this has anything to do with Pocock's *vivere civile* or Wood's organic polity.

But Cato's political science does have much to do with the older Whig political science of Shaftesbury, Sidney, Marvell, and others, including Machiavelli and Harrington, who must be freed from the Pocockian civic humanist interpretation if their relation to Cato is to be clear.[92] He decries many of the same evils they had earlier denounced, the danger of standing armies and the corruption of Parliament among them. It was these features, rather than any direct expression of the Aristotelian idea of the *zoon politikon*, that initially led Pocock to identify Cato as a civic humanist of the neo-Harringtonian variety. Indeed, Cato is a striking example of Pocock's use of his radioisotopes and chain reasoning to establish the links within his tradition of civic humanism—and a striking example of its flaws and dangers.

Cato's concern in the postrevolutionary period, in fact, had much in common with the chief concern of the Whigs in the post-Restoration era. For the most part, Charles II did not exercise powers contrary to the (Whig) constitution, but he nonetheless subverted it, the original Whigs believed, via the informal techniques of "corruption." Cato believed Walpole was doing the same. Cato did not claim that the court was violating formal aspects of the constitution, but rather that the ministry was, again, using informal devices of corruption to threaten the freedom of the nation.

Cato uniformly speaks with praise of the English "mixed form of government." However, "these institutions have provided against many evils, but not against all; for, whilst men are men, ambition, avarice, and vanity, and other passions will govern their actions. . . . They will be ever usurping . . . upon the liberty and fortunes of one another."[93] Those in power will attempt to increase their power. Those in Parliament, who are there to check those in power, can be, in effect, bought off by appeals to their separate and private interests. They forget the public interest, which is also their abiding self-interest, in their pursuit of their "particular" interests. Cato, like the seventeenth-century Whigs of the Exclusion days, sees that informal political mechanisms can subvert the free—that is, non-absolutist—constitutional monarchy. Facing a similar situation, Cato sweeps up the Whig political science and in doing so transforms that political science in a number of important ways. Cato's combination of Lockean political philosophy and the adapted older Whig political science gives his thought the specific qualities that led Bailyn to identify it as different from Lockean theory and led Pocock and Wood to mistakenly identify it as opposed to Lockean theory.

Cato's political thought is genuinely more republican than either the Shaftesbury Whigs' or Locke's had been. But his republican leanings must be properly understood. In the first place, they remain leanings, at most, rather than a firm goal of action. Since circumstances in England are not favorable to the establishment of a genuine republic, Cato concludes that "we have nothing left to do, or indeed which we can do, but to make the best of our own constitution, which if duly administered, provides excellently well for general liberty."[94] His political thought is thus not a call for a new or different constitution, but a presentation of some of the means for making it "duly administered."

Cato's republican leanings, such as they are, have little to do with Wood's or Pocock's preliberal traditions. Cato derives his republicanism directly from a Lockean grasp of the philosophic level of politics:

> The only secret therefore in forming a free government, is to make the interests of the governors and the governed the same, as far as human policy can contrive. Liberty cannot be preserved in any other way. . . . Human wisdom has yet found out but one certain expedient to effect this; and that is to have the concerns of all directed by all, as far as possibly can be.[95]

Here Cato's republican leanings pop out into the open: the regime where "all . . . direct the concerns of all" is surely a republic. Cato here expresses an ideal significantly different from the mixed, nonabsolutist monarchy the Whigs favored and Cato endorsed most of the time. The aspiration to make the interests of the governed and the governors simply identical stands behind Cato's republicanism. He conceives of political society as a device for serving the interests (protection of rights) of the human beings who constitute it; Cato pointedly does not understand political society in the way Whig political scientists did, as a matter of a sharing of political power among the classes or orders of society. Cato thinks in more universalistic and abstract terms.

According to the Lockean theory to which Cato adheres, government exists for the sake of securing the interests of the governed; as both Locke and Cato frequently insist, government is a trust.[96] How better to guarantee that government secures the interests of the governed than to make the two elements the same? In affirming that, Cato does indeed go beyond Locke, who favored some version of the mixed regime. Cato modifies Locke in a republican direction, through without making any real break with Lockean principles, precisely because he takes more seriously the informal mechanisms of constitutional subversion that the Whigs identified and opposed. Cato, like the Whigs and like modern political scientists, is more dubious about constitutional formalism than Locke was; Cato sees dangers to liberty even within a formally free constitution, for the executive possesses resources to turn the guardians of public liberty from their task. He therefore calls for a deeper-going effort to guard against those dangers and points toward a republic as the best means, in an ideal world, to accomplish this goal. Cato modifies both Lockean political philosophy and Whig political science by effecting a synthesis of the two.

Probably that part of Cato's comprehensive political science that most misled Pocock and Wood is his frequent exhortations to virtue and his occasional exhortations to pursue the public good rather than, or even at the expense of, one's individual interest. Both Pocock and Wood derive some warrant for attaching these themes to premodern political traditions from the fact that Cato himself appeals to the examples of the ancients for models of the virtue he recommends.[97]

Like his republicanism, Cato's appeal to virtue, or "public spirit," must be properly understood. In the first place, one must not give it a one-sided emphasis. It coexists in Cato's political thought with two other elements of an apparently different sort. Cato, as we have already seen, is no utopian about the willingness of human beings to submit their own interests to the interests of others—he even doubts the desirability of so doing.[98] Moreover, Cato conceives of politics in the spirit of the new science, as mechanistic and deterministic. "Government is political, as a human body is natural, mechanism: both have proper springs, wheels, and a peculiar organization to qualify them for suitable motions, and can have no other than that organization enables them to perform."[99] But Cato's exhortative appeals to virtue make sense only if the world of politics is not so mechanistic or determinist as he suggests here.

Some may resolve these competing emphases by arguing that Cato is confused, or simply contradictory.[100] This is an advance over the approach to Cato that fails to notice the different elements in his thought, but it does not do full justice to him either. The presence of an exhortative dimension in Cato stands in some tension, perhaps, with these other dimensions but, most important, it enters his thought as a necessary supplement to the more dominant lines of argument we have already discussed. Virtue and public spirit are responses, in the first instance, to problems Cato perceives in the basic Lockean model, difficulties perceived, again, on the basis of his synthesis of Lockean political philosophy and Whig political science. Cato's political science takes its bearings from two partially conflicting insights. Government is a trust, set up to serve the interests of the governed, best achieved by making the interests of the governed and the governors identical. The public interest, the honoring of the trust that is government, is the interest of each and all. Perfectly rational beings would devote themselves to the public good so understood.

Nonetheless, for a bevy of reasons that Cato analyzes in some detail, human beings too often fail to notice the connection between their individual interest and the public interest. They are easily seduced into following separate and partial interests that conflict with the public interest. The directors of the South Sea Company are, for Cato, paradigmatic cases of this, but so are members of Parliament who are bought off from the guardianship of the public interest by "side-payments," payoffs more beneficial to them individually, or at least more tangible, than their attenuated share in the public interest.

> What by artful caresses, and the familiar and deceitful addresses of great men to weak men: what with luxurious dinners and rivers of burgundy, champaigne, and tokay, thrown down the throats of gluttons; and what with pensions, and other personal gratifications, bestowed where wind and smoke would not pass for current coin: . . . I say, by all these corrupt arts, the representatives of the English people . . . have been brought to betray the people, and to join with their oppressors. So much are men governed by artful applications to their private passion and interest.[101]

Cato sees clearly, therefore, that the theoretical convergence of individual and public interest does not always occur in practice, perhaps not even under extremely well-structured institutions, a well-structured institution being precisely the one that makes for that convergence as far as possible. ("The interest of the man must be connected with the constitutional rights of the place.") Exhortations to virtue and public spiritedness come to view at this point as necessary supplements to the system of structural self-interest Cato relies on most of the time. The realm of exhortation responds to the area of slippage between true and apparent self-interest in the large sense, a reminder of the real convergence between the individual's interest and the public interest.[102]

In part, it is an attempt to mobilize another kind of psychological mechanism than calculation of interest, whether long- or short-term. The possibility of the appeal to virtue, as something different from an appeal to enlightened self-interest, depends on one of the modes of self-love Cato identifies. "All men in the world are fond of making a figure in it. This being the great end of all men, they take different roads to come at it, according to their different capacities, opinions, tempers and opportunities."[103] To "make a figure" means for Cato to stand well in the eyes of others—in particular, to be recognized as superior to others. The desire to win the praise of others is thus one of the more or less powerful self-interested motives that move people. That virtue, or dedication to the public good, should win the praise of others is not difficult to explain, for it is surely in the interest of each that all the others subordinate their particular interests to the common interest.[104] Thus Cato, despite his acceptance of an almost Hobbesian psychological account of human nature, appeals to, believes in the truth of, and finds a basis for some efficacy in virtue or public spirit.

Although he sometimes leaves a contrary impression, Cato makes clear in his most systematic statement on the subject that he does not understand it in anything like the classical manner, nor does he in fact decouple it from self-interest. In his essay "Of Publick Spirit" Cato is quite explicit in identifying the limits of his appeal to this virtue: "Publick spirit . . . is the highest virtue. . . . It is a passion to promote universal good, with personal pain, loss, and peril: It is one man's care for many, and the concern of every man for all." But he immediately retreats from this self-abnegating notion of public virtue. "If my character of public spirit be thought too heroic . . . I will readily own, that every man has a right and a call to provide for himself, to attend upon his own affairs, and to study his own happiness. All that I contend for is, that this duty of a man to himself be performed subsequently to the general welfare and consistently with it."[105] Virtue and public spirit are less anomalous within Cato's scheme than they might appear, for they are necessary complements to his more usual reliances.

Cato's position seems confused, or at least confusing, because he can state that liberty is good because without it "life grows precarious"—that is, liberty is important as a means to life, a thought Locke had earlier endorsed—and at almost the same moment he can praise those for whom "love of liberty is beyond the love of life." Cato knows and commends many "heroes of liberty" who willingly risked life for the sake of liberty.[106] Much of his exhortation is meant to encourage the kind of spiritedness in his readers that will, for some causes, continue to produce such willingness. His American readers certainly responded positively to this side of Cato.

Cato seems to say that preservation is the end and liberty important as a means and, at the same time, that liberty is a good for the sake of which preservation can or should be risked. This not only seems contradictory, but the latter of his two positions seems to place him outside or beyond standard images of Lockean bourgeois morality, according to which rational calculation and industry in the pursuit of comfortable preservation appear to be the moral peak. Cato's evocation of apparently non-Lockean moral qualities is not only a response to the tension or difficulty in Lockean philosophy described above, but, more important, an underlining, an italicizing, of a dimension of Locke's position too quickly overlooked in the standard reading of the "bourgeois" Locke.

The bourgeois Locke, or rather, to use Hegel's phrase, the Locke who lays the groundwork for understanding the moral character of the sphere of civil society (the sphere of workers and owners—Locke is not especially a partisan of capitalists), is not the whole of Locke. That self-constituting self that endows human beings with rights that other animate beings lack; that removes human beings from the flux of being and supplies them with stability, unity, and responsibility over time; that genuinely gives them dominion over a world reduced to raw material; that self also removes them from being merely pieces in a mechanistic world, blindly seeking to conserve their own motion in preservation of their lives. They become free beings, able to give shape and form to their lives, able to suspend their desires and act on reason. Freedom is a means to preservation, but it also expresses the unique human differentiation. Human beings stand out from the rest of nature precisely as free, self-directing beings.

As Cato puts it, for human beings liberty is not only "the means of preserving themselves, [but also] of satisfying their desires in the manner which they themselves choose and like best."[107] Human beings are never free simply to disregard desires, especially not the desire for happiness itself, but the very generality of the idea of happiness gives them a large sphere of self-direction. As essentially free beings, humanity always knew that slavery was not only life-threatening—actually, it isn't always life-threatening—but was above all degrading. As Locke himself said in *Two Treatises*, slavery is a "vile" as well as a "miserable" state.[108] Human being is the being capable of freedom and thus destined to be free. Civil and political freedom, even at the risk of life, is the necessary completion or fulfillment of the Lockean philosophy of the self. Cato's importance lies in part in bringing this side of Locke forcefully to the fore, revealing that the Lockean moral orientation is not so unrelievedly bourgeois as it is sometimes taken to be. Cato thus helps to show how, on the basis of the new philosophic and moral understanding characteristic of Lockean modernity, a certain rapprochement with an older moral sensibility is indeed possible. In this sense, Cato does give the impression that he brings into the modern world something very old, but he does so only because there is a deep ground within Lockean modernity for those apparently older moral commitments.

To many, Locke without his traditionalist veneer, the transcendent natural law, seems to leave humanity nothing but comfort-seeking mechanisms, a philosophically problematical and morally repellant conclusion. Cato helps us see how one-sided this understanding of Locke is. It is true that for Locke, human dignity no longer rests on humanity as *imago dei* nor as uniquely rational being. Human dignity lies instead in being a self, and therefore free. Human dignity thus understood paves the way for the new republicanism Cato portrayed and the Americans later attempted to institute.[109]

Unlike classical republicanism, the new republicanism takes its bearings from universal human qualities, that is, personhood, and thus is fundamentally egalitarian. Each human person is recognized as a rights-bearer, a being possessing that which gives and demands value, a being possessing dignity. The new republicanism is not of necessity politically democratic, but Cato reveals something of the dynamic that pushes in that direction in his underlying yearning for a fuller republicanism than was possible in his England.

Unlike classical republicanism, the new republicanism honors labor and the works of the private sphere in general. The sphere of interaction with nature in the service of (comfortable) preservation is not only given more weight within the new republicanism than in the old, but its inherent dignity is respected; labor, production, and even consumption are no longer mere needs of the less-than-human in humanity, the merely animalic, but themselves express human freedom. Only human beings labor, and thereby reproduce in the outer world the deep truth of their inner world—the process of appropriation and transformation by which they become owners of themselves.

Cato is less confused than comprehensive. He brings forward certain implications within Locke that Locke himself had left muted, and he brings together the Lockean political philosophy with the Whig political science, thereby producing a new natural rights republicanism: popular, commercial, pacific but not pacifist, public spirited but not public at core, ambivalent about government as necessary but dangerous, egalitarian but not levelling. In a word, Cato outlines a republic that seeks a tense harmony between private individual liberty and public or political liberty—that is to say, a liberal republic.

Cato's political thought thus has a comprehensiveness and integrity that make it an impressive achievement. When we consider further that both Trenchard and Gordon were fine and spirited writers, able to pass on to a general audience some of the results of the best philosophical thinking of the age, we can well understand how Cato came to be so successful. And with Cato's success, especially in America, we see another step along the path toward Locke's political philosophy becoming, for Whigs, and especially for American Whigs, what Thomas Jefferson called "the common sense of the matter."[110]

Notes

PROLOGUE

1. For example, see Thomas Jefferson to Roger Weightman, June 24, 1826, in *Jefferson*, p. 1517. On divine right theory, see chapter 1 of this book.

2. For a review of the possibilities, consult the historical survey in Tuck, *Natural Rights Theories*; Höpfl and Thompson, "The History of Contract as a Motif in Political Thought," p. 940; Tierney, "Origins of Natural Rights Language," pp. 615–46.

3. Hamilton, Madison, and Jay, *The Federalist* 14.

4. Cf. Lienesch, *New Order of the Ages*, p. 3.

5. Cf. Hoffer, *Revolution and Regeneration*, pp. 14–69.

6. Quoted in ibid., p. 53.

7. Quoted in ibid., p. 55.

8. Jefferson to Weightman, June 24, 1826, in *Jefferson*, p. 1517.

9. Jefferson to John Norvell, June 4, 1807, in ibid., p. 1176.

10. Boorstin, *The Genius of American Politics*, pp. 83–84; Pocock, *Three British Revolutions*, p. 74; Kerber, "The Republican Ideology of the Revolutionary Generation," p. 480; Wood, *The Creation of the American Republic*.

11. Paul Conkin, review of Steven Dworetz, *The Unvarnished Doctrine*, p. 497.

12. Consider Plumb, *The Origins of Political Stability in England*.

13. Schwoerer, *The Declaration of Rights*, p. 3; Jones, *The Revolution of 1688 in England*; Western, *Monarchy and Revolution*. For a less positive account of the accomplishments of the Glorious Revolution, consider Kenyon, *Stuart England*, pp. 245–67; idem, *Revolution Principles* pp. 4–34; Johnson, "Politics Redefined," pp. 692–702; Dickinson, "How Revolutionary Was the 'Glorious Revolution' of 1688?" p. 125. Schwoerer ("The Contribution of the Declaration of Rights to Anglo-American Radicalism," p. 105) calls attention to the current "scholarly fashion" of disparaging the significance of the revolution of 1688–89. I share her opinion that this is an unsound point of view motivated to a large degree by inappropriate comparisons to the (unsuccessful) revolution that preceded it in England in the 1640s or to the revolutions that succeeded it in France and Russia.

14. Quoted in Fink, *The Classical Republicans*, pp. 188–89.

15. Cf. Robbins, *The Eighteenth-Century Commonwealthmen*, p. 57. I shall explicitly discuss the issue of the Lockeanism of the Declaration later.

16. Cf. Schwoerer, "Contribution," p. 117.

17. Cf. Chesterton's contrast between American and English political theory in *What I Saw in America*, p. 16.

18. Dickinson, "How Revolutionary," p. 129.

19. On the difference between the theory of the Glorious Revolution and the Lockean notion of "dissolution of government," see Pocock, "The Fourth English Civil War," pp. 161–64; see also Dickinson, "How Revolutionary," p. 127; Franklin, *John Locke and the Theory of Sovereignty*, pp. 87–126.

20. Schwoerer ("Contribution," p. 225) seems to accept this inference. See also Dickinson, "How Revolutionary," p. 130.

21. See Pocock's important exploration of the theme in *The Ancient Constitution and the Feudal Law*; also Schwoerer, *Declaration*, pp. 37–38, 162. Although the Declaration of Rights echoes the language of the "ancient constitution" in many places, it ought to be noticed that there are important differences as well. Compare "known laws and statutes and freedoms" with the emphasis on "immemorial custom" discussed by Pocock. Consider also Straka, "The Nation Contemplates Its Revolution," p. 44; Dickinson, "How Revolutionary," pp. 127–28.

22. Cf. Franklin, *John Locke*, p. 94.

23. Dickinson, *Liberty and Property*, p. 75; cf. Kenyon, "The Revolution of 1688," p. 47.

24. Schwoerer, *Declaration*, pp. 25, 159–62, 176–77, 206–10, 217–18, 225, 228. Cf. Ashcraft, *Revolutionary Politics and Locke's Two Treatises of Government*, p. 558; Thompson, "The Reception of Locke's *Two Treatises of Government*," p. 188; Kenyon, "Revolution of 1688," pp. 47, 49, 50, 69. For discussion of ambiguities arguably inherent in the very notion of abdication, see Slaughter, "'Abdicate' and 'Contract' in the Glorious Revolution," pp. 323–37; Miller, "The Glorious Revolution," pp. 541–55; Slaughter, "'Abdicate' and 'Contract' Restored," pp. 399–403. Slaughter argues that according to a now obsolete meaning, "abdicate" could (and did for some in 1688–89) mean "depose," "renounce," or "disinherit" in a transitive sense.

25. Thus Schwoerer concludes that "the Declaration of Rights affirmed the ultimate sovereignty of parliament" (*Declaration*, p. 58). I would add "at most" to her conclusion, for she is correct to imply that the document does not recognize popular sovereignty, as the American Declaration does, but that, aside from other hesitations about parliamentary sovereignty, the English documents seem to come closer to affirming the sovereignty of the nation understood as the three estates and *represented* by Parliament. (However, since the nation so understood could hardly act except as a parliament, perhaps this is a distinction without a difference.) See Dickinson, *Liberty and Property*, pp. 81–83, for the Whigs' general "reluctance to locate sovereignty anywhere but in the ancient constitution." Nenner ("Constitutional Uncertainty," pp. 294–95, 297) also doubts the assertion of parliamentary sovereignty. So does Franklin: "The Whigs were no more inclined to invoke Parliamentary supremacy in 1687 and 1688 than they had been in 1680" (*John Locke*, p. 98; cf. p. 90). Also see Dickinson, "Whiggism in the Eighteenth Century," p. 38. For discussion of a very explicit assertion of popular sovereignty in the Convention Parliament, see Nenner, "Constitutional Uncertainty," p. 298.

26. Schwoerer, *Declaration*, pp. 74–78.

27. Straka, *Anglican Reaction to the Revolution of 1688*; Kenyon, *Revolution Principles*, pp. 4–34. Dickinson, "How Revolutionary," pp. 127–28; cf. Goldie, "The Revolution of 1689 and the Structure of Political Argument," pp. 484, 491.

28. As Nenner put it, "Certainly it is true that rather than a run of generalization on the abstract rights of man, the list of claims that emerged from the convention was closely tied to common assumptions about English law and history" ("Constitutional Uncertainty," p. 299).

29. See Zuckert, "Thomas Jefferson on Nature and Natural Rights," pp. 157–63.

30. See Nenner: "The Declaration was being regarded solely as an expression of a

political desire that placed no binding obligations on the crown" ("Constitutional Uncertainty," pp. 298–99).

31. Suárez, *De Legibus* I.ii.5.

32. Schwoerer, *Declaration*, p. 22. See also Frankle, "The Formulation of the Declaration of Rights," p. 269; Nenner, "Constitutional Uncertainty," pp. 304–5.

33. See chapters 4 and 6.

34. See chapter 2.

35. Pocock, *Politics, Language, and Time*, p. 208. Cf. Pocock, *Virtue, Commerce, and History*, pp. 65–66, 217; Frankle, "Formulation," p. 265.

36. Hamilton, Madison, and Jay, *Federalist* 14.

37. Schwoerer, *Declaration*, p. 168; cf. p. 287.

38. Frankle, "Formulation," p. 270. For a thorough survey of the case for and against the Declaration as a contract, see Nenner, "Constitutional Uncertainty," pp. 301–3; Dickinson, *Liberty and Property*, p. 75.

39. Locke, *Two Treatises of Government*, p. 155.

40. Jefferson's original draft is reprinted in Robert Ginsberg, ed., *A Casebook on the Declaration of Independence* (New York, 1966), p. 260.

41. Aristotle, *Politics*, 1252a5–15. Also see Pufendorf, *Elementorum Jurisprudentiae Universalis* III Obs. V. 2–15.

42. Cf. Pangle, *The Spirit of Modern Republicanism*, chapters 15, 18.

43. Aristotle, *Politics*, 1252a25–30. Cf. Locke, *Two Treatises* I 54.

44. Cf. Parry's observation that the historicity of the contract is not crucial to Locke's case, that he is presenting a "rationalist reconstruction" (*John Locke*, p. 99).

45. See chapters 2, 4–5.

46. Wills, *Inventing America*, chapter 11.

47. See Lynn, "Falsifying Jefferson," pp. 66–70; Hamowy, "Jefferson and the Scottish Enlightenment," pp. 503–23; Jaffa, "Inventing the Past," pp. 3–19; Diggins, *The Lost Soul of American Politics* pp. 9, 37, 49, 53–54, 60ff.; Pangle, *Spirit*, p. 37; Dworetz, *The Unvarnished Doctrine*, pp. 16–17. These critics of Wills have presented in some detail the parallels between the Declaration and Locke's text. Below, I present a summary of the main instances, depending in part on Laslett's helpful annotations in his edition of *Two Treatises*:

Declaration of Independence	Locke's *Two Treatises*
"all men are created equal" (final version)	II 54
"all men are created equal and independent" (original draft)	II 6, 7
"laws of nature and nature's God"	I 93, 116, 126; II 142, 195
"to dissolve those bands"	II 219
"to secure those rights"	II 123, 219
"deriving its just powers from the consent of the governed"	II 99
"the right of the people to alter or abolish it, and to institute new government"	II 220, 222
"the frames to which they are accustomed"	II 223
"mankind are more disposed to suffer"	II 230
"long train of abuses"	II 225

A recent, thorough survey of Jefferson's debt to Locke is in Sheldon's *Political Philosophy of Thomas Jefferson*, pp. 41–52.

48. See Hamowy, "Jefferson," for Jefferson's testimonials to Locke's *Treatises*.

49. See Jefferson to Henry Lee, May 8, 1825, in *Jefferson*, p. 1501.

50. Ibid., pp. 511–12, 514, 521–22; also Jefferson to Lee, p. 1501.

51. Wills, *Inventing America*, pp. 238–39.

52. Lundberg and May, "The Enlightened Reader in America."

53. Wills, *Inventing America*, p. 171.

54. Lundberg and May, "Enlightened Reader," pp. 263ff.

55. Ibid., p. 268.

56. Colbourn, *The Lamp of Experience*, pp. 200–232. Cf. Dworetz's review of Colbourn's own use of his surveys, in *The Unvarnished Doctrine*, pp. 40–41.

57. Dunn, "The Politics of Locke in England and America," pp. 74–80. Somewhat along the same lines as Dunn are Handlin, "Learned Books and Revolutionary Action," and Handlin and Handlin, *Liberty and Expansion*, pp. 379–89.

58. Rossiter, *Political Thought of the American Revolution*, pp. 67–70; cf. Bailyn, *The Ideological Origins of the American Revolution*, p. 36; Conkin, *Self-Evident Truths*, p. 101; Koch, *Power, Morals, and the Founding Fathers*, pp. 29, 31.

59. See Zuckert, "The Recent Literature on Locke's Political Philosophy," p. 295.

60. Colbourn, *Lamp of Experience*, pp. 200–232.

61. See Dunn, "Politics of Locke," pp. 69–72. Bailyn (*Ideological Origins*, pp. 43–45) provides further evidence for Locke's early presence in America, as does Miller, in *The New England Mind*, pp. 420, 432.

62. Baldwin, *The New England Clergy and the American Revolution*, pp. 7–8; cf. Newlin, *Philosophy and Religion in Colonial America*.

63. Baldwin, *New England Clergy*, p. 65.

64. Williams, "The Essential Rights and Liberties of Protestants," pp. 56–59.

65. Baldwin, *New England Clergy*, pp. 66–68.

66. Bailyn, *Ideological Origins*, p. 45; Baldwin, pp. 10, 44; Conkin, *Self-Evident Truths*, pp. 103–5.

67. Dworetz, *Unvarnished Doctrine*, pp. 32, 34–35, 44; Lutz, *The Origins of American Constitutionalism*, chapter 11 (Lutz did not survey earlier writings).

68. Dworetz, pp. 43, 45.

69. Rossiter, *Political Thought*, pp. 12, 70.

70. See Bailyn, *Ideological Origins*, p. 35; Robbins, *Eighteenth-Century Commonwealthmen*, passim.

71. Dunn, "Politics of Locke," pp. 74–77.

72. Dworetz, *Unvarnished Doctrine*, p. 28, (italics in original).

73. Dunn, p. 80.

CHAPTER ONE
ARISTOTELIAN ROYALISM AND REFORMATION ABSOLUTISM

1. Jefferson to Roger Weightman, June 24, 1826, in *Jefferson*, p. 1517. On Locke, see *Two Treatises* I 6. Jefferson took the image from Algernon Sidney's, *Discourses Concerning Government* III.33.

2. See, for example, Allen, *English Political Thought*, p. 119.

3. Schochet, *Patriarchalism in Political Thought*, pp. 5, 86. Cf. Dunning, *A History of Political Theories From Luther to Montesquieu*, p. 254.

4. "An Homily against Disobedience and Wylful Rebellion," p. 95.

5. Manwaring, "A Sermon Preached before the King at Oatlands," July 4, 1627, p. 15. On the royalist respect for security of property, see Daly, *Sir Robert Filmer and English Political Thought*, p. 55.

6. James I, *The Trew Law of Free Monarchies* (1598), in *The Political Works of James I*, pp. 64–65, 69. On James's concession of the difference between king and tyrant, see Schochet, *Patriarchalism*, pp. 87–88. On the King's duties, see McIlwain's, introduction to James's *Political Works*, pp. xliv–xlv. On the context for James's thought, see Dunning, *History*, pp. 212–17.

7. Filmer, *Patriarcha*, in *Patriarcha and Other Political Works*, pp. 89–91. On Filmer's relation to other divine right theorists of the seventeenth century, consult Daly, *Sir Robert Filmer*; Schochet, *Patriarchalism*; Kenyon, *Stuart Constitution*, p. 7.

8. For a discussion recognizing some of these distinctions, see Allen, *English Political Thought*, pp. 97–115.

9. Cf. Filmer's judgment on Hobbes in *Observations Concerning the Origin all of Government*, in *Patriarcha*, p. 239; also Manwaring, "Sermon," p. 14; Bramhall, *Serpent Salve*, pp. 87–88. This issue is further complicated by the findings of James Daly ("The Idea of Absolute Monarchy in Seventeenth-Century England," pp. 240–41), who tracked the meanings of "absolute" over the course of the seventeenth century and discovered that in the early years, at least, it did not have a stable meaning of an "absolutist" sort. Indeed, he claims that the identification of absolute with arbitrary power did not occur until the 1640s, and insists that not all royalist thought was absolutist. J. W. Allen (*English Political Thought*, p. 101) goes so far as to conclude that "there are but very few traces in English writings before 1642 of any theory of royal absolutism by divine right."

10. Earl of Salisbury, speech in Parliament, March 8, 1610, in Kenyon, *Stuart Constitution*, p. 12; James I, *A Remonstrance for the Right of Kings, and the Independence of Their Crowns* (1615), in *Political Works*, p. 213. Cf. James, *Trew Law*, p. 69; also Charles I, speech to Parliament, January 25, 1641 (Kenyon, p. 17), in which James's son accepted traditional legal limits on the royal power. Cf. Wootton, *Divine Right*, p. 32; Spelman, *The Case of Our Affaires*, p. 57.

11. Höpfl and Thompson, "The History of Contract as a Motif in Political Thought," p. 933.

12. Kenyon, *Stuart Constitution*, pp. 9–10.

13. "Homily against Disobedience," p. 98.

14. James I, *Trew Law*, p. 69.

15. James I, "A Speech to Parliament," March 21, 1609, in *Political Works*, p. 309.

16. Manwaring, "Sermon," p. 14. Cf. Filmer, "The Freeholder's Grand Inquest," in *Patriarcha*, pp. 135, 142–43, 156–57, 184.

17. Charles I, speech to Parliament, March 17, 1628, in Kenyon, *Stuart Constitution*, p. 81.

18. James I, "Speech to Parliament," p. 309. Cf. the even stronger statement along the same lines in Spelman, *Case of our Affaires*, pp. 95–96.

19. James I, *Trew Law*, p. 63; McIlwain, introduction to *Political Works of James I*, p. xxxix; cf. pp. xli–xliii.

20. Cf. Locke's claim in the preface to *Two Treatises* that Filmer's argument was built wholly on scriptural proofs.

21. Romans 13:1; 1 Peter 2:13–14.

22. Romans 13:3–4. Cf. the very similar point in 1 Peter 2:15.

23. Milton, *The Tenure of Kings and Magistrates*, p. 759. Other anti–divine right interpretations can be found in Palmer, *Scripture and Reason Pleaded for Defensive Arms*, pp. 63–65; Burroughes, *A Brief Answer to Dr. Ferne's Book*, p. 75.

24. See Dworetz, *The Unvarnished Doctrine*, pp. 54–55, 155–72, on the use of this interpretation in America before the revolution.

25. James I, *Trew Law*, p. 64.

26. James I, "Speech to Parliament," p. 307; in *Political Works*, see also the sonnet reproduced on p. 3, which was used by James to preface his *Basilikon Doron* (1599). On James's great familiarity with Aristotle (and classical political philosophy more generally), see the citations in *Basilikon Doron*, in *Political Works*.

27. Schochet, *Patriarchalism*, p. 87.

28. Cf. Aristotle, *Politics* 1252b9–1253a6; idem, *Physics* 192b9–35.

29. Maxwell, *Sacro-Sancta Regum Majestas*, p. 106.

30. Aristotle, *Politics* 1253a20–23. On organic thought in the seventeenth century, cf. Höpfl and Thompson, "History of Contract," p. 931.

31. An especially picturesque version of the nature of the common good in the organismic understanding appeared in Nicholas Breton's sixteenth-century work *A Murmurer*: "If the head (king) of the body ache, will not the heart (the hearts of the subjects) be greatly grieved. . . . Can the eye (the council of the king) of the body be hurt or grieved, and neither the head, heart nor any other members be touched with the pain of it? . . . Can the labourer, the foot, be wounded, but the body of the state will feel it, the head be careful, the eye searchful and hand be painful in the cure of it? And can the commonwealth, the body, be diseased, but the king, his council and every true subject will put to his hand for the help of it?" (quoted in Tillyard, *The Elizabethan World Picture*, pp. 89–90).

32. James I, *Trew Law*, p. 65.

33. Cf. Machiavelli's revealing phrase "the common benefit of each" (*Discourses* I, preface), which captures well the natural rights conception.

34. James I, *Trew Law*, p. 65; idem, *Remonstrance*, p. 234.

35. *Trew Law*, p. 99; cf. *Remonstrance*, p. 234.

36. Aristotle, *Politics* 1253a19.

37. *Trew Law*, pp. 64–65.

38. *Politics* 1254a23–1254b5.

39. Ibid., 1252a30–31, 1255b16–20.

40. Parker, "Some Few Observations upon His Majesties Late Answer," p. 133. Another astute reply to the absolutist implications of the similitudes is Herle's *Answer to Dr. Ferne's Reply*, p. 145.

41. Aristotle, *Politics* 1259b10–11. On Aristotle's doctrine of the naturalness of the political association, see Ambler, "Aristotle's Understanding of the Naturalness of the City."

42. *Politics*, 1260a5–19.

43. Wootton, *Divine Right*, p. 92. One commentator calls the similitude of the body a "well-worn analogy" that had been previously used extensively by James's

teacher, George Buchanan (Burns, "The Political Ideas of George Buchanan," p. 63). Cf. the appearance of one of the similitudes in *Bate's Case* (1606), a legal case involving the power of impositions (Kenyon, *Stuart Constitution*, p. 62). See also *Sir Edward Coke's Case* (1623) (Kenyon, p. 106). Cf. Tillyard, *Elizabethan World Picture*; Walzer, *Revolution of the Saints*, pp. 6, 8, 142.

44. Cf. Foucault, *The Order of Things*, chapter 2.

45. James I, *Trew Law*, p. 66.

46. Aristotle, *Ethics* 1094a27-b10.

47. James I, *Basilikon Doron*, in *Political Works*, p. 3.

48. James I, "Speech to Parliament," p. 307; *Basilikon Doron*, p. 12; *Remonstrance*, p. 234. For a sense of how distant this similitude is from Aristotle's politics, consider his *Politics* 1252b24–27.

49. James I, "Speech to Parliament," pp. 307–8.

50. For medieval precedents, consult Kantorowicz, *The King's Two Bodies*; Höpfl and Thompson, "History of Contract," p. 934 n. 29.

51. Maxwell, *Sacro-Sancta*, p. 107; Morgan, *Inventing the People*, p. 19. Cf. Locke, *Two Treatises* II 6, for a suggestion of the potential blasphemy in the similitude.

52. "Homily against Disobedience," pp. 94–95. Cf. Manwaring, "Sermon," p. 13.

53. "Homily," p. 97.

54. For other expressions of this attitude in the divine right literature, see Bramhall, *Serpent Salve*, p. 54; Spelman, *Case of Our Affaires*, p. 57; Ferne, *The Resolving of Conscience*, pp. 90–91; Maxwell, *Sacro-Sancta*, p. 105; James I, "A Speech in the Starre-Chamber," June 20, 1616, in *Political Works*, p. 333. On Luther and the attitude of obedience, see Nietzsche, *Morgenrote*, p. 207. On divine right theory as essentially concerning the duty to obedience, see Allen, *English Political Thought*, pp. 99–108, 509–19. On Calvin and the attitude of obedience, see Walzer, *Revolution*, pp. 24–25, 28, 35–37, 41, 45.

55. In *The English Poems of George Herbert*, ed. C. A. Patrides (London, 1874).

56. On law and grace in Calvin, see Walzer, *Revolution*, p. 56.

57. Filmer, *The Anarchy of a Limited and Mixed Monarchy*, in *Patriarcha*, pp. 277–78; Figgis, *The Divine Right of Kings*; Maxwell, *Sacro-Sancta*, discussed in Wootton, *Divine Right*, 47–48. Cf. Skinner, *The Foundations of Modern Political Thought*, 2:301; Oakley, "On the Road from Constance to 1688." See also Tyndale, *The Obedience of a Christian Man*, for a statement that brings out the connection between reformist Christianity and obedience. For an alternative view, connecting Filmerean divine right not to Portestantism but to "the extreme republicans," see Dunning, p. 255.

58. Cf. McIlwain's Introduction to James I's *Political Works* p. xxv; Morgan, *Inventing the People*, p. 18; Skinner, "History and Ideology in the English Revolution," p. 173.

59. The best discussion of the relation between Filmer and run-of-the-mill royalist thought is Daly, *Sir Robert Filmer*. Also useful is Schochet, *Patriarchalism*. I disagree with Daly, in that I find Filmer far more "representative" than he does.

60. Locke, *Two Treatises* I 14. Filmer, *Observations Concerning the Originall of Government*, in *Patriarcha*, p. 241.

61. Filmer, p. 241.

62. Filmer, *Observations upon Aristotles Politiques Touching Forms of Govern-*

ment, in *Patriarcha*, pp. 203–4. On Filmer's use of Aristotle, see also *Patriarcha*, pp. 75–80. See also Filmer, *Anarchy*, p. 278.

63. Cf. Walzer: "Zwingli had sacrificed natural law—even as Calvin was to do—to the radical Protestant theory of the Fall" (*Revolution*, p. 40; also see p. 15).

64. For the Calvinist parallel, see Walzer, p. 39.

65. Filmer, *Patriarcha*, pp. 60–61 (emphasis added).

66. Ibid., p. 62.

67. John Calvin, *Sermons on the Epistles of St. Paul to Timothy and Titus* (1579), *A Commentary upon the Epistle of St. Paul to the Romans* (1583), quoted in Walzer, *Revolution*, p. 38; also see pp. 58–59.

68. Filmer, *Patriarcha*, pp. 60–61. For the parallel in Calvin, see Walzer, *Revolution*, p. 38.

69. Cf. Calvin, *Institutes of the Christian Religion* I.v.8–15, I.xvi; on Calvin's political philosophy, see Hancock, *Calvin and the Foundations of Modern Politics*, and Walzer, *Revolution*, p. 35; on the Protestant God, see Hill, *Milton and the English Revolution*, pp. 244–45.

70. See Strauss, *Natural Right and History*; Zuckert, "An Introduction to Locke's First Treatise"; idem, "Locke and the Problem of Civil Religion," pp. 201–3.

CHAPTER TWO
ARISTOTELIAN CONSTITUTIONALISM AND REFORMATION CONTRACTARIANISM

1. Thus I do not follow Michael Walzer in drawing such sharp lines between Lutheran and Calvinist politics. See, for example, his *Revolution of the Saints*, pp. 26–27.

2. James I, "A Proclamation Enjoining Conformity to the Service of God Established," July 16, 1604, in Kenyon, *The Stuart Constitution*, p. 136. On the "conservative" character of James's claims, consider Allen, *English Political Thought*, pp. 3–12.

3. *Bate's Case* (1606), in Kenyon, *Stuart Constitution*, pp. 62–64. A valuable account of the events leading up to the Civil War in terms of the unsettled and ambiguous character of the constitution is in Hume's *History of England*, vol. 1. A very useful summary account of some of the underlying reasons for novel initiatives by the monarchy is Stone's *Causes of the English Revolution*, esp. chapter 2. A very moderate account of the judges' arguments in *Bate's Case* and related cases is in Allen, *English Political Thought*, pp. 13–23.

4. Cooper, "The Fall of the Stuart Monarchy," p. 550.

5. "The Form of Apology and Satisfaction," June 20, 1604, in Kenyon, *Stuart Constitution*, p. 32.

6. Commons Petition of Grievances, July 7, 1610, In Kenyon, p. 72 (emphasis added).

7. "Prohibition del Roy" (1607), in Kenyon, p. 180. The parliamentary reaction severely calls into question Wootton's claim that "Englishmen since 1603 had . . . been willing to accept that they lived in an absolute monarchy" (*Divine Right*, p. 34).

8. "Form of Apology" p. 31.

9. John Pym, "Speech at Manwaring's Impeachment," June 4, 1628, in Kenyon, *Stuart Constitution*, p. 15. Wootton (*Divine Right*, p. 35) is not true to Pym's

thought when he describes him as seeking "a new contract between king and people."

10. Commons Petition of Grievances, in Kenyon, p. 72. Many of the Parliamentary denials of absolute royal power are gathered in the 1620 "Petition of Right," in Kenyon, 82–85.

11. Cf. Pocock, *The Ancient Constitution*, pp. 37, 46, 51–52, 234. Cf. Allen's judgment that doctrines of an original contract had "little or no relevance to thought in England before 1642" (*English Political Thought*, p. 114).

12. Introduction to the Commons Journal, March 19, 1604, in Kenyon, *Stuart Constitution*, p. 10.

13. Canon II, in Kenyon, p. 11. Allen (*English Political Thought*, p. 104) identifies Buchanan as the target of this critique.

14. Pym, "Speech," p. 15.

15. For an early statement that developed both the naturalness of political society and the need for rule, consider Sir John Fortescue, *De Laudibus Legum Angliae*, esp. chapter 13. Fortescue's treatise, written c. 1470, was doubtless a major source of the Parliamentary arguments we are now examining. Cf. Herle, *An Answer to Dr. Ferne's Reply* (1643), p. 145. For general observations on the role of Aristotelian theories in seventeenth century political thought, see Sharp, *Political Thought*, p. 20; Wootton, *Divine Right*, p. 16.

16. Cf. Pocock, *Ancient Constitution*, pp. 21, 31–36, 42–43, 50, 233; Pocock, *The Machiavellian Moment*, pp. 340–48; Sharp, *Political Thought*, pp. 6–9. Cf. Coke in *Calvin's Case*, quoted in Pocock, *Ancient Constitution*, p. 35.

17. Davies, *Le Primer Report des Cases et Matters*, p. 132.

18. Cf. Pollingue, "An Interpretation of Fortescue's *De Laudibus Legum Angliae*," pp. 20–29, 43–44.

19. Cf. Aristotle, *Politics* 1274b30–1275a21, 1275b35–1276a15.

20. Fortescue, *De Laudibus*, chapter 13.

21. On the Aristotelianism of parliamentary thought, see Mayer, "The English Radical Whig Origins of American Constitutionalism," pp. 143–44. On the power of Aristotle in the seventeenth century, see Ashcraft, "Hobbes's Natural Man," p. 1081.

22. Pym, "Speech at Manwaring's Impeachment," p. 15.

23. See the prologue to this book.

24. Pym, p. 15.

25. Fortescue, *De Laudibus*, chapter 4. Contra Pollingue, "Interpretation," pp. 11, 46, and esp. her discussion of law as "expression of rights" with Fortescue's definition of right in chapter 3; in light of which, also consider Pocock's questionable claim that to Fortescue the individual is "primarily a possessor of rights" (*Machiavellian Moment*, p. 335).

26. Aristotle, *Politics* 1252a5, 1252b29.

27. A comprehensive list of Parliament's grievances against the king, financial and otherwise, is contained in Pym's speech of April 17, 1640, reprinted in Kenyon, *Stuart Constitution*, pp. 183–89.

28. Gardiner, *The First Two Stuarts and the Puritan Revolution*, p. 97.

29. Pym, "Speech in the House of Commons," November 7, 1640, in Kenyon, *Stuart Constitution*, 189.

30. The Triennial Act, 16 Car. I c. 1. (1641), in Kenyon, pp. 197–200.

31. "An act for regulating the Privy Council and for taking away the court commonly called the Star Chamber," 16 Car. I c. 10, and "An act for repeal of a branch of a statute primo Elizabeth concerning commissions for causes ecclesiastical," 16 Car. I c. 11 (1641), in Kenyon, pp. 223–26.

32. The Grand Remonstrance (1641), in Kenyon, pp. 207–17.

33. The Nineteen Propositions, June 1, 1642, in Kenyon, pp. 222–27. Weston, "The Theory of Mixed Monarchy under Charles I and After," p. 428.

34. King's speech, January 25, 1641, in Kenyon, p. 17; Allen, *English Political Thought*, p. 411.

35. Parker, *Observations upon Some of His Majesty's Late Answers*, p. 181.

36. A mere two years earlier, Charles had reaffirmed the divine right doctrine, more or less in all its splendor. See Kenyon, *Stuart Constitution*, pp. 166–68; Allen, *English Political Thought*, p. 410.

37. Charles I, *His Majesties Answer to the Nineteen Propositions of Both Houses of Parliament*, p. 173. Pocock (*Machiavellian Moment*, p. 365) gives a slightly different account of the motive behind the *Answer*.

38. Weston, "Theory," p. 426; cf. pp. 436, 437. Cf. Mayer, "Radical Whig Origins," p. 153.

39. Charles I, *His Majesties Answer*, p. 171. A fuller summary of the constitutional doctrine of the *Answer* is in Weston, pp. 428–29.

40. Declaration of the Commons, April 1646, in Sharp, *Political Thought*, p. 36.

41. Charles I, *Answer*, p. 173.

42. Sharp, *Political Thought*, p. 40; Weston, "Theory," p. 430; Allen, *English Political Thought*, pp. 406–12, 483, 507.

43. For an attempt to synthesize the appeal to the ancient constitution as such and the theory of the balanced constitution, see Herle, *A Fuller Answer to a Treatise Written by Dr. Ferne* (1643), p. 151.

44. "A Declaration of the Lords and Commons in Parliament Concerning His Majesty's Proclamation of the 27th of May, 1642," June 6, 1642, in Kenyon, *Stuart Constitution*, p. 226. Cf. Herle, *Fuller Answer*, p. 151. On antecedents, see Skinner, *The Foundations of Modern Political Thought* II.iii.7.

45. These incoherences have been the subject of scholarly notice for some while. Consider Gough, *Fundamental Law in English Constitutional History*; Franklin, *John Locke and the Theory of Sovereignty*, p. 18. The most thorough attempt to supply a rationale for Parliament's position was apparently William Prynne's "The Sovereign Power of Parliaments and Kingdomes" (London, 1643). For a discussion, see Allen, *English Political Thought*, pp. 436–48.

46. "Remonstrance of Both Houses in Answer to the King's Declaration Regarding Hull," May 26, 1642, in Kenyon, *Stuart Constitution*, p. 243. Franklin (*John Locke*, p. 20) identifies this as the clearest statement of a Parliamentary right to resist the king. On the public character of political power, cf. Oakeshott, *On History and Other Essays*, p. 152. A different understanding of the parliamentary position is in Allen, *English Political Thought*, pp. 393–98. For an explanation of the precedents for the distinction between the king's person and his office in sixteenth century Protestant thought, see Skinner, *Foundations*, 2:222–24.

47. Cf. the formulation of the problem of resistance within the theory of mixed

monarchy in Franklin, *John Locke*, pp. 3, 7, 11, 17. On parliamentary hesitations over its radical legal fiction, see Allen, pp. 393–98.

48. Franklin, pp. 17–20, 39, 48–49. Cf. Franklin's similar conclusion regarding one group of Parliamentary writers: "All publicists in the early 1640s were still attached to the existing constitution" (p. 33).

49. Allen, pp. 397–98.

50. Höpfl and Thompson, "The History of Contract as a Motif," pp. 927–28.

51. Gough, *The Social Contract*, pp. 1–3. See also Hampton, *Hobbes and the Social Contract Tradition*; Dunning, *A History of Political Theories*, p. 49.

52. Another important effort to draw distinctions is Lutz, *The Origins of American Constitutionalism*.

53. Höpfl and Thompson, "History of Contract," p. 941. Cf. Gough (*Social Contract*, pp. 96–97), who associates the social contract proper with some of these same ideas.

54. Höpfl and Thompson, p. 942; cf. p. 943. Dickinson (*Liberty and Property*, pp. 74–75) characterizes the debate in terms of an appeal to "an older medieval idea." Also cf. Gough, *Social Contract*, p. 90.

55. Dunn, "The Politics of Locke in England and America in the Eighteenth Century," p. 80. Two other examples of the assimilation of all contractarianisms, one with an English, the other with an American, context, are Furley, "The Whig Exclusionists," p. 29, and Tate, "The Social Contract in America," esp. pp. 378, 385. Höpfl and Thompson cite many other examples.

56. Höpfl and Thompson, "Contract," p. 942; cf. Thompson, "Reception of Locke," pp. 187–88.

57. Henry Ferne, *The Resolving of Conscience*, quoted in Allen, *English Political Thought*, p. 495.

58. Weston, "Theory," p. 434.

59. Herle, *Fuller Answer*, pp. 148–49. On Herle, see Allen, pp. 400–61.

60. Weston, p. 434.

61. Hunton, *A Treatise of Monarchy*, p. 192.

62. Weston, p. 435; Allen, *English Political Thought*, p. 449.

63. Hunton, p. 200. For Hunton's treatment of Parliament's extraordinary powers, see pp. 202–11. On Hunton's parallels to Ferne on the practical question of the day, see Allen, pp. 454–55.

64. Hunton, pp. 177, 183, 192.

65. Ibid., pp. 175–77, 195–211.

66. Ibid., p. 175.

67. Romans 13:5.

68. Hunton, p. 175. On the relation between contractarianism and the Reformation, see Gough, *Social Contract*, p. 84; Patrick Riley, "How Coherent is the Social Contract Traditon?" 543–44.

69. Hunton, pp. 178, 189–90. Cf. Gough (*Social Contract*, p. 89) on the Puritan use of contract "to justify the subordination of the individual to the state, rather than to vindicate his rights against it."

70. For example, Gough, pp. 89–90. Hunton can be read in quite another manner, as a Grotian, for, as will be shown in chapters 4 and 5, Grotian doctrine contained many of the same basic features as Hunton's, including a very similar treatment of

the right of resistance, the original contract, and the moral authority of human will. I am not convinced such a reading would be mistaken, but as opposed to Grotius and the Whig Grotians, Hunton makes much less of natural law and natural theology and much more of biblical theology. Hunton's contractarianism, moreover, is entirely communal and not individual. Nonetheless, Hunton certainly was seen to be relevant by the later Whigs, as witness the fact that his 1643 treatise was reprinted in 1680 and twice in 1689 (Wootton, *Divine Right*, p. 211).

71. This seems to distinguish Hunton from the earlier Catholic contractarian doctrine, such as that found in the Jesuit philosopher and theologian Francisco Suárez. For a discussion of the differences among Christian contractarianisms, see chapters 3–5.

72. Hunton, *Treatise*, pp. 178, 183, 189; cf. p. 191. Consider also Hunton's definition of a "limited contract," p. 183.

73. Ibid., p. 182; cf. p. 177. Emphasis added.

74. Ibid., p. 186; cf. pp. 184, 194. On Herle's similar identification of the fundamental law or constitution with the original contract, see Gough, *Social Contract*, p. 91.

75. Cf. Strauss, *Natural Right and History*, pp. 190–91.

76. Hunton, pp. 185–88, 202–9.

77. Parker, *Observations*, pp. 189–90, 198–213.

78. Ibid., pp. 184–85; see also pp. 207, 210. On contract as itself an analogy, cf. Gough, *Social Contract*, p. 6. On hostility to the familial similitude within Calvinism, see Walzer, *Revolution*, pp. 32–33, 183–98; on the organic similitude, pp. 171–83.

79. Parker, p. 167. On beginning according to method, cf. Aristotle, *Politics* 1252a20–26.

80. Parker, p. 168; Aristotle, *Politics* 1278b5–1279a20. Parker (pp. 168, 176, 186) identifies Machiavelli as sponsor of the view he opposes.

81. Parker, p. 167.

82. Ibid., p. 169. Parker's adaptation of an Aristotelian contractarianism based on *salus populi* points toward a possible link with the similar position of Marsilius of Padua. Cf. *Defensor Pacis*, Discourse I, chapters 4, 9, 12; Allen, *English Political Thought*, p. 429.

83. Parker, p. 210.

84. Ibid., p. 182.

85. Hunton, *Treatise*, pp. 187–88, 195.

86. Parker, pp. 209–10. For Parker's similar arguments regarding the king's powers over Parliament, see pp. 173–75. Cf. Weston, "Theory," pp. 435–36.

87. Parker, p. 202; cf. pp. 211–12.

88. Ibid., p. 181; cf. pp. 188, 194, 200.

89. Ibid., pp. 188, 200. Cf. Allen, *English Political Thought*, pp. 430–31.

90. Cf. Hobbes, *Leviathan*, chapter 46; Filmer, *The Anarchy of a Limited and Mixed Monarchy*, passim, in *Patriarcha*; Allen, pp. 431–32.

91. Parker, p. 200. Parker drew the conclusions for his commitment to supremacy for issues of church government and relation of church and state in *The True Grounds of Ecclesiastical Regiment*, esp. pp. 23–25.

92. Parker, *Observations*, pp. 210, 212. Cf. Tuck's claim that Parker was a "radical natural rights theorist" (*Natural Rights Theories*, p. 147).

93. Parker, pp. 171, 174. Cf. Allen, p. 428.

94. Parker, p. 171.

95. On Parker as a non-Puritan, see Allen, p. 339.

CHAPTER THREE
CONTRACT AND CHRISTIAN LIBERTY

1. "A Declaration of the Parliament House of Commons," January 4, 1649, in Kenyon, *The Stuart Constitution*, p. 324.

2. Ibid.

3. Hunton, *A Treatise of Monarchy*, p. 185; cf. pp. 203, 204.

4. Ibid., p. 186.

5. Parker, *Observations upon some of His Majesty's Late Answers*, p. 210. This rejection of the right to use force against the person of the monarch was the dominant and authoritative position up until 1649, but it was not the only view in the earlier years. Herbert Palmer, for example, rejected the distinction between resistance to the king and resistance to his agents and officers as part of his argument in favor of the rightfulness of resistance (*Scripture and Reason Pleaded for Defensive Arms*). Sharp (*Political Thought of the English Civil Wars*, p. 4) points out, however, that Presbyterians allied with Palmer rejected the actions taken against the king in 1649 on the grounds that they never meant "to bring his majesty to justice." That is, even though there was a much closer connection between Palmer's position in 1643 and Parliament's in 1649, there was still a sense that 1649 represented a major shift from 1643. The Palmerean Presbyterians seem to have remained committed to the mixed monarchy; the logic of that doctrine was better grasped by Hunton, for example, than by Palmer.

6. Hunton, p. 195.

7. See chapters 2 and 4 for discussions of resistance and the original contract.

8. Milton was singled out for disapproval after the Restoration: several of his works were burned in 1660, the faculty at Oxford selected propositions from his books for special denunciation, and numerous royalist writers attacked him in print. See Hill, *Milton and the English, Revolution*, pp. 222–30; Wolfe, *Milton in the Puritan Revolution*, pp. 239–39. In general, on 1660 as a repudiation of everything Milton stood for, see Franklin, *John Locke and the Theory of Sovereignty*, pp. 89–91.

9. Milton, *The Tenure of Kings and Magistrates*, p. 757. Cf. Barker, *Milton and the Puritan Dilemma*, p. 148.

10. Milton, pp. 759–60.

11. Ibid., p. 764. Cf. Milton, *Eikonoklastes*, p. 212.

12. Milton, *Of Reformation in England*, p. 46; idem, *The Reason of Church Government*, pp. 685–86. Cf. Hill, *Milton*, p. 114.

13. Milton, *Tenure*, pp. 754, 755.

14. Cf. Wolfe, *Milton*, p. 213; Sanderson, *But the People's Creatures*, p. 132; Andrew, *Skylock's Rights*, p. 81.

15. Filmer, *Observations Concerning the Originall of Government*, in *Patriarcha*,

pp. 252, 255. For a good account of how Milton went beyond the standard parliamentary writers of the period, see Barker, *Milton*, pp. 145–48; on potentially anarchic consequences, pp. 151–52. On the people and Filmer's critique, pp. 159–62, also Hill, *Milton*, p. 168.

16. Milton, *Tenure*, p. 754. See Bennett, *Reviving Liberty*, esp. pp. 108–14, on the relationship between Milton's "antinomianism" (his interpretation of Christian liberty) and the natural law. Her account fits best with Milton's own vacillation between Christian and natural liberty, as in his *On Christian Doctrine*, pp. 521–41, esp. p. 537. See also Hill, p. 302.; Wolfe, *Milton*, p. 226.; Milton, *The Ready and Easy Way*, pp. 891, 898.

17. Locke, *Two Treatises* II 87, 129–31. For fuller discussion of inalienability of rights in Locke, see chapter 9.

18. Cf. Dunning, A *History of Political Theories*, p. 246: "Liberty, then, was the first and controlling preoccupation of Milton in his political philosophy."

19. Milton, *Tenure*, p. 754.

20. Milton, *On Christian Doctrine*, p. 300; on the errors of the philosophers who ascend only to knowledge of nature, see pp. 400–401.

21. Milton, *Paradise Regained* IV.309–13. On Calvin on the necessary limits of pagan understanding, see Walzer, *Revolution*, p. 37.

22. Cf. Hill, *Milton*, p. 461; but to the contrary, see Dunning, *History*, pp. 242–45. The rhetorical character of Milton's argument in the *Tenure* somewhat obscures the status of his argument. Above all, he aims to persuade of the rightfulness of the trial and execution of the king, and, as a good rhetorician, attempts to use the most effective arguments for his audience that he can deploy. He uses a distinctly latitudinarian strategy in the *Tenure*, and perhaps even more so in *The Ready and Easy Way*. In both places he suggests that he stands on common ground with the ancients, especially Aristotle, but not only the testimony of *On Christian Doctrine*, *Paradise Regained*, and *Paradise Lost* (see Alvis, "Philosophy as Noblest Idolatry in *Paradise Lost*," pp. 263–84), but the substance of his argument makes his suggestion implausible. Many scholars (e.g., Wolfe, *Milton*, pp. 216–47, 391) miss the real foundation of Milton's theory because they misapprehend his relationship to non-biblical thought. (Better is Barker, *Milton*, pp. xv, 123–25, 184, 293.) In the *Tenure* Milton also claims that his position is in accord with the doctrines of all the most approved authors, especially Protestants, and most especially Presbyterians. Despite that claim, and a lengthy appendix intended to make it good, Milton's position differs from standard Protestant political theology, too, as can be seen by a careful comparison of what Milton quotes from his "authorities" and his own doctrine in the *Tenure*, especially on the question of tyranny and the role of lower magistrates in resistance. See, for example, *Tenure*, pp. 753–54: "If the power be of God, it belongs to anyone." Cf. Barker, *Milton*, p. 159. On Milton's use of his Protestant sources, see Hughes's introduction to vol. 3 of Milton's *Complete Prose Works*, p. 122, and articles cited there.

23. See *On Christian Doctrine*, pp. 644, 717–807.

24. On the relation between "property" and "rights" in Locke, see chapter 10.

25. Cf. the alterative account of the generation of inalienable rights from Grotius, in Tuck, *Natural Rights Theories*, p. 143.

26. Milton, *On Christian Doctrine*, p. 353. I have slightly revised the translation to make Milton's point clearer.

27. Ibid., p. 351. Cf. *Paradise Lost* VIII. 325: "The pledge of thy obedience and thy faith."

28. *Paradise Lost* III.98–111, 124.

29. Ibid., VII.625–31.

30. Ibid., XII.67–71.

31. Cf. *On Christian Doctrine*, book 2.

32. Ibid., p. 516.

33. Milton, *Tenure*, pp. 754, 765–66.

34. Milton, *The Doctrine and Discipline of Divorce*, p. 229.

35. Milton, *Paradise Lost* XII.13–37.

36. Cf. Barker, *Milton*, p. 153: "the natural right of the people to break its contract."

37. The role these three central notions play in Milton's political thought stands forth clearly when his position is compared with an earlier work, *Vindiciae Contra Tyrannos*, a sixteenth-century French treatise most often attributed to Phillippe du Plessis Mornay, to which it is often compared and which is frequently seen as an important source for the *Tenure*. (For the comparison, see, for example, Dunning, *History*, p. 242.) The *Vindiciae* was a spirited defense of the right of resistance against tyrannous rulers, and it won the honor of being the best-known and most authoritative statement of Protestant theory on that subject at least up until the publication of Milton's *Tenure*. Like Milton, Mornay presented a version of contractarian theory. The *Vindiciae*'s influence on Milton is fairly clear in several places; for example, Milton's brief sketch of the stages of the development of political society from the first kings to the development of laws and mixed regimes very closely parallels Mornay's similar sketch (cf. *Vindiciae*, pp. 169–70, and *Tenure*, pp. 273–75). Nonetheless, there are decisive differences between Milton and Mornay: (1) Mornay rests his theory on a version of the old Roman law doctrines of natural law (p. 169), according to which natural human liberty is understood to be natural in the sense of the condition shared by all animal beings (pp. 169, 187; cf. *Corpus Juris Civilis*, *Institutes* I.ii pr.2). This is very different from Milton's grounding of natural liberty in man as "image of God"; Mornay did not rely on knowledge derivative from the Bible, as Milton did, and Mornay's "natural liberty" is universal (it applies to dogs and all animals) and purely naturalistic, as Milton's is not. (2) Mornay, likewise, has no role for the Fall. Rather, he accepts the doctrine of the Roman law that the natural liberty as provided by natural law gives way to subjection under the *jus gentium* (law of nations) and human civil law (pp. 169, 188). (3) The different grounding of the two doctrines produces different results in their doctrines of resistance. Mornay adheres to the doctrine as developed by Calvin and Beza, according to which resistance is justified only against tyrants and only by "magistrates" (see pp. 190, 191, 194–97). Milton's rejection of these two limitations has already been detailed. Why Milton refused to follow Mornay in looking to the Roman law is a matter for conjecture; one reason surely had to do with Milton's ideas about the nature of the divine image and its relation to freedom. Another reason may be more negative: Mornay's appeal to the Roman law has difficulties, because he attributed a status to the natural law that

the Roman jurists pointedly did not. For discussion, see Zuckert, "Bringing Philoso-phy Down from the Heavens," pp. 71, 74, 76, 81. Despite its difficulties, the *Vindi-ciae* was hugely influential during the seventeenth century in England; consider, for example, John Lilburne's *Regall Tyrannie Discovered*, cited in Hughes's introduction to vol. 3 of Milton's *Complete Prose Works*, p. 26.

38. Milton, *Paradise Lost*, VIII.403–14, XI.508–10; idem, *On Christian Doctrine*, pp. 395–97.

39. Cf. Hill, *Milton*, p. 64: "Idolatry is a short summary of what he detested"; see also pp. 126, 178–80, 193.

40. Milton, *Paradise Regained* IV.313–15. On what was lost in the Fall, see *Para-dise Lost* XII.180ff.

41. Cf. Hill, p. 158.

42. *Paradise Lost*, XII.25–27.

43. *Paradise Regained* III.109–44. In this context, the interpretation of the "end of time" sponsored by Empson and endorsed by Hill appears as an artifact of fallenness, and therefore contrary to Milton's understanding; see Hill, *Milton*, pp. 296–305.

44. Milton, *On Christian Doctrine*, p. 661.

45. Milton, *Reason*, p. 672; see also pp. 671, 673, 674, 680, 683–84.

46. Milton, *De Doctrina*, p. 461; *Reason*, pp. 656–57, 684; cf. p. 661: "Your prelaty is nothing else but your ambition, an insolent preferring of yourselves above your brethren."

47. Milton, *Tenure*, p. 756; cf. Bennett, *Reviving Liberty*, pp. 34–47.

48. Milton, *Eikonoklastes*, pp. 208, 209; cf. pp. 212, 214.

49. Milton, *A Defense of the English People*, quoted in Wolfe, *Milton*, p. 226. A pamphleteer of the Glorious Revolution captured extremely well this aspect of Mil-ton's thought: "We cannot believe our excellent religion has anything in it of such servile tendency as to incline us to part with our civil liberties and rightful properties. We do not believe Christianity should unman us or that protestancy can make us slaves and beggars" ("A Remonstrance and Protestation of all the good Protestants of this kingdom, against deposing their lawful sovereign king James II [1689], in Somers, *A Collection of Scarce and Valuable Tracts* 10:247.). This Miltonic emphasis on the lack of servility of true Christianity is, on the one hand, an answer to Machia-velli's charge that Christianity effeminated men, and, on the other, the chief basis for Milton's partial synthesis with classical republicanism: Christianity, properly under-stood and practiced, produces a manliness that has something in common with an-cient manliness. In my account of Milton I have deemphasized one theme of some importance, the kind of synthesis or common ground between the politics based on true Christian-biblical principles and classical republicanism. As I have indicated above, I believe Milton was aware of the limits of the common ground, but I do not mean to dismiss this theme as pure rhetoric. A fuller treatment than I can provide here would have to consider how that synthesis works, so far as it does. It is important for Milton, for it provides a link between his "humanist" and "Puritan" motives. I would therefore reverse the emphasis in Walter Berns's otherwise fine essay "John Milton." On Milton's early awareness of the conflict between ancients and moderns, see Hill, *Milton*, pp. 34, 36, 40, 158.

50. Milton, *Ready and Easy Way*, pp. 881, 885–87.

51. Cf. Bennett, *Reviving Liberty*, pp. 59–63, on liberty as the standard of good

rule, even of God's good rule. For an alternative identification of the chief elements and their connections in Milton's political thought, see Barker, *Milton*, p. 141. My disagreement with Barker over the elements of Milton's political thought may account for our differences over the question of the relation between the *Tenure* and Milton's later political writings (see Barker, p. 157). Also see Sanderson, *But the People's Creatures*, p. 137.

52. Zagorin, *A History of Political Thought in the English Revolution*, pp. 111–13; cf. Berns, "John Milton," pp. 442–43; Wolfe, *Milton*, pp. 63, 224, 246; Hill, *Milton*, pp. 160–62.

53. Milton, *Ready and Easy Way*, pp. 888–90; cf. *Paradise Regained* IV.131–42. There is little basis for Hill's claim that this scheme "was far from Milton's ideal solution" (*Milton*, pp. 200, 334).

54. Milton, *Second Defense of the People of England*, p. 352.

55. Zagorin, *History*, p. 111. On Milton's aristocratic leanings, also consider Allen, *English Political Thought*, pp. 334–38.

56. Milton, *Of Reformation*, p. 26; cf. Berns, "John Milton," pp. 451–53; Wolfe, *Milton*, p. 64. I thus disagree with Hill that "liberty for Milton was always largely negative" (*Milton*, p. 128; cf. pp. 262–67).

57. Milton, *Paradise Lost* IV.178–82.

58. For another account of the central tension in Milton's political thought, see Barker, *Milton*, pp. 176–80; Hill, *Milton*, pp. 266–67, 336. For a similar treatment of the ends of political life, see Barker, pp. 300–303.

59. Cf. Locke, *Two Treatises* II 6, 11.

60. Milton, *On Christian Doctrine*, p. 396. See Walzer, *Revolution*, p. 31, for (weaker) parallels in Calvin.

61. Hill, *Milton*, p. 393; cf. p. 396.

62. See Adam's reaction to Michael's account of the scheme of redemption:

> O goodness infinite, goodness Immense!
> That all this good of evil shall produce, and
> Evil turn to good; more wonderful than that
> Which by creation first brought forth
> Light out of darkness.

What Adam finds so wonderful about the scheme of redemption is that in it

> To God more glory, more good will to man
> From God, and over wrath grace shall abound.

Paradise Lost XII.469–73, 477–78. Cf. *On Christian Doctrine*, p. 415.

63. Cf. Strauss, "Progress or Return," in *The Rebirth of Classical Political Rationalism*, pp. 227–30.

64. Herein lies the core of my differences with Walzer's parallel effort to explicate Protestant politics: he sees the Fall at the center of Protestant thinking about politics, while, without denying the importance of the Fall, I find the Creation to be more definitive (cf. Walzer, *Revolution*, chapter 2). Walzer himself brings forward evidence unsupportive of his emphasis on the Fall. Consider, for example, the passage quoted from Calvin, p. 36 bottom. The importance of Creation remains visible in as secular a thinker as Locke (see my chapter 8).

CHAPTER FOUR
WHIG CONTRACTARIANISMS AND RIGHTS

1. Jones, *The First Whigs*, p. 215.

2. Kenyon, *The Stuart Constitution*, p. 361.

3. The Declaration of Breda, April 4, 1660, in Kenyon, pp. 354–58.

4. "An Act for the uniformity of public prayers and administration of sacraments and other rites and ceremonies," 14 Car. II c. 4 (1662), in Kenyon, pp. 378–82; idem, *Stuart England*, p. 183.

5. "An act for the assembling and holding of parliaments once in three years at the least," 16 Car. II c. 1 (1664), in Kenyon, *Stuart Constitution*, p. 382.

6. "An act declaring the sole right of the militia to be in the King," 13 Car. II c. 6 (1661), in Kenyon, *Stuart Constitution*, p. 374.

7. "An act for the well governing and regulating of corporations," 13 Car. II, St. 2, c. 1 (1661), in Kenyon, *Stuart Constitution*, p. 377; "An act for uniformity of public prayers . . . ," in ibid., p. 381.

8. This is not to say, of course, that anti-Catholocism had no presence during the first half of the century. As J. W. Allen observes, "Anti-Catholic sentiment, in 1640, pervaded England so generally that it may be called a national sentiment." *English Political Thought*, p. 312.

9. For narratives of the emergence of the Whigs, see Jones, *First Whigs*; Haley, *The First Earl of Shaftesbury*, esp. pp. 349–50, 352–53, on the character of the early Whigs and on Shaftesbury's role.

10. Thompson, "Reception of Locke," pp. 184–85.

11. Dickinson, *Liberty and Property*, p. 65; idem, "How Revolutionary was the Glorious Revolution?" pp. 127, 131; idem, "The Rights of Man from John Locke to Tom Paine," p. 42.

12. Thompson, p. 185.

13. Ashcraft, *Revolutionary Politics and Locke's Two Treatises*, p. 578, both cites some of the chief purveyors of the old story and summarizes the more recent revision of it.

14. Ibid., p. 184.

15. Dickinson, *Liberty and Property*, p. 58.

16. Kenyon, "The Revolution of 1688," pp. 45, 62.

17. Locke, letter to Edward Charles (c. 1689–90), in Farr and Roberts, "John Locke and the Glorious Revolution," pp. 395–98; Ashcraft, *Revolutionary Politics*, pp. 597–600; cf. Goldie, "The Revolution of 1689," p. 491.

18. Ashcraft, pp. 184, 573; cf. p. 181 n.1.

19. Goldie, pp. 480, 482, 486, 490.

20. Ashcraft, pp. 140, 207. On the Whigs' efforts to make peace with Protestantism, see Horwitz, "Protestant Reconciliation in the Exclusion Crisis," p. 201.

21. "England's Appeal to the Parliament at Oxford" (London, 1681), p. 2.

22. Furley, "The Whig Exclusionists," pp. 21–23; Ashcraft, *Revolutionary Politics*, chapter 5.

23. "Percat Papa," p. 2.

24. Ashcraft, *Revolutionary Politics*, p. 185: Cf. 212–15.

25. Earl of Shaftesbury, speech in the House of Lords, March 24, 1679, in *State Tracts in Two Parts*, p. 24.

26. See, for example, the anonymous pamphlet "A Letter to a Friend in the Country," p. 3.

27. Furley, "Whig Exclusionists," pp. 19, 21. Cf. Jones, *First Whigs*, pp. 214–15.

28. "Letter to a Friend," p. 4; cf. "Percat Papa," pp. 3–4.

29. "Letter to a Friend," p. 3.

30. See, for example, the pamphlet "Vox Populi," pp. 2–3; Hunt, *"The Great and Weighty Considerations,* etc. Considered," pp. 4, 22; idem, "An Answer to a Pamphlet Lately Published," pp. 32–37. Cf. Furley: The Whigs "set great store by the fact that some previous heirs had been excluded by King and Parliament" ("Whig Exclusionists," p. 25, and further examples, p. 26.).

31. "A Letter From a Gentleman of Quality in the Country to His Friend," p. 1.

32. "A Letter to a Friend," p. 3. Cf. Furley, p. 28.

33. "Percat Papa," p. 3. Cf. "Vox Populi," pp. 2–3.

34. Hunt, "*Great and Weighty Considerations*," p. 4.

35. Ashcraft, *Revolutionary Politics*, p. 190; cf. pp. 194, 210.

36. Ibid. p. 210. The tendency to dichotomize appears to stem from Pocock's *The Ancient Constitution*.

37. Hooker, *Of the Laws of Ecclesiastical Polity*, Christopher Morris, ed., (London, 1907), Book I.

38. See, for example, Hugo Grotius, *De Jure Belli ac Pacis* III.iv, vii.

39. Cf. Hunt, "Great and Weighty Considerations," pp. 9, 12.

40. On Grotian methodology, see chapter 5.

41. Goldie, "Revolution of 1689," pp. 490–91.

42. Dickinson, *Liberty and Property*, p. 65

43. Schwoerer, *The Declaration of Rights*, pp. 117–18. Ashcraft identifies Burnet's pamphlet as marked by the very ideas which are also leading ideas in Locke: natural rights, the state of nature, and contract (*Revolutionary Politics*, p. 561). Also see Franklin, *John Locke*, pp. 131–35.

44. Schwoerer, *The Declaration of Rights*, p. 117. Cf. Goldie, "Revolution of 1689," p. 519, on the general role of William in "instigating doctrines."

45. Franklin, *John Locke*, p. 99.

46. Burnet, "Enquiry," p. 1.

47. Ibid., p. 4.

48. Höpfl and Thompson, "The History of Contract as a Motif in Political Thought," p. 941.

49. Burnet, p. 1.

50. Ibid., pp. 6–7.

51. Cf. Schwoerer, *Declaration of Rights*, p. 117.

52. Burnet, p. 1. For differences between Burnet and Locke on the naturalness of family relations, see *Second Treatise*, chapter 6.

53. Burnet, p. 3.

54. Ibid.

55. Ibid., p. 6.

56. Ibid., p. 7.

57. Locke, *Two Treatises of Government* II 95, 116, 119 (emphasis added). An intelligent discussion of Locke on consent in comparison to other seventeenth-century writers is in Wootton, *Divine Right*, pp. 43–45.

58. Burnet, pp. 3–4.

59. For testimony to Grotius's immense influence in the seventeenth century, see Tuck, *Natural Rights Theories*, pp. 3, 58 and passim.

60. Grotius, *De Jure Belli ac Pacis* I.iii.8, I.iv.2, 6; cf. II.iv.8 (rejection of the doctrine of *Vindiciae contra tyrannos*). On Grotius on the alienablity of liberty, see Tuck, *Natural Rights Theories*, pp. 58–81, and Andrew, *Shylock's Rights*, pp. 81–97.

61. Grotius, I.iii.16, 17; I.iv.7, 8. Cf. II.v.30, 31; II.vi.3, 4.

62. Defoe, "Reflections upon the Late Great Revolution," pp. 29, 33, 34, 41, 42, 45–49, 57, 62, 65, 66. Conservative emphases remained in Defoe's later works, even after his writings began to reveal strong Lockean influences; cf. "The Original Powers of the People of England, Examined and Asserted," pp. 135, 136, 157, 158, 160.

63. Julian Franklin (*Locke*, pp. 131–35) takes up the question of whether Locke's *Treatises* had perhaps influenced Burnet in the latter's preparation of the "Enquiry." The *Treatises* was yet unpublished, but both men were living in Holland. Franklin rejects the idea, but not, it seems to me, for the really decisive reasons. He notes, importantly, that Burnet could have taken over his doctrine from Grotius, but he fails to note the differences between Burnet-Grotius and Locke–Declaration of Independence.

64. Thus Goldie says of Locke, "He presented the unacceptable face of Whiggism" ("Revolution of 1689," p. 518). Even in this very conservative form, Burnet's contractarianism may have seemed too radical for his sponsors. Shortly after his "Enquiry," he issued several other pamphlets in which contractarian arguments dropped out. As Goldie suggests, this may also reflect William's efforts to straddle Whig and Tory positions. In this respect, William played his hand much as the Convention Parliament did. See pp. 510–21.

65. In addition to Defoe, consider, for instance, Robert Ferguson's "A Word to the Wise for Settling the Government," in *A Compleat Collection of Papers*. It is perhaps significant that Ferguson was with Burnet (and William) in Holland. On Ferguson, see Höpfl and Thompson, "History of Contract," p. 942; Goldie, "The Roots of True Whiggism," p. 211; Schwoerer, *Declaration of Rights*, pp. 160–61. Consider also William Atwood, *The Fundamental Constitution of the English Government* (1690). On Atwood, see Ashcraft, *Revolutionary Politics*, p. 587. See also Hampden, "Some Short Considerations Concerning the State of the Nation," esp. pp. lxxii–lxxiii. According to Dickinson, the Whigs typically attempted "to conflate the contract theory with the more conservative notion of the ancient constitution" (*Liberty and Property*, p. 71; cf. pp. 72, 77 for explicit contrast to Locke).

66. I am not the first to find a two-sidedness in Grotius's political philosophy that spawned both a conservative and a liberal following. Cf. Tuck, *Natural Rights Theories*, for a sustained treatment of Grotius along these lines. It is also of interest to consider Filmer's discussion of Grotius in his *Patriarcha*, pp. 66, 69, 71, 72, and in his *Observations Concerning the Originall of Government*, p. 271, both in *Patriarcha and Other Political Works*. My conclusion about the essentially un-Lockean character of this group of Whig writings runs counter to the explicit conclusion of Franklin (*John Locke*, pp. 100–101, 108, 119–20, 122) that they (or some of them) were "Lawson-

ians," which Franklin considers Locke also to have been. My difference with Franklin is simple to state: They were Grotians and Locke was not. How George Lawson relates to Grotius I am not in a position to say, other than to note that Franklin concedes Lawson's frequent reliance on Grotius (cf. pp. 53–86). A treatment of Grotius relevant to his relation to Locke is Cox, "Hugo Grotius," pp. 386–95. Franklin (p. 122 n. 71) concedes that his Lawsonians press a theory that Locke did not explicitly discuss, although he believes Locke did or would accept it.

67. Cf. Sexbie, *Killing Noe Murder*, pp. 372, 373, 375, cf. 377, 378. Sexbie's work was actually written in the closing years of the Protectorate, but it, like Milton's *Tenure*, was reprinted at the time of the Glorious Revolution. (Schwoerer, *Declaration of Rights*, pp. 155–56). For other references to Grotius, see "Some Short Considerations Relating to the Settling of the Government" in Somers, *A Collection of Scarce and Valuable Tracts* 10:275; Sidney, *Discourses Concerning Government* I.11; II.7, 24, 27, 30; III.1, 2, 9, 10, 23, 29, 31, 38, 42.

68. Wildman, "A Letter to a Friend," pp. 14, 15. Cf. "Short Considerations Relating to . . . Government," p. 274; Sexbie, *Killing Noe Murder*, pp. 365–73.

69. Humphrey, "Good Advice Before It Be Too Late," p. 21.

70. Ibid., pp. 21, 22. Cf. Robert Ferguson's "A Brief Justification of the Prince of Orange's Descent into England," as discussed in Ashcraft, *Revolutionary Politics*, pp. 567–69; on the evidence of this pamphlet he probably belongs here, with the "left Grotians," rather than with Burnet.

71. "Short Considerations Relating to . . . Government," pp. 274–75. Defoe ("Reflections," pp. 42–51, 63–64) also runs through the Grotian list. See also Sexbie, who draws a more radical conclusion than Grotius, but on Grotian premises (*Killing Noe Murder*, pp. 375–78, and esp. p. 364).

72. "Short Considerations," p. 274; Grotius, *De Jure* II.ix.8.

73. See also Dickinson, *Liberty and Property*, pp. 72–77.

74. Some fine examples of Whig writings that, on balance, appear to betray more of Richard Hooker than of any of the thinkers we have discussed are Hunt's, "*The Great and Weighty Considerations*, etc. Considered," its companion piece "An Answer to a Pamphlet Lately Published," and "A Word Without Doors Concerning the Bill for Succession." See also Sexbie, *Killing Noe Murder*, p. 373; although he shows much Grotian influence, there is something of Hooker in him also. Hooker, along with Grotius, is frequently identified by Whig speakers and writers as an authority (Schwoerer, *Declaration of Rights*, p. 206). On Hooker and Locke, see Zuckert, "Of Wary Physicians and Weary Readers," pp. 59–60; Cox, *Locke on War and Peace*, pp. 49–64.

75. Consider Grotius on punishment under the law of nature (*De Jure* II.xx), and Sexbie's development of Grotius on this theme. Grotius was both more conservative and more radical than the *Vindiciae* on the issue of resistance. He did not accept the argument of the *Vindiciae* that lower magistrates had a general exemption from the duty to obedience; but on the other hand, when resistance was justifiable it was not limited to the lower magistrates (I.iv.6).

76. Grotius, *De Jure*, Proleg. 53, I.i.11. I therefore largely accept Tuck's conclusion (*Natural Rights Theories*, p. 3) that Grotius is the chief source of Whig theory.

77. Franklin, *John Locke*, p. 117.

78. Ibid., pp. 104, 113. Cf. Thompson, "Reception of Locke," p. 188; Nenner,

"Constitutional Uncertainty," p. 295, where he speaks of an "incapacitating fear of extending the revolution too far." On the consequences of Whig hesitancy to follow the radicals, see Ashcraft, *Revolutionary Politics*, p. 598.

CHAPTER FIVE
THE MASTER OF WHIG POLITICAL PHILOSOPHY

1. Cf. Tuck (*Natural Rights Theories*, p. 3), who concludes that Grotius was the chief source of Whig political theory.

2. Lee, *Hugo Grotius*, p. 50.

3. On Grotius as attempting to "protestantize" the natural law, see Dunning, *A History of Political Theories*, pp. 153–54. On Suárez's unpopularity in seventeenth-century Europe, especially in England, see St. Leger, *The "Etiamsi Daremus" of Hugo Grotius*, pp. 106–8. According to St. Leger, Grotius was eager for a good reception both from France's Louis XIII—a fact evident from the dedication of his book—and from the Catholic Church. Grotius did not, however, tailor his book very well to the latter, in that he failed to recognize the "titles" of the Pope (p. 22).

4. See Bellarmine, *De Postestate Summi Pontificis in Rebus Temporalibus*, chapters 2, 3, 6, 13; Suárez, *Defensio Fidei Catholicae et Apostolicae* III.xxiii; Thomas Aquinas, *Commentary on the Sentences of Peter Lombard* II.44 (quoted by Dino Bigongiari, ed., in *The Political Ideas of Thomas Aquinas* (New York, 1953), p. xxxiv).

5. For speculation on why *De Jure* was placed on the Index, see St. Leger, *Etiamsi*, p. 22.

6. "List of Editions and Translations," in Grotius, *De Jure*, 2:877–86.

7. Laslett, introduction, to Locke, *Two Treatises of Government*, pp. 137–38.

8. "List of Editions," pp. 885–86.

9. On Grotius's general fame in Europe, see Dunning: "For twenty-five years before [Hobbes] wrote, Protestant Europe and the most progressive thinkers of all nations had recognized Grotius as the exponent of ultimate truth in political theory" (*History of Political Theories*, p. 301; cf. p. 303).

10. See Lee, *Hugo Grotius*, pp. 35–36.

11. I do not believe this claim to be inconsistent with Grotius's description of his relation to the "controversies of our age." He had not formulated his theory with an eye to these controversies, he said, but "just as mathematicians consider figures separated from bodies, so I have led my mind away from every individual fact in treating law (right)" (*De Jure*, Proleg. 58). Cf. Lee, pp. 56–57.

12. Grotius, *De Jure* II.xv.8. Cf. Giorgio Del Vecchio's recognition of the religious and political necessities that led Grotius "to place law on a more secular foundation" (St. Leger, *Etiamsi*, pp. 32–33).

13. *De Jure*, Proleg. 48.

14. Ibid., Proleg. 50; cf. esp. II.xiii.3 (on God's immutability). For forerunners who develop a doctrine of separation between natural and divine positive law, see Thomas Aquinas, *Summa Theologica* II-II Q 71 A 6 ad 5; Suárez, *De Legibus* II.vi.3. On the mixing of Scripture and the law of nature, cf. Edwards, *Hugo Grotius*, pp. 35–39. For examples of the greater stringency of Christianity than the law of nature,

see *De Jure* II.ii.6; regarding war and the right of self-defense; see III.i.8, 10. Relevant is Grotius's depreciation of oaths, II.xiii.21.

15. *De Jure* I.i.10. See Proleg. 12, on the great difference between the law of nature and the will of God. See also Lee, *Hugo Grotius*, p. 54; Edwards, *Hugo Grotius*, pp. 56–59, 63–64; Ingber, "The Tradition of Grotius and Human Rights," p. 368.

16. *De Jure*, Proleg. 11. According to Grotius, it would be a serious moral fault to grant that there is no God, or that God does not care about human affairs. He apparently did not consider it to be an equally great intellectual fault. Cf. Locke, *Questions Concerning the Law of Nature*, Question I (fol. 9). St. Leger has canvassed the role of Grotius's hypothesis in prior scholastic natural law philosophy; he challenges the view that Grotius was altogether innovatory in positing a natural law perhaps entirely independent of God, and maintains that the Spanish writer Vasquez made an assertion similar to Grotius's, and was probably Grotius's source for the idea (*Etiamsi*, pp. 3, 112, 116, 118, 120, 121, 130–33). St. Leger overstates Grotius's congruence with Vasquez, however, because he considers only the *etiamsi* (pp. 1–2); he therefore may overstate his genuinely helpful challenge to common views about Grotius's innovativeness (cf. pp. 28–30). Grotius's relation to his predecessors is considered later in this chapter.

17. *De Jure*, Proleg. 46.

18. Ibid., Proleg. 28, 32, 36. An important part of his effort was to limit the religious grounds of just war. Cf. II.xx.40, 45, 46; cf. also II.xxv.8, on "pretexts" for war.

19. Ibid., Proleg. 39, 40, 56; I.1.10 (but cf. I.iii.1). On the role of the quest for certainty in Descartes as prompted by Christianity see Heidegger, *Nietzsche*, 4:102–38. The case of Grotius goes a long way toward discrediting Heidegger's account of the origins and character of modernity.

20. Cf. Cook, *History of Political Philosophy from Plato to Burke*, p. 428; Sigmund, *Natural Law in Political Thought*, pp. 61–62. On Grotius's concern for certainty, see his chapter "On Interpretation": not only does he develop the law of nature so as to consist of principles of a clarity and definiteness comparable to mathematics, but he develops a set of rules for interpreting human promises as agreements in order "to establish some degree of certainty," which is necessary for there "to be any binding obligations" (*De Jure* II.xvi.1). Grotius does concede, however, that there are limits to the certainty possible in "moral reasonings" and that there is "much truth" in Aristotle's assertions to this effect (II.xxiii.1). Cf. Samuel Pufendorf's reaction to this concession (*De Jure Naturae et Gentium* I.ii.9).

21. Grotius, *De Jure*, Proleg. 5. Part of Grotius's practical effort was the encouragement of Christian unity against non-Christians; thus his advocacy of a "Christian league" (II.xv.12).

22. Ibid., Proleg. 42: "Among the philosophers Aristotle deservedly holds the foremost place." This is not to deny that Grotius openly deviates from Aristotle—indeed, he does on the very issue of virtue as a mean (see Proleg. 43–44). Nonetheless, the quest for moderation marks nearly every part of Grotius's great treatise; he seeks "a true middle ground" (Proleg. 29). Grotius aims at Aristotelian moderation so far as that is compatible with the kind of certainty he also seeks. That quest for certainty compromises his commitment to moderation, but since it is in the service of oppos-

ing the even greater immoderation of his age's theo-politics, one might say that Grotius chooses the lesser immoderation for the sake of countering the greater.

23. A good discussion of Grotius's distinction between the nature of supreme power (sovereignty) and absolute possession of it is in Cox, "Grotius," p. 392. This distinction allows Grotius to accept the doctrine of sovereignty but to reject the necessary absolutism that might seem to follow from it.

24. Ingber, "Tradition of Grotius," p. 367.

25. Consider Ernst Troeltsche's estimate that Grotius was the first to elevate contract to importance (cited in St. Leger, *Etiamsi*, p. 35).

26. There persists a fundamental uncertainty over Grotius's place in the natural law tradition. Pufendorf, Barbeyrac, and many others following them saw in Grotius "the founder of the modern theory of natural law." Some more recent scholars have emphasized instead Grotius's fundamental continuity with medieval natural law theory. See D'Entreves, *Natural Law*, pp. 50–51 and references therein, and Dunning, *History of Political Theories*, pp. 153–57. Also important are Tuck, *Natural Rights Theories*, chapter 3; St. Leger, *Etiamsi*; Edwards, *Hugo Grotius*. Although I cannot here attempt a systematic statement regarding all the issues in the debate over Grotius's place in the tradition, the attentive reader will probably understand my views as somewhat intermediary between the contesting parties. I believe both parties are correct, in a sense. Grotius did make an important break with the natural law tradition he inherited, but that break was not as fundamental as the further shift away from his position (and the tradition) that characterized later natural rights theory, including, most importantly for this discussion, that of Locke and the American founders. From the perspective of Lockean doctrine, Grotius looks conservative and rather traditional; from the perspective of Thomas or Suárez, Grotius looks innovatory.

27. Suárez, *Defensio Fidei Catholicae* VI.iv.15.

28. For other elements of difference, consult the earlier discussion of Burnet and the "left Grotians," and cf. Suárez, *Defensio* VI.iv.2, 4, 12, 13, 14. For an instructive presentation of Grotius's doctrine, see *De Jure* I.iv.7. Many commentators (e.g., Dunning, *History of Political Theories*, p. 153, and Edwards, *Hugo Grotius*, passim) overstate the similarities between Grotius and Suárez. Edwards (pp. 152–54) concedes the important differences on the right of resistance.

29. Suárez, *De Legibus* III.i.1, 2; cf. III.ii.3.

30. Ibid., III.i.5, 11; III.ii.1, 3.

31. Ibid., III.iii.1; II.xvi.12; III.iv.1, 2, 5.

32. Ibid., III.ii.4. Cf. Thomas Aquinas, *Summa Theologica* I-II Q 90 A 3 ad 2; Q 97 A 3 ad 3.

33. *De Legibus* III.ii.2.

34. Bellarmine, *De Laicis*, chapter 6, quoted in Roger, *Political Philosophy of the Blessed Cardinal Bellarmine*, pp. 51–52. Richard Hooker, too, taught a doctrine very similar to that of Suárez and Bellarmine (*Of the Laws of Ecclesiastical Polity* I.x.4–5). Cf. the conclusion, on the relations of Grotius to the scholastics, in St. Leger, *Etiamsi*, pp. 46–55. In general, see my chapter 8.

35. The failure to appreciate the force of will or convention in Grotius mars James Tully's otherwise thoughtful discussion in *A Discourse on Property* (e.g., p. 82).

36. Grotius, *De Jure* II.xx.7, 40; cf. I.x.10 and II.xx.3, 8, 9. On the relation between

the power to punish and the doctrine of just war, see II.xx.40 and II.xxv.1, 6, 7, 8. On the very different role of the Fall in originating coercive power in Suárez, see *De Legibus* III.i.12. Grotius's clear affirmation of natural equality relates to his discovery of the source of political power in an original individual power (cf. *De Jure* II.xx.4).

37. Suárez, *De Legibus* II.xviii.4, III.iv.4. One must, however, consider the slightly complicating issue of private war. See Grotius, *De Jure* I.iii.1–2, III.iii; Suárez, *Opus de Triplici Virtute Theologico: De Charitate*, Disp. XIII 1.4, on private war, and that disputation generally on just war.

38. *De Jure*, Proleg. 1, 3. Cf. St. Leger, *Etiamsi*, p. 10, on Grotius and the "Machiavellian abyss." For an especially clear case of Grotius's anti-Machiavellianism, cf. III.xxii.5 with Machiavelli, *Discourses* II.12.

39. *De Jure*, Proleg. 5, 6; cf. Cicero, *De Re Publica* III.xxi.

40. See *De Jure*, Proleg. 4.

41. The source for Grotius's version of Carneades appears to be Lactantius, *The Divine Institutes* V.xvi.2–4.

42. *De Jure*, Proleg. 5. Cf. Cicero, *De Re Publica* III.xi; Suárez, *De Legibus* II.ix.8.

43. *De Jure*, Proleg. 5.

44. Ibid., Proleg. 3, 5.

45. The challenges were perhaps not entirely unrelated to each other. Cf. Lactantius (*Institutes* V.xvi.2–13), who endorses the Carneadean critique over and against the defenses of natural right by Plato, Aristotle, and Cicero.

46. See *De Jure*, Proleg. 41.

47. *Corpus Juris Civilis, Institutes* I.ii, *Digest* I.i. Cf. Villey, *Leçons d'histoire de la philosophie du droit*, p. 228. For discussion of the view that *jus naturale* is mere "rhetorical ornament," see Zuckert, "Bringing Philosophy Down from the Heavens," pp. 70–71.

48. Sigmund, *Natural Law*, pp. 24–25; Schulz, *Geschichte der romischer Rechts-Wissenschaft*, p. 88; Aristotle, *Rhetoric* 1373b-1375b. For discussion of the philosophic roots, see Villey, *Leçons d'histoire*, pp. 20, 30–32; cf. Schulz, *Geschichte*, pp. 84–91.

49. *Institutes* I.ii; *Digest* I.i.

50. *Institutes*, II.i.11; I.ii.pr.

51. Cicero, *De Legibus* I.2; *Digest* I.i.2. For brief accounts of the Stoic position, see Sigmund, *Natural Law*, pp. 20–26, and Holton, "Cicero."

52. See D'Entreves, *Natural Law*, pp. 31–32.

53. *Institutes* I.ii.1, 2.

54. See D'Entreves, p. 30.

55. See *Institutes* I.iii; *Digest* I.i.1, 4, 5.

56. *Digest* I.i.1.

57. See Lee, *Elements of Roman Law*, p. 35; Strauss, *Natural Right*, pp. 146–52.

58. *Digest* I.i.6.

59. *Institutes* I.ii.2.

60. The jurists' treatment of the themes of nature and natural right is thus very close to Aristotle's treatment of the same themes. On the coexistence of several notions of nature in Aristotle, see *Politics*, book 1. On the nature of natural right, see *Ethics*, book 5; and cf. Strauss's controversial interpretation in *Natural Right*, pp. 156–63.

61. Cook, *History of Political Philosophy*, p. 434. Cook claims that Grotius deploys "the same distinction" between *jus naturale* and *jus gentium* as the Roman lawyers did. Perhaps also to the point is Dunning's claim that Grotius's theory is more like Cicero than like Thomas (*History of Political Theories*, p. 164).

62. Grotius, *De Jure*, Proleg. 53. See III.ii for examples of natural law provisions the Roman law endorses.

63. Ibid., Proleg. 40, 53.

64. Ibid., Proleg., 30, 37, 38, 40, 56. See II.xv.5, 6 and III.iii.6, 8, 11 for good examples of Grotius's attempts to distinguish the three kinds of law on particular questions. See also the discussion of Burnet in my chapter 4. On the distinction of laws, see Ingber, "Tradition of Grotius," p. 370.

65. *De Jure*, Proleg. 30–1.

66. Ibid., Proleg. 40; cf. I.i.10, III.i.1.

67. Ibid., Proleg. 5.

68. Ibid., Proleg. 6.

69. Ibid.

70. Ibid., Proleg. 11; Aristotle, *Politics* 1278b19–21; cf. 1280a25–1281a6.

71. *De Jure*, Proleg. 7; cf. *Politics* 1253a1–18.

72. See Grotius's definition of the unjust as "what conflicts with the nature of the society of beings endowed with reason" (*De Jure* I.i.2); also Cox, "Grotius", p. 387.

73. *De Jure*, Proleg. 8; I.i.10.

74. Ibid., I iii.

75. See Sabine, A *History of Political Theory*, p. 430.

76. Tuck, *Natural Rights*, p. 81; Cox, "Grotius," p. 394.

77. *De Jure* I.ii.1; II.v.9, 15.

78. Ibid., I.i.12.

79. Ibid., I.ii.1, I.iv.2; cf. I.ii.5. Grotius's comments at II.i.4 and III.i.2 complicate, but do not say anything different from, the passages cited in the text, as, for example, III.i.4 shows. Cf. Suárez, *Defensio Fidei Catholicae* VI.iv.5. Cf. Grotius's interesting discussion of the primacy of social needs over individual rights at II.xxv.3 (the law of nature allows sacrifice of an innocent to an enemy).

80. This is the context of Grotius's use of "state of nature" in II.vii.27.

81. See previous chapters, esp. chapter 4.

82. *De Jure*, Proleg. 10. Cf. Aristotle, *Politics* 1281b38–1282a24, 1282b14–1283a23; *Ethics* 1131a1-b24.

83. Thomas Aquinas, *Summa Theologica* I-II Q 94 A 3; cf. I-II Q 90 A 4.

84. *De Jure* I.i.8.

85. Terminology becomes very difficult at this point, for in the passage in question Grotius contrasts *jus* (right or law) and *lex* (law or statute). F. J. C. Hearnshaw (*Some Great Political Idealists*, p. 100) suggests that Grotius prefers *jus* to *lex* because the former term "connotes 'right' irrespective of its origin," whereas *lex* "suggests statutory enactment." Hearnshaw sees a connection to Grotius's well-known attempt to make the law of nature independent of God's will, as opposed to Suárez, for example, who used the term *lex naturalis*. Hearnshaw's suggestion is persuasive up to a point, but two considerations need to be added to his discussion. First, as Edwards (*Hugo Grotius*, pp. 54–59) nicely shows, Suárez goes very far toward the purely rationalist notion Grotius defends, and Grotius goes far toward the voluntarist

notion Hearnshaw associates (too simply) with Suárez. Secondly, Grotius's terminology relates to his differentiation of *jus* in the strict and proper sense from a more extended sense of *jus*. In making this distinction, Grotius both follows and modifies the Ockhamist tradition wherein the doctrine of right as subjective right developed (cf. Tuck, *Natural Rights Theories*, passim). In Grotius's case, but not so clearly in the case of the earlier Ockhamists, there is the further factor that Grotius means to limit the notions of law in the proper sense to justice which—on etymological grounds, if no other—must have suggested to Grotius the superiority of *jus* over *lex*.

86. *De Jure* I.i.9. See also III.xi.3 for the distinction between different sorts of obligations. Cf. III.i.8, where failure to note adequately the place of obligation is identified as one problem with the Roman lawyers' treatment of *jus gentium*. Also see II.xi.6.

87. Ibid., Proleg. 19, 20; I.i.9.

88. Ibid., Proleg. 8, 9.

89. Ibid., Proleg. 10, 41; I.i.8. Cf. esp. Plato, *Republic* I.

90. *De Jure*, Proleg. 10, 44; cf. I.ii.4 (definition of *civitas*). (Cf. Tuck, *Natural Rights Theories*, pp. 67, 72.) This is the context in which to take up Grotius's critique of Aristotle's treatment of virtue as a mean (Proleg. 44–46).

91. Grotius suggests that his usage is the same as the Roman lawyers', but this claim is quite untenable as a general description of their practice. For a discussion, see Zuckert, "Bringing Philosophy Down," pp. 74–75. The distinction between objective and subjective right is, of course, not to be confused with the similar-sounding distinction casually made between objective and subjective statements, in which the latter are taken to be "merely subjective,", that is, illusory or invalid. A subjective right inheres in a subject, but that casts no doubt on its validity. Compare the distinction between "the naturally right" and "natural rights," drawn by Ewart Lewis in "The Contribution of Medieval Thought to the American Political Tradition," p. 467.

92. Suárez, *De Legibus* I.ii.5. On the primacy of objective right in Roman law, see Villey, *Seize essais*, pp. 149–53; idem, *Leçons d'histoire*, pp. 29–30, 183–88, 224–40.

93. Cf. note 26, above. I thus disagree with the oft-expressed view that Grotius is not original, that he essentially follows Suárez. For a typical expression, see Dunning, *History of Political Theories*, p. 164; also Edwards, *Hugo Grotius*, passim.

94. *De Jure* I.i.8.

95. Thomas Aquinas, *Summa Theologica* I-II Q 94 A 3.

96. Ibid., A 2.

97. Ibid., Thomas explicitly quotes the *Digest* in this context.

98. Ibid.

99. Tuck, *Natural Rights Theories*, pp. 175–76. For a survey of assessments of Grotius's position as founder of modern natural law, see Edwards, *Hugo Grotius*, chapters 2 and 3. On the other side, see Dunning, who argues that Hobbes's system was an undisguised attack on that of Grotius (*A History of Political Theories*, p. 301).

100. Cf. Hobbes, *Leviathan*, chapter 6.

101. Ibid., chapter 46.

102. It is tempting to see Grotius as more or less equivalent to Marsilius of Padua: both thinkers who remained within the broad confines of Aristotelian political philosophy but who were driven to reformulate the Aristotelian philosophy in order to

respond to political deformations produced by Christianity—in Marsilius's case, the deformities caused by papal pretensions, in Grotius's, the deformities caused by the Reformation. Both generated new political doctrines that later became disassociated from their Aristotelian roots and became central elements of modern political philosophy. On Marsilius, see Strauss, "Marsilius of Padua," pp. 276–95. Cf. Dunning, *History of Political Theories*: "Grotius's ethical system is essentially that of Plato, Aristotle, and the Stoics" (p. 164).

103. Grotius, *De Jure* I.i.3; Hobbes, *Leviathan*, chapter 14 (pp. 89–90). On the related theme of the relation between modern doctrines of rights and Grotius, see Ingber, "Tradition of Grotius," pp. 358–65.

104. See Hearnshaw, *Some Great Political Idealists*, p. 82.

105. "See Tuck, *Natural Rights Theories*, p. 73: the law of nature obliges human beings to seek the preservation of social peace, to which end respect for each other's rights is a chief means.

106. *De Jure*, Proleg. 23.

107. Cf. Strauss, *Natural Right*, pp. 163–64. I have deliberately passed over the complex issue of the status of positive laws that are not congruent with natural law. It should be obvious that Grotius does not accept the Thomist notion that civil law is a deduction from natural law (*Summa Theologica* I-II Q 45 AA 1, 2). Ingber's claim that the natural law serves as "the criterion of the validation of the law of nations" ("Tradition of Grotius," p. 374) is problematical if he means that the contents of the two laws must converge in order for the *jus gentium* to be valid. The *jus gentium* (as well as the *jus civile*) often speaks when the natural law is silent—that is, it adds legal requirements where none existed according to nature alone—and in such cases there can be no question of congruence of content. Grotius even usually concedes a kind of validity to positive law that goes against the natural law. Such, he usually says, creates an immunity, if not a perfect right. See *De Jure* I.i.10; II.ii.6; II.xii.22, 26; III.iv.2–3.

108. *De Jure*, Proleg. 30. For Grotius, this science of law was also truly autonomous from political science (Ibid., Proleg. 57).

109. See, for example, Dunning, *History of Political Theories*, pp. 169, 175; Sabine, *History of Political Theory*, p. 429; Friedrich, *Inevitable Peace*, p. 122; Edwards, *Hugo Grotius*, p. 105. These claims are often based on inattentive readings; cf. Dunning, p. 176.

110. *De Jure*, Proleg. 8.

111. Ibid., Proleg. 15.

112. Sabine, *History of Political Theory*, p. 430. See also Ingber, "Tradition of Grotius," p. 366, for a similar claim.

113. *De Jure* II.xi,4. Cf. Edwards's helpful but somewhat different account of obligation in Suárez and Grotius (*Hugo Grotius*, pp. 54–69). On reason and obligation of promise, consider also Grotius's very non-Kantian discussion of deception and truth-telling (*De Jure* III.i.7–22). Ingber makes a helpful observation when he notes that in Grotius the "obligation to keep one's word is no longer, as in St. Thomas's time, the consequence of a universal duty of truth rooted in the natural order, but a rule, a form of self-will, the result of man's ability to associate" ("Tradition of Grotius," pp. 363–66). Ingber's observation (and essay) would be yet more

valuable if he could settle on an understanding of the relationship between "self-will" and "sociability"; the statement just quoted captures his confusion on the question.

114. *De Jure*, Proleg. 17, 21.

115. Cf. Grotius's explicit efforts to show the effectiveness of *jus* (Ibid., Proleg. 19–22).

116. I agree, therefore, with Tuck's claim (*Natural Rights Theories*, p. 58) that Grotius made possible the late-seventeenth- and eighteenth-century theories of rights, but I understand that claim in a very different way.

CHAPTER SIX
A NEO-HARRINGTONIAN MOMENT?

1. Adams, *Political Ideas of the American Revolution*; cf. Becker, *The Declaration of Independence*, passim; Bailyn, "The Central Themes of the American Revolution," pp. 4–6; idem, *The Ideological Origins of the American Revolution*, p. vii; Kramnick, *Republicanism and Bourgeois Radicalism*, pp. 260–88; Lerner, *The Thinking Revolutionary*, pp. 9–10; Shalhope, "Toward a Republican Synthesis," p. 59; Tate, "The Social Contract in America," pp. 370–85; Dworetz, *The Unvarnished Doctrine*, pp. 5–6, 13–38; Matthews, *The Radical Politics of Thomas Jefferson*, pp. 5–6.

2. See Shalhope, "Toward a Republican Synthesis," p. 49; idem, "Republicanism and Early American Historiography," p. 334–35; Diggins, *The Lost Soul of American Politics*, p. 9; Greenstone, "Against Simplicity," p. 455; Sherry, "The Intellectual Origins of the Constitution," p. 326. See O'Brien, "The Framer's Muse," p. 122, for reference to the role of the "republican revival" in recent constitutional studies.

3. Lienesch, *The New Order of the Ages*, p. 5. See also Kramnick, *Republicanism*, pp. 261–63; Shalhope, "Republicanism," p. 335.

4. Appleby, "Republicanism and Ideology," p. 461.

5. Lipset, *The First New Nation*.

6. Appleby, p. 462.

7. Shalhope, "Toward a Republican Synthesis," p. 51; cf. pp. 54, 57, 70–71; Wood, *Creation*, pp. 47, 53; Dworetz, *Unvarnished Doctrine*, pp. 6, 7: "The republican synthesis has completely replaced the Locke model."

8. There are exceptions, esp. Thomas Pangle in *The Spirit of Modern Republicanism* (esp. pp. 28–39); and Diggins in *Lost Soul*. Both Pangle and Diggins are "root and branch" critics of the republican synthesis. Others are revisionists, challenging various features of the synthesis but accepting important parts of it as well; see, for example, Kramnick, *Republicanism*, chapter 6; Appleby, *Capitalism and a New Social Order*. Dworetz, in *Unvarnished Doctrine*, stands somewhere between the revisionists and the others.

9. One scholar who does notice is Greenstone, "Against Simplicity," p. 439.

10. See, for example, Greenstone, pp. 439–40; Diggins, *Lost Soul*, pp. 9–11; Sherry, "Intellectual Origins," pp. 335–40; Lienesch, *New Order*, p. 5. A more sophisticated version is Dworetz, in *Unvarnished Doctrine*, who recognizes real differences between the synthesizers (e.g., pp. 107–8), but who does not take his insights in this regard far enough, continuing to treat republicanism as a single "paradigm."

11. Shalhope, "Republicanism", p. 334. A thorough discussion of pre-Bailyn con-

tributions can be found in Shalhope's "Toward a Republican Synthesis," pp. 51–65; On Bailyn's role, cf. pp. 65ff; Lienesch, *New Order*, pp. 4–5; Pocock, *Virtue, Commerce, and History*, p. 216.

12. Cf. Dworetz, *Unvarnished Doctrine*, p. 23; Matthews, *Radical Politics*, pp. 5–7.

13. Bailyn, *Ideological Origins*, p. vii. Cf. Peter Onuf's judgment that the great achievement of the synthesizers was to redefine the American Revolution as an ideological transformation ("Reflections on the Founding," p. 346).

14. Bailyn, "Central Themes," pp. 4–6; Appleby, "Republicanism in Old and New Contexts," pp. 21–22.

15. Bailyn, pp. 6, 7, 10, 11.

16. Ibid., p. 11; cf. pp. 14–15. For a thoughtful critique of ideology as thus understood, see Lerner, *Thinking Revolutionary*, pp. 1–38. For an appreciation of the shift Bailyn effected in the role of ideas, see Appleby, "Republicanism and Ideology," p. 462.

17. Bailyn, *Ideological Origins*, pp. 22–34; idem, "Central Themes," pp. 7–10.

18. *Ideological Origins*, p. 26. Thus Lienesch overstates the case in claiming that Bailyn ultimately traced the American ideology "to its earliest origins in the classical republican thought of Aristotle, Cicero, and certain of the Greek and Roman historians" (*New Order*, p. 5). Such statements are part of the effort to "paper over the fissures" in the so-called republican synthesis.

19. *Ideological Origins*, p. 31.

20. Ibid., p. 32.

21. Ibid., p. 27.

22. Ibid., p. 30; cf. "Central Themes," p. 10.

23. Ibid., p. 28.

24. Cf. Dworetz, *Unvarnished Doctrine*, pp. 111–13.

25. *Ideological Origins*, p. 45.

26. Ibid., pp. viii, 34.

27. Robbins, *The Eighteenth-Century Commonwealthmen*, esp. pp. 22–56. On the shallowness of Robbins's analysis, see Pocock, *Politics, Language, and Time*, pp. 107–8. A more substantial and yet still inconclusive statement appears in Bailyn, "Central Themes," p. 9.

28. "Central Themes," pp. 7–8.

29. *Ideological Origins*, p. 77. For a fine discussion of Bailyn's ambiguity, see Webking, *The American Revolution*, pp. 163–64.

30. "Central Themes," p. 10. A critique of Bailyn's understanding of Locke's "ambiguous" ideas is in Dworetz, *Unvarnished Doctrine*, p. 10.

31. "Central Themes," p. 9.

32. *Ideological Origins*, pp. 95, 102, 121–22, 144–48; "Central Themes," p. 12.

33. Cf. *Ideological Origins*, pp. 199–200; Wood, *Creation*, p. 200; Greene, "The Ostensible Cause Was . . . the True One," p. 201.

34. *Ideological Origins*, p. 77; cf. pp. 188–89.

35. Webking, *American Revolution*, pp. 13–14; Schmitt and Webking, "Revolutionaries, Anti-Federalists, and Federalists," p. 199.

36. Wood, *Creation*, pp. ix, 18–28.

37. Ibid., pp. 14–16.

38. Ibid., pp. 48, 49; idem, "The Intellectual Origins of the American Constitution," p. 6.

39. *Creation*, p. 50; cf. "Intellectual Origins," p. 6.

40. *Creation*, p. 29. Wood's qualifying "perhaps" must be noted, clearly distinguishing him from Pocock and his followers (cf. p. 14). In "Illusions and Disillusions in the American Revolution," Wood explicitly labeled the Americans as Lockean in their acceptance of "sensationalism" and a (modified) "Lockean environmentalism." Wood's hesitation followed from his clear recognition of the great role of Lockean ideas, which his intimate knowledge of the source material could not allow him to ignore. For example, he spoke of how "meaningful" the "Lockean notion of a social contract" was in the years after 1776 (*Creation*, p. 283). But he did downplay its role before 1776, for reasons we shall see below.

41. "Intellectual Origins," p. 7.

42. Appleby, "Republicanism and Ideology," p. 464. Thus Shalhope spoke more truly than he realized when he looked to Wood as the chief locus of "the republican synthesis" ("Toward a Republican Synthesis," pp. 70–72); cf. Pocock, *Virtue, Commerce, and History*, pp. 216–17.

43. Wood, *Creation*, p. 47.

44. Ibid., pp. 53, 58. For a partially concurrent and partially dissenting understanding of Wood, see Banning, "Some Second Thoughts on Virtue and the Course of Revolutionary Thinking," pp. 197–200.

45. *Creation*, pp. 67, 68, 69.

46. Ibid., pp. 29, 53, 58; cf. Sherry, "Intellectual Origins," p. 336.

47. *Creation*, p. 60.

48. Virtue did play some role in Bailyn; see *Ideological Origins*, pp. 65, 133, 138.

49. Ibid., pp. 24, 61; cf. Sherry, "Intellectual Origins," p. 334. A more nuanced view may be found in McDonald, *Novus Ordo Seclorum*, pp. 37, 39, 82.

50. But cf. Wood's vacillating statements on rights: *Creation*, pp. 4, 10, 20–23, 63.

51. Schmitt and Webking, "Revolutionaries," p. 198.

52. Wood shrank from consistently pressing the differences. He knew the primary materials too well not to see the pervasiveness of the Declaration's alternative conceptions, but he either lamely and inconsistently attempted to integrate these elements into his classical republicanism, or he ignored, as far as he could, the competing data. As Schmitt and Webking point out, he nowhere discussed the Declaration of Independence (Ibid., p. 199). For testimonial to the either/or character of republicanism and the Declaration, see Shalhope, "Toward a Republican Synthesis," p. 59; Lerner, *Thinking Revolutionary*, pp. 9–10; Lutz, "Bernard Bailyn, Gordon S. Wood, and Whig Political Theory," p. 141. But also consider Wood, "Ideology and the Origins of Liberal America," p. 634. See also Agresto, "Liberty, Virtue, and Republicanism," Banning, "Some Second Thoughts," p. 209 n. 22.

53. Wood, *Creation*, p. viii.

54. Ibid., p. 606.

55. Ibid., pp. 606–8, 610.

56. Sherry, "Intellectual Origins," p. 326.

57. Wood, *Creation*, pp. 513, 519 (but cf. pp. 523–24), 543.

58. Bailyn, "Central Themes," pp. 22, 26; more generally, see pp. 18–21, 25, and *Ideological Origins*, chapters 5 and 6.

59. Pocock, "Machiavelli, Harrington, and English Political Ideology in the Eighteenth Century" (1965), in *Politics, Language, and Time*.

60. *Politics, Language, and Time*, pp. 106–7. Cf. Pocock's misleading description of Bailyn in "*The Machiavellian Moment* Revisited," pp. 49–50.

61. Pocock, *Politics, Language and Time*, p. 90; idem, *Machiavellian Moment*, pp. 58, 90; idem, "*Machiavellian Moment* Revisited," p. 49; idem, *Virtue, Commerce, and History*, p. 38.

62. *Politics, Language, and Time*, pp. 112, 114, 128.

63. *Machiavellian Moment*, p. 545.

64. Aristotle, *Politics* 1253a20–23.

65. *Politics, Language, and Time*, p. 85. Cf. Ross, "The Liberal Tradition Revisited and the Republican Tradition Addressed," p. 117. On the adequacy of this interpretation of Aristotle, consider Zuckert, "Aristotle on the Limits and Satisfactions of Political Life."

66. *Machiavellian Moment*, p. 67.

67. *Politics, Language, and Time*, p. 86.

68. *Machiavellian Moment*, pp. 68–71. Cf. Banning, "Jeffersonian Ideology Revisited," pp. 11–12.

69. *Machiavellian Moment*, pp. 71–74.

70. Ibid., p. 75; *Politics, Language, and Time*, pp. 87, 90, 93; *Virtue, Commerce, and History*, pp. 41–43; Pocock, introduction to *The Political Works of James Harrington*, pp. 146–47.

71. *Machiavellian Moment*, p. 212. There is, of course, an implicit rejection of Wood's position in this characterization. It becomes a little more explicit in Pocock's "Between Gog and Magog," p. 342.

72. *Virtue, Commerce, and History*, p. 41.

73. I have emphasized the differences between Pocock and Wood; there are also significant differences between Pocock and Bailyn. Consider Pocock's reinterpretation of the American Revolution in "1776: The Revolution against Parliament," in *Virtue, Commerce, and History*, pp. 73–88.

74. *Machiavellian Moment*, pp. 75–76; *Politics, Language, and Time*, p. 87.

75. *Machiavellian Moment*, pp. 204–5.

76. Pocock, "Virtue and Commerce in the Eighteenth Century," p. 122. An indication of Bailyn's stance toward Pocock's version of republicanism can be garnered from the former's observations on the American attitude toward change. Prior to the 1760s, changes had "often . . . been condemned as deviations, as retrogressions"; but after 1765 the Americans took a very positive attitude toward change. (*Ideological Origins*, p. 20). Bailyn also argued that the "nostalgic" or "reactionary" attitude of Bolingbroke "was simply ignored" in favor of a new progressive attitude ("Central Themes," p. 28).

77. Kramnick, *Republicanism*, p. 167. A concentrated statement by Pocock himself is in "The Myth of John Locke and the Obsession with Liberalism."

78. Pocock, *Virtue, Commerce, and History*, p. 66. Cf. *Politics, Language, and Time*, pp. 107, 144, 145; "Between Gog and Magog," p. 339; *Machiavellian Moment*, p. 335.

79. *Virtue, Commerce, and History*, pp. 40, 45, 49; cf. pp. 59–60, 71.

80. Representative examples of the Pocockian denial of the "end of republican-

ism" thesis are Pocock, *Machiavellian Moment*, pp. 586–92; idem, introduction to *Political Works of Harrington*, pp. 149–50; Banning, "Republican Ideology and the Triumph of the Constitution"; idem, *The Jeffersonian Persuasion*. A review of the controversy over whether and where the republican tradition died is in Onuf, "Reflections on the Founding," pp. 349–50, 352–53. Consider also the exchange between Lance Banning and Joyce Appleby: Banning, "Jeffersonian Ideology Revisited"; Appleby, "Republicanism in Old and New Contexts." See also Lienesch, *New Order*, p. 6.

81. Wood, "Ideology," p. 634. Cf. Appleby, "The Social Origins of American Revolutionary Ideology," pp. 936–37.

82. Locke, *Educational Writings*, p. 400.

83. Jefferson to Thomas Mann Randolph, May 30, 1790, in *Life and Selected Writings*, pp. 496–97; "Minutes of the Board of Visitors, University of Virginia, 1822–25," in *Jefferson*, p. 479.

84. But cf. Strauss, *Liberalism Ancient and Modern*, p. 205.

85. Wood, "Ideology," p. 634.

86. The republican sythesis, moreover, rests not only on the discovery or invention of a "republican" tradition, but on the strenuous reassessment of Locke's role in the political thinking of the eighteenth century. The synthesizers endorse with enthusiasm Dunn, Wills, and other recent inventories that find Locke to have been relatively unimportant both in England and America, a conclusion Dworetz and others have shown to be unreliable. See Prologue.

87. Pocock, *Machiavellian Moment*, pp. 341, 350, 359.

88. Ibid., pp. 365, 383, 384.

89. Pocock, introduction to *Political Works of Harrington*, pp. 136, 144; Davis, "Pocock's Harrington," p. 683. Cf. Pocock, *Politics, Language, and Time*, pp. 108, 130.

90. *Machiavellian Moment*, p. 386. Cf. Goodale, "J. G. A. Pocock's Neo-Harringtonians," p. 238.

91. For pre-Pocock readings of Harrington, consider Tawney, "Harrington's Interpretation of His Age"; Macpherson, *The Political Theory of Possessive Individualism*, chapter 6. Pocock's critique of the quasi-Marxist Harrington seems to be the germ from which the whole of his amazing edifice has risen, for it was a major theme of his first book, *The Ancient Constitution and the Feudal Law* (see pp. 128–47) and the center from which his republicanism interpretation spread out in both directions. His specific response to Macpherson is in *Politics, Language, and Time*, pp. 108–11.

92. *Machiavellian Moment*, p. 390. Cf. *Politics, Language, and Time*, pp. 90–91, 112–13. Pocock's new reading has Harrington saying things about property "more important than anything Locke had to say" (introduction to *Political Works of Harrington*, p. 145). Cf. Sherry, "Intellectual Origins," pp. 333–34.

93. *Politics, Language, and Time*, p. 114. Since my real concern is the Whig opposition tradition, that is, Pocock's "neo-Harringtonians," I do not pursue the question of the validity of Pocock's interpretation of Harrington himself. Many questions have been raised about it, however. J. C. Davis, in "Pocock's Harrington," suggests that Pocock greatly distorts the real Harrington, or at least misses the real tension in the man, a tension constituted by his initial striving for civic virtue and his aspiration to a perfectly successful, machinelike republic, operating quite independently of the

virtue or moral character of its citizens (pp. 695–96). Davis finds Harrington against civic virtue, and finds no basis in him for Pocock's emphasis on man as *zoon politikon* (p. 696). J. R. Goodale, in "Pocock's Neo-Harringtonians," sees the problem in much the same way. He, too, sees the real Harringtonian legacy in terms of a political technology that makes of government "a mere piece of clockwork" (p. 218). Debates, then, that have emerged between republican synthesizers and others over the character of the political thought of the American founding (e.g., *The Federalist*) also exist over the thought of the alleged founder of the tradition, Harrington. These criticisms of Pocock on Harrington seem to me to be, at the least, very weighty. His response to them has been unsatisfactory, for he treats them as though they were a challenge simply to his terminology rather than to his understanding of the character of the thought in question. On Harrington's Machiavellianism, see Mansfield, *Taming the Prince*, pp. 183–84.

94. See *Machiavellian Moment*, p. 450; and cf. Pocock's own characterization of his contribution to the "republican synthesis" in *Virtue, Commerce, and History*, p. 218: "It was a cardinal thesis with him [Pocock] that a persistent emphasis on the armed citizen . . . had entailed as an ideological consequence the ideal superiority of real over personal property, and that this had imparted an agrarian and classical character to eighteenth-century republicanism, infecting it with ineradicable doubts and ambivalences regarding the growth of a world commerce."

95. Pocock's most comprehensive list of neo-Harringtonians is in *Politics, Language and Time*, p. 340: Bolingbroke, Neville, Fletcher, Moyle, Toland, Molesworth, and Trenchard and Gordon.

96. Pocock, *Politics, Language, and Time*, p. 135; introduction to *Political Works of Harrington*, p. 49; *Machiavellian Moment*, p. 385; cf. "*Machiavellian Moment* Revisited," p. 60; *Politics, Language, and Time*, p. 120.

97. *Politics, Language, and Time*, p. 120; cf. p. 135. Cf. Marvell, *An Account of the Growth of Popery and Arbitrary Government*, p. 261: "None will deny, that to alter our Monarchy into a Commonwealth were treason."

98. *Machiavellian Moment*, p. 416; *Politics, Language, and Time*, pp. 133, 136, 138; introduction to *Political Works of Harrington*, p. 129.

99. *Politics, Language, and Time*, pp. 130, 133; "*Machiavellian Moment* Revisited," p. 61. For speculation on the motive for transformation, see *Politics, Language and Time*, p. 128.

100. Introduction to *Political Works of Harrington*, p. 145; *Politics, Language, and Time*, pp. 92, 130–32. See also *Machiavellian Moment*, pp. 406–22.

101. *Politics, Language, and Time*, pp. 90–92, 123, 131; cf. *Virtue, Commerce, and History*, p. 48.

102. See Pocock, "Between Gog and Magog," p. 340; *Virtue, Commerce, and History*, p. 68.

103. *Politics, Language, and Time*, p. 136: "The neo-Harringtonians . . . were making an open attempt (as Harrington had not) to win support from country gentlemen discontented with the progress of Court government." See also pp. 131, 132; introduction to *Political Works of Harrington*, p. 138; *Machiavellian Moment*, p. 420; *Politics, Language, and Time*, pp. 94, 122, 124, 132 (also pp. 136–37, 141, on the historical deficiencies of the neo-Harringtonians).

104. Introduction to *Political Works of Harrington*, p. 129, 146.

105. Ibid., p. 129; *Machiavellian Moment*, p. 406; *Politics, Language, and Time*, pp. 115–16.

106. Cf. *Machiavellian Moment*, p. 415. The pamphlet has sometimes been attributed to John Locke, who at that time was a member of the earl's household. A copy in his hand is the chief piece of evidence for this attribution, for the pamphlet has struck few readers as particularly Lockean in style. The authorship issue is discussed in Haley, *The First Earl of Shaftesbury*, pp. 391–93, and Ashcraft, *Revolutionary Politics and Locke's Two Treatises*, pp. 120–23. On the connections between Shaftesbury and Locke at the time of this pamphlet, see Pocock, *Virtue, Commerce, and History*, p. 65. There are elements in the pamphlet that speak against Shaftesbury's authorship, especially the very flattering references to the earl sprinkled liberally throughout it.

107. *Machiavellian Moment*, pp. 406, 409, 417; introduction to *Political Works of Harrington*, p. 130. Pocock thus conceded in advance the point raised in criticism by Davis ("Pocock's Harrington," p. 697), that Harrington had no "theory of corruption."

108. *Machiavellian Movement*, pp. 406, 411, 412, 414; *Politics, Language, and Time*, p. 119.

109. *Machiavellian Moment*, pp. 406, 414–16. Consider Pocock's summary statement: "The House of Lords, frequent parliaments, and the militia are being enlisted on the same side, that of the mixed and ancient constitution, whose enemy is something Harrington never thought of, the corruption of parliament by patronage and military professionalization. And the militia, to Harrington a new and revolutionary force, is being made ancient, Gothic, and compatible with a hereditary aristocracy— all things he had denied it could ever have been" (*Machiavellian Moment*, p. 416). Also see *Politics, Language, and Time*, p. 117: Harrington's point "was something very far removed from what Shaftesbury was saying."

110. On Pocock's "a priorism," consider *Politics, Language and Time*: "We already know that [Shaftesbury's ideas] required to be expressed in Harringtonian concepts." Pocock has not, however, established that necessity, and it is difficult to imagine an argument that could do so, especially in light of his admission that "few if any of their lordships had read *Oceana* or would recognize the source of his ideas" (p. 117).

111. *Machiavellian Moment*, p. 415; introduction to *Political Works of Harrington*, p. 132.

112. Shaftesbury, "Letter from a Person of Quality," p. lxv. Cf. "A Letter from a Parliament-man to His Friend," p. lxix.

113. Montesquieu, *On the Spirit of the Laws*, book 3; de Tocqueville, *Democracy in America*, esp. vol. 1. In his earliest interpretation of Shaftesbury's speeches, Pocock correctly identified his theme as "the Lords as a *pouvoir intermediaire*," but called this "straight Harringtonian doctrine." (*Politics, Language, and Time*, p. 116). The intermediate-power theme drops out of later versions, perhaps because there is nothing peculiarly or uniquely Harringtonian about that idea, especially not in the way Shaftesbury employs it. Cf. Schwoerer, *No Standing Armies*, pp. 113–14.

114. Pocock, Introduction to *Political Works of Harrington*, p. 131; see also *Ma-*

chiavellian Moment, pp. 413, 416; *Politics, Language, and Time*, p. 124. Cf. Marvell, *Account*, p. 325, for a treatment of the army issue in accord with Pocock's; but see also, pp. 293, 298, 302–3, 306, 315.

115. Better on the standing-army issue in 1675 is Ashcraft, *Revolutionary Politics*, pp. 201–2: The Whigs feared that the king "intended to rely upon the army and the use of force, rather than upon elections and Parliament to support his policies. . . . An insistence upon no standing army, therefore, was second in importance only to the antipopery theme in the Whig campaign for exclusion, and the two themes were frequently intertwined. Thus, one aspect of the meaning of 'popery and arbitrary government' referred to the propensity of Catholic monarchs to rule by 'force,' that is, through a standing army, rather than by 'consent' through a Parliament."

116. For a sketch of the debates over control of the military in the struggles leading up to 1642, see Schwoerer, *No Standing Armies*, introduction and chapters 2–3. Charles I had tried to reform and centralize the militia, efforts that inspired much of the opposition to him. From 1648 to 1660, the army was a regular and decisive participant in politics (chapter 4). Charles II gave statesmen like Shaftesbury reason to worry that he, too, sought to overawe the nation with military force in his recurrent effort to constitute a standing military force (chapters 5–6); that is, there was very good reason for Shaftesbury, Marvell, and the other Opposition writers to fear a standing army and to suspect the Crown of seeking to use it for illicit ends.

117. Ibid., p. 5; cf. pp. 42, 97, 105, 190. She adds another ground for the opposition to standing armies: they entail the arming of the lower classes (p. 13).

118. *Machiavellian Moment*, p. 414; "Letter from a Parliament-man," p. lxix.

119. *Politics, Language, and Time*, pp. 126–27; "Letter from a Person of Quality," pp. lxii–lxiii, lxvii.

120. *Politics, Language, and Time*, pp. 124–27. See also *Machiavellian Moment*, pp. 407–9, 417; introduction to *Political Works of Harrington*, pp. 129–33, 145–46.

121. "Letter from a Person of Quality," p. xlv.

122. Ibid.

123. Ibid., p. lxiii.

124. *Politics, Language, and Time*, pp. 3–41, 273–91; Zuckert, "Appropriation and Understanding in the History of Political Philosophy," pp. 403–24.

125. On the relation between Milton and Marvell, whom Pocock does discuss, see Cherniak, *The Poet's Muse*, pp. 6, 74–79, 101, 102–50.

126. Pocock's explanation for his omissions is unpersuasive. He claims that after the republication of Filmer's works the most pressing task for Whig writers after 1679 was the refutation of Filmer and then, after 1689, the defense of the Glorious Revolution. These were tasks, he claims, not well carried out "in republican terms" (*Machiavellian Moment*, p. 421). The fact, is, however that a writer like Algernon Sidney, devoted to the refutation of Filmer and making arguments that could easily be pressed into service in defense of the revolution, wrote "in republican terms" throughout. Pocock's omissions tend to support the diremption he posits between "liberal" and "republican" modes of thought.

127. Pocock refers to the relevant context in passing (see *Machiavellian Moment*, pp. 409, 412), but his analysis bears few marks of taking it seriously (see also *Virtue, Commerce, and History*, p. 219). Part of Pocock's reason for slighting the context is his tendency not to take the Whig fears very seriously. The original inspiration for his

studies came from his animus against Whig history. Consider his relationship to Butterfield's attack on Whig history (*Ancient Constitution*, pp. viii, 46, 208–9, 250).

128. "Letter from a Person of Quality," p. xxix. Cf. Haley, *First Earl of Shaftesbury*, pp. 387–92; part of Shaftesbury's diagnosis of the aim of Crown policy was based on the king's opening speech to Parliament in 1675 (pp. 373–74).

129. Haley, p. 380.

130. Shaftesbury discerned in the oath a device originated by Archibishop Laud in 1640. "Letter from a Person of Quality," p. lxvi; see also p. xlii.

131. Ibid., pp. xxxix, liv. At the time of the Exclusion Bill, the bishops openly and loudly pressed divine right doctrines against Shaftesbury's efforts to exclude the Catholic James (Haley, *First Earl of Shaftesbury*, pp. 367–68).

132. "Letter from a Person of Quality," pp. lxiv–lxvii. A strong anticlerical air pervades Shaftesbury's pamphlet; see pp. xxxix, lv. Haley makes clear the role of the bishops in the formulation of Danby's policies, in *First Earl of Shaftesbury*, pp. 367–68.

133. "Letter from a Person of Quality," pp. xxxix, liv. See also Schwoerer, *No Standing Armies*, pp. 76, 83, 110–11.

134. "Letter from a Person of Quality," pp. xlii–xliii. Cf. the role of the dispensing power in the Bill of Rights and the conflict leading up to the Glorious Revolution. This is not to say that constitutional issues of a more traditional sort did not figure in Whig political thought—as, for example, in Exclusion-era debates over Parliament's power to regulate the succession. But these were not prominent in Shaftesbury's 1675 statements; instead, one finds there the somewhat new and different thrust of analysis described in the text.

135. See ibid., pp. lxi, lxii. Cf. Marvell, *Account*, pp. 279–82.

136. "Letter from a Person of Quality," p. lxii. According to Haley, Shaftesbury was sensitive to the role of "place men" by at least 1664 (*First Earl of Shaftesbury*, p. 352).

137. Haley, p. 367.

138. "Letter from a Person of Quality," p. lii. This is the one theme in the "Letter" that contains more than a shadow of what would later be Lockean doctrine.

139. Ibid., pp. xlvii–l. Consider also Shaftesbury's position on the case of *Shirley v. Fagg* (Haley, pp. 382–83, 394).

140. Marvell, *Account*, pp. 248, 383.

141. Ibid., pp. 255, 262, 263.

142. See chapter 5. On Marvell's need to present a loyal face, see Cherniak, *Poet's Muse*, pp. 92–93. A different interpretation is in Wallace, *Destiny His Choice*.

143. Marvell, *Account*, p. 252. How plausible Marvell's fears were remains a matter of controversy, but there are scholars who find them generally persuasive, for example, Annabel Patterson: "Knowledge of the secret clauses in the Treaty of Dover has given credibility to Marvell's conspiracy theory" (*Marvell and the Civic Crown*, p. 252); cf. Cherniak, *The Poet's Muse*, pp. 88–97, and in general, Ashcraft, *Revolutionary Politics*.

144. Pocock, introduction to *Political Works of Harrington*, p. 130.

145. Cf. Marvell, *Account*, p. 315.

146. Ibid., pp. 325, 327, 331–32, 337.

147. For two particularly clear instances in which Pocock's interpretative frame-

work produces Marvellean stances quite distant from the original, see *Machiavellian Moment*, p. 409 (cf. Marvell's *Account*, pp. 329–30), and *Politics, Language, and Time*, p. 123.

CHAPTER SEVEN
LOCKE AND REFORMATION OF NATURAL LAW:
QUESTIONS CONCERNING THE LAW OF NATURE

1. See, for example, Kramnick, *Republicanism and Bourgeois Radicalism*, chapters 6, 7; Robbins, *The Eighteenth-Century Commonwealthmen*, pp. 35–36, 84, 100, 187, 249, 340–44; Mayer, "English Radical Whig Origins of American Constitutionalism," pp. 174–75, 190.

2. Even Martyn Thompson, the diagnostician of unicontractarianism, falls prey to the disease when he finds Locke's *Treatises* essentially like earlier works by Tyrell, Sidney, and Pufendorf, who, Thompson says, were in turn very like the earlier writers who served as authorities for them, Grotius and Hooker (Thompson, "The Reception of Locke's *Two Treatises*," pp. 184–85).

3. A recent post-"republican synthesis" survey of the American sources reaffirms the earlier (pre-synthesis) view that the Americans thought as Lockeans: "The historical-textual evidence testifies consistently and often explicitly in the language of 'Locke on Government'" (Dworetz, *The Unvarnished Doctrine*, p. 8; cf. pp. 43–44, 96, 171).

4. Two editions of the work have appeared since 1950: *Essays on the Law of Nature*, ed. von Leyden (1954) and *Questions Concerning the Law of Nature*, ed. Horwitz, Clay, and Clay (1990). The introductions to both editions may be consulted for details on the occasion for Locke's work, and on the manuscript and its fate. I am using the more recent edition, by Horwitz, Clay, and Clay.

5. Locke, *Two Treatises* II 12; cf. Laslett, introduction to *Two Treatises*; Ashcraft, *Locke's Two Treatises of Government*, pp. 100–101.

6. See Diskin Clay, translator's introduction to Locke, *Questions*, pp. 80–81. The editors of this edition and von Leyden agree in seeing Grotius as a source for the *Questions*. Cf. *Essays*, p. 33; *Questions*, p. 47.

7. I am accepting Horwitz's argument regarding the titled but unexplicated *Questions*, that is, that they are part of the work and should be considered when identifying the structure and overall argument of the book. On the other hand, I disagree with both Horwitz and Leo Strauss regarding the structure of the work. The opening paragraph of Question VIII (fol. 82) convinces me that Question XI is part of the third section rather than a separate topic, as Strauss and Horwitz maintain. See Strauss, "Locke's Doctrine of Natural Law," p. 198; Horwitz, "John Locke's *Questions Concerning the Law of Nature*," p. 304 n. 2. On the centrality of these topics to the philosophy of natural law, consider Simon, *The Tradition of Natural Law*, esp. chapter 5.

8. I am citing Locke's *Questions* by the folio number as printed in both the von Leyden and Horwitz editions.

9. See Yolton, "Locke on the Law of Nature," p. 483.

10. Cf. Pufendorf, *De Jure Naturae et Gentium* I.vi.1, 5; II.iii.20.

11. Some of Locke's predecessors, notably Suárez and Pufendorf, make very much the same point. See *Locke*, 2:191, 197.

12. Grotius's treatment of obligation was one of the most frequently criticized elements of his system. Cf. Pufendorf, *De Jure* I.vi.1, 2; Culverwell, *An Elegant and Learned Discourse of the Light of Nature*, pp. 30, 49, 51, 65.

13. Grotius, *De Jure Belli ac Pacis*, I.i.9, 10 (emphases added). The emphasized phrases, and Grotius's general point here, refute Edwards's attempt to assimilate Grotius and Suárez on obligation (*Hugo Grotius*, pp. 56–69).

14. See Grotius, *De Jure*, Proleg. 18, 39.

15. See Tully, *A Discourse on Property*, p. 41.

16. Ibid.

17. Pufendorf, *Elementorum Jurisprudentiae Universalis*, preface.

18. Ibid.

19. Ibid., I Def. XIII.

20. Ibid., II Obs. IV. 3.

21. Horwitz, "John Locke's *Questions*," p. 255.

22. Cf. Pufendorf, *Elementorum* I Def. XIII. 1 (will of superior), 4 (sanctions), 9 (norm for actions), 10 (promulgation). A good discussion of sanctions in other natural law theory is Lehrberger, "Crime without Punishment," pp. 237–57.

23. Cf. Pufendorf, *Elementorum* I Def. XXII. 3, 7.

24. Hobbes, *Leviathan*, chapter 14. Cf. Grotius, *De Jure* II.ii.20.

25. Pufendorf, *Elementorum* I Def. XIII. 14.

26. On conscience, see ibid., II Obs. I. 5–8.

27. For speculation on Locke's reasons for citing Juvenal rather than Paul, see Proietti, "Natural Right(s) and Natural Law," p. 294.

28. Cf. Pufendorf, *Elementorum* I Def. XVI.

29. Singh, "John Locke and the Theory of Natural Law," pp. 106, 112; cf. Drury, "John Locke: Natural Law and Innate Ideas," pp. 531, 542; Hancy, "John Locke and the Law of Nature," pp. 439–40, 448–49; Ashcraft, *Locke's Two Treatises*, pp. 16–17; Polin, *La politique morale de John Locke*, pp. 96–97.

30. See Polin, p. 116.

31. Pufendorf, *Elementorum* I Def. I. 1, Def. XIII. 9, 14.

32. See Horwitz, "John Locke's *Questions*," p. 252.

33. Cf. Culverwell, *Elegant and Learned Discourse*, p. 28.

34. See Strauss, "Locke's Doctrine," p. 198.

35. See Yolton, "Locke," p. 481; Polin, *La politique morale*, p. 102.

36. Polin's failure to notice how Locke's later discussions constitute a reconsideration of his initial disputation greatly mars his otherwise sophisticated and intelligent essay, *La politique morale de John Locke*. Following Locke too unself-consciously, he falls into numerous contradictions. Consider, for instance, pp. 97–103, on the presence of the law of nature to human beings.

37. Aristotle, *Ethics* 1134b25–30.

38. Grotius, *De Jure*, Proleg. 40, I.i.12; cf. II.ix.6 for the a posteriori method in use against the Roman law treatment of *jus gentium*.

39. Von Leyden, in *Locke's Essays*, p. 161 n. 3, and Lindahl, in *A Critical Commentary on John Locke's Essays on the Law of Nature*, p. 126, both note the connec-

tion of Locke's discussion of consensus to Grotius. Lindahl (pp. 113–14) also emphasizes the connection of Question IV to Grotius.

40. See also Locke's consideration of the Grotian qualification that natural law may be found in the consensus of "the most civilized nations" (fols. 66–67).

41. A hitherto unrecognized source for Locke's discussion of consensus, or rather dissensus, is Montaigne's essay "Of Custom, and Not Easily Changing an Accepted Law." Locke takes over from Montaigne the organization of his discussion according to purported consensus in conduct and then in opinion. He also takes over some of the very examples Montaigne uses in his essay—for example, nations where children kill their fathers or where husbands share their wives with others. More generally, Locke's Question VII gives off the same intensely relativistic odor as Montaigne's essay. There is need for systematic study of Locke's appropriation of Montaigne, not only in the *Questions*, but throughout his works. On Montaigne, see Schaefer, *The Political Philosophy of Montaigne*.

42. Cf. Horwitz, "John Locke's *Questions*," pp. 257–58; Strauss, "Locke's Doctrine," pp. 203–4.

43. Thomas Aquinas, *Summa Theologica*, I-II Q 91 A 1.

44. Ibid., I-II Q 94 A 2.

45. Locke, *Essay* I.iii.13.

46. See, for example, Aristotle, *Politics* 1254b26–36.

47. Horwitz, "John Locke's *Questions*," p. 259.

48. Locke, *Essay* I.iii.2; see also Horwitz, p. 268,

49. Pufendorf, *Elementorum* II Obs. III.

50. Grotius, *De Jure* II.xviii.1.

51. On natural sociability, cf. Polin's insightful discussion in *La politique morale*, pp. 104–5, 114–15.

52. Cf. Pufendorf, *De Jure* I.vi.9; Suárez, *De Legibus* II.vi.3; St. Leger, *Etiamsi*, pp. 112, 116, 118, 120–21.

53. See Tully, *Discourse*, pp. 44–45; Polin, *La politique morale*, pp. 96–97, 114, 119, 197. Cf. Polin's failure to assimilate the denial of natural inclinations (p. 113).

54. Pufendorf, *De Jure* I.vi.13.

55. Cf. Lindahl, *Critical Commentary*, p. 81, on the "completely hidden" natural law.

56. Cf. Pufendorf, *De Jure* I.vi.13.

57. For a good summary statement of the implications of Locke's treatment of promulgation, see Lindahl, pp. 128–30.

58. Cf. Descartes, *Meditations on First Philosophy* III. For Cartesian reflections in Locke's proof for the existence of God in the *Essay*, see Zuckert, "An Introduction to Locke's *First Treatise*," pp. 70–71. Cf. how Tully (*Discourse*, p. 39) passes over this argument without notice; cf. Parry, *John Locke*, p. 13.

59. Further indication of the significance of divine inimicality is visible in Locke's parallel formulation in his *Essay Concerning Human Understanding* (IV.iii.18).

60. Cf. Horwitz, "John Locke's *Questions*," p. 285. The sanctions have a more intimate connection than Tully allows (*Discourse*, p. 43). Cf. Parry, *John Locke*, pp. 33–34; Ayers, *Locke* 2:198–99.

61. Locke, *Essay* IV.iii.29; idem, *The Reasonableness of Christianity*, paras. 242–45; cf. Zuckert, "Locke and the Problem of Civil Religion," pp. 196–97; Strauss,

"Locke's Doctrine," p. 210; idem, *Natural Right*, pp. 203–4; Horwitz, "John Locke's *Questions*," p. 285.

62. See Polin, *La politique morale*, p. 114–15 n. 3.

63. Cf. Grotius, *De Jure*, Proleg. 5.

64. For a development of this theme in Locke's later *Essay*, see Ayers, *Locke* 2:185. It is difficult to understand Ayers's judgment that "genuine morality has an authority antecedent to organized society, and cannot be the creation of man for the sake of social harmony" (pp. 185–86); consider all the contrary evidence Ayers himself cites on pp. 186–87.

65. There are remarkable parallels between Locke's critique and David Hume's later dismissal of the "egoistic system." See Hume's *Enquiry Concerning the Principles of Morals*, esp. appendix II.

66. See Lindahl, *a Critical Commentary*, pp. 81, 91.

67. Locke, *Two Treatises* II 34. Grotius was one of those who held the Romans up as a model; See *De Jure*, Proleg. 46.

CHAPTER EIGHT
LOCKE AND REFORMATION OF NATURAL LAW:
TWO TREATISES OF GOVERNMENT

1. See Polin, *La politique morale de John Locke*, pp. 118–19.

2. Patrick Coby discerns a similar movement in the *Second Treatise* ("The Law of Nature in Locke's *Second Treatise*," pp. 299–312).

3. For a consideration of Locke's use of Hooker, see Cox, *Locke on War and Peace*, pp. 41–42; Zuckert, "Of Wary Physicians and Weary Readers," pp. 59–61, and further citations therein; Pangle, *The Spirit of Modern Republicanism*, pp. 132–33, 235–36.

4. Cf. Locke, *Essay on Human Understanding*, III.ix.3, 8; Strauss, *Natural Right and History*, pp. 220–21; Zuckert, "Of Wary Physicians," p. 58; Polin, *La politique morale*, pp. 97, 118. For a hint of the workmanship argument in the more philosophic *Essay*, see IV.iii.18. In the *Essay* there is an attempt to supply a proof for the existence of God (IV.x). For discussion of Locke's proof, see Zuckert, "An Introduction to Locke's *First Treatise*," pp. 70–71.

5. Cf. Tully, *A Discourse on Property*, p. 55

6. Contra Polin, *La politique morale*, p. 119; cf. p. 120, on "necessities and needs."

7. See Simmons, "Inalienable Rights and Locke's *Treatises*," p. 191: "A person has no right to destroy human life, either his own or that of another."

8. See Andrew, *Shylock's Rights*, chapter 4; but cf. Simmons, "Inalienable Rights."

9. See Dunn, *The Political Thought of John Locke*, pp. 120–30; Ashcraft, *Locke's Two Treatises*, pp. 128–29.

10. See Ashcraft, p. 126: "All natural rights are traceable to some specific obligation laid upon individuals by the Law of Nature." See also p. 135: "Lockean natural rights are always the active fulfillment of duties to God." Also see Polin, *La politique morale*, p. 101: "Avant d'être des droits, ce sont des obligations"; also Parry, *John Locke*, p. 40; Lemnos, "Two Concepts of Natural Right," pp. 55–63. An alternative derivation of natural rights from natural duties perhaps more characteristic of the texts cited above is as follows: Every duty to do X implies a right to do X, according

to the principle that one may do what one ought to do. A good presentation of this view is in White, *The Philosophy of the American Revolution*, pp. 147–48.

11. See Ashcraft, p. 101; Pangle, *Spirit*, p. 160.

12. Cf. Locke, *Questions*, fol. 48.

13. On the chief premise of this construct see *Two Treatises* I 52: The one who gives something does not necessarily have a right to take it back. Cf. chapter 7 of this book, on mortality. Cf. Shapiro, *The Evolution of Rights in Liberal Theory*, p. 101.

14. A fuller inventory of Lockean natural laws than is necessary here can be found in Coby, "Law of Nature," pp. 299–300.

15. See *ibid.*, p. 301.

16. Hobbes, *Leviathan*, chapter 14.

17. See, Coby, "Law of Nature," pp. 301–03.

18. See, for example, Ruth Grant, *John Locke's Liberalism*, pp. 69–71; Ashcraft, *Locke's Two Treatises*, p. 130.

19. See Ashcraft, p. 102.

20. Cf. Shapiro's attempt (*Evolution of Rights*, p. 111) to treat Locke's natural law as though it were immanent, contrary to the testimony of both *Questions* and *Two Treatises*.

21. Cf. Ashcraft's different account in *Locke's Two Treatises*, p. 108.

22. Laslett, Introduction to Locke, *Two Treatises of Government*, p. 110 n. 5.

23. Aarsleff, "Some Observations on Recent Locke Scholarship," p. 268n.

24. Skinner, *Foundations of Modern Political Thought*, 2:119.

25. See especially Munz, *The Place of Hooker in the History of Thought*, chapter 3, appendix 1.

26. Thomas Aquinas, *Summa Theologica* II-II Q 64 A 3; idem, *De Regimine Principium* I.4–11. Cf. Skinner, *Foundations* 2:118–19.

27. *Summa* I Q 96 A 4.

28. Suárez, *De Legibus* III.iii.3.

29. Ibid., III.i.5.

30. Ibid., III.ii.3, III.iii.6. On Suárez, see Skinner, *Foundations* 2:157, 181–82.

31. *De Legibus* III.iii.6. Quentin Skinner's claim about Almain requires a brief note. Skinner's own account of Almain is sufficient to show how different the latter is from Locke. According to Skinner, Almain argues that " 'the right of the sword' which a community grants to its ruler in the act of forming a political society must be a right originally possessed by the community itself" (*Foundations* 2:119). This doctrine differs from Locke's in the decisive respect that Locke affirms as "strange" the possession of an original rightful power not in the community but in each individual. In a later discussion (2:157), Skinner appears to have a better grasp of the issue.

32. *De Legibus* III.iii.2; cf. III.i.4, 12. Cf. Locke, *Two Treatises* II 81–83.

33. Cf. Tully, *Discourse*, p. 66: "Although we have no definitive proof that Locke read Suárez, several historians have stressed the similarities between their political philosophies." He cites von Leyden, the first editor of Locke's *Questions*, and Quentin Skinner, among others.

34. Hooker, *Of the Laws of Ecclesiastical Polity*, I.x.4; cf. Augustine, *On the City of God* XIX.13–15, 21.

35. Hooker, *Laws* I.x.1.

36. Ibid., I.x.3, 4.

37. Ibid., I.x.4.

38. Ibid.

39. Ibid.

40. Cf. Eccleshall's insightful comments on the role of private judgment in Hooker's polemics (*Order and Reason in Politics*, p. 25).

41. *Laws* I.x.8.

42. Ibid. I.x.4, 5. Cf. Eccleshall (p. 140): "Hooker posited consent as the legitimating factor of political power [because] he had been influenced by the medieval assimilation of political society to a corporation where authority was held to reside with the collectivity of the members."

43. Cf. Parry, *John Locke*, p. 28, and Locke, *Essay* II.xxviii.6.

44. Hooker, *Laws* I.vii, ix, x.2. Cf. Suárez, *De Legibus* II.vii.7, 8, 10; II.viii.3–5; Cumberland, *De Legibus Naturae*, chapter 1.

45. *Laws* I.ix; cf. *De Legibus* II.vi.13.

46. *Laws* I.ix.2. On eternal rewards and punishments, cf. *De Legibus* II.vi.10, 24, and esp. II.ix.3–4.

47. *Laws* I.v.1.

48. Ibid., I.x.4. On the distance between Locke and Hooker on the state of nature, see Polin, *La politique morale*, p. 105: Locke admits "l'existence de l'homme à l'état de nature, état que n'envisageait pas Hooker pour qui l'homme sortant des mains du créateur, entrait directement dans une société civile et vivait dans un corps politique."

49. See *Laws* I.x.5. Skepticism about the legitimacy of Locke's reliances on Hooker is fully warranted by the recent scholarship on Hooker, for the Hooker scholars find it simply indispensable to get their man out from under the spell of Locke. Most recent Hooker scholars agree with W. D. J. Cargill Thompson ("The Philosophy of the 'Politic Society'") that "Locke's political philosophy [is] essentially incompatible with Hooker's." Indeed, Thompson finds that the proper understanding of Hooker could only begin when people stopped reading him in the manner of Locke:

> Hooker's thought has been handicapped by the "politic use" that has been made of him in the past. For over two centuries his political philosophy was interpreted very largely through the distorting lens of Locke's *Second Treatise*. . . . The manner in which Locke deliberately exploited Hooker's reputation in order to give a semblance of respectability to his own revolutionary argument is now generally recognized. . . . Few myths have proved more difficult to dislodge than the belief that Hooker's views were, in all essentials, identical with those of Locke.

D'Entreves, *The Medieval Contribution to Political Thought*, pp. 125–30; Munz, *Place of Hooker*, esp. pp. 206–7; Eccleshall, *Order and Reason*, pp. 128–30.

50. Cf. the discussion of Locke and Burnet in chapter 4.

51. Hooker, *Laws* I.x.12. Cf. Faulkner, "Reason and Revelation in Hooker's Ethics," p. 684 n. 16. On Hooker's attempt to accommodate the Fall more fully than Thomas had done, consider Suárez's parallel efforts in *De Legibus* III.i.12.

52. Hobbes, *Leviathan* chapter 15.

53. Grotius, *De Jure* II.xx.7. Cf. I.ii.1; I.iii.2; I.x.10; II.xx.3, 8, 9.

54. Ibid., I.iii.2; II.xx.8, 9.
55. Ibid., II.xx.8, 9.
56. Ibid., II.xx.3.
57. Ibid., Proleg. 20.
58. Ibid., Proleg. 6, 13, 18.
59. Ibid., II.xx.40.
60. Ibid.
61. Ibid.
62. Ibid., I ii.
63. See Coby, "Law of Nature," p. 304.
64. See Grant, *Locke's Liberalism*, p. 67; Parry, *John Locke*, p. 58.
65. For discussion, see Zuckert, "Of Wary Physicians," p. 61; Cox, *Locke*, pp. 56–57; Aarsleff, "Some Observations," p. 268; Seliger, *The Liberal Politics of John Locke*, p. 57.
66. See Pangle, *Spirit*, p. 160; Coby, "Law of Nature," p. 304.
67. Goldwin, "John Locke," pp. 479–80. Goldwin's analysis corrects the judgment of standard interpretations like that of Parry, who concedes that the state of nature becomes a state of war and thus "seems" like Hobbes's, but remains assured, on the basis of II 19, that this appearance is false (*Locke*, p. 59; see also p. 111).
68. See Coby, "Law of Nature," p. 305.
69. Grotius, *De Jure* II.xx.28; cf. II.xx.1 (on proportionality), II.xx.4 (on revenge and sociability).
70. Pufendorf, *Elementorum Jurisprudentiae Universalis* II Obs. IV. 16; cf. idem, *De Jure Naturae Gentium*, VIII.iii.10.
71. *Elementorum* II Obs. IV.16.
72. Pufendorf, *De Jure* VIII.iii.7.
73. *Elementorum* II Obs. IV. 4, 16. Despite Pufendorf's incorporation of the right of nature, even he remains more moderate in his view of legitimate force than Locke; see esp. II Obs. IV. 12.
74. Cf. Coby, "Law of Nature," p. 305: Locke's executive power "is little more than Hobbesian natural right dressed up in the splendiferous garb of legal rationalism." Richard Cumberland, author of *De Legibus Naturae* (1672), deserves consideration in this context. The issues raised by his discussion require a far lengthier treatment than they can receive here, however. He shares much with Pufendorf, in that both attempt to reformulate the doctrine of natural law in a post-Hobbesian context. He, more clearly than Pufendorf, attempts to salvage natural law from Hobbes's critique. In our immediate context Cumberland is exceedingly important, for in the course of his confrontation with Hobbes he makes an argument that, I believe, proved to be the germ from which Locke constructed his doctrine of the executive power of the law of nature. Cumberland attempts to salvage the natural law as a genuine law by arguing, among other things, that the power to enforce the law of nature that each can be supposed to possess in a Hobbesian state of nature supplies the sanction necessary to make the laws genuine laws. He insists that Hobbes recognizes such a power, implicitly at least, for Hobbes recognizes a right to war, which would include this power. Cumberland uses this notion of an executive power for the purpose of building a bridge back from Hobbes to his own more traditional notion of the law of nature as a set of precepts aiming at the common good and obligatory for all rational creatures. Locke uses the executive power for the same bridging purpose,

but in the opposite direction. On Locke's relation to Cumberland, see Tully, *Discourse*, p. 6.

75. Grant, *Locke's Liberalism*, p. 67.

76. Pufendorf, *Elementorum* II Obs. V.11.

77. Laslett, in Locke, *Two Treatises*, at II 23. Dunn (*Political Thought*, p. 109n.) denies that Locke concedes the slave suicide as a right. This certainly saves a contradiction, but it does not cohere well with Locke's text. See the end of II 24 for a use of "power" that rules Dunn's interpretation out. A clear recognition of the contradiction and its implications for the workmanship argument is in Pangle, *Spirit*, p. 160. See also Coby, "Law of Nature," pp. 302–3.

78. One interpreter who accepts the indirection argument is Andrew, in *Shylock's Rights*, p. 93.

79. Simmons, "Inalienable Rights," p. 191.

80. Pufendorf, *Elementorum* II Obs. IV.10. Pufendorf's treatment of suicide is more broadly instructive for understanding Locke. Contrary to the conclusion Locke draws from the workmanship argument, Pufendorf concludes that suicide is permissable in the state of nature, in that no one has an obligation to self (ibid.). For the pre-Hobbesian Grotian approach, see *De Jure* I.xvii.2.

81. This forecloses the route Tully took to reconcile the two claims about ownership: "Man's property [in his own person] is the right to use and preserve what is essentially God's property, similar to a tenant's property" (*Discourse*, p. 114). Even on its face this is an implausible solution, because although we might concede that a tenant had certain rights based in contract, the tenant (and Locke) would surely not claim ownership of property, much less a natural right.

82. Cf. Tully, *Discourse*, p. 53.

83. Simmons, "Inalienable Rights," pp. 176, 185–86, 192. Simmons's contention that Locke does not defend inalienable rights turns on the view that human beings do not have a right to those things they cannot give up—for example, their lives. This may be true at the transcendent natural law level of Locke's argument, but even at that level Locke affirms repeatedly that individuals possess a right to life and that they also cannot give up that right. This would seem to justify calling it an inalienable right.

84. Tully, *Discourse*, p. 84.

85. The distinction between a right and the object of the right helps clarify a puzzle about rights that has led some scholars to postulate that the alienability of property accounts for Jefferson's omission of that from his list of rights (cf. White, *Philosophy*, pp. 213–28; Wills, *Inventing America*, pp. 229–39). Whatever may have led Jefferson to skip property, it was not the inalienability problem. For a denial of the significance of Jefferson's omission of a right to property, see Zuckert, "Thomas Jefferson on Nature and Natural Rights," pp. 158–63.

CHAPTER NINE
LOCKE AND REFORMATION OF NATURAL LAW: OF PROPERTY

1. Locke to Richard King, August 25, 1703, in *Correspondence of John Locke*, 8: 58; cf. Macpherson, *The Political theory of Possessive Individualism*, pp. 197–98.

2. See Pangle, *Spirit of Modern Republicanism*, p. 168; C. B. Macpherson astutely notices Locke's reference to his "servant" in II 28, but concludes that Locke must be

"taking the wage relationship entirely for granted" (*Possessive Individualism*, pp. 214–15; cf. p. 217). This is precisely what he is not doing. See also Waldron, *The Right to Private Property*, p. 225.

3. Tully's ingenious account (*Discourse on Property*, pp. 136–45) gets Locke's point exactly backwards because he fails to set the chapter on property in structural context. Cf. p. 137.

4. Laslett, in Locke, *Two Treatises*, at II 25; cf. Tully, *Discourse*, pp. 54, 96.

5. Filmer, *Observations upon Grotius*, pp. 271–74, and *Patriarcha*, pp. 63–66, both in *Patriarcha and Other Political Works*.

6. Cf. Ashcraft, *Locke's Two Treatises*, p. 125.

7. Grotius, *De Jure* I.i.10; cf. Filmer, *Observations upon Grotius*, p. 266.

8. Grotius, *De Jure* II.ii.2; cf. Tully, *Discourse*, p. 80.

9. Grotius, *De Jure* II.ii.2; Pangle (*Spirit*, p. 159) too much collapses the stages of the emergence of property, and thus overstates the biblical character of Grotius's position.

10. Grotius, *De Jure* II.ii.2.

11. Filmer, *Observations upon Grotius*, p. 274.

12. Pufendorf, *De Jure* IV.iv.10–11.

13. Ibid., IV.iv.9.

14. Ibid., IV.iv.2.

15. Ibid., Cf. Waldron, *Private Property*, p. 149.

16. See Filmer, *Observations upon Grotius*, p. 273: "Certainly it was a felicity, that all men in the world at one instant of time should agree together in one mind to change the natural community of all things into private dominion: for without such a unanimous consent it was not possible for community to be altered: for if but one man in the world had dissented, the alteration had been unjust, because that man by the law of nature had a right to the common use of all things in the world; so that to have given a propriety of any one thing to any other, had been to have robbed him of his right to the common use of all things." On Pufendorf's response to the "at one instant of time" issue, see *De Jure* IV.iv.6.

17. Cf. Tully, *Discourse*, pp. 71, 82. Pufendorf's interpretation of Grotius's common right as negative community is plausible and probably correct in the main, but, as he concedes, Grotius does appear to confuse positive and negative community on occasion. See Pufendorf, *De Jure* IV.iv.9.

18. Tully, p. 83.

19. Pufendorf, *De Jure* IV.iv.9. Cf. Tully, *Discourse*, p. 86.

20. Pufendorf, *De Jure* IV.iv.9. Cf. Waldron, *Private Property*, p. 150.

21. Pufendorf, *De Jure* IV.iv.4, 5.

22. Ibid., IV.iv.9; cf. IV.iv.6, on express pacts and division of land.

23. Tully, *Discourse*, p. 74; cf. Goldwin, "John Locke," p. 406: "The original universal common was a state of universal propertylessness"; Waldron, *Private Property*, pp. 155–56, takes very strong exception to Tully on positive commons.

24. See Laslett's note (at II 8) connecting this argument to Pufendorf and Grotius. Laslett points to Blackstone and Barbeyrac as two early commentators who saw the connection of this discussion to Pufendorf (and Grotius).

25. Tully (*Discourse*, p. 79 and passim) makes the puzzling and textually quite indefensible claim that Locke rejects the exclusive property of Grotius and Pufen-

dorf and substitutes an "inclusive right" instead. Tully, following Macpherson, defines private property as "an exclusive right because it is a right of the proprietor to exclude others from that to which the right refers." On the other hand, "common property can be redescribed as an inclusive right because it is a right 'not to be excluded from,' or to be included in, the use of that to which the right refers" (p. 61) Tully's claim here is just another version of his mistake about positive and negative commons. Also see *Two Treatises* II 26, on the exclusivity that must accompany any appropriation. My judgment on Tully parallels that of Waldron, *Private Property*, pp. 140–41: "The theory which Tully attributes to Locke is simply *not Locke's theory*; and the attribution is based on what can only be described as a very seriously defective reading of the *Two Treatises*" (italics in original).

26. See Pangle, *Spirit*, p. 82. Waldron's reflections on this argument are largely misplaced if the specific context is kept in mind (*Private Property*, pp. 168–69). See also Manent, *Histoire intellectuelle du liberalisme*, p. 96.

27. Ashcraft's attempt to displace labor in favor of need as such has remarkably little textual support; compare *Locke's Two Treatises*, pp. 126–27, with Locke's II 27. See also Waldron, p. 139.

28. Cf. Tully, *Discourse*, p. 82: Grotius "cannot articulate a satisfactory natural principle within his framework of a use right and a duty to abstain."

29. Pufendorf, *De Jure* IV.iv.4.

30. Cf. Tully, p. 62: "Since preservation is one of God's goods for man, and hence his natural duty is to bring it about, it follows that he has a natural right to do it." Cf. his conclusion about Locke as a natural law thinker, p. 63. See also Ashcraft, *Locke's Two Treatises*, p. 126: "The basis for their rights claim [to property] is the obligation to preserve themselves by providing for their subsistence." Perhaps, but it is striking that there is no good Lockean text making just this argument.

31. Locke also formulates that principle as "to preserve . . . mankind" (II 6; cf. II 8, 16, 183). This formulation appears to amount to the same as the no-harm principle, however, for Locke consistently treats it as posing negative duties (do not harm) but not positive duties (contribute in some further way to the preservation of others). Thus, there is (at best) a *right* to execute the law of nature to prevent harm, a right initially bounded in such a way as not to be a source of harm. There is no duty to enforce the law of nature (cf. II 8). The negative interpretation of the duty to preserve mankind makes possible the congruence between Locke's transcendent natural law and natural rights. Some scholars have found broader kinds of duties, but they have had to import language into the text that Locke did not put there; see, for example, Tully, *Discourse*, pp. 71, 84.

32. Ashcraft, *Locke's Two Treatises*, p. 126; see also p. 131, where he repeats the same claim. Cf. Tully, pp. 95–96.

33. See Pangle, *Spirit*, p. 162; Goldwin, "John Locke," pp. 489–90. Waldron's extended discussion of the limitations would have been stronger had he connected them to the transcendent natural law, had he treated them in the order Locke presented them and thus picked up on the developing argument Locke is making, and had he noticed the important shift that occurs as Locke shifts his attention from consumables to the means of production (see *Private Property*, pp. 207–18).

34. See Strauss, *Natural Right and History*, p. 236.

35. Consider, for example, the works by Laslett, Dunn, Grant, Tully, and Ashcraft

cited earlier. Cf. the wavering account by Waldron (*Private Property*, pp. 141–47), which is much hampered in its development of the "theological premises" of Locke's property doctrine by its failure to connect up firmly with the workmanship and no-harm argument.

36. For Pufendorf on taxation, see *De Jure* VII.iv.7, 11; VIII.v.4ff.; and on property in general the whole of VIII.v. Pufendorf's allegiance to Hobbesian views on sovereignty takes him even further from Locke and the Whigs than Grotius is; see, for instance, VII.iv.11. Cf. Tully: "In general terms, Locke's theory overthrows all his absolutist adversaries—Grotius and Pufendorf as well as Filmer" (*Discourse*, p. 172). On Locke's theory as resisting the implicaton of political control contained in Grotius and Pufendorf, see Waldron, pp. 152–53.

37. Tully, p. 169; cf. pp. 122ff., and p. 130: "Locke provides a justification, not of private property, but, rather, of the English Common."

38. Waldron's thorough and otherwise thoughtful treatment suffers from his failure to see this shift in Locke's arugment. Consider, for example, *Private Property*, pp. 177–94.

39. Cf. *Locke Essay on Human Understanding*, IV.xix.14.

40. Ashcraft, *Locke's Two Treatises*, p. 134; cf. also Dunn, *Political Thought of John Locke*, pp. 218–19; Tully, *Discourse*, p. 110. Waldron's treatment is very loose, but his conclusion is sound: the importance of labor for Locke "is purely instrumental and the basis of our secular recognition of its importance lies . . . in our common sense realization that we *have to* work in order to survive and flourish" (*Private Property*, p. 147; italics in original).

41. Cf. Pangle, *Spirit*, pp. 163, 166.

42. Cf. Strauss, *Natural Right*, p. 247.

43. Heidegger, "The Question Concerning Technology," pp. 12–19.

44. Cf. Dunn, *Political Thought*, pp. 87–95; Yolton, *Locke and the Compass of Human Understanding*; Locke, *Essay* III.vi.12.

45. Locke, *Essay* II.xii, II.xiv, II.xxxi.6–11, III.vi, III.ix, III.x; cf. Strauss, *Natural Right*, p. 249.

46. Tully, *Discourse*, pp. 116–21. The teaching about the being of the beings forms Locke's deepest reply to the kinds of objection to Locke's "mixing one's labor" argument raised by Waldron in *Private Property*, pp. 184–91.

47. *Essay* II.iv.1, IV.xi.8

48. See Dworetz, *Unvarnished Doctrine*, pp. 115–17; Strauss, *Natural Right*, pp. 237–39.

49. See Goldwin, "John Locke," p. 491; Pangle, *Spirit*, p. 163; also Manent, *Histoire*, p. 98: "Toute la démarche de Locke consiste à abolir les deux limites qu'il a d'abord posées."

50. See Manent, *Histoire*, p. 98.

51. See Macpherson, *Possessive Individualism*, p. 199

52. Cf. Ibid., pp. 211–12, for a different reading.

53. See Waldron's suggestive objections to Locke's point (*Private Property*, pp. 223–24); he needs to make more explicit the model of society and economy he is invoking, however, in order to compare it with the model Locke is taking for granted.

54. Macpherson (*Possessive Individualism*, p. 214ff.) fails to appreciate fully the relation between negative commons, the right of preservation, and labor. This failure leads him into grave errors regarding the "social assumption" of Locke's theory, missing, among other things, Locke's quite self-conscious task of explaining and justifying wage labor.

55. See Ibid., pp. 212–14.

56. See Shapiro, *The Evolution of Rights in Liberal Theory*, p. 14; Manent, *Histoire*, p. 102.

57. See Strauss, *Natural Right*, pp. 242–43.

58. See Pangle, *Spirit*, pp. 169–70; Waldron, *Private Property*, pp. 139, 145–47; Shapiro, *Evolution of Rights*, pp. 83, 126–28, 142.

59. Goldwin, "John Locke," pp. 493–94; Pangle, *Spirit*, p. 168; Strauss, *Natural Right*, pp. 243–45.

60. Hamilton, Madison, and Jay, *The Federalist* 10, p. 79. Cf. Locke, *Two Treatises* II 48; also Pangle, *Spirit*, p. 170: For Locke "property has neither its source nor its purpose in politics. . . . Lockean property does not exist in order to provide the 'equipment' with which man as 'the political animal' may procure fulfillment in civic life and noble leisure." On property in the old republicanism, also see chapter 6 of this book. Cf. Strauss, *Natural Right*, p. 245. On Locke and political economy, see Manent, *Histoire*, pp. 104–7.

61. Hobbes, *Leviathan*, chapter 14 (p. 91).

62. Cf. Locke, *The Reasonableness of Christianity*, para. 14: "the law of reason, or as it is called, of nature."

63. On Hobbes's view of reason as merely calculation or "reckoning," cf. *Leviathan*, chapter 5 (p. 32). For Locke's parallel discussion in his mature philosophy, see *Essay* IV.xvii.

64. In general, see Shapiro's discussion of "the purposes of rights" according to Locke (*Evolution of Rights*, pp. 118–22).

65. Hobbes, *Leviathan*, chapter 14 (p. 91).

66. See Strauss, *Natural Right*, pp. 234, 244–45.

67. Hobbes, *Leviathan*, chapter 15 (p. 101); Locke, *Essay* IV.iii.18.

68. Pufendorf, *De Jure* III.v.1, 3.

69. Ibid., I.i.20.

70. Contra Coby, "The Law of Nature in Locke's *Second Treatise*," p. 306, on the simple collapse of Lockean natural right into Hobbesean natural right; also pp. 307–10, on the merely rhetorical difference between Hobbes and Locke.

71. See, for example, *Leviathan*, introduction (p. 9), chapter 2 (pp. 15, 19); chapter 5 (p. 34); chapter 6 (pp. 37–38). Cf. Strauss, *Studies in Platonic Political Philosophy*, p. 230.

72. See Waldron, *Private Property*, pp. 143–44.

73. Cf. Pufendorf, *De Jure* IV.iv.4, 5.

74. Shapiro, *Evolution of Rights*, p. 124.

75. Locke, *Essay* II.xxvii.8; cf. II.xxvii.20.

76. Ibid., II.xxvii.9, 26. Cf. Allison, "Locke's Theory of Personal Identity," p. 108.

77. Although it is not part of my purpose here to attempt to defend Locke's theory of the self, the person, and personal identity against the many criticisms that have

been raised against it, yet one must note the crucial term Locke deploys: "can," not "does."

78. *Essay* II.xxvii.9; cf. esp. II.ix.4. A different account is in Allison, pp. 108–9.

79. *Essay* II.ix. On perception and thinking, see II.i.1, II.v.2, II.viii.8. On perception as the distinctive feature separating "the animal kingdom, and the inferior parts of nature," see II.ix.11, 15.

80. Ibid., II.xxvii.26.

81. Ibid., 16, 17. See Allison, pp. 120–22, on Locke's theory in relation to Kant's concept of the transcendental unity of apperception.

82. *Essay* II.xxvii.26.

83. Ibid., 10, 14. See Allison, p. 107, on the impetus to Locke's theory in a "skepticism in regard to the nature of the soul"; also see Allison's suggestive comments on person as an "abstract idea" (p. 111).

84. *Essay* II.i.4.

85. Ibid., II.x.1, 2, 8, 10.

86. Ibid., II.xi.1, 4, 5.

87. Ibid., 6, 7; II.xii.1.

88. Ibid., II.xi.9.

89. Ibid., 10.

90. Ibid., 11; cf. IV.xvii.1–2.

91. Ibid., II.vi.2.

92. Ibid., II.xxvii.26. I have adopted Yolton's punctuation of the passages as in his edition of the *Essay* (1961).

93. Ibid., 17; cf. 9, 18, 25, 26 (beginning).

94. Ibid., II.vii.1.

95. Ibid., II.xxi.41. Locke's use of I Corinthians 2:9 in this context is revealing of his view of the Christian promise.

96. Ibid., 42, 62.

97. Ibid., 59.

98. Ibid., II.xxvii.26.

99. Ibid., 17, 18.

100. Locke's doctrine of happiness is considerably more subtle than this, however, and opens out toward other and more pluralistic possibilities for differently shaped human lives. For a brief discussion, see Zuckert, "Thomas Jefferson on Nature," pp. 161–63.

101. *Essay* II.xxvii.17, 18.

102. Ibid., II.xxvii.26.

103. Ibid., II.xxviii.5.

104. Cf. Shapiro's partly convergent and partly divergent conclusion, in *Evolution of Rights*, pp. 121–22.

105. For a discussion, see Zuckert, "Fools and Knaves," pp. 544–64.

106. The failure to sort out these "Lockean paradoxes" accounts for the frequent perception by later scholars of Locke's "confusion" or contradictions. An especially clear (but by no means uncommon) case is Shapiro, *Evolution of Rights*, pp. 102–5.

107. Dworetz, *Unvarnished Doctrine*, pp. 33–34.

108. Ibid., pp. 184–91; Parry, *John Locke*, pp. 14–15; See also Shapiro, *Evolution of Rights*, pp. 145–46.

CHAPTER TEN
LOCKE AND THE TRANSFORMATION OF WHIG POLITICAL PHILOSOPHY

1. Thompson, "Reception and Influence," p. 101.

2. Ibid., p. 107 (italics in original). Thompson cites H. T. Dickinson, J. P. Kenyon, and Julian Franklin. Also see chapter 6 of this book.

3. Ibid., p. 101.

4. Dunn, "The Politics of Locke," p. 56. Cf. Thompson: Dunn's "account exaggerates the lack of response" ("The Reception of Locke's *Two Treatises*," p. 185). Strangely enough, Thompson, too, "exaggerates the lack of response." As Jeffrey Nelson points out, he misses or depreciates many early writings in which *Two Treatises* is noted appreciatively ("Unlocking Locke's Legacy," pp. 101–8). Thompson himself notes the Lockean presence in *Political Aphorisms* (1690), in William Atwood's *Fundamental Constitution* (1690), in James Tyrell's *Bibliotheca Politica* (1692), in William Molyneux's application of Lockean principles to Ireland and Simon Clement's and John Cary's Lockean responses to Molyneux (all in 1698), and in a variety of anti-Lockeans who wrote against the *Two Treatises* in the first decade of the eighteenth century. The last is evidence the book had some weight by then.

5. Ashcraft and Goldsmith, "Locke, Revolution Principles, and the Formation of Whig Ideology," p. 774.

6. Ibid., pp. 774, 789, 793.

7. Ibid., p. 798.

8. On the debate over the historical claim about the original contract, see Pocock, *The Ancient Constitution*. On the theoretical counterattack, consider the power of Filmer's critical attack on Whig doctrines of the original contract.

9. Cf. Pangle, *Spirit of Modern Republicanism*, p. 287 n. 11; and especially Thomas Schrock, "Considering Crusoe."

10. Henry Sacheverell, *The Perils of False Brethren* (1709), quoted in Holmes, *The Trial of Doctor Sacheverell*, p. 65.

11. Ashcraft and Goldsmith, "Locke," p. 789.

12. *An Argument for Self-Defence*, pp. 277–82.

13. Ibid., p. 279.

14. See Schwoerer, *Declaration of Rights*, pp. 59–64, 71–72.

15. *Argument*, p. 280.

16. Ibid., pp. 277, 278. Cf. Locke, *Two Treatises* II 6, 7, 9, 15, 19.

17. *Argument*, p. 280; *Two Treatises* II 131.

18. *Argument*, p. 280; *Two Treatises* II 211–43.

19. Laslett, introduction to Locke, *Two Treatises*, pp. 58–79. On Locke's general caution and secretiveness, see Cranston, *John Locke*, p. xi: "Locke . . . was an extremely secretive man."

20. *Argument*, pp. 277, 278; cf. *Two Treatises* II 136, 138. Cf. Thompson ("Reception of Locke," pp. 187–88, 190): Locke's *Treatises* "were not exactly fitted to perform the task Locke intended when publishing them: the justification of the 1688 Revolution." Instead of the favored "legal and historical" arguments, Locke presented "philosophical arguments." Thompson concludes that "Locke had been led astray, as it were, by rationalist tendencies." Thompson's judgment as-

sumes, of course, that Locke's ambitions in *Two Treatises* were very limited and immediate.

21. The *Argument*'s author uses his common-law authorities in much the same way that Locke used Hooker, emphasizing partial agreements and ignoring important divergences.

22. There are known instances of people who meet these criteria and who were involved, moreover, in the Sacheverell affair. John Somers and Peter King, two Whig lawyer-politicians, who were close to Locke during the postrevolutionary period, fit all parts of this description. King, moreover, as Locke's nephew, had custody of his papers.

23. On Blackstone and Locke, see Storing, "William Blackstone," pp. 622–34.

24. Trenchard and Gordon, *Cato's Letters* 138 (4:281).

25. Charles Bechdelt Realey, "*The London Journal* and Its Authors, 1720–1723," *Bulletin of the University of Kansas* 36 no. 23, *Humanistic Studies* 5, (Dec. 1935), p. 1, quoted in Hamowy, "Cato's Letters," p. 279.

26. Testimony to Cato's later role in English thought is in Bailyn, *Ideological Origins of the American Revolution*, pp. 132, 283 n. 51; Wood, *Creation of the American Republic*, p. 16; Banning, *The Jeffersonian Persuasion*, p. 55; McDonald, "A Founding Father's Library," p. 13; Kramnick, *Republicanism and Bourgeois Radicalism*, pp. 3, 175, 181, 202–5, 228, 236. Cf. Bailyn, pp. 51–52, for limits to Cato's influence. For the publishing history of *Cato's Letters*, see Jacobson, *The English Libertarian Heritage*.

27. The forerunners were Robbins (*Eighteenth Century Commonwealthmen*, pp. 115–25) and Rossiter (*The Political Thought of the American Revolution*, p. 68).

28. Bailyn, *Ideological Origins*, pp. 33–36. Cf. Bailyn, "Central Themes of the American Revolution," pp. 7–10.

29. Bailyn, *Ideological Origins*, pp. 37, 43, 45, 59–60. On the "lifting" from Cato without attribution, also see Maier, *From Resistance to Revolution*, p. 46.

30. Pocock, *The Machiavellian Moment*, pp. 468, 507; Shalhope, "Republican Synthesis," p. 58.

31. McDonald, *Novus Ordo Seclorum*, pp. 47, 70, 77, 89, 93; Hamowy, "Cato's Letters," p. 278; Pangle, *Spirit*, p. 30. There are some recent scholars who question the importance attributed to Cato: "The claims put forward by Bailyn and others on behalf of *Cato's Letters* ... seem exaggerated" (Dworetz, *Unvarnished Doctrine*, p. 44). Dworetz relies to some degree on information presented in Lutz, *The Origins of American Constitutionalism*, pp. 142–146, and Lundberg and May, "The Enlightened Reader in America." See the prologue to this book.

32. *Letters* 38 (2:35, 43).

33. *Letters* 59 (2:221).

34. See *Letters* 128 (4:190, 192–93).

35. See *Letters* 25 (1:184–95), 132 (4:225–36).

36. See *Letters* 13 (1:83–85).

37. See *Letters* 80 (3:119–20), 94 (3:227), 128 (4:195).

38. *Letters* 132 (4:233).

39. Thus Hamowy, in "Cato's Letters," somewhat overstates the case when he finds "no appeals to the ancient constitution nor to the traditional arrangements of English law" (p. 291), but he certainly has the main point right.

40. On Cato's skepticism regarding the principles of Grotian natural law, see *Letters* 108 (4:30).

41. Hamony, p. 291. Cf. Leonard Levy, in Jacobson, *English Libertarian Heritage*, p. vii; Mayer, "English Radical Whig Origins," pp. 189–96.

42. Bailyn, *Ideological Origins*, p. 45.

43. Anyone familiar with *Cato's Letters* knows there is at least one serious difficulty with my attributing a fundamentally Lockean character to Cato's political philosophy. Cato mentions Locke, only twice, although both times in ways that suggest Locke's very great authority for him (105 [3:334], 116 [4:86]). That itself is not decisive, for reasons that should be clear by now. Cato explicitly mentions a number of other political writers, most important of whom is Algernon Sidney. He calls Sidney "an author, who can never be too much valued or read.... [He] has written better upon government than any Englishman, and as well as any foreigner" (26 [1:195]). Moreover, the motifs I identify as particularly Lockean might be argued to be found in Sidney also. Sidney is too complex a political thinker to include in this survey of seventeenth- and eighteenth-century Whig thought, but in the final analysis I think it can be shown that Cato concludes that the best polity is the one geared toward peace, and he doubts the love of glory as a motive for political good. In a word, he favors the prudence of Sancho Panza over the noble aims of Don Quixote (cf. 91 [3:233]; also 74, 93). Sidney, in his *Discourses Concerning Government*, argues for the opposite of these positions: "All governments, whether monarchical or popular, absolute or limited, deserve praise or blame as they are well or ill constituted for making war" (II.23; see also II.22). Both Sidney and Cato are much touched by Machiavelli, but Sidney stays with the Florentine a much longer way than does Cato. The latter opts for Locke's "economic" solution instead (see *Letters* 87 [3:176–84]. A full-scale comparison of Locke and Sidney is required, but that is beyond the scope of this work.

44. *Letters* 45 (2:85); see also 20 (1:131); Locke, *Two Treatises* II 4.

45. *Two Treatises* II 4; *Letters* 45 (2:85).

46. *Two Treatises* II 4; *Letters* 45 (2:85).

47. *Two Treatises* II 19; *Letters* 11 (1:66), 59 (2:218), 60 (2:227).

48. *Two Treatises* II 4; *Letters* 59 (2:216).

49. *Letters* 60 (2:226); *Two Treatises* II, chapter 8.

50. *Letters* 38 (2:35, 41)

51. Jefferson to Weightman, June 24, 1826, in *Jefferson*, p. 1517.

52. *Letters* 15–16 (1:96–111), 99–100 (3:283–300), 52 (2:135–43).

53. Ibid., 60 (2:227), 62 (2:245); cf. 59 (2:216).

54. *Two Treatises* II 131.

55. *Letters* 90 (3:201); cf. Hamowy, "Cato's Letters," pp. 293–94.

56. *Letters* 59 (2:216); cf. 60 (2:228); Locke, *Two Treatises* II 6; idem, *Letter Concerning Toleration*, pp. 26–28. Here, and occasionally elsewhere, Cato uses language reminiscent of Locke's transcendent natural law. He does so less than Locke himself does, however, and raises as many questions for that style of argument as Locke does. In a series of letters perhaps oddly included in a work on politics of this sort, Cato addresses the metaphysical issues involved in claims about divine action and legislation in the human world. The decisive essay is Letter 77 (3:89–99), in which Cato, in effect, denies the possibility, or at least the knowability, of miracles, and thus of

Creation in an argument echoing the discussions in places like Locke's *Discourse on Miracles*. Cato appears to view the theological-political problem in much the same light as Locke does.

57. *Letters* 11 (1:66), 59 (II:216).

58. Ibid., 59 (2:216), 127 (4:181).

59. Ibid., *Two Treatises* II 240.

60. *Letters* 59 (2:217–18); *Two Treatises* II 240–42. Pauline Maier (*Resistance*, p. 36 n. 13) suggests there is some difference between Cato and Locke on the appeal to Heaven, but the texts do not bear out that judgment.

61. *Letters* 59 (2:218); cf. 55 (2:169); Also Locke's *Second Treatise*, chapter 19 as a whole; Maier, pp. 27–28. Other scholars have noted important Lockean features in Cato's thought; see, for example, Pangle, *Spirit*, esp. pp. 32–33, 286 n. 7; Hamowy, "Cato's Letters"; Dworetz, *Unvarnished Doctrine*, pp. 88 (on property), 105–6 (on capitalism), 109 (on closeness to Locke in general); Dickinson, *Liberty and Property*, chapter 5. Dworetz recognizes some of the Lockean themes in Cato but makes the curious claim that Cato is not committed to the Lockean principle of "no taxation without representation" (pp. 88–89). Cato does not spill much ink on this issue, to be sure, but he writes in a different context and with a somewhat different purpose from Locke. The post-1688 constitution securely embodied the principle that only Parliament could raise taxes. "Thanks be to Heaven and our worthy ancestors . . . we have a constitution in which the people have a large share: they are one part of the legislature and have the sole power of giving money; which includes in it everything that they can ask for the publick good," *Letters* 24 (1:181). The peculiar character of Cato's concerns, as in the letter Dworetz notes, will become clear in the next section. He never steps back from his acceptance of the Lockean argument of taxation only with representation. See also *Letters* 60 (2:233), 61 (2:236–40), 70 (3:12, 14).

62. *Letters* 108 (4:24).

63. Ibid., 40 (2:51, 54, 55), 43 (2:71).

64. Ibid., 108 (4:24). For a more detailed working out of a theory of rights almost identical to Cato's, see Zuckert, "Thomas Jefferson on Nature," pp. 152–61.

65. *Letters* 62 (2:245).

66. Ibid., 108 (4:24).

67. Pocock, *Machiavellian Moment*, p. 468; Wood, *Creation*, p. 16; cf. Hamowy, "Cato's Letters," pp. 278, 281; Lienesch, *New Order of the Ages*, p. 65.

68. Steven Dworetz (*Unvarnished Doctrine*, pp. 106–7) makes much of Cato's explicit distancing of himself from the republican or commonwealth tradition. This is, of course, relevant, but Dworetz does not sufficiently consider two facts about Cato's essays. First, whatever Trenchard and Gordon's personal views might have been, it would have been impolitic in the extreme to openly proclaim themselves in favor of a republic. Second, Cato makes a very suggestive argument in Letter 85: whatever "the best government in theory" may be, the limited monarchy is the constitution best suited to English society (3:163). Some of Cato's political principles suggest that he would indeed favor a more republican constitution, in theory.

69. Pocock, *Politics, Language, and Time*, p. 85.

70. *Letters* 33 (2:255).

71. Ibid., Dedication (1:v), 40 (2:50–52), 58 (2:206), 62 (2:245, 247, 249), 77 (3:89), S 2 (4:300); Pocock, *Virtue, Commerce, and History*, p. 41.

72. *Letters* 14 (1:75), 62 (2:249–50).

73. Pocock, *Machiavellian Moment*, p. 390.

74. *Letters* 67 (2:305, 307, 308, 309).

75. Ibid., (2:307–8).

76. Wood, *Creation*, pp. 53, 58, 59, 61.

77. *Letters* 89 (3:192–93).

78. Ibid., 11 (1:66), 62 (2:245), 90 (3:200).

79. Ibid., 90 (3:199–200).

80. Ibid., 31 (1:31): "The study of human nature" leads "for the most part [to] melancholy discoveries . . . of the violent bent of human nature to evil."

81. Ibid., 105 (3:335), 60 (2:230). In general, see Burtt, *Virtue Transformed*, pp. 10–11.

82. Ibid., 39 (2:44), 40 (2:54), 44 (2:77).

83. Ibid., 40 (2:50–51). Cf. Burtt, *Virtue Transformed*, p. 73.

84. *Letters* 40 (2:51–52); Strauss, *Natural Right and History*, p. 251. Cato's presentation of the "restless and selfish spirit of man" reminds a great deal of that other early Lockean presentation of the human self, Defoe's *Robinson Crusoe*.

85. *Letters* 40 (2:55), 108 (4:30).

86. Ibid., 60 (2:231); cf. Hamilton, Madison,and Joy, *The Federalist* 51; Burtt, *Virtue Transformed*, pp. 71–73.

87. Bailyn, *Ideological Origins*, p. 47; cf. Burtt, pp. 69–70.

88. *Letters* 25 (1:184, 192), 33 (1:257).

89. Ibid., 61 (2:237).

90. Ibid., 60 (2:231), 61 (2:236).

91. See chapter 6 of this book.

92. On Pocock's civic humanist Machiavelli, see Sullivan, "Machiavelli's Momentary 'Machiavellian Moment'"; for Pocock's civic humanist Harrington, see chapter 6 n.93 of this book.

93. *Letters* 70 (3:13–14).

94. Ibid., 85 (3:163).

95. Ibid., 60 (2:232).

96. Cf. Burtt, *Virtue Transformed*, p. 81: "Cato's acceptance of Lockean premises plays a crucial role in allowing him to link the pursuit of private interest so successfully to the achievement of the public good."

97. See *Letters* 23 (1:163–77).

98. Thus Burtt goes too far when she claims that Cato "rejects" the institutional solution characteristic of Harrington (*Virtue Transformed*, p. 76).

99. *Letters* 84 (2:150).

100. See Pangle, *Spirit*, pp. 31–33.

101. *Letters* 61 (2:238). Cf. Burtt, *Virtue Transformed*, pp. 78–79.

102. Cf. Burtt, pp. 83–85.

103. *Letters* 43 (2:71).

104. See ibid., 35 (2:14).

105. Ibid. (2:13).

106. Ibid., 62 (3:249–50). Burtt's otherwise thoughtful account of Cato almost altogether omits this side of his thinking; see *Virtue Transformed*, pp. 77–86; but cf. p. 85.

107. *Letters* 62 (2:249).

108. Locke, *Two Treatises* I 1.

109. Cato thus helped bring out aspects of the Lockean doctrines similar to those emphasized by Nathan Tarcov in his important interpretation of Locke's writings on education, *Locke's Education for Liberty*.

110. Jefferson to Henry Lee, May 6, 1825, in *Jefferson*, p. 1501.

Bibliography

Aarsleff, Hans. "Some Observations on Recent Locke Scholarship." In *John Locke: Problems and Perspectives*, edited by John W. Yolton. Cambridge, 1969.

Adams, Randolph G. *Political Ideas of the American Revolution*. New York, 1939.

Agresto, John. "Liberty, Virtue, and Republicanism: 1776–1787." *Review of Politics* 39 (1977): 473–504.

Allen, J. W. *English Political Thought, 1603–1660*, vol. 1, 1603–1644. London, 1938.

Allison, Henry. "Locke's Theory of Personal Identity: A Re-Examination." In *Locke on Human Understanding*, edited by I. C. Tipton. Oxford, 1977.

Alvis, John. "Philosophy as Noblest Idolatry in *Paradise Lost*." *Interpretation* 16 (Winter 1988–89): 263–84.

Ambler, Wayne. "Aristotle's Understanding of the Naturalness of the City." *Review of Politics* 47 (1985): 163–85.

Andrew, Edward. *Shylock's Rights: A Grammar of Lockean Claims*. Toronto, 1988.

Appleby, Joyce. *Capitalism and a New Social Order: The Republican Vision of the 1790s*. New York, 1984.

———. "Republicanism and Ideology." *American Quarterly* 37 (1985): 461–73.

———. "Republicanism in Old and New Contexts." *William and Mary Quarterly*, 3d ser., 43 (1986): 20–34.

———. "The Social Origins of American Revolutionary Ideology." *Journal of American History* 64 (1978): 935–58.

An Argument for Self-Defence. In Somers, *A Collection of Scarce and Valuable Tracts, on the Most Interesting and Entertaining Subjects . . .* , vol. 10. London, 1809–15.

Aristotle. *Ethics*. Edited and translated by H. Rackham. London, 1962.

———. *Physics*. Edited and translated by P. Wicksteed and F. M. Cornford. London, 1963.

———. *Politics*. Translated by Carnes Lord. Chicago, 1984.

———. *Rhetoric*. Edited and translated by J. H. Freese. London, 1959.

Ashcraft, Richard. "Hobbes's Natural Man: A Study in Ideology Formation." *Journal of Politics* 33 (1971): 1076–1117.

———. *Locke's Two Treatises of Government*. London, 1987.

———. *Revolutionary Politics and Locke's Two Treatises of Government*. Princeton, N.J., 1986.

Ashcraft, Richard, and M. M. Goldsmith. "Locke, Revolution Principles, and the Formation of Whig Ideology." *Historical Journal* 26, no. 4 (1983): 773–800.

Atwood, William. *The Fundamental Constitution of the English Government*. London, 1690.

Augustine. *On the City of God*. Edited by David Knowles, translated by Henry Bettenson. Harmondsworth, Middlesex, 1972.

Ayers, Michael. *Locke*. 2 vols. London and New York, 1991.

Bailyn, Bernard. "The Central Themes of the American Revolution." In *Essays on the American Revolution*, edited by Stephen J. Kurtz and James H. Hutson. Chapel Hill, N.C., 1973.

Bailyn, Bernard. *The Ideological Origins of the American Revolution*. Cambridge, Mass., 1967.

Baldwin, Alice. *The New England Clergy and the American Revolution*. Durham, N.C., 1928.

Banning, Lance. "Jeffersonian Ideology Revisited." *William and Mary Quarterly*, 3d ser., 43 (1986): 3–19.

———. *The Jeffersonian Persuasion*. Ithaca, N.Y., 1978.

———. "Republican Ideology and the Triumph of the Constitution, 1789–1793." *William and Mary Quarterly*, 3d ser., 31 (1974): 167–88.

———. "Some Second Thoughts on Virtue and the Course of Revolutionary Thinking." In *Conceptual Change and the Constitution*, edited by Terence Ball and J. G. A. Pocock. Lawrence, Kans., 1988.

Barker, Arthur. *Milton and the Puritan Dilemma*. Toronto, 1942.

Becker, Carl. *The Declaration of Independence*. New York, 1942.

Bellarmine, Roberto. *De Potestate Summi Pontificis in Rebus Temporalibus*. Cologne, 1610.

Bennett, Joan. *Reviving Liberty*. Cambridge, Mass., 1989.

Berns, Walter. "John Milton." In *A History of Political Philosophy*, edited by Leo Strauss and Joseph Cropsey. Chicago, 1987.

Boorstin, Daniel. *The Genius of American Politics*. Chicago, 1953.

Bramhall, John. *Serpent Salve* (1643). In *Political Thought of the English Civil Wars*, edited by Andrew Sharp. London, 1983.

Burnet, Gilbert. "An Enquiry into the Measures of Submission to the Supream Authority" (1688). In *A Compleat Collection of Papers in Twelve Parts, Relating to the Great Revolution in England and Scotland*. London, 1689.

Burns, J. H. "The Political Ideas of George Buchanan." *Scottish Historical Review* 30 (1951): 60–68.

Burroughes, Jeremiah. *A Brief Answer to Dr. Ferne's Book* (1643). In *Political Thought of the English Civil Wars*, edited by Andrew Sharp. London, 1983.

Burtt, Shelly. *Virtue Transformed: Political Argument in England, 1688–1740*. Cambridge, 1992.

Calvin, John. *Institutes of the Christian Religion* (1559). Translated by Henry Beveridge. London, 1962.

"Cato" (John Trenchard and Thomas Gordon). *Cato's Letters: Essays on Liberty, Civil and Religious, and Other Important Subjects* (1723). 4 vols. in 2. New York, 1991.

Charles I, King of England. *His Majesties Answer to the Nineteen Propositions of Both Houses of Parliament* (1642). In *Divine Right and Democracy*, edited by David Wootton. Harmondsworth, Middlesex, 1986.

Cherniak, Warren L. *The Poet's Muse: Politics and Religion in the Works of Andrew Marvell*. Cambridge, 1983.

Chesterton, G. K. *What I Saw in America*. New York, 1922.

Cicero. *De Legibus* and *De Re Publica*. Edited and translated by C. W. Keyes. London, 1977.

Coby, Patrick. "The Law of Nature in Locke's *Second Treatise*: Is Locke a Hobbesian?" In *Political Theory*, edited by Joseph Losco and Leonard Williams. New York, 1992.

Colbourn, H. Trevor. *The Lamp of Experience*. Chapel Hill, N.C., 1965.

Conkin, Paul. Review of Steven Dworetz, *The Unvarnished Doctrine*. *William and Mary Quarterly*, 3d ser., 48 (1991): 496–99.

_____. *Self-Evident Truths*. Bloomington, Ind., 1974.

Cook, Thomas I. *History of Political Philosophy from Plato to Burke*. New York, 1937.

Cooper, J. P. "The Fall of the Stuart Monarchy." In *The New Cambridge History*, vol. 4. Cambridge, 1970.

Corpus Juris Civilis. Edited by Paul Krueger and Theodore Momsen. Berlin, 1922.

Cox, Richard. "Hugo Grotius." In *A History of Political Philosophy*, edited by Leo Strauss and Joseph Cropsey. Chicago, 1987.

_____. *Locke on War and Peace*. Oxford, 1960.

Cranston, Maurice. *John Locke: A Biography*. London, 1957.

Culverwell, Nathaniel. *An Elegant and Learned Discourse of the Light of Nature* (1652). Toronto, 1977.

Cumberland, Richard. *De Legibus Naturae*. London, 1672.

Daly, James W. "The Idea of Absolute Monarchy in Seventeenth-Century England." *Historical Journal* 21 (1978): 227–50.

_____. *Sir Robert Filmer and English Political Thought*. Toronto, 1979.

Davies, Sir John. *Le Primer Report des Cases et Matters en Ley Resolutes et Aiudges en les Courts del Roy en Ireland* (1615). In *Divine Right and Democracy*, edited by David Wootton. Harmondsworth, Middlesex, 1986.

Davis, J. C. "Pocock's Harrington: Grace, Nature, and Art in the Classical Republicanism of James Harrington." *Historical Journal* 24 (1981): 683–98.

Defoe, Daniel. "The Original Power of the Collective Body of the People of England, Examined and Asserted." In *A True Collection of the Writings of the Author of "The True Born Englishman."* London, 1703.

_____. "Reflections upon the Late Great Revolution." London, 1689.

D'Entreves, Alexander Passerin. *The Medieval Contribution to Political Thought: Thomas Aquinas, Marsilius of Padua, Richard Hooker*. Oxford, 1939.

_____. *Natural Law*. New York, 1965.

Descartes, René. *Meditations on First Philosophy* (1641). In *Philosophical Works*, edited and translated by Elizabeth S. Haldane and G. R. T. Ross. New York, 1955.

Dickinson, H. T. "How Revolutionary was the 'Glorious Revolution' of 1688?" *British Journal of Eighteenth Century Studies* (1988): 125–42.

_____. *Liberty and Property*. New York, 1977.

_____. "The Rights of Man from John Locke to Tom Paine." In *Scotland, Europe, and the American Revolution*, edited by Owen D. Edwards and George Shepperson. New York, 1977.

_____. "Whiggism in the Eighteenth Century." In *The Whig Ascendancy*, edited by John Cannon. Bungay, Suffolk, 1981.

Diggins, John P. *The Lost Soul of American Politics: Virtue, Self-Interest, and the Foundations of Liberalism*. New York, 1984.

Drury, S. B. "John Locke: Natural Law and Innate Ideas." *Dialogue* 19 (1980): 531–45.

Dunn, John. *The Political Thought of John Locke*. Cambridge, 1969.

_____. "The Politics of Locke in England and America." In *John Locke: Problems and Perspectives*, edited by John W. Yolton. Cambridge, 1969.

Dunning, William A. *A History of Political Theories from Luther to Montesquieu.* London, 1923.

Dworetz, Steven. *The Unvarnished Doctrine: Locke, Liberalism, and the American Revolution.* Durham, N.C., 1990.

Eccleshall, Robert. *Order and Reason in Politics.* Oxford, 1978.

Edwards, Charles. *Hugo Grotius, Miracle of Holland.* Chicago, 1981.

"England's Appeal to the Parliament at Oxford." London, 1681.

Farr, James, and Clayton Roberts. "John Locke and the Glorious Revolution: A Rediscovered Document." *Historical Journal* 28 (1985): 385–98.

Faulkner, Robert. "Reason and Revelation in Hooker's Ethics." *American Political Science Review* 59 (1962): 680–90.

Ferguson, Robert. "A Word to the Wise for Settling the Government." In *A Compleat Collection of Papers in Twelve Parts, Relating to the Great Revolution in England and Scotland.* London, 1689.

Ferne, Henry. *The Resolving of Conscience* (1642). In *Political Thought of the English Civil Wars,* edited by Andrew Sharp. London, 1983.

Figgis, J. N. *The Divine Right of Kings.* Cambridge, 1896.

Filmer, Sir Robert. *Patriarcha and Other Political Works.* Edited by Peter Laslett. Oxford, 1949.

Fink, Zera S. *The Classical Republicans: An Essay in the Recovery of a Pattern of Thought in Seventeenth-Century England.* Evanston, Ill., 1945.

Fortescue, Sir John. *De Laudibus Legum Angliae* (c. 1470). Edited and translated by S. B. Chrimes. Cambridge, 1942.

Foucault, Michel. *The Order of Things: An Archaeology of the Human Sciences.* New York, 1973.

Frankle, Robert J. "The Formulation of the Declaration of Rights." *Historical Journal* 17 (1974): 265–79.

Franklin, Julian. *John Locke and the Theory of Sovereignty.* Cambridge, 1978.

Friedrich, Carl. *Inevitable Peace.* Cambridge, 1948.

Furley, O. W. "The Whig Exclusionists: Pamphlet Literature in the Exclusion Campaign, 1679–81." *Cambridge Historical Journal* 13 (1957): 19–36.

Gardiner, Samuel Rawlinson. *The First Two Stuarts and the Puritan Revolution.* New York, 1970.

Goldie, Mark. "The Revolution of 1689 and the Structure of Political Argument." *Bulletin of Research in the Humanities* 83 (1980): 473–564.

———. "The Roots of True Whiggism, 1688–94." *History of Political Thought* 1 (June 1980): 195–236.

Goldwin, Robert A. "John Locke." In *A History of Political Philosophy,* edited by Leo Strauss and Joseph Cropsey. Chicago, 1987.

Goodale, J. F. "J. G. A. Pocock's Neo-Harringtonians: A Reconsideration." *History of Political Thought* 1 (June 1980): 237–60.

Gough, J. W. *Fundamental Law in English Constitutional History.* Oxford, 1955.

———. *The Social Contract.* Oxford, 1957.

Grant, Ruth. *John Locke's Liberalism.* Chicago, 1987.

Greene, Jack P. "The Ostensible Cause Was . . . the True One: The Salience of Rights in the Origins of the American Revolution." *Reviews in American History* 16 (June 1988): 198–203.

Greenstone, J. David. "Against Simplicity: The Cultural Dimensions of the Constitution." *University of Chicago Law Review* 55 (1988): 428–49.

Grotius, Hugo. *De Jure Belli ac Pacis Libri Tres* (1625). Classics of International Law, 3, James Brown Scott, general ed. 2 vols. Vol. 1, Latin text, facsimile of 1646 ed.; vol. 2, English text, translated by Francis W. Kelsey et al. Washington, D.C., 1913 (vol. 1); Oxford, 1925 (vol. 2).

Haley, K. H. D. *The First Earl of Shaftesbury.* Oxford, 1968.

Hamilton, Alexander, James Madison, and John Jay. *The Federalist* (1788). Edited by Clinton Rossiter. New York, 1961.

Hamowy, Ronald. "*Cato's Letters*, John Locke and the Republican Paradigm." *History of Political Thought* 11 (Summer 1990): 273–94.

_____. "Jefferson and the Scottish Enlightenment." *William and Mary Quarterly*, 3d ser., 31 (1979): 503–23.

Hampden, John. "Some Short Considerations Concerning the State of the Nation," (1692). In Cobbett's *Parliamentary History of England*, vol. 5, appendix 7. London, 1808.

Hampton, Jean D. *Hobbes and the Social Contract Tradition.* Cambridge, 1986.

Hancock, Ralph. *Calvin and the Foundations of Modern Politics.* Ithaca, N.Y., 1989.

Hancy, James O. "John Locke and the Law of Nature." *Political Theory* 4 (Nov. 1976): 439–54.

Handlin, Oscar. "Learned Books and Revolutionary Action, 1776." *Harvard Library Bulletin* 34 (1986): 362–79.

Handlin, Oscar and Lilian. *Liberty and Expansion, 1766–1850.* New York, 1989.

Hearnshaw, F. J. C. *Some Great Political Idealists.* Freeport, N.Y., 1970.

Heidegger, Martin. *Nietzsche.* 4 vols. Translated by David Krell. San Francisco, 1979.

_____. "The Question Concerning Technology." In *The Question Concerning Technology and Other Essays*, translated and edited by William Lovitt. New York, 1977.

Herle, Charles. *An Answer to Dr. Ferne's Reply* (1643) and *A Fuller Answer to a Treatise Written by Dr. Ferne* (1643). In *Political Thought of the English Civil Wars*, edited by Andrew Sharp. London, 1983.

Hill, Christopher. *Milton and the English Revolution.* Harmondsworth, Middlesex, 1979.

Hobbes, Thomas. *Leviathan* (1651). Edited by Richard Tuck. Cambridge, 1991.

Hoffer, Peter Charles. *Revolution and Regeneration.* Athens, Ga., 1983.

Holmes, Geoffrey. *The Trial of Henry Sacheverell.* London, 1973.

Holton, James E. "Cicero." In *A History of Political Philosophy*, edited by Leo Strauss and Joseph Cropsey. Chicago, 1987.

"An Homily against Disobedience and Wylful Rebellion" (1570). In *Divine Right and Democracy*, edited by David Wootton. Harmondsworth, Middlesex, 1986.

Hooker, Richard. *Of the Laws of Ecclesiastical Polity* (1593). Edited by Christopher Morris. London, 1907.

Höpfl, Harro and Martyn P. Thompson. "The History of Contract as a Motif in Political Thought." *American Historical Review* 84 (1979): 919–44.

Horwitz, H. "Protestant Reconciliation in the Exclusion Crisis." *Journal of Ecclesiastical History* 15 (1964): 201–17.

Horwitz, Robert. "John Locke's *Questions Concerning the Law of Nature*: A Commentary." *Interpretation* 19 (Spring 1992): 251–306.

Horwitz, Robert. *The Moral Foundations of the American Republic*. Charlottesville, Va., 1987.

Hume, David. *An Enquiry Concerning the Principles of Morals* (1752). Edited by P. H. Nidditch. Oxford, 1975.

———. *The History of England* (1754). Indianapolis, 1984.

Humphrey, John, attributed. "Good Advice Before It Be Too Late." In *The Revolution of 1688 and the Birth of the English Political Nation*, edited by Gerald M. Straka. Lexington, Mass., 1973.

Hunt, Thomas. "An Answer to a Pamphlet Lately Published, Entitled A Letter from a Gentleman of Quality in the Country to His Friend, etc." London, 1681.

———. "A Word without Doors Concerning the Bill for Succession." London, n.d.

[Hunt, Thomas.] "*The Great and Weighty Considerations*, etc. Considered." London, 1680.

Hunton, Philip. *A Treatise of Monarchy* (1643). In *Divine Right and Democracy*, edited by David Wootton. Harmondsworth, Middlesex, 1986.

Ingber, Leon. "The Tradition of Grotius and Human Rights." In *Reason in Law*, edited by Carla Farelli and Enrico Pattaro. Milan, 1987.

Jacobson, David, ed. *The English Libertarian Heritage*. Indianapolis, 1965.

Jaffa, Harry V. "Inventing the Past." In *American Conservatism and the American Founding*. Durham, N.C., 1984.

James I, King of England (James VI of Scotland). *The Political Works of James I*. Edited by Charles H. McIlwain. Cambridge, Mass., 1918.

Jefferson, Thomas. *Jefferson*. Edited by Merrill Peterson. New York, 1984.

———. *Life and Selected Writings*. Edited by Adrienne Koch and William Peden. New York, 1944.

Johnson, Richard R. "Politics Redefined: An Assessment of Recent Writings on the Late Stuart Period of English History, 1660 to 1714." *William and Mary Quarterly*, 3d ser., 35 (1978): 691–732.

Jones, J. R. *The First Whigs: The Politics of the Exclusion Crisis, 1678–1683*. London, 1961.

———. *The Revolution of 1688 in England*. London, 1972.

Kantorowicz, Ernst H. *The King's Two Bodies*. Princeton, N.J., 1957.

Kenyon, J. P. *Revolution Principles: The Politics of Party, 1689–1720*. Cambridge, 1977.

———. "The Revolution of 1688: Resistance and Contract." In *Historical Perspectives: Studies in English Thought and Society in Honour of J. H. Plumb*, edited by Neil McKendrick. London, 1974.

———. *The Stuart Constitution, 1603–1688*. Cambridge, 1966.

———. *Stuart England*. Harmondsworth, Middlesex, 1978.

Kerber, Linda K. "The Republican Ideology of the Revolutionary Generation." *American Quarterly* 37 (Fall 1985): 474–95.

Koch, Adrienne. *Power, Morals, and the Founding Fathers*. Ithaca, N.Y., 1961.

Kramnick, Isaac. *Republicanism and Bourgeois Radicalism*. Ithaca, N.Y., 1990.

Lactantius. *The Divine Institutes*. Translated by Sister Mary Evan McDonald, O.P. Washington, D.C., 1964.

Lee, R. W. *Elements of Roman Law*. London, 1956.

———. *Hugo Grotius*. Oxford, 1930.

Lehrberger, James. "Crime without Punishment: Thomistic Natural Law and the Problem of Sanctions." In *Law and Philosophy: The Practice of Theory*, edited by John A. Murley, Robert L. Stone, and William T. Braithwaite, vol. 1. Athens, Ohio, 1992.

Lemnos, Ramon. "Two Concepts of Natural Right." *Southern Journal of Philosophy* 12 (1974).

Lerner, Ralph. *The Thinking Revolutionary*. Ithaca, N.Y., 1987.

"A Letter from a Gentleman of Quality in the Country to His Friend, upon His Being Chosen a Member to Serve in the Approaching Parliament." London, 1681.

"A Letter from a Parliament-man to His Friend" (1675). In Cobbett's *Parliamentary History of England*, vol. 4. London, 1808.

"A Letter to a Friend in the Country: Being a Vindication of the Parliament's Whole Proceedings This Last Session." London, 1681.

Lewis, Ewart. "The Contribution of Medieval Thought to the American Political Tradition." *American Political Science Review* 50 (1956): 462–74.

Lienesch, Michael. *The New Order of the Ages: Time, the Constitution, and the Making of Modern American Political Thought*. Princeton, N.J., 1988.

Lindahl, William C. *A Critical Commentary on John Locke's Essays on the Law of Nature*. Ph.D. diss., University of Dallas, 1986.

Lipset, Seymour Martin. *The First New Nation: The United States in Historical and Comparative Perspective*. New York, 1963.

Locke, John. *The Correspondence of John Locke*. Edited by Edmund S. de Beer. Oxford, 1989.

———. *The Educational Writings of John Locke*. Edited by James Axtell. Cambridge, 1968.

———. *An Essay Concerning Human Understanding* (4th ed., 1700). Edited by Peter H. Nidditch. Oxford, 1990.

———. *An Essay Concerning Human Understanding* (4th ed., 1700). Edited by John W. Yolton. New York, 1967.

———. *Essays on the Law of Nature* (1664). Edited by W. von Leyden. Oxford, 1954 (first publication).

———. *A Letter on Toleration* (1689). Indianapolis, 1983.

———. *Questions Concerning the Law of Nature* (1664). Edited by Robert Horwitz, Jenny Strauss Clay, and Diskin Clay. Ithaca, N.Y., 1990.

———. *The Reasonableness of Christianity* (1692). Edited by George W. Ewing. Chicago, 1965.

———. *Two Treatises of Government* (1690). Edited by Peter Laslett. Cambridge, 1960.

Lundberg, David, and Henry F. May. "The Enlightened Reader in America." *American Quarterly* 28 (1976): 262–71.

Lutz, Donald. "Bernard Bailyn, Gordon S. Wood, and Whig Political Theory." *Political Science Reviewer* 7 (1977): 111–42.

———. *The Origins of American Constitutionalism*. Baton Rouge, La., 1988.

Lynn, Kenneth. "Falsifying Jefferson." *Commentary* 66 (Oct. 1978): 66–71.

Machiavelli, Niccolò. *Discourses on the First Ten Books of Titus Livy* (1532). Edited by Bernard Crick, translated by Leslie J. Walker. Harmondsworth, Middlesex, 1970.

Macpherson, C. B. *The Political Theory of Possessive Individualism: From Hobbes to Locke*. Oxford, 1962.

Maier, Pauline. *From Resistance to Revolution*. New York, 1972.

Manent, Pierre. *Histoire intellectuelle du liberalisme*. Paris, 1987.

Mansfield, Harvey, Jr. *Taming the Prince: The Ambivalence of Modern Executive Power*. New York, 1989.

Manwaring, Robert. "A Sermon Preached before the King at Oatlands" (1647). In *The Stuart Constitution, 1603–1688*, edited by J. P. Kenyon. Cambridge, 1966.

Marsilius of Padua. *Defensor Pacis* (1324). Toronto, 1980.

Marvell, Andrew. *An Account of the Growth of Popery and Arbitrary Government* (1678). In *Complete Works*, edited by A. B. Grosart. London, 1875.

Matthews, Richard. *The Radical Politics of Thomas Jefferson*. Lawrence, Kans., 1984.

Maxwell, John. *Sacro-Sancta Regum Majestas* (1644). In *Political Thought of the English Civil Wars*, edited by Andrew Sharp. London, 1983.

Mayer, David N. "The English Radical Whig Origins of American Constitutionalism." *Washington University Law Quarterly* 70 (1992): 131–208.

McDonald, Forrest. "A Founding Father's Library." In *Literature of Liberty*. Ithaca, N.Y., 1978.

———. *Novus Ordo Seclorum*. Lawrence, Kansas, 1985.

Miller, John. "The Glorious Revolution: 'Contract' and 'Abdication' Reconsidered." *Historical Journal* 25 (1982): 541–55.

Miller, Perry. *The New England Mind: From Colony to Province*. Cambridge, 1953.

Milton, John. *The Doctrine and Discipline of Divorce* (1643). In *Complete Prose Works*, edited by Ernest Sirluck, vol. 2. New Haven, 1959.

———. *Eikonoklastes* (1649). In *Prose Writings*, edited by K. M. Burton. London and New York, 1958.

———. *Of Reformation in England and the Causes That Hitherto Have Hindered It* (1641). In *Prose Writings*, edited by K. M. Burton. London and New York, 1958.

———. *On Christian Doctrine*. In *Complete Prose Works of John Milton*, vol. 6, translated by John Carey, edited by Maurice Kelley. New Haven and London, 1973.

———. *Paradise Lost* (1667) and *Paradise Regained* (1671). In *Complete Poems and Major Prose*, edited by Merrit Y. Hughes. New York, 1957.

———. *The Ready and Easy Way* (1660). In *Complete Poems and Major Prose*, edited by Merrit Y. Hughes. New York, 1957.

———. *The Reason of Church Government* (1642). In *Complete Poems and Major Prose*, edited by Merrit Y. Hughes. New York, 1957.

———. *Second Defense of the People of England* (1654). In *Complete Poems and Major Prose*, edited by Merrit Y. Hughes. New York, 1957.

———. *The Tenure of Kings and Magistrates* (1649). In *Complete Poems and Major Prose*, edited by Merrit Y. Hughes. New York, 1957.

Montaigne, Michel de. "Of Custom and Not Easily Changing an Accepted Law." In *The Complete Essays of Montaigne*, translated by Donald M. Frame. Stanford, 1965.

Montesquieu, Charles Secondat, Baron. *On the Spirit of the Laws* (1748). Edited and translated by Anne M. Cohler, Basia Carolyn Miller, and Harold Summel Stone. Cambridge, 1989.

Morgan, Edmund S. *Inventing the People*. New York, 1988.

Mornay, Phillippe du Plessis, attributed. *Vindiciae Contra Tyrannos* (1579). In *Constitutionalism and Resistance in the Sixteenth Century*, edited by Julian Franklin. New York, 1969.

Munz, Peter. *The Place of Hooker in the History of Thought*. London, 1952.

Nelson, Jeffrey M. "Unlocking Locke's Legacy: A Comment." *Political Studies* 26 (1978): 101–8.

Nenner, Howard. "Constitutional Uncertainty." In *After the Reformation*, edited by Barbara Malament. Philadelphia, 1980.

Newlin, Claude M. *Philosophy and Religion in Colonial America*. New York, 1962.

Nietzsche, Friedrich. *Morgenrote* (1881). In *Werke in Drei Banden*, edited by Karl Schlechta, vol. 1. Munich, 1963.

Oakeshott, Michael. *On History and Other Essays*. New York, 1983.

Oakley, Francis. "On the Road from Constance to 1688: The Political Thought of John Major and George Buchanan." *Journal of British Studies* 2 (1962): 1–31.

O'Brien, David. "The Framer's Muse on Republicanism, the Supreme Court, and Pragmatic Constitutional Interpretivism." *Constitutional Commentary* 8 (Winter 1991): 119–48.

Onuf, Peter. "Reflections on the Founding." *William and Mary Quarterly*, 3d ser., 46 (1989): 341–75.

Palmer, Herbert. *Scripture and Reason Pleaded for Defensive Arms* (1643). In *Political Thought of the English Civil Wars*, edited by Andrew Sharp. London, 1983.

Pangle, Thomas. *The Spirit of Modern Republicanism: The Moral Vision of the American Founders and the Philosophy of Locke*. Chicago, 1988.

Parker, Henry. *Observations upon Some of His Majesty's Late Answers and Expresses*. London, 1642.

———. "Some Few Observations upon His Majesties Late Answer to a Declaration . . ." (1642). In *Political Thought of the English Civil Wars*, edited by Andrew Sharp. London, 1983.

———. *The True Grounds of Ecclesiastical Government*. London, 1641.

Parry, Geraint. *John Locke*. London, 1978.

Patterson, Annabel. *Marvell and the Civic Crown*. Princeton, N.J., 1978.

"Percat Papa; or, Reasons Why a Presumptive Heir or Popish Successor Should Not Inherit the Crown." London, n.d.

Plato. *Republic*. Translated by Allan Bloom. New York, 1991.

Plumb, J. L. *The Origins of Political Stability in England, 1695–1795*. New York, 1967.

Pocock, J. G. A. *The Ancient Constitution and the Feudal Law*. New York, 1967.

———. "Between Gog and Magog: The Republican Thesis and the *Ideologica Americana*." *Journal of the History of Ideas* 68 (1987): 325–46.

———. "The Fourth English Civil War." *Government and Opposition* 23 (1988): 151–66.

———. Introduction to *The Political Works of James Harrington*. Cambridge, 1977.

———. *The Machiavellian Moment*. Princeton, N.J., 1975.

———. "*The Machiavellian Moment* Revisited: A Study in History and Ideology." *Journal of Modern History* 3 (1981): 49–72.

———. "The Myth of John Locke and the Obsession with Liberalism." In *John Locke*, edited by J. G. A. Pocock and Richard Ashcraft. Los Angeles, 1980.

Pocock, J. G. A. *Politics, Language, and Time.* London, 1972.
———, ed. *Three British Revolutions: 1641, 1688, 1776.* Princeton, N.J., 1980.
———. "Virtue and Commerce in the Eighteenth Century." *Journal of Interdisciplinary History* 3 (1972): 119–34.
———. *Virtue, Commerce, and History.* Cambridge, 1985.
Polin, Raymond. *La politique morale de John Locke.* Paris, 1960.
Pollingue, Mary. "An Interpretation of Fortescue's *De Laudibus Legum Angliae.*" *Interpretation* 6 (1976): 11–47.
Proietti, Pamela. "Natural Right(s) and Natural Law: John Locke and the Scholastic Tradition." In *Law and Philosophy: The Practice of Theory,* edited by John A. Murley, Robert L. Stone, and William A. Braithwaite. Athens, Ohio, 1992.
Prynne, William. "The Sovereign Power of Parliaments and Kingdomes." London, 1643.
Pufendorf, Samuel. *De Jure Naturae et Gentium Libri Octo* (1672). Classics of International Law, 17, James Brown Scott, general ed. 2 vols. Vol. 1, Latin text, facsimile of 1688 ed.; vol. 2, English text, translated by C. H. and W. A. Oldfather. Oxford, 1934.
———. *Elementorum Jurisprudentiae Universalis Libri Duo* (1660). Classics of International Law, 15, James Brown Scott, general ed. Vol. 1, Latin text, facsimile of 1672 ed.; vol. 2, English text, translated by W. A. Oldfather. Oxford, 1931.
Riley, Patrick. "How Coherent is the Social Contract Tradition?" *Journal of the History of Ideas* 34 (1973): 543–62.
Robbins, Caroline. *The Eighteenth-Century Commonwealthmen.* New York, 1968.
Roger, Ilu Clement. *Political Philosophy of the Blessed Cardinal Bellarmine.* Washington, D.C., 1926.
Ross, Dorothy. "The Liberal Tradition Revisited and the Republican Tradition Addressed." In *New Directions in American Intellectual History,* edited by John Higham and Paul Conkin. Baltimore, 1979.
Rossiter, Clinton. *Political Thought of the American Revolution.* New York, 1963.
Sabine, George H. *A History of Political Theory.* New York, 1937.
St. Leger, James. *The "Etiamsi Daremus" of Hugo Grotius.* Rome, 1962.
Sanderson, John. *"But the People's Creatures": The Philosophical Basis of the English Civil War.* Manchester, 1989.
Schaeffer, David. *The Political Philosophy of Montaigne.* Ithaca, N.Y., 1990.
Schmitt, Gary, and Robert Webking. "Revolutionaries, Anti-Federalists, and Federalists: Comments on Gordon Wood's Understanding of the American Founding." *Political Science Review* 9 (1979): 195–229.
Schochet, Gordon. *Patriarchalism in Political Thought.* New York, 1975.
Schrock, Thomas. "Considering Crusoe." *Interpretation* 1 (1970): 76–106, 169–232.
Schulz, Fritz. *Geschichte der romischer Rechts-Wissenschaft.* Weimar, 1961.
Schwoerer, Lois J. "The Contribution of the Declaration of Rights to Anglo-American Radicalism." In *The Origins of Anglo-American Radicalism,* edited by Margaret Jacob and James Jacob. London, 1984.
———. *The Declaration of Rights, 1689.* Baltimore, 1981.
———. *"No Standing Armies!" The Anti-Army Ideology in Seventeenth-Century England.* Baltimore, 1974.

Seliger, M. *The Liberal Politics of John Locke*. New York, 1967.

Sexbie, Edward. *Killing Noe Murder* (1657). In *Divine Right and Democracy*, edited by David Wootton. Harmondsworth, Middlesex, 1986.

Shaftesbury, Anthony Ashley Cooper, first earl of, attributed. "A Letter from a Person of Quality to His Friend in the Country" (1675). In Cobbett's *Parliamentary History of England*, vol. 4. London, 1808.

Shalhope, Robert E. "Republicanism and Early American Historiography." *William and Mary Quarterly*, 3d ser., 39 (1982): 334–56.

——. "Toward a Republican Synthesis: The Emergence of an Understanding of Republicanism in American Historiography." *William and Mary Quarterly*, 3d ser., 29 (1972): 49–80.

Shapiro, Ian. *The Evolution of Rights in Liberal Theory*. Cambridge, 1986.

Sharp, Andrew, ed. *Political Thought of the English Civil Wars*. London, 1983.

Sheldon, Garrett Ward. *The Political Philosophy of Thomas Jefferson*. Baltimore, 1991.

Sherry, Suzanna. "The Intellectual Origins of the Constitution: A Lawyer's Guide to Contemporary Historical Scholarship." *Constitutional Commentary* 5 (1988): 323–47.

Sidney, Algernon. *Discourses Concerning Government* (1698). Edited by Thomas G. West. Indianapolis, 1990.

Sigmund, Paul. *Natural Law in Political Thought*. Cambridge, Mass., 1971.

Simmons, A. John. "Inalienable Rights and Locke's *Treatises*." *Philosophy and Public Affairs* 12 (1983): 175–204.

Simon, Yves R. *The Tradition of Natural Law*. New York, 1965.

Singh, Raghnveer. "John Locke and the Theory of Natural Law." *Political Studies* 9 (1961): 105–18.

Skinner, Quentin. *The Foundations of Modern Political Thought*. 2 vols. Cambridge, 1978.

——. "History and Ideology in the English Revolution." *Historical Journal* 8 (1965): 151–78.

Slaughter, Thomas P. "'Abdicate' and 'Contract' in the Glorious Revolution." *Historical Journal* 24 (1981): 323–38.

——. "'Abdicate' and 'Contract' Restored." *Historical Journal* 28 (1985): 399–403.

[Somers, John, collection.] *A Collection of Scarce and Valuable Tracts, on the Most Interesting and Entertaining Subjects . . . Selected from an Infinite Number in . . . Public as Well as Private Libraries, Particularly That of the Late Lord Somers*. 2d rev. ed., edited by Walter Scott. 13 vols. London, 1809–15.

Spelman, John. *The Case of Our Affaires* (1643). In *Political Thought of the English Civil Wars*, edited by Andrew Sharp. London, 1983.

State Tracts in Two Parts: Several Treatises Relating to the Government, Privately Printed in the Reign of King Charles II . . . from 1660–1689. London, 1693.

Stone, Laurence. *The Causes of the English Revolution*. New York, 1972.

Storing, Herbert J. "William Blackstone." In *A History of Political Philosophy*, edited by Leo Strauss and Joseph Cropsey. Chicago, 1987.

Straka, Gerald M. *Anglican Reaction to the Revolution of 1688*. Madison, Wis., 1962.

——. "The Nation Contemplates Its Revolution, 1689–1789." In *The Revolution of 1688 and the Birth of the English Political Nation*, edited by Gerald M. Straka. Lexington, Mass., 1973.

Strauss, Leo. *Liberalism, Ancient and Modern*. New York, 1968.

———. "Locke's Doctrine of Natural Law." In *What is Political Philosophy? and Other Studies*. Glencoe, Ill., 1959.

———. "Marsilius of Padua." In *A History of Political Philosophy*, edited by Leo Strauss and Joseph Cropsey. Chicago, 1987.

———. *Natural Right and History*. Chicago, 1953.

———. *The Rebirth of Classical Political Rationalism*. Chicago, 1989.

———. *Studies in Platonic Political Philosophy*. Chicago and London, 1983.

Suárez, Francisco. *Selections from Three Works: De Legibus, ac Deo Legislatore* (1612); *Defensio Fidei Catholicae et Apostolicae Adversus Anglicanae Sectae Errores* (1613); *Opus de Triplici Virtute Theologico: Fide, Spe, et Charitate* (1621). Classics of International Law, 20, James Brown Scott, general ed. Vol. 1, Latin text, facsimiles from original eds.; vol. 2, English texts, translated by Gwladys L. Williams, Ammi Brown, and John Waldron. Oxford, 1944.

Sullivan, Vickie B. "Machiavelli's Momentary 'Machiavellian Moment': A Reconsideration of Pocock's Treatment of the *Discourses*." *Political Theory* 20 (May 1992): 309–18.

Tarcov, Nathan. *Locke's Education for Liberty*. Chicago, 1984.

Tate, Thad W. "The Social Contract in America, 1774–1787: Revolutionary Theory as a Conservative Instrument." *William and Mary Quarterly*, 3d ser., 22 (1965): 375–91.

Tawney, R. H. "Harrington's Interpretation of His Age." *Proceedings of the British Academy* 27 (1941).

Thomas Aquinas. *De Regimine Principium*. In *The Political Ideas of Thomas Aquinas*, edited by Dino Bigongiari. New York, 1953.

———. *Summa Theologica*. Translated by Fathers of the English Dominican Province. New York, 1947.

Thompson, Martyn P. "Reception and Influence: A Reply to Nelson on Locke's *Two Treatises of Government*." *Political Studies* 28 (1980): 184–91.

———. "The Reception of Locke's *Two Treatises of Government*, 1690–1705." *Political Studies* 24 (1976): 184–91.

Thompson, W. D. J. Cargill. "The Philosophy of the 'Politic Society': Richard Hooker as a Political Thinker." In *Studies in Richard Hooker*, edited by W. Speed Hill. Cleveland, 1972.

Tierney, Brian. "Origins of Natural Rights Language: Texts and Contexts, 1150–1250." *History of Political Thought* 10 (1989): 615–46.

Tillyard, E. M. *The Elizabethan World Picture*. London, 1943.

Tocqueville, Alexis de. *Democracy in America* (1835). Edited by J. P. Mayer, translated by George Lawrence. Garden City, N.Y., 1969.

Tuck, Richard. *Natural Rights Theories*. Cambridge, 1979.

Tully, James. *A Discourse on Property*. Cambridge, 1980.

Tyndale, William. *The Obedience of a Christian Man*. Antwerp, 1528.

Villey, Michel. *Leçons d'histoire de la philosophie du droit*. Paris, 1962.

———. *Seize essais de la philosophie du droit*. Paris, 1969.

"Vox Populi; or, The People's Claim to Their Parliament Sitting, to Redress Grievances, and to Provide for the Common Safety, By the Known Laws and Constitutions of the Nation." London, 1681.

Waldron, Jeremy. *The Right to Private Property.* Oxford, 1988.

Wallace, John. *Destiny His Choice: The Loyalism of Andrew Marvell.* Cambridge, 1968.

Walzer, Michael. *Revolution of the Saints.* Cambridge, Mass., 1965.

Webking, Robert. *The American Revolution.* Baton Rouge, La., 1989.

Western, J. R. *Monarchy and Revolution.* London, 1972.

Weston, Corinne. "The Theory of Mixed Monarchy under Charles I and After." *English Historical Review* 75 (July 1960): 426–43.

White, Morton. *The Philosophy of the American Revolution.* New York, 1981.

Wildman, John, attributed. "A Letter to a Friend Advising in This Extraordinary Juncture, How to Free the Nation from Slavery for Ever." In A *Compleat Collection of Papers in Twelve Parts, Relating to the Great Revolution in England and Scotland.* London, 1689.

Williams, Elisha. "The Essential Rights and Liberties of Protestants" (1744). In *Political Sermons of the American Founding Era, 1730–1865,* edited by Elis Sandoz. Indianapolis, 1991.

Wills, Garry. *Inventing America.* Garden City, N.Y., 1978.

Wolfe, Don M. *Milton in the Puritan Revolution.* New York, 1941.

Wood, Gordon S. *The Creation of the American Republic, 1776–1787.* Chapel Hill, N.C., 1969.

———. "Ideology and the Origins of Liberal America." *William and Mary Quarterly,* 3d ser., 44 (1987): 628–40.

———. "Illusions and Disillusions in the American Revolution." In *The American Revolution,* edited by Jack Greene. New York, 1982.

———. "The Intellectual Origins of the American Constitution." *National Forum* 64 (1984): 5–8, 13.

Wootton, David, ed. *Divine Right and Democracy.* Harmondsworth, Middlesex, 1986.

Yolton, John. *Locke and the Compass of Human Understanding.* Cambridge, 1970.

———. "Locke on the Law of Nature." *Philosophical Review* 68 (1958): 477–98.

Zagorin, Perez. A *History of Political Thought in the English Revolution.* London, 1954.

Zuckert, Catherine H. "Aristotle on the Limits and Satisfactions of Political Life." *Interpretation* 11 (1983): 185–206.

Zuckert, Michael P. "Appropriation and Understanding in the History of Political Philosophy: On Quentin Skinner's Method." *Interpretation* 13 (1985): 403–24.

———. "Bringing Philosophy Down from the Heavens: Natural Right in Roman Law." *Review of Politics* 51 (Winter 1989): 70–85.

———. "Fools and Knaves: Reflections on Locke's Theory of Philosophical Discourse." *Review of Politics* 36 (1974): 544–64.

———. "An Introduction to Locke's *First Treatise.*" *Interpretation* 8 (1979): 58–74.

———. "Locke and the Problem of Civil Religion." In *The Moral Foundations of the American Republic,* 3d ed., edited by Robert Horwitz. Charlottesville, Va., 1986.

Zuckert, Michael P. "Of Wary Physicians and Weary Readers: The Debates on Locke's Way of Writing." *Independent Journal of Philosophy* 2 (Fall 1977): 55–66.

———. "The Recent Literature on Locke's Political Philosophy." *Political Science Reviewer* 5 (1975): 271–304.

———. "Thomas Jefferson on Nature and Natural Rights." In *The Framers and Fundamental Rights*, edited by Robert Licht. Washington, D.C., 1992.

Index

Aarsleff, Hans, 222

Abravenal, 119

Absolutism: Cato's rejection of, 299, 303, 307, 313–14; and divine right theory, 32, 38, 42; and Grotianism, 110, 258; in Hobbes, 274, 276; Lockean rejection of, 218, 233, 244–46, 276, 294, 296; in Parliamentary theory, 51–52, 68, 70, 75, 100; and Suárez, 125; Whig opposition to, 97–98, 103, 116, 172–79, 182, 307, 313–14

Adam, 43–47, 83–92, 217, 219–20, 251, 261–62, 268

Adams, John, 4, 16, 22, 24, 61, 152, 170

Allan, J. W., 59, 63, 67, 73

Almain, Jaques, 222

American Revolution, xiii, xv, 4, 15, 20–25, 152, 158, 162

Ames, Nathanial, 23

Ancient Constitution: assimilation to original contract, 107, 120; Cato's indifference to, 303; inadequacy of, 56–63, 72, 77, 168–69; Locke's indifference to, 295; Parliamentary commitment to, 13, 32, 49–56, 100, 117; Whig commitment to, 173, 178, 182

Anne (Queen of England), 292

Answer to the Nineteen Propositions of Both Houses of Parliament, 59–63, 66, 71–72. See also Mixed Constitution

Appleby, Joyce, 150, 156

Appropriation: Locke and Grotian theories of, 257; Locke on labor and, 254, 265, 270–72, 319; Locke on limits of, 219, 255–57, 266–70; Locke on rights to, 258, 260, 267, 277–78; Locke on the self and, 283–86, 314

Aristotle, 106, 146; and divine right theory, 35–39, 41, 45; and Grotius, xvii, 119, 123, 125, 136, 138–39, 142–43, 145, 149, 194; and Hobbes, xviii, 143; and Hunton, 67, 69, 75; and Locke, 17, 193–94, 196–97, 282, 287; and Milton, 92–93; on naturalness of polity, 13, 17, 36, 45, 63, 67, 136, 138, 155, 160, 203, 223–24, 228, 301, 306,

313; and "old republicanism," 155, 159–62, 166–68, 170, 272, 306; and Parker's contractarianism, 71–73, 75; and theory of ancient constitution, 53–56, 60, 63, 67; and traditional English thought, xv, 49–50, 75, 92–93, 149; and virtues, 41, 69, 138–39, 142, 203, 304; Politics, xv, 17, 53, 61, Rhetoric, 129

Argument for Self-Defense, An, 291–97

Artifice, Government as (artifact): absence in parliamentary and Whig theory, 56, 71, 105, 108–9; in Cato, 301–2, 308; in Declaration of Independence, 3, 6, 10, 12–13, 157; in Locke, 16, 17, 224

Ashcraft, Richard, 104, 256, 290

Atwood, William, 117–18

Augustine, 229

Azor, 126

Bacon, Francis, 23, 203

Bailyn, Bernard: on Locke's influence in America, 21, 152–54; and the republican synthesis, 151–59, 163–65, 182–83, 298, 307, 311–13; and Whig tradition, 24, 182–83, 295, 307

Balance (Constitutional), 61, 72–73, 75, 161, 166, 168–69, 307

Baldwin, Alice, 21–22

Barker, Ernest, 64

Barlow, Joel, 4

Bartolus, 119

Bate's Case (1606), 51, 57

Baxter, Richard, 30

Beard, Charles, 158

Bellarmine, Roberto, xvii, 119–20, 125–26, 226

Blackstone, William, 296

Bodin, Jean, 119

Bracton, Henry de, 300

Burgh, James, 163, 298

Burnet, Gilbert, 79, 87, 106–18, 146

Calvin, John, 47, 49, 121

Carneades: critique of natural right, 127–28, 144, 146, 191, 212; Grotius's response to,

Carneades (*cont.*)
134–36, 139, 146–48; Locke's response to, 212–13; Roman lawyer's response to, 131–32, 134–35, 144

Catholicism (Popery, Roman Church, Romanism): and contractarianism, 42–43; and natural law philosophy, 119, 138, 224, 228; and religious conflicts of the age, xvi, 93, 97, 100, 121, 123, 292; Whig opposition to, 100, 102–3, 179–80

Cato: influence in America, 20, 152, 183; as Lockean, 31, 297–305; and "new republicanism," xix–xx, 166, 182–83, 312–19; and "old republicanism," 305–12. *See also* Gordon; Trenchard

Charles I (King of England), xviii, 23, 31, 33, 43, 56–62, 66–67, 71–72, 77–79, 87, 99–101, 112, 177, 180

Charles II (King of England), 99–100, 106, 177, 313

Cicero, 60, 129–31, 137, 155, 193, 250

Civic Humanism, xiii, xix, 159–63, 166–67, 169–73, 175, 178–79, 182, 298, 306–9, 313

Civil War, xiii, xv–xvii, 4, 15, 30, 51, 63, 78, 90, 93, 98, 103, 122, 153, 166, 174, 176–77

Coke, Sir Edward, 52, 152, 295, 300

Colbourn, H. Trevor, 20–21

Commerce, 270–71, 307–8

Commonwealth, 114, 153

Compact: in Declaration of Independence, 109, 215; in Grotius, 147–48, 194, 205, 215, 233, 241, 245; in Locke, 17, 205, 215, 233, 241, 244–46; and property, 248–54; in Suárez, 124–25; in unicontractarianism, 64–65. *See also* Consent; Contractarianism; Social Contract

Conkin, Paul, 5

Conscience, 192–96, 199–201, 227, 231, 234

Consent: in Burnet, 108–9, 113; in Cato, 300, 303; in Declaration of Independence, 3, 6, 8, 12–13, 61, 82, 85, 105, 108–9, 113, 154, 303; Filmer's rejection of, 47; in Grotius, 135, 138, 148, 258; in Hunton, 68–71, 75–76; in Locke, 17–18, 85, 138, 241, 270, 303; and natural rights, 13; and property, 250–54, 258; in Thomist tradition, 224–26; in unicontractarianism, 41. *See also* Contractarianism; Social Contract

Contractarianism: Catholic, 42–43, 64–65, 71, 79, 98, 106–7, 115–16; in Declaration

of Independence, 110, 113, 123; Filmer's critique of, 45, 81; and Glorious Revolution, 14–5, 98, 101–12; Grotian, xix, 111, 114, 120, 125, 137–38, 178; Hobbean, 137–38; Lockean, 123, 153, 293; Miltonic, 81–83, 92, 101, 110, 113; Parliamentary and Whig, xix, 49–50, 65–76, 82, 98, 101, 110–11, 113–14, 149, 153, 293; philosophical, 65, 78–79, 106–7, 116; unicontractarianism, xiii–xiv, 64–65, 83, 116, 289; varieties of, xv–xvi, 30, 64, 65, 102, 117, 137. *See also* Compact; Consent; Original contract; Social contract

Convention: Carneadean critique of, 128, 212–15; in Grotius, 146–47, 249, 252, 258; in Hooker, 225–26, in Locke, 212–13, 252, 258; in Pufendorf, 252–4, 258; in Roman Law, 131–35

Corpus Mysticum, 54, 125–26, 223–24, 231–33, 301

Corruption, 161, 169, 171–73, 177, 180–81, 307, 313

Creator: in divine right theory, 40, 46; in Miltonic theory, 83–87, 92; as source of natural law, 194, 208, 210, 217, 237, 239, 260, 264; as source of natural rights, 3, 8, 11, 84, 92, 210, 237, 264, 300; in Suárez, 124

Cromwell, Oliver (Cromwellian), xvi, 90, 97, 99, 101

Culverwell, Nathaniel, xvi, 191, 261

Cumberland, Richard, xvi, 222, 261

Danby, Earl of, 171, 175–77, 180

Davies, Sir John, 54

Declaration of Breda, 99

Declaration of Independence, 23, 29, 291; chief doctrines of, 3, 5–16, 154; and classical republicanism, 157–58, 164; compared to *Argument for Self-Defence*, 294–95; compared to Cato, 300–303; compared to Declaration of Rights, 5–15; compared to Milton, 79–85, 89, 91–93; on inalienable rights, 245–46; as Lockean, xvii, 15–9, 24, 48, 154–55; and Parliamentary theory, 50, 55–56, 61, 63, 65, 70–71; and Whig theory, 98, 105, 107, 110, 113–15. *See also* Jefferson

Declaration of Rights, 5–16, 18, 23, 50, 55–56, 64, 71, 104–5, 110, 117

Defoe, Daniel, xvi, 112–14, 290–91

Descartes, René, 203, 239, 265

Deterence, 234–35
Dickinson, H. T., 6, 105
Distributive Justice, 139–41
Divine Right, xv, 3, 29–44, 49–50, 52, 54–55, 59, 61, 63, 69, 71–73, 84, 92–93, 98, 116, 149, 176–77, 299. *See also* Filmer; James I
Dunn, John, 20–25, 29, 65, 289
Dworetz, Steven, 22–24, 288

Education of Cyrus (Xenophon), 140
Elizabeth I, 30–31
Equality: essence of, in parliamentary theory, 55, 71; in Declaration of Independence, 3, 6, 8–9, 12, 84–85; in Declaration of Rights, 6, 8–9; Filmerean critique, 45; in Locke, 16, 18, 217, 219, 221, 248, 293; in Lockean Whig thought, 293, 300–302; in Milton, 84–85, 88; in philosphical contractarianism, 65
Eve, 44, 92, 262, 268
Exclusion Crisis, xvi, 101–3, 106
Executive Power of the Law of Nature, 221, 241; absence in Thomist tradition, 222–30; absence in Grotius, 230–34; and labor, 254–55, 263; in Lockean Whig Theory, 293, 302–3; as path to natural rights, 234–40, 257–58, 267, 274; as source of political power, 83; and suicide, 244–5

Fall, 41–42, 83, 85, 87, 89–90, 212, 226, 229, 260–62
Federalist, The, 3, 61
Ferne, Dr. Henry, 66, 68, 73–74, 111
Figgis, John, 42
Filmer, Sir Robert: comparison to James I, 35, 43, 45; critique of contractarian theory, 81, 248–52, 288; divine right theory, 17, 30–32, 42–48, 100, 112, 244, 288, 301; Locke's critique of, 44, 244, 246, 255, 261; and Reformation, 42–48; and Workmanship argument, 219–20, 241. *See also* Divine Right
Five Knights Case, The (1627), 57
Fortescue, Sir John, 49, 54, 56, 61, 119, 295–96, 300–301
Franklin, Julian, 63, 117
Furley, O. W., 103

Glorious Revolution, 78, 164, 175, 294, 296; and American Revolution, xiii, 4–6, 21, 25; and Locke, 16, 98, 101–2, 105; theorists of, xvi, 106–15, 289, 291, 299

Goldie, Mark, 102, 105
Goldsmith, M. M., 290
Goldwin, Robert, 236
Goodwin, John, 66
Gordon, Thomas, xix, 152, 163, 166, 297–301, 305, 319. *See also* Cato
Gough, John, 64
Grand Remonstrance, 58
Grant, Ruth, 241
Grotius, Hugo: contractarianism of, 87, 11, 113–8, 123–26, 137; and executive power of the law of nature, 230–9, 237–39; as influence on Whigs, xvi, xix, xx, 98, 104–5, 111, 113–15, 150, 175, 178, 182, 290, 294, 299–300; and Locke, 18, 187–99, 201, 204–5, 208–9, 212, 214–8, 241, 244–45, 252–60, 266, 270; new natural law doctrine of, 119–23, 126–49, 165, 221; on property, 119, 146, 248–60, 266, 270; as rights thinking, 3, 139–49, 290; on slavery, 241, 244–45, 287; *De Jure Belli ac Pacis*, 104, 111, 119–21, 123, 127, 191, 230; *De Veritate*, 120

Hamowy, Ronald, 298, 317
Happiness: Cato on, 306–8, 310–11, 317–18; as end of Lockean law of nature, 214, 273; self, person, and possibility of, 279–80, 283–87
Harrington, John: and Anglicization of republican tradition, 159, 167–70; and Cato, 305–7, 313; and neo-Harringtonians, 173–75, 178–80, 182
Hegel, G.W.F., 149, 317
Heidegger, Martin, 264–65
Herbert, George, 41
Herle, Charles, 66–67, 74
Hill, Christopher, 92
Hippocrates, 194, 200
Hoadly, Benjamin, 20, 22, 31, 101
Hobbes, Thomas, 44; absolutism in, 32, 71, 244; and the breakup of Christian Aristotelianism, xvii–xviii, 72, 137; Cato and, 304, 306, 310–11; contractarianism of, 45, 72, 137; and Grotius, 139, 142–43, 145, 191; and Locke, 24, 188, 191, 193, 219–20, 230, 233–34, 236, 272–78, 306; and natural rights, 3, 138–39, 142–43, 192, 209, 238, 272–78, 288; and Pufendorf, 205, 209, 234, 238–39, 277; and quest for certainty, 122
Homer, 170

Hooker, Richard: and Christian Aristotelianism, xvii, 37, 216, 224, 261; on executive
power of law of nature, 224–31, 237, 239;
and Grotius, 104, 237, 239; influence
during Restoration, xvi, 98, 101, 165, 178;
and Grotius, 104, 237, 239; and Locke, 18,
30, 188, 224–31, 237, 239, 295; social contract in, 87
Howard, Sir Robert, 14
Humphrey, John, 114
Hopfl, Harro, 32, 64–65, 71, 79, 83, 115–17
Horwitz, Robert, 192, 204
Hunton, Philip, 30, 66–71, 74–75, 77–82,
93, 103, 105, 113, 116. See also Mixed
Monarchy
Hutcheson, Francis, 19–20

Independents, 99
Inger, Leon, 124
Interregnum, 166

James I (King of England), xiii, 30–40, 43,
45, 51, 72, 93. See also Divine Right;
Filmer
James II (Duke of York): as Catholic, 100,
180; Cato on, 296, 299; and Exclusion,
100, 102–4; and Glorius Revolution, 6–7,
14, 112–13, 115, 292
Jefferson, Thomas: and Cato, 301–2; and divine right theory, 29, 31, 38; and equality,
16; and Locke, 18–19, 23–24, 71, 301–2;
and natural rights philosophy, xiii, 4, 10,
31; and republican tradition, 163, 170;
and Whig tradition, 98. See also Declaration of Independence
Jesuits, 14, 58
Jones, J. R., 98
Judgment of Whole Kingdoms and Nations,
The, 289, 293
Jus Naturale. See Law of Nature
Jus Gentium. See Law of Nations
Juvenal, 193

Kant, Immanuel, 137
Kenyon, J. P., 32, 101
Kramnick, Isaac, 162

Labor: Cato on, 304, 307–8, 311, 318–19;
and construction of the self, 279–80, 282,
285; divine command, 200–202; and
Lockean title to property, 252–57, 263–
66, 268, 271, 278; transformative power

of, 254, 264–65, 269, 272–73, 278, 280,
285
Laslett, Peter, 187, 222, 242, 248–49, 294–95
Law of Nations (jus gentium), 299; Carneadean challenge, 128, 131–32, 147; in
Grotius, 104–5, 123, 126, 135, 140, 147–
48, 190, 205; Lockean critique, 205–6;
philosophic origin of, 129; in Roman Law,
129–33, 135; in Whig theory, 103, 105
Law of Nature: in Grotius, xvii–xix, 98, 105,
111, 114, 116–49, 187–99, 230–34, 249–
52, 255, 258–59; in Hobbes, 272–75; in
Locke's Questions, xviii, 187–215, 217; in
Locke's Two Treatises, 83, 216–75, 287,
293, 295, 318; in Lockean tradition, 293,
299, 303, 307, 318; in Milton, 85–87, 90–
91; in Pufendorf, 191–93, 207, 209, 222,
238–39, 253–55; revival of, xvi, 98; in
Roman law, 129–34, 147, 189; in Whig
thought, 103–11, 114, 116–18, 146, 149,
182
Laws of God (Divine Law), 103–4, 106–7,
119, 125, 137
Laws Properly So-Called (Grotius), 139–43,
146, 149
Levellers, 3, 15, 99, 114
Littleton, 119
Livy, 119, 272
Luther, Martin, 49, 119
Lutz, Donald, 22

Machiavelli, Niccolò, 90, 122, 127, 139, 146,
148, 155, 159, 161–163, 166–68, 178, 203,
221, 305–6, 309, 313
MacPherson, C. B., 269
Madison, James, 3, 14, 170, 272
Magna Charta, 57, 98, 116
Maimonides, 119
Manwaring, Roger, 31, 33, 52–53
Marvell, Andrew, 170, 179–82, 307, 313
Marx, Karl, 167
Mary (Queen of England, Princess of
Orange), 5, 8, 15, 106
Massachusetts Bill of Rights, 9, 16, 245
Maxwell, John, 35, 40, 42
Mayhew, Jonathan, 22
McDonald, Forrest, 298
Militia Ordinance, 62
Mill, J. S., 305
Milton, John, 5; Biblical foundations of
thought, 34, 83, 93, 119, 212; and Chris-
tian Aristotelianism, 261; contractarianism

of, xv–xvi, 30, 78–79, 92, 98, 110, 113, 116; and Declaration of Independence, 80–82, 91; and Filmer, 30, 92–3; influence on Americans, 22, 98; opposition to Restoration, 97; *Paradise Lost*, 85–88; *Paradise Regained*, 84; on resistance, 78–81, 100; *Tenure of Kings and Magistrates*, 79–83, 87–88, 90; *Ready and Easy Way*, 82, 89–90

Mixed Constitution (Regime), 49, 56–65, 78, 307, 313–14. See also *Answer to the 19 Propositions*; Mixed Monarchy

Mixed Monarchy, 46, 62–63, 65–71, 74, 77, 314. *See also* Hunton; Mixed Constitution

Molesworth, Robert, 20

Molina, Luis de, 126

Money, 248, 268–70

Montesquieu, Charles, 154–55, 172

Muggletonians, 99

Natural Inclinations, 142–45, 196, 200–203, 208, 212, 228–31

Natural Law. *See* Law of Nature

Natural Religion, 92, 98, 106, 108–9

Natural Right(s): absence in Declaration of Rights, 5–8, 11–13, 56; absence in Parliamentary theory, 55–56, 61, 70–71, 75, 83–85, 91–92; absence in Whig theory, 101, 105, 108–10, 123; Americans and, xiii, xv, 4–5, 15, 22, 31, 48, 118, 150, 154–55, 157–58, 162–65; Aristotle on, 140, 196; Carneades and, 127, 135; and common good, 36, 56; in Declaration of Independence, 3, 6–8, 11–13, 15, 56, 83–85, 92, 108–10, 123, 164; Grotius and, xvii, 127, 138–40, 144–45, 149, 215; in Hobbes, xviii, 45, 138, 192, 219, 238–39, 272–75; and Hooker, 225–26; inalienability, 218, 245–46; in Locke, xv, xvii, 18, 22, 24, 48, 65, 83–85, 101, 108–9, 123, 139, 149, 155, 163, 165, 182, 192, 214–6, 218–21, 238–39, 242–46, 257–58, 266, 271–88, 302–5, 308–9, 312, 314, 317–18, 319; in Pufendorf, 192, 238–39; and republicanism, xvii–xiv, 151–64, 272; as subjective, 11–12; in Whig opposition writers, 153, 157–58, 162–65, 182, 302–5, 308–9, 312, 314, 317–19

Negative Community, 251–52, 254

Newlin, Claude, 21

Nineteen Propositions, The, 58

Noah, 261

No-Harm Principle, 218, 236–37, 239–40, 242, 255–58, 267, 274, 293

Nozick, Robert, 224

Obligation, xix; in divine right theory, 41, 46, 47; and the Fall, 268; in Grotius, 121, 128, 140, 143, 146–48, 190–91, 194, 204, 208–9, 233, 250, 253; in Hooker, 227; and law, 128, 140, 143, 147–48, 188–91, 198, 207–11, 219, 227, 286; Locke on, in *Questions*, 188–91, 194, 198, 204, 207–11, 213; Locke on, in *Two Treatises*, 219, 242, 253, 257, 262, 268, 273–77; in Parliamentary theory, 64, 68–69, 75; in Pufendorf, 252–53, 275, 277; in slavery, 242; in Whig theory, 109, 115

Organic Theory of Polity: absence in Cato, 301, 305, 312; in Aristotle, 35–36, 54, 61, 72, 159–60, 301; in classical republicanism, 156–60, 163, 182, 308, 312; in divine right theory, 35–36; in natural law tradition, 125; in Parliamentary thought, 54, 61, 72

Original Contract: and constitutional contractarianism, 64–65, 71, 107, 120; contrasted with Miltonic and Lockean contracts, 75, 78, 80, 87, 107, 113, 258–59, 290, 294–95, 299, 303–4; in Grotius, 115, 120, 124, 138, 146, 258–59, 290; in Parliamentary thought, 14–15, 63, 65, 70–71, 75, 78, 82, 101, 103, 120; in Suárez, 124; in Whig thought, 107, 112–13, 115, 117, 120, 146, 182, 299, 303–4

Pangle, Thomas, 298

Parker, Henry, 38, 59, 61, 66, 71–82, 87, 93, 103

Parliament: and American Revolution, 24; and ancient constitution, 51–56; Cavalier Parliament, 98–100; in Civil War, 61–63, 77–78, 81–82; Contractarian ideas, 14–15, 50, 65–76, 78–79; Convention, 3, 13–15, 65, 98, 115; and Declaration of Rights, 11–15; and divine right theory, 32–34, 39–40, 66; Long, 56–57; Rump, 77, 82; Short, 56, 58; Sovereignty, 74; and Whigs, 97–100, 103–4, 115, 169, 171–77, 179–81, 259, 291, 313, 315

Paul, 34, 47, 101, 227

"Percat Papa," 103

Perry, Geraint, 288

Peter, 34

Petition of Right, 57, 176
Plato (Platonism), 119, 139, 141, 250, 272, 287
Plutarch, 138
Pocock, J.G.A., 4, 13, 53, 151, 153, 159–63, 166–75, 177–83, 298–99, 305–8, 312–15
Political Apharisms, 289–91, 293, 297
Polybius, 60, 161, 168
Popery. *See* Catholicism
Popish Plot, 100
Positive Community, 251
Promulagation of the Law of Nature, 192, 195–97, 201, 274
Protectorate, 114, 120
Protestantism: and breakup of Christian Aristotelianism, xv—xvi, 49–50, 79, 92–93, 97–98, 102, 116, 119–22, 149, 219, 229; contractarianism, 30, 50, 70, 75, 79, 92–93; in Declaration of Rights, 7–8; and divine right theory, 42–43, 92–93; fears of Catholics, 98–101, 179–80; influence on Americans, 152. *See also* Reformation
Prynne, William, 61, 66
Pufendorf, Samuel: between Grotius and Hobbes, 191–95, 205, 209, 238–39, 249–52, 258, 275, 277; and breakdown of Christian Aristotelianism, xvii; Locke's break with, 205, 207, 234, 253–54, 258, 270; Locke's use of, 9, 188, 191, 193–95, 204, 207, 222, 242–43, 275, 277, 303
Puritans, 5, 50–51, 67, 97, 152, 226
Pym, John, 52–53, 55–56, 58, 98

Rawls, John, 224
Reformation: and Anti-Catholicism, 102, 180; attitude and contractarianism, 69–71, 92–93, 112; attitude and divine right theory, 34–48, 250; of church, 29–30; and religious conflict, 121–23, 128–29, 144, 166, 189; and transformation of political thought, xv–xvii, xix, 75, 92–93, 102, 119, 121, 128, 144, 146, 189, 223–24, 226, 261. *See also* Protestantism
Republican Synthesis, 150–51, 156, 159, 163–66, 183, 298, 311–12
Republicanism, 80–81, 88–90, 138, 169, 166–70, 175, 181–82, 313–15; classical (old), xiii–xiv, xix, 150–51, 155–59, 161–70, 272, 298, 306, 308, 311 318; natural rights (new), xiii–xiv, xviii–xix, 4, 13, 149, 164, 183, 272, 305, 307–8, 309, 314–15, 318–19

Resistance. *See* Revolution
Restoration, 97–100, 165–66, 168, 176
Revolution, Right of (Resistance): absence in Declaration of Rights, 6–7, 12, 15, 18; absence in Restoration Settlement, 100; in *Argument for Self-Defence*, 294; in Cato, 303–4; in Declaration of Independence, 3, 6–7, 12, 18, 71, 78–80, 109–10, 303–4; in Grotius, 115, 123–24; in Locke, 18, 71, 75, 78–80, 109–10, 218, 294, 303–4; in Parliamentary theory, 56, 61–62, 71, 75, 78–80; in Suárez, 124; in *Vindiciae Contra Tyrannos*, 116
Right to Life (Preservation): in Cato, 307; in Declaration of Independence, 11; in Hobbes, 273; in Locke, 212, 239–40, 244, 254–55, 257, 261, 266, 268–71, 273; in pre-modern tradition, 138, 145
Robbins, Caroline, 153, 159, 162
Roman Church. *See* Catholicism
Romanism, *See* Catholicism
Roman Law, xvii, 3, 111, 117, 129–44, 147, 189, 192, 248
Rossiter, Clinton, 21, 23
Rousseau, J. J., 87, 137, 139
Rutherford, Samuel, 66

Sabine, George, 147–48
Sacheverell, Dr. Henry, 291–92, 296–97
Sade, Marquis de, 277
Sanctions, 128, 140, 192, 221, 227–28, 231, 274
Schmitt, Gary, 157
Schochet, Gordon, 35
Schwoerer, Loas, 5–6, 12, 15, 79
Self-Evident Truths, 3, 6, 8–9, 196
Shaftesbury, Earl of, 101, 103, 166, 170–81, 307, 313
Shalhope, Robert, 298
Shapiro, Ian, 277
Ships Money Case (*Rex v. Hampton*, 1638), 57
Sidney, Algernon, 13, 20, 22, 46, 101, 120, 165, 175, 294, 313
Simmons, John, 243, 245
Skinner, Quentin, 222
Slavery: in Aristotle, 37–38; in Cato, 307, 318; in divine right theory, 37–38; in Grotius, 111, 244; in Locke, 220, 241–46, 318; in Pufendorf, 243; in Roman law, 133; in Whig theory, 110–11, 177, 180

Smith, Adam, 167
Socrates, 134, 139–40
Sovereignty: of Adam, 44, 47, 219; under ancient constitution, 51–2; of God, 42, 48, 68, 208, 211, 219; in Grotius, 115; in mixed monarchy, 67–68; popular, 10, 53–54, 56, 63, 65, 68, 75, 81, 101, 111; parliamentary, 74; and rights, 238, 245, 276, 285, 310; in Whig theory, 107, 115
Spiolage Rule, 256–57, 266–68
Spinoza, Benedict, 122, 276
Standing Army, 162, 169, 171–73, 177, 292, 295–96, 307
State of Nature: absence in Grotian theory, 108, 137–38, 150, 234; absence in parliamentary theory, 56, 65; in Declaration of Independence, 9, 83, 108, 137, 150, 301–2; in Hobbes, 138, 220, 230, 236, 275–76, 306, 311; in Locke, 17–18, 65, 83, 108, 138, 150, 153, 206, 217, 220, 222–24, 228–30, 233–41, 246, 253, 274–77, 286, 301–4; in Lockean tradition, 293, 301–4, 306, 311; in Thomist tradition, 223–24, 228–30, 234
State of War: in Cato, 306, 311; in Hobbes, 138, 230, 236, 270, 306, 311; in Locke, 220 236–37, 241–42, 244, 248
Stoicism, xvii, 130 134, 136, 139, 141–42, 144–45, 193
Strauss, Leo, 269, 311
Suárez, Francisco: on executive power of the law of nature, 223–24, 226; relationship to Grotius, xvii, 119–20, 230–31; on resistance, 124; on right, 141; on source of political authority, 124–26, 226, 301
Subjective Right, 141. See also Natural Right(s)
Suicide, 219, 221, 241–46, 257, 276

Terence, 127
Thirty Years War, 122–23
Thomas Aquinas (Thomism): on executive power of the law of nature, 126, 222–34; and Grotius, 119, 126, 129, 139–46, 198, 230–4; law of nature, 139–46, 193, 196, 198, 200–203, 208, 214, 216; and Locke, 193, 200–203, 208; synthesis of biblical and philosophical, xvii, 37, 92, 119–20, 261; on virtue, 139–46, 304
Thompson, Martyn, 32, 64–65, 71, 79, 83, 115–17

Tocqueville, Alexis de, 150, 172
Toland, John, 5
Tories (Toryism), 6, 9, 101
Trenchard, John, xix, 152, 163, 166, 297–300, 303, 305, 319. See also Cato
Tuck, Richard, 142
Tully, James, 251, 265
Tyranny, 22, 34, 75, 80, 88, 101, 299, 305, 311

Van Schaack, Peter, 24
Vazquez, Fernando, 126, 129
Victoria, Francisco de, 126, 129
Vindiciae Contra Tyrannos, 116–17, 134
Virginia Bill of Rights, 16, 23, 245
Virtue: in Cato, 304, 309, 311–12, 315–17; in Grotius, 141–43; in Locke, 198–99, 204, 206, 214; in republican synthesis, 156–59, 161, 163, 169–70, 174, 178, 181–82, 214, 311, 315–17
Voltaire, 152
Vox Populi, Vox Dei, 289, 293

Walpole, Sir Robert, 297, 313
Webking, Robert, 157
Weighman, Roger, 10
Weston, Corine, 60, 67
Whigs: American, 5, 18–19, 24, 29, 31, 155, 157, 319; emergence of, 97–103, 166; and Glorious Revolution, 5–7, 21, 25, 29, 106–18, 289, 299; and Grotius, xviii, 105, 111, 114, 120, 123, 137, 146, 149–50, 165, 187, 210, 259, 290–91; and Locke, xvii, 25, 107–11, 187, 216, 259, 274, 288, 290–91, 293, 300, 302–4, 307; opposition, 153, 155, 157–59, 162–63, 170, 297–300; political science, xix, 165, 172, 175–83, 313–15; tradition, xiii, xv, 21, 25, 29, 31, 45, 47, 64–65, 78, 90, 97–120, 162, 216, 288–91, 300, 302–4, 309
Wildman, John, 114, 116
William (of Orange) (King William III), 5, 8, 15–16, 102, 106, 112, 291, 296, 299
Williams, Elisha, 22
Wills, Garry, 19–23
Wood, Gordon, 4, 51, 155–64, 182–83, 305–6, 308–15
Workmanship Argument, 217–19, 221, 239–40, 243–44, 255, 257, 262, 264, 269, 288

Zagorian, Perez, 90